Ethnicity and Crime: A Reader

Readings in Criminology and Criminal Justice series

Series editor Sandra Walklate

Forthcoming titles:

Gender and Crime: A Reader
Karen Evans and Janet Jamieson

Crimes of the Powerful: A Reader
Dave Whyte

Victims and Victimisation: A Reader
Brian Williams and Hannah Goodman Chong

Ethnicity and Crime: A Reader

Basia Spalek

Open University Press

Open University Press
McGraw-Hill Education
McGraw-Hill House
Shoppenhangers Road
Maidenhead
Berkshire
England
SL6 2QL

email: enquiries@openup.co.uk
world wide web: www.openup.co.uk

and Two Penn Plaza, New York, NY 10121-2289, USA

First published 2008

A catalogue record of this book is available from the British
Library

ISBN-13: 978-0-335-22379-4 (pb) 978-0-335-22378-7 (hb)
ISBN-10: 0-335-22379-6 (pb) 0-335-22378-8 (hb)

Library of Congress Cataloging-in-Publication Data
CIP data applied for

Typeset by RefineCatch Limited, Bungay, Suffolk
Printed in Great Britain by Bell and Bain Ltd, Glasgow

Contents

Series editor's foreword

This is the first collection of readings to be published as part of a new McGraw-Hill/Open University Press series, 'Readings in Criminology and Criminal Justice'. The purpose of this new series is to offer a student-friendly approach to the key issues and debates currently pre-occupying the discipline of criminology. Despite the proliferation of textbooks claiming to offer wide coverage of criminology and the criminal justice system, such books inevitably do not do justice to the needs of the undergraduate curriculum beyond year one. The intention of this series is to fill this gap. Indeed, the changing nature of the criminology undergraduate market makes its own claims for readily available material. These changes take two forms. The first is in relation to the sheer number of students now engaging in criminology programmes either as a single honours or a joint honours programme. The second lies with the nature of programme delivery: the modular system means that in order to deliver a course of an appropriate standard, tutors require readily available and easily accessible material to support this course delivery. A readily accessible collection of readings that address the core features of the criminology curriculum provides an essential starting point for students and tutors alike, especially in the light of the increasing number of journals and other outlets which may not be that easily accessible or subscribed to by all libraries, electronic developments notwithstanding. Lack of availability of a wider range of material has a detrimental effect on the discipline and the student experience. The intention of this series is not only to fill these kinds of gaps, and as a result do better justice to the debates in the discipline, but also to provide the opportunity for the nominated editors, and the series itself, to make a mark on the discipline, by stretching and contributing to the boundaries of criminological debates in the kinds of reading that are chosen. This collection by Basia Spalek achieves just this.

Divided into five parts, this reader draws together both classic and contemporary work. Part 1 addresses the historically contentious 'race and crime' debate by paying particular attention to the extent to which racial discrimination within the criminal justice system contributes to the wider (questionable) relationship between race and crime. Spalek is keen to point out in her presentation of these readings the underlying tension that exists between the demands for social order in which (post)modern societies are implicated, and the increasing recognition of the fluid nature of the (post)modern condition. It is her contention that a critical reading of the debates presented here demand a critique of the Enlightenment project itself, out of which debates around modernity and the notion of the 'racial other' was itself born. Such a critique requires that academics, policy makers and practitioners work reflexively and these twin concerns with the Enlightenment project and reflexivity run through Spalek's discussion of the rest of this collection. Part 2 presents readings that address the racialisation of crime in its social, political and cultural context. This part encourages the reader to think critically about the complex interaction and interplay between ethnicity, age, gender, sexuality and class. The way in which these variables operate, and the contexts in which one of them may be more salient than others, is a key problematic for criminology generally but is particularly problematic for the 'race and crime' debate. Understanding which dimensions of this interaction that criminologists have made visible and have kept invisible and under what circumstances this has happened, adds an important critical edge to what claims can and cannot be made by researchers in this area. In this part of the book Spalek introduces the importance of understanding the concept of 'identity', and especially faith identity, which she argues that in the post 9/11 era should not be collapsed into the category of either race or ethnicity. This theme is also taken up in Part 3 of this collection. The readings in Part 3 consider the relationship between race, ethnicity and victimisation. In this part Spalek introduces us to work that not only considers the experiences of people from ethnic minorities and victims of crime, but also considers the far-reaching consequences of those experiences. In this context her selection of readings brings to our attention the notion of 'spirit injury' as being significant in understanding the full impact of racism and sexism on minority ethnic women, especially important in the context of religious hate crimes. The importance of reflexivity is endorsed in the final two parts of the book. Part 4 considers the importance of self and discipline reflexivity whilst Part 5 examines the theme of ethnic identities, institutional reflexivity and crime. The readings in Part 4 encourage us to think about what counts as 'real knowledge': whose voices are listened to, why, and how is that listening constructed? In order to answer these questions it is important to think about the presumptions surrounding Whiteness that infuse the knowledge construction process both at a disciplinary and individual level but are especially important if we are concerned to make meaningful interventions in the social world that aim to embrace the concerns of ethnic minority groups. This latter issue of intervention is explored in Part 5. In this part questions pertaining to 'institutional reflexivity' are taken as the central theme for critical examination, pointing out that concepts like community participation and community engagement should not be taken as given.

This collection presented by Basia Spalek takes us on a very important intellectual journey. Her choices impeccably situate questions around ethnicity and crime within the bigger questions of modernity/post-modernity, identity and reflexivity, who can know things, what it is that can be known, and how that knowledge is constructed. In a world in which increasingly people from ethnic minorities occupy, and are made to occupy, social, cultural, and identity spaces, in which they are both the fearful and the feared, the questions that are posed by this reader are both important and timely for all of us whether academic, student, policy maker or practitioner. This intellectual journey is one on which we should all travel if we are serious about addressing the problems that face the contemporary social world. I am certain that this reader will make a significant contribution to that process.

Professor Sandra Walklate
Eleanor Rathbone Chair of Sociology
University of Liverpool
November 2007

Publisher's acknowledgements

The authors and publisher wish to thank the following for permission to use copyright material:

Jefferson, T., Walker, M. and Seneviratne, M. (1992) 'Ethnic Minorities, Crime and Criminal Justice: a study in a provincial city' in D. Downes (ed.) *Unravelling Criminal Justice*. London: Macmillan.

Holdaway, S. (1997) 'Some Recent Approaches to the Study of Race in Criminological Research' *British Journal of Criminology* Vol. 37 (3), by permission of Oxford University Press.

Hood, R. (1992) Chapter 12, 'Discrimination in the Courts?' in *Race and Sentencing*. Oxford: Clarendon Press.

Agozino, B. (2003) 'The Enlightenment and Euro-American Theories of the Judicial Process' in *Counter-Colonial Criminology: a critique of imperialist reason*. London: Pluto Press.

Lea, J. and Young, J. (1993) Chapter 4, 'The Race and Crime Debate' in *What is to be Done about Law and Order?* London: Pluto Press.

Gilroy, P. (1987) 'The Myth of Black Criminality' in P. Scraton (ed.) *Law, Order and the Authoritarian State: readings in critical criminology*. Milton Keynes: Open University Press.

Poynting, S. and Mason, V. (2006) 'Tolerance, Freedom, Justice and Peace?: Britain, Australia and Anti-Muslim Racism since September 11th 2001' *Journal of Intercultural Studies* 27 (4).

Alexander, C. (2000) Chapter 1 'Introduction', *The Asian Gang*. Oxford: Berg Publishing.

Goodey, J. (2007) 'Racist Violence in Europe: challenges for official data collection' *Ethnic & Racial Studies*.

Rai, D. K. and Hesse, B. (1992) 'Racial Victimization: an experimental analysis' in B. Hesse, D. K. Rai, C. Bennett and P. McGilchrist (eds) *Beneath the Surface: Racial Harrassment*. Aldershot: Avebury.

Bowling, B. (1999) Chapter 7, 'Racism and Victimisation' in *Violent Racism: victimisation, policing and social context* (revised edition). Oxford: Oxford University Press.

Mama, A. (2000) 'Woman Abuse in London's Black Communities' in K. Owusu (ed.) *Black British Culture & Society*. London: Routledge.

Modood, T. (1994) 'Political Blackness and British Asians' *Sociology* Vol. 28 (4), by permission of Sage Publications.

Phillips, C. and Bowling, B. (2003) 'Racism, Ethnicity and Criminology: developing minority perspectives' *British Journal of Criminology* 43, by permission of Oxford University Press.

Ferber, A. (2003) 'Constructing Whiteness: the intersections of race and gender in US White Supremacist Discourse' in B. Perry (ed.) *Hate and Bias Crime: a reader*. London: Routledge.

Spalek, B. (2005) 'Researching Black Muslim Women's Lives: a critical reflection' *The International Journal of Social Research Methodology* Vol. 8 (5).

Kalunta-Crumpton, A. (2004) 'Criminology and Orientalism' in A. Kalunta-Crumpton and B. Agozino (eds) *Pan-African Issues in Crime and Justice*. Aldershot: Ashgate.

O'Byrne, M. (2000) 'Can Macpherson Succeed where Scarman Failed?' in A. Marlow and B. Loveday (eds) *After Macpherson: policing after the Stephen Lawrence Inquiry*. Lyme Regis: Russell House Publishing.

Heer, G. (2008) '(In)visible Barriers: the experience of Asian employees in the probation service' *Howard Journal of Criminal Justice*.

The publisher directs the reader to the original publications for a full list of references.

Every effort has been made to trace the copyright holders, but if any have been inadvertently overlooked the publisher will be pleased to make the necessary arrangement at the first opportunity.

Introduction
by Dr Basia Spalek

Issues in relation to 'race' and ethnicity have generated substantial, and ever-growing, interest from, and within, a multitude of academic, research and policy contexts. Such is the richness and complexity of this work that any attempt to convey it succinctly is fraught with difficulties. As such, the *Reader in Ethnicity and Crime* consists of a collection of works that serve to best capture the main themes that arise from within this vast area of work. It is important to stress that the organisation and contents of the *Reader* themselves comprise a framework through which to view and think about developments and issues in relation to 'race'/ethnicity and crime. Therefore, the *Reader* is not to be taken as a chronological presentation of the material, but rather, it is to be viewed as the construction of five sections that serve to encapsulate the large volume of work in this field of study, simultaneously generating broader questions about contemporary and future developments. It is important to highlight that although some of the suggested readings are more than 20 years old, they nonetheless contain issues and themes that are implicit within, and also explicit to, current work. Therefore, older, as well as newer, works are reprinted in the *Reader* as both are key to gaining a greater awareness of the trajectory that important debates have taken, and both serve to encapsulate ethnicity in relation to crime.

Structure

The *Reader in Ethnicity and Crime* is divided into five parts: 'Race and crime', racial discrimination and criminal justice; The racialisation of crime: social, political and cultural contexts; Race, ethnicity and victimisation; Self and discipline reflexivity: ethnic identities and crime; and Ethnic identities, institutional reflexivity and crime. Each of these sections contain recurring and overlapping themes, and they include many different ways of thinking about 'race'/ethnicity in relation to crime, reflecting, and being underpinned by, theoretical approaches that might be labelled as positivist, critical race analyses, left realist approaches, feminist, as well as postmodern, perspectives. These different positions engage with the issue of 'race'/ethnicity in relation to crime in significantly different ways, and they bring with them many questions, which generate considerable debate and controversy. It is important to note that although some theoretical positions and approaches become more dominant than others at particular points in time, these positions co-exist, and continue to shape, and are shaped by, research, policy and theorising in this area.

Part 1 begins by referring to what has been commonly referred to as the 'race and crime debate'. Prison statistics consistently show that Black, particularly African Caribbean, men and women are over-represented in penal institutions, and so questions have been raised about Black people's offending rates and any discriminatory treatment that they might experience at various points throughout the criminal justice system. Part 1 highlights the elusive nature of 'race'/ethnicity – being socially constructed phenomena – so that statistical data in relation to crime and criminal justice is partial and incomplete, and subject to many inherent biases.

Part 1 also draws attention to a deeper dynamic at play: the interaction of two contradictory, yet inter-related, mechanisms associated with the conditions of late modernity. Arising out of, and being located within, the framework of modernity, is an 'imperative of order' (Lash, 1994): the use of 'race' and ethnic monitoring procedures within the criminal justice system, the targets that agencies are expected to meet in terms of minority ethnic employee representation or in relation to boosting minority ethnic communities' confidence in criminal justice, and the search for uncovering and documenting direct and indirect forms of racial discrimination, bear testimony to the belief that progress can be made in terms of reducing 'race effects', including racial discrimination, through the application of logical procedures that are underpinned by social scientific approaches and rationale. It might be argued that the multitude of studies statistically exploring racial discrimination as a phenomenon bear testimony to the power of Enlightenment philosophy transcending the modern pursuit of, and claims to, knowledge; the implication here being that by using (better and more sophisticated) scientific methods so as to conceptualise and measure racial discrimination, then it might be possible to implement strategies that can be used to reduce and ultimately eliminate this phenomenon. At the same time, standing in contradiction to, but also interacting with, this imperative are characteristics linked with postmodern processes: an acknowledgement of the fluidity, and situated nature, of knowledge claims, including an acknowledgement of the socially constructed nature of 'race'/ethnicities. Increasing reflexivity within academia, as well as in social and policy contexts, is apparent, involving a critique of Enlightenment values associated with modernity, particularly as modernity itself has been linked to the creation of racial hierarchies which helped to institutionalise slavery, as well as helping to instigate the Holocaust, through dehumanising those classified as 'racial others'. Reflexivity within academic and criminal justice fields is a theme that also features in other parts of the *Reader*.

Part 2 focuses upon the broader social, political and cultural contexts to 'race'/ethnicity and crime. This part highlights that the context of crime with respect to minority communities is highly politicised, so that at different points in the criminal justice system, at different periods of time, different communities will become more prominent in policy, research and media arenas, influencing the extent and type of state intervention and control. Whereas in the 1970s and 1980s relations between the police and Black communities deteriorated, with police perception of the Black population as being a potential threat to order and stability, as potential trouble makers, feeding into the aggressive and intimidating policing of Black communities, in a post-September 11th 2001 context, when many terror attacks have been committed around the world by violent extremists, Asian men, in particular young Muslim men, have attracted attention, where they have been viewed as constituting a 'problem group' (Alexander, 2000), as 'evil' and a 'fifth column enemy within' by media, politicians, the security services and by agencies of the criminal justice system (Poynting and Mason, 2006). A theme highlighted in the *Reader* is that whereas 'race'/ethnic identities have, over the last three decades or so, attracted much research attention, lying at the forefront of criminological enquiry, faith identities have largely been overlooked. It is important to highlight, however, that religious identification is a more important aspect of self-identity for individuals belonging to minority ethnic groups than for white groups. For example, according to findings from the Home Office Citizenship Survey (2001), in contrast to the 17 per cent of White respondents who said that religion was important to their self-identity, 44 per cent of Black and 61 per cent of Asian respondents said that religion was important. For Muslims, religion was ranked second only after family in terms of the importance to their self-identity (O'Beirne, 2004). O'Beirne (2004) has stressed that religious affiliation and ethnicity should be considered together rather than separately when carrying out research and when making policy decisions. Beckford, Gale, Owen, Peach and Weller (2006: 8) have argued that 'the religion dimension should not be completely collapsed into ethnicity and vice versa'. Therefore, faith identities, and their inclusion in research and policy fields, is a theme that features throughout the *Reader*.

Part 2 also highlights tensions between class-based approaches to 'race'/ethnicity and crime, and those approaches that give a greater focus to 'race' issues, the debates here being linked to debates highlighted in Part 1 in relation to the elusive nature of 'race'/ethnicity, and 'race'/ethnicities as constituting social constructs. For some researchers, 'race' is an ideological construct that obscures economic relations of power, so that with regard to the issue of criminality amongst Black communities factors such as social deprivation, poverty, low educational attainment and unemployment are more important than 'race'. Other researchers, on the other hand, stress that 'race' is a

construct, or indeed a hegemonic discourse, through which exclusion and criminalisation are manifest. As a result, 'race' might be thought of as a cultural
resource through which social life is experienced and from which identities and
resistances are built, and imperialism and colonialism might be thought of as
the broader contexts within which to place issues in relation to 'race'/ethnicity
and crime.

Part 3 focuses upon the experiences of minority ethnic communities as
the victims of crime. Victimisation by race and religious hate crime is explored,
these being areas that are attracting significant research and policy attention,
particularly as it has been suggested that hate crimes impact not only upon
direct victims, but also upon the wider communities that individuals belong to.
Indeed, if communities may be imagined as well as real (Castells, 2004), then
the effects of a particular incident of hate crime may have far-reaching consequences. Part 3 further stresses that an experience of victimisation is influenced by an individual's 'race'/ethnic, including their faith and other, identities;
however, it seems that all too often, victimological work has homogenised
victims, failing to take into consideration diversity amongst the victims of crime.
Nonetheless, cultural, religious, and other, factors are increasingly featuring
in accounts of victimisation, particularly from those accounts that are underpinned by critical black perspectives. For example, when studying the victimising
experiences of minority ethnic women, critical black feminists have introduced
the concept of 'spirit injury' in order to explain and to try to understand the full
impact of racism and sexism upon women's lives (Davis, 1997; Williams, 1997).
The theme of the suppression of social difference and the homogenisation of
knowledge claims within the discipline of criminology, as well as within the sub-
discipline of victimology, also features implicitly, as well as explicitly, in other
sections of the Reader.

Part 4 conceptualises developments taking place within the criminological
and victimological fields in relation to 'race'/ethnicity by drawing upon the
notion of 'reflection', as outlined by Lash (1994). Reflection is a constituent
part of reflexivity in late modernity, whereby individuals, collective groups and/
or institutions intentionally and rationally reflect upon the part that they play in
the perpetuation of identified social problems as well as reflecting upon ways in
which they can intervene and act so as to minimise harms (Lash, 1994;
McGhee, 2005). In relation to criminological and victimological knowledge production around 'race'/ethnicity, researchers are questioning the applicability of
the terminology used to categorise minorities, so that, for example, the racial
classifications of Black, Asian and so forth have been extensively critiqued. At
the same time, researchers' reflection involves debates in relation to the
racial/ethnic identities of the researcher and the researched, and how these
influence the research process. Moreover, the issue of the marginalisation of
minorities' experiences and claims to knowledge is increasingly being reflected
upon, with some researchers arguing that perspectives within criminology/
victimology have insufficiently taken into consideration the voices and individual,

as well as group collective, experiences of minorities, including, for example, African voices and perspectives, as well as Muslim and other faith identities. Other hidden communities include traveller communities, asylum seekers, people of dual heritage, white minority ethnic groups and rural minority ethnic households. For example, according to James (2006: 471), sedentarism is a norm that underpins mainstream society, serving to construct traveller communities as deviant. New Travellers in the countryside are often seen as violators of a rural idyll, and police employ guerrilla tactics to manage them (James, 2006). Asylum seekers and newly arrived immigrants will be unfamiliar with the criminal justice system of their host country, and so are likely to be reluctant to contact police. Women trafficked from other countries for sexual (or domestic) slavery are also unlikely to go to the authorities out of fear (Fawcett Society, 2004).

Implicit within this work is a critique of the legitimation of knowledge claims that arise from scientific approaches, as these are associated with the characteristics of objectivity and impartiality (Walklate, 2003) and therefore are seen as 'real knowledge'. Claims that come from other sources, like personal experience for example, are thereby delegitimised and consigned to the category of the 'Other'. Individual and community claims must therefore be legitimised, and one example of the ways in which claims are legitimated is when these are taken up by senior establishment figures such as by those in the judiciary or by Members of Parliament. An example that might be drawn upon here is that of the Stephen Lawrence Inquiry, which heard accounts from local monitoring groups, churches and activists regarding experiences of racist violence, the weakness of the police response and oppressive policing practices (Phillips and Bowling, 2002). It might be argued that the claims of these groups/individuals were legitimated only when Sir William Macpherson, a high-ranking judge who headed the Inquiry, published his report (the Macpherson Report) in which he concluded that the criminal justice system is perceived by minority ethnic communities as biased against them, and that moreover, the police are institutionally racist. So it would appear that individual and group collective accounts need to be legitimised so as to be taken seriously, in this instance when their claims are taken up by those who hold positions of power or respectability, who, it might be added, are often White. Indeed, Whiteness is a further theme highlighted in the *Reader*. Whiteness studies have emerged, setting out the changing contours of white power and privilege, suggesting that white people's experiences form the basis around which norms are created and around which minorities' lives are judged. Therefore, featured in the *Reader in Ethnicity and Crime* is a critical discussion of the category of 'whiteness' as consisting of what is considered to be 'normal', 'neutral' or 'common sense', serving to oppress Black and Asian, as well as other, minority groups.

Part 5 pursues the theme of reflection, applying this to the criminal justice context, focussing specifically on agencies of the criminal justice system. Given that in late modernity, identity is increasingly a source of meaning through which experience is mediated (Lyon, 1999), reflection within the criminal justice system involves the acknowledgement, monitoring, as well as engagement with, and minimisation of harms in relation to, social identities. With respect to 'race'/ethnicity, agencies of the criminal justice system routinely assemble information to help monitor disadvantage, so as to ensure that their policies and practices are not disadvantaging minority ethnic communities, as exemplified by publications arising from Section 95 of the Criminal Justice Act 1991, entitled 'Race and the Criminal Justice System: Statistics under Section 95 of the Criminal Justice Act 1991'. Institutional reflection can also involve the pursuit of a 'representative democracy' (Lash, 1994), whereby criminal justice institutions open themselves up to the communities that they serve, with the lay public engaging with, as well as critiquing, rival forms of expertise. Therefore, phrases such as 'community participation' and 'community engagement' are often found in government and criminal justice policy documents. Institutional reflection might also involve agencies of the criminal justice system reflecting upon the ways in which different racial and ethnic identities are represented in their workforces.

Summary

The above paragraphs set out the structure of the *Reader in Ethnicity and Crime*, providing some of the background context to the work that will be featured here. Clearly, many issues arise from within the study of 'race'/ethnicity and crime, spanning the areas of crime, victimisation and criminal justice. The following five Parts of the *Reader* will present between two and five extracts from suggested readings as well as listing suggested further reading material.

PART 1

'Race and crime', racial discrimination and criminal justice

The over-representation of Black people in prison, particularly those of African/ Caribbean heritage, has generated much research attention. Questions have been raised about Black people's offending rates and any discriminatory treatment that they might experience in the criminal justice process. Turning to the issue of crime rates within Black communities, Phillips and Bowling (2002) have stressed that any statistics generated by criminal justice agencies only provide partial information about the nature of offenders because individuals who have been diverted from the criminal justice system are not likely to feature in any statistics generated here. Indeed, the vast majority of people who commit crime are never processed by the criminal justice system. As a result, arrest statistics, or indeed any other kinds of criminal justice-generated statistics, do not provide conclusive evidence that Black individuals are prone to greater criminality than their white counterparts, even though individuals from Black communities might be over-represented in these statistics. Other sources of data in relation to criminality come from self-report delinquency studies, where individuals are shown a list of dishonest or criminal activities and are asked to indicate which activities they have engaged in. According to Phillips and Bowling (2002), self-report delinquency studies show rather mixed results. Although some studies indicate that Black and White young people have similar rates of offending, whilst Asian people report lower rates, other studies suggest that individuals from minority ethnic backgrounds might be more likely to conceal their offending, however, these studies have been criticised for their conceptual and methodological underpinnings (see Phillips and Bowling, 2002, for more discussion).

The discussion above hints at the difficulties of empirically measuring and establishing 'race' effects in relation to criminal justice. Police stop-and-search patterns have generated considerable discussion, as these patterns show an over-representation of particular racial groups, leading to questions being raised about whether police use racial profiling when deciding who to stop and search, or whether social and economic factors help account for any over-representation. The first suggested reading featured in the *Reader* is a study by Jefferson, Walker and Seneviratne (1992), who carried out a comparative study of African Caribbeans, Asians and Whites, aged 10–35, in areas of Leeds in relation to police arrest data, stop data and outcome of arrest. Their findings include that over the whole of Leeds, African Caribbean males (10–35-years-old) had a higher arrest rate than Whites, with Asians being close to Whites. However, when arrest rates were related to area of residence, the question of over-representation became more complicated. In blacker areas (classified as those areas where there were more than 10% non-White households) Whites had a higher arrest rate than African Caribbeans for the younger age group (11–21), and Asians had a lower rate than both African Caribbeans and Whites. For the older age group (22–35), differences were small. In whiter areas (classified as those areas where there were less than 10% of non-White households) African Carribeans had a higher arrest rate, with the Asian rate being much closer to that of Whites. The issue of the complexity of empirically establishing racial discrimination in relation to police stop and search is evident in contemporary research. Here studies have highlighted that when the ethnic composition of the available population (that is, available in public places to be stopped and searched), rather than the residential population, of a particular area is taken into account then there appears to be no general pattern of racial bias in stop-and-search tactics (Waddington, Stenson and Donn, 2004; Rowe, 2004). Moreover, Waddington et al. (2004) argue that ethnic patterns in stop and search should be compared with racial patterns as ethnicity includes cultural differences that are manifest through behaviour and lifestyle, potentially leading to different levels of exposure to police stop and search. The theme of complex local processes and their relation to 'race'/ethnicity is a theme that also features in other work, as evidenced by the studies of Taylor, Evans and Fraser (1996) and Webster (1997). Researchers have also focussed upon the issue of rural racism, where it has been argued that rural minority ethnic households have tended to feel isolated, both geographically and socially, and lack the kind of in-built formal and informal networks that numerically significant urban minority ethnic communities have developed. Rural minority ethnic groups may also feel marginalised from local village life due to their visible and cultural differences from the white 'norm' (Chakraborti and Garland, 2004).

Moving away from the issue of stop and search, the next suggested reading in this part is an article by Holdaway (1997). Holdaway (1997) pursues the theme of the difficulties associated with empirical analyses that attempt to measure racial discrimination, arguing that any statistical analysis is limited because the assumption that 'race' is a discrete phenomenon, being separate from wider social contexts, is questionable and so researchers engaged in empirical studies of race and crime should take more note of the theoretical assumptions underpinning their work. Indeed, nonracial factors such as area of residence, type of housing owned and so forth, should not be viewed straightforwardly as extra-racial variables, since these are linked to wider social, economic and political processes which themselves are linked to the racialised segregation of Black and Asian groups. For Holdaway (1997), there is a need to find a conceptual framework to analyse adequately the phenomenon of 'race' and to embed it within the institutional and organisational contexts within which it is articulated. Holdaway (1997) uses two case studies of Black and Asian police officers to highlight how processes of racialisation are perhaps more adequately researched through mundane processes that constitute organisational life: police occupational culture and the policies instigated by chief officers.

It might be argued that the inability to establish conclusively racial discrimination in the criminal justice system has led to people's perceptions of racism being an object of study and policy concern. For example, a 2005 study, carried out for the Department of Constitutional Affairs, has focussed on investigating whether, and the ways in which, members of minority ethnic communities who have appeared in the criminal courts perceived their treatment to be unfair or discriminatory and how this might have affected their trust or confidence in the criminal courts. The findings here include that between a quarter and a third of minority ethnic defendants believed that their treatment by the criminal courts had in some way been unfair (Shute, Hood and Seemungal, 2005: 129).

The third suggested reading in this part is Hood's (1992) examination of racial bias in the sentencing process, probably one of the most well-publicised and classic studies, which appears to provide conclusive evidence of racial discrimination. Hood (1992) examined the sentencing decisions of all minority ethnic men at five Crown Courts in the West Midlands and compared these with an equivalent sized sample of white men, consisting of 2884 cases. 433 minority ethnic and white women offenders were also focussed upon (Hood, 1992: 35). Hood's findings reveal that African Caribbeans made up 21% of those found guilty at Birmingham and 15% at Dudley Courts, although they accounted for less than 4% of the general male population in the age range 16–64. Asian males were convicted only slightly more often than would be expected in the population at large. Moreover, there were significant variations between the proportions of minority ethnic individuals sentenced to custody at different Crown Courts (Hood, 1992: 194). When factors such as the offender's previous criminal record or the seriousness of the offence were taken into account, Hood (1992: 199–200) found that the probability of a black male defendant being given custody was 5% higher than a white male, with the probability in one Crown Court being substantially larger, amounting to an increased probability of 23%. Furthermore, Asian defendants who had pleaded not guilty received longer sentences than white defendants. Hood's (1992) study, therefore, points towards there being racial discrimination in the sentencing process.

The paragraphs above help to illustrate the kinds of difficulties involved in empirically establishing racial discrimination, and the types of discussions that have been generated here. Whilst it might be argued that improvements in data collection and analysis are needed so as to better reflect and represent minority communities' experiences (Phillips and Bowling, 2003; Shute et al., 2005), this position fails to engage critically with, and to deconstruct, the dominance of Enlightenment values associated with modernity, which are deeply problematic when researching Black, as well as other minority communities, where 'minority community' might be viewed as constituting those individuals and groups that comprise the 'Other' – those that lie outside of, and challenge, taken-for-granted assumptions and norms that underpin Western culture (Taylor, 2004).

According to Garland (2002), modern criminology has been shaped significantly by what he calls the 'Lombrosian' project. For Garland (2002: 8), the Lombrosian project refers to 'a form of inquiry which aims to develop an explanatory science, based on the premise that criminals can somehow be differentiated from non-criminals'. Lombroso (1876) attempted to distinguish different types of humans and to classify them through biological and racial difference, constituting a form of criminal anthropology. For Lombroso (1876), the 'atavistic criminal' was a person biologically inferior, representing a human evolutionary throwback (White and Haines, 2000). Furthermore, the list of physical attributes that Lombroso (1876) identified as being characteristic of the criminal were based on dark skinned Sicilians, who were racially profiled and subject to social control and seen as the main source of criminality in Italy during this time (Agozino, 2003). Although in Britain, psychiatric and medico-legal frameworks influenced early criminological work (these being distinctly different from a Lombrosian perspective), these nonetheless consisted of the adoption of a scientific approach to the study of criminality (Garland, 2002). Indeed, Morrison (1995) highlights how rationality and scientific study are key characteristics of criminology.

It might be argued that the application, and predominance, of a (social) scientific approach to 'race' is problematic when viewed from a perspective that actively engages with, and acknowledges, the harms caused under the guise of Enlightenment philosophy and the so-called 'civilising' process of modernity. Modernity has been linked to the creation of racial hierarchies which have helped to construct, and to dehumanise, racial 'Others'. For Bauman (1989), modernity helped to create the conditions for the Holocaust. The classification of Jewish peoples as racial 'Others', helped create the conditions in which millions of individuals were murdered. According to Phillips and Bowling (2002; 2007), although slavery ended in Britain in 1807 and in the US in 1833, the legacy of racist Enlightenment theories and approaches lived on through imperialism and colonial practices as constituted within Asia, Africa and the West Indies, and indeed stretching to white working-class groups in Ireland and England.

Not only have Black communities and other 'racial minorities' historically occupied a subordinate status, the 'Other', in relation to Whiteness within discourses linked to Enlightenment and the Age of Reason, but moreover, as vividly portrayed by Gilroy (1993) in the *Black Atlantic*, individuals belonging to the African Diaspora have critiqued and rejected modernity and have used their own discourses from which to practise resistance, and from which to explain and account for their actions. According to Gilroy (1993: 68), a 'discourse of black spirituality' has been used to legitimise and choose death over slavery, which would appear to be at odds with logic and reason characteristic of Western thinking in modernity. The final suggested reading in this part consists of a chapter by Agozino (2003), which looks at European theories of judicial process. Here, Agozino highlights that classicism emerged at the height of the slave trade; however, although it challenged the arbitrary nature of punishment in medieval Europe, its principals and insights were not used to challenge the slave trade. Moreover, although the Enlightenment challenged the privilege of divine right, it denied that those colonised possessed the moral capabilities to reason about what is wrong and what is just. For Agozino (2003: 9), 'European theories of social control used the colonised for laboratory experimentation before being reflected back to internal colonies in Europe'.

Suggested essays

Jefferson, T., Walker, M. and Seneviratne, M. (1992) 'Ethnic Minorities, Crime and Criminal Justice: a study in a provincial city' in D. Downes (ed.) *Unravelling Criminal Justice*. London: Macmillan, pp. 138–164.

Holdaway, S. (1997) 'Some Recent Approaches to the Study of Race in Criminological Research' *British Journal of Criminology* Vol. 37 (3): 383–400.

Hood, R. (1992) Chapter 12, 'Discrimination in the Courts?' in *Race and Sentencing*. Oxford: Clarendon Press, pp. 179–192.

Agozino, B. (2003) 'The Enlightenment and Euro-American Theories of the Judicial Process' *Counter-Colonial Criminology: a critique of imperialist reason*. London: Pluto Press, pp. 13–39.

Further reading

Bowling, B. and Phillips, C. (2002) *Racism, Crime and Justice*. Harlow: Longman.

Eze, E. (1997) *Race and the Enlightenment: a Reader*. Oxford: Blackwell.

Fitzgerald, M. (1993) 'Racism: establishing the phenomenon' in D. Cook and B. Hudson (eds) *Racism & Criminology*. London: Sage, pp. 45–63.

Gilroy, P. (1993) Chapter 2, 'Masters, Mistresses, Slaves and the Antinomies of Modernity' *The Black Atlantic: modernity and double consciousness*. London: Verso, pp. 41–71.

Kalunta-Crumpton, A. (1999) *Race and Drug Trials*. Aldershot: Avebury.

Shute, S., Hood, R. and Seemungal, F. (2005) *A Fair Hearing? ethnic minorities in the criminal courts*. Devon: Willan Publishing.

1

Ethnic minorities, crime and criminal justice: a study in a provincial city
by Tony Jefferson, Monica Walker and
Mary Seneviratne

Introduction

The issues posed by race and criminal justice in Britain are contentious, none
more so than the longstanding conflict between the police and black people.
Though this achieved its most dramatic exemplification in the riots of the
1980s, the warning signs had long been in place. Much has been written
about the issue, and who, or what, is to blame. Factors such as the 'lawlessness of black youth', 'deprivation' and 'police racism' are just the three most
prominent ascribed causes in a wide-ranging debate (cf. Benyon, 1986). Less
dramatically, other moments in the criminal justice process – the decision to
caution or to charge, for example – have also come under critical scrutiny.

The truth is, however, that the resulting picture remains contradictory
in parts, blurred or missing in others and, perhaps in consequence, highly
contested. Reiner (1985), for example, has drawn attention to the way obser-
vationally based findings contradict the 'discriminatory pattern [of policing]
suggested by the quantitative work' (p. 171); and Walker (1987) to the latter's
methodological problems. The result is that you can find similar evidence
(for example, that Blacks are more likely than Whites to be stopped, arrested,
and so on) given different interpretations. Our study is an attempt to clarify
matters.

In making the decision to do a comparative study of Afro-Caribbeans
(hereinafter called Blacks), Asians (from the Indian sub-continent) and
Whites, we were following a common methodological approach designed to
uncover any differences in treatment, since these are one possible indicator of
discrimination. Within this broad strategy, we intended to tackle five main
problems raised by studies of this sort. The first concerned the issue of 'over-
representation': were Blacks over-represented (in relation to their numbers)
in any part of the statistics produced by the Criminal Justice System? The
second was that of interpretation – if so, why? (cf. Reiner, 1989).

The Metropolitan Police (MPD) has consistently found, over many years, Black over-representation in London's arrest figures. In 1986, for example, 17 per cent of those arrested were black though they constituted only 5 per cent of the general population (Home Office, 1989). Moreover, Stevens and Willis (1979) have shown this over-representation applies to all age and offence groups. However, the meaning of this over-representation was unclear since no controls for the social and economic factors which might explain it had been made. We felt this could be rectified by comparing arrest rates of those living in the same (small) areas which broadly share similar social and economic environments. This would require recording the race of each person arrested and the enumeration district in which he lived, and then comparing rates within areas.

As for the outcome of arrest in terms of cautions, convictions and sentences, the picture was unclear. First, there was little data on those released without prosecution or acquitted. Secondly, the sentencing data, which suggested that Blacks and Whites with similar offences and criminal records have the same chance of a custodial sentence (see, for example, Mair, 1986) seemed confusing when set against the over-representation of black people in custody (see, for example, Home Office, 1986). Thirdly, the cautioning data was similarly confusing, with Landau's finding in London of black juveniles being less likely to be cautioned (see, for example, Landau and Nathan, 1983) contradicted by the work of Farrington and Bennett (1981), who found no racially based differences in cautioning rates. Once again there were methodological problems, with class and factors such as whether parents were prepared to accept the caution inadequately considered.

Some of these difficulties, we felt, might stem from the tendency to focus only on a particular, isolated moment of the criminal justice process. We decided to tackle this by following through (statistically) our sample from arrest to sentence, and by supplementing this with observations conducted at key decision-making sites (for example, cautioning/sentencing) in the process, and interviews with relevant participants.

Fourthly, there was the issue of 'London bias'. Since all the published arrest data, and much of the other, referred to London, this did pose the question of the provincial experience. We decided, in consequence, to focus upon Leeds as a sort of check on the generalisability of the London experience.

Finally, there was the general problem of comparability. In 1983, the Policy Studies Institute (PSI) published its survey of the general population of London (Smith, 1983). One of the issues it raised was the relationship between experiences of the police and attitudes towards them. Though these were found to be correlated, it was also found that experiences of being stopped could not by themselves account for the more hostile attitudes of black youth (Smith, 1986). We wanted to see if similar results would emerge in the provinces, and whether controlling for area, as did Tuck and Southgate (1981) in their Moss Side, Manchester, survey, would make any difference.

In other surveys the samples have been representative of those living in large areas (populations of over 100,000) so that many of the white sample came from areas containing more in the higher social classes. The comparison with non-whites has been therefore between those living, in the main, in different circumstances.

In order to obtain more meaningful comparisons our survey concentrated on black, Asian and white males living in the areas of Leeds where most of the non-white people live. These are the areas which have more than 10 per cent of the population non-white, and contain about 58 per cent of the Blacks in Leeds, 55 per cent of the Asians, but only 6 per cent of the Whites. This enabled us to compare the experiences of the police of those living in the same small areas and to relate these to attitudes. The sample was clearly not representative, particularly of Whites in Leeds. However, comparisons were between groups living in similar circumstances. In every part of our research we confined ourselves to the group most involved in the criminal justice system, namely, males aged 10 to 35.

In the following sections we describe the methodology and results of the five main aspects of our research. These are (1) arrest data, (2) stop data, (3) outcome of arrest, (4) observation and interviews, (5) survey. In the main, only statistically significant results will be mentioned. These are followed by a summary and our overall conclusions, the latter discussed in the light of the five problems identified above.

Arrest rates

With the co-operation of the West Yorkshire Police we obtained the race (as perceived by the police), sex, age, offence and address of every person stopped or arrested in Leeds for six months in 1987.

To compare arrest rates within areas we recorded the enumeration district (e.d. – about 150 households) where each person arrested lived, and the base population of each race in each e.d. The best estimates we could get of the latter were from special tabulations from the 1981 census which gave us the numbers where the head of household was born in the Caribbean or Africa (expected to be black), the Indian sub-continent (expected to be of 'Asian' appearance) or elsewhere. The age groups available were 5–15 and 16–29 in 1981. We thought this would provide reasonable estimates of those aged 11–21 and 22–35 in 1987. Since many of the numbers involved were very small or zero, it was necessary, in carrying out the analysis, to group together e.d.s and, in many of the areas not near the centre of the city, to use whole wards in order to obtain enough non-whites. (For details of the problem and assumptions involved, see Walker, 1992).[1]

An initial examination showed that Blacks were over-represented, with an arrest rate of 7 per cent as against only 3 per cent of the whole population (not nearly so large a difference as in London, however, with 17 per cent as against 5 per cent). Asians were roughly proportionately represented, as in London, and Whites slightly under-represented. Blacks and Asians tended to have higher proportions arrested for violence and theft, whereas Whites had more for burglary and damage (for full details, see Walker *et al.*, 1990).

A breakdown by age group showed a similar picture, with Blacks having a higher rate than Whites in both age groups. As would be expected, rates are higher for the younger group (see Table 1.1).

In our analysis controlling for areas, we classified all e.d.s according to whether they contained less or more than 10 per cent non-white households.[2] For convenience these are called 'whiter' or 'blacker' areas, and the arrest rates for the two groups are given by age and race in Table 1.2. In the blacker areas we found Whites had higher rates than Blacks and Asians, in the younger age group, but in the whiter areas Blacks had a higher rate than Whites in both age groups. (These differences were statistically significant.)

A more detailed analysis of the black and white rates (summarised in Table 1.3) revealed that the black rate decreased with increasing 'blackness' whereas the white rate increased. It was also found that the white rate was significantly correlated with the unemployment rate and the percentage of

Table 1.1 Race distributions and arrest rates by age group (all words together)

	Age 11–21				Age 22–35			
	Black	Asian	White	N = 100%	Black	Asian	White	N = 100%
Population (%)	3.5	5.3	91.2	37,165	3.1	3.7	93.3	51,245
Persons arrested (%)	5.7	3.4	90.8	2,669	6.0	3.7	90.3	1,590
Rates (no. arrests per 100 pop.)	11.7	4.7	7.2	7.2	6.3	3.1	3.0	3.1

Table 1.2 Arrest rates[a] by age group and area type

Ratio[b]	Age 11–21				Age 22–35				All males: 11–35	
	Black	Asian	White	All	Black	Asian	White	All	Population	%
<10%	15.0	5.0	6.9	7.0	8.9	3.2	2.9	3.0	79,235	90
>10%	8.9	4.4	13.3	9.9	4.4	2.4	3.9	3.7	9175	10
All areas	11.7	4.7	7.2	7.2	6.3	3.1	3.0	3.1	88,410	100

Notes:
[a] Rate = (total number arrested in all relevant areas/total estimated population in these areas) × 100.
[b] Ratio = (all black households + all Asian households)/all households.

Table 1.3 Arrest rates[a] related to census variables (Blacks and Whites)

	Arrest rates				Census data					
	Age 11–21		Age 22–35		% Privately rented		% Unemployed		No. of households	
Ratio[b]	Black	White	Black	White	Black	White	Black	White	Black	White
<2%	16.5	5.4	6.1	2.4	5	4	7	18	420	90,900
2–10%	11.1	8.3	9.0	3.2	15	13	25	19	1,055	76,820
10–33%	9.5	12.6	4.1	3.6	10	27	21	27	500	4460
>33%	7.8	14.4	4.6	7.3	3	26	41	39	915	1340
All areas	11.7	7.2	6.3	3.0	9	9	24	19	2,890	173,520

Notes:
[a] Rate = (total number arrested in all relevant areas/total estimated population in these areas)
      × 100.
[b] Ratio = (all black households + all Asian households)/all households.

privately rented households of Whites in the area, and this was not the case
for Blacks. For Asians none of these variables was significant. Whites had significantly more in privately rented accommodation (one indication of a more
transient population) than the Blacks, and the correlation with the arrest rate
is in keeping with an earlier finding in Sheffield (Baldwin and Bottoms,
1976). So, for Whites there was a fairly comprehensible relationship between
certain indices of poverty and deprivation and the arrest rate. However, since
this was not the case for Blacks, another explanation for these arrest rates is
needed. (Data on social class from the census were not sufficiently accurate
to be useful, as they were based on a 10 per cent sample.)

There is no doubt that the high black rates in the whiter areas are difficult
to explain, but it is worth pointing out that these are very large areas (mainly
wards with over 6000 households). In the wards with less than 2 per cent
non-white the number of blacks was small and only 49 Blacks were arrested.
This means that any misperception of race by the police or miscoding disproportionately amplifies percentage differences. Moreover, if there has been
even a small change in the black population since the 1981 census data on
which our estimates are based, this too will have had a disproportionate effect
on our figures. However, as we saw earlier (note 1) the changes we know of
suggest only a higher black arrest rate. Having said that, a personal investigation by the researchers into the areas where those arrested lived revealed
that both white and black arrestees in the whiter areas lived in poor-quality
housing in small groups in large 'white' wards.

What this analysis shows is that it is necessary to examine areas of residence in detail before any conclusion can be drawn either about a tendency
of the police to discriminate against black people or about black people being
more 'criminal'. However, explanations of the differences found remain to be

explored. The characteristics of the three races are different in some respects even though they live in the same small areas. The survey (see below) in the blacker areas confirmed that more white people lived in privately rented accommodation and showed that they had lived in the area a shorter time. But they also appeared to have fewer in social classes 4 and 5 than the blacks, and had higher educational attainments. This was the case even when students were excluded from the analysis. These demographic characteristics make the higher white arrest rate in the blacker areas even more striking.

It has to be remembered that the arrest data reflect all the factors affecting the perception and reporting of offences by the public, and the police decision-making involved – factors that for many years were regarded as making any interpretation of 'official' statistics dubious. In the present context, for example, an explanation of the comparatively low black arrest rate in the blacker areas could, perhaps, be ascribed to the possibility that many offences are intra-racial and Blacks may be more reluctant to report them to the police. This latter tendency emerged from our survey, which revealed that whilst Blacks had a slightly lower victimisation rate than Whites, they also reported a lower proportion. It could also be that the police are more reluctant to record intra-racial offences, though we have no evidence on this point.

Stop and search

While arrests by the police arise, in the main, as a result of the reporting of offences by the public, 'stop and search' is entirely due to police proactive behaviour.

The Police and Criminal Evidence Act (PACE, 1984) requires a record to be made of every compulsory stop and search carried out; in West Yorkshire the numbers appear fairly small. For example, while in London about 7.6 'stops' (persons and vehicles stopped and searched) were made per 1000 population, the corresponding figure in West Yorkshire was about 0.8 (1987 data). This suggests one significant difference between London and a provincial force.

We obtained details of all stops (323) recorded in the six sub-divisions of Leeds in the same six-month period as for arrests. There were cases involving 303 males where the race was recorded, 18 of whom were black, 14 Asian and 271 white. Over half the stops were in one police sub-division (Chapeltown), which has a high non-white population, and nearly two-thirds involved a search for drugs. About a quarter of those stopped were arrested (for all races) and these accounted for about 1 per cent of all arrests.

Overall, the analysis in relation to residence revealed that blacks were over-represented in the whole city (blacks 7 per cent; Asians 3 per cent; whites 90 per cent), to about the same extent as for arrests. Further analysis also showed a similar pattern. The black stop rate, for all ages and areas together, like the arrest rate, was about double the white rate. Young

Table 1.4 Stop and search rates[a] (males)

Ratio[b]	Age 11–21			Age 22–35			All		
	Black	Asian	White	Black	Asian	White	Black	Asian	White
<10%	8.1	3.6	3.5	4.3	2.5	1.6	6.0	3.0	2.2
>10%	4.4	0	9.9	2.5	0.9	6.5	3.3	0.5	7.6
All	6.1	1.6	2.6	3.3	1.6	1.8	4.6	1.6	2.1

Notes:
[a] Rate = (total no. stopped and searched in relevant areas)/(no. resident in areas) × 1000.
[b] Ratio = (all blacks households + all Asian households)/all households.

males had a higher stop rate than older males; and for both age groups in the 'blacker' areas whites had a higher rate than blacks and Asians, whilst in the 'whiter' areas blacks had a higher rate than whites and Asians (see Table 1.4).

The results of our survey, in the blacker areas, are described later but it is worth pointing out the correspondence between both sets of data (see Table 1.7). Though we asked for the (higher) number of car and street stops (not only searches) in the previous 12 months, none the less differences between races were of the same order.

Outcome of arrest

We intended to follow up all non-Whites and a sample of Whites (total about 1500) arrested. This involved inspection of returned police files. Unfortunately, only about half had been returned during the time available for inspection. As the files of cases where there was no further action (NFA) and for those cautioned would usually be returned quickly, we think we have good estimates of these. We decided it was important, however, also to obtain accurate estimates of the numbers (and outcome) of those dealt with in the Crown Court, and we were able to obtain this data from the Probation Service. The data of the remaining cases – just over one-third of all adults – are those tried in the magistrates' courts.

Our analysis of juvenile files revealed that on average about 8 per cent had 'no further action' with no difference between races. After removing them, however, it was found that a higher proportion of Asians – 72 per cent – were cautioned for all offence groups (see Table 1.5). Although these were juveniles, as many as 14 per cent of Blacks were tried in the Crown Court, with Asians and Whites having significantly less at 7 per cent – which still seems high (see Table 1.5). A detailed examination of the records showed that six of the 12 Blacks were probably arrested in one incident, and some of these were charged with robbery and public-order offences. In this and the

Table 1.5 Outcome of arrest (juveniles)

	Black	Asian	White
Intended sample	95	56	280
% no further action	9	4	8
Total dealt with	86	54	261
Of these:			
% cautioned	31	72	41
% Magistrates' Court trial	54	20	52
[followed up]	[11]	[9]	[19]
[not followed up][a]	[43]	[11]	[33]
% Crown Court trial	14	7	7

Note:
[a] These figures are estimates and probably include a few cautioned or having no further action whose files had not been returned by July 1988 (see text).

other cases it was not clear if there was a co-defendant aged 17 or over which would justify trial in the Crown Court.

The pattern for adults was not dissimilar (see Table 1.6). In this case Asians had significantly more (at 15 per cent) with 'no further action', though the cautioning rates of the remainder (on average 6 per cent) did not differ between races. (This figure was considerably lower than that for the whole of West Yorkshire, which was 15 per cent.) Once again, as for juveniles, significantly more Blacks were tried in the Crown Court. These

Table 1.6 Outcome of arrests (adults)

	Black	Asian	White
Intended sample	255	126	756
% no further action	7	15	9
Total dealt with	237	107	687
Of these:			
% cautioned	4	5	7
% Magistrates' Court trial	57	66	62
[followed up]	[21]	[30]	[23]
[not followed up][a]	[36]	[36]	[39]
% Crown Court trial	39	29	31
% acquittal rate (all courts)[b]	12	6	4

Notes:
[a] These figures are estimates and probably include a few cautioned or having no further action whose files had not been returned by July 1988 (see text).
[b] Owing to the incomplete follow up of magistrates' court cases these figures may be inaccurate (and probably under-estimates).

findings are consistent with that of a study of the London courts (Walker, 1988, 1989).

This research did not undertake a sentencing study because necessary details (for example, number of charges, offences taken into consideration, and so on) were not incorporated. So only a selective overview will be given.

Since only 8 black, 5 Asian and 43 white juveniles were sentenced in the magistrates' courts, a detailed analysis was not carried out. Altogether 19 (or 34 per cent) had a custodial sentence; the offences sentenced covered the whole range, with theft predominating. Of the 30 sentenced in the Crown Court just half the Blacks and Whites received custody, and three of the four Asians.

For adults in the magistrates' courts, data on previous convictions were available. We found that Blacks and Whites averaged approximately three whereas Asians averaged under one. There were corresponding differences in the proportions with no previous convictions. However, in the Crown Court proportionately more Blacks than Whites had no previous convictions. A regression analysis of sentences, taking into account offence type and previous convictions, found that the type of sentence for the three groups did not differ significantly in either court, nor did the length of custodial sentences.

Overall the proportions given custodial sentences in the Crown Court did not differ significantly and averaged 60 per cent. It was mentioned earlier that for adults (as well as juveniles) a greater proportion of Blacks were tried in the Crown Court. This was the case for each main offence group. Offences were examined in detail to see if these would explain this difference. Only a small percentage (7.5 per cent) were indictable-only and had to be tried in the Crown Court. This was the same for each race. Triable-either-way offences are either tried in the Crown Court because magistrates feel they are too serious to try or because the defendants elect for jury trial. However, we found no differences between races, with 25 per cent of defendants electing for Crown Court trial and 75 per cent being sent by magistrates.

It seems, then, that there is no obvious reason why there are proportionately more Blacks tried in the Crown Court, though there are slightly more indictable-only, slightly more where magistrates decide and slightly more where the defendant so chooses. But the fact that more black defendants are tried in the Crown Court, where the chances of a custodial sentence are higher, can help to explain the increasing over-representation of black people in prison. The percentages receiving immediate custody in the Crown Court were not significantly different and were similar to a national figure of 52 per cent. In the magistrates' courts the national figure (1987) for indictable offences given custody was 7 per cent – a figure slightly higher than ours.

Acquittal rates in our study do not appear to be consistent with London figures, particularly in the Crown Court. At 12 per cent for Blacks in both the magistrates' courts and the Crown Court, this was significantly higher than Asians and Whites in both the magistrates' courts (where they averaged

5 per cent) and in the Crown Court (3 per cent). In London, by contrast, in both courts Blacks had only slightly more acquitted (by about 1 per cent). The magistrates' courts figures are similar to those for London (7 per cent; Walker, 1989), but the Crown Court figure for London is far higher than the Leeds figures, being nearer to 25 per cent. Once again, these differences may be pointing to significant regional differences.

Observations and interviews

Analysing statistical data reveals certain facts requiring explanation – in our case, the differences found between the races in arrest rates, juvenile cautioning rates, adult 'NFAs', acquittal rates and Crown Court trials. Searching for possible explanations may involve collecting and analysing new statistical data or utilising other forms of data, such as observations and interviews. During this aspect of the research, we were able to observe 135 cases of non-white and matched white defendants in court, and to interview ten of the solicitors involved who had some dealings with non-white clients. We observed a Case Referral Panel (which decides on the cautioning of juveniles) in action, and also interviewed panel members. The hope was that this supplementary data might help to explain some of our statistical findings, such as why Asian juveniles were more likely to be cautioned and Blacks more likely to go to Crown Court and to be acquitted.

We observed the Chapeltown Panel in action on four occasions, and witnessed 23 cases being discussed; 12 blacks, 8 whites and 3 Asians. Nothing in our observations, nor in the subsequent interviews, revealed any evidence of racial bias in the decision to prosecute or caution. Panel members were certainly aware of the problem of racism and thought it might be operating elsewhere in the criminal justice system. But all felt that their own Panel did not discriminate, and our own observations – limited though they were – support that.

A similar finding emerged from our court room observations and follow-up interviews. We observed 135 cases (about half being non-white, mainly black) in the magistrates' courts; very few (of any race) involved contested trials. The overall impression was that the bureaucratic routine predominated; that is, that cases proceeded (usually after one or several adjournments) according to an invariant formula and produced predictable outcomes. 'Interruptions' to this bureaucratic routine took the form of comparatively harsh or comparatively lenient benches (harshness or lenience being a subjective impression of the observers when judged against the mundane 'norm'). For our purposes, the important point was that such 'interruptions' to the routine happened regardless of race; a harsh bench remained harsh for the duration of its sitting whoever happened to be in front of it – and the same was true of lenient benches.

The ten solicitors (one Asian) interviewed did not say anything to disturb these impressions substantially. Some individuals thought the courts 'bent over backwards' to be fair to racial minorities, others that Blacks are more likely to plead 'not guilty' – both of which, if true, point towards an explanation of the higher black acquittal rate. We shall return to this question later, in our concluding discussion. But, overall, the feeling was that there was no systematic bias in the courts, even though the sample thought black clients tended to feel they were being discriminated against – a viewpoint which connects with some of our survey findings, to which we now turn.

The survey

The aim of the survey was to investigate and compare the experiences of the police of Blacks, Asians and Whites, and to relate this to their attitudes to the police and to crime in their areas. The main survey was of males aged 16–35 but we included a sample of boys aged 10–15 for comparative purposes.

To make our comparisons more meaningful we confined our sample to those living in areas (enumeration districts) with 10 per cent or more non-White households, based again on the 1981 census. We achieved interviews with 171 black, 199 Asian and 271 white adults, and 64 black, 117 Asian and 44 white boys.[3]

It should be borne in mind that the respondents cannot be regarded as representative of Blacks, Asians and Whites in the whole of Leeds, since the areas sampled contained 58 per cent of Blacks in the city and 55 per cent of Asians but only 6 per cent of Whites. However, comparisons between races are between those living in the same small areas and differences which exist therefore are more likely to be due to race *per se* than to differences in environment. Because of our sampling design we would expect our adults to be different from those of other surveys, mainly in London, which have sampled very large areas. This obviously affects the usefulness of making other than very general comparisons with other surveys.

We shall anticipate the detailed results which follow by drawing attention to the finding that *in these areas* Blacks and Whites were similar in many respects in their experiences of the police, but were consistently different from Asians. However, Blacks tended to disapprove of the police more than Whites, and Asians were much more approving. The overall impression is that attitudes to the police of both the Blacks and Whites tended to be negative or hostile. As far as the boys were concerned, although many of the differences were not statistically significant, there were indications that responses and differences between races were similar to the adults'.

Experiences of the police

There were two main types of experience of the police, respondent-initiated – such as phone calls to the police asking for help or reporting a crime – and police-initiated, where police suspected the respondent of an offence, for example. We shall examine the latter, more important group first.

Four types of police-initiated contacts were investigated: persons being stopped in a vehicle; persons being stopped when on foot (in the street); house searches; and arrests. People were asked about whether any of the first three events had occurred in the last 12 months, and about arrests in the last five years. For any of these events there was a follow-up questionnaire.

It was found that Whites (50 per cent) had significantly more who had had at least one type of contact than both Blacks (35 per cent) and Asians (28 per cent). The total number of such contacts was also higher for Whites. We also looked at the number of *different* types of contact ('STOPTYPES', ranging from 0 to 4) and found Whites had significantly more than Blacks who, in turn, had significantly more than Asians (see Table 1.7).

These results differ considerably from those of the Policy Studies Institute which found that Blacks were stopped considerably more often than Whites (Smith, 1983). This could be because the study was for the whole of London, while ours was only in the 'blacker' areas of Leeds, containing the more deprived Whites. Moreover, the London study was carried out before PACE (1984) with its stricter requirements for recording stops. However, our results clearly do not show discriminatory stopping of Blacks.

The pattern for those initiating a contact with the police, by phone or otherwise, showed surprising similarity. The proportions contacting the police in the last 12 months were: Blacks 65 per cent, Asians 50 per cent and Whites 71 per cent. Again Asians had significantly less than Blacks and Whites (who did not differ). Full details are given in Table 1.8 where the percentages saying they were 'satisfied' with the contact are also given. Almost two-thirds in each category for each race said they were, except for 'approaches in the street' where less than half were satisfied.

Also given in Table 1.8 are the proportions who had been victims of offences and the proportions of those who had reported them to the police.

Table 1.7 Contact with the police (police-initiated)

% experiencing one or more	Black	Asian	White
Car stop (one year)	21	17	24
Street stop (one year)	8	6	16
House search (one year)	5	1	4
Arrests (5 years)	14	6	20
Any of these	35	28	50
Mean number of stops, etc.	1.15	0.36	1.34
Number of different sorts of stops, etc. (0–4) (STOPTYPES)	0.50	0.30	0.65

Table 1.8 Contact with police (respondent-initiated)

	Contacting police			Satisfied or v. satisfied (% of those contacting)		
	Black	Asian	White	Black	Asian	White
% made 999 calls	12	22	9	67	53	76
% made other phone calls	13	19	24	74	68	67
% called in at police station	26	24	28	67	64	69
% approached police in street	14	6	19	35	44	42
% contacted police any form	65	50	71			
Contacts (mean number)	1.4	2.7	2.5			
% of these ever dissatisfied	15	24	18			
% of these ever satisfied	45	53	58			
Satisfactory contacts (mean)	.38	.33	.55			
% victims of offence	23	37	42			
% of victims who reported to police	38	60	46			
% overall reporting victimisation	9	22	19			

(These would, in the main, be included in the earlier contacts.) Significantly more Asians than Blacks reported the offences, with Whites in between. Overall the proportion of all Blacks who reported being victims of offences was only 9 per cent, less than Whites (19 per cent) and Asians (22 per cent). In answer to other questions it was found that significantly fewer Asians had been annoyed with police or wanted to complain about them. Blacks did not differ from Whites in this respect.

In summary, Asians had fewer contacts of any type with the police and Whites more police-initiated ones, but also more satisfactory self-initiated ones. Blacks were less willing to report offences.

Attitudes to the police

There were several aspects of attitude to the police which were explored and we found consistently that Asians had a more favourable attitude than Blacks but were, in some responses, similar to Whites. On the other hand, in comparing Blacks and Whites, in some aspects Blacks had a less favourable attitude, while in others they were much the same.

Twenty-five per cent of Blacks thought there were too many police in their area – significantly more than Asians and Whites, who averaged 7 per cent. On the other hand, the percentages saying 'not enough' all differed significantly (Blacks 28 per cent, Asians 61 per cent and Whites 47 per cent).

We presented a set of statements about the police, such as: 'the police try to help the community'; 'the majority of police in Leeds do a good job'; 'there are quite a lot of dishonest policemen in Leeds', and asked respondents if they broadly agreed or disagreed. From this we obtained a score we called 'disapproval'. On the score, based on five items,[4] all the races differed significantly, Blacks being most disapproving and Asians least.

Several questions were asked about police malpractice (these items being the same as those of the Policy Studies Institute survey). Asked if some groups of people were particularly likely to be stopped by the police, about two-thirds of Blacks and Whites thought so, but only slightly over one-third of Asians. When asked which groups, two-thirds or more of these in each race said 'non-Whites' (Blacks 75 per cent; Asians 72 per cent; Whites 66 per cent). Similar results were obtained for answers to 'Are all people treated fairly and equally?', with even more (Blacks 80 per cent; Asians 76 per cent; Whites 74 per cent) of those answering 'no' to the question identifying 'non-Whites'.

Four other questions asked about perception of the police: whether they used pressure in questioning people; whether police took accurate records of evidence; whether they used unnecessary violence; and whether they made up evidence. On average just over half of both Blacks and Whites thought these types of malpractice occurred, but only a quarter of Asians. An overall score was obtained from these six items and was called 'perception of police': the score for Blacks and Whites was identical (3.5) and significantly higher than that for Asians (1.7).

Our last main item investigating attitude to the police concerned whether people thought they would report offences they had witnessed, help identify the culprit and give evidence in court, three such hypothetical incidents being described. We called this 'co-operation'. The incidents were a robbery, vandalism and a traffic accident. For the robbery, significantly fewer Blacks said they would co-operate, at each stage, than Asians and Whites, who did not differ, and this was the case for each incident. Co-operation was consistently high for the traffic accident and lowest for the vandalism item. Only 48 per cent of Blacks would report the latter to the police, with 81 per cent of Asians and 66 per cent of Whites. Except on this item, Asians and Whites tended to have similar (and high) proportions willing to co-operate. Their overall scores did not differ significantly and were higher than that for Blacks. Full details are given in Table 1.9.

We have pointed out that the three race groups have had different experiences of the police, so we investigated whether the several measures of attitude to the police were correlated with experiences. We found the best measure of police-initiated experiences was the number of different types of experience (called STOPTYPES) which varied from 0 to 4. The correlations were almost all significant – the greater the number of STOPTYPES, the more unfavourable the attitude. This is illustrated in Table 1.10. It can be seen that the attitude scores increase steadily for each race group for disapproval and perception (unfavourable) and decrease for co-operation, as the number

Table 1.9 Co-operation with police (% yes)

	Black	Asian	White
If you saw:			
someone knock a man down and take his wallet would you			
(a) tell police	75	96	92
(b) help identify culprit	64	90	87
(c) give evidence in court	51	80	83
youths smashing a bus shelter would you			
(a) tell police	48	81	66
(b) help identify culprit	41	74	61
(c) give evidence in court	35	65	53
somebody badly hurt in a traffic accident would you			
(a) tell police	95	99	98
(b) help identify culprit	85	94	96
(c) give evidence in court	73	86	93
Total score (0–9)			
co-operation	5.4	7.5	7.1
definite non-co-operation	1.1	0.6	0.6

of STOPTYPES increases. However, it is interesting that for each line showing the number of STOPTYPES, differences between races are maintained. In particular, even when people have not been stopped at all, Blacks have higher 'disapproval' scores than Whites, who are higher than Asians; Blacks and Whites have a worse perception of police malpractice than Asians, and Blacks are less co-operative than Asians and Whites. It is clear that these attitudes and their differences cannot be 'explained' simply by whether or not the police had stopped them – indeed it would be surprising if they could.

A more detailed examination of the responses has been carried out using the follow-up questionnaires, and any expression of annoyance and dissatisfaction about police behaviour was scored. It was found that this was more highly correlated with the attitude scores than simply the number of stops and STOPTYPES, except for Asians, where the actual number of stops and so on was more significant. For Blacks and Whites, therefore, it wasn't so much the fact of being stopped that annoyed them as the way the police dealt with this – not everyone was dissatisfied who had been stopped. However, differences in the scores of disapproval and co-operation between Blacks and Whites were still significant, even controlling for these measures of dissatisfaction.

Examination of the details of why people had been annoyed by the police or wanted to complain revealed that of both Blacks and Whites a few had had very unpleasant experiences that could not be dismissed as minor insults. Very few of the unpleasant experiences of Blacks seemed to be related overtly to racism. Because of this it was interesting to note, as mentioned earlier, that

Table 1.10 Score related to number of types of stops, etc.

No. of	% Distribution (STOPTYPES)			Disapproval score			Perception score			Co-operation score		
	Black	Asian	White	Black	Asian	White	Black	Asian	White	Black	Asian	White
0	65	75	50	17.6	15.2	16.0	3.1	1.5	3.2	5.6	7.7	7.2
1	25	21	38	18.1	16.7	16.6	4.0	2.3	3.6	5.9	7.2	7.3
2 or more	11	4	13	19.9	17.6	17.7	4.8	3.4	3.9	2.9	5.0	6.3
N = 100%	171	199	271									
Correlation				0.31	0.31	0.20	0.19	0.31	(NS)	-0.22	-0.32	-0.18
Mean All	0.50	0.30	0.65	18.0	15.6	16.5	3.5	1.5	3.5	5.4	7.5	7.1

nearly as many Whites as Blacks (on average about 45 per cent and 53 per cent respectively) thought the police discriminated against non-Whites.

Demographic characteristics and 'way of life'

We asked respondents about their age, occupation, how long they lived in the area, whether they lived in owner-occupied accommodation or whether it was rented (council or private). We also asked about their 'way of life', whether they had gone out each evening of the previous week, their transport, their destination and time of return. Many of these factors differed between race groups, and some were significantly correlated (but never highly) with the factors discussed earlier.

Asians went out on fewer evenings than Blacks and Whites (1.5, 2.6, 2.9 respectively), were home earlier (80 per cent by midnight, but only 48 per cent of Blacks and 57 per cent of Whites), tended to use cars and to visit friends or relatives (while Whites tended to have gone to pubs). Only for Whites did we find that those who had gone out more tended to have been stopped more. For all races, however, there was a significant correlation (of about $r = 0.20$) between number of evenings out and having been annoyed by the police.

The main findings regarding other demographic characteristics were that among Asians there were more married (42 per cent) than among Blacks and Whites (who averaged 26 per cent), and Whites had more single people who were not living with parents (56 per cent). This was partly accounted for by more being students, but even excluding these, Whites had more living in privately rented accommodation. This is consistent with the census data reported in subsection 1 above. Also linked to this is the fact that 52 per cent of Whites had lived in the area less than three years, compared with about a quarter of Blacks and Asians. For Whites and Asians, excluding students, those in privately rented accommodation tended to have a less favourable attitude to the police.

Whites had fewer in Social Classes 4 and 5 (semi-skilled and unskilled), with 44 per cent compared with 61 per cent of Blacks and Asians, while Blacks had more unemployed (42 per cent compared with a mean of 23 per cent for Asians and Whites). Whites tended to have more academic qualifications, nearly half having 'A' levels or above, compared with 15 per cent of Blacks and 24 per cent of Asians.

It is apparent, therefore, that there are many differences between the race groups regarding social status, but it is not easy to see how these would be linked to their experience of and attitude to the police. As they are living in the same small areas, differences in these variables seem more likely to be related to their race than to other factors.

The relationships between the percentage of non-Whites in the areas and various measures of attitude and experience were investigated. The only variable showing a trend with 'blackness' was 'co-operation'. Those living in 'blacker' areas tended to be less co-operative and this was the case for each race group.

Concern about crime

To obtain a wider picture we investigated experiences of crime as victims, feelings of safety in the streets, worries about particular crimes, whether these were seen as a problem in their area, and also, in the attitude questionnaire, opinions about crime and criminals.

In the main, Blacks showed less concern about crime. Only 10 per cent thought it unsafe to walk alone in the area after dark, compared with 31 per cent for Asians and 21 per cent for Whites (all differences being significant). Among the oldest in the survey, those aged 31–35, as many as 54 per cent of Asians thought it unsafe, but only 16 per cent of Blacks and 24 per cent of Whites. (Other studies including this item have usually included women and older people, both of whom tend to feel less safe.)

Respondents were asked if they thought that burglary, vandalism, street fights, mugging and 'crime' were problems in their area. On average (over five items) 30 per cent of Blacks, 37 per cent of Asians and 36 per cent of Whites thought these a big problem. However, for 'sex attacks on women' and 'women pestered', Whites had significantly more (averaging 24 per cent) than Blacks and Asians (average only 12 per cent).

Another question concerned worries about crimes: burglary, robbery and vandalism. In this case, more Asians appeared to worry (on average 53 per cent saying the items were 'a big worry'), Blacks and Whites were equal with about 36 per cent saying this.

The general picture, again, is that Asians differ from Blacks in their concern about crime, and that Whites are more concerned than Blacks on some items ('safety', 'problems') but are similar to Blacks regarding 'worries'.

Summary of main survey

Within our sample of areas with 10 per cent or more non-Whites, Blacks and Whites tended to be similar in many respects and Asians different. Whites had slightly more police-initiated contacts (stops, and so on) than Blacks, and Asians less. Blacks and Whites both had about 60 per cent who believed the police behaved badly, compared with 30 per cent of Asians. About half of Blacks and Whites thought the police discriminated against non-Whites.

For Blacks it was found that for all three measures of attitude to the police (disapproval, perception and co-operation) older people had a more favourable attitude than younger people. This was also the case for Asians (excluding perception) but not for Whites. However, Blacks overall had a more disapproving attitude to the police than Whites, with Asians, again, being less disapproving. Blacks felt less co-operative towards the police, regarding witnessing an offence; Whites and Asians did not differ in this respect.

Although all the measures of attitude to the police were related to stops and so on, and Asians were stopped less and Whites more than Blacks, differences between races on attitude were consistent regardless of the number of stops.

On the whole, Blacks were less, and Asians more, fearful and worried about crime than Whites.

The boys

The boys' questionnaire was fairly short and was answered by 225 boys. Several items were of the same type as those given to the older group, and although few differences were statistically significant, they tended to be in the same direction as for the men, with Blacks tending to be least favourably disposed and co-operative, and Asians most. Direct experience of the police regarding stops affected just over a quarter in all races – perhaps surprisingly high, considering their age.

This small survey is of very considerable interest and suggests either that the attitudes found among the older group have been already implanted from their experiences while they were children, or that the older group have influenced the younger ones in their attitudes. The boys' actual experience of the police would be expected to be fairly slight, but may have had wider repercussions.

Summary and conclusions

This study has shown that over the whole of Leeds black males (aged 10–35) have a higher arrest rate than Whites, with Asians being close to Whites. An analysis looking at two age groups (11–21 and 22–35) and area of residence of those arrested has revealed that there were differences between areas with more than 10 per cent non-White households (the 'blacker' areas) and those with less than 10 per cent (the 'whiter' areas). In the blacker areas Whites had a higher arrest rate than Blacks for the younger group, and for this group Asians had a lower rate than both Blacks and Whites. For the older group, differences between races were small in these areas. In the whiter areas Blacks had a higher arrest rate, with the Asian rate again close to that of Whites for both groups. The pattern with regard to 'stop and search', though less clear, was broadly similar.

The analyses of arrest outcomes showed that Asian juveniles received relatively more cautions than the rest, and more Blacks were tried in the Crown Court. For adults, Asians had more with no further action, and Blacks had a higher proportion tried in the Crown Court and more acquittals. However, sentencing in the magistrates' courts and the Crown Court did not differ between races.

Observation and interviews relating to the processes involved did not reveal any obvious forms of discrimination.

The survey (in areas with more than 10 per cent non-Whites) revealed that Whites had slightly more negative experiences (stops and so on) of the police than Blacks, while Asians had less. However, Blacks tended to be more hostile to the police than Whites, although both groups thought the police discriminated against non-Whites. Asians tended to be more favourable to the police and more afraid of crime. The boys' survey to some extent revealed similar attitudes.

Finally, we need to go back to the problems identified at the outset and consider, briefly, whether our results have clarified matters and what still needs to be done.

Over-representation

For our purposes, the most important point to emerge is that when arrest rates are related to area of residence, the question of 'over-representation' becomes very complicated. This alone vindicates our decision to compare 'within-area' rates. In the blacker areas, it would appear to be the high white arrest rate that needs explaining. Since this was also correlated with certain indices of disadvantage and deprivation (high unemployment, high numbers in privately rented accommodation), the explanation might appear to be straightforward: more deprivation, more offenders, more arrests. And, indeed, the greater transience of the white population – that is, more living in private rented accommodation, and for shorter periods on average, than the black – is in line with this sort of explanation. However, arrest rates are a complex product of offending behaviour, reporting and recording practices and, in the case of proactive crimes, levels of police activity. Taking police activity: we know that areas with high rates of recorded offences tend to attract more police attention than those areas with relatively low rates – which is to say, simply, that we know police attend more to 'crimes of the poor' than to 'crimes of the powerful'. So could the high white arrest rate be explained, at least partially, in terms of levels of police activity? Unfortunately, our arrest rates were based on *where suspected offenders lived*, not *where offences took place*. So, unless these coincided in Leeds, with areas containing large numbers of offenders also having high offence rates (which has been found elsewhere, cf. Baldwin and Bottoms, 1976), our particular study could not shed light on the role of police activity, even supposing, with our purely statistical approach, we were in a position to do so.

We could, of course, approach this from the 'other side' and seek to explain the comparatively low black arrest rate in these same areas. It should first be emphasised that, in a strict sense, the two groups are not commensurable since these areas contain over 50 per cent of the Blacks and Asians living in Leeds and only 6 per cent of the Whites. However, Blacks in these areas were generally more disadvantaged in terms of unemployment, class and educational attainments; that is, they had more 'offender-related' characteristics, except for the greater transience of the white population. That suggests we need to look to differences in reporting behaviour by the public and/or differences in police recording and reporting activity. It could be that Blacks are reluctant to report crimes committed by other Blacks – a possibility that ties up with our survey finding that Blacks report less crime. On the other hand, police may take crimes against Blacks less seriously and therefore fail to record them as offences; or they may be more circumspect generally with Blacks in these areas, preferring – in the interests of better community relations, for example – informal resolutions to arrests. Singly, or together, these sorts of explanations are compatible with the notion of black 'no-go' (to the police) areas.

The other side of this particular equation is the notion of whiter areas being 'out of bounds' to Blacks. This could only begin to explain the high black arrest rate in the whiter areas (if this was not simply attributable to certain methodological limitations mentioned earlier) if such areas were also those where the offences were committed (which we do not know). This needs to be seen in conjunction with stereotypes of the criminal since, otherwise, we might expect higher Asian rates too in 'whiter' areas. Our evidence is not sufficient to decide such matters. But what is clear is that the relationship between crime, policing, race and arrests needs far more careful unravelling than it usually receives. The fact that Asians were *not* over-represented in any areas only endorses the need to make careful distinctions.

Outcome of arrest

The outcome-of-arrest study revealed that Asians were more likely to be cautioned (juveniles) and to have had 'no further action' (adults) and that Blacks had a higher acquittal rate and more tried in the Crown Court for each main offence group.

The higher acquittal rate for Blacks, together with the higher use of cautioning and NFAs with Asians, suggests a number of possible explanations. It may be that non-Whites are more readily arrested, on lesser evidence, and this is later 'rectified' by caution, NFA or acquittal. Or, in the case of Asians, it could be that the police decide, despite the evidence, that Asians are less in need, once arrested, of a 'deterrent' court appearance because of their more tractable disposition or because of a belief that offenders will be dealt with adequately in the community. Our survey evidence certainly confirms a more conforming set of Asian attitudes to the police. In the case of Blacks, we first thought that their higher acquittal rates might be connected with the higher numbers going on to Crown Court, since Crown Courts have higher acquittal as well as custodial rates. However, since the higher Black acquittal rate holds true for both types of court, this cannot provide a sufficient answer. It may be, then, that their higher acquittal rates result from a more combative attitude in relation to the criminal justice system – a greater willingness to plead not guilty; or, it could be that Blacks are charged on the basis of weaker evidence; or it could be that, in order to combat any possibility of racism, the courts require a higher standard of proof to convict. The first and last of these possibilities were mentioned by some solicitors in interview. However, in the absence of further evidence at this stage, the matter must remain open.

The significance of Blacks having more Crown Court trials bears on the question of the importance of taking a processual approach, to which we now turn.

The importance of a processual approach

Comparative sentencing studies, as we mentioned earlier, have shown virtually no differences in the sentences meted out to Blacks and Whites, once offence seriousness and previous convictions are controlled for. Our study confirmed this. But we also found significantly more Blacks being tried in the Crown Court. Since such trials are much more likely to produce custodial sentences, this fact, we concluded, must be implicated in the gradual build-up of Black prisoners. Additionally, we should not forget the significantly higher arrest rates for Blacks which must also contribute to this build-up. From our point of view, both show how important it was to look at the whole process. Had we focused purely on the moment of sentencing, the reason for the over-representation of Blacks in prison would have remained obscure. To shed further light on the matter, however, requires a closer look at two decision-making moments. First, we found no differences between the race groups in terms of the proportions of each taking the various routes to Crown Court trial: charged with fully indictable offences, sent by magistrates, election by defendant; this requires a closer examination of the various decisions underlying each route. Secondly, we need to take a closer look at an earlier stage – the decision to charge – to see whether, of those arrests leading to a charge, Blacks are likely to be charged on lesser evidence than Whites or Asians. Once again, though our study has identified the importance of this decision-making moment, it was not designed to go further.

London and provincial differences?

The picture in Leeds appears to be broadly similar to that in London, in that we found in the city as a whole some over-representation of Blacks in the police statistics for arrests and stops. However, we found that area of residence – a factor not utilised in the London studies – made a considerable difference. It may be that the comparatively low level of recorded stops in the Leeds statistics, mostly for suspected drug offences, and the comparatively high resulting arrest rate, suggest that stops are not generally used in conjunction with 'saturation' policing tactics in the way they clearly have been, on occasions, in London (cf. Scarman, 1981). Thus the notion of discriminatory stopping, so prevalent an issue for Blacks in London, appears, if at all, in a far more muted form in our provincial case-study.

Comparability, attitudes and equality

A full comparison with PSI and British Crime Survey data has yet to be tackled. Moreover, two differences between our study and that of the PSI should be noted. Our survey compared Blacks, Whites and Asians living in the same areas, whereas the PSI sample were from the whole of London. This suggests that the experiences of the three race groups in their sample were probably more dissimilar than those in ours, owing to overall very wide differences between the races in their social circumstances and areas of residence. Secondly, the PSI measure of attitude was the same as our measure of perception – which we found did not differ between Blacks and Whites. None the less, our findings – of more negative Black attitudes which could not be explained solely by experience – do echo those of the PSI. This suggests, possibly, a general, national dimension to Black antipathy to the police which is over and above particular, local experiences. This may also help explain the finding from our interviews with solicitors that Blacks feel discriminated against even when, to all intents and purposes, they appear to get similar treatment. This disjunction – between attitudes and experiences – raises difficult questions about what constitutes equality. Comparative studies of this sort are premised – implicitly anyway – on the idea that equal, in the sense of similar, treatment is the desired policy goal. However, what the above suggests is that the depth of feeling – of oppression and injustice – may be so powerful in some disadvantaged ethnic minorities that the indignities, resulting from the bureaucratic indifference and a host of other interactional factors which befall most if not all of those caught up on the wrong side in the criminal justice system, are felt more keenly. It may well be the case that those processes contain a subtle (or not so subtle) racial dimension that the questionnaire and statistical approach, supplemented with observations of purely formal settings, is not equipped to pick up.

The result of all this may be that the goal of ensuring equal treatment should be replaced by that of appropriate treatment, a point Pinder (1984) makes in looking at the issue of race and probation work. In this case, it means taking attitudes of Blacks seriously on their own terms, not simply in terms of whether these 'truly' reflect their experiences, or whether their experiences – as judged objectively (that is, statistically) by others – are different from those of the majority population. The goal, from this perspective, is a turnaround in Black attitudes, from negative to positive. And this will only be achieved when the felt sources of discontent are fully identified and transformed. Finally, we should not overlook the very different, more positive attitudes of Asians. Given this, there can be no justification in studies of this sort for failing to distinguish between Blacks and Asians.

Notes

1   Recent estimates obtained from a survey by the Leeds County Council indicate that our estimates of the white population in all areas and Blacks in the non-white areas are fairly accurate, but our estimates of Blacks in the whitest areas are too low. Asians appear to have been underestimated throughout.
2   This cut-off point was taken because it was anticipated that only areas with more than 10 per cent non-white would have large enough base populations of non-whites to enable arrest rates to be calculated sensibly.
3   For full details of the sampling scheme, response rate and numbers in the strata, and questionnaire, see Walker *et al.* (1990). The places of birth of the head of the 'Asian' households were: Pakistan 43 per cent, India 26 per cent, Bangladesh 5 per cent, others 26 per cent.
4   For full details see Walker *et al.* (1990). Items included in the 'disapproval' scores were developed by R. I. Mawby.

References

Baldwin, J. and Bottoms, A. E. (1976), *The Urban Criminal: A Study in Sheffield* (London: Tavistock).
Benyon, J. (1986), *A Tale of Failure: Race and Policing*, Policy Papers in Ethnic Relations no. 3 (Warwick: University of Warwick).
Farrington, D. P. and Bennett, T. (1981), 'Police cautioning of juveniles in London', *British Journal of Criminology*, 21, 123–35.
Home Office (1986), *The Ethnic Origin of Prisoners*, Home Office Statistical Bulletin 17/86 (London: Home Office).
Home Office (1989), *Crime Statistics for the Metropolitan Police District, Analysed by Ethnic Group, 1987*, Home Office Statistical Bulletin 5/89 (London: Home Office).
Jefferson, T. (1991), 'Discrimination, disadvantage and policework', in E. Cashmore and E. McLaughlin (eds), *Out of Order?* (London: Routledge).
Landau, S. F. and Nathan, G. (1983), 'Selecting delinquents for cautioning in the London Metropolitan Area', *British Journal of Criminology*, 23, 128–49.
Mair, G. (1986), 'Ethnic minorities, probation and the magistates' courts: a pilot study', *British Journal of Criminology*, 26, 147–58.
Piner, R. (1984), 'Probation work in a multi-racial society', unpublished ms, University of Leeds, Applied Anthropology Group.
Reiner, R. (1985), 'Police and race relations', in J. Baxter and L. Koffman (eds), *Police: The Constitution and the Community* (Abingdon: Professional Books).

Reiner, R. (1989), 'Race and criminal justice', *New Community*, **16**(1), 5–21.

Scarman, Lord (1981), *The Brixton Disorders, 10–12 April 1981*, Cmnd 8427 (London: HMSO).

Smith, D. (1983), *Police and People in London. 1: A Survey of Londoners* (London: Policy Studies Institute).

Smith, D. (1986), 'West Indian hostility to the police in relation to personal experience', unpublished MS.

Stevens, P. and Willis, C. (1979), *Race, Crime and Arrests*, Home Office Research Study no. 58 (London: Her Majesty's Stationery Office).

Tuck, M. and Southgate, P. (1981), *Ethnic Minorities, Crime and Policing*, Home Office Research Study no. 70 (London: Her Majesty's Stationery Office).

Walker, M. A. (1987), 'Interpreting race and crime statistics', *Journal of the Royal Statistical Society*, A, **150**, 39–56.

Walker, M. A. (1988), 'The court disposal of young males by race, in London in 1983', *British Journal of Criminology*, **28**, 442–60.

Walker, M. A. (1989), 'The court disposal and remands of White, Afro-Caribbean and Asian men (London 1983)', *British Journal of Criminology*, **29**, 353–67.

Walker, M. A. (1992), 'Arrest rates and ethnic minorities: a study in a provincial city', *Journal of the Royal Statistical Society, A* (forthcoming).

Walker, M. A., Jefferson, T. and Seneviratne, M. (1990), *Ethnic Minorities, Young People and the Criminal Justice System*, main report to Economic and Social Research Council, Ref. E06250023. Centre for Criminological and Legal Research, University of Sheffield.

2

Some recent approaches to the study of race in criminological research

Race as social process

by Simon Holdaway*

Abstract

In this paper, recent approaches to the study of race and criminological subjects are reviewed. First, regression analysis is discussed
and criticized for its tendency to conceptualize race as a discrete
phenomenon, unrelated to the social contexts within which it is
manifest. The problem here is an under-theorization of race. Next,
the concept of 'Other', which has been employed by sociologists
who work within what has been called the 'new racism' themes of
research, is criticized for a lack of grounding in systematic evidence
and neglect of the mundane world. Race is here over-theorized.
Using data from two studies of the employment experience of black
and Asian police officers, an analysis of processes of racialization
grounded in the occupational cultural contexts of policing is
advanced to illustrate a preferred approach to the study of race.

Questions about the relationship between race and crime have been raised
again by the British police.[1] Sir Paul Condon, Commissioner of the Metropolitan Police Service, one of the very few chief officers to have stated publicly his outright rejection of racialized prejudice and discrimination within
the ranks he commands, wrote recently to a number of 'community leaders'
inviting them to a briefing to launch, 'an important police operation to combat street robbery'. Central to Condon's letter, which included recognition
that street robbery is related to social conditions beyond the control of the
police, was, as he put it, the very sensitive 'fact' that, '. . . very many of the

---

* Reader in Sociology, Sheffield University, Department of Sociological Studies.
[1] The word 'race' is sometimes enclosed in marks as a convention, to indicate that it is a social
construct. I avoid this as an unnecessary, stylistic fashion. The terms black and Asian used in this
paper refer to people of Afro-Caribbean and South Asian (usually Indian) sub-continent origins.

perpetrators of muggings are very young black people, who have been excluded from school and/or are unemployed' (The Runnymede Trust 1995*b*: 1).

Newspaper headlines about 'black muggers' followed. Some were sympathetic and some critical of Condon's ideas, echoing the reception his Commissioner predecessors received when they similarly, and often with less sensitivity, entered the public arena of debate about race and crime.[2] The clearest criminological echo from this episode, however, is perhaps the controversy that followed the Metropolitan Police submission to the 1977 Home Affairs Select Committee hearings on police race relations. At that time 'The Met' produced evidence reporting the results of an internal, statistical study indicating that a disproportionate number of street robberies in London were committed by black youths (Newing and Crump 1974; Lea and Young 1984). Similarly, the basis for Condon's recent comments was an internally conducted, unpublished study of victims' descriptions of their attackers in which about 80 per cent said that their assailant was a black male in his teens or early twenties.

Condon's reliance on and use of statistical data could provide criminologists with an opportunity to comment about the dubious reliability of victims' perceptions of their attacker; the inadequacies of the research design used; and a host of other methodological points. One could turn for assistance about these and related matters to the chapter about race and criminological subjects in *The Oxford Handbook of Criminology*, where most of the pertinent studies are reviewed and their shortcomings identified, save one (Smith 1994). In that review, and more generally in the relevant criminological literature, there is an absence of critical consideration of how we can most adequately conceptualize the phenomenon 'race'. Furthermore, there is within criminology a related lack of debate about the theoretical foundations upon which most empirical studies of race and crime are based.[3]

When theoretical concerns have informed the study of race and crime, over-arching, grand concepts of social structure and ideology have tended to dominate enquiry. The prior 'logic' of particular social structures and/or associated theoretical arguments has taken analytical precedence over the sensitive use of empirical evidence. An assumption has been made that relationships between wider social structures, institutions and organizations are harmonious. There has been a tendency to over-theorize, to reify race and dislocate it too sharply from the everyday world (Schutz 1967). The need is to find a conceptual framework to analyse adequately the phenomenon of race and to embed it within the institutional and organizational contexts within which it is articulated.

[2] For a brief résumé of this point see The Runnymede Trust (1995*a*, *b*).
[3] I deal with research in Britain. Similar points could however be made about the research in other European and in North American societies.

In this paper recent, major criminological approaches to the study of race are reviewed—there are basically two—and criticized.[4] The argument will not be concerned solely with the race and crime debate, and it will not be a review of the available statistical evidence leading to agreement with Robert Reiner's conclusion that, 'It is inconceivable that this approach could ever conclusively establish racial discrimination' (Reiner 1992: 5). My starting point is the virtually uncontested acceptance in sociological research that race is a social construct. A clear research theme should therefore be precisely about how race is constructed within institutions and organizations.

The concept of 'racialization' is central here, premised on an acceptance that race is socially constructed and that the research task is to describe and analyse social processes that create and sustain its forms (Smith 1989; Omi and Winant 1994; Small 1994). This has led some sociologists to the study of migration and labour market processes within capitalist societies. 'Racialization' is here understood as a grand, over-arching concept (Miles 1982, 1989, 1993). Processes of racialization, however, are also and, from the perspective I will advocate, more appropriately researched in relation to mundane processes and related ideas that are part of organizational life. There is a research task to analyse how race is constructed and sustained within the routines of organizational life. Data from two studies of the occupational experience of black and Asian serving police officers and resigners will be used to explore the analytical utility of this perspective within a criminal justice organization.

Regression analysis

Regression analysis has become one of the means and probably the standard one of analysing the extent to which racialized factors are part of an explanation of offending and victimization rates amongst different ethnic groups. It has been used, for example, in major, national studies of victimization, local studies of offending, and of sentencing (for example, Walker 1987; Skogan 1990; Hood 1992; Mayhew et al. 1993). Regression analysis is not a theory but it is a methodology, a set of assumptions about the nature of social phenomena and, related, how they should be studied. Social theory and research methods cannot be neatly separated.

The rationale for regression analysis is well known. Many 'extra-racial' factors, area of residence and housing type, for example, that can be associated with differential rates of offending, of criminal victimization, and so on need to be distinguished from *the* racial factor. Once this differentiation of factors is completed and, as far as is practical, all relevant variables are

---

[4] This paper is not a review of all recent criminological publications about race and crime. No doubt other approaches could have been selected. I have chosen two major, dominant themes of research about race and crime and do not claim that my choice is exhaustive. Variations of the quasi-systems approach can be found, for example, in the work of Lea and Young and Solomos (Lea and Young 1984; Solomos 1993).

controlled, it becomes possible to express statistically the extent to which the race of an offender is significant within an explanation of the commission of an arrestable offence, a theft for example. The essential research task is the isolation of race from all other factors.

Social scientists have their own criticisms of regression analysis (Bryman and Cramer 1990). These are not relevant to my argument because they leave the theoretical neglect of race intact. My central point of criticism is that in regression analysis and all that precedes it in the design of a sample, the refinement of a questionnaire and in the analysis of data, an assumption is made that race is an object that can be studied. There is no better illustration of Durkheim's premise that 'social facts should be treated as things' (Durkheim 1982). From this stance the social world is rendered into a form that allows its complexity to be amenable to systematic study; the extent to which race is relevant to a criminological research analysis can be measured; it is possible to express numerically and subsequently in prose the salience of race to a research question.[5] Regression analysis therefore deals with the outcomes of action—a stop in the street, an arrest, a victimization. Social processes that constitute an action are ignored. Race is reified and conceptualized as a discrete factor, only related to other discrete parts of an explanation in statistical terms.

A number of severe analytical limitations flow from this approach to the study of race. First, it is inadequate to conceptualize race as a discrete variable, an object arrested in time and space that can be disconnected from other apparent, objective 'non-racial' explanators. Area of residence, type of housing owned, type of tenure, all factors that have been isolated in research for the purposes of regression analysis, cannot be regarded straightforwardly as extra-racial variables. Type of housing, type of tenure, and so on should be related to the history and racialized segregation of black and Asian people in Britain. If inner city areas are consistently high crime areas and this is where largish numbers of black and Asian people live, it follows that their residence in a high crime area is of relevance to the rates of criminal victimization they experience. If we then ask why they settled in inner city areas in the first place, and document the historical processes that led to such a pattern of residence, we are faced with constraints related to the racialization of the residential and employment prospects of black and Asian people (Rex and Moore 1967; Rex 1973; Smith 1989). These at first sight disparate but, under a sociological eye of analysis, interrelated factors frame relationships between groups defined by racialized criteria. They constitute and sustain the structure of racialized relations within contemporary Britain.

Secondly, there is an assumed link in regression analysis between objective factors identified by research—objective because they are the 'product' of

---

[5] This is of course but part of a wider critique of positivism.

a formal, rational analysis—and the everyday behaviour of people. The British Crime Survey, for example, assesses the relative risks of victimization for different offences amongst various ethnic groups, Asians and Afro-Caribbeans in particular (Mayhew *et al.* 1993). A series of snapshots, linked in album format by a research report, describe patterns of risk of victimization for black, Asian, white and other groups. Here, race is operationalized in people's lives if, as an object in its own right, it is associated with particular offences committed on particular people who are defined by racialized criteria. The assumption is that in people's minds race is equally discrete, operationalized within their lives when directly perceived to be present in something that happens to them and/or when directly associated with their action.

This understanding of victimization risks is misleading because it fragments the social world, compartmentalizing it into discrete moments rather than a stream of lived, reflected upon, enduring consciousness (Bowling 1993). Individuals who have experienced victimization do not place their concerns and worry about what has and in the future might happen to them into neatly packaged, discrete parcels of experience (Merry 1981). They relate their victimization to other spheres of their life, to other misfortunes they have suffered, to any sense of unfairness they might harbour. They discuss their experience with family, friends, colleagues at work; they mention it in various fora and listen to the responses, explanations and, no doubt, frustrations of others who may have also been victims of crime, or heard about the same or similar events at first or second hand.

An individual's experience of victimization is but one aspect of their consciousness of crime, of their sense of personal safety and fate within a locality and a society. Individual experience flows back and forth, perhaps creating unease and misapprehension, even fear of similar happenings in the future. From this perspective the experience of victimization among black and Asian people is a thread running through other social contexts within which race is articulated.

Recognizing the racialized character of manifold relationships that have led many individuals and, by implication, groups to an experience of disadvantage, hurt and frustration, it is not surprising to find that fear of victimization is amplified; that the racial element of a victim's account of one or more crimes is heightened, perhaps even constructed from minimal evidence. This does not mean that, as one famed paper about the use of drugs suggested, 'fantasy can become reality' (Young 1971). It does suggest, however, that the experience of victimization lived by the members of minority ethnic groups coheres around a greater number of reference points than the single crime to which they have been subjected (Walklate 1992). Immediate, more distant, rumour-based and many other types of information and knowledge are relevant to the encapsulation of criminal victimization within experience.

We therefore need to learn much more about the ways in which the personal experience of being a victim of crime and the general victimization of black and Asian people are relevant to individual and collective identities, and to action. This does not necessarily mean that the black and Asian experience is uniform. Neither does it mean that it is wholly distinct from the experience of white victims. Research in this area, however, would help us to understand how racialized relations structure and provide meaning for, in Schutz's terms, a 'life world' and, therefore, how processes of exclusion draw contours of racialized relations within contemporary Britain (Schutz 1967). Before we can do this, however, we need to conceptualize race as constructed through social processes within the everyday world. We need to understand how processes of racialization are moulded within the mundane world to form what we recognize as 'race'.

Finally, in regression analysis, race is not conceptualized as a phenomenon that is constructed through routine practices by people working in organizations by, for example, the unreflective, routine use of policy that discriminates indirectly on racialized grounds.[6] Rather, race is understood as an objective fact with a status of its own. An explanation of racialized discrimination is concerned precisely with its direct effect on individuals and groups, not its indirect and interrelated effects through what at first sight do not appear to be racialized routines of institutional and organization life. The notion of 'indirect discrimination' makes little or no sense from the standpoint of regression analysis (Fitzgerald 1993).

Race cannot therefore be straightforwardly isolated as a discrete, statistical variable. Its relevance to the analysis of victimization, and to any other subject of research, should be demonstrated by systematic research methods —there is no argument about that. However, the tendency of much criminological research to objectify race and to regard it as a discrete variable within the criminal justice system fails to take adequate account of the historical and continuing social structural, cultural and other constraints that sustain racialized relations pertinent to risks of victimization. Furthermore, the use of regression analysis fails to place race within the world of mundane social relationships, extracting it from the everyday to the reified world of criminological positivism.

Race as ideology and structure

The other, dominant criminological approach to the study of race I want to consider rejects its objectification as a discrete phenomenon and the fragmentation of the social world through regression analysis. The notion of race as a social construction is central here and, indeed, race is conceptualized as an ideological ruse, which is to say that it serves an interest of a dominant group. The extent to which discourse constitutes race or has a realist basis, however, differentiates forms of this approach.

[6] See Reiner (1985: 133–5) for a discussion of different types of discrimination.

Paul Gilroy's rejection of all statistical analysis of race and crime as 'empiricist haggling' is a hallmark of this stance and, within a wider subject field, of the 'new racism' (Gilroy 1982, 1983, 1987; Goldberg 1988; Cohen and Bains 1993). Gilroy repudiates a realist understanding of phenomena: reality is constructed by discourse alone, with primary attention given to the ways in which, for example, images of black youth, sometimes connotative and sometimes denotative, have constituted the apparently factual.

In this argument, race and 'crime' have no status other than discourse, the meaning of which lies beneath their surface appearance. Gilroy, for example, has presented what he calls 'an archaeology of representations of black law-breaking' (1987: 73) which in the first instance deconstructs the related notions of law and legality that express and represent the idea of a nation-state and national unity.

> The subject of the law is also the subject of the nation. Law is primarily a national institution and adherence to its rules symbolises the imagined community of the nation and expresses the fundamental unity and equal-ity of its citizens ... The changing patterns of their portrayal as law-breakers and criminals, as a dangerous class or underclass, offer an opportunity to trace the development of the new racism for which the link between crime and blackness has now become absolutely integral. (p. 74)

Symbols powerfully extend contentious meanings beyond the immediate context to which they refer and Gilroy's argument is that on the one hand a bricolage of race has effectively excluded blacks from inclusion in the common definition of British society—'there ain't no black in the Union Jack.' The other and for Gilroy, crucial aspect of this analysis is that, within the space between exclusion and response, black youth have created a cultural solution to secure a collective identity with the potential to sustain a politically con-scious community. 'Collective identities spoken through race, community and locality are, for all their spontaneity, powerful means to co-ordinate action and create solidarity' (pp. 246–7).

There is far more to Gilroy's argument than I have been able to present here. At the heart of his work is a critique of Marxist notions of class as the basis of an analysis of black communities and the consciousness of black people. Culture is not a direct reflection of a material base, the base/superstructure relationship as Marxists put it, or in the last instance deter-mined by class conflict (Althusser 1971). Race may have no biological base but it is nevertheless the 'material' to construct a dynamic culture with its own integrity. Both crime and race are socially constructed and should not be reified as, for example, in the realist criminology of Jock Young or the positiv-ists' assumption that phenomena can be measured, which contextualizes adequately 'the social'. Race is complexly constructed, significantly through the discourse of public figures and, although there is no close analysis of this relationship in Gilroy's work, its impact on the common-sense of white people. A 'new racism' therefore appears in many different cultural forms, mediated through political rhetoric, law, notions of nation, community and national identity, from which black people are implicitly excluded.

A significant influence on the development of Gilroy's ideas has been the work of Birmingham University's Centre for Contemporary Cultural Studies, especially their *Policing the Crisis* (Hall *et al.* 1978). In some ways this was the forerunner of his theoretical writings because its authors also sought to understand why, in the middle of the 1970s, there had been the presentation of black youth as criminal and associated with mugging. At root, the thesis of *Policing the Crisis* is that during the 1970s Britain faced an economic recession requiring a scapegoat. The scapegoat, which was black youth, diverted attention away from and thereby bolstered public confidence in a social order that, 'in reality', was tied to a capitalist economy in crisis. This argument, therefore, placed questions about the meaning of black youth within a wider analytical framework and, crucially, asked, 'Why at this particular historical juncture of this particular society were black youth presented as 'muggers'? The preferred answer was that in the final instance, and at the particular time of crisis documented, the economy provided a framework within which it was necessary for a scapegoat, an Other, to be found. The Other was black youth.

There seems little daylight between this analysis and any other postulating a clear continuity between economic structures and dominant, pervasive ideas. Relationships between the two are certainly more flexible and complex than would be found in a crude, fundamental Marxist analysis. As far as the basic structure of the argument is concerned, however, system needs are constantly in the ascendancy and ideas about race are orchestrated accordingly. This is why Stuart Hall and his colleagues have been vulnerable to the findings of critics who have carefully combed their evidence and found it inadequate, inappropriate or wrongly interpreted (for example, James 1978; Waddington 1986). The needs of Hall's theory and therefore the needs of the economic system analysed have required a particular interpretation of data.

If we return to Gilroy's work and ask why the ideas about black youth and black culture changed in the periods he analysed a less certain answer is given, partly because he is not interested in a quasi-causal analysis, resisting any reification of phenomena. The idea of an economic system that orchestrates discourse is anathema to him. There is, however, the glimmer of an answer signalled by his rather strange capitalization of 'the Other'. Any notion of social inclusion requires a comparator, an exclusionary idea. 'The Other', an assemblage of exclusionary characters, the promiscuous, the drug taker, the welfare scrounger, the young black, fulfils this function.

Tony Jefferson, one of the authors of *Policing the Crisis*, has also extended recently the original argument of his co-authors by employing the concept of 'Other' (Jefferson and Walker 1992, 1993; Jefferson 1993). His argument is that an 'Other', in the shape of a scapegoat for class division and related social inequalities, has been constructed around the empirically verifiable but nonetheless contrived, ideological categories of 'young', 'male', 'working class' and 'black' (Jefferson and Walker 1992; Jefferson 1993). 'The Other' is needed if within British society the structure of power is to hold within its necessary boundaries of social and economic order. These pertinent ideological categories are complex constructions and their fragmentation by regression analysis simply distorts the key point that:

> for a whole host of historical and contemporary reasons, to be young, male and 'rough' working class is to be inordinately at risk of criminalization. The importance of *that* fact is in danger of being lost in a debate centred on whether young black males are currently over-represented amongst the criminalized.
>
> (Jefferson 1993: 39)

In a number of papers, Jefferson has sketched the historical processes through which different groups have been criminalized and, in the case of black youth, racialized (Jefferson and Walker 1992, 1993; Jefferson 1993). His analyses have been grounded mostly in statistical evidence from a study of police and minority ethnic group relations in Leeds, though he has been careful to point out that his statistics can go no further than a description of factors that need to be cast into an explanation encompassing:

> a larger issue—the question of who is to be 'cast out' as the criminal Other. It is this form of racism that seems critical in the crime debate, especially in a time of deepening recession and a widening gap between the 'haves' and the 'have nots'.
>
> (1992: 40)

These types of analysis of race and criminalization that are exemplified by Gilroy's and Jefferson's work are very different from the studies based on regression analysis. They seek to deconstruct common notions of race and then reconstruct them within a sociological analysis of the wider, one might say structural, processes that create and sustain them. For Jefferson, race seems to be epiphenomenal: it is an ideological construct needed by the society in which it is manifest. The essential and prior task here is to engage an analysis of political economy that allows a criminologist to identify when and how consent to policing and a particular notion of social order has been sustained within different historical periods.[7] Once that general

---

[7] For a general discussion of political economy and analysis of crime, of which Jefferson's work is but one example, see Taylor (1994).

framework of analysis has been established, the particulars of research flow from it.

For Gilroy, race is a powerful discourse, at once exclusionary and criminalizing but a valid and firm basis of a racialized politics and of community organization. Race is socially constructed but it is 'real' as a principle for action. There is little analytical reliance, if any, on political economy in Gilroy's account, with primary attention given to dominant discourses as phenomena in their own right.

Gilroy and Jefferson share the view that we should analyse 'racisms', manifested, refracted and articulated in many different forms. Racialized exclusion is based implicitly or explicitly on criteria related to age, gender, notions of nationalism, community membership, legality, citizenship, and many other processes and forms. Agreement about their essential elements is less secure, however, though for Jefferson they are based on the needs of particular economies.[8]

Both writers are dismissive of regression analysis, although Jefferson writes as an insider at this point, having conducted a large-scale analysis of arrest and related rates. Both are concerned with the public implications of signifying groups and phenomena defined by racialized criteria. Race may appear object-like but it cannot be measured and understood through statistical analysis alone.

Critique

A basic problem of Gilroy's and Jefferson's analytical approach is the lack of conceptual clarity afforded to the central concept, 'the Other'. Both of them reject Marxist and other forms of functionalist analysis because they do not capture the changing phenomenal forms of racism or, particularly for Gilroy, race is rendered wholly to the status of an epiphenomenon. Yet these writers insist that a wider structural analysis, with the concept of 'Other' as central, should prevail.

The reasons for this insistence are not clear. Is 'the Other' preserved as an analytical category because every category of social exclusion logically requires a category of inclusion to which it can be compared? Is 'the Other' necessarily criminalized or are other forms and processes of social exclusion as pertinent? Is it a metaphorical ruse and therefore illuminating as an illustrative device, wrongly interpreted as if it is actually present and functional within any society? Is it merely a sociological fashion, new jargon and therefore a new form of words to re-express instrumentalism? Or is it functionally necessary for all or particular societies, perhaps classified by types of economy, to retain an 'Other', to cast out

---

[8] See David Mason (1994) for a rather different point about essentialism, one that has been the subject of debate in sociology rather than criminology.

groups which threaten acceptable levels of social order? These questions have not been clarified but one is left with the strong impression that the latter interpretation is closer to the truth than any other. Until this point is clarified we cannot assess adequately the analytical power of 'the Other' as a concept.

A related and crucial point is that there is in these analyses an assumed, pliable audience that behaves more or less, though usually more, in harmony with the apparent yet unexplicated need to create a criminalized 'Other'. In *Policing the Crisis* it is the hegemonic needs of capital that articulate the function fulfilled by 'the Other'. The same analysis is evident in Jefferson's recent papers, in which the balance between police law enforcement, para-military policing and community policing, all related to the policing and criminalization of black people, is directly aligned to the need to sustain a particular form of social order.

The anthropology implied by these accounts is unreflective, indeed, at times it is slavish. Gilroy, for example, assumes that the category 'black' and an associated consciousness of race are in equal measure applicable to Asian people (see Modood 1992, 1994). All are one. Jefferson assumes that hege-monic needs articulate policing straightforwardly and, therefore, senior and rank-and-file officers' ideas about race, youth, and so on. Other research sug-gests that the relationship is in fact far more complex and diverse (Manning 1977; Fielding 1988).

The tendency in these types of analyses, in contrast to regression analy-ses of race within the criminal justice system, is to over-theorize. Rather than understand social structures and related processes of criminalization and racialization as a framework for criminological analysis a virtual straitjacket is created. A slippery concept, 'Other', is placed centre stage, which means that we cannot falsify the analysis adopted because there are no criteria to decide whether or not social exclusion is in any context practised on racialized grounds. Although Jefferson argues that the categories of young, black and male are interrelated, he does not define the particular contexts in which they become relevant for police officers. Any encounter between police and black youths can be explained by a pervasive and ill-defined concept of 'Otherness'.

Finally, we reach the same point of criticism that was made about regres-sion analysis. The social world is here objectified—more acting upon than enacted by people in their everyday life (Manning 1980; Weick 1982). Race is a social construction, that much is one of the starting points for the analysis of 'the Other'. However, processes that construct and sustain race are removed from the lives of people working in or coming into contact with criminal justice organizations. They are placed at the service of system imperatives and, ergo, people oblige. The Commissioner of the Metropolitan Police Service, whose briefing and operation to deal with black youth committing crime were mentioned at the beginning of this paper, presumably, *necessarily* functioned in this way, at this historical juncture, to criminalize and racialize black youth.[9]

Racialization within the police workforce

The published body of criminological literature does not offer adequate examples of research about race and criminological subjects of the type I want to promote. To elucidate the approach I have in mind I will therefore draw on findings from two studies of black and Asian police officers serving in or who have resigned recently from English constabularies (Holdaway 1991, 1993).[10] This means that my discussion will move away from the bulk of the published criminological studies, which have been concerned with race, offending and the reaction to offending. My objective is to explore further the concept of racialization and to do so within the context of empirical research. A new focus on racialized relations within the police workforce does not distract from this purpose.

One of the studies to be used was concerned with black and Asian resigners' reasons for resignation from their constabulary. Erstwhile officers from five constabularies in England and Wales were interviewed. The other study was of the occupational experience of black and Asian officers serving in the same constabularies (Holdaway 1991, 1993). Twenty-nine resigners and 30 serving black or Asian officers were interviewed during these two projects. Using a structured interview schedule, questions probed black and Asian officers' and resigners' experience of working with peers, and related matters. In the resigners' project a partly matched sample of white resigners was also interviewed and data from these interviews will be used at appropriate points.

The general finding from these two research studies is that, though in some senses phenomenally distinct, race is not a discrete category of the police occupational culture. Mundane features of the rank and file occupational culture, and of chief officers' policy for that matter, have sustained processes of racialization affecting the working lives of black and Asian officers. Race and, therefore, processes of racialization within the police workforce have to be placed within the distinct organizational and related occupational-cultural context of policing and police work. For the purposes of illustration and in the interests of brevity I only use data concerned with the employment experiences of black and Asian officers. Two well-documented

[9] I am in agreement that this and similar, past statements and acts by chief police officers have denoted and connoted black people with the meaning of race—but how and why this is done is far more complex than the explanations offered by the criminologists reviewed would proffer.

[10] The two projects were funded by the Home Office and I am grateful for their assistance with the research, as I am for the co-operation of all the officers involved. The views expressed here are entirely my own. The term 'black' describes people of Afro-Caribbean origin and Asian people with origins in the Asian sub-continent. We are here referring to officers who were all born in England.

features of the occupational culture are discussed, team membership and stereotypical thinking.

Team membership

Rank-and-file officers define police work as team work (Holdaway 1983, 1992). The policing of public order and some other situations certainly require officers to work together as a team. When an officer is in danger a mutual commitment to help each other is shared by colleges (Waddington 1987). Most uniform officers work on a shift, which might also be regarded as a team of members with interdependent skills.[11] The bulk of police work, however, is undertaken by an officer working alone.

Rank-and-file officers extend these notions of team membership in rather different directions. For them, team membership implies acceptance of the rank-and-file definition and practice of police work; the values that underpin it; and the perpetuation of 'common-sense' ideas about the public and how it should be policed, including stereotypes of members of minority groups, not least minority ethnic groups within the workforce. This does not mean that an officer joining a shift from training school who places primary emphasis on, say, community-based crime prevention, will be subjected to something akin to cloning. The point is that most colleagues' benchmark for the assessment of police competence incorporates attitudes and beliefs about minority ethnic groups, including black and Asian colleagues.[12]

Team membership is a mundane feature of the rank-and-file occupational culture of relevance to all officers. One of its consequences, however, is the racialization of the workforce. Membership of the work group implies a significant measure of acceptance of the rank-and-file culture, including its racialized elements, which makes it difficult for a black or Asian officer to build wholly agreeable relationships with colleagues.

We can observe clearly rank-and-file ideas about team membership relevant to black and Asian officers when they are overcome by an officer. Various routes can lead officers into closer team membership; in the following incident it is by an (unrealized) acceptance of an occupational trait with a higher status than one relevant to race. An ability to use physical force to protect a colleague is such a trait and in this illustration we see a black officer finding a

[11] The Association of Chief Police Officers has recently placed considerable emphasis on the notion of police work as team work, by which they mean a formal, interdependent team of officers who bring their various skills and knowledge to bear upon the myriad problems that constitute police work. The implications of this view for the racialization of relations within the workforce, however, have not yet been considered by the Association. See ACPO Quality of Service Committee (1993).

[12] The extent to which the occupational culture *per se* or its core forms, the basis of rank and file ideas about work and action is a subject of debate among researchers (see Fielding 1988). For debate about the occupational culture see Manning (1977), Chan (1996), Holdaway (1987).

greater measure of acceptance among colleagues, precisely because he has demonstrated his physical prowess when dealing with an offender.[13] The officer quoted found himself more closely integrated into his team of colleagues after he demonstrated he could 'handle himself'. The irony of his transition is that his integration into the police team was facilitated by a reclassification from one stereotype to another. At first he was classified as a black person and subjected to the exclusion experienced by his ethnic peers. Once integrated he became the officer who could deal with difficult situations requiring physical force.[14]

At first he talked during an interview about colleagues' assumptions that he and his parents were born in Jamaica, that all black people are unintelligent, and that derogatory, racialized language is commonplace and acceptable within the workforce. The situation then changed.

> But then finally another one of these breaks. One night there was quite a bad disturbance in the town centre and we actually had to wade in. One of the officers was overpowered so to speak and he was getting a damn good pasting. Now, because I had done quite a lot of self-defence and I'd done quite a bit of martial arts I didn't find any problems. I was able to dig him out and get him back to the van. And from that point onwards I was one of the lads . . . That was it. I was one of the lads because I'd actually gone out and proved myself in a situation and they thought, well that's it for us, he's one of the lads. And from that point onwards I was always being dragged off, 'Oh we need someone to come with us. Call Bob, go and find Bob, wherever is he, go and find Bob'. You know, if I was sat at the station desk doing something else, 'Can I have Bob to come with me please?'

Membership of a police team and acceptance into it also extends beyond the working day, to socializing after work and the implicit expectation lodged in the occupational culture that officers will congregate for a drink.[15] Probationer constables joining their shift in a pub after work are eased into membership of the team of colleagues; an invitation to socialize signifies that closer team membership is being offered. The problem for some Asian officers, however,

---

[13] I am not arguing that all colleagues at this officer's station placed the same degree of credibility on defensive skills or that the officer's skills are entirely unrelated to police work. If I argued thus the occupational culture would be presented as a stereotype.

[14] There is also perhaps a weaving of this idea with the notion that black men are good fighters. It is also the case that situations like this are not just of relevance to minority ethnic officers. The point is that mundane features of the occupational culture racialize relations between police colleagues and between the police and the public.

[15] Other occupations also have unwritten rules about the use of alcohol and a willingness to consume alcohol is part of a broader value placed on its consumption. There is nothing about this point that is intrinsic to the police. There may be another, more guarded acceptance of black and Asian officers related to their willingness to work within black and Asian communities to gather evidence and make arrests.

is that for religious reasons they do not consume alcohol. Although the same point can be made about some white officers, it is more likely to be the case among Asians. This makes the 'drinking route' into team membership difficult because although it is perfectly feasible to drink non-alcoholic beverages in a public house it seems hardly usual for police officers. This Asian officer described how he believed abstinence had contributed to his experience of policing.

> Even those I had a good rapport with probably wanted to draw a line and after a tour of duty that was it. I mean, after a while I talked of going to pubs and things. Some people would obviously have social occasions in their homes and things and I wasn't invited to some of these things— because 'What's S going to do, he doesn't drink, he's not going to have a piss-up'. I felt a little bit isolated at that time.
>
> I tried a hell of a lot to, or I feel I tried a hell of a lot to integrate myself. The first Christmas that we were there, for example, we were on duty. 'Ok, what are we going to do this Christmas?' People were starting to talk. I can prepare quite nice stuff so I prepared an Indian meal for everybody. I got my parents to do this, bought it out of my own pocket. I didn't get them to pay. We had a really fantastic meal and it was a good time. Everybody enjoyed it. So I wanted to say 'Look, I want to join in with you.' I tried as far as possible but as time went on . . .

Team membership, defined by criteria related to the rank-and-file definition of police work and policing rather than routine work demands, is a stock feature of the occupational culture. The strength of team spirit among officers wavers according to the context within which they interact and their notion of team does not exclude the pursuit of rivalries and differences. The interview data, however, indicate that black and Asian officers are team members in some senses but also that the extent of their membership is very limited. Importantly, their differentiation from full or significant membership was a factor that contributed to the racialization of the workforce.

Stereotypical thinking

The essence of a stereotype is a rigid, one-dimensional presentation of a more diverse and multi-faceted phenomenon. Stereotypes differ from 'typifications', which are rounded and therefore somewhat inaccurate summaries of information about people, situations, places and so on (Schutz 1967). The complexity of the social world requires us to simplify information to some extent, to disregard in some measure evidence that is contrary to our own beliefs, to justify the relationship between our ideas and actions with a retrospective gloss of constancy rather than inconsistency. Conversation would be endlessly laced with qualifications if we did not use typifications routinely. Typifications, however, are not stereotypes, which are more simple, rigid and virtually irrefutable, except in extreme situations.

Police work presents officers with complex and ambiguous situations which they have to understand, often in a short period of time. A stock of information and knowledge combines with the exigencies of the situation, presenting an officer with a decision to find, as Bittner has put it, 'an unknown solution to an unknown problem' (Bittner 1967). Typifications are the stock in trade of police work and their relationship to stereotypes is a close one (Chatterton 1992; Keith 1993; Manning 1977; Norris et al. 1992). In this setting, I argue, stereotypical thinking and the racialization of relationships within the police workforce are enhanced.

Being particularly rigid, stereotypical ideas are difficult to challenge and they become entrenched within organizational thinking, which is the case with the police occupational culture. When researchers have asked serving black and Asian officers about their occupational identity they have stressed that they regard themselves as police officers who happen to be black or Asian. Their colleagues, however, regard them rather differently, as black and Asian people who happen to be police officers and therefore as different from the mainstream (Wilson et al. 1984; Metropolitan Police: Analysis Team 1990). Stereotypical ideas about black and Asian people dominate and are a virtual preoccupation among white officers. Indeed, in a recent report of a thematic inspection of equal opportunities within the constabularies of England and Wales it was argued that, from the perspective of many white rank-and-file officers, to be a police officer is to be white (Her Majesty's Inspectorate of Constabulary 1992).

In the most routine of situations race as a social category of differentiation seems to be of immediate relevance to white officers. This is a black officer describing his colleagues who regularly talked about black and Asian people in derogatory terms.

> I would say, 'I don't think you should be saying that' and those people that said, 'Sorry, I didn't know you were there' would say, 'Well you know what it's like, you get used to it.' 'Well get un-used to it then', I would say, 'you wouldn't like it if I said, "You so-and so", I mean how would you feel if I said that to you?' . . . They like to put people in boxes. If someone was black they could call them some derogatory name but instead they put us in boxes. They were just trying to identify us with the sort of person that was socially deprived or any person that's black. But I should say they should just give it a bit of thought before they open their mouth and that's what I told them. I don't know, I sort of give up. I never got any sort of commendation because I'd said that. Nobody takes any notice.

Stereotypical thinking is a stable, mundane feature of the occupational culture. The line between typifications and stereotypes is a fine one. My argument is that in police work, with its emphasis on the speedy identification and retention in memory of people, places, events, and so on, typifications can easily and often do become stereotypes. Within the rank-and-file's work, stereotypical thinking leads to processes that facilitate the articulation and, indeed, amplification of racialized prejudice and, possibly, discrimination.

Race and racialization

The concept of racialization points us towards mundane social processes that construct and sustain race as a meaningful phenomenon. It implies an anthropology incorporating the reflective capacity of mind and the interaction between self and others' definitions of phenomena that might be denoted or connoted as racial (Jenkins 1994). Further, it directs us to consider wider structures of taken for granted, sedimented meanings that constrain the phenomenal forms of racialized phenomena. The illustrations from the employment experience of black and Asian serving officers and resigners indicate that there is not a separate, discrete aspect of the occupational culture assigned or functioning to articulate race. Race is interwoven with and articulated through the mundane typifications and, more usually, stereotypical perceptions that are basic to the occupational culture of the police rank and file. They, therefore, point us towards an interactional conceptualization of race with its construction within the routines of everyday life as the focus of research attention.

As far as research about crime and race is concerned, for example, the concept of racialization directs our attention away from the question, 'What is the relationship between race and crime?', to ask, 'How do some crimes, the contexts within which they have occurred and the people who have or are said to have committed them come to be associated with, directly or indirectly, the category of race?' 'What are the social processes that have led these events and people to be connoted and, or denoted with the meaning "racial"?' In turn, we should ask how criminal justice personnel and those who come into contact with them sustain processes of racialization; what are the consequences of their reflection upon and response to their categorization as 'racial'? The research question is therefore not so much, 'What do black offenders do?' as 'What do black offenders do that leads those who respond to them, including people from all racialized groups, to denote and connote the social world with the meaning of race?' How is the context of their action, an offence, victimization, stop in the street, prosecution, appearance in court, and so on, racialized?[16] How is the phenomenon 'race' constructed within the everyday world? If the response to these questions is that some criminologists have addressed

---

[16] See Small (1994) for a discussion of the consequences for adopting the concept of racialization for the study of racialized relations. Small, however, does not discuss the mundane settings that are stressed in this paper.

them, the criticisms of dominant approaches to the study of race made in this article signal a failure within criminology adequately to grasp the analytical implications of conceptualizing race as social process and to locate it within the everyday world of criminal justice organizations and personnel.

Race cannot be isolated as a discrete variable. Criminologists should seek to document mundane features of the social world that at first sight do not appear to be racialized but, when analysed within an inductive, theoretical framework, are found to be directly and indirectly relevant to the construction of race as a social phenomenon. The constraints of deductive theory in which race is objectified as a need of a social system and conceptualized as an 'Other' are equally perilous. This approach to the study of race avoids the trap of fragmenting the social world into manageable chunks solely for analytical purposes. An attempt is made to identify social processes that construct race but, once deconstructed, the same phenomenon is reified. Too much is assumed about the social articulation of action, which is over-determined.

There are signs that some criminologists are beginning to recognize the value of both statistically based and more qualitative studies of race (Fitzgerald 1993).[17] Their arguments, however, are usually framed in terms of adding on qualitative work after statistical variations for minority ethnic groups have been secured. The basic argument informing this article is that research should in the first instance base its methods on the status of the phenomenon studied. If race is a social construct, and we know that it is, our methodology should not objectify it. There should be consistency between theory and methods of research.

It would be interesting, for example, to respond to Sir Paul Condon's recent comments about race and crime referred to at the beginning of this article by a study of the social context he and his advisers perceived they were addressing. This would include the organizational and more widely derived information that moulded the racialized elements of his ideas into matters of perceived public concern. It would also seek to identify how and why he and other personnel attributed the meaning of race to the events that drew their attention. We could then look at the statistics used in his analysis in a new light, seeing them as part of a process of racialization that need not have denoted the race of those said to be responsible for offences committed. We would not understand the statistical evidence used as in any sense separate from the analysis of the social construction of race.[18]

---

[17] Roger Hood's recent study of the sentencing of minority ethnic offenders in fact ends its extensive statistical analysis with the conclusion that there is a need to research the culture of the court room and the occupational work of judges (Hood 1992).

[18] This also means that 'race' is constructed and sustained in interaction between majority and minority ethnic groups. The notion of power lying within the analysis is not that of a zero-sum game, in which white people are constantly in the ascendancy. The extent to which members of minority ethnic groups racialize phenomena is a subject that has been neglected in social science research.

None of this suggests complacency about the harm crime does to people; attention is not distracted from researching the extent of crime. It does suggest, however, that criminological research concerned with race should theorize the mundane, everyday world of crime and criminal justice organizations; that it should, to use David Matza's term, appreciate the meaningful nature of the social world and, therefore, the phenomena studied (Matza 1969).[19] Present research tends to under or over-theorize race, to objectify the everyday rather than analyse how phenomena, in this case race, are constructed and sustained within it.

References

ACPO, Quality of Service Committee (1993), *Getting Things Right*. London: Association of Chief Police Officers.

Althusser, L. (1971), *Lenin and Philosophy*. London: New Left Books.

Bittner, E. (1967), 'The Police on Skid Row', *American Sociological Review*, 32/5: 699–715.

Bowling, B. (1993), 'Racial Harassment and the Process of Victimisation', *British Journal of Criminology*, 33/2: 216–30.

Brown, J. and Savage, S. C. (1992) 'Policewomen's Career Aspirations: Some Reflections on the Role and Capabilities of Women in Policing in Britain', *Police Studies*, 15/1: 13–19.

Brown, J. and Fielding, J. (1993), 'Qualitative Differences in Men and Women Police Officers' Experience of Occupational Stress', *Work and Stress*, 7/4: 327–40.

Bryman, A. and Cramer, D. (1990), *Quantitative Data Analysis for Social Scientists*. London: Routledge.

Chan, J. (1996), 'Changing Police Culture', *The British Journal of Criminology*, 36/1: 109–34.

Chatterton, M. R. (1992), Controlling Police Work. Strategies and tactics of the lower ranks—their past and future relevance. Paper presented at conference 'Social Order in Post Classical Sociology', University of Bristol.

Cohen, P. and Bains, H. S., eds. (1993), *Multi-Cultural Britain*. Basingstoke: Macmillan.

Durkheim, E. (1982), *The Rules of Sociological Method*. London: Macmillan.

Fielding, N. (1988), 'Competence and Culture in the Police', *Sociology*, 22/1: 45–65.

Fitzgerald, M. (1993), 'Racism: Establishing the Phenomenon', in D. Cook and B. Hudson, eds., *Racism and Criminology*. London: Sage.

---

[19] This paper is about 'race'. However, much of the argument could be applied to the construction of gender relationships within the police and within other organizations. Indeed, the research reported could act as a comparative base from which it might be possible to identify common processes of social exclusion, relevant to a range of groups. Jennifer Brown, Frances Heidensohn and Judith Hunt have published research findings about women police officers that suggest such an approach would be fruitful (for example, Brown 1992, 1993; Heidensohn 1992; Hunt 1984). As far as the articulation of race within occupational cultures is concerned, it may be that comparative research within different types of occupations would reveal that my argument is about occupational cultures *per se* as much as it is about the occupational culture of the police.

Gilroy, P., ed. (1982), *The Myth of Black Criminality*. London: Merlin.

Gilroy, P. (1983), 'Police and Thieves', in Centre for Contemporary Cultural Studies, *The Empire Strikes Back: Race and Racism in Britain*. London: Hutchinson.

Gilroy, P. (1987), *There Ain't No Black in the Union Jack*. London: Hutchinson.

Gilroy, P. (1993), *The Black Atlantic*. London: Verso.

Goldberg, D., ed. (1988), *Anatomy of Racism*. Minneapolis: University of Minneapolis Press.

Hall, S. *et al.* (1978), *Policing the Crisis*. London: Macmillan.

Heidensohn, F. (1992), *Women in Control? The Role of Women in Law Enforcement*. Oxford: Oxford University Press.

Her Majesty's Inspectorate of Constabulary (1992), *Equal Opportunities in the Police Service*. London: Home Office.

Holdaway, S. (1983), *Inside the British Police: A Force at Work*. Oxford: Blackwell.

Holdaway, S. (1987), 'Discovering Structure: Studies of the Police Occupational Culture', in M. Weatheritt, ed., *The Future of Police Research*. Aldershot: Gower.

Holdaway, S. (1991), *Recruiting a Multi-Racial Police Force*. London: HMSO.

Holdaway, S. (1992), Culture, Race and Policy: Some Themes of the Sociology of the Police. Paper presented at conference, 'Social Order in Post Classical Sociology', University of Bristol.

Holdaway, S. (1993), *The Resignation of Black and Asian Officers from the Police Service. A Report to the Home Office*. London: Home Office.

Holdaway, S. (1996), *The Racialisation of British Policing*. Basingstoke: Macmillan.

Holdaway, S. and Rock, P. (1996), *The Social Theory of Criminology*. London: UCL Press.

Hood, R. (1992), *Race and Sentencing*. Oxford: Clarendon Press.

Hunt, J. (1984), 'The Development of Rapport through the Negotiation of Gender in Fieldwork among Police', *Human Organisation*, 43/4: 37–49.

James, D. (1978), 'Police Black Relations: The Professional Solution', in S. Holdaway, ed., *The British Police*, 66–82. London: Edward Arnold.

Jefferson, T. (1993), 'The Racism of Criminalization: Policing and the Reproduction of the Criminal Other', in L. R. Gelsthorpe, ed., *Minority Ethnic Groups in the Criminal Justice System*, 26–46. Cambridge: Cambridge University, Institute of Criminology.

Jefferson, T. and Walker, M.A. (1992), 'Ethnic Minorities in the Criminal Justice System', *The Criminal Law Review*, 83–95.

Jefferson, T. and Walker, M.A. (1993), 'Attitudes to the Police of Ethnic Minorities in a Provincial City', *British Journal of Criminology*, 33/2: 251–66.

Jenkins, R. (1994), 'Rethinking Ethnicity: Identity, Categorization and Power', *Ethnic and Racial Studies*, 17/2: 197–223.

Keith, M. (1993), *Race, Riots and Policing: Lore and Disorder in A Multi-Racist Society*. London: UCL Press.

Kohn, M. (1995), *The Race Gallery: the Return of Racial Science*. London: Cape.

Lea, J. and Young, J. (1984), *What Is to Be Done about Law and Order?* Harmondsworth: Penguin.

Manning, P. (1977), *Police Work*. Cambridge, MA: MIT Press.

Manning, P. K. (1980). *The Narc's Game: Organisational and Informational Limits to Drug Enforcement*. Cambridge, MA: MIT Press.

Mason, D. (1994), 'On the Dangers of Disconnecting Race and Racism', *Sociology*, 28/4: 845–58.

Matza, D. (1969), *Becoming Deviant*. Englewood Cliffs, NJ: Prentice-Hall.

Mayhew, P., Aye Maung, N. and Mirlees-Black, C. (1993), *The 1992 British Crime Survey*. London: HMSO.

Merry, S. E. (1981), *Urban Danger: Life in a Neighbourhood of Strangers*. Philadelphia, PA: Temple University Press.

Metropolitan Police: Analysis Team (1990), *The Metropolitan Police Seminars Looking into Recruiting and Retention of Officers, Particularly Black and Asian Officers: Analysis of Data from Seminar July 1990*. London: Metropolitan Police.

Miles, R. (1982), *Racism and Migrant Labour*. London: Routledge and Kegan Paul.

Miles, R. (1989), *Racism*. London: Routledge.

Miles, R. (1993), *Racism After 'Race Relations'*. London: Routledge.

Modood, T. (1992), *Not Easy Being British: Colour, Culture and Citizenship*. London: Runnymede Trust and Trentham Books.

Modood, T. (1994), 'Political Blackness and British Asians', *Sociology*, 28/4: 859–76.

Newing, J. and Crump, R. R. (1974). Footpad Crime and Its Community Effect in Lambeth, unpublished report. A7 Division, New Scotland Yard.

Norris, C., Fielding, N., Kemp, C. and Fielding, J. (1992), 'Black and Blue: An Analysis of the Influence of Race on Being Stopped by the Police', *British Journal of Sociology*, 43/2: 207–24.

Omi, M. and Winant, M. (1994), *Racial Formation in the United States*. London: Routledge.

Reiner, R. (1985), *The Politics of the Police*. Brighton: Wheatsheaf.

Reiner, R. (1992), 'Race, Crime and Justice: Models of Interpretation', in L. Gelsthorpe, ed., *Minority Ethnic Groups in the Criminal Justice System*, 1–25. Cambridge: The Institute of Criminology, University of Cambridge.

Rex, J. (1973), *Race, Colonialism and the City*. London: Routledge and Kegan Paul.

Rex, J. and Moore, R. (1967), *Race, Community and Conflict*. London: Oxford University Press.

Schutz, A. (1967), *Collected Papers 1: The Problem of Social Reality*. The Hague: Martinus Nijhoff.

Skogan, W. G. (1990), *The Police and Public in England and Wales*. London: HMSO.

Small, S. (1994), *Racialised Barriers*. London: Routledge.

Smith, D. J. (1994), 'Race, Crime and Criminal Justice', in M. Maguire, R. Morgan and R. Reiner, eds., *The Oxford Handbook of Criminology* (pp. 1041–1118). Oxford: Clarendon Press.

Smith, S. J. (1989), *The Politics of Race and Residence: Citizenship, Segregation and White Supremacy in Britain*. Cambridge: Polity.

Solomos, J. (1993), 'Constructions of Black Criminality: Racialisation and Criminalisation in Perspective', in D. Cook and B. Hudson, eds., *Racism and Criminology*. London: Sage.

Taylor, I. (1994), 'The Political Economy of Crime', in M. Maguire, R. Morgan and R. Reiner, eds., *The Oxford Handbook of Criminology*, 469–510. Oxford: Clarendon Press.

The Runnymede Trust (1995a), 'Fleet Street Survivors,' *The Runnymede Bulletin*, July/August, pp. 4–5.

The Runnymede Trust (1995*b*), 'Echoes Over The Years', *The Runnymede Bulletin*, July/August, p. 1.

Waddington, P. A. J. (1987), 'Towards Paramilitarism? Dilemmas in Policing Civil Disorder', *British Journal of Criminology*, 27: 37–46.

Walker, M. (1987), 'Interpreting Race and Crime Statistics', *Journal of the Royal Statistical Society*, A150, pt.1: 39–56.

Walklate, S. (1992), *Victimology: The Victim and the Criminal Justice Process*. London: Unwin Allan.

Weick, K. (1982), 'Enactment Processes in Organisations', in B. Straw and G. Salanick, eds., *New Directions in Organisational Behaviour*. Malabar: Robert E. Krieger.

Wilson, D., Holdaway, S. and Spencer, C. (1984), 'Black Police in the United Kingdom', *Policing*, 1/1: 20–30.

Young, J. (1971), *The Drugtakers*. London: Paladin.

3
Discrimination in the Courts?
by Roger Hood

This study has confirmed what has for long been suspected, namely that, to a very substantial degree, the over-representation of Afro-Caribbean males and females in the prison system is a product of their over-representation among those convicted of crime and sentenced in the Crown Courts. The best estimate that it is possible to make from this study is that 80 per cent of the over-representation of black male offenders in the prison population was due to their over-representation among those convicted at the Crown Court and to the type and circumstances of the offences of which black men were convicted. The remaining 20 per cent, in the case of males but not of females, appeared to be due to differential treatment and other factors which influence the nature and length of the sentences imposed: two thirds of it resulting from the higher proportion of black defendants who pleaded not guilty and who were, as a consequence, more liable on conviction to receive longer custodial sentences.

From Crown Court records it was not possible to shed much light on the circumstances and factors which might produce a higher rate of convictions amongst the black population, but there were some clues which are worthy of further investigation. A higher proportion of black people were charged with offences which could only be dealt with on indictment at the Crown Court: considerably more being charged with robbery, often of the kind normally referred to as 'mugging'. One should not minimise the distress caused by such behaviour, especially when women are the victims, nor the general sense of unease which it breeds, but as a form of violent or property crime it is often not more serious in its consequences than grievous bodily harm or housebreaking, both of which can be dealt with summarily if the court and defendant consent. This would not, of course, have meant that all of these black defendants would have accepted summary trial. The reason is that considerably more of them had, early on in the procedure, signified their intention to plead not guilty: 46 per cent of blacks and Asians compared with

34 per cent of whites charged with robbery. Nevertheless, the unavailability of discretion to deal with these offences either-way inevitably brings more black defendants into the arena of the Crown Court and its greater propensity to inflict a custodial penalty.[1]

Black offenders were also disproportionately involved in the supply of drugs, usually cannabis, and these convictions regularly arose from police activity rather than from a complaint by citizens. This is not the place to open the debate about the seriousness of illegal dealings at street level in cannabis. It is only to say that if these offences were excluded the proportion of black males dealt with at the West Midlands courts would have been 13.7 rather than 17.2 per cent, equivalent to 20 per cent lower. By contrast, excluding such cases amongst whites and Asians would have reduced their number by only 0.6 and 0.9 per cent respectively. Of course, it is impossible to say whether these persons would have committed other offences but it is incontrovertible that the continued legal proscription of cannabis and the insistence that trading in it, even on a small or moderate scale, is an offence which should always be committed to the Crown Court for trial,[2] is a substantial factor influencing the number of black persons in the prison population.

Furthermore, black defendants were at a disadvantage both because of decisions they made and decisions made about them during the processing of cases before they appeared for sentence. They were more likely to be remanded in custody by magistrates who committed them for trial, even taking into account the seriousness of the charges against them and other factors which might legitimately have had an effect on the decision whether to give bail. They were much less likely to have had a social inquiry report prepared on their background, mainly because a considerably higher proportion of them signified their intention to plead not guilty, but also because fewer who pleaded guilty were reported on, although, the reasons for this are not known.

Being already in custody, pleading not guilty, and not having a report were all associated with a higher probability of receiving a custodial sentence or with a lengthier sentence. And all of them, of course, limit the possibilities for effective pleas in mitigation. Those who have been in custody have less

---

[1] See, Carol Hedderman and David Moxon, *Magistrates' Court or Crown Court? Mode of Trial Decisions and Sentencing* (1992), Home Office Research Study No. 125. This study showed, after cases had been matched on nine variables, that 'custody was used almost three times as often and sentences were, on average, about two and a half times longer in elected cases than in comparable cases at Magistrates' Courts. In other words, the Crown Courts impose more than seven times as much custody as do Magistrates' Courts for cases having similar characteristics', at p 37.

[2] In his Practice Note: (Mode of Trial Guidelines), the Lord Chief Justice Lord Lane laid down that supply or possession with intent to supply a class B drug should be committed for trial 'unless there was only small scale supply for no payment' *The [1990] 1* WLR, 1439 at 1442.

opportunity to show that they have been of exemplary behaviour or have sought to make amends by, say, entering regular employment since they were charged with the offence. Those who deny the offence cannot suddenly, on being found guilty, convincingly express remorse. For those without social inquiry reports there is often insufficient information on hand to put the offence in its social context and no opportunity to take advantage of a specific proposal from a probation officer for an alternative sentence to custody. It would appear, therefore, that ethnic minority defendants were inadvertently subjected to a form of indirect discrimination at the point of sentence due to the fact that they chose more often to contest the case against them. Because of the way that the system works to encourage guilty pleas through a 'discount' on sentence, which has been shown to produce a substantial reduction,[3] and because it is the policy of the Probation Service not generally to make social inquiry reports on those who intend to contest the case against them, black defendants obviously put themselves at greater risk of custody and longer sentences.

No criticism should be levelled against the judges on this issue: they were, of course applying the policy as laid down by the Court of Appeal. And there would, of course, be resistance to changing the policy of giving a substantial credit for guilty pleas given the pressure on the workload and costs of the courts and the judicial desire to be able to respond to expressions of genuine remorse. Nevertheless it is time to consider all the implications of a policy which favours so strongly those who plead guilty, when ethnic minorities are less willing to forgo their right to challenge a prosecution. For, as Andrew Ashworth has argued, 'there are grave dangers of injustice in its practical operation'.[4]

Some headway may be made in dealing with this problem after Section 3(1) of the Criminal Justice Act 1991 comes into effect on 1st October 1992.

---

[3] See D. Moxon, *op. cit.*, p 32. D. A. Thomas's, *Current Sentencing Practice* (1983 continuing), Section A 8.2., states that the Court of Appeal has approved reductions of between one quarter and one third. As mentioned above, at fn 5 p 125, the average discount for male adults in the West Midlands appeared to be about a third. Recently (June 1992), a Working Party of the General Council of the Bar (Chairman Robert Seabrook QC) has suggested that the amount of discount should be linked to the stage at which the defendant decided to plead guilty. Those who notified their intention to do so at the committal stage would get a minimum of 30 per cent discount; those who did so before the first listing of the case in the Crown Court would get a minimum of 20 per cent; and those who only decided to plead guilty between the first Crown Court listing and arraignment in court would only be eligible for a minimum of 10 per cent. This is intended to decrease the number who change their plea at a late stage, causing 'cracked trials' and administrative inconvenience. *The Efficient Disposal of Business in the Crown Court* (1992), p 38. It would be important to monitor any ethnic differences before putting such a proposal into effect.

[4] Andrew Ashworth, *Sentencing and Penal Policy* (1983), at p 314. For a more recent discussion see the new edition of Professor Ashworth's book *Sentencing and Criminal Justice* (which was published as this report was in Press): (1992), pp 130–133.

This will make it mandatory for the court to obtain and consider a pre-sentence report (the designation for a new style of social inquiry report) when the court is considering the imposition of a custodial sentence on either of the grounds laid down by the Act: namely, the seriousness of the offence and one other offence associated with it, or, where the offence is a violent or sexual offence, the protection of the public from serious harm from the offender. However, the Act does make an exception to this requirement where 'the offence or any other offence associated with it is triable only on indictment' and the court considers that a pre-sentence report would be 'unnecessary'.[5] This provision was inserted so that reports would not have to be prepared in cases which were inevitably bound for custody. But the evidence of this study suggests that if this exception is used for a wider range of indictable-only offences, it will bear far more on black and Asian defendants than on whites in the Crown Court. There is a danger that it will not address sufficiently the issue of indirect discrimination in the amount and type of information available to judges in deciding whether or not a custodial sentence should be imposed.

This research has also revealed a rather complex pattern of racial disparities in the sentences imposed. It should be recognized that there was no evidence of a 'blanket' race or colour discrimination against all ethnic minority defendants, male or female. In most respects, Asian offenders did not fare worse than whites nor did all Afro-Caribbeans. Whether they did or did not depended on a number of factors: the seriousness of the case, age, employment status, whether they had pleaded not guilty, and, above all, the court centre to which they had been committed for trial the judge before whom they appeared for sentence, some of whom appeared to sentence a considerably lower proportion of black defendants to custody than would have been expected. At Coventry, for example, white defendants were much more likely to receive a custodial sentence than whites dealt with elsewhere in the West Midlands, particularly at nearby Birmingham. On the other hand, although blacks at Coventry more often got a custodial sentence than blacks at Birmingham, they were more leniently treated than either whites or Asians at Coventry.

Taking the total number of male cases dealt with over the whole of the West Midlands, and controlling for the nature of the offences and several other legally relevant variables, the apparent differences in the proportionate use of custody between white, black and Asian males dealt with by these courts was considerably reduced from 8 percentage points to about 2.5 points. Thus, a relatively small difference remained. Depending on the basis of the comparison, a black offender had a probability of receiving a custodial sentence about 5 to 8 per cent higher than a white offender. Asians, on the other

---

[5] For a very useful discussion of this Sub-Section see Martin Wasik and Richard D. Taylor, *Blackstone's Guide to the Criminal Justice Act 1991* (1991), pp 22–23.

hand, had about a 4 per cent lower probability. Given the number of cases which appeared before these courts in the course of a year, these differences were sufficiently large to be to the disadvantage of a considerable number of black defendants especially when combined with the longer sentences imposed on the higher proportion of them who had pleaded not guilty.

But does this amount to evidence of discrimination? Or, to put it another way: is the evidence consistent with a pattern of discrimination rather than a residue of unexplained variation?

It is true, of course, that no statistical study can control for all the variables which might affect differences between cases. But it has to be recognised that the analysis carried out for this inquiry was based on a substantial number of cases, used multivariate techniques to control for the influence of some 15 legally relevant variables, and used a variety of bases for making comparisons: a risk of custody score based on all cases, disaggregated to show court and race variations; a score based on the white cases only so as to compare the weight given to variables for whites with their weight when applied to blacks; a score based solely on the Birmingham cases, so as to compare the weights given to variables by that court to the weights attached to the same variables at other courts. All these scores produced the same pattern of results and very similarly sized differences. And, as a further check, a probability of custody score was devised using an entirely different statistical method, a method widely in use by the probation service in devising risk of custody indices. This, too, produced similar results. It is difficult to imagine what other legally relevant variables not already taken into account could explain the fact that for every 100 black males sentenced to custody at Birmingham about 130 black males were given a custodial sentence at the Dudley courts, and even more at Warwick or Stafford.

It is, of course, always hazardous to move from correlation to explanation. But the marked differences in the apparent treatment of black and white offenders amongst those who had been sentenced at one of the Dudley courts needs some interpretation, particularly because there was a much lower proportion of blacks sentenced to custody in the neighbouring Birmingham Crown Court. Nevertheless the fact that a similar high custody rate for blacks was observed at Warwick and Stafford suggests that there may be nothing unique about the Dudley courts.

The judges who were relatively severe on black offenders compared with whites dealt with a higher proportion of the cases at the Dudley courts than at Birmingham, but on aggregate the other judges at the Dudley courts—taken together—were also comparatively more likely to sentence black offenders to custody than colleagues at Birmingham. There were other indices of a different sentencing pattern. Black defendants at the Dudley courts got a sentence greater than that recommended by a probation officer much more often than did blacks at Birmingham. Moreover, blacks at the Dudley courts received sentences generally further up the scale of penalties; and if they were recommended for probation or community service they were more likely to get a more severe penalty than was a white defendant.

In attempting to understand what may have produced this divergent pattern, it was at once noticeable that the differences were greatest not in the mid to upper band of cases where difficult decisions were being made about whether to use custody or not, but in the range of cases at the lower end of the scale of severity. There was strong evidence to suggest that factors which would have been regarded as mitigating the seriousness of the case if the defendant was white were not given the same weight if the defendant was black in the cases dealt with at Dudley courts. Yet, they were given a similar weight for black offenders dealt with at Birmingham. For instance, blacks at the Dudley courts were sentenced to custody in a significantly higher proportion of cases whether they were employed or unemployed, whether they were under 21 or over 21, whether they had only one prior conviction or 2 or more, whether they pleaded guilty or not guilty.

A much higher proportion of the black offenders at the Dudley courts (amongst those in the lower band of seriousness) who had been convicted with at least one other black defendant were sentenced to custody at the Dudley courts. Here the difference between the observed and expected rate, given the nature of the cases, was so big that it explained half of the difference between the observed and expected rate of custody for all black cases at the Dudley courts. An examination of these cases failed to find any distinctive differences between them and cases where whites had been convicted with other whites. Nor were the black cases at Birmingham, where custody was, in contrast, rarely used, substantially different in character. It appears reasonable to assume that the judges at the Dudley courts viewed these cases in a different light to those involving groups of whites. While it is true that there were slightly more black offenders who were committed with other black offenders at the Dudley courts than at Birmingham, there were substantially more whites at the Dudley courts who had been convicted alongside other whites. Furthermore, blacks were sentenced more often to custody than either whites at the Dudley courts or blacks at Birmingham when they were the sole offender. On the whole, there was nothing to suggest that the judges who dealt with the Dudley courts' cases were confronted with a worse impression of black criminality than were the far more lenient judges at Birmingham. On the contrary, black defendants were a lower proportion of the caseload of the Dudley courts, and the seriousness of the cases dealt with, as measured by their risk of custody score, was no different from the cases at Birmingham.

Could it be that black offenders sentenced at the Dudley courts had been less well served by the pleas of mitigation made on their behalf? There was no way of measuring the performance of barristers and probation officers, but this hypothesis seems implausible for a number of reasons. First, a higher proportion of blacks at the Dudley courts than at Birmingham pleaded guilty

(83% v 75%) and had social inquiry reports available about them (63% v 56%): both factors which are an aid to mitigation. Secondly, as already mentioned, it was in the less serious range of cases, where mitigation would normally be more readily accepted, that the largest differences between the use of custody for blacks and whites existed. Thirdly, the fact that the sentences imposed on blacks at the Dudley courts were of greater severity than those recommended by probation officers where the defendant was black rather than white, or was a black dealt with at Birmingham, also suggested that it was not the quality of the mitigation, but the different practice of the Dudley courts when faced with a black defendant, that accounted for the racial differences observed.

It is therefore apparent that the failure to find a large overall difference in the use of custody for blacks, whites and Asians in the West Midlands as a whole was a product of the fact that by far the largest proportion of cases in the sample had been dealt with at Birmingham Crown Court, a court with no overall racial bias in its sentencing patterns as far as use of custody was concerned. Leaving Birmingham aside, there were substantial racial differences in the sentencing patterns of the other courts and it seems inconceivable that similar variations would not be found in other regions of the country. It would not need very many courts to behave as the Dudley courts and Warwick and Stafford appear to do, for it to have a considerable impact on the proportion of black offenders in the prison system: especially when one bears in mind that not only are they more readily sentenced to custody but, because they are more likely to contest the case, they have longer sentences to serve. Furthermore, it seems that if they are not given a custodial sentence they are more likely, and much more likely in some courts, to receive a suspended sentence of imprisonment or a community service order which puts them more at risk of being sentenced to custody if they should re-offend.

When one contrasts the overall treatment meted out to black Afro-Caribbean males one is left wondering whether it is not a result of different racial stereotypes operating on the perceptions of some judges. The greater involvement of black offenders in street crime and in the trade in cannabis, their higher rate of unemployment, their greater resistance to pressures to plead guilty, and possibly a perception of a different, less deferential, demeanour in court may all appear somewhat more threatening.[6] And, if not threatening, less worthy of mitigation or punishment. It was significant that being unemployed increased the risk of a black male getting a custodial sentence, but not, in general, for a white or an Asian offender. In contrast, the

---

[6] This was not something that could be investigated without interviews with judges, but the Oxford pilot study of Crown Courts suggested 'that the defendant's demeanour and "attitude" in court were regarded as legitimate and indeed significant matters to be taken into count', Andrew Ashworth et al., *Sentencing in the Crown Court* (1984), *op cit.*, pp 22–23.

better financial and employment status of the Asians and their more socially integrated households, when judged by white standards, as well as the fact that they were much more likely to be first-time offenders, may have meant that they were probably able to present themselves as less threatening, and more worthy of mitigation than either whites or blacks. Only in respect of the length of sentences received by those who were sentenced to prison did Asian adult males fare worse. But without research which would allow the investigation of judicial attitudes towards, and perceptions of, racially related differences in crime patterns and in cultural responses to the criminal justice system, all this for the moment must remain speculation. It cannot be doubted that such a programme of research is now needed.

The findings regarding women will surprise many, especially given the very large over-representation of black women in penal institutions. The evidence in general supports the so-called 'chivalry' or 'paternalistic' hypothesis that judges give much more weight to mitigating features of the case in sentencing women offenders, whether white or black. No differences were found between the use of custody, of alternatives, or in sentence length between white and black women when variables relating to the seriousness of the offences were controlled for. Black women were just as likely as the whites to have had a social inquiry report prepared about them prior to sentence and were no more likely than the whites to have been given a sentence greater than that recommended by the probation officer. Furthermore, compared with black men, black women were dealt with relatively leniently just as white women were dealt with leniently compared with white men. Nevertheless, when a particularly disadvantaged group were singled out—those who had various attributes which could be associated with failure to conform to female stereotypes—a relatively high proportion of them were sentenced to custody: yet, no more blacks than whites and no more females than males. One thing is certain. If considerations relating to their gender did not mitigate the punishment of women, and they were treated as men are, there would be many more in custody than at present.[7]

What conclusions of a practical kind can be drawn from this study? First, that the research has revealed a complex picture of the way in which race appears to have affected the pattern of sentencing. In doing so, it has led to some uncomfortable conclusions for those whose duty it is to sentence offenders. It will not be possible any more to make the claim that all the differences in the treatment of black offenders occur elsewhere in the criminal justice system. At least some of it occurs in the courts, and more often in

[7] In the United States, where Sentencing Commissions have sought to establish equality in the treatment of men and women, there is evidence from Minnesota that sentencing severity for women increased to the level for males within three years of the establishment of the Guidelines (I am grateful to Professor Michael Tonry for this information). Overall, the State and Federal Incarceration rates for women have been growing at a much faster rate than for men. See 'Female Prison Population Growing Faster than Males' *Overcrowded Times* May 1991, p 3.

some localities than others. Much will be achieved if judges recognise this. One aim of studying sentencing by empirical methods is to help stimulate reassessment of attitudes and judicial responses. Previous research has shown how unaware judges may be of their own practices, let alone those of their colleagues.[8] It may be that some are not yet sufficiently sensitive to the way in which racial views and beliefs may influence their judgement. If this research can stimulate such self-awareness and re-evaluation it will have made a modest contribution towards the positive self conscious appreciation of the need to take the question of race seriously which the Judicial Studies Board has now recognized by the setting up of its Ethnic Minorities Advisory Committee.

Secondly, this study draws attention to the way in which the criminal process may contribute to indirect discrimination against black people. There is clearly a need to consider the implications of the policy which favours so strongly those who plead guilty, when ethnic minorities are less willing to let a prosecution go unchallenged. This has implications, in particular, for the range and value of the information available to the courts in deciding whether or not to impose a custodial sentence as well as the type of non-custodial sentence. And, for the reason already mentioned, it will be necessary to monitor carefully the way in which the courts exercise their discretion, under the Criminal Justice Act 1991, to pass sentence without a pre-sentence report when the case is one triable only on indictment.

Thirdly, there are obvious implications relating to the duty placed on the Secretary of State by Section 95 (1)(b) to 'publish such information as he considers expedient for the purpose of . . . facilitating the performance . . . [by persons engaged in the administration of criminal justice] . . . of their duty to avoid discriminating against any persons on the grounds of race or sex or any other improper ground.' To do this it will be essential for the Crown Courts to monitor the ethnic origin of all persons appearing before them. If the self-reflection on sentencing performance mentioned above is to be achieved, information on sentencing dispositions, analysed by ethnic origin, should be communicated to each judge and to the court as a whole annually. Only then will it be possible to detect whether sentencing patterns which might prove to be unfavourable to any ethnic minority are becoming established. Judges may regard this as an unnecessary imposition, or even as a slight on their integrity and impartiality. But in all walks of public life, servants of the Crown are being expected to monitor their performance, both with regard to its quality and to its evenhandedness with respect to ethnicity and gender. There can be no good reason for judges to be excepted from this demand. Indeed it is essential if the principle promulgated by the Judicial Studies Board in its Report for 1987–1991 is to be made a reality:

[8] See Andrew Ashworth *et. al.*, *Sentencing in the Crown Court, op. cit.*, pp 50–56.

It is axiomatic that no court should treat a defendant differently from any other simply because of his race or ethnic origin. Any court that exhibited prejudice against a defendant from an ethnic minority would be failing in its basic duty to treat all defendants before it equally

When this research was originally envisaged, it was hoped to sample a large number of cases at each of the various stages of the criminal process. For the reasons already explained this proved to be an impossible task with the resources available. It is therefore recommended that a study should be set in train, officially supported by all the agencies in the criminal justice system, which would follow a large number of cases in all the major areas where there are sufficient concentrations of ethnic minorities, as they progress from arrest to final disposition in the courts. Only when this flow of cases is properly monitored will it be possible to identify the points at which any discrimination may occur and to quantify their cumulative effect on the number and proportions of ethnic minorities who eventually enter the prison system.

4

The Enlightenment and Euro-American theories of the judicial process
by Biko Agozino

The influence of the Roman Empire on the evolution of European penology is all too obvious. Many legal historians would emphasise the role of the Roman emperors, as well as Napoleon and German legal scholars in laying the foundation of the Romano-Germanic family of law which dominates continental Europe today. However, when it comes to modern European imperialism and the imposition (of often perverted western ideas about 'crime and punishment' on the rest of the world, and the heroic resistance to this) of a largely puzzling *criminal* justice, conventional criminology is curiously silent. This conspiracy of silence may be due to criminology's complicity in the imperialist project. The silence could also be partly due to the questionable nature of *criminal* justice in the face of resolute resistance to colonial injustice in contrast to the *relative* legal consensus among the ruling capitalist classes of Europe.

From your reading of history, you must be familiar with the sociocultural contexts within which the Enlightenment movement developed and from which the movement broke away to found modernity. The pre-Enlightenment period was the era of supernatural explanations for power and misconduct – kings ruled because they had divine right to rule and people became deviant as a result of demonic possession from which they had to be exorcised and purified if possible, or destroyed in order to be saved in the hereafter. The demonic judicial process was characterised by public executions for serious 'offenders' or sinners, pillory and shame for cheats, the centralisation of judicial authority in the hands of religious officials, public administration of punishment in the community and, above all, a phallocentric bias against pagan women, who were executed as witches (Pfohl, 1994). In this sense, the Enlightenment, or *Iluminismo* in Portuguese, was a progressive movement in social thought, aimed at the liberation of individuals from despotic rule by the forces of nature, religious orthodoxy and political traditionalism in Europe.

Piers Beirne analysed how a Frenchman was wrongly executed in 1761 for the murder of his son who had in fact committed suicide. Three years later, Beccaria published anonymously his best-seller, *Treatise on Crime and Punishment*, condemning the arbitrary power exercised by judges and calling for the rational application of the law based on the principle of equality. He also called for the abolition of the death penalty because, according to him, the right to take life was not one of the rights that individuals possessed in a state of nature and so was not a right that people ceded to the state to be exercised on their behalf under the social contract. However, his insistence that punishment should be made to fit the crime provided his supporters with an excuse to retain capital punishment as the only penalty that fitted certain crimes. At the same time, his opponents were powerful members of the justice system and the Church who ridiculed his idea of equality before the law and convinced the Pope of the need to ban his treatise for almost 200 years (Beirne, 1993). The execution of a single innocent Frenchman counts for more in the conventional history of criminology than the genocidal trans-Atlantic slavery in which millions of Africans were destroyed or the genocide of Native Americans and Aboriginal Australians by European *conquistados*.

The European slave trade was the testing ground for the Enlightenment's credentials as a liberatory thought, but as Gilroy (1993), Fanon (1963) and Rodney (1972) – all descendants of enslaved Africans – have shown, *Iluminismo* was pathetically blinded by what Retamar (1979) calls the 'black legend'. According to the myth of the black legend, Spain was blamed by Britain and France for giving a bad name to imperialism due to its more brutal form of the civilising process. However, Retamar argues: 'If anything distinguishes the Spanish conquest from the depredations of Holland, France, England, Germany, Belgium or the United States . . . it is not the proportion of crimes – in this they are all worthy rivals – but rather the proportion of scruples.'

The conquest of the New World and the development of European slavery systematised the persecution of people simply because they appeared different, long before this experiment was extended to the 'witches' of Europe. The European enslavement of Africans and the massacre of Native Americans began in the fifteenth century, but it was in the seventeenth century that the rarely enforced medieval criminal category of 'witchcraft' became a massive force of moral panic that saw millions of mostly women murdered. European enslavement of Africans and the genocidal conquest of Native Americans started before the witch craze, but all three forms of persecution continued together for many years. In fact, the Salem witch hunt was blamed on Tituba, a kitchen slave from Barbados, who was the first to be tried and murdered for allegedly bewitching young girls, who were crawling on all fours, and barking like dogs, at a time when the Royal Charter of the Puritans had just been revoked, giving rise to widespread economic stress and uncertainty (Pfohl, 1994: 26; Wilson, 1993).

It was at the height of the slave trade that classicism emerged to challenge the arbitrary nature of punishment in medieval Europe, but this insight was not extended to enslaved Africans who were arbitrarily victimised, even when they did no wrong. However, it was not until the height of colonialism in Africa and Asia that Europe discovered the new 'science' of criminology as a tool to aid the control of the Other – a supposed advancement on classicist philosophies of justice. This was also the time that the Marquis de Sade was writing about the pleasure of inflicting pain on innocent people, a metaphor for imperialism, except that the sadist did not live on the surpluses of sadism. However, talk of retribution and utilitarianism could well become a metaphor for the campaign by people of African descent demanding reparations for the crimes of slavery and colonialism, except that Marx rightly critiqued the gangster philosophy of Jeremy Bentham, who suggested that everyone was a calculating philistine, maximising profits and minimising losses, like the bourgeoisie, without regard to morality (Marx, 1954: 609–10). In other words, the demand for reparations is not a search for profit from slavery by people of African descent, but a search for justice which would be incomprehensible to the utilitarian Bentham, who saw the common people as objects to be manipulated with carrots and sticks instead of recognising them as active subjects who are making their own principled history. As Cæsaire put it, with his compelling poetic prose that says a lot about criminology without any need to name the discipline:

> Security? Culture? The rule of law? In the meantime, I look around and wherever there are colonizers and colonized face to face, I see force, brutality, cruelty, sadism, conflict, and, in a parody of education, the hasty manufacture of a few thousand subordinate functionaries, 'boys', artisans, office clerks, and interpreters necessary for the smooth operation of business ... Between the colonizer and colonized there is room only for forced labor, intimidation, pressure, the police, taxation, theft, rape, compulsory crops, contempt, mistrust, arrogance, self-complacency, swinishness, brainless elites, degraded masses.
>
> (Cæsaire, 1972: 21)

Enlightened retribution and Utilitarianism

The Enlightenment came about to challenge the privilege of divine right as well as the ideology of revealed knowledge among Europeans while denying that the colonised had the rational faculty to reason about what is just and what is cruel. In the place of divine right, moral philosophers like Hobbes (1650), Locke (1690), Rousseau (1762), Kant, Hegel and others insisted that a social contract was the best possible foundation for civil democratic rule, which must be informed by rational principles rather than by unverifiable claims of revelation. Yet under the slave trade and colonialism, democracy was completely denied, the social contract was nonexistent and whole populations were treated as criminals without human rights. Cesare Beccaria's (1804) publication is credited with laying the foundation of the classicist school of criminology by synthesising the principles of the (Hobbesian) social contract, which referred to political rule in general, and applying them directly to crime and punishment. According to him, men have the right to use punishment to deter one another from wrecking the social contract into which they have freely entered. Again, the emphasis is on the power of European men to punish others but, given that the enslaved and the colonised did not freely enter into any social contract, what was being administered to them is better understood as victimisation, especially when they were completely innocent.

According to Beccaria, punishment is justifiable only if it is not arbitrary (and it was certainly arbitrary under slavery and colonialism), if it is calculable (the pain caused by colonialism is beyond calculation though slave law often tried to calculate the quantity of torture that could be imposed at a time; see James, 1980), if it is applied to all offenders equally, irrespective of their social circumstances (slavery and colonialism punished the innocent as though they were offenders), and if it is proportional to the amount of pain caused by the crime. What sort of punishment would be proportional to the crimes of slavery and colonialism for which people of African descent are deservedly demanding reparations?

The French Revolutionary Penal Code of 1791 was apparently based on these Beccarian principles of inflexible rationality yet Napoleon refused to recognise the Haitian revolution of that year until his army was defeated by Haitian forces led by Toussaint l'Ouverture (James, 1980). Then Napoleon tricked this leader of the Black Jacobins, as James called them, to Paris for a peace treaty only to kidnap him and torture him in prison until his death. The impractical nature of the inflexible Penal Code resulted in neoclassical revisions to the Code in 1810 and 1819 to make allowance for the mitigating circumstances of age and premeditation, but still without recognising slavery as a crime against humanity. (That declaration waited almost 200 years until the World Congress against Racism in 2001, a conference that was boycotted by America and threatened by Europe because the issue of reparations for the crimes of slavery and colonialism was tabled for discussion along with the injustice of Israeli colonisation of Palestinian territories.) In England, insanity was added as a defence following the case of McNaughten who was charged in 1843 with the murder of Mr Drummond, secretary to the Prime Minister, Robert Peel (who organised the first professional police force). McNaughten claimed that it was Peel that he intended to kill because God had asked him to do so on the ground that the Prime Minister worshipped the devil and that he was running a government of Evil Tories. The fact that McNaughten was a political activist in the Chartist movement against the alienation of labour by the industrial revolution was ignored by the prosecution (Pfohl, 1994). Given his Irish name, he could have been an anti-imperialist too but the jury was satisfied with the insanity plea.

Before these neoclassicist reforms, Jeremy Bentham had found the archaic state of eighteenth-century English common law repugnant in the same way that Beccaria found the continuation of harsh demonic control in Europe repulsive. In his books, Bentham (1789) closely followed Beccaria in attempting to find an answer to the Hobbesian question of why society is possible in spite (but also because) of the love of private pleasure and dislike of personal pain (except when it is the sadistic pain inflicted on others under slavery and colonialism). Although Bentham and Beccaria are in agreement with Hobbes that European men are basically hedonistic bastards, they differ in the sense that Beccaria would want punishment to serve the purpose of retribution, whereas Bentham would add the utilitarian principle of deterrence to the purpose of punishment.

A review of the philosophy of punishment shows that the punishment of the innocent (the colonised, for instance) is treated as a fantastic tale found only in fiction and analogies. For example, a strong objection to the Benthamite utilitarian philosophy of punishment by Beccarian retributivist philosophers is that utilitarians would permit and even encourage the punishment of the innocent if this could be seen to have the utility of promoting order (a common colonial tactic). For example, if a white woman is allegedly raped by a black man in a colonial situation, the hypothetical example goes, it would be utilitarian to punish any black man, even if he is innocent, in order to satisfy the public desire for revenge and avert a race riot in which many more black people might be attacked and killed. Note that there is no hesitation on the part of this hypothesis that the rapist was a black man for, under the colonial situation, the native is synonymous with the offender.

Rawls (1969) attempted to solve this hypothetical case (without doubting whether the allegation that the rapist was black is true or false) by assuming that:

1   The punishment of the innocent in such a circumstance would not promote law and order and therefore would not be utilitarian, especially if it is known that the person punished was innocent. So,
2   Such a punishment can work only if it remains a secret and for it to remain a secret, there must be a special institution for 'telishment' whose job it would be to manipulate the public and control information about telished individuals and cases. In this sense, the punishment of the innocent would not be punishment but telishment and because the conditions for the establishment of institutions for telishment are impossible, telishment can only be hypothesised but never practised.

Rawls's assumptions are flawed by the fact that knowledge of innocence is never universal and collective, but often sectional and partisan. Under the colonial situation, people who are known by many to be innocent could remain under 'punishment' (Nelson Mandela, for instance) if the people who believe them to be innocent lack the power to effect or secure their acquittal. On the other hand, people who are widely known to be guilty could escape punishment because the people who know of their guilt lack the will or the power to prove their guilt and effect or secure their punishment. In other words, the sophisticated attempt to define conditions for telishment is an unnecessary diversion from the fact that existing institutions do 'punish' the innocent and attempt to conceal their innocence or even with public knowledge of their innocence, without having to rely on a philosophical institution for telishment.

Anthony Quinton (1969) comes close to recognising that 'punishing the innocent' is not only a logical contradiction or hypothetical hair-splitting, but also a historical problem that faces real people. Among moral philosophers, he is one of the few who agree that suffering can be inflicted on innocent people, but he insists that this cannot be called punishment. According to Quinton, such suffering should properly be described as 'judicial terrorism' or 'social surgery'. As he puts it, 'If we inflict suffering on an innocent man and try to pass it off as punishment, we are guilty of lying since we make a lying imputation that he is guilty and responsible for an offence' (Quinton, 1969: 58–9).

Quinton is right in observing that the punishment of the innocent is not punishment, but judicial terrorism. However, by making judicial terrorism equivalent to social surgery, he seems willing to let the judicial terrorists off too lightly by suggesting that their actions are equivalent to surgical life-saving operations. By saying that those who inflict suffering on the innocent are guilty simply of lying or perjury, he trivialises the problem of victimisation as mere punishment (VAMP) by suggesting that it is no more than a logical problem of imputation.

This book will show that the preoccupation with the punishment of offenders (POO) is only partly valid when applied to class, race and gender relations, especially under colonialism. It is not the case that punishment is proof of an offence, nor that all offenders are punished. However, since punishment is usually conceptualised as a predict of the offender, it is necessary to develop a different vocabulary for the phenomenon of the 'punishment' of the innocent (POTI). It is necessary to go beyond descriptive vocabulary to show the nature which such victimisation assumes in its impact on people with variable power and material resources corresponding to class, race and gender relations. It is not enough to explain this away as a pitfall along the penal paths of progress, or as irrationalities within largely rational bureaucratic systems, or as mistakes to be corrected with the payment of financial compensations, or simply as repressive fetishes for domination and exploitation (Agozino, 1997a).

I am convinced (and you are welcome to disagree) that the judicial process does not only punish offenders and protect 'victims'. The system sometimes also criminally victimises. A classic example of such systematic victimisation is the Dreyfus Affair which occurred in France at the end of the nineteenth century. (See Finkelstein (2001) for an account of what he calls 'the classic case of miscarriage of justice . . . a full understanding of the triviality, the prejudice, the casual cruelty and the clannishness which sent a wholly innocent man to isolation on a Caribbean rock, kept him there for five years, and with a lack of scruple and a tenacity worthy of a better cause checked every move to re-open the case.') Douglas Porch (1995) contends that the case was insignificant in itself, but became prominent because it could be used to clarify ideological boundaries in the revolutionary and counter-revolutionary struggles of the time and the role of the French secret service in imperialist wars since then.

The anti-Semitism that was widespread in France, as in other European countries, at that time was expressed by the opponents of Alfred Dreyfus, who was framed as a spy and who was nearly lynched after his conviction. However, the notoriety of this individual case should not blind us to the fact that it was one among many that may or may not be well known today. For example, King Ja Ja of Opobo, Nigeria, was not even offered a trial by the British Merchant Navy, which deported him to slave labour in the Caribbean for opposing European domination of trade in the Niger Delta. Moreover, many other cases did not involve single individuals but whole groups and categories of people, as can be seen in the history of the judicial process under slavery, colonialism, fascism and authoritarian populism (Hall, 1988; Hillyard, 1993). In other words, what Stuart Hall calls the perspective of articulation is useful for understanding how punishment, victimisation and welfare practices are relatively articulated, disarticulated and rearticulated like race–gender–class articulation. This also suggests that the judicial process is articulated with other criminal/civil justice processes in such a way that the analysis of one benefits from a comparative reference to the others.

The principles of classicism are recognised by Taylor et al. (1973), Gouldner (1971) and many others as polemics by the rising bourgeois class against the privileges of the landed aristocracy. These same principles have equally been criticised for advocating formal equality between men without also advocating substantive equality, without which the former would be more or less empty words. The Enlightenment has also been criticised for concentrating on the rights of man and the rationality of man, with the underlying assumption that women are irrational and therefore undeserving of equal justice. This is recognised by many as an extension of critical race studies which have challenged the presumption that rationality is exclusively possessed by Europeans and that 'other cultures' are still ruled by tyrannical nature (Kingdom, 1992; Gilroy, 1993). The Enlightenment can therefore be likened to gangster philosophy – the idea that the people robbed, raped and murdered by the mob are fall guys, mugs and fools, while the Mafia are the wise guys or good fellas. Hence, Soyinka (1988) suggested to the Nobel Institute that works by the Enlightenment philosophers should carry a health warning to African readers: 'BEWARE, THIS WORK CAN DAMAGE YOUR RACIAL SELF-ESTEEM.'

These are valid claims, except that Enlightenment philosophy was prescriptive rather than descriptive. Kant (1964) would say that it was the Age of Enlightenment rather than the Enlightened Age. In other words, the universal man, equality before the law, individual freedom and even rationality were not decreed into existence by the Enlightenment, but were proclaimed as worthy goals of the movement towards increasing happiness. For example, the Enlightenment called for rationality and science, but the Enlightenment philosophers were not scientists themselves, they were philosophers offering what West (1993) calls 'prophetic thoughts' on the need for scientific knowledge of ways to improve human conditions. The problem with the conventional versions of positivism is that there is nothing positive or progressive about their reactionary, repressive ideology. It is for this reason that critical thinkers distance themselves from August Comte and his idiosyncratic version of positivism as social engineering. Apart from the assumption that eliminating people who are different from the white supremacist, patriarchal imperialists would make society more positive or better or happier, positivism wrongly assumed that only empiricism is acceptable as a scientific method. As a consequence, anything that is not observable, like surplus labour, the square root of minus one (the unknown 'X' in mathematics which Malcolm X adopted to replace the name imposed on his family during slavery) or race–class–gender relations would be ruled out of analysis by empiricist positivism.

The Enlightenment was not simply prescriptive, it was also descriptive in the sense that it too easily idealised the existing hierarchies of race, class and gender and represented these inequalities in power relations as evidence of the survival of the fittest. Apart from the fact that the Enlightenment philosophers described their own studies of history, philosophy, law, arts and language as 'scientific' in the sense of being rational and objective, the Enlightenment denied rationality to the poor, women and people of other cultures who were supposedly still ruled by nature and instincts rather than by reason and (Christian) civilisation. Similarly, the Enlightenment was too confident of the goodness of rationality, as if anything that is reasonable (to a white, middle-class man) is necessarily good. Uncritical faith in science and rationality is what distinguishes the Enlightenment, which was largely blind to enslavement, from a postmodern world which is conscious of the crimes of Nazism and apartheid as the collective victimisation of mostly innocent people, a collective victimisation that was articulated as a penalty for the subaltern 'offender' by the dominant collective offender. The ethic of collective responsibility exposes the ethic of individual responsibility as another prophecy of the Enlightenment that has not been religiously fulfilled.

Many writers, such as Emile Durkheim (1965), Max Weber (1905), Karl Marx (1980) and more recently Peter Fitzpatrick (1992), have pointed out that the demographic explosion in Europe in the eighteenth century, the burgeoning in scholarship initiated by the reformation of the Church and developed by improved means of communication, the French Revolution and the rise of modern states, the decline of feudal economy, the rise of mercantilist capitalism and the industrial revolution did not completely destroy the fatalism of the Middle Ages. Rather, the rituals and discourse of demonology, such as swearing on the Bible to tell the truth in court, remained an aspect of the judicial process. At a deeper level, the traditions of adjudication which were developed under feudalism, such as the jury system and the inquisitorial versus the adversarial systems of adjudication, were retained by the various European jurisdictions and transplanted to non-European cultures through conquest and trade.

The rational ideal type and Orientalism

Max Weber (1979) provides an account of these contrasting models of the judicial process in the language of the Enlightenment. His ideal types of judicial administration are effectively two models of the judicial process – the bureaucratic or 'rational' (Enlightenment) model and the traditional or 'irrational' (pre-modern) administration of justice. The bureaucratic model is more successful, according to Weber, because of its technical superiority. It has precision, economy, consistency, co-ordination and speed. It executes justice in a 'professional' way because cases are decided 'without regard to persons'. If this bureaucratic authority is applied consistently, it would level out social differences, but this is not always the case because bureaucracy is diverse in form and context. Modern bureaucracy differs from medieval attempts at bureaucratisation due to the relative 'calculability of its rules'. Needless to add that the bureaucratisation of justice was the primary goal of every colonial administration as it codified the law and tried to appear neutral in the adjudication of cases between European exploiters and the victimised.

In the Middle Ages, according to Weber, the reception of Roman law proceeded with the bureaucratisation of juridical administration. Adjudication by rationally trained specialists took the place of tradition or irrational presupposition. Weber contrasted rational adjudication on the basis of rigorously formal legal concepts with adjudication based on sacred traditions without any clear basis for concrete decisions. In the latter, cases are decided either on the basis of 'charismatic justice' – revelations by oracles – or as Khadi justice, which is non-formalistic and value-laden (Islamic law), or as empirical justice, which is formalistic but based on 'precedents' (English common law). According to Weber, contemporary England still has a broad substratum of the legal system which is similar to Khadi justice – untrained Justices of the Peace, for example. Continental jury systems operate similarly in practice, according to Weber, because jurors are not trained experts who understand the rational rules of an ideal bureaucracy. Democratic principles of adjudication are not necessarily the same as rational principles, according to Weber, because a democracy might lack the precision of formalistic adjudication. American and British courts are still largely empirical, even though they are not less democratic than continental European jurisdictions with a codified law, according to him. It is not clear how much of this is a sign that Weber was a patriotic German who believed that his country's system was the best and how much of it could be attributed to what Edward Said called Orientalism, or the idea that everything non-western is inferior.

Centrally organised lawyers' guilds, according to Weber, resisted codification in England and rejected Roman law because they produced judges from their ranks, kept privileged legal education in their hands as highly developed empirical technique and fought off the threats of ecclesiastical courts and university legal theorists to codify the laws of England and Wales. This instance of English resistance to legal imperialism is completely absent in the history of colonial criminology, probably because decolonisation resulted in the orderly replacement of colonialism with neocolonialism. Capitalism succeeded in England (and in the colonies by extension), Weber contends, largely because the courts and trial procedure denied justice to the poor (and the colonised). Modern judges are not vending machines of justice, however; they are still biased to some extent, especially under colonialism. Public opinion and popular justice still impinge on the rational administration of justice (but not necessarily the public opinion of the colonised, which is completely ignored). Weber's contribution was intended as a corrective to the traditional study of law, the study of 'dogmatics' or exegesis – the interpretation of statutes. Rational/irrational ideal types are, however, misleading because Weber must have meant regular/irregular. But even so, the rule that an oracle should decide is just as regular as the rule that the appeal court should decide.

Bauman (1989) has pointed out that there is nothing in Weber's theory of rationality to prevent the emergence of a phenomenon like Nazism (and colonialism, we might add). Such a phenomenon does not appear simply as irrational traditional forms of the administration of justice, but represents the application of science, legal rationality, medicine and the industrial revolution systematically to enslave or eliminate innocent people. In fact, Weber pointed out that rationality does not necessarily guarantee democracy, but he had no doubt that rationality was superior to judicial processes that took personal circumstances and the background of the actors into consideration in adjudication.

Weber's modernist sociology of law appears to be a defence of the principles of the Enlightenment at a time when they were increasingly coming under sustained attack. At the time the moral philosophers were developing their theories of social control, the French philosopher August Comte was already calling for progress beyond philosophy to what he called a positive science of society. According to him, such a science would be the queen of all the sciences and the practitioners would serve as the high priests of society by finding solutions to the social problems that plagued society. One of the earliest criminological writers to take this call for positivism seriously was the Belgian astronomer Adolphe Quetelet, who argued that the reason why crime is regular in frequency from place to place and from time to time has nothing to do with free will. Rather, according to him, crime is determined by forces such as socio-economic conditions and environmental factors. By implication, better social organisation would result in eliminating social ills such as crime. He was writing in the 1820s at a time when middle-class fear of the 'dangerous classes', or what Victor Hugo called *les misérables*, was so high that the state was developing statistics as a way of keeping the people under surveillance. Quetelet argued that social reform was what was needed to tackle what he called the social mechanism of crime not classicism, with its unverifiable emphasis on free will.

The expansion of prisons and the methods of statistical record-keeping by the state helped to constitute a specialised discipline for criminologists in Europe. If Quetelet and the criminologists that followed him had extended their focus to slavery and colonialism, they would have exposed the basic fact that crime control is not the principal aim of widening the net of social control. In this book, I am not arguing that criminologists deliberately tried to serve colonialism with their knowledge; rather, *Counter-Colonial Criminology* will show the extent to which criminology was underdeveloped due to its lack of awareness of colonial criminology.

One of those who followed the positivism of Quetelet was the Italian prison physician Lombroso, who shifted in the 1860s from the sociological determinism of the former to advance what has come to be known as biological determinism. According to Lombroso and his followers, those who are critical of Quetelet for expressing scepticism about free will miss the point that some people are biologically predisposed to criminality as a result of their low level of evolution. Applying Darwin's theory of natural selection to moral conduct, Lombroso observed that his experiments on dead criminals revealed that their skulls were deformed like the skulls of rodents. He concluded that criminals were atavistic throwbacks to an earlier stage of evolution and, much like Quetelet, concluded that rather than punish them under the ideology of free will, they should be treated for their deformities. He went on to say that born criminals can be easily identified by physical stigmata which made 'criminals, savages, and apes' stand out (Lombroso, 1911). The difficulty for him was that his list of stigmata mirrored the characteristics of dark-skinned Sicilians, who were racially profiled in the popular imagination and in official social control as the main sources of criminality in Italy.

Although Lombroso later revised this crude biologism, his views agreed with commonsensical notions of pure blood and nobility and so he remained influential, especially because he was the first to conduct a 'scientific' experiment in criminology. This 'father' of scientific criminology later influenced people such as Charles Goring, who observed in eugenic terms that the English convict in 1913 appeared to inherit criminality because crime ran in families. Quetelet could have offered an environmental explanation to such family crime records, but it was the view of Lombroso that supported the practice of transporting habitual criminals to the British colonies to prevent them from marrying and reproducing their type among the master race at the height of empire. This crude ideology was later to influence the Nazi propaganda that Jews were an inferior race that must be exterminated to save the master race from genetic pollution.

Whose conscience is the collective conscience under colonialism?

Underlying Weber's theory, like that of Emile Durkheim (1973), and in fact underlying all theories of the Punishment Of Offenders (POO), is the assumption that it is only offenders who are punished and so the history of Victimisation As Mere Punishment (VAMP) remains relatively untheorised, perhaps due to the blindness to slavery and colonialism in criminological theory. Even in victimology, VAMP is unrecognised because the sub-field follows the individualist Enlightenment criminological framework of POO theories to conceptualise the victimised as an *individual* 'victim' (Agozino, 1997a).

Durkheim was anxious to distance sociology from the atomistic explanations of biology and psychology by returning to the Comtean call for a social science *sui generis*, as attempted by Quetelet. According to Durkheim, the answer to the Hobbesian question of order is that every society has a collective conscience which regulates morality to ensure that social control is not too strong and deviance not too common, otherwise anomie would result. Just as Weber divided society into a dual typology of the rational and the irrational, Durkheim, at about the same time, divided society into mechanical and organic types of solidarity. He argued that the division of labour within society is what leads to increased specialisation and increased differentiation of roles but also to increased integration of the differentiated units and upgraded adaptation of the society that is evolving from pre-industrial mechanical solidarity to modern organic solidarity. He observed that one way to study the evolution of any society is by focusing on the system of punishment in that society. According to him, 'quantitative change' is identifiable in the history of penal justice because penal intensity is greater, the closer a society approximates mechanical solidarity – and the more absolute power is. 'Qualitative changes' are characterised by varying terms of imprisonment which, depending on the seriousness of the offence, become the only normal means of social control.

Durkheim recognises that absolutism, or unlimited governmental power over citizens who have no rights and who are treated like private property, could result in obstructions to the qualitative dynamic (though he failed to use colonial policies to illustrate this). Nevertheless, he argued that imprisonment is impractical under the ethic of collective responsibility of mechanical types of solidarity and that prisons ensured certainty of penalty for individual offenders in organic-type solidarities. (Again he failed to speculate on whether this was why European colonial administrations preferred to use genocide as a penal policy against largely innocent people who were presumed guilty by association.) According to him, increasing sympathy for and sensitivity towards human suffering cannot explain the qualitative dynamic towards imprisonment simply because such a humanism could also lead in the opposite direction of increasing intensity in punishment (especially under the colonial situation where the life of one European was judged superior to the lives of millions of natives). Durkheim impoversihed his theory by failing to utilise the resources available to him through the French Colonial Office and relied instead on inaccurate travellers' tales about South Pacific societies which were presumably under mechanical solidarity. Consequently, he arrived at a less than satisfactory theory that argues that the evolution of criminal law tautologically causes penal evolution by becoming less sacred. The rational principle in operation, according to Durkheim, is that it would be contradictory to punish offences against human dignity in the victim by violating the self-same human dignity in the offender and so deviance increasingly demands less severe penalty (although the reverse was the case in the colonies). The historical inaccuracies in Durkheim's theory have been well summarised by Garland and there is no need to rehearse them here, except to say that even Garland (1990) was silent on the colonial dimensions.

Colonialism proves that repressive sanction is also characteristic of organic forms of solidarity. The examples of slavery, apartheid and fascism illustrate further that whole groups of people have been rationally repressed as if they were guilty of unspecified crimes – rational because it was in the interest of Europeans to do so. The crimes of fascism were internationally judged and punished, notably at Nuremberg, and yet some of those crimes may have been initially committed while carrying out orders to discipline and punish the Other. Moreover, what Durkheim saw as a more humane qualitative change could now be seen to be more quantitative in terms of the lengths of imprisonment rather than simplistically as more humane alternatives to imprisonment. Similarly, what he saw as quantitative change could be said to be qualitative in terms of the severity of punishment which is more difficult to quantify than prison sentences.

Durkheim's collective conscience is more like a hegemonic moral order in the sense that Antonio Gramsci used the term. According to Gramsci (1971), hegemony is the intellectual and moral leadership of a class which makes it possible for that class to rule not only by force and not without force at all, but also with coerced consent. This class hegemony has since been applied to race and gender hegemony by many writers. It is the rationalist conceptualisation of the most individual of attributes, conscience, in terms of the collective society, that prevented Durkheim from interrogating the dysfunctional aspects of penal justice. However, his emphasis on the popular, emotional dynamics of punishment provides an insight into why punishment is popular and why politicians are able to mobilise public opinion around issues of law and order, even under colonialism. Durkheim's call for the energy of the collective conscience to be kept at a moderate level in order to allow both good and evil geniuses to emerge and flourish in any normal society can also be seen as part of the campaign for liberatory social policy which the Enlightenment thinkers advocated, but which was under threat from biological and psychological positivists who were unwittingly calling for the final solution to the problems of difference, deviance and defiance.

Liberal sociologists in America, including Robert Parks (former personal assistant to Booker T. Washington) and his colleague at the University of Chicago, Anthony Burgess, borrowed the social structural theory of Durkheim and moved away from the anthropological criminology of the Italian School. According to the Chicago School, crime is not caused by the nature of individuals but by the social environment in which they live. They observed that crime was concentrated in inner city areas of Chicago even though different waves of immigrants from different cultural backgrounds moved into the poor housing available in the inner city and then moved to the suburbs while crime remained relatively high in this zone. Their students, including Shaw and Mckay, applied this ecological theory to juvenile delinquency and concluded that the cause of delinquency is social disorganisation, which happens to be more pronounced in inner city areas. Although these liberal scholars were well intentioned in their attempt to persuade policy-makers to tackle the dreadful poverty that poor immigrants are forced to endure, their emphasis on the crimes of the poor and their lack of interest in the crimes of the powerful resulted in racial–class–gender profiling of inner city youth.

The Durkheimian emphasis on individual freedom was continued in America by Robert K. Merton, who used the concept of anomie to explain why crime is prevalent in a liberal society. According to Merton (1938), a liberal capitalist society like America lays emphasis on the American Dream, according to which anyone can succeed if they work hard. However, according to Merton, anomie arises when there is a lack of fit (or unequal emphases) between cultural goals – the American Dream – and the legitimate means of achieving those goals – equal opportunities. As a result of the unequal emphases, individuals adapt in five main ways to their perception of relative deprivation of access to the legitimate means to the cultural goals.

The good guys, according to Merton, are the conformists – those who succeed by using the legitimate means of hard work to achieve the American Dream (Bill Gates, for example).

The rebels are those who reject the cultural goal of the American Dream and substitute their own dream of total liberation from capitalism while rejecting the institutionalised means of achieving the American Dream, substituting the Malcolm X philosophy of 'by any means necessary' (for example, the Black Panther Party of the 1970s).

The ritualists are those who know that by working hard they will not achieve the American Dream, but they work hard anyway (the masses of American citizens who work from 9 a.m. to 5 p.m. and sometimes work at two jobs to make ends meet).

Then come the retreatists, who reject the American Dream and the legitimate means of hard work, but fail to replace them with goals of their own or means of their own. The Hippies of the 1960s are an example, though they had their own goals of universal love and their own means of permanent partying.

Finally, Merton identified individuals he called the innovators. These are the clever ones who believe in the American Dream but are aware that working from 9 to 5 will not get them to the Promised Land. These individuals adapt to anomie by adopting their own means to the goal of the American Dream. According to Merton, these are the individuals who are more likely to adopt criminal means. The Mafia are an example of innovative individuals.

Merton's emphasis on liberty and individualism is what makes his theory very popular in postcolonial locations, where few writers call for equal opportunities as a way of stemming the epidemic of crime in societies where inequalities are simply scandalous. However, Merton has been severely critiqued for assuming that the modes of adaptation are individual whereas most forms of adaptation, criminal and otherwise, happen to be group activities. The more powerful critique of Merton, however, comes from the countercolonial theory of Steven Box (1983), who states that the facts do not fit the Mertonian assumption that the poor are those most likely to become criminal due to their relative deprivation. In the colonial situation, for example, the conformists could be mass murderers who massacre whole villages, especially when there is organised resistance to forced labour and forced seizure of surplus produce and forced taxation without representation. Although the nationalists could fit into the category of innovators, they are treated as conformists under the colonial situation and this is probably prophetic since bourgeois nationalists accepted the cultural goal of colonialism – the domination of their own people – and the colonial means of force, except that their own is a neocolonial means of exploitation. Yet the genuine rebels who rejected the colonial goal and the colonial means and substituted their own genuine nationalist goals and nationalist means (Ho Chi Minh, Frantz Fanon, Kwame Nkrumah, Amilcar Cabral, Samora Machel, Agostino Neto, to name but a few) cannot be classified as common criminals following Merton's theory. The problem is that this was hardly what Merton meant by rebellion since these men were revolutionaries and not simply domesticated rebels without a cause. Box's theory is instructive for *Counter-Colonial Criminology* because of its convincing assumption that it is power, not poverty, that explains most crimes, be they the crimes of the rich or the crimes of the poor. If it is relative deprivation that causes criminality, why is it that top government officials, multinational corporations, dictators and wealthy drug barons continue to commit crimes despite their incredible privileges? The answer is that, like the criminal organisations that ran colonial empires, they have the power to do as they wish and, as Box, following Lord Acton, states: power corrupts and absolute power corrupts absolutely. This same theory of power or relative power rather than relative deprivation explains why some poor desperadoes offend against other poor people – because, as one disco record repeats monotonously, they've got the power.

Merton was severely criticised by Cloward and Ohlin (1960) who observed that unequal opportunities also exist in illegitimate activities and so it does not follow that anyone who cannot go to college automatically qualifies as a gang leader. Their theory of social disorganisation and delinquent subcultures, however, retained the Mertonian prejudice against the working poor. Edwin Sutherland (1949) tried to correct some of these blind spots in criminological theory by advancing the view that criminal behaviour is learned in the same way that lawful behaviour is learned. He observed that white-collar crime should not be ignored by criminologists and that his theory of differential association offered a satisfactory explanation for all types of crime, although he too focused on individuals' crimes and ignored imperialist crimes.

In an address to the Ghana National Assembly on 22 March 1965, Kwame Nkrumah analysed white-collar crime in the colonial situation with specific reference to the Congo:

In the five years preceding independence, the net outflow of capital to Belgium alone was four hundred and sixty-four million pounds.

When Lumumba assumed power, so much capital was taken out of the Congo that there was a national deficit of forty million pounds.

Tshombe is now told the Congo has an external debt of nine hundred million dollars. This is a completely arbitrary figure – it amounts to open exploitation based on naked colonialism. Nine hundred million dollars ($900,000,000) is supposed to be owed to United States and Belgium monopolies after they have raped the Congo of sums of 2,500 million pounds, 464 million pounds, and 40 million pounds. . . . But the tragic-comedy continues. . . . To prop up Tshombe, the monopolies decided that of this invented debt of $900 million, only $250 million has to be paid. How generous, indeed! . . . The monopolies further announce a fraudulent programme to liquidate so-called Congolese external debts of 100 million pounds. Upon announcing this, they declare Congo is to

be responsible for a further internal debt of 200 million pounds. . . .
Despite political independence, the Congo remains a victim of imperialism and neo-colonialism . . . [but] the economic and financial control of
the Congo by foreign interests is not limited to the Congo alone. The
developing countries of Africa are all subject to this unhealthy influence
in one way or another. (Nkrumah, 1967: 198–200)

While Nkrumah is right that these fraudulent practices continue with
impunity, there is very little criminological interest in the phenomenon. As
chapter 9 will show, African novelists are more likely than criminologists to
explore the crimes of the powerful. Historians and general social theorists
are more likely than criminologists to express interest in such events. For
example, Adam Hochschild (1998), a literary theorist, catalogued the genocidal crimes of Belgian colonial officials in the Congo in the way that creative
writers such as Mark Twain did when the crimes were being committed.
Only dependency theorists like Offiong (1980: 163–4) come close to this
issue by critiquing apologists of imperialism who assert that the French domination of Burkina Faso today and the US involvement in the assassination of
Patrice Lumumba are part of the politics of 'containing communism'.
Offiong argues that there are exploitative economic interests involved in
imperialist domination and that it is not domination for the sake of domination. He goes on to analyse how the American multinational company ITT
and the CIA plotted the overthrow and assassination of Salvador Allende in
Chile in the early 1970s.

Third World criminologists who have studied fraud concentrate on
desperate individuals in the Third World who try to con greedy people
in the West. The unhealthy influence that Nkrumah referred to can therefore be extended to criminological influences by which western experts and
ambassadors are invited to prescribe solutions to the presumed crime-
proneness of the poor while saying absolutely nothing about imperialist
crimes. Criminologists might object to this analysis and maintain that they
are interested only in knowledge for the sake of knowledge, but critical criminologists would accept that knowledge and power serve each other intim-
ately. However, Nkrumah has been criticised by Rodney (1974) for expelling
critical members from his ruling party and surrounding himself with syco-
phants until he was overthrown by the bourgeois army, like Lumumba before
him. C.L.R. James also criticised Nkrumah for sacking the country's Chief
Justice for passing a judgement that Nkrumah did not agree with (James,
1982), warning that such an error could pave the way for fascist rule in
Africa.

Aimé Cæsaire (1972: 10) stated that 'Colonialists may kill in Indochina,
torture in Madagascar, imprison in Black Africa, crack down in the West
Indies. Henceforth the colonised know that they have an advantage over
them. They know that their temporary "masters" are lying . . . [colonialism is

not] an attempt to extend the rule of law'. To drive home the point, Cæsaire quotes a white supremacist passage which reads like something from Hitler's *Mein Kampf*. But it was actually written by a certain Renan, a 'liberal' French intellectual who was interested in moral and intellectual reformation following the second imperialist world war which should have taught the French better about the injustice of fascism:

> The regeneration of the inferior or degenerate races by the superior races is part of the providential order of things for humanity. With us, the common man is nearly always a *déclassé* nobleman, his heavy hand is better suited to handling the sword than the menial tool. Rather than work, he chooses to fight, that is, he returns to his first estate. *Regere imperio populos*, that is our vocation. Pour forth this all-consuming activity onto countries which, like China, are crying aloud for foreign conquest. Turn the adventurers who disturb European society into a *ver sacrum*, a horde like those of the Franks, the Lombards, or the Normans, and every man will be in his right role. Nature has made a race of workers, the Chinese race, who have wonderful manual dexterity and almost no sense of honor; govern them with justice, levying from them, in return for the blessing of such a government, an ample allowance for the conquering race, and they will be satisfied; a race of tillers of the soil, the Negro; treat him with kindness and humanity, and all will be as it should; a race of masters and soldiers, the European race. Reduce this noble race to working in the *ergastulum* like Negroes and Chinese, and they rebel. In Europe, every rebel is, more or less, a soldier who has missed his calling, a creature made for the heroic life, before whom you are setting *a task that is contrary to his race* – a poor worker, too good a soldier. But the life at which our workers rebel would make a Chinese or a fellah happy, as they are not military creatures in the least. *Let each one do what he is made for, and all will be well.* (quoted in Cæsaire, 1972: 16)

Such imperialist reasoning might be dismissed by criminologists as having nothing to do with their scientific discipline, but in the early years of the discipline, this was the type of propaganda that criminologists produced in the service of imperialism. Initially, it was known as criminal anthropology and was well respected until the Holocaust dealt it the most effective critique by following it to its logical conclusion. However, before the Nazis came to power, anthropologists such as Ernest Albert Hooton were looking for the biological basis of criminality in the 1930s. Following Lombroso's theory of the born criminal, while trying to improve the measurement tools of anthropometry which he believed to be more advanced compared to the research of Lombroso, Hooton (1939) measured 17,000 people in the US to determine whether they had any of the 125 characteristics that supposedly disposed people to criminality. In conclusion, Hooton recommended that it is desirable to control 'the progress of human evolution by breeding better types and by the ruthless elimination of inferior types, if only we are willing to found and to practice a science of human genetics' (quoted in Barkan, 1992: 106–7). Needless to add that the Nazis were more than willing, and many states in America, with the support of the Supreme Court, forcibly sterilised tens of thousands of citizens who were deemed feeble-minded.

In 2001, a decorated Vietnam war veteran and former US Senator, Bob Kerry, confessed that the troops under his command massacred innocent civilians during the war, but pleaded that it was a mistake in the heat of battle rather than a deliberate war crime. This started a national debate on the extent of the culpability not just of Bob Kerry, but of the whole of the US in the crimes committed against the people of Vietnam. As usual, criminologists have not had a word to say about this controversy, leaving journalists such as Chang (1997) to be the best criminologists on similar questions about Japanese imperialist crimes in China. Richard Falk (2001), a professor of international law at Princeton University, analysed the controversy in *The Nation*. According to him, the US would contribute more to the promotion of international law if the crimes against the Vietnamese people were no longer denied or excused but acknowledged and reparations paid. He draws an analogy between the Nuremberg War Crimes tribunal and the war crimes committed in the name of America. Instead of condemning the war crimes simply because the war was not won, as the popular media tended to do, Falk urged more honesty and the admission of guilt. Instead of continuing with the arrogant spirit of denial and ridicule that greeted the Vietnam war crimes tribunal headed by Bertrand Russell in 1967, Falk recommended implicitly that America should negotiate a plea bargain. He suggested that an admission of guilt should be extended to the crimes committed against African Americans during the centuries of slavery. Meanwhile, criminologists have continued to bury their heads in the sand of administrative criminology, completely ignoring the relevance of such debates to the development of theoretical criminology.

Similar criminological work was abandoned to Edward Herman, a professor of finance, and Noam Chomsky, a professor of linguistics, who came very close to developing a theory of crimes of the state, with the propagandist mass media as accomplices, in their book *Manufacturing Consent* (1988). As they put it: 'A propaganda system will consistently portray people abused in enemy states as worthy victims, whereas those treated with equal or greater severity by its own government or clients will be unworthy' (Herman and Chomsky, 1988: 37). This charge applies to the imperialist logic of conventional criminology which ignores imperialist crimes. The mass media report events with obvious ideological biases, but criminologists are yet to summon the courage to address the imperialist crimes committed in Biafra, Vietnam, Laos, Cambodia, El Salvador, Nicaragua, the Middle East, Rwanda and South Africa, to mention but a few examples. Following the 11 September

2001 attack on the World Trade Center and the Pentagon, as well as the plane that crashed in Pennsylvania on its way to further attacks, criminologists are falling over each other to develop courses on terrorism. Only a few criminologists are addressing the forces that have resulted in the globalisation of terrorism (Onwudiwe, 2000). Some criminology departments even advertise on the internet that crime is now the leading social problem and so there are many more employment opportunities for criminology graduates.

From the micro-physics of power to the bifurcation thesis

The long quotation from the imperialist ideologue Renan, cited above, reminds criminologists of the policy of transportation through which Europe shipped its prisoners to the colonies to act as the conquering hordes of imperialism. Today, the prisons of Europe, Australia and North America are exploding with surplus populations that cannot be off-loaded to a penal colony. Yet, the prisons resemble the slave plantations and the penal colonies given the increasing disproportionate warehousing of minority individuals behind their walls. At the same time, criminologists continue to write like the apologists of imperialism by pretending that all they seek in their research is the truth, the whole truth and nothing but the truth, refusing to recognise the fascist uses that criminological knowledge serves in unequal societies.

Exceptions include Foucault (1977) and his followers, who strongly argue that there is a knowledge–power axis in every discipline but who remain silent about the outrageous foundation of criminology on the bloody soil of imperialism. Every knowledge gained is gained in a power relationship and every knowledge relevant is exercised in specific power relationships. What distinguishes one knowledge from another is not truth or falsehood as such, but the varying power resources available to those who possess and exercise them in varying degrees and those who contest them relatively. However, Foucault shares with Durkheim a focus on the individual offender, on what he called the 'micro-physics of power', and the puzzling silence on imperialist power to punish and the consequent resistance (although Durkheim tried to avoid the atomisation of what he saw as social facts). We will see in this book that criminological modernity is not always concerned with the micro-physics of power but with the macro-physics of intergroup power relations and how these are juridistically represented – especially under colonialism.

Mathiessen (1983) has analysed a contested piece of law reform in Norway to show that in the future whole groups and categories could come under the disciplinary power of the judiciary. However, he also noted that the proposal was dropped, along with the originating minister, and so it was not put into practice. In this book, we will come across instances of such net-widening within the judiciary itself as a reality rather than as a future prospect. This is in agreement with the Foucauldian dispersal thesis of

Cohen (1985), who identified the imminent reversal of the tendency towards individualisation which Foucault had identified as a feature of modern exercises of disciplinary knowledge and power. According to Cohen, the following processes are taking place in penal policy (although he could have used the well-documented history of colonialism to illustrate his points more clearly and correct the false assumption that all these things are happening mainly to offenders):

1 a blurring of the boundary between institutional and non-institutional penalty;
2 a widening of the net to include those who would escape judicial power previously;
3 a thinning of the mesh, greater intervention in the community to discipline more offenders; and
4 penetration of more informal networks by state agents.

Bottoms (1983) has argued, with his bifurcation thesis, that an exclusive focus on discipline, repression and oppression when looking at the criminal justice system is misleading. He applied Durkheim's second law of penal evolution, 'the law of quality', and found that punishment is not always disciplinary, although punishment for serious or violent crimes takes the form of disciplinary punishment – prison and supervised probation, for example. Non-disciplinary penalties – fines, suspended sentences and compensation orders – are given for less serious offences. The bifurcation thesis contradicts Durkheim's second law because imprisonment is falling at the expense of the fine, community service and the growth of compensation and related matters, whereas Durkheim predicted that the deprivation of liberty and liberty alone would become increasingly the main penal form under organic types of solidarity. It is difficult to know if all of the penal forks identified by Bottoms are exclusively disciplinary; it could more easily be said that they are all disciplinary to some extent. Moreover, the assumption is that it is penal policy that is bifurcating into disciplinary and non-disciplinary penalties, that it is penalty that is bifurcating into itself. It seems more convincing to say that what is bifurcating is criminal justice policy as a whole and not just penal policy.

Social enquiry reports help to diagnose and differentiate individual offenders according to their social circumstances. While this is a challenge to Weber's impersonal bureaucratic rationality, it seems to derive from the sociological positivism of Durkheim. In a similar way, the adoption of psychiatric detention orders and expert witnesses could be said to be the result of theories of individual positivism, which Lombroso (1876) pioneered. Apart from these two policy implications, positivism seems to have had little impact on the Weberian bureaucratic administration of justice. This field is dominated by classicism and neoclassicism, which supply the ideologies of individual responsibility, just deserts, free will rationality with a few exceptions and punishment as a duty different from the treatment that positivistic determinism recommends in the area of sociological research where it remains the dominant framework. This synthesis of classicist and positivistic principles in the administration of justice results in the penal welfare strategies identified by Garland (1985). The penal welfare strategies in turn reflect Bottoms' bifurcation thesis. However, Garland (2001) returned to Foucault for an explanation of why European and American penal policies have moved away from welfarism and seem to be reversing the process of civilisation that was notable in the past. He found European social theories incapable of explaining the history of present penal policies, but failed to consult the Third World theories of Fanon, Cæsaire, Nkrumah, Cabral, Rodney, Soyinka, Ngugi, Achebe, James, Hall, Said and others, who have interpreted these processes as being closer to the theories of imperialism that Foucault ignored.

Becky Tatum (1996) has argued that the 'colonial model can be used as a theoretical explanation for the over-representation of African Americans in crime, victimization and delinquency statistics'. She applies Fanon and other theorists to explain the marginalisation and alienation of African Americans in terms of their domination by another racial group that reaps huge material benefits from the colonial type of relationship. The frustration of African Americans is expressed in Mertonian terms of mimicry by some, misplaced aggression by others and resistance by yet others. However, she concludes that internal colonialism is a better explanation of the political, economic and social domination of African Americans and their behavioural adaptation (Mertonian) to such subjugation due to the elimination of the foreign element of colonial domination in American society. In a different context, I used internal colonialism theories to go beyond the bifurcation thesis and move towards a trifurcation thesis by recognising victimisation as a neglected feature of penal policy, especially with reference to black women and to the need to decolonise victimisation (Agozino, 1997a).

A Japanese colleague, Minoru Yokoyoma, agreed with the thrust of my argument at a session of the American Society of Criminology in San Francisco, November 2000. He added that western criminology has since colonised Japanese criminology by relatively monopolising the training of young criminologists who return to Japan to apply western theories uncritically. However, the Orient has a unique contribution to make to criminological theory which has only recently been recognised by western criminologists. This is the concept of criminology as peace-making, which is influenced by Buddhism among other spiritual, feminist and critical ideas opposed to imperialist war-mindedness (Pepinsky and Quinney, 1991). The limitation of the peace-making approach is that it focuses on the relationship between one individual victim and an individual offender. It is not clear how to make peace with imperialism or with a criminal state at the individual level without capitulating to imperialist reason. It is also true that peace is something that imperialists love – colonial peace treaties remind us of the fact that cowboys smoked peace pipes with the Indians before massacring them to steal their land. Peace and justice, but is there room for love in criminology? Is it possible to have real peace and justice while institutionalising white supremacist, patriarchal, imperialist hatred and intolerance of multiculturalism? Ho Chi Minh (1924) stated, almost echoing the African American classic of Ida B. Wells-Barnet (1892), what the Chicago School conveniently ignored in their obsession with broken windows in the inner cities:

> It is well known that the black race is the most oppressed and most exploited of the human family ... What everyone does not perhaps know, is that after sixty-five years of the so-called emancipation, American Negroes still endure atrocious moral and material sufferings of which the most cruel and horrible is the custom of lynching. (Ho Chi Minh, 1924)

How satisfactory are the accounts of these theoretical perspectives in explaining how the judicial process has worked in the history of postcolonial countries?

PART 2

The racialisation of crime: social, political and cultural contexts

Crime constitutes a site through which political debates about 'race' issues have emerged and through which power struggles have been played out. According to a key study by Hall, Critcher, Jefferson, Clarke and Roberts (1978), *Policing the Crisis*, a moral panic around 'mugging', underpinned by police perception of the Black population as being a potential threat to order and stability, as potential trouble makers, has fed into the aggressive and intimidating policing of Black communities. Hall *et al.* (1978) have argued that Black communities experience a position of 'secondariness' through a combination of 'race' and class. Hall *et al.*'s study (1978) explored the nature of the moral panic around 'mugging', with the researchers here arguing that policing Black communities during the 1970s became synonymous with policing the economic and social crisis during this time. As economic recession deepened, the social control of urban 'trouble-spots' was tightened through intensified street policing, impacting particularly on Black youth.

Researchers holding a critical race perspective have argued that linking the issue of crime to the 'race'/ethnicity of the offender is damaging as this helps to propagate racist viewpoints of Black communities as being disorganised both politically and socially. High arrest rates should rather be viewed as the result of police prejudice rather than high criminality (Bridges and Gilroy, 1982). Moreover, the police are to be viewed as the agents of imperialism, and so some members of Black communities are engaged in an anti-colonialist struggle with the authorities (Sivanandan, 1981). The first suggested reading in this part consists of a chapter written by Lea and Young (1993), who, taking a left realist position, criticise critical race perspectives for being idealist because they fail to acknowledge the impacts of crime upon Black communities. Lea and Young (1993) argue that crime rates within Black communities must be taken seriously as much crime is intra-class and intra-racial so that crime has a very real impact upon Black communities. Social deprivation and unemployment, as well as racial discrimination, can lead to a minority engaging in crime.

For Lea and Young (1993: 124), 'the notion that some sort of cultural Geist accompanies immigrants from the colonies to the imperialist city and is directly available to the second-generation sons and daughters of immigrants born in the city is profoundly idealist'. According to Pitts (1993), higher levels of offend-ing are associated with communities that feature the following characteristics: poverty, low educational attainment, unemployment, as well as having a young age profile; and so 'race'/ethnicity may not in itself be a significant factor.

The second suggested reading in this part consists of a chapter written by Gilroy (1993), who criticises approaches on the left of the political spectrum, arguing that these obscure the centrality of 'race' and leave unacknowledged the dynamics, and importance of, politicised 'race' identities, so that 'race' might be viewed as a cultural resource through which communities are created and through which resistance can be produced. Gilroy (1993: 112) views the work of left realists Lea and Young (1993) as dangerous, prompting 'specula-tion as to why it is only black poor who resolve their frustration in acts of criminality'. Lea and Young's (1993) work must be viewed within a broader context, where Black culture has been scrutinised and demonised by state authorities, where Black communities have been viewed as being contamin-ated by the alien predisposition to criminality. Gilroy (1993: 107) has argued that the policing of Black communities cannot be separated from a wider con-text of popular racism and nationalism, whereby the extension of police power and the recruitment of law in political conflicts has become commonplace. Moreover, the policing of Black areas might be characterised as militaristic, underpinned by policing theory that legitimates the view that Black com-munities are disproportionately prone to crime.

More recently, Asian men, in particular young Muslim men, have attracted political, social and research attention. In the UK, the publication of *The Satanic Verses* by Salman Rushdie in 1989 led to Muslims highlighting their social and economic exclusion, using blasphemy as an issue around which to raise politi-cal awareness of these broader concerns (Modood, 2003). Whilst Asian men have traditionally been viewed by the authorities, as well as by wider society, as law-abiding and peaceful, more recently, and particularly in the aftermath of the attacks on the World Trade Center on September 11 2001, young Muslim men have been viewed as constituting a 'problem group' (Alexander, 2000), as 'evil' and a 'fifth column enemy within' by media, politicians, the security services and the criminal justice system (Poynting and Mason, 2006). The terrorist attacks of September 11th 2001 and July 7th 2005 have propelled Muslim political activism further, due to very real concerns about the inappropriate targeting of young Muslim men in police stop-and-search and arrest activities, as a result of new anti-terror laws. Moreover, the terror attacks have brought to crisis point core tenets of the liberal democratic state relating to notions of citizenship and individual rights in multi-ethnic and multi-religious contemporary democratic societies. In the UK, following the July 7th bombings in London in 2005, there has been considerable discussion within media and political arenas about the extent to which second or third generation Muslim men, particularly South Asian men, have been assimilated into British culture.

Poynting and Mason (2006) argue that in both Britain and Australia, Muslim immigrants and their families who had been subjected to racism over several generations, experienced an exacerbation of such othering, and indeed, criminalisation, after September 11th 2001. For Poynting and Mason (2006), the demonisation of minorities based on 'colour' or 'race' has metamorphosed into a demonisation of Muslims. Their chapter highlights how both Australia and Britain have conducted, since 9/11, high profile security and police raids on mosques and the private homes of Muslims, which have functioned to construct a manifest and imminent dangerousness among the communities concerned. In both Britain and Australia, a moral panic around Muslim communities can be discerned, involving not only the state authorities but also the media.

The role of the media in propagating racist stereotypes has been extensively documented. Vocabulary in newspaper headlines and articles, for example, often links law and order issues to 'race' and, more recently, religion, particularly Islam. Although blatant racism may have declined over the last two decades, minorities continue to be represented as a threat or a problem in the press, with minority ethnic communities being associated with issues like crime, conflict and intolerance (Ferguson, 1998). According to Imtoual (2008), the Australian media tend to represent Islamic gender relations as disordered, dysfunctional and disturbing, as being characterised by violent, over-sexed men and submissive, abused women. The final suggested reading in this part is a chapter by Alexander (2000), part of which focusses upon the media-created moral panic surrounding Asian youth. According to Alexander (2000: 3), racialised representations of Asian youth in the media obscure broader, more complex youth identities, arguing that 'race' has become a substitute for analysis. Alexander (2000) further discusses the social construction of the Asian gang as the new Asian folk-devil. Moreover, for Alexander (2000), the rising interest in religious identities, and particularly in Muslim identities, has a number of important consequences for the study of Asian youth.

Suggested essays

Lea, J. and Young, J. (1993) Chapter 4, 'The Race and Crime Debate' in *What is to be Done about Law and Order?* London: Pluto Press, pp. 105–134.

Gilroy, P. (1987) 'The Myth of Black Criminality' in P. Scraton (ed.) *Law, Order and the Authoritarian State: readings in critical criminology*. Milton Keynes: Open University Press.

Poynting, S. and Mason, V. (2006) 'Tolerance, Freedom, Justice and Peace?: Britain, Australia and Anti-Muslim Racism since September 11th 2001' *Journal of Intercultural Studies* 27 (4): 365–392.

Alexander, A. (2000) Chapter 1 'Introduction', *The Asian Gang*. Oxford: Berg, pp. 1–26.

Further reading

Agozino, B. (1997) *Black Women and the Criminal Justice System*. Aldershot: Ashgate.

Gilroy, P. (1987) *There Ain't No Black in the Union Jack*. London: Hutchinson.

Hall, S., Critcher, C., Jefferson, T., Clarke, J. and Roberts, B. (1978) *Policing the Crisis: mugging, the state, and law and order*. London: Macmillan.

Modood, T. (2003) 'Muslims and the Politics of Difference' *Political Quarterly* 74 (1): 100–115.

Sim, J., Scraton, P. and Gordon, P. (1987) 'Introduction: Crime, the State and Critical Analysis' in P. Scraton (ed.) *Law, Order and the Authoritarian State: readings in critical criminology*. Milton Keynes: Open University Press.

Spalek, B. (2005) 'British Muslims and Community Safety post-September 11th' *Community Safety Journal (Special Edition) Race, Ethnicity and Community Safety* Vol. 4 (2): 12–20.

Wardak, A. (2000) *Social Control and Deviance: A South Asian Community in Scotland*. Aldershot: Ashgate.

5

The race and crime debate
by John Lea and Jock Young

The repeated issue by the Metropolitan Police of crime statistics involving ethnic distinctions for a particular type of street crime, commonly called mugging, has once again raised the question of race and crime. The overwhelming response from the left has been, correctly, to deplore the one-sided, political nature of these statistics and to see them as consistent with an attempt to fuel an atmosphere of moral panic in which the issues raised by the Scarman Report and the Greater London Council's campaign for a democratic police authority can be safely ignored. It has given rise to an extreme reaction in the gutter press; for instance, the *Sun* ran a headline BLACK CRIME SHOCK and carried *without* inverted commas the statement: 'Blacks carried out twice as many muggings as whites in London last year' (23 March 1983). Let us state now the extremely strong objective reasons for being highly sceptical about statements such as that out of 19,258 cases of robbery and violent theft in London, 10,960 were carried out by blacks.

(1) They focus on only one type of crime out of a whole catalogue of serious offences. Robbery and violent theft only account for about 3 per cent of all serious crime. They ignore the fact that whites are more likely to commit the vast majority of serious crimes and present us with the image of the 'black criminal'.

(2) Many of these crimes are of an amateurish and minor nature, but the phrase 'robbery and violent theft' suggests something of a more extreme nature. In a Home Office Research Study of mugging, for example, it was found that 54 per cent of those mugged suffered minor injuries such as cuts and bruises, and only 3 per cent needed to stay in hospital for longer than twelve hours (*New Society*, 25 March 1983).

(3) The category 'robbery and violent theft' is a very flexible one and blends with other offence categories such as 'theft of personal property'. By allocating crimes from the latter to the former, inflated figures can easily

occur. The exercise of police discretion can quite easily alter the amount of a particular crime by changes in recording practices. A recent study, for example, suggests that precisely such a manipulation occurred in the claim that there was a dramatic rise in street crime in Brixton in 1981 (Blom-Cooper and Drabble).

(4) They ignore the fact that mugging is a very indistinct category and that only about one third of all robbery and violent theft fit the conventional notion of it. This was put well in a Runnymede Trust Bulletin:

Mugging is not, however, an offence known in law and the term is not normally used by police. To the public it usually means a theft, in the street, which is accompanied by violence. But the Metropolitan Police category of robbery and other violent thefts includes 'snatches' where the victim is neither threatened nor injured (7,330), robberies from business premises open to the public (2,684), and 'other robberies' which are not street robberies (2,860). This leaves 5,889 robberies which would fit in with the popular meaning of 'mugging', only 31 per cent of the figure bandied about in the press, and only 0.9 per cent of the total recorded serious offences. (No. 143, p. 8)

(5) It does not present us with the ethnic origins of the victims of crime, thus serving to feed the illusion that black crime is predatory upon white. Of course, most crime is intra-racial and intra-class.

(6) It does not allow for the fact that police statistics are *in part* a function of police prejudices. It presents the figures on ethnic divisions as objective reflections of reality.

All in all, we have an extremely slanted portrayal of the crime problem which, no doubt, contributes considerably to the build-up of racial fears in the non-black community. It is a blatant example of the type of moral hysteria about crime which has occurred throughout the century. The main preoccupation during the fifties and sixties was the crime of lower-working-class youth, and now attention has been shifted on to young blacks.

Even if the figures were totally accurate – and we have seen that this is an impossibility – it is a priority that they be presented in context, to allow the audience to understand their true significance. Figures do not speak for themselves and there are plenty of racist 'contexts' into which they will inevitably be slotted if the presenters of the statistics 'naively' inform us that they are only giving the public 'the facts'. It is vital, therefore, that we debunk this strategy and provide accurate interpretations to counter the moral panic over crime which serves to fuel racism.

But a common reaction on the left and among liberal commentators has been significantly different from this. Instead of scrutinizing the figures impartially and providing a context in which they can be understood, they have engaged in a wholesale dismissal of the evidence, often in a very contradictory fashion. They have either questioned the validity of any connection at all between race and crime (e.g. Bridges and Gilroy), or argued that the problem is irrelevant as such crime is insignificant by comparison with the 'crimes of the powerful' (e.g. Harman). Bridges and Gilroy suggest that any link between crime rates and ethnic background is purely a function of police prejudice and that any discussion to the contrary gives 'intellectual support to racist stereotypes of the black community as socially and politically disorganized' (p. 35). Such a position, quite apart from the vacuous definition of racism involved, appears to associate critical discussion with silence. As if silence can eliminate the fear of crime, or blank denial rid us of racial prejudice! It is precisely such silences that have placed the left continually on the defensive and guaranteed the hegemony of the right over the terrain of law and order. A challenge to this long established domination by the right must begin with the simple recognition that crime is a pressing problem for the poor and for the black community, and that the control of crime is a vital issue for socialists.

As we have argued, in all industrial societies a small minority of the oppressed sections of society are brutalized into criminality. But because crime is produced by the system, it does not follow that crime is some sort of crypto-political struggle against the system. Bridges and Gilroy refer evasively to the 'social and political character' of working-class black crime (p. 35). One might as well argue that dying of asbestos poisoning, undoubtedly a disease produced by industrial capitalism, is some sort of political activity. The notion of crime as a kind of politics rests on a few myths that need to be dispelled. Working-class crimes are predominantly intra-class and intra-racial. A poor person is more likely to rob a poor person than a rich person, a black is more likely to assault another black than a white, and a white more likely to attack a white than a black. Eighty per cent of crimes of violence involving serious injury and 62 per cent of those causing slight injury are intra-racial (see Stevens and Willis).

The high crime rate of certain minority segments of the black community is directed to that community. Street culture is, on the one hand, expressive and liberative, and on the other, individualistic, macho and predatory. Hustling is not a pursuit of angels; only the most unmitigated romantic would believe this. 'Hyenas and wolves of the street' was how Malcolm X referred to street criminals, and George Jackson in his prison letters wrote to his mother about intra-racial crime in his community:

The men can think of nothing more effective than pimping, gambling and petty theft. I've heard men brag about being pimps of black women and taking money from black women who are on relief. Things like that I find odious, disgusting.

And as a matter of fact, socialists ever since Engels have consistently viewed the vast majority of crime as serving to destroy the community, as something that has to be resisted. Yet these idealists tend merely to invert the imagery of the mass media. If the mass media say that crime is a danger then it obviously is not!

Both the mass media and the left share one thing: they overwhelmingly concentrate on inter-racial crime. Inter-racial crime is a minor, albeit very serious, phenomenon; within this category a substantial proportion occurs because of overtly racist reasons. Thus a recent Home Office study attributes one quarter of all inter-racial crimes to racist motives. In absolute terms these represent only a 0.25 per cent of recorded crime, but what is of significance is the victimization rate for minority groups. The rate for Asians was fifty times that for white people, and that for blacks thirty-six times (see *Racial Attacks*, Home Office, 1981). We have no doubt that this is a gross underestimation and that the police response to racial persecution is severely inadequate. What we must note, however, is that the criminal victimization rates *as a whole* are considerably greater. Furthermore, the left, although correctly focusing on racist incidents, seems, quite incorrectly, unable to see the existence of crime outside this category.

A startling illustration of this shortsightedness is the following quote from *Policing London*, commenting on the Metropolitan figures and the study we have just mentioned:

> Though they possess the information, the Met did not publish at the same time figures which show what proportion of the victims of these crimes are also black. The Home Office report on *Racial Attacks* (November 1981) indicated that, with regard to offences such as violence against the person and robbery: 'The incidence of victimization has been much higher for the ethnic minority populations, particularly the Asians, than for white people. Indeed the rate for Asians was 50 times that for white people and the rate for blacks was over 36 times that for white people.' (*Policing London*, No. 1, July–August 1982, p. 3)

Now, to any reader this remark could only be read as suggesting that serious criminal victimization was fifty times greater for Asians, and thirty-six times greater for blacks, than for whites. This is precisely what has been repeated in several other articles. Of course, these figures do not refer to the total extent of criminal victimization by ethnic groups. They do not even refer to inter-racial attacks. What they do refer to, as we have already noted, is inter-racial attacks where there is 'strong evidence or some indication' of a racist motive. As a matter of fact, the criminal victimization of blacks in the very restricted category of robbery and violent theft alone (about 3 per cent of all serious crime) is over ten times greater than for *all* serious crime against blacks of an overtly racist nature; for Asians the figure is fourteen times. This is not to deny the problem of racist attacks. *On the contrary*, police inactivity with regard to such outrages is a scandal. Our point here is simply that the left, while quite rightly pressing for police involvement in combating such crime, turns a blind eye towards the existence of a massive amount of crime against blacks and the working class.

Inter-racial crime, involving blacks against whites, is a minor phenomenon. Mugging is far from being an exclusively black crime – yet it is also one of the *few* crimes where there is some evidence of a substantial, if still minor, racial component (Pratt). The mass media have picked upon an atypical black crime and portrayed it as the *typical* crime, while at the same time grossly overestimating its seriousness. It is, in fact, largely without serious violence, involves small sums of money and it is the amateurish crime of young boys and adolescents. But its impact should not be underplayed. £5 stolen from an old age pensioner is of far greater significance than £500 stolen from Woolworths, which is why the former, rightly, creates more alarm and disgust than the latter. Mugging, regardless of whether the perpetrator or victim is white or black, is a despicable crime but one which must be seen in perspective. It must neither be exaggerated, in an alarmist fashion, nor ignored as a matter of petty importance.

Intra-racial crime and intra-class crimes are of massive proportions, but because much of the left is locked in a debate with the mass media they are simply not seen. Thus, for ideological reasons, real problems facing the community are quite simply ignored and a ground-swell of anxiety allowed to build up. Both intra-racial and inter-racial crime are demoralizing and divisive within the black community and the working class. The fact that most working-class crime and black crime is directed against the working-class and black communities, coupled with the situation where such communities are less likely to receive adequate police protection than the rich, should be the starting-point for the left. The need is surely for more efficient police protection responsive to the needs of the working class and the groups within it.

If unemployment and deprivation brutalized into criminality a minority of the poor in certain cultural and political circumstances, why is there such a problem for writers on the left to accept the proposition that the accentuation of such deprivation through the additional mechanisms of racial discrimination results in higher crime rates? The claim that the higher recorded rate for certain types of crime for young blacks is purely and simply a product of police prejudice is open to a number of objections. We will examine these in detail later in the chapter but the following four points form an incontestable basis:

(1) Such a claim makes the assumption that the 'real' crime rate for all social groups is the same. This is tantamount to the suggestion that the black community does not in reality suffer any additional ill-effects from racial discrimination.

(2) The recorded rate for a range of Asian crimes is consistently lower than the white rate (Stevens and Willis). Police racism would have to manifest very strangely indeed to be entirely responsible for such results.

(3) The crime rate for the first generation of West Indian immigrants recorded in the 1960s was lower than the general rate (Lambert). Either real changes in the crime rate within the black community have occurred or the police were exercising positive discrimination for over a decade in favour of the black community!

(4) The argument for higher crime rates for black youth is only made for certain types of crime. The police do not claim, for example, that blacks have a higher rate for burglary than whites, or for bank robbery. The issue centres around street crime (see Scarman Inquiry Minutes, Day Two).

Shadow boxing and the debate about race and crime

In 1982 we referred in an article to the fact that there seemed to be real differences in the crime rate between different ethnic groups. We argued that of all the groups on the receiving end of social deprivation – black, Asian and white – blacks most acutely experience the combination of social deprivation and lack of political power, within the established framework, to change their situation as a group. We argued that this combination of economic and political marginalization lay behind the high crime rate within and around the black community, which affected a minority of the community and only sporadically. Crime was a negative manifestation of this discontent, whereas the uprisings of 1981 were an extremely positive response to deprivation. Moreover, we argued that the degree of deprivation experienced by black youngsters in British society was not a product of their being 'aliens' within Britain. On the contrary, it was the very cultural assimilation of these black Britons that made their deprivation all the more acute. Because they had assimilated so well – both in terms of aspirations and expectations – they felt the impact of discrimination and prejudice all the more acutely.

Our work has received an extremely hostile response from certain quarters. Thus Paul Gilroy commented:

> Various factions of the left movement, increasingly marginal to popular concerns, have recently glimpsed, in the intensity of feeling around questions of law and order, a means to gain proximity to the working class. (1982, p. 50)

We were accused of being 'ready allies of the police' (Bridges and Gilroy, p. 35); of giving 'intellectual support . . . to racist stereotypes of the black community' (ibid.); of capitulating to 'the weight of racist logic' (Gilroy, 1982, p. 52); of reproducing 'pathology . . . in polite social democratic rhetoric' (ibid., p. 53) and of being 'a couple of trendy sociologists who advocate harassment and mugging by the racist police force' (J. Crutchley, in a letter to *Marxism Today*, September 1982, p. 47).

Our astonishment was increased by our awareness of the contrast with the situation in America. For instance, here is a comment from two prominent American liberals writing on race relations:

> If a careful, detached scholar knew nothing about crime rates but was aware of the social, economic and political disparities between whites and negroes in the United States, and if this diligent researcher had prior knowledge of the historical status of the American negro, what would be the most plausible hypothesis our scholar could make about the crime rate of negroes? Even this small amount of knowledge would justify the expectation that negroes would be found to have a higher rate of crime than whites. And the data at hand would confirm this hypothesis. (Wolfgang and Cohen, pp. 30–31)

Even American radicals would not deny the greater crime rate of blacks compared to whites. Nor would they deny the dire problem of intra-racial crime in the black community. It is difficult to stand in black Harlem and not deplore the way the community destroys itself. It is almost impossible to be romantic about the extent of crime and believe it is part of the colonial struggle against White America. Rather, as all black activists are ready to point out, it is a product of oppression.

In Britain our critics seem to fall into two categories: liberal and orthodox left on the one hand, and on the other, those people, highly critical of the labour movement, who see the black struggle as special and pioneering. The first position is in essence defensive: it argues that the imputation of a high crime rate to certain immigrants is racism and that everything must be done to debunk such a 'myth'. At the same time it tends to hold the contradictory notion that because of poverty and racism immigrant groups are driven into crime. One could sum the stance up as: 'Of course there isn't a higher black crime rate and even if there is it would scarcely be surprising!' In every sense this position is ideological in that its role is totally propagandist and inflexible. It could, in fact, never admit that there was a higher rate; its role is to defuse arguments that are 'racist' enough to suggest it. And, more importantly, it has never worked its way through the contradictory nature of its suppositions because it sees any critical position as being, at the very least, closet racism. The second position, which superimposes itself on the first, is more sophisticated and much more on the offensive. It does not work its way through the contradiction, but as an ideology it scarcely worries about being contradictory. It is this version that has made most of the running and which we will tackle first.

Despite the level of unthinking abuse levelled at us, it became apparent that there was an implicit coherence in the patterns of criticism. Strangely, we encountered a peculiar *déjà vu* in the sense that the position on crime taken up by our critics – and reflecting a largely untheorized position prevalent on the left – was that of the radical criminology of the late 1960s and early 1970s. During the last ten years a considerable amount of work has been done to reconstruct the original but sometimes naive left idealism of the original formulations of radical criminology and to remove its more obvious theoretical inadequacies. It was thus something of a surprise that these ghosts should choose to resurrect themselves and return, in the guise of a debate on race and crime, claiming to be a new, updated version of a critique of radical criminology! Let us briefly reiterate the main features of the new criminology of the 1968–1972 period:

(1) *Crime as proto-revolutionary:* Crime was viewed as a misconstrued but proto-revolutionary activity. Radical criminology played down the extent of crime within the working class and focused on crime between the social classes.

(2) *Crime statistics as a result of police prejudice:* Radical criminology maintained an extremely critical stance towards the official crime statistics. The high proportion of working-class and black crime within the figures was seen more as the result of police prejudice than of actual behavioural differences between the social classes.

(3) *Panic over crime as a fabrication:* Left idealism saw the official crime rate as used – intentionally or otherwise – by powerful groups such as the police and the media to create a 'moral panic', to mislead the public as to the real social problems they faced, and to divert attention away from the crimes of the powerful – including the police – towards seeing the poor as the main threat. This served as part of a conspiracy to blame the poor for poverty and to portray the rich and powerful as the protectors of society against crime. The war against crime was seen, largely, as an ideological smokescreen behind which the police could siphon off resources in their mobilization against the working class.

In this type of criminology there was a contradiction – which has now revealed itself anew in the writings of our critics – between poverty as an obvious cause of crime, and the crime statistics as constructed by and reflecting simply the activities of a prejudiced police force. There was little attention in such thinking to the simple fact that both could be true: that crime could be a product of poverty *and* that the poor, as a group, could be more susceptible to arrest. Such simple additions were anathema to the either–or dichotomies so characteristic of such theorizing. Over the more recent period, radical criminologists have realized that it is impossible to have it both ways. If crime is one of the consequences of social oppression and deprivation of the poor, then the higher crime rate for the poor cannot simply be a function of police prejudice. Furthermore, criminologists have come to realize the essentially contradictory nature of crime, economically, socially and politically. Thus, in 1975, one of the present authors noted that:

> Crime and deviancy, from a socialist perspective, are terms which encompass an uneven array of activities and behaviours – at times behaviours which are quite inimicable to socialism; at other times rebellions against property and repression which are as justifiable in their consequences as they are primitive in their conception. Forms of illogicality exist within the working class which are adaptive, collective in their accomplishment and progressive in their function: objects 'fall off the back of lorries', factory property metamorphoses as property within the home. Forms of deviancy occur as attempts to create unhampered and liveable space; the tyranny of the workplace and conventional sexuality being left momentarily behind. Marihuana and booze, pub life and gay bars, black music and white rhythm-and-blues – a tenderloin of the city where a sense of 'the possible' breaks through the facticity of what is. But just as one must discriminate actively between crimes which are cultural adaptions of the people, and crimes which derive from the brutalization of criminal and community alike, so we must clearly distinguish between the contradictory nature of many of these adaptive manifestations. Deviance will contain both positive and negative moments; the breakthrough from repression is distorted and beguiled by the reality from which it springs. (Young, 1975, pp. 90–91)

At the same time the American criminologist Tony Platt wrote:

> The political solution to 'street' crime does not lie in *mystifying* its reality by reactionary allusions to 'banditry' nor in *reducing* it to a manifestation of 'lumpen' viciousness. The former is utopian and dangerous because it defends practices that undermine the safety and solidarity of the working class (and glorifies spontaneity and putchism); the latter objectively legitimates the bourgeoisie's attack on superexploited workers especially black and brown workers . . . Pimping, gambling rackets, illegal drug operations, etc., are just as damaging to working-class communities as any 'legal' business which profits from people's misery and desperation.
>
> But we must be careful to distinguish organized criminality from 'street' crime, and the 'lumpen' from the superexploited sections of the working class. Most 'street' crime is not organized and not very profitable . . . The conditions of life in the superexploited sections create both high levels of 'street' crime *and* political militancy. The urban black community, for example, is hit the hardest by 'street' crime, but it is also the locus of tremendous resistance and struggle – as witnessed by the civil rights movements, the ghetto revolts of the 1960s and the anti-repression struggles of today. (p. 26)

Thus, in very pronounced terms, radical criminology has made clear its position on the problem of working-class crime. It explicitly eschews *both* romanticism *and* the law-and-order campaigns of the conservative variety. But it notes quite urgently that there is a substantial element in street crime which is merely the poor taking up the individualistic, competitive ethos of capitalism itself and that its consequences are anathema to the standpoint of socialist concerns.

Now, it would be incorrect to suggest that such strictures cleared the debate on the left of such romanticism about crime. There have always been people unwilling to confront these problems except through rose-coloured spectacles, and this tendency is perhaps stronger in Britain than elsewhere. But the key to the re-emergence of this position in such a strident form was race. The debate over the nature of lower-working-class crime has been transposed to a debate over black crime. Accusations of a high black crime rate were seen as racist and the denial of such an occurrence as a defence of the black community. From this standpoint the duty of all anti-racists was to show how the crime statistics were exaggerated and constituted a smoke-screen while on another, more combative level, the image of an illicit colony growing up within the host country was evoked in which crime was seen as a form of resistance or anti-colonial struggle. This is well captured by two left-wing writers, Friend and Metcalf, who write:

> The establishment of these black neighbourhoods opened up for some the possibility of surviving by alternative means, by a process of hustling involving activities such as gambling, undeclared part-time work, ganja selling, shoplifting, street crime, housebreaking and distributing stolen goods. Sections of the white working class have long chosen to survive through similar strategies, demonstrating in their communities a collective contempt for work discipline, concern for and dependence on the goodwill of an employer or outside authority. (p. 156)

They go on explicitly to identify the crimes of young people as a direct challenge to capitalism with black youth being in the forefront of such a struggle:

> During the seventies the challenge to property relations and the smooth re-production of capitalist social relations increasingly came from working-class youth in general. The decade began with a fairly narrow set of youth singled out for attention – skinheads, hippies, student militants and blacks. There followed constant rumblings about vandalism, hooliganism and truancy and from 1976 onwards both media and state were glancing anxiously at the militancy and self-organization of Asian youth. By the end of the decade politicians, media and the state functionaries were talking of youth as a whole as being a 'problem'. The number of

crimes recorded as committed by young people rose throughout the period . . .

This progression has not, of course, been unconnected to the structural unemployment which was hitting black youth at the beginning of the period and is now bearing down on all working-class youth. Loss of income through unemployment debars youth from almost all recreational and cultural activities which have to be bought in the marketplace and inevitably leads to problems of social control. As vandalism has become a routine recreational activity for younger kids and teenagers alike, thefts have risen and truancy has reached a level where one London borough estimates between 450 and 600 kids skip school every day. (ibid., pp. 161–2)

We wish to argue that such an approach commits a cardinal error. The challenge to property which such young people evinced was directed not so much at capitalism as at the working class – both white and black. And the social relations which were threatened were, very often, not those of capitalism but of the working-class community around them.

The 'anti-colonial struggle' in the inner city

The image of crime as a proto-revolutionary struggle is made to fit a particular view of race and immigration: a view of the alien colony within the imperialist city. This is well summed up in the title of a book recently produced by the Race and Politics group of the Centre for Contemporary Cultural Studies: *The Empire Strikes Back*. The image is that of a colonial culture, steeped in resistance, existing in the heart of the Empire. The traditions of anti-colonialism dormant in the first generation of immigrants are resuscitated in the youth of the second generation. Thus such areas as Railton Road in Brixton or Saint Paul's in Bristol represent the toehold of a colonial people fighting back against imperialism. The frontline is a colony *within* the host country. The culture that has grown up there is the vanguard of Afro-Caribbean culture – it is the culture of survival which every now and then breaks out into the open as resistance. Crime, from this perspective, is *part of* the continuing fightback of a downtrodden people against their colonial oppressors.

From this perspective the police are not merely 'an intrusion into that society, but a threat, a foreign force, an army of occupation – the thin end of the authoritarian wedge, and in themselves so authoritarian as to make no difference between wedge and state' (Sivanandan, 1981, p. 150).

Not only the culture but the form of policing itself originated in the colonies. As Courtney Griffiths put it (p. 10): 'Police practices and attitudes towards black people in the UK have a history originating in the conditions of imperialism'.

The 'white left' fail to understand the nature of such resistance. Paul Gilroy, for instance, is 'unable to accept . . . the assertion that all sections of the population are united in their opposition to street crime' (1983, p. 150). He presumably believes that a substantial minority of the black population support such activities. As to the *genuine* fightback, such as during the riots of summer 1981, the belief that these occur because of a lack of political organization is seen as incorrect. The 'black communities' response [is not one] of "alienation" or "political marginalization" but of organized resistance, albeit in terms drawing on traditions of anti-colonial struggle which do not necessarily fit with the Left's perceptions of politics' (Bridges and Gilroy, p. 35). Furthermore,

> We must also realize that forms of political action and organization developed in previous struggles offer no guarantees of efficacy in new circumstances and relations of force. The ahistorical fetishism of organizational forms which have outlived their adequacy in the dogmatic prescriptions of omniscient bureaucrats and party officers is both a fetter on progress and a set of blinkers preventing useful analysis of the present. (Gilroy, 1981, p. 220)

Lastly, concomitant with this position is a belief that all the various immigrant groups – but Asians and West Indians in particular – share common responses to their situation in Britain. This is because of their postulated common anti-colonial heritage and their uniform experience of discrimination in this country.

An attempt can be made to sum up at this point the main principles of the colony-within-the-imperialist-city approach to race:

1 A *minimization* of the differences between the various immigrant groups' cultures.
2 A *maximization* of the differences between immigrant groups and the native culture: in the case of West Indians this involves an attack on notions of acculturation – a minimization of the impact of British culture in the Caribbean and a maximization of the importance of its African roots.
3 A *minimization* of the social problems occurring within immigrant cultures *despite* the recognition of the deleterious impact of colonial oppression. As a consequence a degree of relativism enters into the discussion of family structures, relationships between the sexes, inter-generational disputes, etc. All of these, of course, are highly controversial areas.

This represents a perspective on race within which discussion about crime is only one aspect of a much wider debate. However, because of the moral panic in the mass media concerning race and crime, the problem of immigrant criminality has become a central cockpit for both right and left. Furthermore, as Paul Gilroy says:

> Because of their capacity to symbolize other relations and conflicts, images of crime and law-breaking have had a special ideological importance since the dawn of capitalism. If the potential for organized political struggle towards social transformation offered by criminality has often been low, images of particular crimes and criminal classes have frequently borne symbolic meanings and even signified powerful threats to the social order. This means that 'crime' can have political implications which extend beyond the political consciousness of criminals. The boundaries of what is considered criminal or illegal are elastic and the limits of the law have been repeatedly altered by intense class conflict. It is often forgotten that the political formation of the working-class movement in this country is saturated with illegality. The relation of politics to 'crime' is therefore complex. These points should be borne in mind if socialists are not to rush into the arms of the right in their bid to 'take crime seriously'. (1982, p. 47)

The political context of the debate

Let us briefly outline our political differences with authors such as Gilroy and Bridges. The most clear exposition of their politics is Lee Bridges' diatribe against the Labour Movement in the recent *Sage Relations Abstract*. Bridges' political position can, we believe, be summarized in four propositions:

(1) The state and all its institutions, but notably the police and the media, are monolithically racist. This racism is an aspect of the functional relationship between state policy and the 'logic' of capital.
(2) Current concerns with crime, rather than reflecting real social problems, are part of a moral panic orchestrated by the state in the interests of capital accumulation. There is no real rise in black crime – there is merely an increased victimization by the police of blacks as scapegoats.
(3) The only real resistance to this process comes from the black movement, which is not concerned with the problem of crime as it affects the black community but is oriented towards the employment of essentially anti-colonialist techniques of defensive struggle against the racist state.
(4) The 'white left' is marginalized from this struggle although it makes periodic attempts to co-opt black politics and issues.

The position that we represent, which has come to be labelled the 'new left realism about crime' and against which Bridges directs his polemic, starts from a different set of propositions concerning the state and the nature of the problem of crime. The practical political orientation of this tendency is towards the left of the Labour Party. The main ingredients of the position can be summarized as follows:

(1) The state as an institution does not start simply from the 'logic' of capital. The state is concerned above all with the reproduction of social relations. This involves *both* securing a stable framework for the process of capital accumulation *and* attempting to minimize some of the more destructive results of the latter. Thus, during the 1970s state policy on race relations was contradictory, involving attempts both to secure immigrants as a low-wage labour-force *and* to achieve a degree of integration sufficient to forestall a repetition in Britain of the American riots of the late sixties (Lea).

(2) Integration policies were thrown into disarray by the onset of economic recession. Massive unemployment and the attempts by capital to alter the composition of the working class have resulted in such phenomena as the weakening of the working-class community, and a growing alienation from the Welfare State and the social democratic politics that sustained it. An increase in political racism within the working class has been one response to this situation.

(3) Another response has been increased crime. Increases in crime rates are one manifestation of the destructive effects of recession upon working people. Moral panics concerning crime have a resonance precisely because they accord with the perceptions and fears of ordinary working-class people. There is an increase in black crime as a consequence of economic deprivation and police harassment. As Stuart Hall and his colleagues put it (p. 390):

> The position of black labour, subordinated by the processes of capital, is deteriorating and will deteriorate more rapidly, according to its own specific logic. Crime is one perfectly predictable and quite comprehensible consequence of this process – as certain a consequence of how the structures work, however 'unintended', as the fact that night follows day.

(4) Likewise, recent changes in policing policy cannot be seen simply as orchestrated from above. The move to what we term 'military' policing has to be seen as a response to real social problems, a complex interaction between the structure of state organs such as the police and the forms of response institutionally available to them, and the changes in the structure of the working class resulting from de-industrialization. Consequently, struggles to change state policy in the direction of democratic control of social policy must also be aimed at re-strengthening forms of local community rather than taking the latter for granted. As was made clear in Cowell (ed.), *Policing the Riots* (p. 152):

The whole point about democratic accountability of the police to properly elected and constituted police authorities . . . is that it can be part of a process whereby a political culture is established in the communities and extended into new areas.

A subcultural approach to race and crime

In contrast to the 'colonial' approach, we would argue for an approach which stresses the fact that human beings continually *create* solutions at the level of culture and subculture to the material experience with which they are con-fronted. Men and women make their own cultural history, but they do so out of the cultural traditions they carry with them and in historical situations and environments not of their own choosing. What characterizes the view of our critics is its misunderstanding of the process whereby peasants and workers from the colonies and former colonies find themselves in the labour markets of the imperialist metropolis. The notion that some sort of cultural *Geist* accompanies immigrants from the colonies to the imperialist city and is dir-ectly available to the second-generation sons and daughters of immigrants born in the city is profoundly idealist. The continuity of imperialism consists in the transition from the status of ex-slaves, peasants, etc., in the colonies or ex-colonies, to that of an exploited 'ethnic minority' condemned to low wages and long and unsocial hours of work in the metropolis in occupations vacated by native labour. This process is accompanied by a high degree of racial hostility and discrimination from all social classes in the imperialist city, and in today's economic circumstances very high rates of unemployment for the minority communities. The means whereby the immigrant communities and especially the second-generation children of immigrants *adapt* culturally and emotionally to this process is complex and contradictory involving elements both of assimilation to the culture of the 'host' country and of rediscovery or reconstruction of elements of the culture and political experience of the countries from which the first generation of immigrants came. The main ingredient of the response of the second-generation descendants of immi-grants to the social and economic deprivations which they face in metro-politan society is certainly not describable as the simple transfer of 'traditions of anti-colonial struggle'.

The history of an immigrant group is, of course, important. But immi-grant communities must be understood in terms of their real histories, not ones imposed upon them to fit in with some political preconceptions. The conflation, for instance, of the West Indian and Asian experiences under the general rubric of anti-colonial struggle and a common experience of prejudice scarcely does justice to the very different traditions, experiences and actual outcomes involved. Subcultures constantly evolve; they do not merely propagate a cultural essence such as 'the anti-colonial experience' from generation to generation. This is particularly important to understand when such extraordinary transitions and upheavals as migration are concerned. At a minimum, therefore, we must distinguish between (a) the culture of the country from which migration takes place, within which there are often diverse subcultures, (b) the particular subculture of those who migrate, and (c) the subcultures which grow up as part of the process of adaption to the country of immigration. The link from (a) to (c) is tenuous. To believe, for example, that the activities of second-generation West Indian youth are simply the enactment of a resuscitated home culture of the West Indies denies the extremely different conditions in Britain compared to those of the West Indies. It also blatantly denies creativity and innovation to the youth. It denies the way in which immigrant groups are heterogeneous, not only inter-generationally but also intra-generationally. The same predicament may produce a diversity of solutions: witness Pentecostalism, Rastafarianism, hustling, and respectability, among blacks (see Pryce). To take one's favourite subcultural solution as indicative of the vanguard or even of the whole group just because it fits certain political preconceptions is a common problem which we must constantly be aware of.

Subcultures emerge as adaptions to problems faced by individuals and groups, but such adaptions do not necessarily bring a solution to the problem which is either tenable or in the interests of the group as a whole. Often the response to injustice is itself individualistic and competitive and may bring harm to the people involved. To believe that the reaction against injustice is of necessity just and effective is a common mistake of the optimist. The relation between politics and subculture is itself complex. History is rich with examples – and the anticolonial struggle is one of them – of how groups with profoundly differing cultural practices can unite around common political aims (for example, the unity between blacks and Asians in the struggle for colonial independence in the West Indies). The problem is not, therefore, to deny politics in favour of 'mere' cultural habits, but to avoid the reverse: the ossification of subcultural *adaptions* to injustice into the status of political *struggles* against it. Nowhere is this problem clearer than in the case of criminality.

Crime is one aspect, though generally a small one, of the process of *cultural adaption to oppression*. While a fetish is not to be made out of legality – class struggle may involve the violation of laws whose only purpose is to defend the particular interests of ruling élites and to criminalize anyone who challenges their power – neither must it be thought that all criminal acts by oppressed groups advance the struggle for emancipation. In reality the issue is not criminality *per se* but responses to suffering which further debilitate and brutalize the sufferers, as opposed to those which advance the struggle for justice.

There is no reason whatsoever to assume that unintegrated ethnic cultures are more likely to generate instability and discontent than a situation of cultural homogeneity. In fact, the reverse is probably true. The first generation of immigrants entering this country in the 1950s and 1960s more often than not had lower expectations of living standards than the indigenous population because comparisons were still predominantly being made with conditions in the country of emigration. Under these circumstances cultural diversity is a factor working against instability and discontent. It is the second generation, born in this country of immigrant parents, educated to have equal job expectations by the school, and consumer demands by the mass media, that begins to see itself, when compared with the native population of the same age, as manifestly unequal. If discrimination remains entrenched in the practices and attitudes of the majority of the population, then it is not the separateness of cultures but the process of their homogenization, through the school and the mass media, that gives rise to discontent.

Secondly, it is a mistake to see the culture of many black youths in Britain today as derived from their parents. Take 'West Indians' as an example. What we are witnessing among 'West Indian' black youth is the development of a culture of discontent resulting precisely from the visibility of deprivation, a visibility highlighted by the very process of integration into British standards and expectations of life. The street culture of black youth of West Indian parentage is *not* a hand-down from the previous generation of immigrant parents as the conservative thesis of 'alien cultures' would suggest. Rather, it is an improvised culture based on the import of elements from the West Indies by kids most of whom either have never been there or left when they were very young. Indeed, such culture is widely disapproved of by the older generation of West Indian immigrants and it is, furthermore, a minority and deviant subculture within the West Indies itself.

So the conservative thesis has got it badly wrong: the 'alien' culture feared by conservatives grew not out of the values of the previous generation of immigrants but out of the process of cultural assimilation itself, a process in which a new generation of young people have assimilated the expectations of the majority culture, only to be denied them in reality. The question arises at this point of the differences between Asian and West Indian youth. As a result of discrimination, the unemployment rate for ethnic minority youth in general has risen at a much faster rate than for their white counterparts. But between youth of West Indian and Asian parentage there are two differences which have the effect of comparatively insulating the latter from the process of relative deprivation. Firstly, by comparison with West Indian youth, Asians have a more substantive opportunity structure within their own community. This is due to the larger size of the professional and business class in the Asian community. Secondly, the distance between Asian culture and indigenous British culture is greater than that between the latter and West Indian culture. Assimilation to indigenous British standards and aspirations has thus probably been a more rapid process for youth of West Indian parentage, and hence relative deprivation is felt more acutely, with the consequent fostering of a deviant counter-culture. There are other factors at work here which will be mentioned later.

Actually, the most 'alien' or way-out cultures are, in fact, often the most innocuous. For example, the Hasidic Jews among the ethnic groups, or hippies among youth cultures, are, probably, the most distant from mainstream conventions. It is subcultures involving crime and delinquency which, because they are closest to our wider values, have the greatest criminal impact on our lives. And this includes not only lower-working-class delinquents, but also criminals, whose lives are so conventional that they would heartily deny that their illegalities were really criminal.

Part of the wrath which Paul Gilroy and his associates vented on us stemmed from this analysis of the predicament of second-generation West Indian youth in Britain. We argued that their disquiet stemmed from their similarity to native white youth. The culture of West Indian youth, unlike that of various Asian immigrant communities, was close to that of the British, and their socialization through British schools made it even more so. It was the degree of *assimilation* which made them – quite rightly – discontented when they compared themselves, in terms of opportunities, with their white schoolmates, and not their alienation from British culture. Bridges, Gilroy, and a large part of the Race and Class Collective argued the opposite: that West Indian kids had carried with them cultural notions of the anti-colonial struggle. Like conservatives, but for the opposite reasons, they conceived of black youth as exhibiting an alien culture. However much their parents, as immigrants, had been quiescent, the youth had revived the tradition. For us, however, the 'frontline' was a creation of those black youths who had assimilated, yet at the same time seen themselves rejected by British society through racial discrimination and deprivation. These kids have created their own cultural means of surviving that rejection, by reviving half-warm memories of the Caribbean, and this culture has to be understood both in terms of its creativity and of its disorganization, in terms of its being a black British rather than an undiluted Caribbean culture carried genetically from a widely differing society. Like all poor and marginalized groups throughout history, black youth has developed a contradictory subculture, part collective resistance and part criminality and disorganization. The contradictory nature of such subcultures – and the same goes for those in white youth cultures, such as punks or skinheads – must always be kept in mind. They can be both progressive and divisive, both rebellious and reactionary. Hence the one-sided readings that occur either by radicals who, through rose-tinted glasses, see only positives, and the conservatives, whose jaded glance notes merely the negative.

By pointing to the differences in crime rate between Asians and Afro-Caribbeans we were seen to be 'driving a wedge' between the two communities, despite the fact that the vast majority of authorities are in agreement on this issue. Most recently, Mawby and Batta, in their painstaking study of crime published by the National Association for Asian Youth, came to this conclusion, as does every single research study that we can trace. This is not to make insidious comparisons at all, it is merely to record the differences that culture makes to experienced deprivation. As Jefferson and Clarke (pp. 37–8) put it:

> We wish to distinguish firmly between West Indian and Asian communities in Britain, in terms of their differing cultures. Asian teenagers do not experience the worst effects of structural and racial inequalities since they remain within the strong, self-contained Asian culture, primarily contained in family and religion.

The shaky nature of evidence to the contrary is summed up by Gilroy's rather desperate remark (1982, p. 177):

> Of course, since police rely heavily on intelligence from outside their own ranks to catch criminals or even to detect their crimes, and Asian people have every reason to steer clear of a force which assumes them to be illegally resident rather than take their grievances seriously, there may be some much simpler reason for the low rates of reported crime.

The fact that Asians have a very high rate of criminal victimization which is reported to the police (over four times that of blacks or whites in certain categories of offence) belies this point, however true it may be that they have a totally justifiable suspicion of the police.

Subcultural theory and racism

Accusations of racism have, as we have noted, been made against our argument. It is therefore necessary to demonstrate that subcultural theory is quite innocent of such accusations. Moreover, subcultural theory enables us to locate embarrassing similarities between genetic theories of crime and the notions of cultural continuity such as those exhibited in the 'colonial-struggle-in-the-metropolis' approach discussed above.

For subcultural theory the behaviour of a particular group relates to its specific history and the opportunities and constraints which that brings. Subcultural theory is opposed to any notion of 'natural' criminal tendencies of a particular group whether this be established in a genetic, racist fashion or by means of a cultural essence transmitted relatively unaltered over time. Nowadays the belief in a pre-written genetic script determining the behavioural characteristics of a group has little audience. Culturalist theories have a more pervasive influence, however. From the latter standpoint the essential characteristics of a group are seen to be determined by cultural traditions whose 'essence' can be discovered by the discerning analyst. Thus a Jewish propensity for finance is discovered, or an African propensity for rhythm identifiable in contemporary black America. Such theories abound in the discussion of ethnic groups and their history, and stretch from music (jazz as the direct expression of an African culture in America) to politics (Jews as innately quiescent in the face of adversity), and embrace all those writers, of the right or left in politics, who see the behaviour of second-generation immigrants as a cultural replay of their ancestry.

The point is not to deny cultural legacies and traditions but to emphasize that they are constantly changed, reinterpreted and reworked in the face of changing circumstances. The immense variations of human behaviour cannot be accounted for in terms of the genetic script or the cultural essence. Those who a generation ago were talking of Jewish quiescence in response to persecution presumably now speak of the innate aggressiveness of Jewish culture. The relationship between one generation and the next is a process of *reworking* rather than a process of *transmission*. A group in a new set of circumstances or environment reconstructs, adapts, and innovates, culturally as in other aspects of existence. Aspects of the new environment are combined with the appropriation of often contradictory elements of the past in the process of the creation of a new subcultural adaption to a new environment. A New York Jew is both a Jew and a New Yorker.

As far as crime is concerned it is very useful to look at the work of the Chicago School of Urban Sociology, which charted the progress of immigrant groups through the city of Chicago. They started from the observation that certain areas of the city invariably had high crime rates, and that these areas were close to the city centre, in the poorer neighbourhoods. Delinquency rates progressively decreased as one moved from the urban centre out towards the suburbs.

As each immigrant group arrived they moved into this cheap inner-city area – the zone of transition – while the group already there began the trek to the suburbs. Irish, Germans, Jews – each moved through this zone of migration, adapted to the high delinquency rate of the area and began to lose its delinquency as it moved 'over the tracks' towards the suburbs. What the Chicago School demonstrated was that delinquency was not the perquisite of any one ethnic group alone, but that of any group placed in certain predicaments. It is not common, for example, in Britain today to think of Jews or Italians as having high crime rates. Indeed, the opposite is true. Yet at the beginning of the century in London this was the case. Witness this extract from Arthur Harding's description of Whitechapel:

> Edward Emmanuel had a group of Jewish terrors. There was Jackie Berman. He told a pack of lies against me in the vendetta case – he had me put away . . . Bobby Levy – he lived down Chingford way – and his brother Moey. Bobby Nark – he was a good fighting chap. In later years all the Jewish terrors worked with the Italian mob on the race course . . . The Narks were a famous Jewish family from out of Aldgate. Bobby was a fine big fellow though he wasn't very brainy. His team used to hang out

in a pub at Aldgate on the corner of Petticoat Lane. I've seen him smash a bloke's hat over his face and knock his beer over. He belonged to the Darby Sabini gang – that was made up of Jewish chaps and Italian chaps. He married an English lady – stone rich – they said she was worth thousands and thousands of pounds. He's dead and gone now. (Samuel, pp. 133–4)

A proportion of poor people everywhere have turned to crime. But not to the same extent. The Chicago School was too mechanical in its linking of constant adversity with a constant rate of crime. Different ethnic groups react differently to deprivation, whether it be, for example, unemployment, poor education or bad housing. As Terrence Morris commented on the Chicago School:

> Although Chicago's immigrant groups were concentrated in the deteriorating interstitial areas of the city, and delinquency and deterioration correlate positively and highly, it remains that the Negroes and Italians produced delinquency out of proportion to their numbers when compared with other ethnic . . . groups. (pp. 86–7)

This is not to say that blacks and Italians, due to a cultural essence or to genetic predisposition, inevitably have higher crime rates. The crime rate is *neither* wholly a function of the material conditions – the areas with their unemployment, bad housing, etc. – *nor* of a particular culture, but a complex interaction between the two. Subcultures arise out of material conditions, but at the same time the culture a group carries with it into a new situation will influence how the new material conditions will be experienced, enjoyed, tolerated, suffered, or actively fought. The existing culture will provide a major *part* of the raw material out of which a new cultural adaptation will be worked.

In concluding this stage in the discussion we wish to underline three of the points we have tried to make above. Firstly, as regards crime, one cannot have it both ways. Street crime cannot be seen as having a 'social and political nature' which links it to the tradition of anti-colonial struggle if at the same time it is maintained that the crime statistics are purely a function of police prejudice. Secondly, the culture of second-generation black youth in Britain today is not simply a transmitted culture embodying an unbroken tradition of anti-colonial struggle. It is, rather, a complex entity involving assimilation to native British culture, the received cultural adaptions of the first generation of immigrants, and a process of innovation and cultural construction attempting to make sense of, and survive in, the harsh conditions of racist Britain. For some the political rediscovery of the anti-colonial struggle has been a way of trying to make sense of their position in Britain. For many, shifting in and out of criminality and hustling have become forms of adaption to the same problems. Finally, the fact that criminality will be used as an ideology by ruling élites in attempts to legitimize the repression of groups meeting their displeasure does not entail that street crime is some form of politics. Those who refer to the 'social and political nature' of the criminality of a minority of black youth have yet to demonstrate its contribution to the struggle for social justice as opposed to the demoralization and weakening of that struggle. We can only echo the words of Stuart Hall and his colleagues

> The fact is that there is, as yet, no active politics, no form of organized struggle, and no strategy which is able adequately and decisively to *intervene* in the quasi-rebellion of the black wageless such as would be capable of bringing about that *break* in the current false appropriations of oppression through crime – that critical transformation of the criminalized consciousness into something more sustained and thoroughgoing in a political sense. (pp. 396–7)

6

The myth of black criminality
by Paul Gilroy

*The Police must win . . . but we must never be seen to win easily. If policemen
all loaded down with special equipment went to a demonstration and arrested
1,000 people and no policemen were injured, why the critics would be coming
out of the woodwork. It's like a good cricket match: we must thrash the other
side, but our public likes us much better if we come from behind to do it.*
Deputy Assistant Commissioner George Rushbrook
Metropolitan Police

The last decade has witnessed 'law and order' moving steadily to the centre of
the political stage. As the national crisis has deepened, the extension of police
power and the recruitment of law in political conflicts have become commonplace. The rule of law and maintenance of public order have appeared in
forms which involve a racist appeal to the 'British Nation'[1] and have become
integral to maintaining popular support for the government in crisis conditions. Indeed the recent history of 'law and order' is scarcely separable from
the growth of popular racism and nationalism in the period following Enoch
Powell's[2] famous intervention. Powell's wide-grinning piccaninnies have
grown up, and with the onset of their adulthood, potent imagery of youthful
black criminals stalking derelict inner-city streets where the law-abiding are
afraid to walk after sunset[3] has been fundamental to the popularization of
increasingly repressive criminal justice and welfare state policies.

Because of their capacity to symbolize other relations and conflicts,
images of crime and law-breaking have had a special ideological importance
since the dawn of capitalism.[4] If the potential for organized political struggle
towards social transformation offered by criminality has often been low,
images of particular crimes and criminal classes have frequently borne symbolic meanings and even signified powerful threats to the social order. This
means that 'crime' can have political implications which extend beyond the
political consciousness of criminals. The boundaries of what is considered

criminal or illegal are elastic and the limits of the law have been repeatedly altered by intense class conflict. It is often forgotten that the political formation of the working-class movement in this country is saturated with illegality. The relation of politics to 'crime' is therefore complex. These points should be borne in mind if socialists are not to rush into the arms of the right in their bid to 'take crime seriously'.

Black crime and the crisis

In contemporary Britain, the disorder signified in popular imagery of crime and criminals, to which law and order is presented as the only antidote, has become expressive of national decline in several ways. At best, a lingering environmentalism makes a causal link between crime and unemployment or the deterioration of the inner cities. At worst, discussion of crime becomes subsumed by the idea that the rule of law, and therefore the Nation itself, is somehow under attack. Here alien criminals[5] take their place alongside subversive enemies within[6] and self-destructive defects in the national culture.[7] Race is, however, always dominant in the way this decline is represented. The left's failure to appreciate how the racism of slump and crisis is different from the racism[8] of boom and commonwealth, has meant that they have not grasped how notions of black criminality have been instrumental in washing the discourse of the nation as white as snow and preparing the way for repatriation. The imagery of alien violence and criminality personified in the 'mugger' and the 'illegal' immigrant has become an important card in the hands of politicians and police officers whose authority is undermined by the political fluctuations of the crisis. For them, as for many working-class Britons, the irresolvable difference between themselves and the undesired immigrants is clearly expressed in the latter's culture of criminality and inbred inability[9] to cope with that highest achievement of civilization – the rule of law.

The centrality of race has been consistently obscured by left writers on police and crime, often too keen to view 'racism' as a matter of individual attitudes adequately dealt with under the headings of prejudice and discrimination, and the struggle against it as an exclusively ideological matter far removed from the world of class politics.

In answer to this tendency, it is our contention that recognition of the contemporary importance of racial politics allows a number of important analytical and strategic issues to take shape. It is not only that a left movement which makes rhetorical commitment to viewing the law as an arena of struggle can profit from careful attention to the methods and organizational forms in which various black communities have won a series of legal victories whilst simultaneously organizing outside the courtroom, though the history of such cases, which span the 12 years between the Mangrove 9[10] and the Bradford 12, does merit careful inspection. It is rather that taking the experience of black communities seriously can transform 'left-wing' orthodoxy on the subject of the police and thereby determine a change in the orientation and composition of the struggle for democratic local control of police services. It is fruitless, for example, to search for programmatic solutions to 'discriminatory police behaviour' in amendments to the training procedure when professional wisdom inside the force emphasizes a racist, pathological view of black familial relations, breeding criminality and deviancy out of cultural disorganization and generational conflict.[11] If this racist theory is enshrined in the very structure of police work, it demands more desperate remedies than merely balancing the unacceptable content against increased 'human relations' training. However, left-wing writers have tended to ignore the well-documented[12] abuse of the black communities by the people which stretches back to the beginnings of post-war settlement in sufficient volume to have made a considerable impact on their critical view of the police. This history not only shows the manner in which police violate the letter and the spirit of the law in their day-to-day dealings with blacks. It is sufficient to prompt the questions about the kind of law which deprives 'illegal' immigrants of their rights of habeas corpus, restricts their rights of appeal, operates retroactively, and bids its special branches to round them up whilst sanctioning vaginal examinations and dangerous X-rays of other would-be settlers.[13]

Lack of attention to other important issues has similarly reduced the value of left analysis of police and crime. The continuing war in the six counties of Northern Ireland has had profound effects on the police service in the rest of the UK. These go beyond the simple but important idea that operational techniques, methods of surveillance and even structures of criminal justice refined in that experience are being progressively implemented in Britain.[14] The appointment of Sir Kenneth Newman to the Metropolitan Commissionership indicates the official premium placed on lessons learned there, but the fact that senior policemen routinely study General Frank Kitson's *Low Intensity Operations*[15] and Colonel Robin Evelegh's *Peace Keeping in a Democratic Society, the Lessons of Northern Ireland*,[16] more accurately conveys the transformation of policing theory which has followed the impact of counter-insurgency planning. It has been argued[17] that theories of 'community policing' most clearly represent the fruits of this relationship, and though we cannot go into this in detail here, several basic points can be made. Counter-insurgency theory not only stresses the need to combat domestic subversion,[18] but also the annexation and synchronization of social and welfare-state institutions under police control. Though all of Kitson's methods are not readily transferable to the current situation on mainland Britain it is clear that his definition of subversion includes activities which are neither illegal nor alien to the political traditions of the working-class movement in this country. 'It [subversion] can involve the use of political and economic pressure, strikes, protest marches, and propaganda.'[19] General

Kitson has recently been appointed Chief of Land Forces in the UK. It is also worth pointing out that it is the liberal ex-police chief John Alderson who has been credited with pioneering the study of counter-insurgency theory on the senior command course at Bramshill Police College.[20] Kitson's emphasis on the psychological dimension to law enforcement and peace-keeping operations 'psyops' is echoed in Alderson's stress on the imagery and language of police politics:

> We need a climate to be created in which we [the police] are seen not as potential enemies, but as potential friends and, dare I use the word, brothers. You have to start talking like that. You have to use expressions like that. The rhetoric of leaders and administrators is critical.[21]

If policing by consent is the fundamental principle of the British approach, crisis conditions dictate that policemen have ceased to merely pay lip-service to this idea, they now recognize that consent must be won, maintained and reproduced by careful interventions in popular politics.

It has been suggested that the use of computers in Northern Ireland has made a considerable impact on the British police in its own right. Here too there are lessons which have been learned from maintaining law and order in the six counties.[22]

Popular politics of law and order

Various fractions of the left movement, increasingly marginal to popular concerns, have recently glimpsed in the intensity of feeling around questions of law and order a means to gain proximity to the working class. These theorists[23] take note of the fears of crime and violence which have been amplified by the entry of police chiefs into media politics. But rather than view these fears as themselves produced by a novel situation in which the police have begun to derive their ideological authority from a direct relationship to the police, and their political legitimacy from an increasingly acceptable voice in matters of social policy, this fear is taken as an unproblematic reflection of the reality of crime in working-class communities. There is not the slightest acknowledgement that police are in a good position to mould and even create public fear in such a way as to justify an increase in their powers. This is a serious lapse in view of the fact that they state intellectuals have begun to abandon the idea that detecting and preventing crime can be the principal object of police work, arguing instead, that[24] 'the fear of crime . . . is perhaps only marginally related to the objective risk of becoming a victim and that people who feel well policed are well policed'.[25]

One consequence of this is that the public, particularly the black public must be re-educated[26] in more realistic expectations of the police and their capabilities. We shall explore the way in which this shift has transformed the

politics of policing below, but it must be immediately related to an understanding of the manner in which chief constables have become media per-
sonalities and also to the personalization of their office which has followed
Sir Robert Mark's reign at Scotland Yard. It is remarkable that the left has
accepted the over-polarization of debate around the contrasting police per-
sonalities of James Anderton and John Alderson.[27] Alderson has himself
warned that this simplistic view 'obscures more than it reveals'. There is also
evidence to suggest that the police in Devon and Cornwall are as capable of
the excesses of 'fire-brigade'[28] policing as their brother officers in Manchester.
This makes nonsense of the view of community policing as a miraculous
cure-all for urban ailments and the symptoms of economic crisis. Alderson's
much publicized solutions to the problems of a society 'in which the only
permanence is change' appear attractive when contrasted to the crudities of
operation 'Swamp 81', but the reality of community policing is rather more
complex in theory let alone in practice, than the optimism and enthusiasm
of some left commentators would suggest. It is not always appreciated, for
example, that 'community policing' is not planned to be an alternative to
other 'more dramatic'[29] modes of police work, but rather a 'complementary
strategy' designed to 'bring the reactive and preventive roles of the police
service into a balance appropriate to long-term aims and objectives'.[30]

A senior officer from the West Midlands, where Alderson's ideas have
been put to the acid test of the inner city, dispels the idea that community
policing alters the fundamental orientation of aims of the police officers who
practise it: 'We are not always the nice guys . . . these are good sound operational PCs in uniform doing an operational PC's job, but they are doing it
more effectively . . . We're not trying to create a force of social workers or
make claims we are getting involved in welfare. It's very much policing.'[31]

In his evidence to the Scarman inquiry, Brixton's home-beat policeman,
John Brown,[32] provided further insights into the relationship between the
'criminal intelligence' gained in the practice of 'penetrating the community in
all its aspects' and the more reactive and aggressive styles of policing. Brown
explains that he not only guided the Special Patrol Group round his own beat
during their tour of duty in Brixton, but also that in the past he aided officers
from a neighbouring district in collecting the names of demonstrators
engaged in an entirely lawful and non-violent trade union dispute. When
asked if this could be described as intelligence gathering, Brown replied, 'No
it is not that'.

Illusions about the nature of policing theory revealed in a naive view of
community policing are compounded by an innocent faith in the evenhandedness of police practice on the ground. Ian Taylor, for example, criti-
cizes the left as conspiratorial in their approach to policing issues and 'proves'
this by suggesting that the police have been systematically curtailing the
military activities of the fascist right, and calling for bans of their marches.
That the gun-running activities of the right can be exposed on prime-time

television without the police prosecuting the individuals responsible makes nonsense of Taylor's first claim.[33] The nature of blanket bans which restrict all protest, and which cannot therefore be regarded as victories, invalidates his second. On this last point, it is remarkable how little critical comment has greeted Lord Scarman's recommendation that the Public Order Act 1936 be amended so that the police must be notified in advance of any procession or demonstration.[34]

The left's failings in relation to law, police and crime go far beyond poor analysis of the immediate situation or misunderstanding of the Scarman Report. However, discussion of the conflicts of summer 1981 and the political responses to them can illustrate more general failings with great clarity.

In a series of influential articles, John Lea and Jock Young[35] have argued that the source of the summer riots lay, not in matters of police harassment and abuse, but in the political marginalization of inner-city communities. Their analysis is disabled by a startling ignorance of police–community relations. Worse than this, the view of the black communities which they advance shares a great deal with the most conservative explanations of the conflict. They view West Indian life as characterized by pathological family relations and a high degree of generational conflict, but these are not presented as the sole source of black criminality. Discrimination, disadvantage and economic alienation clash with inappropriate aspirations derived from the internalization of 'British values' (sic) and this also generates the 'propensity' to crime. Thus the relation between race and crime is secured, not directly, as in the biological culturalism of Conservative explanations, but at one remove which is equally dangerous, particularly as it prompts speculation as to why it is only the black poor who resolve their frustration in acts of criminality. To present 'black crime' as a primary *cultural problem* whether forged in the economic 'no man's land' between deprivation and restricted opportunity, or secured in a spurious social biology, is a capitulation to the weight of racist logic. This suggests a total discontinuity between the cultures of black and white youth which is inappropriate given the multiracial character of the riots, and becomes openly visible when Lea and Young trace the roots of urban British street crime to a 'minority and deviant sub-culture within the West Indies'.

The emphasis on black culture legitimates the idea that any black, all blacks, are somehow contaminated by the alien predisposition to crime which is reproduced in their distinctive cultures, specifically their family relations. Police theorists have already made the link between supposedly 'Victorian' conceptions of discipline in the West Indian home and the growth of Rastafarian inspired criminality:

> This unfortunate break-up of family association has seen the formation of substantial groups of young blacks leaving home and banding together in numerous squats and communes, unemployed and completely disillusioned with society. Most of them have donned the Mantle

of Rastafarianism, or more precisely the criminal sub-cult of the dread-lock fraternity.[36]

Young and Lea do little more than reproduce this pathology in polite social democratic rhetoric.

Their political solution to police–community conflict is built on the pos-sibility of instituting what they described as 'consensual policing'. This, they explain, is a situation in which 'the policeman is in and with the community'. They refer to the breakdown of this relationship, implying therefore that it existed in the past, yet are unable to cite a single concrete historical instance of where or when this model of social harmony has actually existed. Their related view of the police officer as a friendly or avuncular figure, acceptable to the urban working class bears scant relation to the numerous instances of conflict between working-class communities and the police which appear to have extended well into this century. Their view is also unable to accom-modate the practice of forms of social crime in urban working-class com-munities, particularly by young people,[37] let alone patterns of intra-class struggle which have often involved forms of property crime.[38]

Young and Lea present the militarization of inner-city policing as a straightforward, if undesirable, response to rising levels of 'street crime' in inner areas. There is no acknowledgement of the possibility that broader imperatives of social control and public order have been transformed by crises of political representation and in the economy. The neat scenario which presents rising street crime as the cause and police militarization as the effect, places the blame for this state of affairs squarely on the shoulders of a minor-ity of deviant blacks. It is posited at the expense of engaging with the history of police–community relations, particularly in so far as this relates to the black communities. Supt Lawrence Roach,[39] sometime head of the Met's Com-munity Relations Branch, has revealed how the development of specialist community relations policing has arisen out of the exigencies of policing the blacks; police theorists' views on the functions of communities in police strategy[40] also suggest that techniques devised in policing black areas can provide a new paradigm for policing cities in crisis conditions.

Significantly, prior to their defeat by black youth at the Notting Hill Carnival in 1976, Metropolitan Police evidence to the Commons Select Committee described a situation in London where, during the preceding 12 months, forty incidents 'carrying the potential for large scale disorder' had developed out of police attempts to arrest black youths. The pattern of this conflict dates back to the early 1970s, landmarked by notable cases of police–community conflict in Notting Hill (1970), Brockwell Park (1973), Stockwell, Cricklewood, Dalston, Hornsey and Brixton (1975). However, London was not unique in the scale of street-level conflict between the police and the black communities. In Birmingham, the massive stop-and-search operation which sealed off the Handsworth area following the murder of a policeman in July 1975 involved the arrest of 600 blacks though only one was charged. (The officer had been stabbed after setting his dog on a young woman outside the Rainbow Room Club.) In Leeds, the bonfire-night confrontations in Chapeltown occurred annually from 1973 to 1975. The summer of 1976 saw well-documented conflict in Manchester, Birmingham and at least four different parts of London.[41]

The combined weight of these 'isolated incidents' is sufficient to transform the picture presented by Young and Lea, restoring in the process a determinancy to the dynamics of police–community conflict which is obscured by their idea of black 'counter-culture' or 'unintegrated ethnic culture'. The systematic application of militaristic and reactive policing to black areas the length and breadth of Britain undermines any view of consensual policing – black streets have never enjoyed the benefits of this police policy. Furthermore, the nature of these police operations is not adequately grasped by reference to 'discrimination' or the 'prejudice' of individual officers. They are systematic and, in police terms, rational, as a complex body of specialized policing theory informs them and legitimates the view of blacks as disproportionately prone to criminality.

Black political organization against police abuses has frequently exhibited a unity between people of Asian and Afro-Caribbean descent,[42] yet most left-wing writers on the subject seem curiously keen to introduce a pernicious contradiction between the interests of the two communities with regard to law and order. Several authors have identified an implicit Asian demand for more rather than less police activity,[43] albeit of a rather different type from that which they have come to expect from the British police. This suggestion, which derives its plausibility from the twin racist stereotypes of the quiescent Asian victim and the criminally inclined West Indian street youth, has been achieved at the expense of historical record. Young and Lea, Taylor and Frith all cite the rioting outside the Hamborough Tavern in Southall, 1981 as an example, and each views this incident as violence of a different order from that experienced elsewhere. Their suggestion that the militant Asian youth did not know what they were doing when they attacked police and skinheads alike is derisory. It is impossible to grasp the meaning of the 1981 riots in Southall without careful attention to previous confrontations there. In 1976, after the death of Gurdip Singh Chaggar, and again in 1979 during the police riot there, Asian youth acquired their own grievances against the local police whose abuse of the black community had been catalogued as early as 1973 by Dr Stanislaus Pullé. It is therefore more plausible to suggest that their assault on the police was not an inarticulate demand for more bobbies on the beat, but a sign of their deep anger, created by years of harassment, and a powerful statement to the effect that like their sisters and brothers in the Afro-Caribbean communities, militant Asians viewed community self-defence as the legitimate answer to racist violence. It is worth recalling that the initial response by officers at a police disco in Hammersmith to the news that rioting had started was to sing 'there ain't no black in the Union Jack'.[44] They were silenced by their senior officers.

The central argument here is that the question of black crime must be approached in a historical fashion, and in a context supplied by the overall pattern of police–community conflict in conditions of deepening crisis. In conclusion, there are several general points about the priorities and structure of police practice which need to be brought into the discussion. There is strong evidence to suggest that emphasis on particular crimes can engineer what appear to be crime waves of these offences, not only because of heightened police sensitivity to these crimes, but also as a result of changes in police practice.[45] It is certainly plausible that 'mugging' has constituted a self-fulfilling prophecy of this type. Blom-Cooper and Drabble[46] have recently shown that the Met's manipulation of the compound categories in which their statistics are recorded can be used to support this view. Young and Lea are not alone on the left in their tendency to take critical crime statistics at their face value.

E.P. Thompson[47] and Ian Taylor, among others, have also been disinclined to question these figures. It is important that the left clarify its views of officially recorded crime rates, particularly as a growing number of police thinkers and right-wing ideologists proceed unimpeded by the idea that they are an accurate reflection of crime actually experienced.

The Police Federation magazine, hardly noted for its radical politics, recently argued: 'no informal person regards the existing criminal statistics as the most reliable indicator of the state of crime'.[48] More significantly, inspector Peter Finnimore's essay 'How should police effectiveness be assessed', winner of the 1980 Queen's Police Gold Medal Essay Competition, attacked statistics not only as a guide to the level of crime, but also as a measure of police activity: 'It is difficult for experienced police officers to concede that skilful police work has relatively little effect on overall crime levels, but it must be realised that no criticism is implied by such a view.'[49]

In addition to this, the fact that official surveys of the victims of crime have consistently returned findings[50] which are completely at odds with the idea that crime itself rises when 'crime rates are soaring', should draw comment from the left. None of these authors appear to be aware of this. Finnimore is correct to insist that the issue of objective knowledge of crime leads directly to whether it is within the capacity of police to prevent or deter. Most recent left thinkers subscribe to what Home Office researchers have called the 'rational deterrent' model.[51] Young, Lea and Taylor, though they are correct to emphasize that the flow of information from communities is the main source of police knowledge, balance this by the idea that in exchange for the information the police will prevent crime. They are particularly concerned with the everyday forms in which it is experienced by working-class communities. This view of police capability is debatable to say the least, for two distinct, but related reasons. Scrutiny of the history of policing in Britain,[52] particularly its cities, suggests that everyday crimes in which the working class are the victims have never been of major concern to police; and secondly, the proliferation of private scrutiny firms described by Hilary Draper[53] suggests that the police may not even have been very successful in protecting the property of the bourgeoisie. Recognizing these limitations to their capacity, police chiefs and senior Home Office researchers have begun to raise the question of whether police are capable of deterring or preventing criminal activity. Assessing recent British research into the effectiveness of policing, R.V.G. Clarke and K.H. Heal from the Home Officer Research Unit conclude: 'The crime prevention value of a police force rests less on precisely what it does than on the symbolic effect of its presence and public belief in its effectiveness'.[54] Sir Robert Mark, who uses these arguments to justify a greater police concern with public order and anti-terrorist crime, puts the same point with characteristic bluntness: 'A great deal of crime is simply not preventable. Even the biggest police force that society could want or afford to pay would be unlikely to have any significant effect on the numbers of thefts, burglaries, or on crimes of violence between people who know each other.'[55]

This points to the need for more imaginative and bold initiatives from the left on the issue of law and order. Contemporary 'socialist' thinking on crime and police is dominated by pathological and environmentalist explanations wedded to a practice of progressively greater demands on a criminal justice system in which formal, legal equality sits uneasily on real inequality and relations of power and domination. In crisis conditions, police have increasingly separated the crime detection/prevention side to police activity from its political and ideological requirements.

Afterword

This essay was completed at the end of 1982. It could not be merely updated without wholesale revision and I believe that it has value in its original form which betrays the conflicts and anxieties of the period. Since its completion the danger to which it points in many respects has been realized. Left and right increasingly have come to share a common view not merely of the problem of inner-city crime, but more disturbingly of the issue of race itself in which crime plays a central role. Black law-breaking supplies the historic proof that blacks are incompatible with the standards of decency and civilization which the nation requires of its citizenry.

If the term 'new racism' retains any value as a shorthand it points to the intersection of left and right around common definitions of the meaning of 'race' in terms of culture and identity. This emphasis and the convergence it allows is significant for the degree to which it transcends the otherwise opposed positions of formal politics. Crime in which blacks are involved for left and right alike is intrinsically un-British and alien. More than this, certain categories of crime are now identified not merely as those which blacks are most likely to commit, but as crimes which are somehow expressive of the ethnicity of those who carry them out. For example, in their book *What is to Be Done about Law and Order?*, published under the imprint of the Socialist Society, Lea and Young, writers against whom the original polemic of this article was aimed, have referred to the origins of street crime in the 'residual ethnic factor' in black urban life.[56] Similarly, the riots of autumn 1985 were dismissed by the right as 'a cry for loot rather than a cry for help' and by the parliamentary left as 'barbarous acts of criminality' which betrayed, in Lea and Young's phrase, 'the absence of any *viable* tradition of ethnic politics' (my emphasis). It is not that blacks lack the means to organize themselves politically but that they do so in ways in which are so incongruent with Britishness that they are incapable of sustaining life! Their distance from the required standards of political viability is established by their criminal character. Thus black crime and politics are interlinked. They become aspects of the same fundamental problem – a dissident black population. Street robberies and street protests are elided into a single phenomenon: 'street crime'. This is defined both by its context and by the cultural ties which invest that context with meaning.

The riots of 1985 were 'race riots' not because they were carried out largely, though by no means exclusively, by blacks but because in the folk grammar of contemporary racism, the type of events they were told white Britain something about the nature of 'race' and its problematic relation to authentic substantive Britishness.

The left position on 'race' and crime criticized in the article is, far more than I realized at the time of writing, a symptom of a wider political crisis. These socialist academics think that they are writing the social policies of the next Labour government. The notion of class on which their Labourist dream depends is being experienced by the majority of the population as a contingent and meaningless fact. Class relations are changing profoundly and new antagonisms are being created in urban areas between a pauperized, permanently workless layer and the young urban cadres of the professional and managerial class who are colonizing the inner city as gentrifiers. The fear of crime speaks above all to the anxieties of this latter group. It offers a spurious means to connect their experience of vulnerability and victimage to the lifeworld of other-city residents with whom they have absolutely nothing in common.

The Labourist politics of law and order is defined by its populist character. The populist potential of the crime issue, as a cynical means to repair Labour's failing relationship with its traditional supporters in the urban areas, has grown and been made concrete in the work of local authorities who, like Roy Hattersley in the run up to the 1983 election, effectively accuse police chiefs like Kenneth Newman of having stolen Labour's policies on crime. Putting 'bobbies back on the beat' has become a shibboleth of this new Labourism. Only the right has had the intellectual honesty to query the facile equation of more police with less crime. Islington in north London has sought to rehabilitate its own image in the popular press as a bastion of the 'loony left' through carefully constructed interventions into law and order politics. These have included a joint drive by the borough and the police to increase black recruitment.

One last issue arises from the article which needs to be identified and dealt with. It concerns the mythical status of black criminality. By calling the article 'The Myth of Black Criminality' I did not intend to suggest that blacks did not or could not commit crimes or to invoke a pastoral definition of the black communities or the inner cities as places where crime did not occur. I sought instead to refer the reader to the images and representations of black criminality which seemed to me to have achieved a mythic status in the lexicon of contemporary race politics.

Asserting the disproportionate involvement of blacks in some categories of crime masks rather than disposes of significant problems in measuring their participation. The validity of official statistics and survey methods in the analysis are not the least of these difficulties. Britain's black population is a poor one and it would be remarkable if their law-breaking was not related in some way to their poverty. Banal formulae which emphasize an untheorized concept of 'marginality' in place of the more familiar notion of deviance simply deprive blacks of the opportunity to be seen as other than reactive monads incapable of considered behaviour in the active mode. Their reduction of politics to mere policy does nothing more than offer Labour's municipal bureaucracies the lazy comfort of simple solutions to their intractable problems. The possibility of a direct relationship between ethnicity, black culture and crime is an altogether different and more complex issue which requires detailed historical investigation and which is likely to end, as previous attempts to quantify crime itself, only in raising further yet more speculative questions.

Acknowledgement

This is an updated version of a paper which was published in *Socialist Register*, 1982.

Notes

1 S. Hall *et al. Policing the Crisis*, London, Macmillan, 1978.
2 Enoch Powell's speech Wolverhampton, April 1968, reprinted in, 'Freedom and reality', London, Paperfront, 1969.
3 *The Sun*, 13 September 1978, is typical of the imagery referred to, there are many other examples.
4 See *Crime and the Law. The Social History of Crime in Western Europe*, V.A.C. Gatrell, B. Lenman and G. Parker (eds.), Europa, 1980; especially chapters by Larner, Weisser and Davis.

5 P. Worthsthorne, *Sunday Telegraph*, 29 November 1981.
6 James Anderton, *Manchester Evening News*, 16 March 1982.
7 Alfred Sherman, 'Britain's urge to self-destruction', *Daily Telegraph*, 9 September 1976.
8 Martin Barker's excellent *The New Racism*, London, Junction Books, 1981, is an exception to the left's failures. See also Errol Lawrence, 'The roots of racism' in *The Empire Strikes Back*, London CCCS/Hutchinson, 1982.
9 Sir Kenneth Newman's views on the biological base of West Indian anti-authoritarianism can be found in the American *Police* magazine for January 1982 (Vol. 5, No. 1). See also speech by Basil Griffiths, vice-chairman of the Police Federation, reported in *Police Review*, 28 May 1982.
10 See A. Sivanandan *A Different Hunger*, London, Pluto, 1982 (especially his account of Asian and Afro-Caribbean struggles in the chapter *From Resistance to Rebellion*). Also see copies of *Race Today* for the period.
11 Paul Gilroy, 'Police and Thieves' in *The Empire Strikes Back, op. cit.*
12 Derek Humphry, *Police Power and Black People*, London, Pan, 1972; Gus John, *Race and the Inner City*, Runnymede Trust, 1972; Dr S. Pullé, *Police/Community Relations in Ealing*, Runnymede/Ealing CRC, 1973; Joseph Hunte, 'Nigger Hunting in England', West Indian Standing Conference, 1964; Institute of Race Relations, *Police against Black People*, 1978.
13 Paul Gordon, *Passport Raids and Checks*, Runnymcdc Trust, 1981.
14 Paddy Hillyard, 'From Belfast to Britain: Some critical comments on the Royal Commission on Criminal Procedure', *Politics and Power*, 4, 1981; K. Boyle *et al.*, *The Legal Control of Political Violence*, NCCL, 1980.
15 Gilroy, *op. cit.*
16 London, Faber, 1971.
17 C. Hurt, 1978.
18 Kitson, *op. cit.*
19 Kitson, *op. cit.*
20 *Time Out*, 5 September 1976, p. 3; *Searchlight*, November 1976.
21 *Police Review*, 19 March 1982.
22 Duncan Campbell, 'Society under surveillance', in P. Hain (ed.) *Policing the Police*, Vol. 2, London, John Calder, 1980.
23 The tendency referred to is exemplified by the recent works of Jock Young, John Lea and Ian Taylor. Taylor's *Law and Order Arguments for Socialism* is the fullest exposition of this position, Macmillan, 1981. His article in *New Socialist*, 2, November–December 1981 also merits attention. Young and Lea also published in *New Socialist* January–February 1982. See also *Critical Social Policy*, vol. 1, no. 3, and *Marxism Today*, August 1982.

24 R.V.G. Clarke and K.H. Heal, *Police Journal*, vol. LII, no. 1, January–March 1979.
25 John Alderson, Chief Constable's Report, 1980.
26 Sir David McNee, Commissioner's Report, 1981.
27 One instance of this is the way in which Alderson was interviewed in *Marxism Today*, April 1982; also M. Kettle, *Marxism Today*, October 1980.
28 The case of David Brooke is particularly interesting, see *The Guardian*, 12 May 1981.
29 See Alderson's evidence to the Scarman Inquiry, 'The case for community policing', p. xii.
30 Supt. David Webb, 'Policing a multi-racial community', unpublished paper, West Midlands Police, 1978.
31 Supt. A. Lievesley, *Police Review*, 7 March 1980.
32 Scarman Inquiry, Day 6, 22 May 1981.
33 'Guns for the Right', *World in Action*, Granada, July 1981; See also *Searchlight*, August 1981.
34 Scarman Report, para. 8.63.
35 See note 23.
36 Webb, *op. cit.*
37 Stephen Humphries, *Hooligans or Rebels, an Oral History of Working Class Childhood*, Oxford, Basil Blackwell, 1981.
38 Jerry White, 'Campbell Bunk, a lumpen community in London between the wars', *History Workshop*, 8, Autumn 1979.
39 Supt. L. Roach, *Police Studies*, vol. 1, no. 3, 1978.
40 John Brown, 'The function of communities in police strategy', *Police Studies*, Spring 1981 and *Police Review*, 31 July 1981.
41 *Race Today* is the best single source of information on these confrontations; for Southall see Campaign Against Racism and Fascism (CARF), *Southall the Birth of a Black Community*, IRR, 1981.
42 The examples of BASH (Blacks Against State Harassment) and Southall's People Unite are the most obvious; Sivanandan cites numerous others in his article '*Resistance to Rebellion*' in *A Different Hunger, op. cit.*
43 All those in note 23, plus Simon Frith in *Marxism Today*, November 1981.
44 *Searchlight*, October 1981.
45 E. Schaffer, *Community Policing*, London, Croom Helm, 1980, p. 17.
46 *British Journal of Criminology*, vol. 22, no. 2, April 1982.
47 'The state of the nation', reprinted in *Writing by Candlelight*, London, Merlin, 1979.
48 *Police*, February 1982.
49 *Police Journal*, January–March, 1982, vol. LV, no. 1, March 1982.
50 See Home Office Statistical Bulletin, 12 March 1982. R.E. Sparks, M.R. Glenn and D.J. Dodd, *Surveying Victims*, N.Y. Wiley, 1978.

51 Clarke and Heal (eds.), *The Effectiveness of Policing*, Aldershot, Hants, Gower, 1980.
52 For example, David Jones, *Crime, Protest, Community and Police in Nineteenth Century Britain*, London, Routledge & Kegan Paul, 1982.
53 *Private Police*, Brighton, Sussex, Harvester Press, 1978.
54 See note 24.
55 *Police Review*, 12 March 1982.
56 For a more detailed consideration of these issues see my '*There Ain't No Black in The Union Jack': The Cultural Politics of Race and Nation*, London, Hutchinson, 1987.

7

Tolerance, freedom, justice and peace? Britain, Australia and anti-Muslim racism since 11 September 2001

by Scott Poynting and Victoria Mason

Abstract

Since 1 September 2001, Muslim minorities have experienced intensive 'othering' in 'Western' countries, above all in those US-led anglophone nations which invaded Afghanistan and Iraq to prosecute their 'war on terror'. This chapter examines the cases of Britain and Australia, where whole communities of Muslims have been criminalised as 'evil' and a 'fifth column' enemy within by media, politicians, the security services and the criminal justice system. Although constituted by disparate ethnic groups, the targeted communities in each of these nations have experienced similar treatment in the state's anti-terrorist measures, as well as ideological responses and everyday racism, making comparable the two cases.

Introduction

Since 11 September 2001, ethnic minorities associated with Islam have experienced increased negative attention from the police and security forces in countries allied with the United States.[1] In the United Kingdom and Australia, this has been particularly so, and these are the two cases considered in this chapter. We argue that the ethnic targeting, and indeed racial profiling, involved in this process invokes an 'othering' of the communities concerned and a racialisation of security threats. This is akin to the previously existing racialising of crime and of asylum-seekers in both nation-states. Thus September 11 marks a drastic upsurge, but not the beginning, of this process. Certainly, the increased attention from police and security agencies to the

[1] The authors would like to thank Dr Mike Sutton and the Centre for Study and Reduction of Hate Crime at Nottingham Trent University for their hospitality to Scott Poynting there as a Visiting Scholar, February–June 2005, when this chapter was largely researched and written.

racially targeted groups since 9/11 has not, according to accounts from the ethnic and religious communities concerned, involved a positive increase of paying attention to their reports and experiences of racial hatred, abuse and victimisation, nor of acting on these in a non-discriminatory way. These processes have only intensified, moreover, following events which have occurred since 9/11: the October 2002 Bali bombings, the July 2005 London bombings and the October 2005 bombings in Bali.

In the case of both nation-states considered here, the minority 'other' underwent a transition in representation and also in identity over the foregoing decade or so before 9/11. Thus in the UK there was a shift from mainly 'Pakistani' or 'Asian' identification, to identification in terms of religion: from Asian Other to Muslim Other. This transformation took place both in racialising labels and in the construction of identity (Modood, 1997: 154–72; Modood, 2005: 4, 122, 155–61; Poynting, Noble, Tabar and Collins, 2004). In Australia, the transition was from 'Lebanese' or 'Arab Other' to Muslim Other. Thus the racialised minorities concerned were increasingly represented (and identified) in these terms, from the Salman Rushdie affair of 1989 and the Gulf War of 1991 against Iraq, to the communal disturbances in Bradford, Burnley and Oldham in northern England in early 2001, to the moral panics over supposed 'ethnic gang rape' in Sydney in 2001–2 (Anti-Discrimination Board of New South Wales, 2003; Poynting *et al.*, 2004; Gleeson, 2004; Warner, 2004) and over so-called 'boat people' seeking asylum in Australia, culminating in the Tampa Crisis in August 2001 (Poynting, 2002; Deen, 2003, Lygo, 2004; Poynting *et al.*, 2004; Poynting and Mason, 2005).

As Pnina Werbner (1997) points out, the conflicts inherent in racialised labelling lead, through ongoing moral panics, to shifts in, and limits to, identification and belonging: 'The pathological ambivalences of racism or xenophobia are the very motor that drives polarising processes forward through a series of agonistic moral panics, towards violent exclusions, assimilations and denials' (Werbner, 1997: 19). Part of this polarisation and moral panic has been the increasing currency of ideas of Arab and Muslim populations comprising a possible 'fifth column' threat within both the UK and Australia. The idea of the 'fifth column' – of the 'enemy within' who cast up new questions about citizenship, identity, and loyalty during times when their country of residence is seen to be in conflict with their country of origin – is not new: the term was first coined during the Spanish Civil War. Fears that clandestine groups would attempt to subvert the nation from within resulted in both Britain and Australia interning individuals of 'questionable loyalty' during World War I and World War II. The extension of the idea of the 'fifth column' specifically to Arab and Muslim populations in these countries started to gain momentum in the wake of the Salman Rushdie incident and the 1990–1991 Gulf War, where race and religious relations and issues of who constituted a 'loyal' citizen were brought to the surface and polarised (Abbas, 2005: 13–14; Kepel, 1997: 138–43).

As Ghassan Hage notes, questioning the loyalty of particular individuals within the nation demonstrates the 'incompatibility between the state's formal acceptance of new citizens and the dominant community's everyday acceptance of such people' (1998: 50). Zlatko Skrbis defines this as there being various 'gradations' of acceptance and belonging within the formal citizenship discourse, and the tension between what he calls the 'formal' and 'social' status of citizenship:

> Formal citizenship is static, whereas its social status is charged with normative and ever-changing notions of what constitutes the acceptable attributes of citizenship and belonging. It is in the domain of social citizenship where the notions of 'appropriate' and 'inappropriate', 'right' and 'wrong' . . . play a defining role.
>
> (Skrbis, 2006: 182)

Two caveats must be made before proceeding. Firstly, since this chapter is primarily about the empirical manifestations of the assembling of this 'Muslim Other' in Britain and Australia, there is not space here for a nuanced, concrete examination of the moral panics in which this folk-devil has been constructed. Such an examination can be found in Alexander (2000a; 2000b) in the case of the UK, in Poynting et al. (2004) which refers to the post 9/11 'Arab Other' in the case of Australia, and Collins et al. (2000) in the case of 'ethnic gangs' in Australia. Secondly, this is not the place for a theoretical study of how a religious 'other' can be racialised. Others have undertaken that task, including Miles (1993: 133, 138–9, 143–8); Miles and Brown (2003: 30–32), Kushner (2005), with the most obvious case being that of the racialisation of Jews. Brah (1996) has also addressed the question, and Hage (2005) has conducted an exemplary analysis of how Lebanese Maronites racialise Muslims as Arab and Other in racialising themselves as White and European.

Within this framework, the contemporary racialisation of Muslims, we contend, offers ideological justification – what Barbara Perry (2001: 179–223) calls 'permission to hate' – to both everyday and egregious acts of racial hatred against these ethnic and religious communities. This increases virulently in incidence after 9/11, and then the bombings in Bali in 2002 and 2005 (Poynting and Noble, 2004) and in London in 2005. Furthermore, we argue that the highly publicised and politically manipulated state raids on 'terror suspects' and crackdowns on communities linked with them, and their ensuing discriminatory treatment in the criminal justice system (and its 'anti-terror' analogues), from incarceration and interrogation without charge under anti-terror provisions and laws, to indefinite confinement, to condoning maltreatment of the detained at home and collaborating in their torture abroad, lends ideological and moral licence to racist anti-Muslim hate crime. Indeed, they can be seen as a form of state hate crime in themselves (Poynting, 2005).

In the post-9/11 climate, some would argue that increased measures to protect the nation are necessary. And indeed the police must police – and will do so in any functional state. Yet police and security forces should not abuse, harass, intimidate, bash, or falsely arrest or prosecute. Such unlawful actions by definition erode the rule of law, and in practice undermine people's confidence in the state and its criminal justice and enforcement systems. To the extent that the police, courts, military, security services and other repressive apparatuses of the state resort to such measures on a racially, ethnically or religiously discriminatory basis, the state itself – its functionaries, its institutions and above all its processes – are implicated in racialisation. This is of vital significance in understanding, in more radical analyses, how the state operates in the concrete conjunctures where such patterns are observable – we outline some in this chapter – but it also has important consequences for the perceived legitimacy of the state among the sectors of the population so targeted (Dreher, 2005). Of course the police must focus their attention on suspect individuals or cohorts, perhaps even justifiably using ideal-typical suspect 'profiles', but this is certainly not the same as deeming whole populations, whole communities, to be suspect by virtue of a racialised profile. Nor are victims less worthy of police assistance, protection, investigation and other duties, by virtue of being 'othered' into categories ideologically associated more with suspects than with victims.

The construction of the Muslim Other as the pre-eminent folk-devil in both the UK and Australia, took place against the backdrop of concerted and corrosive right-wing ideological attacks on multiculturalism over a decade or more since the 1990s, as the 'political correctness' of elites out of touch with the concerns of ordinary (read white, Anglo) people. Thus, it is useful to preface our account with a brief comparison of multiculturalism in the two countries.

Multiculturalisms

In Australia, multiculturalism had been more entrenched, since it had formed government policy with bipartisan support from the major parties since the early 1970s, when the policy was borrowed and adapted from Canada (Cope and Kalantzis, 2000: 326–7; Lopez, 2000: 164–5) to address the manifest failures and unsustainability of the earlier assimilation approach to ethnic affairs instituted after the abandonment of the White Australia policy in the 1960s. By 1981, as a result of the post-war labour immigration program, 20.7% of Australia's population was born overseas, and almost 20% who were born in Australia had at least one parent born overseas (Collins, 1991: 32). The immigrant population was very diverse, with around one hundred ethnic groups and 80 immigrant languages. In 1981, only 37% of the foreign-born population came from Britain and Ireland (Castles, Kalantzis, Cope and Morrissey, 1992: 25). Under these circumstances, Immigration Minister Snedden's vision in 1969 had been sheer fantasy:

> We have a single culture. If migration implies multicultural activities within Australian society, then it was not the type Australia wanted. I am quite determined we should have a monoculture with everyone living in the same way, understanding each other and sharing the same aspirations. We do not want pluralism (cited in Hartley and McDonald, 1994: 11).

By the 1970s, it was apparent that persistent social inequalities faced by immigrants of non-English-speaking background (such as in education, the labour market, and political and cultural representation) were continuing. People who had moved half a world away and made enormous sacrifices to make a better life for their children, found that this second generation also were being systematically disadvantaged. The larger and earlier (and therefore more settled) immigrant communities, notably Italians and Greeks, had begun to organise politically and culturally, and to exercise a 'migrant vote' as well as a political voice. Australian multiculturalism was not a mere well-meaning plan of social engineers, it was won by struggle and achieved in compromised settlement.

Australian multiculturalism always had two main thrusts. One was in the direction of equity and social justice, towards eradicating the existing inequalities which operated along ethnic lines (which also frequently were, or were complicated by, class lines). The second was the equal right to practise and maintain different cultures, with equal respect and value being accorded to these, as well as some state resourcing of their maintenance (such as of languages, for example). The 'carefully defined limits' which accompanied the right to 'cultural identity', however, always included a commitment to Australia's 'democratic institutions' and the 'rule of law'.

Conservative governments in Australia have tended towards the second element of multiculturalism, and eclipsed the first, such that the objective of 'social justice' had actually disappeared from the 1999 version of the National Agenda on Multiculturalism (produced by the National Multicultural Advisory Council, appointed in 1997 by the new Howard government). Under governments of both ilks there has been, in the name of multiculturalism, some trivialising of culture which reduced it to the superficial spectacle of celebrating exotic food and folkloric dance (cf. Werbner, 2005: 760): an approach which left multiculturalism prey to lambasting by cultural conservatives. There has also become instituted (through both main political parties) a multicultural politics of 'ethnic leader' patronage and the conditional delivery of sorely needed community resources in return for political quiescence or blocs of votes (Tabar, Noble and Poynting, 2003): again an easy target of right-wing anti-multiculturalist attacks.

In Britain, multiculturalism came later, was more contested (from both the right and the left), and appears to be 'colour coded' in a manner shared by the United States. Official statistics in Britain today categorise the population as White, Black, Asian and 'Other', in a way which 'whitens', say, Arabs, Afghans, Iranians and Turks. In Britain in the 1970s, as in Australia, 'Multiculturalism emerged as a result of the realization, originally in the USA, and then in Britain, that the melting pot doesn't melt, and that ethnic and racial divisions get reproduced from generation to generation' (Anthias and Yuval-Davis, 1992: 158). Multiculturalism has never been entrenched in government policy in Britain, however, to the extent in which it has in Australia. British multiculturalism has been a philosophy, a cultural politics, but not a defining set of national principles.

The demographics are different, and they are accounted for differently. In Britain, 'ethnic minorities' comprise 7.9% of the population, according to the National Statistics (2001): 4% Asian or Asian British, 2% Black or British (about half from the Caribbean and half from Africa), 0.4% Chinese, 0.4% 'Other ethnic groups' and 1.2% 'Mixed'. These are officially equated with 'Non-White'; if you are 'White' you are not counted as an 'ethnic minority'.

Nick Pearce (2005), Director of the Institute for Public Policy Research, sums up the principles of British multiculturalism as:

> a description of practices which are common to many progressive democracies: race equality strategies, public recognition of cultural diversity, and sensitivity, within the framework of public law, to religious beliefs.

This embraces the two elements we identified in Australian multiculturalism, but the first one, that of equality, has in Britain been couched largely in terms of racial equality and race relations. As Tariq Modood (e.g. 2005) has consistently pointed out, such parameters cannot adequately grasp inequalities that discriminate against, or systematically 'other', cultures or religions rather than 'race'. Anthias and Yuval-Davis (1992: 158) describe what we might call 'transatlantic multiculturalism' as follows:

> Multi-culturalism constructs society as composed of a hegemonic homogeneous majority, and small unmeltable minorities with their own essentially different communities and cultures which have to be understood, accepted and basically left alone . . . in order for the society to have harmonious relations.

They point to this form of multiculturalism being congenial to 'the first generation of "Race Relations Experts" ' (Anthias and Yuval-Davis, 1992: 158). Elements of this form of multiculturalism, which were to be found in Australia in the measures introduced after the Galbally Report in 1978, were strongly criticised as exacerbating and solidifying inequalities along ethnic lines (Jakubowicz, Morrissey and Palser, 1984). The second of the two elements, that of cultural sensitivity and belonging, is succinctly stated by Bhiku Parekh, one of the foremost proponents of British multiculturalism, and Chair of the Commission on the Future of Multi-Ethnic Britain, set up in 1998 by the Runnymede Trust:

> ... since citizens have differing needs, equal treatment requires full account to be taken of their differences. . . . Equality must be defined in a culturally sensitive way and applied in a discriminating but not discriminatory manner. . . . Every society needs to be cohesive as well as respectful of diversity, and must find ways of nurturing diversity while fostering a common sense of belonging and a shared identity among its constituent members.

Note that the mention of cohesiveness and shared identity is made in the context of multiculturalism being under attack for divisiveness and erosion of national identity – in Britain as in Australia. Note, also, that the principle of differential provision to meet differing needs equitably has always been under attack in Australia as well, and that the respect for cultural diversity there enshrined in policy has often featured more in rhetoric than in practice.

Demographic background

Australia's 2001 census recorded 281,578 Muslims: around 1.5% of the population. They live predominantly in capital cities, especially Australia's two largest and most ethnically diverse cities, Sydney and Melbourne, with 48% and 31% of Australian Muslims respectively. Of the 102,566 Australian-born Muslims, about 30% recorded Lebanese ancestry and about 18% Turkish ancestry (HREOC, 2004). Large-scale immigration from these backgrounds began in the 1970s, when Australia's post-war immigration programme needed sources beyond Europe. Some 36% of Australian Muslims were born in Australia; 28% in the Middle East or North Africa, 16% in Asia, 9% in Europe, 4% in Africa (excluding North Africa) and 3% in Oceania (excluding Australia). Their language backgrounds include, in addition to English: Arabic, Turkish, Persian (Farsi), Bosnian, Indonesian, Bengali, Malay, Dari, Albanian, Hindi, Kurdish, and Pashto (HREOC, 2004).

The 2001 census enumerated 1,558,890 Muslims living in Great Britain, or 2.8% of the population (bearing in mind that 7.8% of respondents did not state a religion or 'no religion'). Largely deriving from post-war labour immigration from former colonies, the vast majority of the Muslims within Britain are of South Asian, East African and Middle Eastern origin (Khan, 2000: 38; Lewis, 1994: 13–16). Some two-thirds originate from Pakistan, Bangladesh and India (Peach, 2005: 20). Approximately half of these

Muslims have been born in the United Kingdom (Smyth, 1996). Muslim communities have historically been located in the so-called 'urban heartland' of Britain in areas such as London and the cities and big towns of the Midlands and the north of England (Peach, 2005: 28; Khan, 2000: 38).

The British backlash after 9/11

With Osama bin Laden's *al Qaeda* network being rapidly blamed and then soon claiming responsibility for the airliner attacks in the USA on 11 September 2001, 'Islamophobia'[2] and racist violence against Muslims across Europe increased substantially. Britain was no exception. While continental Europe saw a marked and widespread resurgence of far-right and anti-immigrant political groups, Britain also experienced virulent campaigns and local election victories by the right-wing, racist British National Party (BNP) (Kundnani, 2003).

Of the European nations, the United Kingdom responded the most extremely to the events of 9/11 in terms of legislation – invoking a State of Emergency in order to pass the controversial Anti-Terrorism, Crime and Security Act two months after 9/11. When declaring the 'state of emergency', Home Secretary David Blunkett admitted that he invoked this measure as a technical means to derogate from the European Human Rights Convention (Young, 2001). This draconian response may in part have been a reaction to Britain being labelled as a so-called 'haven' for 'terrorists', as a result of media coverage given to radical Islamic leaders and organisations in Britain who publicly expressed sympathy for *al Qaeda* and who have been accused of recruiting for its network (Dhondy, 2001; Moussa, 1998; Burke, 2002a, 2002b; Wazir, 2002b). These figures included Omar Bakri Muhammad and Abu Hamza from London mosques, and the *Al-Muhajiroun* organisation (Wazir, 2002a, 2002b; Harris, Wazir and Burke, 2001; Burke, 2002a, 2002b).

The notion that a threat was posed to Britain by groups supporting *al Qaeda* stemmed from the belief that September 11 constituted an attack on the ideals of the 'West' as a whole, rather than a single attack on the US specifically. Prime Minister Tony Blair pronounced in a joint press conference with US president, George W. Bush:

> There may be some who think that Britain would gain from standing back from this struggle, even some who believe that we, and the United States, and our allies have somehow brought this upon ourselves. Let

---

[2] The term was '. . . coined in the late 1980s, its first known use in print being in February 1991, in a periodical in the United States. The word is not ideal, but is recognisably similar to "xenophobia" and "Europhobia", and is a useful shorthand way of referring to dread or hatred of Islam – and, therefore, to fear or dislike of all or most Muslims' (Runnymede Trust, 1997: 1).

us be very clear. America did not attack al-Qaida on September 11, al-Qaida attacked America, and in doing so attacked not just America, but the way of life of all people who believe in tolerance, and freedom, justice and peace.

(Blair, 2003)

Though recognising the enmities attracted by the alliance which saw Britain participate in the 1991 Gulf War and the blockade of Iraq, the popular ideology surrounding this notion also draws on the controversial 'clash of civilisations' paradigm from which Blair attempted to distance his government. Not all political leaders and public opinion-makers have been so careful. While maintaining that Islam was not the enemy, Opposition Leader Iain Duncan Smith told the Conservative Party conference in October 2001, 'When civilisation is attacked, civilised nations must spring to each other's defence' (Smith, 2001). He asserted:

The terrorists who attacked America also have us in their sights. Not because of what we in Britain have done but because of what we and America stand for. Britain and the United States have become the enemy because we are beacons of democracy and champions of freedom.

(Smith, 2001)

Even a cursory assessment of the Arab and Islamic populations within Britain shows that individuals such as radical cleric Abu Hamza represent a very small minority within the British Islamic communities. Indeed, the majority of Muslim spokespeople in Britain were very vocal in denouncing the 9/11 attacks, and made it clear that pro-*al Qaeda* views and actions were not representative of British Muslims. Yousef Bhailok, spokesperson for the Muslim Council of Britain, said: '[the people supporting 9/11] are not rational people . . . their extreme views are certainly not the views of the Muslim community or indeed any part of our civilised society' (cited in BBC News Online, 2001e).

Of the 17 people found guilty in the UK since 9/11 of terrorist acts (as at June 2005), however, only four of the twelve whose ethnic backgrounds are known are Muslim, according to Massoud Shadjareh, chair of the Islamic Human Rights Commission (Dodd and Travis, 2005). Shadjareh commented:

The war on terror has had a devastating effect [on British Muslims]. . . . We have become targets of the security apparatus and are seen as an enemy within unjustifiably. This has resulted in a backlash against the Muslim community. We have become the hidden victims. People are having to live, being terrorised, in the name of the war on terror.

(Campbell, Norton-Taylor and Dodd, 2005: 12)

The pre-existing notion of these communities as constituting a 'fifth column' prior to 9/11, coupled with media coverage of individuals such as Abu Hamza (Cook, 2003), resulted in an amplification in Britain demonising Muslims as the dangerous Other. The immediate consequence of this was a range of attacks against Arab and Islamic people and communities within Britain (Jones, 2001; BBC News Online 2001a, 2001b, 2001c, 2001d; Hill, 2001; Ferguson, 2001). In the two years to July 2003, there were 674 reported incidents of anti-Muslim attacks, with many more (and probably most) going unreported. Some 51% of reported cases were serious and violent crimes, and 28% were verbal and written abuse, according to the Islamist *Khilafah Magazine* (2003).

In the immediate aftermath of 9/11, for example, graffiti scrawled on a mosque in north-east England read 'Avenge USA – Kill a Muslim now'. Mosques received threats, vandalism, desecration with pigs' heads and actual bomb attacks; many more mosques did not report attacks, fearing retribution. Schools and pre-schools were attacked, including an arson attempt in Surrey while children and teachers were inside. Businesses and private homes of Muslims were subjected to vandalism; Muslim graves were desecrated. A large number of beatings of Muslims occurred. Many Muslim women wearing the *hijab* were vilified and physically harassed. Representing just a few examples, a teenage girl of South-Asian descent was attacked with a baseball bat by two youths and a young Muslim woman was bashed with a hammer on the head and body by a white man on a crowded tram in Manchester. In one particularly vicious attack, an Afghani taxi driver was attacked by three passengers in West London, leaving him a quadriplegic (Jones, 2001; Human Rights Watch, 2002).

While Kenan Malik (2005) argues that the evidence from such statistics and accounts 'does not amount to a climate of Islamophobia', Hage (2003: 247) points out, 'Violent racists are always a tiny minority. However, their breathing space is determined by the degree of ordinary "non-violent" racism a government and culture will allow'. Despite official British government rhetoric condemning such attacks, the actions undertaken by the British government served to reinforce the idea of Muslims as a 'fifth column' to be feared.

Since 9/11, Muslims in Britain face disproportionate police 'stop-and-search' measures and targeting. From 2002 to 2003, the stop and search of Asian people (a category which also includes Hindus and Sikhs and other non-Muslims, who together comprise 45.3% of the Asian or British Asian population who stated a religion) in the UK increased by 285% (calculated from Peach, 2005: 22; Hayes, 2004). From 2002–3 to 2003–4, counter-terrorism stop and searches increased by about 40%, to almost 30,000.

Other steps taken by the government included the blanket banning of 16 Islamic organisations and the rushing through parliament in December 2001 of the controversial 'Anti-Terrorism' legislation. Over 500 Muslims have been arrested in the UK under the prior Terrorism Act 2000, yet only two of these were convicted by January 2004 (Islamic Human Rights Commission, 2004). The Anti-Terrorism Crime and Security Act 2001 (ATCSA) contained sweeping measures that were criticised by civil libertarians as being draconian and as undermining basic democratic rights[3] (Horsley, 2001; Hyland, 2001; Young, 2001; Human Rights Watch, 2001a, 2001b, 2001c; Sampson, 2001; Dyer, 2001; Morris, 2001; Bright, 2001; McDonald, 2002; Ahmed, Barnett and Bright, 2001; Ahmed, Barnett and Bright, 2001).

Under the 2001 Anti-Terrorism law, which has been called Britain's 'Guantanamo Bay law' (*Guardian*, 2004) 16 men, all Muslims, were arrested and imprisoned without charge or trial in Belmarsh high security prison. Upon detention, they were denied access to lawyers or family. Amnesty International reported that the detainees were locked in for 23 hours a day and were not allowed daylight. They were denied prayer facilities, and subjected to humiliating body searches by women (Islamic Human Rights Commission, 2004). Detainees spent over three years in Belmarsh, until the government was obliged to release them into home imprisonment in early 2005. This was as a result of a decision by the Special Immigration and Appeals Commission (SIAC), later upheld by the full bench of the nine law lords, that the detention of the men was unlawful and breached the European Human Rights Convention. Under pressure of a March 2005 deadline imposed by the law lords' decision, the Government proposed new legislation involving confinement and deprivation of liberties which stopped short of incarceration. With the opposition under pressure of the forthcoming election and unwilling to be cast as soft on terrorism, the Prevention of Terrorism Act 2005 was passed.[4]

Islamophobia increased following the 7 July 2005 terror attacks on the London underground which killed 52 people and injured approximately 700. The discovery that the perpetrators of the attacks were all British-born and raised began a spate of worrying about 'home-grown' terrorists and

[3] The central measures of the Act include: the power to intern indefinitely any non-citizen suspected of involvement in terrorist activities (and deny those interned the right of appeal to a normal court of law); restricting the right to seek asylum; granting police enormous powers to access people's personal information (including tax returns) and broadening the ability of government agencies to exchange information about individuals, greatly curtailing internet privacy, for example. The original passing of the Act itself was conducted in a manner that allowed it to be renewed without the full assessment of the British Parliament (Young, 2001; Hyland, 2001).

[4] The Act provides for home detention with curbs on visits and meeting people, electronic tagging, curfews, regular reports to police stations, and police or security searches at any time, as well as enabling the Home Secretary to restrict individuals' movement and communications (no mobile phones or internet), on suspicion of their involvement in terrorism-related activities, with little (and no independent) judicial review and minimal parliamentary review of the legislation. This can be without sufficient evidence to charge the suspected individuals with any breach of the law, and without their knowing what information is being acted upon.

the propensity for second-generation (mainly young and male) people of Muslim background to be radicalised and recruited by terror networks.

According to the UK Monitoring Group (which publishes accounts of racist incidents), attacks on Muslims in Britain started immediately after the terrorist attacks. Within the first day of the bombings, a schoolboy in Devon was assaulted and told it was retribution for the bombings; there were attempted arson attacks on houses of families of South-Asian descent in Middlesex and West London; racist graffiti defaced a mosque and Pakistan community centre in Edinburgh and even a Sikh temple in Kent was – presumably mistakenly – attacked (monitoring Group, 2005).

Within three weeks of the bombings, hate crimes, particularly against Muslims, had increased six-fold (BBC, 2005). In their report on the impact of the terrorist attacks, the European Monitoring Centre on Racism and Xenophobia (EMCRX) noted that rates of 'hate crime' in London had increased by 5% and over 200 calls had been made to the Merseyside Racial Monitoring Unit helpline in the first six weeks after the London attacks. Days after the attacks the British National Party started a leaflet campaign that showed a photograph of the bombed bus with the slogan 'maybe it's time to start listening to the BNP' (EMCRX 2005: 15–19).

While EMCRX praised efforts by the government and police to prevent reprisals against the general Muslim community, in early August 2005 the government decided that further anti-terrorism measures were needed. The Terrorism Bill of October 2005 was described by Amnesty International (2005) as containing 'further sweeping and vague provisions that undermine the rights to freedom of expression and association, the right to liberty, the prohibition of arbitrary detention, the rights to the presumption of inno-cence and fair trial'. One proposal was to introduce as a crime the vague notion of 'glorification of terrorism'. This lack of legal clarity, remarked Amnesty (2005), could arbitrarily restrict human rights such as freedom of expression.

Reservations about the new security measures were underlined by the execution-style killing, shortly after the bombings, of Jean Charles de Men-ezes, an innocent 27-year-old Brazilian electrician on his way to work on a London Tube train. He was mistaken for a terrorist by special police, and, under 'shoot to kill' orders, shot dead with seven bullets to the head. Tariq Ali (2005: 64) surmises that 'a premeditated execution was ordered'. He asks rhetorically whether such 'taking out' is employed '[a]s a deterrent in a coun-try where capital punishment is forbidden'. He reasons that such 'public execution' cannot possibly deter suicide bombers, it can only put off dark-skinned people from taking the Tube. The Brazilian, it had been reported, had South-Asian appearance.

British involvement in torture and killing of Muslims abroad

There is also now mounting evidence that the British military in Iraq has been involved in widespread abuse of civilians, apparently (at best tacitly) sanctioned by the chain of command, and in several cases causing death (Carrell, 2005a). An Iraqi hotel attendant, Baha Moussa, died on 14 September 2003 after allegedly being badly beaten in British military cells. While four soldiers faced charges over this, none faced charges over the torture and assault of the eight civilians arrested along with Mr Moussa (Carrell, 2005a; Shiner, 2005). Four other soldiers were charged with having abused and handcuffed a 17-year-old Iraqi youth, and thrown him into a river, where he drowned (Dodd, 2004; Carrell, 2005a; Shiner, 2005). A 53-year-old Iraqi schoolteacher also died after a vicious beating, allegedly at the hand of British troops. Some ten cases of torture are pending hearing (Shiner, 2005). British soldiers court-martialled for binding, beating and tormenting civilian captives at 'Camp Breadbasket' in Iraq claimed that they were acting under orders.

Britain acted somewhat more expeditiously and effectively than Australia, however, to secure the release of its nationals from Guantanamo Bay, where US military torture is now well documented (Carrell, 2005b: 1, 4; Shiner, 2005). Nevertheless, three British citizens who were interned there have claimed that 'they were repeatedly punched, kicked, slapped, forcibly injected with drugs, deprived of sleep, hooded, photographed naked and subjected to body cavity searches and religious humiliations'. They report that 'there was never any suggestion on the part of British interrogators that this treatment was wrong' (BBC News online, 2005). Australian Guantanamo detainee, David Hicks, who has made corroborated claims to have been 'rendered' and tortured under US military custody (*Four Corners*, 2005), was also interrogated at Guantanamo by MI5, according to documents the British intelligence agency themselves produced in the British High Court (Crabb, 2006).

The anti-Muslim reaction in Australia

As in Britain and as also had occurred during the 1991 Gulf War, Australia also experienced an upsurge of racially based attacks on Muslims and those of 'Middle Eastern appearance' after 9/11. Numerous Muslim women wearing their *hijab*, or traditional headscarf, in public places were assaulted, abused and had strangers of both genders trying to rip their veil away. There was an outbreak of incidents of people in Muslim dress or of 'Middle Eastern appearance' being spat upon or more violently assaulted in streets, shops and on public transport, of incidents of arson, vandalism, threats, harassment and other racist attacks directed by 'white-thinking' people against these newly discovered enemies within. It was as if, as Ghassan Hage (2002b) has put it, there were now manifold 'borders' internal to the nation rather than around its edges to be patrolled against the non-Christian, non-Western, 'third-world looking' (Hage, 1998) outsiders who might endanger the Australian good life from within the nation.[5]

By the end of September 2001, a bilingual (English and Arabic) Anti-Racism Hotline in New South Wales had logged well over 300 calls (Brown, 2001: 2); by the time it finished operating on 9 November, there were about 400 responses recorded. It needs to be recognised that the number of incidents actually tallied in this way is a measure only of the 'tip of the iceberg': that is, those with knowledge of the hotline and with the most motivation and means to complain. This is borne out by a survey of 186 Arab and Muslim Australians in Sydney and Melbourne conducted in 2003 for the Human Rights and Equal Opportunities Commission (Poynting and Noble, 2004), in which 87% of the Muslim respondents said they had experienced racism, abuse or racist violence since 9/11, with three-quarters saying they had experienced more such racism since that date: 39% saying 'a bit more' since September 11 and 37% saying 'a lot more'. Yet of those surveyed, only 6.5% had reported incidents of racism, abuse or violence to the police, and even fewer to other instrumentalities or community organisations. The most common reason offered (by 33% of respondents) was that they did not think anything useful would come of it. They had good reason to think so: of those who did complain, 70% were dissatisfied or very dissatisfied with the outcome. The state thus not only arguably induces hate crime by modelling it, as we argue below, but also generally neglects or declines to bring the perpetrators to justice when hate crime is committed by individuals.

Other official bodies, such as (federally) the Human Rights and Equal Opportunities Commission (HREOC) and (statewide) the New South Wales Anti-Discrimination Board (ADB), and the Victorian Multicultural Commission (VMC), as well as religious and ethnic community organisations, also received and recorded a plethora of such complaints. The evidence points to a pre-existing base level of incidence of such attacks and an underlying tendency just waiting for an immediate cause to provoke them. The range of types of racist attack, moreover, remains continuous: only the intensity surges. This upsurge was widely reported in the media (Jopson, 2001; Brown, 2001; PM, 2001; Burke and AAP, 2001). There was an intensification of existing, ongoing and everyday forms and patterns of racism (Poynting and Noble, 2004).

In one instance, a middle-aged housewife and her daughter were attacked by 'a group of Australians' in a Sydney supermarket. Their veils were snatched from their heads and they were beaten, with the daughter

---

[5] In the hierarchy of otherness set up in compounding these categories, we might compare the exclusion of Hage's 'third-world looking' other with what Sivanandan (2001) has identified as 'xeno-racism'.

suffering a broken arm (AAC Racism Register, 2001). A 17-year-old school student of second-generation Lebanese background was verbally abused and her veil was ripped off on a tram in Melbourne; she was later cut with a knife at a tram stop, threatened by a group with baseball bats, had a brick through her window and a fire set in her front yard (Poynting and Noble, 2004). Places of worship, schools, workplaces, shops and streets were all sites of racist attack (HREOC, 2004). There was vilification and menace by internet, radio, telephone and mail. A busload of Muslim schoolchildren was set upon with stones and bottles in Brisbane.

The spate of anti-Muslim racist attacks continued long after September 2001, and resurged following the October 2002 Bali bombings in which 88 Australians were killed and many more seriously injured. With these bombings, carried out by the Indonesian Islamic militant group *Jemaah Islamiyah*, Australia found itself directly touched by Islamist terrorism for the first time. This precipitated another cycle of anti-Arab and Muslim violence including the firebombing in Melbourne of the Umma Islamic Centre, and the vandalising in Sydney of the Rooty Hill Mosque, an Islamic school, and the home of a Muslim cleric (*The Age*, 2002; Fickling, 2002b).

As recently as May 2005, a school bus belonging to an Islamic College in Perth was completely destroyed in an arson attack (AAP, 2005a; *ABC News Online*, 2005). It bears repeating that such outbreaks of racial hatred and vilification have been an upsurge, albeit a dramatic one, against a background of anti-Arab and anti-Muslim racist attacks that existed in Australia well before 11 September. As Ghassan Hage (2001: 241–2) puts it, with the recent racism directed at Middle Eastern 'boat people' and so-called 'Lebanese rapist gangs', '"September 11" happened right after "June, July and August 11, 12 and 13"'.

Security raids

In late September 2001, the Australian Security Intelligence Organisation (ASIO), accompanied by the Australian Federal Police (AFP) and New South Wales police with 'intimate local knowledge', raided approximately 30 suburban households and workplaces in Sydney. They brought the media with them and publicised the raids (Trad, 2001; Kidman, 2001: 4–5). All those raided were Muslims, and the Australian tabloid media provided justification, as well as publicity:

> The perpetrators of the September 11 attacks were young Middle-Eastern Muslim men. Bin Laden's followers are young Middle-Eastern Muslim men. So it is young men of Middle-Eastern Muslim background who will be targeted in Sydney, many of them Australian citizens, who were born here.
>
> (Devine, 2001: 28)

Whatever other purposes were intended, the raids were clearly meant to be a public gesture. They were also plainly designed to intimidate. In one case, a mother of two young children, complained (as did others raided) that a gun was put to her head and she was made to lie on the floor. She said 'police turned the residence "upside down" and interrogated her in front of her family'. The raids were 'backed by armed teams of the State Protection Group' and there were dozens such raids around the country (Watson, 2001: p.15).

After the Bali bombings in October 2002, ASIO and AFP operatives again mounted raids on suburban homes of Muslim citizens – this time mainly Australians of Indonesian origin in Sydney, Perth and Melbourne (Poynting *et al.*, 2004). *AM* (2002a) reported that 'a key to the raids' was that men in the targeted families had attended lectures of visiting religious leader Abu Bakar Bashir, who was suspected of being the spiritual leader of *Jemaah Islamiah*. As with the 2001 raids, there have been (at June 2005) no charges laid and no arrests made on terrorism-related matters – though there was an arrest over a visa infringement.

Once more, the ethnic profiling brought terror to the communities being targeted. Muslim leaders said the raids had 'caused hysteria and fear that anyone in the community could be targeted'. Sheik Fehmi Naji, Imam of the Preston mosque in Melbourne, said that many Muslims were upset about the blaming of their community for the Bali bombing (*Age*, 2002).

Such swoops serve an important function in the maintenance of the prevailing hegemony: the coercion behind the consent, in Gramsci's (1971) famous formulation. The effect goes well beyond those raided. The raids were clearly intended to send an intimidatory message to whole communities to which those raided belong. For that very reason, the media were taken in tow in both the 2001 and 2002 raids. On several occasions the media identified the families concerned, and they were consequently subjected to vigilante-style harassment. As the raids were inefficient and probably counter-productive for intelligence-gathering purposes, and no-one raided was charged for terrorist offences; this can hardly have been their underlying purpose unless they were extremely bungled. They did function to reassure the white, Christian 'mainstream' that something was being done about these terrorists or terrorist sympathisers in our midst, and to frighten the targeted communities into keeping a low profile. The mainstream media literally went along with this. This, too, is a form of terror, as is the gentler form of persuasion in the shape of fear of the ubiquitous enemy.

One everyday effect of what could be seen as hate crime at the level of the state (Poynting, 2005) is that it seems to license the more recognisable forms of hate crime perpetrated by individuals and groups of individuals. If the state is assaulting, harassing and vilifying Muslims as the enemy in the war on terror, and thus terrorising whole communities, then perhaps white-thinking citizens feel justified in personally attacking this enemy wherever they might encounter them. One victim of a veil-tearing assault and verbal abuse, an Australian-born, Lebanese-background medical professional in her mid-20s, told researchers for HREOC of her attackers: 'They obviously felt powerful or something, 'cause they felt that they could speak like that to us, and do all that, and no one would do anything to them' (Poynting and Noble, 2004). From the reports of approximately 200 other respondents, they would probably have been right that no-one would do anything to the perpetrators. That is to say, in the rare cases where victims report racist hate crimes to state authorities, their perception is that no action was taken. The state thus not only arguably induces hate crime by modelling it, but also generally neglects or declines to bring the perpetrators to justice when hate crime is committed by individuals.

Anti-terror laws

Though the raids detailed above were plausibly claimed by Minister Downer to be within existing law, federal and state governments saw the need for further legislation effecting anti-terrorist measures. The Australian Security Intelligence Organisation Legislation Amendment (Terrorism) Bill 2002 provided for the capacity hitherto unknown under Australian Commonwealth law to arrest a person on suspicion, merely for interrogation. According to Justice John Dowd, a judge in the Supreme Court of NSW, people could be held for up to seven days under the proposed legislation, and when released, 'can be detained on a new warrant . . . in the lobby of the building as they leave' (*Lateline*, 2002a). The whole family of a 'person who may have information that may assist in preventing terrorist attacks or in prosecuting those who have committed a terrorist offence' could be detained in this manner (*Sydney Morning Herald*, 2002: 12; *Lateline*, 2002a). 'People of interest' may be so held for a week under the legislation, without charge, without legal representation, without appearing in court, and without the right of silence (Morris, 2002: 9; *Lateline*, 2002b). The 'safeguards' regarding the issue of warrants were virtually valueless, in Dowd's experience, since warrants are almost always issued when security or police services make a case for them. Justice Dowd argued that in 'an atmosphere of hysteria', 'Muslims stood to become the first victims of the new laws' (Morris, 2002: 9).

The Islamic Human Rights Commission (2002) saw this law as modelled on the UK anti-terror laws. As in the British case, there were some very token concessions made to civil liberties objections, but with the opposition cowed, the ASIO Legislation Amendment (Terrorism) Act was passed in 2003. Certainly, in addition to the above provisions, the new raft of legislation proscribed membership of 17 'terrorist organisations'. As in the British case, every one was a Muslim organisation. Draconian though these laws were, they were further strengthened and supplemented by new laws after the July 2005 London bombings, including reintroduction of laws against sedition, a crime which had not been prosecuted in Australia since the Cold War and the Vietnam War.

Australian complicity in torture

Australian citizen, Mamdouh Habib, who was finally released from Guantanamo Bay without charge at the end of January 2005 after more than three years in detention, was kidnapped unlawfully in Pakistan and handed over to US forces. They 'rendered' him to Egypt to be interrogated under torture (Wilkinson, 2005a: 9) and from there he was taken to the US base in Guantanamo, where he was subjected to further torture (McLean, 2005). Pakistani president Pervez Musharraf has said that the Australian government must have known of his country's handing Habib over to US forces, since this notification was always Pakistan's practice in such cases (AAP, 2005b). The Australian government denied any knowledge about Habib's transfer to Egypt, but has conceded that ASIO and AFP officers were in Pakistan to see Habib. The commissioner of the AFP told an Australian Senate hearing that US officials advised the AFP in Islamabad that Habib was detained in Pakistan. Habib claims (with a witness) to have been interrogated by US officials in Pakistan in the presence of an Australian official; the Government does not deny this. Habib says the Australian officer was also at the airport when he was bound and gagged and taken by plane to Egypt. A former CIA lawyer believes it likely that the agency would have informed Australia of this transfer (*Dateline*, 2005). Habib also claims that information from materials taken from his home by ASIO was passed on to those who interrogated him under torture of 'unspeakable brutality' in Egypt (Wilkinson, 2005a, 2005b).

Habib claimed to have been in Pakistan looking for a suitable Muslim school for his several children. He was there legally. As someone who had called attention to himself in the Sydney Muslim community, for example by wearing t-shirts showing support for Osama bin Laden, and was wont to public arguments and known to be a disturbed personality, he is an unlikely operative of an organised terror machine. When public knowledge emerged of his detainment in Guantanamo (along with that of fellow Australian David Hicks, alleged to have been captured fighting in Afghanistan alongside the Taliban), the Australian government claimed that they could not ask for their repatriation to Australia, since there was no evidence of their having broken any laws, and they would have to be released. Habib indeed eventually was released after his return to Australia in 2005, though under heavy security surveillance and subjected to mysterious house break-ins and an unsolved stabbing under the noses of ASIO (Nicholson, 2005; AAP, 2005c). For several years the Australian government merely accepted the assurances of American officials that Habib and Hicks were in good health and being treated well in Guantanamo, despite the obviousness of what was happening there. Visiting Australian officials turned a blind eye to their condition and treatment.

David Hicks is a working-class white Anglo Australian who converted to Islam. He was certainly maltreated in Afghanistan and Guantanamo, and claims to have been tortured (*Four Corners*, 2005). He is, however, still imprisoned at Guantanamo, awaiting trial by a military tribunal subject to a series of legal appeals, so as yet we have not heard much of his own account of his treatment. The Australian government still appears to be doing little to seek his repatriation, despite the illegality of his detention. Habib himself was only returned to Australia when the US found inconvenient the emergence in court documents, and thus in the media, of horrifying details of his torture in both Egypt and Guantanamo.

Beyond complicity with Guantanamo abuse, Australian military and security services personnel were (at best) complicit with the keeping of 'ghost detainees' at Abu Ghraib and with interrogations at Camp Cropper, near Baghdad airport, where torture and killings are also known to have occurred (Wilkinson, 2005c; Fisk, 2003). Major George O'Kane brushed aside the Red Cross report about torture at Abu Ghraib (Wilkinson, 2005c). Another Australian military officer seconded to the US military became aware of 'ghost detainees' at the prison, in contravention of international law, and allegedly only reported the matter after the Abu Ghraib outrage became public knowledge (Wilkinson, 2005c). One Australian intelligence officer, Rod Barton, interrogated Iraqi scientists at Camp Cropper, where he witnessed facial bruising of two prisoners and became aware of the mysterious death of another (Wilkinson, 2005c). The Australian government attempted to cover up both O'Kane's and Barton's involvement, and then prevaricated, saying, for instance, that the 'interviews' were not 'interrogation' (Manne, 2005).

Dissent

The anti-Muslim racism demonstrated in the wake of 9/11 in both the UK and Australia did not go entirely unchallenged. In the UK hundreds of thousands of people took to the streets to demonstrate against the planned military action against Iraq, and opposition to jingoistic Islamophobia in the 'war on terror' was part of their protest. Conservative police estimates placed the numbers marching on one day alone in London – 16 February 2003 – at 750,000 people (BBC, 2003). As discussed earlier, dissent also came from unlikely sources such as the House of Lords, with the Law Lords forcing the hand of the government in regards to unlawful detention under the 2001 anti-terrorism legislation.

In Australia, small opposition parties such as the Greens and the Democrats (these now being practically defunct following the 2004 federal elections) were very vocal in condemning the government's unlawful and inhumane treatment of refugees and opposing Australia's involvement in the wars in Afghanistan and Iraq. Public opposition to government policies, particularly in relation to refugees, was reflected in the 'protest' votes received by the Greens during the 2001 election, where their vote doubled to nearly 5% (Dellit, 2001). Whilst such dissenting voters were still in the minority, this was a significant indicator of opposition to the stance of the government.

Strong opposition to government policies in relation to refugees, the 'war on terror' and human rights in Australia were also expressed by human rights and refugee advocate groups such as 'A Just Australia' and the 'Justice Project' with members of the latter including former Prime Minister Malcolm Fraser. Many in the legal profession in Australia also spoke up against the injustices they saw, such as high-profile QC Julian Burnside.

Public protest in response to Australia's participation in the 'war on terror' matched levels not seen since the nuclear disarmament marches of the 1980s, or the protests against the Vietnam War of the 1960s and 1970s. Hundreds of thousands of Australians marched against Australia's involvement in the US-led military incursions into Afghanistan and Iraq (*BBC Online*, 2003). There was also questioning of, and opposition to, the dominant discourse following 9/11 and great division over how to view and react to the Bali bombings (Fickling, 2002a; Mason 2004). This was demonstrated particularly when members of the government insinuated a linkage between the Bali bombings and Australia's involvement in the then-proposed war against Iraq (Fickling, 2002a).

Andrew MacIntyre notes that many Australians refused to support a war in Iraq as a knee-jerk reaction to the Bali bombings and protested what they saw as the political exploitation of the tragedy:

> My guess would have been that the dominant effect [of the Bali bombings] would have been, if not a rallying around the flag, then at least a coming together, but I'm not sure that's what we're seeing . . . People understand that Saddam Hussein is a bad guy who could do some terrible things, but they are wary of going into a discretionary war (cited in Fickling, 2002a).

How these dissenters were encoded by their respective governments, however, speaks volumes. In Australia, those who marched and protested against the war in Iraq were accused by Prime Minister Howard of giving 'encouragement to the leadership in Iraq' (Jones, 2003). This questioning of the 'loyalty' of such Australians was firmly framed within George Bush's paradigm of being either 'with us' or 'against us' in the war between 'good and evil.' Similarly, in a speech at the United Nations' 60th-anniversary summit in New York, Tony Blair expressed unity with President Bush, saying, 'Terrorism won't be defeated until our determination is as complete as theirs, our defence of freedom as absolute as their fanaticism, our passion for democracy as great as their passion for tyranny' (Gawenda, 2005).

Conclusion

We have seen how, both in Britain and Australia, the Muslim immigrants and their families who had been subjected to racism over several generations, experienced an exacerbation of such othering, and indeed, criminalisation after 11 September 2001. They had experienced a similar heightening of racism a decade earlier during the Gulf War against Iraq: the racism, be it individual, institutional, or indeed state racism, was not new (nor, of course, unique to these groups), but underwent a marked upswing with these critical events of 11 September and the Bali and London bombings. Nevertheless, the form of racism in these (and many other 'Western') countries had been undergoing a transition, since about the time of the Iranian revolution in 1979, but certainly since the *Satanic Verses* controversy. Contemporaneously, with the rise of the 'New Racism' (Barker, 1981), we have seen a transform-ation of such a demonised 'other' in Britain from being othered as 'coloured' (phenotype) or Asian (a continent of origin, mainly imagined as the Indian subcontinent, involving orientalised others) to their othering as Muslims (Peach, 2005: 18). At about this time, the term Islamophobia was coined in the US, and was imported to Britain in the early 1990s. Similarly and contemporaneously in Australia, where the majority of Muslims are of Arab – and most of these of Lebanese – background, there has been an analogous shift from racial to cultural othering, and a move from Arab or Lebanese, or more generally 'Middle Eastern', as racialised other, to 'Muslim' as the diabolised figure of danger and threat.

In response to 9/11 and the bombings in Bali and London, both Britain and Australia passed draconian new legislation designated as 'anti-terrorism' measures, which was condemned by civil libertarians and senior members of the judiciary as a dangerous erosion of legal rights. The Australian laws were said to be modelled on the British ones, and both sets bore a more than passing resemblance to the US 'PATRIOT' Act. The new laws explicitly targeted membership or aid to (respectively 16 and 17) specific organisa-tions labelled as 'terrorist': all were Muslim. Both countries participated in the US-led coalitions which attacked, occupied, and ultimately set up puppet governments in Afghanistan and then in Iraq, arguably making real the threat of terrorist attack, particularly given that the London bombers appar-ently committed the atrocious acts in response to UK involvement in Iraq (Sivanandan, 2006: 4–5).

Both countries have conducted, since 9/11, high-profile security and police raids on mosques and private homes of Muslims, which have func-tioned to construct a manifest and imminent dangerousness among the communities concerned. In both Britain and Australia, Muslim communities have subsequently, with the aid of the media, been diabolised in cycles of moral panic. These cycles have corresponded with spates of vilification and violent racist attacks on members of the communities concerned, who understandably believe that their labelling and targeting by the media and politicians is a cause of the attacks. In neither nation has such crime been adequately monitored or dealt with by the criminal justice system, in the experience of the communities victimised. Finally, both states have been involved or complicit in what could arguably be characterised as Islamophobic hate crime abroad, such as unlawful deprivation of liberty, mistreatment, and even torture and killing. The state terror of the raids on Muslim others at home, and the latter hate crimes abroad, arguably lend a sort of moral licence and impetus to Islamophobic hate crime attacks within each nation.

References

AAC (2001) *Increase in Racial Vilification in Light of Terror Attacks: Sep 2001*. Melbourne: Australian Arabic Council [unpublished xerox].

AAP (2005a) 'Perth Islamic school bus set ablaze', *Sydney Morning Herald Online*. http://www.smh.com.au/news/National/Perth-Islamic-school-bus-set-ablaze/ 2005/05 [sic].

AAP (2005b) 'Govt knew Habib to be handed over: claim', *Sydney Morning Herald Online*, 8 June. http://www.smh.com.au/news/National/Govt-knew-Habib-to-be-handed-over-claim/2.

AAP (2005c) 'Habib stabbed near his home', *Sydney Morning Herald Online*, 23 August. http://www.smh.com.au/news/national/habib-stabbed-near-his-home/ 2005/08/23/1124562857727.html.

Abbas, T. (2005) British South Asian Muslims: before and after September 11. In T. Abbas (ed.) *Muslim Britain: Communities under Pressure*. London: Zed Books, pp. 3–17.

ABC News Online (2001) 'Australian Muslims urge racial tolerance as children attacked', 12 September. http://abc.net.au/.

ABC News Online (2005) 'School bus gutted by fire', 17 May. http://www.abc.net.au/ news/items/200505/1369884.htm?wa.

Adams, G. (2005) 'I have been in torture photos, too'. Appendix Two in T. Ali *Rough Music: Blair/Bombs/Baghdad/London/Terror*. London: Verso, pp. 95–98.

Age (2002) 'Muslims Condemn "Heavy-Handed" Tactics', *Age* (1/11/02). http:// www.theage.com.au/articles/2002/10/31/1036026979308.html.

Ahmed, K., Barnett, A. and Bright, M. (2001) 'Britain placed under state of emergency', *Observer*, November. http://www.observer.co.uk/Print/0,3858, 4296620,00.html.

Ahmet, P. (2005) 'Turkish-speaking communities in Britain: a rude awakening', *IRR News*, 8 March. http://www.irr.org.uk/2005/march/ak000010.html.

Alexander, C. (2000a) *The Asian Gang: Ethnicity, Identity, Masculinity*. Oxford: Berg Publishers.

Alexander, C. (2000b) '(Dis)Entangling the "Asian Gang": Ethnicity, Identity, Masculinity'. In B. Hesse (ed.), *Un/settled Multiculturalisms: Diasporas, Entanglements, Transruptions*. London: Zed Books, pp. 123–147.

Ali, T. (2005) *Rough Music: Blair/Bombs/Baghdad/London/Terror*. London: Verso.
AM (2002a) 'More ASIO raids expected', *AM*, ABC Radio, 31 October.
AM (2002b) 'Downer unapologetic over ASIO/AFP raids', 1 November.
Amnesty International (2005) 'UK: Human rights under sustained attack in the "war on terror" '. http://news.amnesty.org/index/ENGEUR450502005.
Anthias, Floya and Nira Yuval-Davis (1992) Racialized Boundaries: Race, Nation, Gender, Colour and Class and the Anti-Racist Struggle. London: Routledge.
Anti-Discrimination Board of New South Wales (2003) *Race for the Headlines: Racism and media discourse.* Sydney: Anti-Discrimination Board of NSW. http://www.lawlink.nsw.gov.au/adb.nsf/pages/raceheadlines.
Barker, M. (1981) *The new racism: conservatives and the ideology of the tribe.* London: Junction Books.
BBC News Online (2001a) 'Scottish Muslims describe fears', 19 September. http://news6.thdo.bbc.co.uk/low/english/uk/scotland/newsid_1553000/1553409.stm.
BBC News Online (2001b) 'Muslim community targets racial tension', 19 September. http://news6.thdo.bbc.co.uk/low/english/uk/scotland/newsid_1553000/1553409.stm.
BBC News Online (2001c) 'Extra police to protect Muslims', 21 September. http://news6.thdo.bbc.co.uk/low/english/uk/newsid_1555000/1555162.stm.
BBC News Online (2001d) 'Muslim leaders debate race hate', 19 September. http://news.bbc.co.uk/hi/english/uk/newsid_1552000/1552001.stm.
BBC News Online (2001e) 'UK to monitor Islamic group', *BBC News*, 19 September. http://news.bbc.co.uk/hi/english/uk/newsid_1552000/1552682.stm.
BBC News Online (2003) ' "Million" march against Iraq war', *BBC News*, 16 February. http://news.bbc.co.uk/2/hi/uk_news/2765041.stm.
BBC News Online (2004) 'Britons allege Guantanamo abuse', *BBC News*. http://news.bbc.co.uk/go/pr/fr/-/1/hi/world/americas/3533804.stm.
BBC News Online (2005) 'Hate crimes soar after bombings', *BBC News*, 4 August. http://news.bbc.co.uk/2/hi/uk_news/england/london/4740015.stm.
Bhailok, Y. (2001) cited in *BBC News Online*, 'UK to monitor Islamic group', 19 September. http://news.bbc.co.uk/hi/english/uk/newsid_1552000/1552682.stm.
Blair, T. (2003) Downing Street transcript of joint press conference with US president, George Bush, 20 November, *Guardian Unlimited*. http://politics.guardian.co.uk/iraq/story/0,12956,1089630,00.html.
Brah, A. (1996) *Cartographies of Diaspora: Contesting Identities*. London: Routledge.
Bright, M. (2001) 'Liberty Watch: Introduction', *Observer*, 30 September. http://www.observer.co.uk/Print/0,3858,4267256,00.html.
Brown (2001) 'Arabic festival cancelled for fear of attack by bigots', *The Australian*, 10 October: 2.
Burke, J. (2002a) 'Terror video used to lure UK Muslims', *Observer*, 27 January. http://observer.guardian.co.uk/print/0,3858,4343906–108997,00.html.
Burke, J. (2002b) 'AK-47 training held at London mosque', *Observer*, 17 February. http://observer.guardian.co.uk/print/0,3858,4357814–108997,00.html.
Burke, K. and AAP (2001) 'Muslim women, children targeted', *Sydney Morning Herald*, 14 September, p. 8.
Calvert, J. (2002) 'Knife torment charge', *Melbourne Herald*, 9 March.
Campbell, D. (2005) 'The ricin ring that never was', *Guardian*, 14 April, p. 25.

Campbell, D. and Norton-Taylor, R. (2005a) 'Cleared ricin suspects face deportation', *Guardian*, 14 May. http://www.guardian.co.uk/print/0,3858,5193695–111274,00.html.

Campbell, D. and Norton-Taylor, R. (2005b) 'Jury anger over threat of torture', *Guardian*, 21 May, p. 1.

Campbell, D., Norton-Taylor, R. and Dodd, V. (2005) 'Words of warning backed by little clear evidence', *Guardian*, 23 April, p. 12.

Carrell, S. (2005a) 'Four soldiers face charges over death of Iraqi in British custody', *Independent on Sunday*, 6 March, p. 2.

Carrell, S. (2005b) 'US guards at Guantanamo tortured me, says UK man', *Independent on Sunday*, 24 April, pp. 1, 4.

Carrell, S. and Whitaker, R. (2005) 'Ricin: The plot that never was', *Independent on Sunday*, 17 April, pp. 6–7.

Castles, S., Kalantzis, M., Cope, B. and Morrissey, M. (1992) *Mistaken Identity: Multiculturalism and the Demise of Nationalism in Australia*, third edition. Sydney: Pluto Press Australia.

Collins, J. (1991) *Migrant Hands in a Distant land: Australia's post-war immigration*, second edition. Sydney: Pluto Press Australia.

Collins, J., Noble, G., Poynting, S. and Tabar, P. (2000) *Kebabs, Kids, Cops and Crime: Youth, Ethnicity and Crime*. Sydney: Pluto Press Australia.

Cook, I. (2003) 'Behind the News. Abu Hamza: Hooked by the press', *Ouch!* http://www.bbc.co.uk/ouch/news/btn/hamza.shtml.

Cope, B. and Kalantzis, M. (2000) *A Place in the Sun: Re-creating the Australian way of life*. Sydney: HarperCollins.

Cowan, R. and Campbell, D. (2005) 'Detective murdered by an obsessive loner', *Guardian*, 14 April, p. 9.

Crabb, A. (2006) 'Hicks trained with shoe bomber, MI5 says', *Sun-Herald*, 19 March, p. 5.

Daily Telegraph (2001a) 'Carr warns against ethnic hate attacks', *Daily Telegraph*, 14 September, p. 8.

Daily Telegraph (2001b) 'Act of War: Islam backlash continues', *Daily Telegraph*, 15 September, p. 10.

Daily Telegraph (2002) 'Like scenes from a movie', *Daily Telegraph*, 31 October, p. 7.

Dateline (2005) 'The Extraordinary Rendition of Mamdouh Habib', SBS Television, 9 March. http://news.sbs.com.au/dateline/index.php?page=transcript&dte=2005–03–09&headin.

Deen, H. (2003) *Caravanserai: Journey Among Australian Muslims*, second edition. Fremantle: Fremantle Arts Centre Press.

Dellit, A. (2001) 'Greens Capture Humanitarian Vote', *Green Left Weekly*, 21 November. http://www.greenleft.org.au/back/2001/472/472p3.htm.

Devine, M. (2001) 'Where security counts, tolerance goes two ways', *Sun Herald*, 11 November, p. 27.

Dhondy, F. (2001) 'Our Islamic Fifth Column', *City Journal*, Autumn 2001, *11*, 4. http://www.city-journal.org/html/11_4_our_islamic.html.

Dodd, V. (2004) 'Soldiers arrested after Iraqi beaten and drowned', *Guardian*, 26 August.

Dodd, V. (2005) 'Doubts grow over al-Qaida link to ricin plot', *Guardian*, 16 April.

Dodd, V. and Travis, A. (2005) 'Muslims face increased stop and search', *Guardian*. http://www.guardian.co.uk/print/0,3858,5138540–111274,00.html.

Dreher, T. (2005) *Targeted: Experiences of Racism in NSW after September 11, 2001.* UTS Shopfront Monograph Series, No. 2. http://www.shopfront.uts.edu.au/news/targeted.pdf.

Dyer, C. (2001) 'Top judge's human rights warning', *The Guardian*, 28 September. http://www.guardian.co.uk/Print/0,3858,4266113,00.html.

Dyer, C. (2005) 'UK treatment of terror suspects "inhuman" ', *Guardian*, 10 June, p. 5.

European Committee for the Prevention of Torture and Inhuman or Degrading Treatment or Punishment (2005) *Report to the Government of the United Kingdom on the visit to UK carried out by the CPT form 14 to 19 March 2004.* Strasbourg, 9 June 2005. http://www.cpt.coe.int/documents/gbr/2005–10-inf-eng.htm#_Toc105559309.

European Monitoring Centre on Racism and Xenophobia (2005) *The Impact of 7 July 2005 London Bomb Attacks on Muslim Communities in the EU*, November. http://eumc.eu.int/eumc/material/pub/London/London-Bomb-attacks.pdf.

Ferguson, E. (2001) 'Britain's defiant minority: British Muslims are refusing to be scapegoats for the September 11th attacks', *The Observer*, 7 October. http://www.observer.co.uk/Print/0,3858,4272058,00.html.

Fickling, D. (2002a) 'Australians fear Bush link backlash: Public failure to rally round flag foxes experts', *The Guardian*, 16 October.

Fickling, D. (2002b), 'Mosque attacks leave Muslims fearing backlash', *The Guardian*, 18 October.

Fisk, R. (2003) 'The ugly truth of Camp Cropper: A torture story to shame us all', *Counterpunch*, 24 July. http://www.counterpunch.org/fisk07242003.html.

Four Corners (2005) 'The Case of David Hicks', ABC Television, 31 October. Reporter: D.   Whitmont.   http://www.abc.net.au/4corners/content/2005/1494795.htm.

Gawenda, M. (2005) 'Blair and Bush call for unity against terrorism', *Sydney Morning Herald*, 16 September. http://www.smh.com.au/news/world/blair-and-bush-call-for-unity-against-terrorism /2005/09/15/1126750077150.html.

Gillan, A. (2005a) 'Five soldiers took 22 pictures', *Guardian*, 19 January. http://www.guardian.co.uk/print/0,3858,5106635–103550,00.html.

Gillan, A. (2005b) 'Iraq abuse soldiers have sentences cut', *Guardian*, 2 June, p. 4.

Gleeson, K. (2004) 'From Centenary to the Olympics, Gang Rape in Sydney', *Current Issues in Criminal Justice 16*, 2, November.

Gramsci, A. (1971) *Selections from the Prison Notebooks of Antonio Gramsci.* New York: International Publishers.

Guardian (2004) 'Ancient Liberties', editorial, 17 December.

Hage, G. (1998) *White Nation: Fantasies of white supremacy in a multicultural society.* Sydney: Pluto Press.

Hage, G. (2001) 'Postscript: Arab-Australian belonging after "September 11" '. In *Arab-Australians Today: Citizenship and Belonging.* Melbourne: Melbourne University Press, pp. 241–248.

Hage, G. (2002a) *Against Paranoid Nationalism: Searching For Hope in a Shrinking Society.* Sydney: Pluto Press.

Hage, G. (2002b) Anthrax-politics, *Canberra Times*, 31 January.

Hage, G. (2003) *Against Paranoid Nationalism: Searching for Hope in a Shrinking Society.* Sydney: Pluto Australia.

Hage, G. (2005) 'White Self-Racialization as Identity Fetishism: Capitalism and the Experience of Colonial Whiteness'. In K. Murji and J. Solomos (eds) *Racialization: Studies in Theory and Practice*. Oxford: Oxford University Press, pp. 185–205.

Harris, P., Wazir, B. and Burke, J. (2001) 'We will replace the bible with the Koran in Britain', *Observer*, 4 November. http://observer.guardian.co.uk/islam/story/0,1442,587375,00.html.

Hartley, R. and McDonald, P. (1994) 'The Many Faces of Families: Diversity among Australian Families and its Implications', *Family Matters* 37, April, pp. 6–12.

Hayes, B. (2004) 'The "War on Terror" as a "war on freedom and democracy" '. http://www.statewatch.org/news/2004/dec/hayes-terrorism.htm.

Head, M. (2002) 'Violent police raids', *Guardian* (Sydney) 6 November. http://www.cpa.org.au/garchve5/1116asio.html.

Hill, A. (2001) 'Muslims refuse to be victims of racism', *The Observer*, September 30. http://www.observer.co.uk?Print/0,3858,4267201,00.html.

Hillyard, P. (2002) 'In Defence of Civil Liberties'. In P. Scraton (ed.) *Beyond September 11: An Anthology of Dissent*. London: Pluto Press, pp. 107–113.

Horsley, W. (2001) 'Analysis: Muslims in Europe', *BBC News Online*, 11 October. http://news.bbc.co.uk/hi/english/world/europe/newsid_1594000/1594066.stm.

HREOC (2004) *Isma – Listen: National consultations on eliminating prejudice against Arab and Muslim Australians*, Human Rights and Equal Opportunity Commission. http://www.hreoc.gov.au/racial_discrimination/isma/report/index.html.

Human Rights Watch (2001a) 'Commentary on the Anti-Terrorism, Crime and Security Bill 2001', 16 November. http://www.hrw.org/backgrounder/eca/UKleg1106.htm.

Human Rights Watch (2001b) 'UK Anti-Terrorism Bill Undermines Fundamental Human Rights Protections', 16 November. http://www.hrw.org/press/2001/11/UKBill1116.htm.

Human Rights Watch (2001c) 'UK: New Anti-Terror Law Rolls Back Rights', 14 December. http://www.hrw.org/press/2001/12/UKBill1214.htm.

Human Rights Watch (2002) 'United Kingdom: Human Rights Developments'. http://www.hrw.org/wr2k2/europe21.html.

Hutton, W. (2004) 'Why the West is wary of Muslims', *Observer*, 11 January. http://observer.guardian.co.uk/comment/story/0,693,1120615.html.

Hyland, J. (2001) 'Britain: Parliament passes draconian anti-terror legislation', *World Socialist Web Site*, 20 December. http://www.wsws.org/articles/2001/dec2001/lord-d20_prn.shtml.

Ingram, A. (2005) House of Commons Hansard for 9 February 2005: column 1512W.

Islamic Human Rights Commission (2002) 'Urgent Alert: Australia to Pass Draconian Anti-Terrorism Laws based on UK models', 26 February. http://www.ihrc.org.uk/show.php?id=244.

Islamic Human Rights Commission (2004) 'Briefing: Anti-Terrorism, Crime and Security Act 2001'. http://www.ihrc.org.uk/show.php?id=938.

Jakubowicz, A., Morrissey, M. and Palser, J. (1984) *Ethnicity, Class and Social Policy in Australia*. Sydney: Social Welfare Research Centre, University of New South Wales.

Jones, G. (2001) 'Muslims targets in terror backlash,' *CNN News*, 19 September. http://www.cnn.com/2001/WORLD/europe/09/19/gen.muslim.attacks/.

Jones, T. (2003) 'PM accuses anti-war protesters of siding with Saddam', *Lateline*, 20 February.

Jopson, D. (2001) 'Muslims harassed, and it is women who bear the brunt', *Sydney Morning Herald*, 20–21 October, p.18.

Kepel, G. (1997) *Allah in the West: Islamic Movements in America and Europe*. Stanford: Stanford University Press.

Khan, Z. (2000) 'Muslim presence in Europe: The British Dimension – Identity, Integration and Community Activism', *Current Sociology*, 48 (4), October: 29–43.

Khilafah Magazine (2003) 'Islamophobia – The product of a Clash of Civilisations'. http://www.khilafa.com/home/category.php?DocumentID=7941&TagID=24.

Kidman, J. (2001) 'ASIO swoop in hunt for BinLaden link: Muslim woman claims gunpoint interrogation', *Sun-Herald*, 30 September, pp. 4–5.

Kundnani, A. (2003) 'The BNP in the local elections', *IRR News*, http://www.irr.org.uk/2003/may/ak000004.html.

Kushner, T. (2005) 'Racialization and "White European" Immigration to Britain'. In K. Murji and J. Solomos (eds) *Racialization: Studies in Theory and Practice*. Oxford: Oxford University Press, pp. 207–225.

Lateline (2002a) 'Dowd and Brandis on anti-terror legislation', 26 November. Transcript accessed at: http://www.abc.net.au/lateline/s735539.htm.

Lateline (2002b) 'Proposal to boost ASIO powers has judges worried', 26 November. Transcript accessed at: http://www.abc.net.au/lateline/s735537.htm.

Lewis, P. (1994) *Islamic Britain: Religion, Politics and identity among British Muslims*. London: I.B. Tauris.

Lopez, M. (2000) *The Origins of Multiculturalism in Australian Politics 1945–1975*. Melbourne: Melbourne University Press.

Lygo, I. (2004) *News Overboard: The tabloid media, race politics and Islam*. Adelaide: Southerly Change Media.

Malik, K. (2005) 'Islamophobia Myth', *Prospect Magazine*, 10 February. http://frontpagemag.com/Articles/Printable.asp?ID=16735.

Manne, R. (2005) 'An evasion of the truth', *Age*, 2 February. http://www.theage.com.au/news/Robert-Manne/An-evasion-of-the-truth/ 2005/02/21/ 1108834727646.html#.

Mason, V. (2004) 'Strangers within the lucky country: Arab-Australians post September 11' in 'September 11: Global Impacts', *Journal of Comparative Studies of Africa, Asia and the Middle East*, Vol 24, No 1.

McDonald, H. (2002) 'Bin Laden's victory: we are bowing to terrorism if we jeopardise our civil liberties', *Observer*, 6 January. http://www.observer.co.uk/Print/0,3858,4329997,00.html.

McLean, T. (2005) 'Prostitute used in Habib torture: lawyer', *Sydney Morning Herald*, 27 January.

Miles, R. (1993) *Racism after 'Race Relations'*. London: Routledge.

Miles, R. and Brown, M. (2003) *Racism*, second edition. London: Routledge.

Modood, T. (1997) ' "Difference", Cultural Racism and Anti-Racism'. In T. Modood and P. Werbner (eds) *Debating Cultural Hybridity: Multicultural Identities and the Politics of Anti-Racism*. London: Zed Books, pp. 154–172.

Modood, T. (2005) *Multicultural Politics: Racism, Ethnicity and Muslims in Britain*. Edinburgh: Edinburgh University Press.

Monitoring Group (2005) 'The Monitoring Group examines racist attacks and events since the London bombings on the 7th July 2005'. http://www.monitoring-group.co.uk/this%20week/after_7_7/after_the_london_bombing.htm.

Morris, B. (2001) 'Are civil liberties at risk? – yes, says Bill Morris: Tighter Security Measures will make life even more difficult for refugees', *The Observer*, 30 September. http://www.observer.co.uk/Print/0,3858,4267174,00.html.

Morris, L. (2002) 'Backlash building over security laws', *Sydney Morning Herald*, 27 November, p. 9.

Morris, L., Cameron, D. and Cornford, P. (2002) 'Police told man: you are one of J', *Sydney Morning Herald*, 1 November, p. 7.

Morris, R. and Rowlands, L. (2002) 'Father denies link to feared group', *Daily Telegraph*, 31 October, p. 7.

Moussa, A. 'Who are the UK based militants?', *Al-Ahram*, 3–9 September 1998, n393.

MPAC (2005) 'Hazel Blears: Muslims will have to face reality!'. http://www.mpacuk.org/content/view/397/103/.

Muir, H. (2005) 'Report reveals hierarchy of hate', *Guardian*, 7 March. http://www.guardian.co.uk/print/0,3858,5141905–110414,00.html.

Nagel, C. (2002) 'Constructing difference and sameness', *Ethnic and Racial Studies*, 25 (2): 258–287.

National Statistics (2001) 'Religious Populations'. http://www.statistics.gov.uk/cci/nugget.asp?id=954.

Nicholson, B. (2005) 'Habib burgled as PM says he may yet be charged', *Age*, 8 February, p. 3.

Peach, C. (2005) 'Britain's Muslim Population: An Overview'. In T. Abbas (ed.) *Muslims in Britain: Communities under Pressure*. London and New York: Zed Books, pp. 18–30.

Pearce, N. (2005) 'Goodbye to Multiculturalism, but welcome to what?' Parliamentary Brief, 1 December. http://www.ippr.org.uk/articles/archive.asp?id=1835&fID=55.

Perry, B. (2001) *In the Name of Hate: Understanding Hate Crimes*. New York: Routledge.

Phillips, R. (2001) 'Escalating attacks on Muslims and Arabs in Australia', World Socialist Website, 20 September. http://www.wsws.org.

PM (2001) 'Australia's Islamic Community Victims of Racial Tension', *PM* programme, Australian Broadcasting Corporation radio, 14 September (reporter Lachlan Parker).

Poynting, S. (2002) ' "Bin Laden in the Suburbs": Attacks on Arab and Muslim Australians before and after 11 September'. *Current Issues in Criminal Justice, 14*, 1, July, pp. 43–64.

Poynting, S. (2005) 'Hate Crimes of the State?: Some Anti-Muslim instances since 2001'. In R. Julian, R. Rottier and R. White (eds) *TASA 2005 Conference Proceedings*. Hobart: The Australian Sociological Association.

Poynting, S. and Mason, V. (2005) 'The Resistible rise of Islamophobia: Anti-Muslim Racism in the UK and Australia before 11 September 2001'. Unpublished paper.

Poynting, S. and Noble, G. (2004) *Living with Racism: The experience and reporting by Arab and Muslim Australians of discrimination, abuse and violence since 11 September 2001*. Report to the Human Rights and Equal Opportunity Commission, April. http://www.humanrights.gov.au/racial_discrimination/isma/research/index.html.

Poynting, S., Noble, G., Tabar, P. and Collins, J. (2004) *Bin Laden in the Suburbs: Criminalising the Arab Other*. Sydney: Institute of Criminology.

Rath, T. (2001) 'Arabs around world face backlash: Racial attacks spread across the globe', *The Daily Star*, Beirut, 15 September.

Risen, J. and Van Natta, D. (2003) 'Bases the target in ricin plot theory', *Sydney Morning Herald*, 25 January.

Roberts, B. and Smith, J. (2004) 'Imgram wriggles out of torture apology', *Mirror. co.uk*, 14 May. http://www.mirror.co.uk/news/allnews/tm_objectid=14239084&method=full&siteid=50143&headline=ingram-wriggles-out-of-torture-apology-name_page.html.

Rolston, B. (2002) 'Resistance and Terror: Lessons from Ireland'. In P. Scraton (ed.) *Beyond September 11: An Anthology of Dissent*. London: Pluto Press, pp. 59–66.

Runnymede Trust (1997) *Islamophobia: A challenge for us all*. London: Runnymede Trust.

Sampson, A. (2001) 'Terror must not lead to torture: Human rights are the foundation on which civilisation still rests', *Guardian*, 9 November. http://www.guardian.co.uk/Print/0,3858,4295354,00.html.

Shiner, P. (2005) 'Our military won't find itself guilty', *Guardian*, 6 May.

Sivanandan, A. (2001) 'Poverty is the new Black', *Race and Class 43*, 2, pp. 1–5.

Sivanandan, A. (2006) 'Race, terror and civil society', *Race and Class 47*, 3, pp. 1–8.

Skrbis, Z. (2006) 'Australians in Guantanamo Bay: Gradations of Citizenship and the Politics of Belonging', in N. Yuval-Davis, K. Kannabiran and U. Vieten (eds) *The Situated Politics of Belonging*. London: Sage.

Smith, I.D. (2001) Speech to Conservative Party Conference, Blackpool, 10 October. http://www.conservatives.com/tile.do?def=news.story.page&obj_id=18115&speeches=1.

Smyth, G. (1996) 'On Mohammad's side: radical young British Muslims have lost faith in Westminster and are following a route of their own', *New Statesman*, June 21, v125, n4289.

Sydney Morning Herald (2002) 'Other threats to freedom', *Sydney Morning Herald*, 28 November, p. 12 [editorial].

Sydney Morning Herald (2003) 'CIA looks into possible al Qaeda link to ricin plot', *Sydney Morning Herald* 29 January. http://www.smh.com.au/articles/2003/01/12/104.

Tabar, P., Noble, G. and Poynting, S. (2003) 'The rise and falter of the field of ethnic politics in Australia: The case of Lebanese community leadership', *Journal of Intercultural Studies 24*, 3, pp. 267–287.

The Age (2002) 'Firebugs threaten mosque attacks' 17 October. http://www.theage.com.au/articles/2002/10/17/1034561262558.html?from=storyrhs.

Trad, K. (2001) 'The ASIO raids on Muslims: Statements on behalf of victims' (unpublished). Sydney. Lebanese Muslim Association.

Warner, K. (2004) 'Gang rape in Sydney: crime, the media, politics, race and sentencing', *Australian and New Zealand Journal of Criminology*, vol. 37, no. 3, pp. 344–361.

Watson, R. (2001) 'ASIO raids home', *Sunday Telegraph*, 30 September, p. 15.

Wazir, B. (2002a) 'The Talibanising of Britain proceeds', *New Statesman*, 11 February, p. 32.

Wazir, B. (2002b) 'Essex boys sign up for "holy war" ', *Observer*, 22 February. http://observer.guardian.co.uk/waronterrorism/story/0,1373,656223,00.html.

Werbner, P. (1997) 'Introduction: The Dialectics of Cultural Hybridity'. In T. Modood and P. Werbner (eds) *Debating Cultural Hybridity: Multicultural Identities and the Politics of Anti-Racism*. London: Zed Books, pp. 1–26.

Werbner, P. (2005) 'The translocation of culture: "community cohesion" and the force of multiculturalism in history', *Sociological Review*, pp. 745–768.

Wilkinson, M. (2005a) 'Australian official saw torture, Habib alleges', *Sydney Morning Herald*, 7 January, p. 9.

Wilkinson, M. (2005b) 'ASIO fed information to my torturers, says Habib', *Sydney Morning Herald*, 9 March.

Wilkinson, M. (2005c) 'Military Lawyers a law unto themselves', *Sydney Morning Herald*, 30 April. http://www.smh.com.au/news/World/Military-lawyers-a-war-unto-themselves/ 2005/04/29/1114635747833.html.

Young, H. (2001) 'David Blunkett holds liberty and the judges in contempt', *Guardian*, November 15.

8

Introduction to *The Asian Gang*
by C. Alexander

Details have emerged this week about a recent flare up between black and Asian youths at the Thomas More School . . .

Police had to call on support from the Territorial Support Group to deal with the tension that erupted last month.

Superintendent Daniel Hirons told the Police and Community Consultative Group that a fight broke out between black and Asian pupils in the school canteen.

Police returned to the school later that day, but the pupils went home without any incident. The following day, a black youth was attacked by fourteen Asian youngsters and sustained a fractured elbow and a bump on his head.

Police patrols were stepped up and were called to deal with several stand offs between youths on the nearby Stoneleigh Estate.

Things came to a head when officers patrolling Abbey Street came across youths making petrol bombs – with six already prepared.

Police called in the TSG to ensure a large presence to deter any more trouble, particularly when large groups of youths were seen roaming the estate.

Superintendent Hirons told the SPCCG: 'We must get the message across to young people that they should not be taking the law in to their own hands.

They risk damaging the quality of life for everyone where they live if they continue to behave in this way.' (Local Press Report, Summer 1996)

At 7.30 p.m., Friday 25 October 1996, the lights went up on the stage at the Clifton Community Centre, South London. To the sound of Josh Winks' techno-track, *A Higher State of Consciousness*, ten young men walked into the spotlight and introduced themselves. They were Stoneleigh Asian Youth Organization[1]; this was *Style and Culture '96*.

Taking place as part of a wider series of events to celebrate Black History Month, *Style and Culture '96* was a fashion show and cultural display by a group of predominantly Bangladeshi young men. The models were all aged 14–15 years old, members of a project for Asian young men based in a South London borough. With the support of three semi-professional Asian models, their full-time youth worker, Yasmin Ullah and her staff team (including myself), these young men took control of the lighting, music and stage management, helped choreograph the walks, modelled and compered the show. The clothes were a combination of the group's own designer labels, and traditional and designer Asian wear donated by stores in Brick Lane and Green Street. The result of over six months of research and preparation, and two months of practice, nervousness and foot-faltering, confusion and increasing self-confidence, the fashion show lasted an hour and a half, enacting a dramatic mixture of routines to an audience of jubilant and noisy, if slightly astonished, brothers and sisters, youth and community workers, friends and neighbours. *Style and Culture '96* was, in every sense, a 'community' event. And it was a triumph.

A week or so later, I found myself on a housing estate in East London, at 7.30 in the morning, in the cold and rain, dressed for summer, on the set of a new British film. I was there with Yasmin, who had been contacted at the youth club by a casting agency in desperate search of Asian extras, particularly women, for an unspecified project. The film, it transpired later, was a 'love story/thriller', about a teenage girl who joins 'a gang', but then falls in love with a teacher and runs away to Yorkshire with him. The intricacies of the plot eluded me but my role, as I shivered in the requested 'traditional *costume*' was obviously to provide background ethnic colour – literally and figuratively – for one of the gang scenes. In search of an authentic inner-city environment, which fully reflected the depravity of youth gang subculture, the film crew chose to locate in a condemned, though still inhabited, block on one of the poorest housing estates in London. Even this was obviously, however, not quite 'authentic' enough, so the crew had imported three 'yoof' skateboarders from a public school in Hampshire and a burned-out estate car for added atmosphere. It was a strange feeling, being transformed from an anthropologist with a morning to spare and her own 'costume', to a marker for inner-city deprivation; an experience I, perhaps rather naively, had not expected and not one with which I was entirely happy. The film did not seem to draw much support from the crowd of Bengali young men who gathered around, either, watching with a mixture of bemusement and vocal derision as their homes and lives were transformed into gangland fantasy.

What struck me more forcibly was the continuity between this fantasy masquerading as cutting-edge reality and the current popular and media obsession with inner-city youth. Amongst the clamour of anger, accusation and recrimination that characterizes the recent series of moral panics over youth gangs, girl gangs, Triads, bullying, exclusions, violence against teachers and failing schools, events such as *Style and Culture '96* become something of a sideshow. Or perhaps more accurately, are rendered simply invisible, supplanted by a series of snapshots and soundbites characterized by an unremitting negativity that requires only a burned-out car in the foreground to ensure its authenticity.

What my stint as an Asian extra also made me acutely, and rather painfully, aware of was the way in which markers of 'race' have become – or perhaps I mean remained – a symbol for all of these concerns. Indeed, it could be argued that the phantasm of 'race' is what binds these new moral panics together, and provides the continuity with their earlier incarnations. 'Race' has become so completely synonymous with ideas of moral and social decline as to become invisible; an absent-presence, the power of which is so much assumed that it no longer needs to be overtly articulated. The silent racialization of images of urbanization, poverty, and particularly of 'problem' youth, acts as unquestioned cause and sufficient explanation – a necessary marker of contemporary life and more so of contemporary social breakdown. Rather than a participant in a multi-cultural, multi-racial landscape, I had become instead a representation of all that was wrong with it, an easy but potent signifier of urban decay, social anomie and cultural atrophy. I had become a folk-devil.

A couple of weeks later still, an article in the London *Evening Standard* formally proclaimed the arrival of this new folk-devil – 'Asian Teenage Gangs Terrorising London' (13 November 1996). Here are all the hallmarks of 'authentic' gangland London – youths wielding weapons, alienated from their families, their community and British society, locked into a cycle of meaningless violence, low self-esteem and self-destruction. Headteacher Michael Marland thus warns of 'a new underclass of illiterates, who have acquired a habit of violence', creating what the article describes as an 'almost apocalyptic vision of unrest'. And if the talk of 'nihilistic . . . violence' echoes a Powellian 'rivers-of-blood' style philosophy, then it also plays silently into the same images of racial and cultural conflict.

The evocation of racialized representations of Asian youth, and particularly of Asian young men, has served both to focus media and public attention on this new 'problem' group and obscure a wider, more complex understanding of youth identities and identifications. Images of hooded young men on council estates have fed on well-established tropes of racial alienation and cultural difference to create a potent symbol of disorder that seemingly requires no further explanation – 'race' has become a substitute for analysis.

The same processes are at work in the opening article, taken from a local newspaper. The article concerns a series of encounters between some black young men and some of the Bengali young men from the SAYO project, which took place over several weeks a few months prior to the fashion show. The actual details of these encounters will be considered in a later chapter. What is of interest here is the way in which notions of 'race' and 'difference' are inscribed in the article and used as an implicit rationale for the events.

'Race' is used overtly throughout the piece only as a form of group label; it is significant that it is the 'racial' identifications 'black' and 'Asian' that form the primary identification for the two groups, which were in reality formed around a relatively narrow subset of friends from school and the local area. In addition to these labels, however, 'race' is articulated through a series of racialized codes focused on disorder and lawlessness. Emotive and meaning-laden language such as 'flare up', 'tension', 'stand offs', 'erupted', conjure up a vision of urban unrest, a vision consolidated through the image of 'large groups of youths roaming the estate', petrol bombs at hand and only held in check through the intervention of the Territorial Support Group. And if this sounds like the Bradford riots, it wasn't – it was a series of loosely connected, sporadic and small-scale, admittedly sometimes violent, but intensely personal and personality-led, fights between a very specific group of fourteen- and fifteen-year-old young men.

The effect of this silent racialization is to render obsolete any more complex or alternative explanation for these events. No reason or context for the fights is given in the article nor, in its own terms is it deemed necessary: the spectre of 'race' with its implications of absolute and hostile difference, conflict and 'nihilistic . . . violence' is left to speak for itself – at once cause, effect and justification.

Of youth and the new Asian folk-devil: the rise of 'the Asian gang'

What both the local newspaper report and the *Evening Standard* article reflect is a growing concern with the 'problem' of Asian youth – and more specifically, with the 'problem' of *Muslim young men*. If they share the same well-established tropes of racial alienation and social breakdown that created, and continue to create, moral panics over Rastafarian drug dealers, black rioters, muggers and Yardies (Hall, 1978; CCCS, 1982; Gilroy, 1987; Alexander, 1996), what they also reflect is a new cultural formation.

It is revealing, and perhaps more than a little ironic, that these same shared markers were until comparatively recently used as a form of distinction between the African-Caribbean and Asian communities. Where the former were racked with tales of culture conflict, generation gap, lack of parental control, alienation and despair, Britain's Asian communities were held to be, by contrast, holistic and coherent, alien and incomprehensible perhaps, but peaceable, law-abiding, successful and – the odd scare about illegal immigration aside – largely unproblematic (Benson, 1996).[2] A *Guardian* article (13 September 1991) states:

There is worse poverty today in some Asian communities. But very poor

Asians, however desperate their material plight, have a sense of their own worth; they connect to a tradition, a history and a culture.

Indeed, it is in this very coherence – the assumption of absolute and unchanging difference – that both the strength and the weakness of Asian communities and cultures is held to reside. As an article in the *Daily Mail* (28 July 1993), intriguingly titled 'Can Asians Recivilise our Inner Cities?' argues:

> One does not encounter among them [Asian communities] that moral, spiritual and cultural vacuum in which so many of the native young now live. Indeed, the very closeness of Asian families often gives rise to terrible and tragic problems when parents seek to keep alive the traditions that they remember from their upbringing in India and Pakistan while their children, *surrounded by a different culture*, seek to enjoy the *freedoms of British youth.* (emphasis added)

Leaving aside here the opposition of 'native young' and implicitly alien Asian families, not to mention the questionable freedoms of British youth, the article displays a more profound ambiguity about the Asian presence in Britain. On the one hand, the invocation of strong cultural values and traditions are seen as a positive contribution to society, overtly challenging wider social decay, whereas on the other, they are seen as constituting a source of internal oppression for the young. The coalescence of strength and oppression has been most noticeably focused in relation to Asian young women, where public concerns particularly over arranged marriage systems have served as a critique of an assumed patriarchal absolutism (CCCS, 1982: 75). It is worth noting that although concerns over African-Caribbean communities have been primarily fixated on black young men, Asian young men have been largely invisible until three or four years ago, the presumed beneficiaries of a rigid system of male hierarchy and privilege.

However, written into this attribution of cultural homogeneity and particularity are the seeds of its inevitable atrophy, a sense of cultural displacement and anachronism, which has been easily reinvented as contemporary assertions of 'nihilistic . . . violence' amongst Asian communities.

                                                 ★ ★ ★

On the wall of the office of SAYO there is a poster, one of a series entitled 'Common assumptions and stereotypes about the Asian community'. The poster is a cartoon, depicting two Asian men, one with goatee beard and Muslim headwear telling the other, 'I suppose with you being Gujerati and me being Bangladeshi and being born and brought up 4500 miles apart, you can forgive them for thinking we're the same'. In the wake of the *Satanic Verses* furore and the Gulf War, this perception of homogeneity has undergone something of a sea change (Samad, 1996). The attention generated by these events has had two broad effects; firstly, it has led to a division in the perception of previously undistinguished Asian communities (Modood, 1992) and secondly, it has brought the issue of youth to the foreground.

Although in some quarters this change has been welcomed as liberating and a belated recognition of the diversity of Asian cultures (Modood, 1992), it has also created a perceptual split along religio-cultural lines, which has more damaging implications. Attention has thus become focused on religious difference, which has in turn become a marker for differential social success or failure. Tariq Modood, for example, has contrasted Indian 'achievers' with the disadvantaged 'believers' (1992: 43), an emergent Muslim Pakistani and Bangladeshi 'underclass' given its most notorious embodiment in the 1993 *Panorama* documentary *Purdah in the Underclass*.

The reification of Islam as one of the key markers of difference in contemporary British racial discourse has proved pervasive and politically potent, providing the impetus for renewed public debates around immigration, integration and the requirements of citizenship. Voicing these concerns in the aftermath of the Rushdie affair, John Patten was quoted in the *Times*:

> The last few months have been difficult ones for British Muslims. The issue of race relations has been thrown into sharp relief and all of us have had to think deeply . . . about what it means to be British, and particularly about what it means to be a British Muslim.
>
> (5 July 1989, in Solomos, 1993: 224)

Increasingly it seems that what it means to be a British Muslim is definably solely in terms of negativity, deprivation, disadvantage and alienation. It is worth noting here that the term 'Asian' in relation to negative images and stereotypes has become synonymous with Muslim communities, again drawing on the notion of an emergent Pakistani and Bangladeshi underclass. An *Independent* article of July 1995, warning of an 'Asian crime "timebomb" ' suggests, 'that the country is on the verge of an outbreak of disorder caused by Asians'. Recent Home Office research pins this to 'A demographic timebomb of Pakistani and Bangladeshi youths [which] is likely to explode and could shatter the belief that Asians are more law-abiding than white or black people'.[3] As an inevitable corollary to this, images of cultural dysfunction have grown apace, most notably in regard to young men, who were at the visual and perceptual front-line of both the anti-Rushdie protests and the demonstrations against the Gulf War.

In the wake of angry demonstrations in Tower Hamlets following the racial attack on Quddus Ali in September 1993, Vivek Chaudhary points to the 'discovery' of Asian youth:

> The press claim to have discovered something new – that Asians are at last fighting back. But active resistance has been an integral part of the

history of our community ... from Southall to Smethwick, from Bradford to Brick Lane ... the rolecall of resistance is endless,

(*Guardian*, 16 September 1993)

Through the lens of the media, however, 'resistance' has become increasingly synonymous with criminality and upheaval, with the breakdown of perceived traditional values and the growth of a pathologized culture of alienation and confusion. As part of this, representations of 'the Asian community' have moved from a concern with a uniformly victim status to that of perpetrator – a reinvention of passive recipient to active combatant which has simultaneously, and significantly, transformed the gendered markers of imagined Asian identities. Concerns have thus increasingly focused on the public activities of young men – the youth in the streets (Keitha, 1995) – rather than the more domestic, 'private' concerns of young women.

An *Independent* article (20 April 1992) captures the beginning of this transformation. Its author writes:

The East End is fast becoming a neighbourhood of ghettos, a breeding ground of intolerance and violent frustrations ... Racial violence has been increasing for several years, but *the Asian gangs are a new phenomenon*, and the increasing frequency of their confrontations is a sign, many fear, of things to come. (emphasis added)

The links between 'race', violence, urban decay, ghetto life, the underclass, poverty and criminality are made explicitly here. On the one hand the article asserts socio-economic justifications, 'The new East End is, like its predecessors, a product of poverty', while simultaneously conjuring images of racial/ ethnic specificity on the other – these are, as the title of the piece makes clear, 'new rivalries'. Integral to both is the construction of 'the Asian Gang', with its inevitable links with notions of tribalism, violence and criminality, 'Every estate has its gang ... They fight to protect not only their territory but their rights to steal.'

Two years later, the transformation seems complete. A *Sunday Times* feature of 21 August 1994, a week after the death of Richard Everitt in Camden, for example, reports that sixty per cent of racial attacks in Oldham are perpetrated by Asians on whites. Leaving aside tangible problems in the reporting and registering of what constitutes a 'racial attack', the article is significant in its representation of Asian youths as newly active, and newly threatening, agents in the public arena. Again, racialized images are at the forefront of the piece, notably making a direct comparison with African-American gang subculture, with all its implications of extreme violence, nihilism and danger:

The gangs, predominantly youngsters from Bangladeshi families, take their inspiration from Afro-American culture. Mimicking gangs in L.A., they wear hooded jackets and baggy jeans and listen to rap and ragga music. An increase in drug taking and dealing among young Asians has happened in tandem.

Besides criminalizing by association a large section of contemporary mainstream youth culture and style in an extraordinary manner, the article draws on the assumptions of Asian cultural particularity discussed earlier as the most salient – not to mention the most readily available – explanation. Hitherto holistic cultures are thus portrayed as breaking down in the face of implicitly superior Western values and freedoms, playing into familiar tropes of cultural difference and inevitable tensions. The same article reports:

> Police and community groups are increasingly alarmed by an upsurge in inner-city violence, led by *traditionally well-behaved* Asian youths. Detectives blame the disturbing rise in crime on the disintegration of family life in Asian homes as children refuse to obey their elders. (emphasis added)

The ongoing criminalization of Asian youth, and especially Muslim youth, can be traced in recent years to two significant events – the murder of Richard Everitt in 1994, and the 'riots' in Bradford in the following year.

Richard Everitt was stabbed and killed in South Camden in August 1994, by a group of Asian young men, one of whom, Badrul Miah, is now serving a life sentence for murder.[4] The attack was understood and represented in the media as a motiveless racial attack in an area that has become notorious for high levels of racist incidents and tensions between the white and predominantly Bangladeshi communities. Significantly, it is the same area that the *Evening Standard* article represents two years later as the crucible of 'nihilistic intra-Bangladeshi violence', and the coverage of the Everitt murder contains all the seeds of this later portrayal. The explanations for the attack in the broadsheet newspapers are a compelling mixture of culture clash, inter-generational conflict and social and economic breakdown, with a strong emphasis on a 'between two cultures' identity crisis amongst Bengali young men. These young men are constructed as caught between an oppressive and rigid parental culture at home and a ghettoized subculture of poverty outside, with its incumbent implications of youth deviance, criminality and violence.

Several months prior to the Everitt incident, the *Sunday Telegraph* reported on the high incidence of violence between black and Asian pupils in South Camden schools, pointing to tensions between the now more successful African-Caribbean community and the less successful Bengali community. The article notes 'In response, the Bangladeshis have formed *vigilante gangs to protect their own*' (emphasis added), continuing ominously, 'Members of the "Drummond Street" gang are known for their proficiency in martial arts' (20 April 1994). Later articles, in the wake of Everitt's death, build up a more dramatic picture of these Bengali 'gangs'[5] – the Drummond Street Posse, the Brick Lane Gang, the Chalk Farm Posse – asserting 'Young Bangladeshis are acquiring many of the characteristics of a common inner-city youth culture' (*Telegraph*, 21/8/1994).

A letter to the *Observer* newspaper from Jonathan Stanley, an officer for Camden's Race Equality Unit fleshes out this picture:

> The first generation of Bengalis born in the area are now reaching adulthood. Their formative influences largely coincided with those which shaped the values of their white peers: television, school, poor quality housing, inner-city streets, long term unemployment. It is unsurprising that they are prepared to react to violence in the same way as their white counterparts.
>
> (19 August 1994)

In a twist on the 'culture-of-poverty' thesis, an article in the *Daily Mail*, entitled 'youths combine *the worst of both worlds*' (16 August 1994), blames this crisis on racism, which causes Asian young men to deny their cultural identity and turn instead to a pathologized youth culture:[6]

> The unremitting propoganda of English culture deriding the Asian one has produced a generation of Asian youth combining the worst of the Western model – disrespectful of authority, nihilistic, violent . . . The result has been a crisis of Asian culture where the authority of the old has all but collapsed.

The duality of this representation, between the image of the Asian 'alien' on the one hand and marauding youth gangs on the other, marks out the creation of the Asian youth folk devil. The tension between 'race' and 'class' explanations are a constant feature of media accounts and their conflation provides a powerful icon for a plethora of social problems and dangers, real or imagined.

The same mixture of cultural crisis and class conflict is found in coverage of the so-called 'Bradford riots', which took place over two nights in June 1995. The disturbances were directly triggered by police reaction to a complaint about Asian youths playing football in the streets, during which the officers involved were said to have mistreated two Asian women (*Independent*, 12/13 June 1995). However, the events were held to be more widely significant as signaling a crisis in the community. Where Bradford had been in the spotlight several years earlier, during the *Satanic Verses* furore, when it was portrayed as reactionary and anachronistic, the community now appeared in the throes of cultural and social breakdown. Or as one article put it, 'a picture began to emerge yesterday of a community struggling to come to terms with itself and *modern* Britain' (*Independent*, 12 June 1995, emphasis added).

The image of a backward, tradition-bound culture struggling in the face of progressive Western values provides the parameters within which theories of generation gap and culture conflict are forged. The *Independent*, for example, reports, 'Senior police last night blamed a generation gap in the Asian community, saying that young people were alienated from their parents and cultural leaders' (12 June 1995). Another article, on the same day, states that in addition to issues of police harassment and high levels of unemployment, 'Another important factor is the breakdown of the influence of the family and community as many third and fourth generation British Asians have adopted Western values and aspirations' (Bennetto, 1995). The disturbances thus become both effect and symbol of youth alienation and a racialized cultural incompatibility – a situation made more overtly threatening with the overarching spectre of religious fundamentalism, a legacy of the *Satanic Verses* affair. Yasmin Alabhai Brown reports:

> The result is unexplored territory for young Asians – adrift from the values of their elders, immersed in an Islam which is essentially a reaction, out of step with the liberal values of secular society and yet enamoured of its amoral materialism, while being denied the means to fulfill the modern dream. (*Independent*, 13 June 1995)

What is conveniently lost within this discourse is any sense of alternative explanation. As happened in the wake of the riots in Brixton and elsewhere in the 1980s, notions of identity crisis serve as an effective disavowal of responsibility and an emblem of innocence. As Norman Bettison, Assistant Chief Constable of West Yorkshire Police altruistically asserts, 'The police is *simply* the anvil on which the youth is beating out its frustration and anger' (*Independent*, 12 June 1995, emphasis added). Similarly, *The Times* argues of the events leading up to the confrontation:

> Although it was a mundane police task, it quickly led to disturbances, fuelled by *festering tensions* among British-born Asians and reflecting a *generation gap* within the Asian community. (12 June 1995, emphasis added)

The article continues:

> All these factors have created a widening gulf between British-born Asians and their elders, for whom their way of life, with their interest in *Bhangra* music and contemporary fashion, is *alien*. (12 June 1995, emphasis added)

It is a short conceptual step to the representation of 'nihilistic . . . violence' and of 'vicious schoolboy tribal wars' in the *Evening Standard* article referred to earlier. The article replays all the hallmarks of cultural dysfunction – of meaningless expressions of frustration by uncontrollable and unemployable young men of 'poor peasant stock', whose parents are illiterate, who live in overcrowded and substandard housing (presumably by choice – cf. CCCS, 1982) and whose command of English is poor. The article asserts:

> The evidence is clear that Bangladeshi youth are turning violently against each other – almost as if their prowess in a brawl and their collective strength offer the only prospect of status and self-esteem. (13 November 1996)

Here too is the evocation of inner-city/ghetto youth subculture – of gangs like the Drummond Street Posse, or the Lisson Green Posse, of territory and turf wars, of knives, knuckle dusters, belts and baseball bats, of Lucozade bottles and anonymous teenage boys with covered faces and macho poses recounting tales of former victories and future challenges.

And if all this scene seems to need is a burned-out estate car and a couple of skateboarders to make it complete, then perhaps this ought to give us pause for thought.

Imagining 'the Asian Gang': ethnicity, masculinity and the problem of black youth

It would perhaps provide a little comfort – to academics at least – to hold up 'the Asian Gang' as simply the latest example of media mythmaking and popular panic. Nevertheless, the creation of 'the Asian Gang' outlined above draws upon and reinscribes a number of well-established tropes of racialized identities that have assumed the status of 'common sense' as much in academic understandings as in the more fertile ground of media and popular imagination. 'The Asian Gang' then brings together conventional academic wisdom around what it means to be 'black'[7] and young and male to legitimate the formation of this new folk devil. Although, as usual, academia has been a little slow in jumping on this particular bandwagon – though the signs are that this is about to change (Goodey, 1999; Macey, 1999) – it has in one sense laid the crucial foundations for this new creation; Dr. Frankenstein to the monster, as it were. Though perhaps few would claim parentage of this particular invention, it is nevertheless true that the portrait sketched above rehearses truisms that now stand as Truths – self evident and incontrovertible – as often found in contemporary sociology as in its more popular incarnations.

The thumbnail sketch drawn above centres its arguments on three interwoven strands: ethnicity, masculinity and youth. Each of these facets is posited in and of itself as constituting a problem – the coalescence of all three leads to prophecies of social doom. Each facet also has a well-established status *as problem* within the social sciences; while not wishing to rehearse the history and breadth of this scholarship here, I want to draw out some broad themes that reflect on the imagination of 'the Asian Gang' and that act as the conceptual baseline for the present study. Though they are here considered as largely distinct strands, these three dominant themes are in reality intricately enmeshed and mutually corroborative; some of these coalitions will hopefully become apparent and can be re-read into the imagination of 'the Asian Gang'.

Ethnicity

As Sue Benson has convincingly argued (1996), studies of Asian communities in Britain have been largely dominated by an anthropological gaze, which has constructed these groups as homogeneous, bounded and autonomous entities (Shaw, 1988; Werbner, 1990; Ballard, 1994). Attracted by the supposed culture-rich/culture-bound nature of Asian collective identity, the emphasis has been on 'difference', which has placed diverse Asian groups as the cultural 'Other'. This has focused attention on Asian 'ethnicity' as the primary marker of self-definition and of boundary maintenance (Barth, 1969), in which culture is transfixed and reified as the only authentic form of identity creation and solidarity. This in turn has had two significant effects: firstly, it has denied the structural positioning of Asian communities within a racialized discourse of inequality and oppression; and secondly, it has paved the way for the fragmentation of Asian identity around the notion of multiculturalism and the celebration of 'difference' (Benson, 1996; Eade, 1996).

The celebration of 'difference' has led to the increasing fragmentation of Britain's Asian communities, proliferating a range of separate and bounded 'ethnic bubbles' (Gates, 1992) in which the emphasis has been on 'culture' as the primary source of collective identification; what Modood refers to as 'one's mode of being' (1992: 55). The central symbol of this multi-culturalist rainbow vision is 'community', in which individual subjectivity blends seamlessly with collective ideals of culture, ethnicity and belonging, and in which there is seemingly little room for contact or change, and less for conflict or confusion. The ethnicity-as-cultural-tapestry approach presupposes the existence of internal homogeneity and external difference, in which boundaries are absolute and uncontested, yet which fit neatly and exactly within the framework of the British nation. As I have argued elsewhere (Alexander, 1998), however, the assertion of 'difference' has brought unintended consequences, not least in the reinscription of Asian identities as implacably alien and unassimilable – as outside the nation. The emergence, in particular, of Muslim sensibilities in the aftermath of the *Satanic Verses* affair, the Gulf War and the Bradford riots has not only championed the cause of diversity but also reformulated the boundaries of British citizenship and nationhood along religio-cultural lines. Rather than dealing the intended death blow to dualistic anti-racist perspectives, the result has been to replace black/white divisions with one of British/Muslim, with Muslims placed as the new social and cultural pariahs – and increasingly as the new objects of desire for academic research.

The comparatively recent focus on religious identifications amongst Britain's ethnic minority communities has resulted in some ambiguous manifestations. Where in 1996 Benson could, with some justice, caricature research on race and ethnicity along the 'Asians have culture; West Indians have problems' dichotomy (Banks, 1996), the appearance of religion centre stage has muddied the picture, with 'Asians' being divided along a non-Muslim/Muslim culture/problem axis and African-Caribbeans falling out of the picture altogether. Where ethnicity theorists have largely decided to treat religion as synonymous with ethnicity, and continued to write about 'Sikhs', 'Muslims' and 'Hindus' as distinct *cultural* communities (Baumann, 1996), or have privileged one or other dimension (Modood (1992, 1997), for example, writes about 'Muslims', while Werbner and Anwar's 1991 collection privileges 'ethnic' groups), others have seized on the problematic and problem-oriented dimension of emergent religious identities. Across Europe, and across the social and political sciences, the rush to categorize, analyse, interpret and understand these 'Muslim voices' has led to what Glavanis (1998) has termed a 'neo-Orientalist' perspective. In Britain, concerns over Islamophobia (Runnymede Trust, 1997), or alternatively, religious fundamentalism have concurred in the positioning of Islam at the centre of political and academic discourse as Public Enemy Number One – Britain's Most Unwanted, as it were.

The interest in religious identities, and particularly in Muslim identities, has a number of important consequences for the study of Asian youth, and particularly the imagination of 'the Asian Gang'. Firstly, it has precipitated the focus on youth as the adherents of the new 'fundamentalism', and has given new life to the 'culture conflict' theory of Britain's black communities. Jacobson, for example, has written (1997) of the distinction between 'ethnicity' and 'religion' amongst young British Pakistanis, in which the former is associated with the traditional and tradition-bound cultures of their parents and rejected, whereas religion is embraced as an 'alternative' self-definition tying the individual into a global, culture-free identity (cf. also Gardner and Shakur, 1994). Secondly, this new religious identification is most usually understood as the manifestation of this culture conflict, representing a defensive and usually hostile reaction to racism with which the parental culture is unable to fully contend. Like Rastafari before it, Islam thus stands as a psychological barricade behind which Pakistani and Bangladeshi young people (usually young men) can hide their lack of self-esteem and proclaim a fictional strength through the imagination of the *umma* (Gardner and Shakur,

1994; Jacobson, 1997; Macey, 1999).[8] Thirdly, and integral to this depiction, is the increased concern about 'the Muslim underclass', which places Pakistani and Bangladeshi communities at the top of a reformulated hierarchy of oppression, notably vis-à-vis other South Asian groups (Modood, 1992; Modood et al., 1997); focusing, in Modood's evocative phrase, on the material and cultural distinction between the 'achievers' and the 'believers' (1992: 43). This has further marginalized Muslim youth as the unwilling and resentful heirs of a culture of disadvantage, and as the perpetrators of a burgeoning 'Asian' criminality (Modood et al., 1997; Webster, 1997).

The focus on Islamicization has, moreover, underscored the longer standing sense of threat posed by 'the enemy within' (Gilroy, 1987; Saeed, Blain & Forbes, 1999; Halliday, 1999). In this sense, the emergence of Islamophobia, or anti-Muslimism (Halliday, 1999) is less a new phenomenon than a translation of earlier concerns around the presence of black communities in Britain or Europe. The current academic fascination with Islam/ Islamophobia/Fundamentalism has, however, served to dislocate Muslims from this broader (if not longer) history of black/Asian struggle (Brah, 1996), and concentrated more on the authenticity debate than its implications for the structural positioning of Muslim groups within a racialized discourse. What the focus on religion shares with its precursors is the evocation of fixed boundaries and absolute identities, in which religion, ethnicity and culture are naturalized and essentialized, and become, in effect, synonymous with 'race' (Gilroy, 1992). Muslims have then, ironically, become the new 'black', with all the associations of cultural alienation, deprivation and danger that come with this position.

Masculinity

One crucial by-product of the resurgent interest in Muslim identities, particularly in relation to the imagination of 'the Asian Gang' is the regendering of Asian identities. Largely because of the anthropological monopoly on Britain's 'ethnic' (as opposed to 'racial') minorities, with its unfaltering assertion of bounded and internally homogeneous cultures, Asian communities in Britain were considered as previously unthreatening, law abiding and unproblematic[9] – a portrait that erased the role of both racial inequality and violence, and resistance in the formation of community identities (Brah, 1996; Sivanandan, 1981/2). The only critique of this perspective came from black feminists, concerned with the role and experience of Asian women within these struggles (Wilson, 1978; Brah, 1996). At the same time, however, it was upon assumed gender relations that the few moral panics about Asian communities were hung, notably, and most sensationally, concerns over arranged marriages for young women. Where Britain's African-Caribbean communities were constructed as male – with the incumbent associations with threat and violence (Alexander, 1996) – Asian communities were largely imagined as female, with the resulting focus on the gendered and sexualized arenas of family and marriage (CCCS, 1982), most notoriously around immigration legislation and virginity testing.

As argued above, recent years have seen the regendering of Asian communities as much in the academic imagination as in the media and in the popular imagination. The shift, then, has been from a focus on 'women' as the subjects of study towards 'gender relations', in which women are positioned as the objects of control and legislation. Glavanis has argued (1998) that gender relations play a central part in Orientalist and neo-Orientalist perspectives on Asian cultures, especially in the representation of the inherently patriarchal and sexist nature of Muslim societies (Sahgal and Yuval-Davis, 1992). Where, until recently, these concerns remained largely 'private', invisible and unremarked, concerns over Muslim young men and 'the Asian Gang' have cast the spotlight on the public performance of masculinities. This has signalled a shift in the perception of Asian masculinities, traditionally visioned as passive and hyper-feminized, towards an association with violence and a highly visible hyper-masculinity (Alexander, forthcoming).

Asian men are comparative latecomers to the race to 'unwrap' masculinity (Chapman and Rutherford, 1988). It can be argued that the field of masculinity studies has always been concerned with the problematization of masculine identities, and that Asian men are simply the latest inheritors of a tradition that almost instinctually positions them as 'problem'. The breakdown of perceived patriarchal authority, notably in the arenas of family and employment, have led to the redefinition of masculinity, most potently captured in the notion of 'masculinities in crisis'. The position of working-class young men is particularly fraught:

> Male redundancy has created cultures of prolonged adolescence in which young male identities remain locked into the locality of estate, shops and school . . . Violence, criminality, drug taking and alcohol consumption become the means to gaining prestige for a masculine identity bereft of any social value.
>
> (Rutherford, 1988: 7)

The foundation for gang mythmaking is already present here, and the association of masculinity-in-crisis, criminality and working-class youth is crucial. For Muslim young men, the correlation of ethnicity/religion with perceived underclass status is an additional nail in the coffin; a series of associations clearly traceable in the media representations discussed above. This already tenuous stance is undermined further, however, by the racialization of Asian masculinities, which places them as triply in crisis, triply deviant, and triply dangerous. As I have argued elsewhere (Alexander, 1996; forthcoming) the equation of black male identities solely with 'race' has served to focus concerns on violence, criminality and control, inscribing a hyper-visibility of black masculinity, which disguises a more profound invisibility (West, 1993). Black masculinities are then positioned uncritically as 'subordinated' to hegemonic ideals (Connell, 1987, 1995), as always already flawed and inevitably failing (hooks, 1992). Violence, criminality and hyper-sexuality are posited as the alternatives to the fulfilment of patriarchal responsibilities and control, to 'real' male power. It is no accident, then, that the representation of 'the Asian Gang' above should draw explicit comparisons with African-American 'gang' subculture, with its associations with ghettos, drugs, black-on-black violence and 'nihilism' (West, 1994). It is interesting, moreover, that the concern over 'Islamic fundamentalism' is usually understood as a *male* issue and interpreted as a reaction to racial hostility and loss of patriarchal authority, a way of gaining self-esteem and a sense of individual and group control.[10]

Goodey (1999), for example, has recently argued that 'Islamophobia' can be seen as a reaction of white male hegemony against 'new-found' assertiveness on the part of Asian young men. The move from 'victim' to 'aggressor' has served to homogenize and demonize Asian men externally, but it also, according to Goodey, works internally to threaten Asian young men by promoting intra-group tensions and fear. Goodey conflates this new assertive form of male identity unproblematically with the expression of violence and with 'fundamentalist' Islam, and places these young men as oppositional to dominant white society. She thus cites Webster (1997) who posits a range of Asian male identifications from conformist, ethnic brokers and experimenters to vigilantes and Islamists (again the typology is reminiscent of Pryce's 1979 work on African-Caribbean young men), stating 'vigilantes and Islamists are more predictive of aggressive behaviour and a negative public image' (Goodey, 1999). Recognizing in part the role of representation in the re-imagination of Asian identities, Goodey ultimately rests the blame on the actions of Asian young men themselves, moving from 'image' to reality without noticing, and privileging the white hegemonic gaze as interpreter and legislator:

> The interest and apparent 'problem' with Asian youth, for the white majority, arise when an image has been drastically changed from 'passive' to 'aggressive' in combination with the recent ascendancy of Islamophobia on the world stage. The development of a 'tough' identity of and by Asian youth may assign them a degree of power where there previously existed a sense of powerlessness, but in the eyes of the white population, this can pose a threat against their order and against them. Nowhere is this more the case than when Asian youth are aggressive, violent and apparently racist towards the white population.
>
> (Goodey, 1999)

Macey similarly equates Pakistani male identity in Bradford as emerging out of a 'culture of poverty', adopting a 'gangsta fashion . . . of disenchanted urban American youth gangs' (Taj, 1996, cited in Macey, 1999), and centred on a lifestyle of drug dependency, violent crime and prostitution – a portrait almost identical to the media images outlined above. For Macey, however, this new male identity cannot fully be explained by deprivation and exclusion; it has a cultural twist that is aimed at the oppression of Pakistani women and that, by implication, delegitimizes any political claims – an assertion of misogyny that perhaps echoes the concerns over black cultural misogyny and homophobia in the United States. Macey blames this new, 'Islamic' identity for exacerbating racial exclusion and increasing generational and gender hostility (Macey, 1999: 852); for promoting 'public disorder' and violence, and excusing private harassment and violence against Asian women. However it is explained, excused or demonized, it seems all are agreed on one thing – Asian men are out of control and in trouble.

Youth

Implicit, though often unstated, in the problem-oriented approach to both ethnic/religious identities and masculinities is generation; that is, that the groups most often positioned as 'in crisis' are young people, particularly, of course, young men (who are largely synonymous with the term 'youth'). Although the category 'youth' has been a popular focus of study since the 1950s, particularly the notion of subcultures and resistance through rituals, black youth have largely been absent from this canon, perhaps because of the complicating and seemingly constraining factor of 'race'. Where it has been present, black youth style and expressive cultures have been positioned as defensive, negative and oppositional, with an emphasis on authenticity and exclusion (Hebdige, 1976; Cashmore, 1979). By extension, black youth have been perceived as outside mainstream society, and hostile towards it, defined through what might currently be termed 'social exclusion' and marginalization. Asian young people have, until very recently (Sharma, Hutnyk and Sharma, 1996) been completely invisible, except as perhaps reluctant brides and runaways. Asian young men have simply never featured.

As Giroux (1996) has argued, the category 'youth' itself denotes a specific set of associations focused on crisis, making the seamless association of deviance, violence and threat.[11] He cites Hebdige:

> In our society, youth is present only when its presence is a problem. More precisely, the category 'youth' gets mobilised in official documentary discourse, in concerned or outraged editorials or features, or in the supposedly disinterested tracts emanating from the social sciences at those times when young people make their presence felt by going 'out of bounds', by resisting through rituals, dressing strangely, striking

bizarre attitudes, breaking rules, breaking bottles, windows, heads, issuing challenges to the law.

(in Giroux, 1996: 3)

The 'rebel without a cause' naturalization of youth resistance has been more recently re-problematized through economic and social structuring, which has left large sections of young people – male and female – at the margins of work and social participation, extending the transition to adulthood and throwing up new challenges, particularly in the formation of working-class masculine identities (cf. Rutherford, 1988).

While it could be argued that the category of youth is in transition, both extending its boundaries and diversifying internally, with an emphasis on youth style and consumption patterns (Giroux, 1996), the representations of black youth have proved remarkably resilient to change. Black youth have remained then the epitome of oppositional youth culture, defined through disadvantage and alienation. Black youth masculinities, even more so than their white working-class counterparts, have been cast through the appeal to peer group as the last remaining source of security and self-esteem, what Mac An Ghaill refers to as 'the building of a defensive culture of masculine survival against social marginalization' (Mac An Ghaill, 1994: 187). Importantly, Giroux has noted that where white male youth identities are read against a wider backdrop of structural and economic changes, black male identities are seen as hermetically seated, self-referential and destructive, a product of a 'culture of poverty' (Giroux, 1996). Explanations for black youth behaviour are thus placed on black communities themselves rather than wider forces – a culturalist, blaming-the-victim perspective that is clearly discernible in the media accounts of 'the Asian Gang', and also in the account of black masculinity discussed above. At the same time, black youth are seen as turning against the culture of their parents, precipitating a 'culture conflict' or 'generation gap', which is often lived through as gendered hostility. Mac An Ghaill (1996: 191) brings this cauldron of pathologies together in his account of African-Caribbean young men:

> For young black men's racially subordinated masculinity there are potential intergenerational tensions . . . one way of attempting to resolve these tensions was to displace onto their mothers and sisters their experiences of social inferiority as men in the wider society.

There are tangible echoes here with the account offered by Macey (1999) and also with Goodey's account of emergent youth masculinities (1999). Although many studies of Asian communities tend to reify community, and render youth invisible (Werbner, 1990), where they do appear, usually as an afterthought (Shaw, 1988, 1994), generation is experienced as conflict and as threat (Anwar, 1994), a product of cultural overdetermination, on the one hand, and failing masculinities on the other.[12]

The primary source of black youth identities, almost by default, becomes the peer group – the repository of self-esteem, security and status. Which brings us rather neatly back to the association of youth cultures with deviance, and slides easily into the evocation of 'the Gang'.

The idea of 'the Gang' is, in many ways, the archetype of the intersection of all these dimensions – 'race'/ethnicity, masculinity and youth – the ultimate symbol of crisis, deviance and threat. Klein (1995), for example, has noted in his description of *The American Street Gang*, that 'gang' identity is largely defined as black, male youth. He argues that 'gangs' tend to be self identified groups of ethnically/racially homogeneous, almost exclusively African-American or Hispanic, men with an average age of twenty years. In addition, they are urban, territorially based and with an involvement in criminal activity and a strong association with violence (although Klein does not see this latter attribute as a defining characteristic). Although the British history of 'gang' activity traditionally differs, with its somewhat romanticized notion of East End villains, it can be argued that, as with the concept of 'mugging' before it (Hall et al., 1978), the notion of 'Gang' has been re-inflected through this American discourse, to present the idea of 'the Gang' as an already raced entity, standing for the dangerous 'Other' in contemporary British society. Although little, or no, research work has been carried out on 'gangs' in Britain in recent years, the term is used widely and uncritically in relation to black and Asian youth identities, and increasingly to denote any group of black and Asian young men. The term works not only to naturalize and criminalize group identities, but it also serves as a substitute for analysis, particularly where ethnicity or 'race' is privileged as the primary group marker and offered as a self-explanatory motivation for conflict (Keitha, 1995) or control.

(Mis)representing Asian youth: invisibility and the iconoclasm of style and culture

Ironically, in the blinding glare of recent media and academic reimagination, Asian youth have been rendered effectively 'invisible', which Cornel West, in another context, has described as, 'the relative lack of [cultural and political] power to present themselves and others as complex human beings and thereby to contest the bombardment of negative, degrading stereotypes' (West, 1993: 210). The adherence to an unflinching cultural absolutism has led to the reification of racial/ethnic identities as mono-dimensional icons, which carries with it the belief in absolute choices 'between' cultures, experiencing the characterization of change as distortion and the emergence of new syncretic forms of identification as a loss of authenticity. The creation of a folk devil demands simplicity at the expense of any recognition of humanity, with all the complexity, contradiction and uncertainty that this entails.

What I am not asserting is a rose-tinted, Pollyanna style approach to youth – inner-city, Asian, Bengali or otherwise. For many of Britain's Bengali and Pakistani communities there are very real problems of unemployment, overcrowded and substandard housing, exclusions from school and racial harassment. There is violence too, but these conflicts often carry with them a complex local history and set of understandings that should not be simply dismissed as a catharsis for the culturally dispossessed. To imagine, however, that these problems can adequately account for the lives and experiences of an individual or an entire community is to project a set of cultural pathologies that brings us back to the realms of unreconstructed ghetto fantasies.

Of course, neither the desire nor the capacity to define a community or a generation in exclusively negative terms necessarily makes it so; nor does it come close to exhausting the creativity and potential of most young people. And it was in this resilience that, for me, the real significance of *Style and Culture '96* lay. The young men involved were, on one level, the same youths whose lives have been too easily reduced to caricature and dismissed; they have been uniformly labelled as gang members, criminals and bullies, defined as disruptive, suspended from school, targeted by police, and regarded with an uncomprehending horror by some older members of their community. When they walked on stage, it was in the face of an almost blanket negativity, an expectation of failure of which they were all too aware.

Yet these are the same young men who are now three-quarters of the way through their Duke of Edinburgh's bronze award; who pored over books about Bangladeshi history, religion and language for their cultural display; who practised routines for nearly two months; and who turned up on the day with white boxer shorts, a neat row of shirts fresh from the dry cleaners and – the biggest sacrifice of all – no hair gel. And if at times none of them felt they would make it, the motivation to show what they were capable of, given the chance, overrode everything else. On the night they were foot-perfect, acne-free and, when they walked on in traditional Bengali dress, they brought the house down.

For Stoneleigh Asian Youth Organization, *Style and Culture '96* issued a challenge – to see them for whom they are and what they could achieve; to look beyond easy images and convenient stereotypes to see the real, and complex, picture. The show demonstrated at once a knowledge and celebration of the culture of their parents, acknowledged its continuity and, perhaps more importantly, enacted its changes. It refused easy categorization and played out the paradoxes of being young and male and Bengali and Muslim and British without apology, without problematization, and with Definite Attitude. It was not about one evening, or about an award, but about their lives. It was about 'culture' but not an imagined culture that could be neatly labelled and pathologized. It was a vibrant fusion of tradition and change, of Bollywood remixes and jungle music, of *kabbulis* and Moschino jeans, of Islam and dry slope ski-ing, football and hairgel.

For me, *Style and Culture '96* captured the energy, creativity and imagination of Bengali youth expression as it is lived, in all its contradictions and frustrations and strengths and joys. It was a dramatic and positive enactment of potentialities, of cultural syncretism and of emergent identities amongst this group of Bengali young men, their friends and families and their communities, both local and 'imagined' (Anderson, 1993). It was with this potentiality, this syncretism and these hybridized identities that the present study is concerned. Focusing on a small group of Bengali young men, the study hopes to explore the fissures and fusions of emergent youth identities. In counterposing the fashion show with media representations of Asian youth as a means of introduction, I have hoped to draw attention to one of the dominant themes of the work – the ongoing, constitutive and often creative tension between external imaging and internal identification. The aim is not simply to replace 'false' representations with 'true' pictures, but to unravel the complex interplay of elements in the articulation of identities.

The work thus hopes to challenge monodimensional, essentialist accounts of Asian youth identities, and 'identity crisis' through an exploration of their more fluid and dynamic performances, transgressions and negotiations. However, this is not to insert in this space a perhaps more fashionable, but no less simplistic, account of a celebratory hybrid culture, captured in the notion of 'the new Asian cool' – a free-for-all One-World mixture of Talvin Singh, bindis and henna tattoos (Banerjea, forthcoming). It is rather to argue for a more nuanced, local and historically situated account of identity formation, which encapsulates often contradictory processes of continuity and change, constraint and agency, solidarity and diffusion, representation and re-imagination.

To this end, I have chosen to present this work as an in-depth, textured and highly personal account, which explores the process of identity formation at a level of analysis usually overlooked – or considered theoretically questionable, if not actually morally reprehensible – by academic research. This is not to make claims for the authenticity of experience over theoretical abstraction, but to assert the significance of time- and place-specific research, which acknowledges the contours of the research encounter and the located and embedded nature of identity construction. In focusing on 'the Asian Gang' – or perhaps more accurately '*not* the Asian Gang' – the aim is to disentangle some of the processes at work in creating the mythology of 'the Gang', the role of these representations in interpreting and constraining Asian youth identities and experiences, and the challenges or alternatives pursued – or not – by these young men at a particular time and place in their lives. Chapter Two describes the process of research, the frictions and transitions of the research encounter, the role of innocence and subjectivity in the study, and its status as 'fiction'. Chapter Three paints in the background and setting of the study, exploring the nexus of 'deprivation' and 'threat' which marks out the creation of 'the Muslim Underclass' and its relation to the history of the Stoneleigh

Estate and the SAYO project. Chapter Four returns to the events of 1996, referred to in the opening extract, and explores the role of racialized representations in the mythmaking around 'the Asian Gang', its local incarnation and its contested history. Chapters Five and Six explore the performance of masculinity in these encounters; firstly, in the formation of peer group identities and friendship, and secondly, in the re-imagination of community through notions of authority, hierarchy and respect between 'brothers'. Chapter Six also explores the articulation of age, gender and sexuality in the relationship with 'sisters'. The conclusion reflects on the process of research and of 'writing fiction', and re-examines understandings of 'ethnicity', 'identity', 'masculinity' and 'the Gang' in the light of the present work.

A note on terminology

Although this study is entitled *The Asian Gang*, the subjects of the study are all Bengali young men. The term Bengali, rather than Bangladeshi, Muslim, Asian or British Asian, is used throughout the work in reference to the young men since this was the label most used by themselves. Although most did describe themselves as 'Muslim' this tended to be in more specific circumstances, when discussing religion or the representation of Islam in the media. 'Black', 'Asian', 'Muslim' or 'Bangladeshi' are terms used more as generic labels in relation to external constructions of identity, other academic work in the field, or as a convenient shorthand in referring to more inclusive formations of identity, or a particular structural positioning.

Notes

1 All place and personal names have been changed to maintain confidentiality and anonymity.

2 The notion of Asian communities as 'unproblematic' refers here to the commonsense perception of Asian communities as unthreatening to the public sphere. It is true, however, that Asian (especially Muslim) cultures have always been perceived as outside, and opposed to, the values of Britishness, with the persistence of demonologies around illegal immigration, domestic violence and deviant sexualities. There is, in addition, a 'hidden history' of fears around the activities of Asian youth/ communities which are more generally subsumed into the discussions of black (African-Caribbean) youth and resistance/criminality, and are thereby rendered invisible (but cf. Sharma, Hutnyk and Sharma, 1996; Bains, 1988).

3 In the following account, it should be noted that 'Asian' usually refers exclusively to Muslim groups.

4 Ko Banerjea has pointed out to me that the conviction of Badrul Miah is regarded by many as 'unsafe' and that it was acknowledged by the

sentencing judge that Miah was being left to shoulder the blame for those (unknown) individuals who had actually carried out the attack. The newly formed notion of 'joint enterprise' was used by the prosecution to secure the conviction – a manipulation of the British legal system that suggests an urgent desire to contain the Asian threat – by any means necessary. This can also be seen to relate to the construction of Asian communities as outside the normal imagination of Britishness (and British justice). An instructive contrast might be drawn with the handling of the Stephen Lawrence case and the resistance to any legal innovation (or action) to deal with his murderers.

5 An *Independent* headline (dated 1 November 1995) after the sentencing of Badrul Miah reads '*Gang leader* gets life for killing boy' (my emphasis). The article goes on to describe Miah as 'leader of a ten strong Asian *mob.*'

6 Here, as throughout, interesting comparisons can be drawn with the demonization of African-Caribbean youth.

7 Although currently rather unfashionable, the following section uses the label 'black' to refer to both African and Asian descent young people. While noting Modood's (1992) critique of the term in relation to Asian groups, it is used to denote the process of racialization at work in the construction of African-Caribbean and Asian youth identities. The argument marks differences where appropriate.

8 It is significant, I think, that 'Asian gangs' are most usually conceptualized around religion, either Muslim (Pakistani or Bangladeshi) or Sikh.

9 The same reservations are made here as in note 2 above.

10 Again, comparisons can be made with the interpretation of black subcultures such as Rastafari which have been (mis)understood as a reaction to social marginality and the lack of self-esteem, cf. Mac An Ghaill (1994).

11 It is true, of course, that subcultural theory has its origins in the sociology of deviance and criminology (cf. Cohen, 1955; Downes, 1966 etc.).

12 Cf. Alexander (1998, forthcoming) for a fuller discussion of these issues.

PART 3
Race, ethnicity and victimisation

Victimisation by race and religious hate crime constitutes a significant, and expanding, area of study. Data in relation to the extent and impact of race/religious hate crime is generated through a number of different sources, including official crime statistics, national crime surveys, local crime surveys, local monitoring, community and support groups, as well as public inquiries (Bowling and Phillips, 2002). Racist victimisation and religious racism are under-reported phenomena, and so any statistics that we have reflect only a minority of experiences. Goodey's (2007) article, reproduced in this *Reader*, examines official data collection on racist violence in European Union (EU) Member States. Goodey (2007) argues that current official criminal justice data collection practices in EU Member States are limited, although the UK is held up as an example of good official data collection on racist violence (although, even in this case, she argues that there is still scope for refinements to be made to data collection practices). In England and Wales, under the Crime and Disorder Act 1998, race hate crime legislation was enacted which introduced higher penalties for offences that are racially aggravated. Similarly, under the Anti-Terrorism Crime and Security Act 2001, a religiously aggravated element to crime has been introduced, which involves imposing higher penalties upon offenders who are motivated by religious hatred. The definition of a racist and religiously racist incident, as proposed by the Macpherson Report (1999), is used; this being, 'any incident which is perceived to be racist by the victim or any other person'. This indicates a significant shift in terms of police crime recording practices, as police officers have traditionally used an evidential approach that seeks to corroborate allegations rather than automatically accepting victims' accounts. This approach might be viewed as having the potential to address widespread concerns that police officers, acting as gatekeepers, can deny that incidents are motivated by racism, even though victims and witnesses are certain of their racist components (Rowe, 2004). Goodey (2007) further argues that although the 'racist incident' recording mechanism in England and Wales presents a 'best practice' example in its generous application, there is perhaps scope for reconsidering its long-term relevance in practice with respect to its impact on criminal justice resources and for its effectiveness as a tool for monitoring and responding to racist crime.

The second suggested reading in this part is a chapter by Rai and Hesse (1992), who discuss the limitations of crime surveys and the limited insights of existing research on racist victimisation. Their work comprises an experiential analysis of the dimensions to racial victimisation. Rai and Hesse (1992) argue that the spread of racial harassment is landmarked by forms of White territorialism, which is a principal cause of incidents and events in particular places over time. Rai and Hesse (1992) further examine the role of local agencies in responding to the victims of racial harassment.

The third suggested reading in this part is a chapter by Bowling (1999). Bowling (1999: 196) explored racist victimisation in a borough of London, illustrating that 21 per cent of African and Afro-Caribbean women, 19 per cent of Asian men, 18 per cent of Asian women and 17 per cent of African and Afro-Caribbean men had experienced some form of racial harassment, in comparison to 8 per cent of white men and 7 per cent of white women. Incidents included 'low level', 'persistent' incidents such as criminal damage, graffiti, abusive behaviour, as well as more serious incidents such as physical assault and arson, so that the experience of racist violence might be conceptualised via a 'continuum of violence'. According to Bowling (1999), victims of racist violence might move house, might avoid certain places (for example, football matches, the pub), and they might invest in crime prevention techniques such as shatterproof glass and fireproof mailboxes. Collective responses to victimisation from within communities may also occur, such as movements opposing racist organisations such as the National Front or the British National Party. Indeed, a study by Webster (1997) shows that young Asian men defending particular parts of territory in Keighley, West Yorkshire, was a way in which these men responded to racial hostility and violence. Bowling (1999) also argues that attempting to break down the dynamic of violent racism into a series of incidents, and separating these from their wider context, is problematic.

Another dimension to consider when exploring victimisation in relation to 'race'/ethnicity is that of the process of victimisation itself and how cultural factors, which may be linked to particular 'racial' identities and ethnicities, can shape and significantly influence this. Within victimological work, although differences between victims have been acknowledged, these have been insufficiently explored or addressed, so that studies have traditionally tended to homogenise victims and their reactions. Nonetheless, a growing body of work includes a focus upon, and an acknowledgement of, 'racial'/ethnic identities in relation to victimisation. For example, a study by Neville, Oh, Spanierman, Heppner and Clark conducted in 2004 reveals that race and cultural factors contribute to post-rape recovery. Cultural attributions about why they were attacked were stronger in Black women than in their White counterparts. The

Jezebel image, a race-gender stereotype of Black women as sexually loose, which has been identified by Black feminist academics, appeared to be internalised by the Black women taking part in this study and identified as a reason why they were raped. Neville *et al.* (2004) argue that the more powerfully that this image was internalised, the greater was the victim's self-blame, and the lower the level of their self-esteem.

Feminist research looking at domestic violence against minority ethnic women suggests that there is a substantial and significant cultural context to the offending that takes place, and to victims' experiences, their understandings and their survival strategies. Mama's (2000) work, the final suggested reading in this part, is key. Mama conducted the first detailed survey of domestic violence as experienced by Black women, between 1987 and 1988. Mama's (2000) findings include the fact that some men might invoke 'tradition' or 'religion' to justify their violent actions, and that the justification for battering some women was that they were too Western. For Mama (2000), as the religious texts of the main world religions do not advocate violence against women, men are appropriating religion in their relationships with women. Women also often referred to 'tradition', in that they had tried to conform to idealised notions of a dutiful wife. Mama's (2000) work also highlights that extended families are likely to have a more significant role in minority ethnic women's experiences of victimisation, and these may sometimes intervene positively, although they can also sometimes make the situation worse. More recently, a study by the Fawcett Society suggests that some Black women experiencing domestic violence may be reluctant to report their experiences to the police due to having previous experiences of racism against themselves or the perpetrator (Fawcett Society, 2004).

Suggested essays

Goodey, J. (2007) 'Racist Violence in Europe: challenges for official data collection' *Ethnic & Racial Studies* (July).

Rai, K.D. and Hesse, B. (1992) Chapter 5, 'Racial Victimisation: an experiential analysis' in B. Hesse, K. D. Rai, C. Bennett and P. McGilchrist (eds) *Beneath the Surface: racial harassment*. Aldershot: Avebury, pp. 158–195.

Bowling, B. (1999) Chapter 7, 'Racism and Victimisation' in *Violent Racism: victimisation, policing and social context* (revised edn). Oxford: Oxford University Press, pp. 166–168, 181, 191–216, 221–233.

Mama, A. (2000) 'Woman Abuse in London's Black Communities' in K. Owusu (ed.) *Black British Culture & Society*. London: Routledge, pp. 89–110.

Further reading

Bowling, B. and Phillips, C. (2003) 'Racist Victimisation in England and Wales' in D. Hawkins (ed.) *Violent Crime: assessing race and ethnic differences*. Cambridge: Cambridge University Press, pp. 154–170.

Chahal, K. and Julienne, L. (1999) *We Can't All Be White!* Joseph Rowntree Foundation. York: York Publishing Services.

Garland, J. and Chakraborti, N. (2004) 'Racist Victimisation, Community Safety and the Rural: issues and challenges' *British Journal of Community Justice* Vol. 3 (2): 21–32.

Iganski, P. (2002) (ed.) *The Hate Debate*. London: Profile Books Ltd.

Shorter-Gooden, K. (2004) 'Multiple Resistance Strategies: how African American women cope with racism and sexism' *Journal of Black Psychology* Vol. 30 (3): 406–425.

Sibbitt, R. (1997) *The Perpetrators of Racial Harassment*. London: Home Office.

Yarrow, S. (2005) *The Experiences of Young Black Men as Victims of Crime*. London: Office for Criminal Justice Reform.

9

Racist violence in Europe: challenges for official data collection

by Jo Goodey

Abstract

This article critically examines official data collection on racist violence in European Union [EU] Member States. Academic and legal definitions of "racist violence" are offered, in a European-wide context, before the article explores the current state of data collection on "racist violence", both official and unofficial, in the European Union. Drawing on evidence reported by the European Monitoring Centre on Racism and Xenophobia [EUMC], the article presents a stark introduction to the limitations of current official criminal justice data collection practices in EU Member States. In contrast with most Member States, the UK is held up in the article as an example of good official data collection on racist violence (although, even in this case, there is still scope for refinements to be made to data collection practices). Towards the end, the article looks at the challenges for official data collection on racist violence across the EU, such as different data collection traditions and legislative barriers. In response, the article introduces a range of recommendations to meet the challenge for effective data collection on racist violence in the EU.

Introduction

'Racism' and 'racist violence' are universally condemned by all European governments, yet legal definitions and criminal justice responses to racist violence vary greatly between countries. As a reflection of this, official criminal justice data collection on racist violence is either absent or inadequate in most European countries, and, where data do exist, are not directly comparable between countries as different recording practices are used. Given the absence of comprehensive, publicly available and comparable data on racist crime and violence in much of the EU, this article focuses on the need for improvements to be made in official data collection in this area. The article draws on evidence presented by the European Monitoring Centre on Racism and Xenophobia [EUMC], which became the European Union Agency for Fundamental Rights on 1 March, 2007 [FRA], in its comparative overviews of official data collection on racist violence in [EU] Member States[1], and critiques existing data collection for failing to adequately monitor and respond to racist violence. The barriers that are in place against effective data collection on racist violence are introduced in the article, and suggestions are made towards the end about how they can be challenged. The article refers extensively to data collection practices in England and Wales as, at present, these offer a number of 'best practice' examples.

Defining and interpreting manifestations of 'racist violence'

Racist violence, like racism, has no universal definition in law, nor is there any consensus from sociology as to what the term encompasses. Herein lies the first stumbling block when trying to describe and analyse the manifestation of 'racist violence' in different countries. In the EU, the absence of a common definition and response to racist violence is a reflection of Europe's diverse legal and social cultures. World War II has also had a lasting impact on how certain European countries, such as Germany and Austria, define and approach the problem of 'racism' and racist violence. Yet, given the absence of a universal response to and definition of racist violence, it is useful to attempt to outline what is understood and encompassed by the term racist violence before we can begin to explore the nature and extent of racist violence in the EU.

Academic readings of racist violence

Racist violence, like violence, encompasses anything on a continuum from verbal aggression and damage to property, through to murder and genocide (Bowling and Phillips 2002, p. 39). Racist violence is not only manifested as brutal violent acts against the individual, but emerges in the form of everyday occurrences, which have the potential for violence, and which have a steady and negative impact on vulnerable individuals and communities. Racist violence can be interpreted in any number of ways according to 'who' is doing the interpreting – victim, offender, witness, police, prosecutor, male or female, 'black' or 'white' (Johnson 1998). In other words, no two people, and currently no two European jurisdictions, define and respond to racist violence in the same way. For example, while Witte (1996) defines racist violence as 'the (threat of) violence in which victims are "selected" not in their capacities as individuals, but as representatives of imagined minority communities based on phenotypical characteristics, and/or religious, national or cultural origin' (Witte 1996, p.11) – so interpreting racist violence from the standpoint of violent racist offenders – Bowling (1998) employs the various terms adopted by different British governmental and non-governmental agencies in an effort to expose the place and meaning of racist violence for each agency.

Theories of racist offending and violence, like theories of crime, draw on a range of explanatory variables (Blee 2005); for example, legal scholars tend to focus on individual incidents and offenders' motives, while twentieth-century historians have drawn on Germany's economic collapse when seeking to explain the rise of National Socialism. At a basic level, three strands for describing and analysing racist crime and violence can be tentatively identified; namely (EUMC 2005, pp.187–193 (print version)):

1   meta explanations, which draw on dominant theoretical explanations for offending, and adopt these theories to explain violent racist offending;
2   meso explanations, which can be read as contextual readings of why racist violence occurs among certain groups and in certain settings; and
3   micro explanations, which are explanations for violent racist offending that rest with the individual.

As an illustration, meta explanations for racist hostility are often based on (economic) competition theory (Blalock 1967), which suggests that the most economically marginalized members of society feel threatened by real or perceived competition for scarce resources (Olzak 1990), such as welfare benefits, from 'outsiders'. Competition theory refers also to non-economic competition, both real and perceived, for other 'resources' – such as political and cultural competition. In a similar vein, the size of a country's minority or incoming immigrant population is often held to be a trigger for racism and racist violence. However, the explanatory value of theories that are embedded in the idea of competition falls somewhat short when we consider that racist violence emerges in times of economic prosperity and political stability, and when immigrant populations are not increasing or changing their profiles (Goldhagen 1997). At the same time, there is no straightforward connection between economic, political and social conditions 'in practice' and how people subjectively experience and interpret these conditions. In this regard, although we can be told that the economy is booming and people's 'quality of life' is improving, the individual or the group may experience or interpret these conditions differently. In turn, more abstract concerns about insecurity, risk and threat, which are difficult to measure and are not necessarily related to competition, may play equally into the hands of racist sentiments. Having said this, there is no neat correlation between what people think and say, and what they actually do. In other words, insecurity and resentment against 'outsiders' does not necessarily evolve into violent racist action.

Alongside broad meta explanations for the emergence of racist hostilities, meso explanations take elements of meta explanations and relate them to localised events or contexts that act as triggers for racism and violent racist acts – from localized 'race' riots to countrywide inter-ethnic hostilities (Tilly 2003). In this regard, violent racist acts are contextualized in time and place, and are interpreted with respect to specific localized conditions (Chakraborti and Garland 2004). Inter-community hostilities at the local level often take place against the backdrop of international hostilities that are based on ethnic and religious differences (here one thinks of the on-going Israel-Palestine conflict and the fallout from 9/11), and provide the context in which to understand localized racism and violent racist acts. Knowing the history and culture of local communities, with respect to periods of inter-community conflict and intolerance, can help to make sense of, but not condone, violent racist acts in certain settings (Webster 1997; Ray and Reed 2005; Wells and Watson 2005).

Finally, micro explanations of racist violence focus on offenders' characteristics or personality as an explanation for racist ideas, behaviour and offending. While explanations that focus on individual pathologies are currently discredited, some scholars have resurrected this research in another direction by adopting a social-psychological approach for understanding the manifestation of racist riots (Horowitz 2001), or by looking at the inter-linkages between social theory and psychoanalysis when attempting to understand racism and 'fear' related to 'otherness' (Clarke 2003). Other micro readings of racist violence explore individuals' social-economic biographies (Blee 2002) and current circumstances, with references again to meta theories, as explanatory backdrops for racist offending (Ray, Smith and Wastell 2003)[2]. Still other micro-level analyses of racist violence can draw on social constructivism to examine the meanings – including the racist meanings – that individuals attach to the social world and 'others'; meanings which are informed by the cultural contexts they inhabit (Gergen and Gergen 2003). In turn, seemingly mundane but nonetheless important factors should not be overlooked when seeking to explain violent racism as something that is not just the prerogative of extremists. For example, over-consumption of alcohol or the number of young males in a local population are just two factors that correlate with violent offending, which can include racist violence.

Where sociology and criminology are unable to offer universal definitions and explanations for racist violence, it could be expected that the law, which in its most abstract is constructed as a neutral 'science', might offer a definition of racist violence that can be shared between countries. Yet, examining evidence from different European countries, it is clear that the law is often no better positioned than sociology to respond to the problem of racist violence.

Working legal definitions of racist violence

Most European jurisdictions have no specific legal definition of racist violence. Because of this, there is no common working legal definition of racist violence or racist crime in Europe. The absence of a common definition reflects the diverse legal and criminal justice cultures that exist in Europe, which, in turn, reflects each country's political, social, economic and cultural heritage. However, on 19 April 2007, after six years of discussion, EU justice and interior ministers have finally agreed to EU-wide legislation to fight racism and xenophobia in the form of the Council Framework Decision on Combating Racism and Xenophobia.[3] The Framework Decision calls on Member States to punish the incitement of violence or hate based on a person's or group's race, colour, religion, descent or ethnic origin; but it only goes so far towards legislative 'harmonization' in the EU as it includes a number of opt-out clauses for Member States – e.g. with respect to Holocaust denial.

A range of legislative responses to racism, xenophobia and discrimination, which incorporate elements of racist violence, can be identified in European jurisdictions; from laws which set out to protect the Constitution, and which are adopted in an effort to prohibit the activities of extremist political groups (typically in those European countries with a National Socialist/fascist past), through to broad-based hate crime legislation that encompasses a range of harms against the individual or the group to which the individual belongs, or is perceived to belong (according to race, ethnicity and religion, as well as gender, sexuality and disability). While different legal options are in place to punish a range of racist offences, violent racist crime consistently goes unpunished.

In many European Union jurisdictions the police (and prosecutors) are not given the legal means or the incentive, where the legal means exists, to proactively record crimes as *racist*, including violent crimes, outside of a narrow range of crimes that are pre-defined as 'racist' or 'anti-Semitic', such as racist and anti-Semitic propaganda by banned political parties. As a result, 'everyday' violent racism, if it is reported and prosecution is pursued, is usually dealt with as violent crime, rather than as violent *racist* crime. In turn, where 'racist motivation' is recognized in law, and where a charge of 'racist motivation' is pursued, the onus in many European jurisdictions is on the victim to prove the defendant's racist motivation, rather than for the defendant to disprove it where a victim or third party alleges it. Because of this onus of proof, coupled with the absence of legislative and practical possibilities for recognizing, specifically, 'racist' crimes, the reality of getting a successful conviction for a *racist* offence is largely impossible or rare.

Within the European Union, the working definition of a racist incident in England and Wales is, currently, the most generously defined. This definition, which was forwarded in the MacPherson Report into the investigation of the death of Stephen Lawrence, states that a 'racist incident' is 'any incident, which is perceived to be racist by the victim, or any other person'[4]. Although it is easier to generously define a racist 'incident' than a racist 'crime', which has more stringent criteria for admissibility of evidence, the victim-centred interpretation of a racist incident, as used in England and Wales, means that more potentially racist incidents are being captured at the initial reporting stage than would be the case if police-centred interpretations were relied on. However, there is some indication that the purpose for which this generous working definition was intended – to identify incidents of racist crime against vulnerable ethnic minority groups in society – is being 'misused' as a significant number of reports of racist victimization emanate from the majority white population. Yet, given that many of these reported incidents go on to be recorded as 'crimes' by the police would appear to vindicate the suggestion that the system is being misused.

In comparison, other EU Member States do not have the same generous recording *practices* from which to identify and tackle a range of racially and religiously aggravated (violent) criminal offences. However, what a number of Member States do have in place, and which is not at the forefront of legislation in England and Wales, are legal responses that specifically tackle the actions of extreme right-wing political parties and neo-Nazi/fascist movements. As a reflection of these different approaches, between broad-based applications of legislation relating to racist and religiously aggravated crime and a more narrowly defined focus on extremism, data collection on racist violence and related offences, as this article will show, is more extensive in the UK than in other European Member States. However, as some critics have pointed out (MacNamara 2003; Hall 2005), generous application of laws can also serve to strain limited police resources as law enforcement agencies are instructed to respond equally, initially, to all public reports of racist incidents. This may have the unintended impact of diluting the meaning of a 'racist' incident as too many petty offences are encompassed within a 'catch-all' system. To this end, although the 'racist incident' recording mechanism in England and Wales presents a 'best practice' example in its generous application, there is perhaps scope for re-considering its long-term application in practice with respect to its impact on criminal justice resources *and* for its effectiveness as a tool for monitoring and responding to racist crime.

Sources of information on racist violence

Our knowledge about the extent and nature of racist violence is determined by available data. As the above illustrates, legislative parameters, working criminal justice definitions, and application of the law in practice sets the stage for what can be collected on racist violence by official agencies. This article focuses its critique on official data collection mechanisms, but apart from official data sources there exists a range of unofficial sources that can supply information, and sometimes data, about racist crime and violence; for example: unofficial data and reports from non-governmental organizations (NGOs), such as the European Network Against Racism [ENAR], along with academic researchers. To this one can add the work of inter-governmental organizations such as the Council of Europe's European Commission against Racism and Intolerance [ECRI], the European Union's Monitoring Centre on Racism and Xenophobia [EUMC]: and now the FRA and the Organisation for Security and Cooperation in Europe [OSCE] through its Office for Democratic Institutions and Human Rights [ODIHR]. In turn, sporadic media reports on racist violence, which tend to focus on particularly violent incidents or significant incidents involving a number of people, offer the only widely available source of public information on manifestations of racist crime in a number of countries.

Reports by EUMC[5] provide an important source of information in the EU on racist crime in Member States. What is abundantly clear from the EUMC's work is that no two Member States have the same mechanisms in place to collect official data on racist crime and violence. Not only are different government institutions given the task of data collection, but what they collect and, most importantly, the volume and quality of their data collection differs enormously. Because of this, no two Member States produce data on racist violence that are directly comparable.

This state of affairs largely reflects differences in the legislative approach to racist crime and associated activities in the Member States, and the emphasis that is given over in practice to recording racist crimes or incidents. As an illustration: in The Netherlands the National Discrimination Expertise Centre focuses on 'offences' related to 'discrimination', with this approach modelled on the UN Convention on the Elimination of all Forms of Racial Discrimination. In comparison, in Austria, the Ministry of Interior and the Ministry of Justice focus their official data collection mechanisms on prohibited extremist acts or acts that threaten the constitution. In France, the Ministry of the Interior provides a breakdown of 'threats' and 'acts' that are racist, xenophobic and anti-Semitic in nature. In the UK, the Home Office publishes information on racist and religiously aggravated incidents and, in turn, crimes (Home Office 2006). In comparison, some EU countries publish limited information on a handful of court cases under different offence categories. While, in Cyprus, Greece, Italy, Malta, Portugal and Spain there has not been any systematic annual official data collection on racist crime and violence, or associated activities (although data are, on occasion, sporadically collected and made public).

Where official data sources on racist violence are inadequate, one might expect that non-governmental agencies and research institutions fill this knowledge gap. However, according to the EUMC's 2005 report on racist violence in the 'old' fifteen EU Member States[6], where official data on racist violence are absent or lacking in quality, it is often the case that unofficial research on racist violence is also absent or lacking. So, where there is a tradition of official data collection on racist crime and violence in, for example, Germany and the UK, there is also a range of unofficial research and data collection. In comparison, in Italy and Malta, for example, where official data are inadequate, there is also a limited range of unofficial data sources when compared with other Member States.

The explanation for the above lies in a number of factors, chief among which is, first, whether racist violence and crime is focused on as a social problem in each Member State and, second, the extent to which each country has a tradition of social science data collection. Where governments publicly recognize the problem of racist crime and violence, and invest efforts into identifying and effectively responding to it, a climate is created for other non-governmental institutions to actively research racist crime and violence. At the same time, Member States with a strong tradition of social science research and data collection appear more readily placed to collect information on a range of social phenomenon, including racist violence. Other factors add to the degree of attention given over to racist crime and violence in each Member State, such as the political representation and 'voice' of ethnic minority and immigrant groups, or the focus of media attention on racist crime and violence as a problem.

Finally, where legislation and official mechanisms are in place that, theoretically, allow for data collection on racist crime and violence, there is no guarantee that the public will use these mechanisms to register incidents. The majority of racist violence, as 'everyday' incidents which are not the work of extremists, is brought to police attention by the public and not through police intelligence work. If the public are unwilling to report racist victimization to the police, for a variety of reasons including the belief that the police will not respond to racist crime seriously, the police are unable to record incidents. In turn, victims of racist victimization will see the police as disinterested in racist crime because of their failure to record incidents. As a result, under-reporting and under-recording are part of a cyclical relationship that underestimates the 'true' extent of racist crime. In comparison, reporting to the police can serve to enhance police recording practices, which facilitates the public perception that the police are taking racist victimization seriously and, hence, may encourage more people to report racist incidents. In countries with a victim-centred and service oriented approach to policing, where people are encouraged to report to the police, one can expect to find higher recorded figures for racist crime. With this in mind, the next section looks at what official sources currently tell us about the extent and nature of racist crime and violence in EU Member States.

The extent and nature of racist crime and violence

Official data on racist crime and violence

Looking at the highest official figures for 'racist crime' in 2005 in each of the EU's twenty-five Member States, (N.B. – this article was written prior to the accession of Bulgaria and Romania to the EU in January 2007), where this information is available, a striking pattern emerges (FRA online InfoBase[7]). For example, while the Home Office recorded 57,902 racist incidents and 37,028 racially or religiously motivated crimes for England and Wales in the twelve-month period 2004–05, and Germany, with the next highest figures, recorded a total of 15,914 crimes under the category 'politically motivated – right wing', France recorded a total of only 974 racist, xenophobic and anti-Semitic acts and threats in 2005. In comparison, in 2005, there was no comprehensive, publicly available criminal justice data on racist violence and crime in the following Member States – Cyprus, Greece, Italy, Malta, Portugal and Spain. In turn, other Member States only record and prosecute a very limited number of cases; for example, Hungary recorded eleven cases in 2005 and Slovenia eight cases.

Looking at available data it must be remembered that each Member State has a very different recording system in place. Different labels are assigned to racist acts, which largely reflects the way in which each legal system defines a racist act, and the point at which each act is counted in relation to each stage of the criminal justice system. For example, racist incidents, which are recorded in England and Wales, count the point at which the public reports an act as racist, while racist crimes count the point at which the criminal justice system recognizes a racist incident as a crime, and is the normal starting point for recording in other jurisdictions. Most Member States only divulge limited data that relate to certain points in time at which counting takes place. Because of this, figures do not reveal the attrition rate between public reporting of racist acts, police recording of incidents as crimes, and prosecution and sentencing disposals. As a result, no two countries have directly comparable data.

Although some might argue that it is meaningless to compare different data sources when trying to measure the extent of racist violence in the EU, comparison of official data collection *mechanisms* is a useful way of critiquing the effectiveness of each mechanism as a tool for gathering information on and prosecuting racist offences. In this regard, those Member States with high recorded levels of racist crimes and violence can be assessed as having effective data collection mechanisms, whereas those Member States with extremely low or non-existent data can be assessed as having ineffective data collection mechanisms. What is abundantly clear, when looking at available information (EUMC, Annual Report 2006), is that information about racist crime, and associated activities, is not evenly spread across the European

Union, and that most Member States are failing to collect data. The limited research evidence from non-criminal justice sources, where it exists, indicates that official data collection on racist violence severely underestimates its extent. In England and Wales the government's British Crime Survey [BCS], with its booster sample of ethnic minorities, currently presents the richest alternative data source in the EU, at the level of the individual Member State, on minorities' experiences as victims of crime; which estimated, for the period 2002–2003, that the number of racially motivated incidents in England and Wales was 206,000. In comparison with official criminal justice data, the British Crime Survey shows that official records might be underestimating the real extent of racially motivated incidents by a factor of four to eight times. If we accept that England and Wales are not exceptional in their experiences of racist crime and violence, then this critique can be more strongly levelled at other Member States where there appears to be gross under-recording of racist crimes.

Trends in racist violence

As illustrated, direct comparison of data between Member States is a dangerous exercise if we want to know the true extent of racist crime. A more meaningful exercise is to compare data for a single country over time. Providing that data collection mechanisms do not change within a given period, direct comparison of figures for individual countries allows us to look at trends in reports and records of racist crime.

On the basis of official criminal justice data sources for the period 2000–2005, the FRA notes that only eleven of the EU25 produced robust enough data for each of these years allowing for a comparison of trends (FRA online InfoBase). Drawing on FRA produced data, which calculates a mean average of year-by-year percentage changes in recorded figures, it can be seen that eight of the eleven Member States experienced an overall upward trend in recorded racist crime in the period 2000–2005; namely: Denmark, Germany, France, Ireland, Poland, Slovakia, Finland and the UK (referring to data for England and Wales only). In comparison, three Member States – Czech Republic, Austria and Sweden – showed a downward trend; with Austria's downward trend being extremely slight (minus 0.2 per cent).

Looking at trends in official data for each country tells us something about whether there is an actual increase or decrease in reported or recorded racist incidents. However, significant changes in recorded crime should be interpreted cautiously. Member States with consistently low absolute recorded figures, such as Denmark and Ireland, can report dramatic percentage changes on the basis of very few numbers (respectively, plus 70.9 per cent and plus 21.2 per cent in the period 2000–2005; FRA online InfoBase). In the same way, Member States with large absolute recorded figures, such as England and Wales, can report relatively minor percentage changes on the basis of thousands of reports (plus 4.2 per cent, 2000–2005; FRA online InfoBase). Also, significant changes in trend patterns can reflect changes to the law and corresponding recording practices. For example, Germany introduced a new registration system in January 2001 – the Criminal Investigation Registration System: Politically Motivated Criminality [KPMD-PMK]. As a result, data prior to 2001 cannot be compared with data from 2001 onwards. Similarly, the appointment of a new Minister of Interior or a new chief of police may contribute to changes in recording practices, which makes it important to have a full picture of political and social changes in a country when seeking to analyse trends in official data.

At the same time, when trying to explain racist violence in a European context, incidents often increase and decrease against certain targets and communities in tandem with notable events, both at home and abroad, that act as a catalyst for racist violence and inter-ethnic conflict. In France, according to the EUMC report on manifestations of anti-Semitism (EUMC 2003), there was a significant increase in anti-Semitic violence and threats in 2002 (of the 1,317 racist, xenophobic and anti-Semitic threats and acts reported in 2002, over 900 were anti-Semitic) compared with the same period in 2001, which directly corresponded with a peak in heightened tensions between Israel and Palestine in April 2002.

The failure to monitor racist violence

Although many Member States have official mechanisms in place that, in theory, could collect data on racist crime, it is apparent that these mechanisms are failing at a number of levels to do just this. The limits of the law, both on paper and in its application, which in turn is reflected by policing and criminal justice cultures that do not prioritize racist violence and its victims, serves to hinder comprehensive and effective data collection.

A narrow focus on extremism?

Member States can claim that they have mechanisms in place to record racist violence and associated criminal activities, but on closer inspection it is apparent that these systems are often wanting in practice because (a) their data collection is limited and (b) it is often focused on certain banned activities or groups – as defined narrowly in law. For example, reflecting the legacy of the Holocaust, Austria and Germany understandably concentrate a large part of their policing efforts on the activities of the extreme right, as do, to a lesser extent, Denmark, Italy and Sweden (although Italy does not publish official data on an annual basis). As a result, it is something of a self-fulfilling exercise that in Austria and Germany racist activities are found to be the domain of the extreme right. In comparison, the UK does not focus its policing activities on the extreme right, but instead has adopted a wide-ranging working definition of a racist incident that is reflected by generous data collection practices. Although it may be the case that the extreme right are responsible for the bulk of racist, xenophobic and anti-Semitic offences in those countries that concentrate their policing efforts on extremist activities, this cannot be definitively accepted on the evidence of highly subjective police data alone (Blee 2005).

Like the media, research and official data collection on racist violence in a number of Member States is often focused on the most serious events, and is particularly attracted to the activities of right-wing extremists (Virtanen 2002). As a reflection of this, agencies and reporting watchdogs, like the FRA, are often asked to comment on whether racist crime by right-wing extremists is increasing or decreasing. While these groups undoubtedly represent a significant problem in many countries, and particularly in those European countries that have a National Socialist past, they do not represent the full spectrum of racist violence as it is perpetrated and as it is experienced by victims (EUMC 2005, pp.175–176, print version).

Focusing on victims

If we accept that the majority of ordinary crime is not detected by police-led intelligence work, then we have to acknowledge that the public play an essential role in reporting crime and assisting the police with their investigations. If we also accept that a significant percentage of racist crime is not committed by extremists, and is manifested often as low-level incidents, such as damage to property, then the role of victims in reporting racist incidents, which cannot be identified by police-led intelligence, is apparent. However, given that police forces are reliant on victims to report crime, this knowledge is obviously not enough to instil a sea-change towards victim-centred policing, let alone victim-centred policing in the area of racist crime and violence.

Somewhat controversially, it can be suggested that the narrow focus on right-wing extremism by some European police forces, or the complete absence of any official data collection on racist crime in some countries, is, perhaps, as much to do with predominant ideas about appropriate police work (Walklate 1995; Rowe 2004; Oakley (EUMC) 2005) as it is to do with the present day activities of extremists or the needs of victims. Certain crimes, such as violence against women, have traditionally not been seen as appropriate and important areas for police work. Ordinary and everyday racist violence, from harassment to graffiti, has also suffered from a low profile image in policing work. However, in Britain, violence against women and racist violence have increasingly come to play a prominent role in police work. These changes can be attributed to a number of factors that coalesced in 1980s and 1990s Britain, chief among which was the rise of victim-centred policing and criminal justice (Crawford and Goodey 2000; Rock 2004; Goodey 2005), and, with respect to racist crime and violence, the fallout from the MacPherson Report into the investigation of the death of Stephen Lawrence.

Areas of crime that were traditionally not thought of as part of police work, such as domestic violence, gradually moved centre-stage as priority areas for policing in 1990s Britain. As a reflection of this rise in victim-centred justice, alongside calls for equal justice from minority ethnic communities, racist crime and violence has also moved closer to the centre of policing work in the UK. However, it was the MacPherson Report into police mismanagement of the investigation into the death of Afro-Caribbean teenager Stephen Lawrence, with its commentary about 'institutional racism', which forced the Metropolitan Police to adopt radical changes in their response to reports of racist crime and violence.

Data collection and ethnic classification

At the same time as victims of crime and victims of racist crime were afforded increasing recognition in Britain, there was a corresponding change in the use of ethnic categories for statistical purposes. To this end, it should be remembered that an 'ethnic' question was only inserted in the UK census in 1991, which until then had collected information about parents' country of birth (Simon 2004). With the introduction of ethnic categorization in the UK census, government departments, from education through to employment, have gradually adopted ethnic monitoring as a means for quantifying instances of discrimination, and have been aided in this with the introduction of new anti-discrimination legislation – most notably the Race Relations Act 2000. Data collection on ethnicity has also infiltrated policing practices, and has been prioritized by successive governments in response to calls for monitoring police stop and search practices, or 'ethnic profiling' (Rowe 2004; Goodey 2006).

While the UK closely resembles the US in its categorization of people according to their ethnicity, in comparison, most European countries do not collect data on ethnicity. The reasons for this are myriad, but are primarily related to two factors; namely: a desire to avoid the misuse of ethnic data, and cultural precedents about citizenship. It is usually said that the sinister uses to which ethnic data were put under National Socialism are a reminder to Member States, which were either part of the Nazi regime or under its control, not to collect ethnic data. Resistance to ethnic monitoring also reflects deeply held ideas about citizenship, and what it means to be, for example, 'Austrian', or 'German', or 'French'. In the case of France, ethnic classification is prohibited on the grounds that French citizens, regardless of their 'ethnicity' or 'race', are all equal before the law. In this context, classification on the basis of ethnicity is, in itself, seen as a discriminatory practice that can exacerbate negative references to differences between citizens.

Alongside these arguments against ethnic classification, it should not be forgotten that while most European countries do *not* collect data on ethnicity, most *do* collect comprehensive data on people's nationality, country of birth, parents' country of birth and/or spoken languages. And all Member States keep registers on non-citizens according to their nationality. In other words, a form of 'ethnic' monitoring by proxy currently exists in the EU. Examples in support of ethnic categorization can also be drawn from other non-EU countries where ethnic or racial data collection was used in the past for purposes of segregation, such as the United States, but where it is now routinely collected in an effort to identify continuing discrimination and as a gesture to right the wrongs of the past (Simon 2004). Similarly, it can be readily suggested that the principle of equality before the law cannot be established without the availability of evidence that can confirm or refute whether the law is actually working equitably in practice. In this case, statistical data collection on ethnicity is a means by which laws can be effectively tested.

Strict European laws on personal data protection (Goldston 2001), such as the Council of the European Union's 1995 Directive on Data Protection, are often cited as the legal basis for *not* collecting data on ethnicity – including data on criminal justice, victimization and ethnicity. However, while data protection laws *do* prohibit the identification of *individuals* on the basis of their ethnicity (without their prior consent) they do *not* prohibit the collection of anonymous ethnic data for the purposes of statistical research. In support of statistical data collection on ethnicity, the European Community's Racial Equality Directive (2000/43/EC) and its Employment Equality Directive (2000/78/EC) were followed in the same year by a Community Action Programme with the aim of fighting discrimination on the grounds of, among other things, 'racial or ethnic origin, religion or beliefs'. At the heart of the Programme was the desire to increase understanding of discriminatory practices, and to do this by supporting the development of methodologies and indicators to assess the effectiveness of anti-discrimination policy and practice. In other words, the Programme advocated measurement of discriminatory practices in public services through the collection of appropriate statistics, including statistics that are able to identify ethnicity.

Remedying the problem of inadequate data collection

If European governments are serious in their desire to challenge racist crime and violence, mechanisms should be put in place to monitor the extent and nature of these crimes. Only with comprehensive data collection can Member States gain a more accurate picture of the extent and nature of racist victimization as it impacts on victims. If we accept that policing is only as good as its intelligence sources, then it is apparent that the policing of racist crime and violence is not a priority in most Member States and is failing to meet the needs of victims.

Legal reform and data collection

One approach for remedying the current problems of inadequate and non-comparable data collection on racist violence in the EU is to promote legislative and criminal justice reform at the level of the EU. The Commission's Framework Decision on Combating Racism and Xenophobia has put the first (limited) EU-wide legislation in place for punishing racist and xenophobic crime as criminal offences. But for the effectiveness of this legislation to be measured in practice, with respect to its impact on vulnerable minority ethnic groups, the law on ethnic data collection would have to be reformed in many Member States, which, as illustrated, is a contentious area.

If EU-wide legislative reform is not forthcoming, then legislative reform at the level of individual Member States is another option to pursue. Individual Member States can learn from each others' legislation in areas related to racist crime and violence, and data collection. But, rather than impose current 'best practice' examples from England and Wales, which reflect a particular Anglo-Saxon and common law approach to ethnic monitoring and criminal justice, Member States with similar legal cultures should be 'matched' when suggesting lessons for reform. Although knowledge and practical know-how about 'good practices' in jurisdictions with very different legal and criminal justice cultures is always useful, reform is more likely to occur if Member States do not feel that a particular model is being imposed on them, and if they are able to gain insights from similarly matched legal cultures that face similar challenges.

Legal reform can only improve data collection on racist violence if legislation is accompanied by practice initiatives. Mechanisms need to be established at the level of individual countries, and regions within countries, that ensure that the police and other agencies, such as examining magistrates, are aware of legislative change and have the necessary resources to hand to implement the law, which, ultimately, should be reflected in improved data collection. Herein, the practical needs of agencies and victims should be taken into account when establishing criteria for 'good practice' in data collection. In turn, any legislative and criminal justice reforms in the area of racist crime and violence, and corresponding data collection, need to be rigorously followed up to ensure that initiatives are working in practice.

Yet suggestions 'on paper' for improving criminal justice data collection mechanisms for recording and responding to crime, in general, and racist crime, in particular, are difficult to achieve in practice. As Jenness and Grattet (2005) point out in their article about the practical application of hate crime legislation by the Californian police, the role of the 'law-in-between' – that is, police organizational cultures and structures – is crucial in determining if and how legislative reform is applied by officers on the ground. Herein, Jenness and Grattet highlight the significant role that environmental factors play in influencing police practice with respect to hate crime enforcement; namely, the important role of communities and victim lobby groups. This point is taken up in the EUMC's report on Policing Racist Crime and Violence (2005) with respect to the role that civil society and dedicated NGO groups can play in informing and working with the police to combat the problem of racist crime.

Research initiatives and data collection

Alongside reforms to the criminal law and criminal justice practice, governments should also explore the possibility of data collection on racist violence through other channels. To this end, crime or victim surveys on ethnic minorities and immigrants' experiences of criminal victimization could offer an alternative cross-check to official data collection on racist crime and violence. As illustrated by the British Crime Survey, a great proportion of criminal victimization, against both the main population and ethnic minorities, goes unreported. As a result, even the most effective official data collection mechanisms are unable to capture the 'true' extent of criminal victimization. Combined knowledge from official data collection mechanisms and crime survey data can reveal whether policing resources are correctly placed to meet the challenges of racist violence and the particular needs of its victims. To this end, the EUMC (now the FRA) launched a pilot victim survey in 2006 to explore selected ethnic minorities' experiences of criminal victimization and policing in six EU Member States.

In addition to quantitative victim survey data collection, qualitative academic and NGO research should be promoted and, importantly, funded by governments. Where quantitative victim surveys can paint a broad picture of the extent and nature of crime and racist crime against minorities, qualitative research can provide detailed information about the characteristics of both victims and offenders, and can look in detail at the impact of racist crime on individuals and communities. In-depth qualitative research with victims and offenders can also play a critical role in assessing whether policies are having their desired impact. Victim-centred research, of both a quantitative and qualitative nature, can explore any differences between victims' expressed and real needs, and the kind of service they are offered in practice by the police, other criminal justice agencies, and victim support agencies (where these exist).

Finally, the role of the Ombudsman and other national observatories should not be overlooked when exploring ways in which to improve data collection on and responses to racist crime and violence. In many Member States where official criminal justice data collection on racist violence is lacking or absent, the Ombudsman and other national observatories can play an important role in collecting complaints and information about racist incidents. And, as agencies that have a critical role to play in monitoring and responding to complaints against government action or inaction, the Ombudsman should be supported in its role as an additional source of information on racist incidents.

End comment

This article has addressed some of the challenges faced by official data collection on racist crime and violence in the EU; challenges that are reflected in the inadequacy of many Member States' policing responses to racist violence and crime (Oakley (EUMC) 2005). It is also apparent, when looking at existing mechanisms for recording and responding to racist violence and crime in the EU, that many of the 'old' EU Member States are no better placed to manage the problem of racist crime than the 'new' Member States that joined the EU in 2004.

The evidence referred to in this article paints a shocking picture of the inadequate mechanisms for data collection on racist crime and violence in most Member States. The message that this inadvertently promotes is that racist crime and violence is not considered to be a priority issue for policing and criminal justice in most Member States. Although a legal basis exists in each Member State to punish racist crime, either under special laws or within the framework of the criminal law, it is apparent that the law 'in the books' is not reflected in the application of the law in practice.

Until there is the political will to recognize racist crime and violence as a serious social problem, Member States will continue to neglect data collection in this area. Current EU legislation can only go so far in promoting reform at the level of individual Member States. The example of EU legislation on data protection illustrates how well-intentioned laws, which can be used to collect anonymous data on ethnicity, are subject to re-interpretation by individual Member States. Arguably, only when victim-centred criminal justice reforms are prioritized in individual Member States, and when ethnic minorities and immigrants are recognized as victims of crime (as opposed to their populist portrayal as offenders), will effective counting mechanisms for racist violence be put in place throughout the EU.

Notes

1   EUMC (2005) 'Racist Violence in 15 EU Member States', Vienna: EUMC; also EUMC Annual Reports, chapters on racist violence and crime (http://fra.europa.eu).

2   Research by Ray, Smith and Wastell (2003) interviewed 64 violent racist offenders, as part of a national UK government-funded ESRC research programme on violence, and identified dominant characteristics that were shared between offenders – such as unemployment or employment in low-skilled, insecure and badly paid jobs; absence of qualifications;

and convictions for similar racist offences as well as convictions for other non-racist offences.

3   COM (2001) 664 final – Proposal for a Council Framework Decision on Combating Racism and Xenophobia.

4   MacPherson Report (1999), Chapter 47, paragraph 1.

5   The European Monitoring Centre on Racism and Xenophobia (EUMC) was an Agency of the European Union. Its mandate was to collect reliable, objective and comparative data on different manifestations of racism and xenophobia, including racist violence and crime. The work of the Centre was extended on 1 March 2007 as it was transformed into the FRA. The Agency has National Focal Points (NFPs) in each Member State, which are responsible for its core data collection tasks. The EUMC's 2005 report on Racist Violence in 15 EU Member States and the EUMC's/FRA's Annual Reports are based on data supplied by these NFPs.

6   EUMC (2005) 'Racist Violence in 15 EU Member States', Vienna: EUMC, pp. 168–170, print version (http://fra.europa.eu/factsheets).

7   FRA – See online InfoBase data on the racist violence 'European Union' – http://fra.europa.eu/factsheets

References

Blalock, H. 1967 *Toward a Theory of Minority Group Relations*, New York: Capricorn Books

Blee, K. 2002 *Inside Organized Racism: Women in the Hate Movement*, Berkely: University of California Press

Blee, K. 2005 'Racial Violence in the United States', *Ethnic and Racial Studies*, 28(4), pp. 559–619

Bowling, B. 1998 *Violent Racism*, Oxford: Clarendon Press

Bowling, B. and Phillips, C. 2002 *Racism, Crime and Justice*, London: Longman

Chakraborti, N. and Garland, J. (eds) 2004 *Rural Racism*, Cullompton: Willan

Clarke, S. 2003 *Social Theory, Psychoanalysis and Racism*, Basingstoke: Palgrave

Crawford, A. and Goodey, J. 2000 *Integrating a Victim Perspective within Criminal Justice: International debates*, Dartmouth: Ashgate

European Monitoring Centre on Racism and Xenophobia (EUMC) 2005 *Racist Violence in 15 EU Member States*, Vienna: EUMC

European Monitoring Centre on Racism and Xenophobia (EUMC) 2003 *Manifestations of Anti-Semitism in the EU 2002–2003*, Vienna: EUMC

Gergen, M. and Gergen, K. J. 2003 *Social Construction: A Reader*, London: Sage

Goldhagen, D. 1997 *Hitler's Willing Executioners: Ordinary Germans and the Holocaust*, New York: Vintage Books

Goldston, J. 2001 'Race and ethnic data: A missing resource in the fight against discrimination' in *Ethnic Monitoring and Data Protection: The European Context*, Budapest: Central European University Press, pp. 19–41

Goodey, J. 2006 'Ethnic Profiling, Criminal (In)Justice and Minority Populations', *Critical Criminology*, 14(3), pp. 207–212 who lead relatively crime-free lives which may, if they are unlucky be punctuated by becoming the victim of an assault, a burglary, a theft or some other crime'. This denies a reflection of the social reality of other forms of victimization. Even where conventional crime surveys have attempted to include these experiences, they have been confronted by the 'quantification' problem. For example, the British Crime Survey assigns a top value of 5 'discrete events' to recurrent crime in a victim's life. But this disconnects rather than connects a process.

Feminist research has been particularly critical of the traditional methodological approaches in crime surveys. Stanko (1985) argues that much of the violence against women is hidden from crime surveys, and suggests that the concept and reality of gender stratification has to be given credence to reveal its influence in women's lives. Many feminist writers (see Hall, 1985; Mama, 1990) have analyzed the reality of women's experiences through the formulation of focused questions which inquire into the range of male violence. Interestingly, the local crime surveys, initiated by the Middlesex Polytechnic criminologists, claim to recognize feminist criticisms and to have an approach which embraces the process experienced by the victims. But this apparent modification is negligible when we consider the status of racial harassment in their research. The criticisms of Sim et al. (1987) are relevant here. They suggest that the so-called 'realist criminology' under-pinning this survey approach conceptualizes 'crime (as) a particular problem in deprived inner-city areas; it is predominatly intra-class and intra-racial; it is a reflection of those most basic of capitalist values, individualism and acquisitiveness . . .'. One problem with this approach is the idea that if crime goes unchecked, it will divide the working class community, it thus assumes a notion of homogeneity which is unsullied by victimization inscribed in differences of gender, race, sexuality, employment and so on. Specific victimization experiences appear to have no categoric, experiential identity in the local crime survey. This ignores for example the historical and geographical experience of violation encountered by Asian and Black communities in their encounters with 'white Britain'. It is not surprising then that local crime surveys can so easily trivialize the crime of racial harassment.

The second Islington Crime Survey (Crawford et al., 1990), provides a typical example of this. The research presents a detailed analysis of crimes in the London Borough of Islington but singularly fails to examine the nature of racial harassment. Instead it contains a vague gesture to its presence through a reference to 'racial tension' which itself is subsumed under the general category 'public abuse'. In effect the survey marginalizes and obscures racial victimization. This is perhaps all the more surprising given the high number of racial incidents recorded by the police in Islington during 1987–1989. We cite this simply because of the trend, developed in the latter part of the 1980s, when policy makers became increasingly influenced by local crime surveys. Although these surveys purport to examine crime in general they invariably

Goodey, J. 2005 *Victims and Victimology: Research, Policy and Practice*, London: Longman

Hall, N. 2005 *Hate Crime*, Cullompton: Willan

Home Office 2006 *Statistics on Race and the Criminal Justice System* (2005), London: Home Office

Horowitz, D. 2001 *The Deadly Ethnic Riot*, London: University of California Press

Jenness, V. and Grattet, R. 2005 'The Law-In-Between: The Effects of Organizational Perviousness on the Policing of Hate Crimes', *Social Problems*, 52(3), pp. 337–359

Johnson, M. 1998 'Gender, race and rumors: re-examining the 1943 race riots', *Gender and History*, 10(2), pp. 252–277.

Macnamara, B.S. 2003 'New York's Hate Crimes Act of 2000: Problematic and Redundant Legislation Aimed at Subjective Motivation', *Albany Law Review*, Vol. 66, pp. 519–545

Macpherson, W. 1999 *The Stephen Lawrence Inquiry, report of an inquiry by Sir William MacPherson*, London: HM Stationery Office, Cm 4262-I

Oakley, R. (EUMC) 2005 *Policing Racist Crime and Violence*, Vienna: EUMC

Olzak, S. 1990 'The political context of competition: lynching and urban racial violence, 1882–1914', *Social Forces*, 69(2), pp. 395–421

Ray, L. and Reed, K. 2005 'Community, mobility and racism in a semi-rural area: Comparing minority experience in East Kent', *Ethnic and Racial Studies*, 28(2), pp. 212–234

Ray, L., Smith, D. and Wastell, L. 2003 'Understanding racist violence', in E.A. Stanko (ed.), *The Meanings of violence*, London: Routledge, pp. 112–129

Rock, P. 2004 *Constructing Victims, Rights: The Home Office, New Labour and Victims*, Oxford: Clarendon

Rowe, M. 2004 *Policing, Race and Racism*, Cullompton: Willan

Simon, P. 2004 *Comparative Study on the Collection of Data to Measure the Extent and Impact of Discrimination within the US, Canada, Australia, Great Britain and The Netherlands*, European Commission Directorate General for Employment, Social Affairs and Equal Opportunities; see: www.europa.eu.int/comm/employment _social/fundamental_rights/pdf/pubst/compstud04_en.pdf

Tilly, C. 2003 *The Politics of Collective Violence*, Cambridge: Cambridge University Press

Virtanen, T. (ed.) 2002 *Youth and Racist Violence in the Nordic Countries*, www.abo.fi/ ~ tivirtanen/(14/10/04)

Walklate, S. 1995 *Gender and Crime*, London: Prentice Hall

Webster, C. 1997 *Local Heroes: Racial Violence Among Asian and White Young People*, British Criminology Conference, Leicester, July 1997

Wells, K. and Watson, S. 2005 'A politics of resentment: shopkeepers in a London neighbourhood', *Ethnic and Racial Studies*, 28(2), pp. 261–277

Witte, R. 1996 *Racist Violence and the State*, London: Longman

10

Racial victimization: an experiential analysis

by Dhanwant K. Rai and Barnor Hesse

Many attacks on Asians and West Indians are attacks in the street when there is clearly no background of a prior argument or misunderstanding. In such incidents strangers may simply approach others and hit them, kick them, throw stones at them or even use knives and bottles to assault them.

(Walmsley, 1986)

research has only just begun to scratch the surface of the geography of racist violence and of organized resistance by black people.

(Jackson, 1987)

All victims have the right to specialist advice and support.

(Mawby and Gill, 1987)

Asian and Black people have persistently been the victims of racial harassment in Britain (see Gordon, 1990a). Despite this the nature and reality of that experience continues to be questioned and disputed. Particularly alarming is the fact that the varied and connected experiences of racial victimization are all too easily forgotten in the welter of competing policy discussions and debates. But as should be evident the experiences of racial harassment is uniquely traumatic principally because these apparently random incidents have a potentially life-long continuity. There is in other words little or no refuge from racial harassment where it has developed and become entrenched in the locations where people live, travel or work over a period of time. This is particularly so where it continues to go unchecked and when support for the victims is often no more than a 'good idea' in the minds of agencies best placed to help but who are ultimately ineffective. What does it mean to experience constant and recurrent verbal abuse, damage to property, personal injury and even the prospect of death as a result of racial harassment? What is racial victimization? These questions are not usually subject to

detailed analysis. But in the absence of posing these questions ishing the needs and rights of victims of racial harassment. In t discuss the limitations of crime surveys and limited insigh research and argue that the victims of racial harassment shou stood *as* victims of crime. This brings us into conflict with the cu 'victimology'. But it is within the context of social geography tha an experiential analysis of the dimensions involved in racial victin argue that the spread of racial harassment is also 'landmarked' *white territorialism* which in turn are a principal cause of incidents in particular places over time. We describe these experiences as *ra ization scenarios*. This is the second dimension to the patternin harassment. Finally we comment on the role of 'local' agencie response to victims of racial harassment, highlighting the impo victims rights.

Crime surveys, research and racial victimization

Crime surveys are now dominant in public policy analysis of general ization. Emerging in the 1960s in the USA and in the late 1970s in t initially they were designed to investigate and quantify the 'dark fig crime (i.e. the level of unrecorded crime). These surveys highlight the crimes that go unreported and why, the experiences of victimization ar fear of crime. In the UK the British (National) Crime Survey, conduct the Home Office was introduced in 1982 and followed up in 1984 and 1 During the 1980s criminologists associated with Middlesex Polytec pioneered various local crime surveys. However, while crime surveys provide firmer indications of the extent of particular crimes than is availa from officially recorded crime statistics either nationally, regionally or loca they incorporate a number of methodological problems which cast seve doubt on their capacity to 'measure' crime effectively. Walklate (1988:2 argues that crime surveys concentrate on conventional crime, that is, 'crin against the person (meaning for the most part "street crime") and crime against property'. Other criminal activity which results in personal dehuman ization (e.g. racial harassment, anti-Gay violence, domestic violence against women) is not usually considered in its own specific terms. Much of the reason for this lies in the incapacity of the crime survey to capture victimiza tion experiences which are processual, that is, regular occurrences; they simply cannot quantify this. The cyclical and multiple features of particular forms of victimization are therefore not reflected in crime surveys. Genn (1988:90–91) suggests, 'this failure stems primarily from the general orienta tion of victim surveys and partly from the inherent limitations of the social survey method as a means of understanding complex social processes'. The British Crime Survey, for example, conceptualizes crime as a discrete event. Implicit in this characterization, argues Genn 'is potential victims as people *invisibilize* the specific crime of racial harassment. The point is there is no such thing as crime in general and specific experiences of victimization, demand specific consideration.

Nevertheless it is possible to derive from a small range of research some valuable observations on racial victimization. First there is the *range of its incidence*. For example, the Newham Crime Survey (1987) emphasized its *persistent nature*. It described how 116 victims reported 1550 incidents of racial harassment over a period of one year. Secondly there is its *impact on people's living conditions*. For example, the CRE report (1987a) on racial violence and harassment in housing, *Living in Terror*, described how the plight of victims is exacerbated when their homes, the traditional place of safety, are transformed into dangerous places to be. Thirdly there is the *traumatic experience of reporting racial harassment*. This was considered by the Home Office (1989:89):

> We have frequently been told that some junior police officers do not appear to appreciate that racial motivation can transform an otherwise apparently trivial incident into something that is particularly distressing for the victim. We have also been told of (police) officers who cause offence by dismissing as unfounded the victim's assertion that the incident was racially motivated.

This undoubtedly contributes to the large reservoir of under-reporting we discussed in Chapter 4. Fourthly, there is the *recurrent experience of victimization*. For example, the 1988 British Crime Survey (Mayhew et al., 1989:27) commented:

> Afro-Caribbeans and Asians certainly reported many offences against them which they saw as having a racial basis. Being threatened because of race is very common; both Afro-Caribbeans and Asians were also often racially assaulted. For Asians, evidence or suspicion of a racial element in property offences is relatively frequent.

In addition the British Crime Survey noted that Asian and Afro-Caribbean people were more likely to become victims of crime than white people. Many of these experiences were conveyed in evidence to our Inquiry, however what became apparent through analysis is that the *experiential* content of racial harassment is patterned in social and *spatial* terms which mark it out as a distinct form of victimization. This has largely been ignored by victimological research which has so far failed to examine the extent of social variations in the experience of 'personalized' crime. In addition some of its more unhelpful concepts have filtered into the discourse of common sense which exerts its own influence on policy makers.

The problem of victimology

The study of victimology (i.e. the relationship between the victim and the offender) is a relatively recent development (Walklate, 1988). Its origins can be traced back to the works of Menderson and von Hentig in the 1940s in the USA (Maguire and Pointing, 1988). These early works were primarily concerned with understanding why crime was committed. Attempts to explain the offender's motives extended to understanding the behavioural relationships between the offender and the victim. The analytical question which arose was: 'how did the victim contribute to the enactment of crime?'. This meant, studying the victim's behaviour. A series of misguided investigations followed. One system for understanding the victim's behaviour, developed by von Hentig, was constructed from a typology of thirteen categories, based on psychological and sociological variables which could be related to situations or persons. These categories included: youth, women, the elderly, immigrants, the depressed. Although they were not based on empirical evidence, von Hentig argued that people from any of the categories were more likely to create circumstances in which victimization occurred. Mendelson however went beyond these descriptive categorizations. He created six classifications and assigned 'values' to them. He introduced the notion of 'guilt' and 'innocence' in terms of the victims own complicity in their victimization. This was developed even further in the idea of 'victim precipitation', formulated by Wolfgang in 1958. The dominant logic of these early researches suggested absurdly that victims produced their own victimization rather than the converse. This is a legacy of misreading that continues to influence contemporary policy thinking. For example Kelly and Radford (1987) argue that notions of 'victim precipitated rape' and 'victim blaming' are clearly evident in studies of sexual abuse and domestic violence. These concepts not only reflect commonly held assumptions about sexual violence against women (e.g. the idea that 'women ask for it'), they also fail to take account of women's accounts of their experiences. A similar misreading distorts the diagnosis of racial victimization. Although this has generally been overlooked in the victimological literature it is common for racial victimization to be blamed on the fact that 'they' are here or 'they' are taking our jobs or 'they' refuse to live like 'us'.

Another influential development in victimology is the 'life style' model. This places personal victimization within a framework of life style or 'daily routines' in order to understand recurrent patterns of victimization. The model suggests people live within constraints, 'structural' (e.g. housing conditions, employment, etc.) and 'characteristic' (e.g. age, race, sex, class, etc.). Through adaptation to these constraints they construct a daily routine to their lives. It is in living these routines that they expose themselves to various risks of being victimized. These range from the time that people spend in public areas to the geography they share with the offenders (see Walklate, op. cit.). Smith (1986) discusses how variables in the life style model may be used as indices of risk: for example the size of the household provides a measure of the extent to which guardians are available to protect person and property; unemployment status provides an indicator (timewise) of exposure to risk. Arguably, the life style model also locates responsibility (the degree may be variable) with the victims (i.e. expose themselves to 'crime situations'). Although it may not be possible to alter to a life style of 'no risk' to victimization (e.g. people have to go to work, do shopping, engage in other daily routine activities) the life style model has influenced policy makers current ideas on 'target' hardening. This suggests the more difficult a 'target' is made, the less likely it will risk victimization. The 'target' referred to is confusingly interchangeable between person and property. Thus advice is available in Metropolitan police literature on crime prevention, to keep doors and windows secured with effective bolts – to harden the 'target'. The same idea is conveyed in advice to women (e.g. to avoid using isolated bus stops – see Home Office, 1991). Similar advice has also been made available to Asian, Black and other Ethnic Minority people, to reduce their risk of being racially victimized. The obvious difficulty is that the life style model, while providing a framework to establish a pattern in which property crime occurs, is unable to deal with specific crimes against the person because these have never been its focus. For example, domestic violence is a crime that occurs repeatedly in the home but the life style model can only encapsulate the public arena. Similarly, racial harassment, a recurrent crime with its own distinct dynamics and apparent random occurrences (see Chapter 4) cannot be explained simply within a framework of life style and daily routines. (A lot more might be gained by examining the life styles of the perpetrators of racial harassment.)

Although it may be argued that these victimological ideas, contain some plausible elements, they are nevertheless the source of two major deficiencies in current thinking on victims of crime. The first is a tendency to see crimes against specific persons (i.e. different communities) in the same terms as crimes against property or crimes for financial gain. At this point a second deficiency arises, this is the propensity to 'blame the victims' for their victimization. A great deal of policy analysis, whether concerning victimization or crime prevention, has reinforced these notions considerably. As Walklate (op. cit.:105) has argued in a slightly different context:

> It becomes difficult to envisage, for example, how concepts like 'victim precipitation' or 'life style' can be maintained. These concepts have been constructed with an individualistic bias. They need to be reconsidered in a form which locates victimization in a structural setting rather than an individualistic setting. This means that the explanations offered by victimology need to embrace a view that victimization can occur as a result of processes above and beyond particular individual action or personality.

While there is a need to expand and transform the conventional parameters of victimology, to cover variable and structural concerns, particularly where questions of personal violation or social dehumanization are major issues, this cannot be achieved solely within the confines of that discipline. Our analysis of the specificity of racial victimization suggests that additional perspectives are necessary to re-think the human experience of crimes which recurrently find expression in personal violations. This brings us to the terrain of 'social geography'.

Geography and victimization

At this stage it is necessary to see how we can advance beyond the limited insights of existing research. We want to argue that ideas drawn from social geography are crucial to an understanding of the *constitutive experiential features* of racial victimization. In a previous Chapter we argued that racial harassment has a local geography (and history) which shapes the terrain for connected, diverse and recurrent *scenarios* of victimization over time. These important experiential contours are usually ignored by policy makers who have failed to perceive, let alone attach any significance to, overlapping patterns of racial victimization and their spatial forms of inscription. In this section we develop this discussion by arguing that a social geography of victimization needs to establish a sense of the relationship people are 'positioned' to have with their social environment and then move to question what makes people feel safe or threatens their idea of security.

Elements of a social geography

How far the themes of victimology have begun to influence social geography is unclear, but a great deal of attention has been devoted to the geographical analysis of crime (Smith, 1986; Cater and Jones, 1989; Evans and Herbert, 1989). Despite its often exclusive reliance on legal definitions of 'offending' and the 'offender', which in turn lends credence to the individuation of 'crime' as a discrete event or criminality as a 'career', it is possible to tease out those elements that could inform (or point to difficulties in) a geography of victimization. Antecedents are the first pre-occupation here. Studies in the incidence of crime or delinquency had their geographical 'origins' in the so-called 'cartographic school'. This was pioneered in France during the mid-nineteenth century and subsequently imitated in Britain. As Cater and Jones (op. cit.:79) have noted, 'the sharp regional variations in offence rates disclosed by the early map makers supplied the first systematic evidence that criminality is space-specific'. It is at this point perhaps that the trajectories of a *potential* geography of victimization and an *actual* geography of crime diverge. As we shall argue they are contiguous rather than co-extensive analytical strategies.

Examining the background to the accentuation of geography in the analysis of crime reveals how conceptions of offending or breaking the law tend towards conceptions of 'space' or 'location' in which victimization occurs as a categoric event rather than an uneven, open-ended process. Consequently it is the spatiality of property (offences) rather than (offences against) the person which determines the criminological focus on victimization. In common with various strands in victimology, the social dimensions of a legal conception of property crime are applied inappropriately to a spectrum of crimes against the person. Arguably this has its roots in the urban ecological analyses of the Chicago school of ethnography in the United States during the 1930s. They spawned the other, more dominant strand in geographical approaches to crime. Particularly emphasizing 'spatiality' they developed an invariable focus on the 'areal co-variance between criminality and various aspects of the built and social environments' (ibid.:81). Leaving aside the difficulties of sustaining and defining an ecological analysis of the 'symbiotic' relation between crime and its environment (see Taylor et al., 1973:114), the general idea of environmental influence on the incidence of crime has continued to orchestrate the composition of many geographical analyses (see Evans and Herbert, op. cit.).

Within criminology generally much of the work undertaken has utilized what has been described as the 'opportunity/motivation rubric' in analyzing the pattern and incidence of crime (see Cater and Jones, op. cit.:90). Increasingly geographers have emphasized the opportunity dimension in two aspects of space or the environment: 'distance' and 'architectural form'. The question of distance concerns the extent to which property crimes are committed near the offender's residence, where for example, information about potential targets may be readily available. Although this suggests that the 'geography of offences' is connected to the 'geography of offenders', it is recognized that the two are not necessarily isomorphic. Complimenting this approach the issues involved in architectural design and urban landscape draw attention to the extent to which the built environment determines the potential accessibility of a target to criminalization. The problem with both approaches for an analysis of victimization is that the social and spatial experiences of personal violations appear incidental to the concerns about property crime. A tendency to see the 'victim' as an adjunct to the 'crime' persists even when victimization is the acclaimed focus of study. For example, despite the mushrooming of victim surveys during the 1980s, it is instructive to note that 'the technique has not been extensively applied to the spatial patterning of victimization' (ibid.:104). As we have argued above victim or crime surveys have generally attempted to quantify the extent of crime incidents reported/unreported to the police and the extent to which different groups are victimized by crime. The crux of the analytical problem here lies with privileging the construction of 'crime' as a measurable, quantifiable entity and as a discrete category. The resulting statistical patina dissipates the 'actual' experience of victimization. Thus Kelly (1987:48) has argued that the victimization involved in sexual harassment must be seen as a 'continuum' because:

> there are no clearly defined and discrete analytical categories into which women's experiences can be placed. The experiences women have and how they are subjectively defined shade into and out of a given category such as sexual harassment, which includes looks, gestures and remarks as well as acts which may be defined as assault or rape.

If we understand Kelly's concept of 'continuum' in spatial as well as experiential terms then there is much in her observations that bear comparison with other crimes against specific persons. Within this context the 'official' category of crime is an insufficient basis for thinking about victimization. Not only does it portray and skew the experience of personal victimization (refracted through the dominant image of property crimes), as individualistic and uni-dimensional. It obscures 'sequence and simultaneity' (Soja, 1989:28) in victimization by reducing the spatialized continuum to the 'displaced' event. The 'official' recognition of the victimization of Asian and Black communities, women and Gay people provides numerous examples of the mystification of the experiential and the spatial. With these ideas in mind then, we want to argue that elements of a geography of victimization could emerge through two related forms of analysis. The first would stress the role of 'space' (e.g. environment, place) in the continuum of crimes against specific persons within the local 'ethnoscape' (Appadurai, 1990); and the second would examine the awareness of these experiences through the concept 'spatial security'. The methodological rationale of both analyses is encapsulated in Jackson and Smith's (1984:194) contention that social geography should emphasize:

> how people convey meaning to space as part of their negotiated identity; how social interaction is under-pinned by spatial differentiation; and, perhaps most ambitiously, how space mediates between social interaction and social structure.

It is within this context we make a number of theoretical remarks in the following sections which may assist in developing useful tools of analysis.

Local ethnoscape

It is important to understand how particular demarcations of space (the street, the estate, the neighbourhood), become embroiled in particular strategies of 'social dehumanization'. Analysis at this level therefore needs to distinguish ' "people" variations with specific types of "people" at greater risk' (Herbert,

1989). But how can this be conceptualized? Appadurai (op. cit.:299) uses the term 'ethnoscape' globally to describe the 'landscape of persons who constitute the shifting world in which we live'. We can apply this equally strategically in a 'local' sense where, irrespective of long-term demographic transformations, (transient) permanence rather than (permanent) transience is the most striking characteristic of the everyday populace at any point in time. Thus for us the local ethnoscape which characterizes a neighbourhood or different regions of a city, consists of variously segmented population gatherings which 'landmark' a sense of 'place' both in relation to defining where 'we' are and to whom 'we' are. The local ethnoscape is constructed as permanence not simply through the recurrence of particular individuals 'here or there', but through the proportional repetition of particular categories of person (e.g. race, class, ethnicity, age, etc.) in the local geography of 'transient congregations'. These include public-transport populations, supermarket populations, residential populations, pedestrian populations, school populations, in short, any regular, 'landmarked' population gathering dispersed across an administratively bounded space. It is the immediacy and accessibility of these 'transient congregations' which for us defines the 'local' context. It is here that people see 'who' is around or 'who' surrounds them, here that people reflect (on) who they are and see reflections of themselves or their social 'differences'. This is the lived 'spacing' of 'community' where social encounters may reinforce or challenge ethno-margins and ethno-centres in the social landscape, where the power to dominate and the domination of power is variously expressed through the 'authority' of race, gender, sexuality, class and so on.

There are many different explanations for the emergence of specific victimizations (e.g. racism, sexism, homophobia). The question of ethnoscape is important because its fluidity and composition may enable us to understand how different (e.g. race, gender, sexuality and class) popular investments are engaged in struggles, in the production of 'imagined communities' (Anderson, 1983). Initially this may be a useful way of thinking about the spatialization of racial victimization. For example the 'multi-cultural society' (one image of the ethnoscape), has a quintessential contestability that 'marks' not only distinct regions and specific localities of Britain but the very idea of Britain itself. It is a precarious 'building block' of an 'imagined world' (Appadurai, op. cit.: 298) in which the ethnoscape's 'non-white' constituents, (i.e. its margins) in the clusterings of day to day encounters, may be subjected to interrogation, disruption and violation. Elements of this racist logic have been amplified by Cohen (1988:28) where he writes:

> The construction of the ethnic majority in Britain has depended on the intervention of two key terms – people and nation. One of the peculiarities of the English is the way these terms have been coupled together as part of a tradition of democratic resistance to the governing class – whilst

at the same time becoming actively racialised and being used to marginalise ethnic minorities within society.

The generality of this analysis, that is victimization predicated on the contingencies of marginalization, can be extended to include other forms of social dehumanization. It requires we recognize that the local ethnoscape is embedded in a 'plurality of cultures and the multiplicity of landscapes with which those cultures are associated' (Jackson, 1989:1). Its construction is constantly a precarious mediation of innovation and conservatism. Populations at greater risk of victimization may simply be those whose autonomy and expressiveness of life style, simply by virtue of their 'different' social existence, or assertion of self-determination, challenges and resists the oppressiveness of dominant cultures within the ethnoscape and the latter's codification as somehow representative of the 'people'.

Spatial security

People's awareness of their various (i.e. race, gender, sexuality) 'positionings' within the local ethnoscape is obviously implicated in their comprehension of personal safety. In this regard there is much to be learned from feminist research in the area of violence against women which can point to how physical and social space is conceptualized and negotiated in terms of security. Stanko (1990) suggests that women devise routine precautionary strategies to limit the every day possibility of violence. This involves women in the lived experience of preparing themselves to anticipate male harassment and violence and actively engages them in the negotiation of their own security. Stanko's (op. cit.:6) description of this clearly has a wider, albeit differential application:

> We gather experiences of safety and danger and come to perceive situations as safe or as dangerous through our own accumulated experience. We also come to understand our own effectiveness in assessing likely peril.

However, the capacity to 'negotiate danger' requires in many respects 'negotiating power' (ibid.:8). This suggests any adequate analysis should not ignore the wider unequal relations of power in 'society', in particular those of class, race, gender and sexuality. These are 'not mutually exclusive but interactive' (Hanmer, Radford and Stanko, 1989:6). For us this means while it is important to focus on specific forms of victimization, an analysis of people's awareness of spatial security must recognize the 'different' power relationships instituted in the socially constructed 'positionings' of people within the ethnoscape (i.e. society). Despite the undoubted advances of feminist research it has often failed to achieve this, for example Mama (1990:4) argues:

Black feminists in the West have demanded that race, religion and culture be incorporated into the analysis of violence against women. In doing so they have begun to articulate an approach which challenges the ethno-centricism and essentialism of the approaches that have been generated by those Western feminists who have focussed too narrowly on patri-archy and sexual oppression, and therefore failed to consider class, racial and cultural oppression.

Specific forms of violation need to be seen in the wider context of connected and distinctive instances of social dehumanization. Where racial harassment is concerned, this is the basis of the analysis which goes 'beyond Anti-racism' (see Introduction). Only once we have grasped the relation of 'equivalence' (Laclau and Mouffe, 1985) between contested social differences can we begin to develop the focus of a geography of victimization.

In analytical terms a geography of victimization could also be resourced from a number of concepts recently developed by Giddens (1990). Although specifically designed for 'global' analyses, themes such as 'security versus danger' and 'trust versus risk' can be used to formulate ways of discussing peoples' spatial awareness of 'local victimization profiles'. These include the 'particular portmanteau of threat or dangers' (ibid.:100) which characterize various types of victimization. Understanding the extent to which different sectors of the population have trust or confidence in the social environment broadens the frame for analyzing the contextuality of victimization. It also reveals the social differentials in the quality of routine spatial security. Follow-ing Giddens (op. cit.:36) security may be defined as:

> a situation in which a specific set of dangers is counter-acted or min-imised. The experience of security usually rests upon a balance of trust and acceptable risk. In both its factual and its experiential sense, security may refer to large aggregates or collectivities of people – up to and including global security – or to individuals.

The desire for spatial security is quotidian, its attainment is premised on trust which in turn is routinized through reliability in the face of a continuum of social contingencies. However if, as Giddens (ibid.:54) suggests, trust is deployed in 'environments of risk' where varying levels of security are pos-sible, the question arises, in what specific circumstances does trust palpably lapse? And how is this to be understood? These questions can be answered briefly by returning to the central theme of this book. It should be apparent from our analyses in previous Chapters (1–3) that racial victimization can so easily rupture the balance of day-to-day existence. By fragmenting the experience of living into a series of 'anxiety situations' it momentarily and persistently splinters the touchstones of social interaction. Resulting in what can best be described as 'spatial insecurity'. This characterizes the 'local' disruption people feel in their sense of safety or well-being and in 'the constancy of the surrounding social and material environments of action' (ibid.:92). Racial victimization is a particularly complex form of this disruption. Its analysis raises important questions concerning the racial experience of location.

White territorialism

If we accept that the general sense of local 'ethnoscape' and social settings within a bounded jurisdiction is shaped by the interventions of diverse local populations, how then do we construe the particular sense of racially contested space which generates racial harassment? For us it is the relationship between white identity, racism and territory. This is what we need to explore in order to conceptualize the experiential or subjective impact of the logic of racial harassment, that is, its inscription in victimization. In other words we need to consider these issues in terms of the *relationship of the perpetrators of racial harassment to their location*. What then is the rationale of these recurrent forms of racist social behaviour in various places and locations over time? Bonnerjea and Lawton (1988:23) in a study of racial harassment in the London Borough of Brent provide an observation which is extremely relevant to our present discussion. They argue:

> part of the attempt to establish the meaning of racial harassment requires the concept of 'territory'. *In particular it is white people's concept of territory which seems to be the problem.*

> (emphasis added)

The concept of 'white territory' is relatively unexplored in much of the literature on racial harassment, yet its salience is evident in the connectedness of the victimization experiences. If racism generally exhibits a logic of social regulation and exclusion (see Introduction), then racial harassment in particular seems geared towards a territorial logic of expulsion, periodically accelerated by tactics of personal violation and even extermination (whichever is calculated to remove or eject the 'non-white' territorial presence). It is important to be clear about how we are thinking of territoriality, in one sense it is,

> best understood as a spatial strategy to effect, influence, or control resources and people, by controlling area: and, as a strategy, territoriality can be turned on and off. In geographical terms it is a form of spatial behaviour. The issue then is to find out under what conditions and why territoriality is or is not employed.

> (Sack, 1986:1–2)

In another sense the imperatives of territoriality should always be seen as a means to some end (see Smith, 1990). What then is the context and objective of 'white territorialism'? A rhetorical digression may be useful here: Consider the discursive resonances wrought by expressions like 'Pakis go home', 'go back to your own country', 'alien cultures swamping British identity', 'immigrants colonizing Britain', 'blacks ghettoizing the inner-city' or more recently 'Islamic fundamentalism sweeping the nation'. At least two things should be apparent from these spatial obsessions. Firstly there is heightened anxiety about these 'subordinate', 'other' populations resisting regulation and getting out of 'our' control; and secondly, there is a sense in which 'our' British identity (for 'our' read 'white') is under threat because 'our right' to dominate is being questioned; this is the expressive logic of the desire for racial exclusion. The point is, however disorganized or under-elaborated, the rationale of a cumulative racial harassment is the resistance to any diminishment in the authorial claims of a particular white identity to sovereign inscription in any layer of the social landscape or 'ethnoscape' in Britain. This is similar to Gilroy's (1987:48) observation that the 'black presence is thus constructed as a problem or threat against which a homogenous, white, national "we" could be unified'. A subsiduary of this is the localization of racial victimization.

This emphasizes why the concept of 'territory' should be integral to the analysis of racial victimization. In particular it suggests that racial harassment expresses, in the eyes of its perpetrators, a sense of proprietorial relation to social space *as white territory*. This has been observed by other commentators. For example, Husbands (1982) in an analysis of racism in the East End of London during the period 1900–1980 observed that 'attacks tend to cluster in areas where black people form a small minority of the population, *but appear to be challenging the territorial preferences of whites*' (emphasis added). This also provides the background to Smith's (1989:162) discussion of the relationship between space and racial harassment:

> where such violence is particularly localized and intense, it may also be read as an expression of territoriality – as a popular means of asserting social identity, of defending material resources and of preserving social status. Racial attacks is (sic), from this perspective, a segregationist as well as an exclusionary practice, effected to keep or force black people out of particular urban neighbourhoods.

The linkage between territoriality, the assertion of an imperial white identity and racial harassment is a complex one, yet it is possible to argue that it is mediated by customary social behaviour among various individuals and groups in white communities who regard themselves in a racial or cultural terms to be *defending their space against change and transformation*. This persistently victimizes Asian and Black people, in so far as their cultures, demands, values and life styles are perceived as a threat to the exclusive dominance of white identities in the local ethnoscape or the social environment. It is only against this background that the complexity of racial victimization itself can be mapped.

Racial victimization scenarios

Racial victimization is a complex phenomenon. In addition to its territorial imperatives and settings, our analysis suggests it points to many levels of experiences in a process that is always open ended. The actual incident may appear to be opportunistic from the perspective of the perpetrator (or even the researcher) but the impact on the victim is not transient, it cannot be dismissed as having a low probability of recurring. These are some of the characteristics of burglary victims or victims of street theft and may be termed the *simple* structure of victimization. In contrast, racial victimization, in common with other *crimes against specific persons* (e.g. violence against women, child abuse, anti-Gay violence) is not really carried out for personal financial gain, it seems to be an attempt to exert control over or violate the conduct and life style of the subject victimized. Typically this attempt at control or violation is exemplified through various forms of violence and abuse. In addition the different rationales involved in different types of crimes against specific persons are equally complex.

As we have suggested throughout this book the apparent random distribution of racial harassment incidents seem to have the sense of *déjà vu* attached to them, particularly in the light of their persistent recurrence in particular locations. Also, it should be evident from the contextual analyses in Chapters 1–3 that the experience of harassment *as* victimization has various experiential dimensions. It is the patterned connection between these in the lives of the communities which are its focus, that for us invokes the image of scenario to describe what Asian and Black people are able to perceive in their locality even prior to so-called 'first hand experience' (see Chapter 4). This is the basis of the *complex structure of racial victimization*. We have attempted to identify at least four empirical dimensions in the construction of its scenario. Each is based on our contextual analysis of the scope of experiences in Waltham Forest.

Multiple victimization

Racial harassment may be experienced by Asian and Black people in a variety of verbal and physical violations which strike both person and their property. Many different forms of abuse may be experienced simultaneously by individuals and families. Often name calling progresses to physical assaults and damage to property, with severe consequences to the victims. In addition, it is fairly common for people to experience various forms of racial harassment in different places. We received evidence from school children of all ages, including those under five, describing their experiences, and from their parents who escorted them to and from school. Name calling from white peers in schools was frequent (many took this as a form of 'expected behaviour'). When walking on the streets between school and home, they were subjected to more verbal abuse and intimidation. Children also recalled in their evidence how their homes were racially harassed, for example racially abusive literature was occasionally pushed through their letter boxes. The potential for, if not actual subjection, to multiple victimization was a continual prospect. This *multiple* victimization, with its *potential for escalation*, is in effect directed at whole communities, although it targets its victims at random.

Cyclical victimization

Racial harassment is experienced by its victims as repetition. It has a cyclical quality, that is, victims are subjected to racial harassment over varying time periods, for example, every day, every week, every month, every few months or every few years. This cyclical feature of racial victimization also implies that within the time periods of its recurrence, it confronts different Asian and Black individuals and families at *apparently random moments*. Its impact can have profound long term psychological effects on its victims, these are often ignored or underestimated by the statutory agencies. Eventhough the persistent nature of racial harassment affects the whole family. For example for four years an African-Caribbean family experienced racial victimization from their neighbours. Stones, food, rubbish and excrement were thrown into their garden. The consistency of this victimization reduced the mother from a 'confident' person to a 'nervous wreck'. The effects on the children were equally devastating. Their two year old child developed skin rashes and their ten year old child continually asked his mother 'why don't they like us mummy?'.

In the evidence we received, verbal abuse, racial epithets like 'Wogs', 'Pakis', 'Black Bastard', 'Blackie', 'Golliwogs', 'Niggers', were described as continuous experiences. The overwhelming indication was that the victims grudgingly accepted this almost as a way of life for them. For example a teacher described how when an Asian parent was racially abused she said, 'don't worry, I don't want to make a fuss, it's always happening'. Asian and Black people in Waltham Forest were often subjected to physical assaults in public places, this included being spat upon, jostled in the streets, pelted with eggs and other items and even harassed by the police. The recurrence of life threatening racial attacks like arson left its victims profoundly distressed and anxious. A young African-Caribbean woman with small children was the focus of arson attacks despite moving house twice. The first time her flat was arsoned, 'it (the fire) wouldn't go out', and none of her neighbours helped. During another incident, her children were watching television when a sock soaked in petrol was set alight and pushed through her letter box. These horrifying experiences left the family traumatized. The children developed anxiety related problems (e.g. sleep walking and bed wetting). While the mother's concept of a safe property was transformed to include the possibility of escape as a major prerequisite. The cyclical features of racial victimization mean that Asian and Black peoples' fear of being harassed is extremely high, and the prospect of the crime actually taking place is almost equally high. While other forms of crime create genuine fear among people, sometimes high levels of fear, the actual probability of these crimes is often relatively low, even when under-reporting has been taken into account. In contrast the fear of recurrent racial victimization is often a product of *personal experience* in the surrounding locations.

Secondary victimization

The impact of racial harassment on its victims can have severe effects on the social behaviour of Asian and Black communities with regard to their social environment. Like any other crime, when it takes place, many Asian and Black people are inclined to report the incidents to the police and other statutory agencies. But, as we have seen, the response they receive is often less than helpful. The problems associated with reporting appear to be two-fold. Firstly there is the difficulty of actually persuading an agency like the Council or the police to consider a case in terms of racial harassment, and secondly, there is the issue of getting the agency to respond effectively. Both these problems present dilemmas which may lead to victims choosing not to report.

Our research revealed many examples of the frustrations felt when reporting traumatic experiences. These included instances where the victims had even identified the perpetrators to the police who still failed to take action. One family subjected to continual racial victimization from their neighbours frequently reported the perpetrators to both the Council and the police. The response of the police was to question the family's understanding of their responsibilities to the law, despite the family's willingness to give evidence in court. An intervention from Waltham Forest CRC to pressurize the police to respond produced the following comments in a letter from the Chief Superintendent:

> Rest assured that we will continue to keep the situation under review. In the meantime, perhaps Mr. Y could be encouraged to provide the police with some tangible assistance if he needs to call us to his premises in the future, he should be aware that his evidence and possible personal appearance would be necessary in any court proceedings. He seems reluctant to accept this fundamental requirement of the law at present.

Other evidence suggested the police were uninterested when called unless there was evidence of some physical damage. According to one witness, 'if we don't say yes, then the police don't bother coming out again'. Victims experiences of the Council were similar. Often they were simply not believed. One case described to us concerned an Asian woman who reported a racial attack to the Housing department. She was told by a Council officer, 'Asian people deliberately tell lies because they want to move'. Adverse comments like these discourage people from reporting. Often people were asked for extensive evidence. We were told 'the onus of proof is always on the victim'. This comes close to establishing a tacit precedent where victims are expected to undertake their own detective work to provide further evidence to substantiate their complaint. Despite this context, people did report to agencies and continued to do so repeatedly. It was more than evident that the role played by statutory agencies compounded the initial victimization.

Spatial victimization

It should be apparent that the previous dimensions of the racial victimization scenario, directly influence the relationship of Asian and Black peoples lives to their social environment. One result of this appears to be that Asian and Black people form *mental maps* of the distributions of racial harassment (see also Chapter 4). This suggests that people begin to perceive social spaces in 'racially' particular ways. That is, as locations which allow freedom of movement and those which inhibit; and locales which are 'no go areas' or are relatively safe to live. In this sense the movements of people are shaped by the *mental maps* they 'carry in their heads'. Not only do settlement patterns sometimes illustrate this, but the functional use of space is also affected. The cumulative effect of these perceptions, based on real experiences, creates conditions where Asian and Black communities adjust themselves to being forced to live in and contest an unsafe social environment.

The impact this has on Asian and Black people's life styles can be significant. Their social behaviour may be restricted in the local environment because they have to live with not only ineffective responses from statutory agencies when reporting their experiences, but the reality of the harassment recurring. Several witnesses described these experiences as: 'living under siege', encountering a 'total erosion of self confidence', finding themselves 'turning into nervous wrecks' and having their capacity to live 'normally' severely undermined. As a consequence the spatial mobility of people becomes restricted. Not only does this interfere with everyday life (e.g. going shopping, going to work, etc.), it also restricts access to the use of public facilities. Some people felt unsafe using public parks. For example, Sikh Sangat East in their evidence told us of situations where elderly people sitting in the parks and speaking in their own language were tormented with racial abuse like 'speak in English' and 'go back to your own country'. In addition they informed us:

Children get verbally abused when playing in parks. Some members have talked about how they take their children to the park, white kids call them commonly 'Pakis', subsequently parents do not take children to the park.

Even apparently innocent social activities like walking in the streets can be intimidating and frightening. A group of Asian women informed us that they only go out when it is absolutely necessary, for example, when accompanying children to and from school, or to do the shopping. On these occasions they went out collectively in small groups of twos or threes. In matters of victimization, the social landscape is never neutral.

The relevance of local agencies

In general we discovered very little service provision to victims of racial harassment in Waltham Forest. In the evidence, it was clear that victims did not know where to go for help or who could give effective assistance. A number of community organizations confirmed this predicament. For example, the Joint Council for Afro-Caribbean Organizations (JCACO) described 'the added problem of the fact that it is not clear, to whom victims should or can report racial harassment' while Walthamstow Constituency Labour Party (Lloyd Park and Higham Hill Branches) stated:

A common theme from those who feel that they have suffered racial harassment is their sense of isolation. There is no authority to which Asian families feel they can turn with confidence for help in resolving their difficulties.

Those who did approach some agencies, found themselves shunted around and repeatedly attempting to consult an agency without any satisfactory help. In Chapters 2 and 3 we analyzed the ineffective impact of the police and local Council as statutory agencies, in this section we consider agencies in the voluntary sector. Statutory agencies often fund voluntary organizations to fill the gaps in local service provision. In addition voluntary organizations have a legitimate role in putting pressure on statutory agencies.

The voluntary sector

The situation in Waltham Forest's voluntary sector was hardly encouraging. As we describe in later sections the Victim Support Scheme did not offer any specific service to victims of racial harassment; a similar neglect affected other agencies. For example the Citizens Advice Bureau was not only described as unhelpful but characterized as a 'military type regime' by one witness. Other witnesses described experiences of receiving inappropriate help (e.g. one was advised to take out a private prosecution and another was advised to seek help from our Inquiry). The CAB cited their lack of experience in dealing with racial harassment due to few enquiries and also commented:

> it would seem that the incidents of racial harassment reported to us are low for several reasons. For example, the Citizens Advice Bureau may not be seen to be as 'appropriate' for this type of problem as other agencies, such as (the) CRC, also a victim may feel that such crimes are insoluble, thus being deterred from seeking help altogether, finally many of the victims of this type of harassment may feel less able *for reasons of language and culture* to seek help.
>
> (emphasis added)

Leaving aside this inexplicable excursion into cultural explanations, our evidence suggests that what significantly deterred people from seeking help was that like other agencies the CAB did not offer a 'serious' service to victims of racial harassment. Other organizations gave similar explanations for not dealing with racial harassment. MIND, the organization that deals with people with mental disabilities, said they had no evidence to submit to our Inquiry as racial harassment had not arisen in the organization or been reported to them. While Waltham Forest MENCAP, who deal with children and adults with 'mental handicaps' wrote to say they had no reported cases of racial harassment. They suggested this was:

> because our agency specialises in giving information and advice on the area of mental handicap, benefits, services available etc.

Evidence received from Waltham Forest Association for People with Disabilities (WFAPD) suggested they were aware of a number of incidents of harassment of people with disabilities. They informed us that their representatives on various bodies sought 'to ensure that agencies which provide support or advice to such people are aware of the particular concerns disabled people may have in such situations, help they may need and of particular sources that help'. However they went on to explain that the cases they referred to:

> (had) not involved disabled people who are ethnic minority members of the local community. We feel however that such people may be particularly vulnerable to harassment.

The striking facts to emerge in the evidence from these and other specialist organizations in the voluntary sector are: an inability to understand racial harassment and its impact on victims or the role the particular organization could play in responding to the problem; a reluctance to acknowledge a responsibility for dealing with racial harassment; and a reluctance to countenance the existence of racial harassment either by publicizing what the organization could offer or by encouraging people to report incidents. It was particularly worrying that organizations which offered a specialist service (e.g. MENCAP, MIND, WFAPD), catering for the needs of people with mental and physical disabilities and advocates on their behalf, considered racial harassment to be a marginal concern in the lives of Asian and Black people. The absence of policies and procedures to deal with racial harassment and the sense of their 'waiting' to hear from victims implied that services from these organizations were dependent on the idiosyncratic views of the workers approached.

The only organization that dealt with cases of racial harassment in a significant way in the voluntary sector appeared to be the Community Relations Council (CRC). It offered limited practical advice and acted on behalf of victims when dealing with other agencies. Generally most community organizations did not offer a direct service regarding racial harassment, but acted as referral agencies. Apart from advising the police and the Council when they knew some victims would not approach these public agencies directly, it seemed there was little further help the CRC could provide. Perhaps it can be argued that funded organizations, which are specialist advice agencies should ensure their publicity clearly states what they can do for victims of racial harassment. If so this would require that their staff were adequately trained, aware of the need to address the issue and familiar with the role of other agencies in providing additional specialized help (e.g. practical support). In particular, we would argue that local Councils should consider making this a part of the funding conditions, especially with regard to agencies like the Victim Support Scheme who have a clearly defined brief to help victims of crime (see later sections).

Asian, black and ethnic minority organizations

The first point of contact for many Asian and Black people when seeking advice is often a relevant community organization. In Waltham Forest, these catered mainly for the specific cultural needs of the people they served. Some also provided a basic advice service in a sensitive manner and in appropriate languages. Many of these organizations were funded by the Council. Although they ranged from small grant aided 'support groups' run by volunteers to larger organizations with considerable salaried staff, the emphasis was usually on catering for the specific needs of their communities, and/or undertaking advocacy work. The evidence we received came from a variety of organizations. For example, the East London Harmony group met monthly as a support group to discuss racist incidents. They pursued these cases by putting pressure on other agencies to act. The Victim Aid Action group offered some initial advice, and referred cases to the Council and the police. While the Bangalee Women's Welfare Project wrote in their evidence that they 'Do not have the means to deal with cases directly'. This depicts the general response from many small community organizations. These organizations either provided a very basic advice service or did not deal with cases of racial harassment, referring them to other agencies (e.g. the police, the Council). A lack of resources in the Asian, Black and Ethnic Minority organizations put severe pressure on their ability to respond to the demands of dealing with racial harassment. The absence of an identifiable agency in the voluntary sector to deal with the problem, meant that these organizations, like many individuals who gave evidence, were *dependent on the Council and the police to take appropriate action*. This was often with fore-knowledge that very little would be done by them. Sikh Sangat East informed us that they advised people to go to the police but knew no action would be taken. The Joint Council for Asian Organizations, described specific experiences with the Council following referrals as entailing, 'varying degree of responses depending on the advice of (the) person dealing with it'. While the Victim Aid Action Group stated: 'We have not seen any assistance available to victims of racial harassment in the Borough'. These were remarkable revelations. They confirmed that traditional advice agencies, like the local CAB and the Council's Aid Centre, were simply incapable of providing a response to meet the needs of the victims of racial harassment. What is perhaps more significant is that no reference was made to the Council's telephone 'hotline' service on racial harassment, nor to the Victim Support Scheme. Asian and Black community organizations clearly seem to have been frustrated, under pressure and unable to help their communities effectively. This was in part due to the reluctance in the wider voluntary sector to take racial victimization seriously.

Service provisions to victims of crime

In the UK, attempts to address the needs of racial harassment victims cannot be disentangled from the thinking which informs initiatives generally designed for victims of crime. Various forms of service provision exist for victims of crime. Although these are not based on any well defined victimological theory, it may be useful to consider van Dijk's (1988:166) work which suggests four 'ideologies' to describe the trend within the victims movement across different countries. He describes these as 'victimagogic' ideologies and defines them as ideologies 'about the best ways to give treatment, guidance or support to crime victims'. He argues they should be seen as objects for social analysis and research which could be used as a basis to develop a unified theory grounded in victimological research.

On the basis of van Dijk's four ideologies, it is possible to describe the provisions available in the UK. These can be categorized through the 'care' ideology, the 'rehabilitative' ideology, the 'retributive' or 'criminal justice' ideology and the 'abolitionist' ideology. The 'care' ideology emphasizes provision for victims of crime by the community, and generally perceives the problems they face as stress, psychological trauma or economic need. Victim

Support Schemes provide this service in the UK. The 'rehabilitative' ideology, looks at measures which can 'treat' the offender. These can include victim-offender confrontations, in which the interests of the victim are often neglected. Here, crime is perceived as a conflict between two parties, the offender and the victim. Mediation schemes fall into this category. The 'retributive' or 'criminal justice' ideology encapsulates the idea that the offender must be punished according to the seriousness of the crime and the damage to society. Increasingly, there are moves to get the offender to compensate the victim. In the UK, this is reflected in compensation orders. Compensation is also available to crime victims from the Criminal Injuries Compensation Board (CICB). Finally, the 'abolitionist' ideology, favours the treatment of the offenders on the principles of civil law, arguing that the criminal justice system should intervene as minimally as possible. It suggests that mediation, reparation, aid to victims and crime prevention should be left to neighbourhood groups and other social networks. Some of this emphasis is currently found in the UK, particularly in crime prevention strategies (see Chapter 2). Below we discuss three structured provisions for victims of crime and consider whether they can meet the needs of victims of racial harassment.

Victim support schemes

Initiated in the mid 1970s, Victim Support Schemes have been one of the fastest growing organizations in the voluntary sector. Their role is to provide short-term help for crime victims. They have four key features: they are independent organizations, employ full-time co-ordinators, rely on carefully selected and trained volunteers and are a 'front-line' crisis service agency. Most, but not all schemes are affiliated to the National Association of Victim Support Schemes (NAVSS), which was founded in 1979. The NAVSS co-ordinates the Victim Support Schemes, and publishes guidelines on their establishment. It also requires VSSs to have independent management committees which should consist of at least one representative from the police, probation or social services, a voluntary organization or church and scheme volunteers. The policies adopted by individual schemes determine their referral system (i.e. which crime victims they service). The exclusion of certain categories of victim is partly attributable to the result of police referral practices which are based on police perceptions of who needs the service. Generally victim support schemes are heavily reliant on the police for referrals (sometimes exclusively). But police referrals are not necessarily effective or efficient (Mawby and Gill, 1987). Not only do the police act as *gatekeepers*, their representation on the management committees creates ambiguity in the 'independent' nature of the victim support schemes. They can have a disproportionate influence on the conduct of the schemes. Furthermore, where victims have suffered police harassment, the schemes may be reluctant to acknowledge such incidents and therefore not offer appropriate support.

This is pertinent to Asian, Black and Ethnic Minority communities. Often these communities are reluctant to have dealings with the police because of their experiences, and would be apprehensive in seeking help from an organization that is seen to be so closely linked with the police.[1]

We are unable to comment in detail on the Waltham Forest Victim Support Scheme as they did not submit evidence to the Inquiry. Nevertheless, our own research indicated that the local Victim Support Scheme did not offer specific support to victims of racial harassment. There appeared to be no comprehension in the organization regarding the needs of victims of racial harassment and an undisguised reluctance to improve the situation. This was all the more remarkable given the organization's vehement opposition to the establishment of a 'hotline' telephone service in 1986 for victims of racial harassment (see Chapter 1). This suggested the scheme was unwilling to engage the issues involved in racial harassment and perhaps explained why the scheme as constituted was unable to offer a distinct and sensitive service to victims of racial harassment. In 1991 the scheme published a leaflet on racial harassment, this adopted a definition of racial harassment similar to that of the police.[2] It advised victims to take precautions to avoid victimization. The leaflet's advice was similar to that offered by the police on preventing property crime. It also advised victims of racial harassment to gather information about their perpetrators to help police investigations. There was no conception of the impact of racial victimization.

Interestingly, the scheme had ignored even the problematic recommendations from the NAVSS project report on racial harassment (see Kimber and Cooper 1991). This research examined how victim support schemes could provide an effective service to racial harassment victims. Based on three demonstration projects observed from 1988, regular evaluation was carried out until the production of the final report. The report's major conclusion was that 'racial harassment should become an essential and integral part of mainstream victim support work' (ibid.:89). It makes various recommendations on how this may be achieved, for example, training for staff and volunteers, designating specific workers to take a lead role, developing equal opportunities policies; and it offers pragmatic advice to victim support schemes on how to offer a relevant service.

The NAVSS report however presents a weak analysis. Firstly, in the elaborate process that each project went through to formulate a definition of racial harassment, they encompassed without distinction all communities except the (generally) majority (white) British population. The lumping together of all 'minority communities' fails to understand the specific racial victimization processes and the social impact on victims which may affect the nature of a relevant service provision. This also suggests, incorrectly, that racism is somehow experienced as a consequence of 'minority' status. Secondly, an extensive analysis of statistics in the report omits any clear findings which leaves us to question the validity of such work. An example of this is the information it presents concerning the year (in months) when racial harassment took place in the three Boroughs. Are we to think that racial harassment is seasonal? Thirdly, the report, recognizing the difficulties that victim support schemes have in obtaining referrals from and forming links with Asian, Black and Ethnic Minority communities, reflects on this in a peculiar way. It suggests 'the ways in which the "politics of race" are manifested at the local level is clearly a major issue for victim support schemes wishing to extend their work in the field of racial harassment' (ibid.:78). The researchers advise that if the 'politics of race' is high on the agenda of local groups, then victim support schemes will find it difficult to form links with them. The logic implied here is unfathomable, what exactly is meant by the 'politics of race' and how can a high or low value be assigned to it? Generally, one of the main considerations of Asian, Black and Ethnic Minority communities is to challenge racial exclusion and it is inconceivable to think that the 'politics of race' will not be constitutive of their organizational agendas. By default this argument seems to recommend the position prior to the research. In analytical terms then the report makes very little contribution. But it is arguable, that its recommendations for victim support schemes could be useful in initiating or progressing work in this area. Whether schemes will implement these recommendations remains to be seen. If the example of Waltham Forest is anything to go by, the results may be disappointing.

Mediation schemes

A second form of community intervention has emerged in the form of mediation schemes. These are based on the belief that it is desirable to empower the community to handle its own conflicts rather than to have this responsibility arrogated by professionals. Although they deal largely with neighbourly disputes, some do extend their work to other sorts of conflicts (e.g. within families, between social groups, within organizations, etc.). The schemes are usually located in community bases, employing scheme co-ordinators and using volunteers from the local community to act as mediators in non-directive roles. Like VSSs, the volunteers are trained. Although mediation schemes may vary in their emphasis or practice of service provision, the technique employed can be generalized as follows. Usually one party will approach a mediation project and the details of the case will be taken by them if they think they can help, the second party will then be approached with the consent of the first party. The concerns of the first party will be conveyed to the second party and the project will attempt to mediate a settlement agreeable to both. Disputants enter into negotiations voluntarily, have to abide by the schemes rules and may abandon negotiations at any time. A settlement may be reached through the mediator, by both parties meeting face to face or not at all. The schemes vary in the number of mediators used, the number of meetings held with each party, availability of advice and support to one party if the other party refuses to enter negotiations, etc. Mediation schemes are relatively new in their formation, and there is little knowledge available about how racial harassment is tackled. It appears that where the mediators of a scheme think that a case of racial harassment can be dealt with in the comparable terms of a neighbourly dispute, then the case will be handled accordingly, while more complex cases would simply not be taken on. In effect the neighbour dispute is the problem *par excellence* that mediation schemes have been designed to resolve (Marshall and Walpole, 1985).

Where racial victimization is concerned, mediation schemes are inappropriate for two main reasons. Firstly, a relationship of inequality exists between the two parties. In cases of racial harassment, it is likely that the less powerful party (e.g. Asian and Black people), will be constrained to accept the best deal possible and not the most fair settlement, while the more powerful party may well concede as little as possible. The second main problem is concerned with how racial harassment is tackled. As we argued in Chapter 2 the police utilize discretion in dealing with racial harassment specifically as a crime. By defining racial harassment as a neighbourly dispute as distinct from a crime, the police may be influenced to treat these cases similarly by making referrals to mediation schemes. Asian and Black people may find that they are bargaining for their basic human rights in the mediation process. For both reasons, mediation schemes are wholly unsatisfactory forms of provision where racial victimization is concerned.

Compensation to victims

(i) Compensation orders We have discussed above schemes that offer support to crime victims outside the legal system. The provision available within the legal system is in the form of compensation orders. The Criminal Justice Act (1972) gave courts a general power to order compensation to be paid to victims by convicted offenders as part of their sentence. However, within a year, it was found that the use of compensation orders was made more widely in offences against property than where personal injury was involved (Rock, 1990:279). Problems in the computation of compensation for personal injuries contributed to their low use. Applications for compensation orders are the responsibility of the prosecution on behalf of the victim. Research by Shapland et al. (1985) found that often this was not done. As victims are usually not present in courts, and few know about the existence of the compensation orders, in most cases, victims did not receive any compensation from offenders. The Criminal Justice Act (1988) now requires the courts to give reasons where compensation orders are not made. This may be seen by some as a way towards improving compensation order awards. However, Duff (1988) argues that there are fundamental problems with the compensation orders which need addressing. He suggests that of the three relationships that exist in the judiciary system, between state and offender,

victim and offender and state and victim, the criminal justice system is exclusively concerned with the state-offender relationship. As such, the system is concerned with deciding the appropriate penal measure for the offender. Compensation orders take a secondary role and are adapted to fit in with the criminal justice system rather than being integral to its infrastructure. A number of difficulties arise here: firstly the criminal courts make compensation orders on the basis of what the offender can afford. The sum has to be a realistic amount and if payable by instalments, which should not last very long. Thus the awards are often 'meagre' amounts compared to the loss the victims may have suffered. Secondly where the convicted offender receives a prison sentence, they are almost never able to pay compensation because their source of income ceases, unless the order is to come into effect after the sentence in which case again, it has to be a realistic sum. Thirdly there are problems concerning evidential matters as awards are made whatever seems appropriate in the light of the evidence available. This poses particular difficulties in cases of personal injury. Victims are not usually present in the court and there is often no information available about the victim's loss. Criminal courts also find it problematic to compute compensation in these cases as their focus is on issuing penal sentences. Fourthly, victims have no right of audience in court to give evidence about their loss. Victims cannot apply for a compensation order to be made in their favour, nor can they appeal against a decision. Generally, the judicary is of the view that the criminal courts should concentrate on the 'state-offender relationship' and that the civil court can deal with the 'offender-victim relationship'. However in the latter system, legal aid is usually not available and for the victim to pursue compensation in the civil courts can be an expensive undertaking. Victims of racial harassment can rarely take advantage of compensation orders unless the victimization they are subjected to corresponds with some other offence triable in court. Racial harassment per se is not a criminal offence. We described in Chapter 2 the problems associated with the police in their recording and investigation of cases of racial harassment. Very few of these go to court. Even though the compensation order is less than a satisfactory arrangement for victims of crime its existence benefits some victims of crime. However for victims of racial harassment even this seems inaccessible.

(ii) Criminal Injuries Compensation Board (CICB) This was created in 1964 to provide state compensation to victims of violent crime (whether the offender was caught and/or not convicted). The government at the time accepted the principle that victims of violent crime should be eligible for some compensation for personal injury at the public expense (Rock, 1990:82). However the government also made it clear that the state was not liable for injuries caused to people by acts of others. The CICB provides ex-gratia payments based on strict criteria. It sets a minimum level of award below which compensation is not payable (for less serious injuries). It carefully scrutinizes any share of

responsibility of the victim in the commital of the crime. It also takes into account the 'conduct' of the victim, by checking previous convictions. Although the Criminal Justice Act 1988 has given victims a statutory right to apply for compensation, there is no right to sue the CICB to challenge the amount awarded or the refusal of an award. The service is 'discretionary' and not a 'right'.

The Board has been variously criticized, we discuss this here. The Board is limited to provide compensation to victims of violent crime only, and this Duff (op. cit.) argues is a fundamental problem. The 'victim-state' relationship is confined to a narrow conception of victims of crime, particularly to victims of violent crime (defined by the CICB). This Walklate (op. cit.) suggests is because governments can embrace greatest public 'sympathy' in this area and be seen to be doing something for the victims. Implicit is the 'notion of public responsibility and sympathy for the victim, suggesting that the state is not responsible but feels a sense of responsibility' (ibid.:114). The Board uses its discretionary power to assess eligibility of the claimant on the basis of their 'conduct' and 'innocence'. Although this may be a concern to avoid fraudulent claims, the idea embraces the traditional distinction between the deserving and the non-deserving found in the traditional welfare system model (see Williams, 1989). The CICB has the power to check the claimants past convictions, which will have a bearing on their award. The award may be refused or reduced depending on the severity of the convictions. The CICB also requires that the claimant, 'must be able to convince the Board that you were not in any way responsible for the incident in which you were injured' (CICB, 1990:para 6(c):28). The onus clearly lies with the victim to prove his/her innocence. Furthermore, the CICB has to be satisfied that the victim had informed the police about the crime at the earliest possible opportunity, and had co-operated fully with the police throughout the investigation of the case which can include making a statement, attending an identification parade, naming the assailant, attending court. Failure to comply with this requirement also prejudices the application. The most damning criticism lies in the fact that few victims are aware of the scheme's existence (Shapland et al., 1985; Walklate, op. cit.; Rock, 1990). Ironically, the largest single profession to claim compensation is the police (Rock, op. cit.). Duff (op. cit.:153–154) concludes:

> . . . it is possible for this broad and controversial discretionary power to exist because of the lack of definition of the state-victim relationship; there is no satisfactory theoretical premise which demands that crime victims be compensated and, as a result, there is no legally enforceable right to compensation. Furthermore, the fact that the only reason given for compensating crime victims is that they attract public sympathy demands that compensation be withheld from those who might be perceived to be 'undeserving'.

When we consider victims of racial harassment, we can immediately see a number of problems with the scheme. Asian and Black people often do not report racial victimization to the police because they perceive or experience the police as insensitive. This would clearly prejudice their application. The CICB's requirement for claimants to prove their innocence may pose problems for Asian and Black people in cases of racial victimization. We have seen in Chapter 2 how victims are often not believed by the police, and as the police view influences the CICB's decision, Asian and Black victims may well lose out. Finally, while knowledge of the CICB is generally absent in the public domain, this may be exacerbated in the Asian and Black communities.

Mapping victims rights

Most legal systems are concerned with the prosecuting and sentencing of offenders while victims play a minimal role of giving evidence in courts. Although the effects of crime are suffered by the victims, their general neglect in the criminal justice system has led to the development of victims rights movement. As a result, movements in various countries across the world, some more organized (e.g. USA, Canada) than others (e.g. UK) have raised the issue of the victims rights. However it was not until 1985 that the General Assembly of the United Nations adopted a charter of victims rights. Waller (1988) comments that the charter, 'is an impressive landmark in establishing the need for action to provide equitable justice for victims across the world'.

The United Nations Declaration established four major principles for victims of crime:

(a) Access to judicial and administrative procedures (how victims should be treated fairly and their views considered).
(b) Restitution (payment for harm by offender to victim).
(c) Compensation (from government funds where restitution from offenders is not enough).
(d) Assistance to victims (need for support from agencies concerned with health and mental health care, social services, policing and justice).

The World Society of Victimology has campaigned for the implementation of these principles across the world. In 1987, it brought together a number of leading countries, including the UK to recommend improvement and expansion in victim assistance. However it was not until February 1990 that the UK produced a 'victims charter'. Before discussing this, we compare briefly developments in victims rights in the USA, Canada and UK.

USA

Although legislation exists in the USA to protect the interests of victims, two major pieces of federal legislation have had a considerable overall effect. These are: the Federal Victim Witness Protection Act of 1982, which promoted restitution by courts; and the Federal Victims of Crime Act 1984 which levied a special tax on federal offenders and enabled the use of fines to provide funds to federal states for the development of victim assistance networks and compensation programmes. This work continues to progress in many states in the USA.

Canada

Legislation exists in the form of Justice of Victims of Crime Act 1986 to implement the principles from the UN declaration. Many of the victim assistance programmes are based on 'needs assessment'. Regular surveys of victims needs are carried out and new services are created to fill any identified gaps. Most of the victim assistance programmes are located in police departments, based on the recognition that victims usually contact the police first.

UK

In contrast to the USA and Canada, victim assistance is largely provided by volunteers from Victim Support Schemes usually funded by the Home Office and local authorities. The 1982 Criminal Justice Act gave magistrates the powers to order compensation from offenders to victims. Since 1964, state compensation has been available to victims of crime (see above for discussion of these services). Interestingly, the UK through its Victim Support Schemes has not pursued the USA or Canadian path of establishing more connections with the criminal justice system (Shapland et al., op. cit.). For example, victim assistance programmes in those countries enable victims to provide witness statements which may influence the sentencing of the offender. Traditionally the Victim Support Schemes have chosen not to intervene in the criminal justice system (Maguire and Corbett, 1987).

Victim's Charter

Rather belatedly in 1990, the Home Office published a 'Victim's Charter' subtitled – 'A statement of the Rights of Victims of Crime'. This document was hastily produced to coincide with the European Victims Day on 22 February. The Charter's attempts to raise victims rights as an issue fails miserably. Divided into three sections, developments, current services and a list of questions to consider to assess the standards of the criminal justice system, it makes no reference to the United Nations Declaration of the four principles established for victims of crime. The Charter provides no background information as to how it is 'linked' to the European system, except that it now has reciprocal compensation arrangements with four other European countries. While its claims to be 'A statement of the Rights of Victims of

Crime' is confusing. Although some improvements have been made in the criminal justice system, when we compare these to the UN principles, the overall treatment of victims of crime seems inadequate. This can be seen if we consider it with reference to the four principles of the UN Declaration.

In relation to the first principle, access to judicial and administrative procedures, the Charter hardly attempts to comply. It fails to state clearly if this should be available as a right to the victim or as a discretionary information service provided by the police. If anything the emphasis seems to be on the latter, reinforcing police discretion.

As an interesting contrast the Government has made some improvements in the area referenced by 'restitution', the second principle of the UN Declaration. The Criminal Justice Act 1982, enabled victims to be compensated by convicted offenders. The problem with this, however, was that compensation orders were infrequently used. To improve their usage the Criminal Justice Act 1988, required magistrates to give reasons if they had not considered payment from the offender to the victim in 'suitable cases'. The knowledge of this provision, however, is not widely available.

If we consider the third principle, compensation, the Charter stipulates that the Government provides state compensation to victims of crime. Other than acknowledging the administrative difficulties, experienced by the CICB (e.g. long delays in payments and promising to increase staff to meet the backlog of work) it gives no consideration to structural problems in the scheme. A failure to tackle these problems will continue to offer a less than satisfactory service to victims of crime.

Finally, when we consider the fourth UN Declaratory principle, assistance to victims, the Government takes great pride in describing the Victim Support Schemes which 'offer comfort and practical advice'. The Charter gives information about the systematic increase in funding of these schemes from £1.5m in 1987/88 to over £2.5m in 1988/89 and approaching £4m in 1989/90, with an estimated £4.5m for 1990/1991. The Charter boasts that over 350 schemes cover England and Wales and over 10,000 volunteers are involved. However at an annual meeting of the National Association of Victim Support Schemes in 1991, the Director commented that the Government had failed to provide funding to some schemes and as a result they were experiencing financial difficulties. More significantly the Director announced, 'We are still waiting for improvements promised 18 months ago in the first victim's charter' (*The Guardian*, 26 July 1991).

The Government's attempts to consider the rights of victims have been resoundingly effete. It would not be surprising if a general withdrawal of the service provision emerged. The Charter is particularly problematic in so far that it offers no evaluation of statutory service provision and it provides no specification of the 'rights' victims can claim under the criminal justice system. Curiously the Charter poses a set of questions to consider in the improvement of the services. But there is no indication as to how the improvements will be considered and implemented. As well as failing to meet the exemplary criteria of the United Nations principles, the Charter is hollow in areas close to the interest of this study. For example, while it is encouraging to see the Charter make reference to the treatment of victims of rape and domestic violence and the progress made in this area, victims of racial harassment are conspicuously absent. The Charter fails to acknowledge their existence even when it refers to fair treatment:

> Victims should always be treated fairly and without adverse discrimination. Consistently with this, the services will give particular consideration to victims who are especially vulnerable such as children, victims of sexual or violent crime, and those who are severely shocked by their experience.
>
> (op. cit.:8)

Once again racial victimization is submerged, beneath the surface of official acknowledgement. By totally ignoring victims of racial harassment, the Charter echoes the 'state of affairs' which results in a skeletal service provision (e.g. Victim Support Schemes) and disparaging treatment by the criminal justice system.

(Neglected) needs of the victims of racial harassment

Given the scope of racial victimization outlined in this Chapter, we need finally to consider the type of victim 'support' raised in our evidence as important in terms of basic needs. In general terms the needs of victims of crime have always been an area of neglect, this neglect has been compounded where victims of racial harassment are concerned. For example, Shapland et al. (op. cit.) conducted a major longitudinal study of victims in the criminal justice system. They claimed that very little was known about what victims think despite the rapidly expanding interest in victims. As an attempt to remedy this situation, over a period of three years in Coventry and Northampton, they analyzed a sample of victims from the initial reporting of the case to its outcome. They considered the following offences: physical assaults; offences involving physical violence and property loss; sexual assaults. Although the sample contained a few Asian and Black victims, no reference was made to racial victimization in the study. Despite this absence, the study's recommendations do retain some interest and may be relevant to the needs of the victims of racial harassment. Shapland et al. argue:

> Victims should have an accepted role within the system such that their contribution is acknowledged by the professional participants. This implies that victims need to be treated with care and respect by police officers, prosecutors, court officials and compensation agency personnel.

Their recommendations are made under five categories; (a) provision of information to victims about their case through the system; (b) a more thoughtful attitude towards the needs and difficulties of victims in the investigation and prosecution; (c) consideration for victims at courts; (d) compensation and (e) victim support services. Cooper and Pomeiye (1988) made similar observations when they assessed the needs of the victims of racial harassment based on the National Association of Victim Support Schemes project in Camden in 1986. They argued that the needs of the victims of racial harassment were similar to the needs of other victims of crime.

In our research, we were able to identify four categories of needs (see Figure 10.1 below). While three are significantly compatible with those discussed above, the fourth is equally important.

1. Action against perpetrators	*proper investigation of reported cases *penalty/prosecution of identified perpetrators *regular information about the progress of the case of victims

2. Protection
    personal safety
 	
    physical security
	
	*immediate intervention to secure personal safety of the victim e.g. injunctions, prosecution, alternative accommodation
	*immediate repairs to property
	*provision of grants for security equipment

3. Practical assistance and advice	*legal matters *victims rights *welfare rights *insurance and compensation *liaison with agencies
4. Emotional support	*empathy *counselling – sensitive, available in community languages, easily and safely accessible geographically

Figure 10.1: Needs of the victims of racial harassment

It should be evident that these needs raise similarities with other forms of personal victimization (e.g. domestic violence and sexual assaults). However, needs are immaterial unless they are met with a strategic material response from responsive public agencies.

Notes

1   A project report on racial harassment undertaken by the Polytechnic of North London for the National Association of Victim Support Schemes (Kimber and Cooper, 1991), based in three Victim Support Schemes, Camden, Newham and Southwark makes similar observations.
2   This was subsequent to the local publication of our research findings in 1990.

11
Racism and victimization
by Benjamin Bowling

Methodological approach

In order to explore violent racism as a process, a methodological approach is required which takes account of all moments in the crime process, can capture the dynamic of repeated victimization, and provides geographical, social, historical, and political context. Qualitative as well as quantitative research methods are required to procure an holistic analysis (Bell and Newby, 1977; Walklate, 1989, 1990).

One approach which has been useful in criminology and other spheres is the case study. According to Yin, 'a case study is an empirical inquiry that: investigates a contemporary phenomenon within its real-life context; when the boundaries of the context are not clearly evident; and in which multiple sources of evidence are used' (1989: 23). These features lend themselves to an empirical, holistic, and processual account of crime. Surveys alone can try to deal with phenomenon and context, but by dint of the need to limit the number of variables to be analysed, their ability to investigate context is extremely limited (*ibid.*). Context, history, and process can best be captured using evidence from sources such as historiographical material, in-depth interviews, and observation as well as official records and surveys. In British criminology, case studies have produced some excellent descriptive and theoretical studies (e.g. Smith and Gray, 1983; Grimshaw and Jefferson, 1987).

A case study combining a survey with other methods of inquiry offers the possibility for explanation. Explanation—asking how and why—requires tracing processes over time as well as describing frequencies and incidence. Narrative accounts provided by people interviewed in the survey using in-depth interviews offer some insight in this regard. They offer the opportunity for the research subjects to describe their experiences in their own terms. As a means to understand offending, victimization, and state intervention, the actions and experiences of the social actors involved, and the points at which they intersect are indicated. Starting with historical context, data were collected on the events involved in the commission of the offence, its immediate aftermath, and long-term consequences for those involved. Qualitative accounts of the subjective reality of each actor in particular instances aim to flesh out the skeletal descriptions provided by the survey.

Providing a multi-facetted account of the expression and experience of violence offers the potential for evaluating the effectiveness of policing and the criminal justice system. By charting the moments at which criminal justice agents intervene in the processes of racism, violence, victimization, and survival, the impact of their police and court action can be assessed. The police and criminal justice system appear only fleetingly in survey descriptions, and yet both victim and offender may have to interact with them over an extended period (totalling hours, if not days and weeks) after the event.

The way ahead

Reading Baudrillard's view of opinion polls or social surveys (during 1989 when analysing survey data collected in North Plaistow) drew my attention to the sense in which statistical simulation does not necessarily increase certainty about the nature of social reality, and indeed may induce uncertainty about the idea of social reality itself. Baudrillard likens opinion polls to meteorology, noting the 'indecisiveness of their results, the uncertainty of their effects, and their unconscious humour' (Baudrillard, 1989: 211). The idea that survey data might 'destroy the political as will and representation, the political as meaning, precisely through the effect of simulation and uncertainty' shook my hitherto acceptance of the axiom of modern social survey research expressed succinctly by Orwell. I saw only the methodological flaws in surveys, their imprecision, uncertainty, the imperfect way in which commercial research agencies conduct their work, and above all the creation of de-contextualized statistics, stripped of meaning. This view was reinforced when I saw a *Sun* report of a 'race relations poll' headlined 'Send us back say British's blacks', which purported to show that '[s]even out of ten British black people are in favour of repatriating immigrants'.[1] That a survey could produce such a social 'fact' is surely what Baudrillard refers to as 'statistical pornography' (Baudrillard, 1989: 211).

However, working in a government-funded action-research setting does not allow the researcher the luxury of opting out into the hyper-reality of postmodernism. Survey data are there to be used as best they can as tools in administrative practice. On reflection, the survey was neither designed, conducted, analysed, nor written up as well as it could have been. But the data were used nonetheless. Since drafting a report on the survey in 1990, further analysis of the quantitative data and an exploration of the limited qualitative data recorded in the survey have been possible. I am now of the view that survey data are of value, but that they must be seen alongside other forms of data and set in a historical and political context. Using numbers complemented with individual narratives of victims, the police, and others, set in historical context, it is possible to 'tell relevant stories' about racism, violence, and policing.

Violence is like the 'white noise' of society. The incessant and myriad attempts to express an emotion, communicate a desire, or exert power over others may seem to the casual viewer like the hiss and crackle of a badly tuned television set. It is possible to see how, superficially, violence might be considered random, inexplicable, and unfocused. Survey research, like a tuner, attempts to distinguish signal from noise. It records moments of human experience in both digital and narrative forms and through tabulation and cross-tabulation seeks to reveal patterns of social action and interaction. Drawing on a victimization survey, official records, interviews with officers from local statutory agencies, and detailed case studies, this Chapter gives voice to experiences of violence and shows how they are patterned by 'race' and racism. The Chapter describes the extent and nature of violent racism, who the victims and perpetrators are, and where and when incidents occur. It examines how violence impacts on those who are targeted and explores the relationship between experiences of violence and the broader context of racist discourses and exclusion.

The North Plaistow Racial Harassment survey

A component of the initial data-gathering of the North Plaistow Racial Harassment Project was a victimization survey. The survey was based on a random sample of 751 residents of the study area and a 'booster sample' of Asian residents, giving a total sample size of 1,174. These interviewees completed a short *general questionnaire*, which covered several general issues relating to crime and racial harassment and then ascertained whether the respondent had suffered a racial incident. This sample forms the basis for the analysis of the prevalence and incidence of the problem.

Of the 163 respondents who mentioned a racial incident, 114 (70 per cent) completed a *victim questionnaire*. It was intended that up to three incidents would be recorded in detail for each victim. In the event, not all subsequent incidents were recorded. The total number of incidents recorded in detail was 158. These form the basis for the analysis of patterns of incidents, the effects suffered, etc. The fieldwork was carried out by Harris Research using 'ethnically matched' interviewers during May and June 1989.

The views of survey respondents

Views about the locality

By almost any 'objective' criterion, North Plaistow is not the best place to live. In terms of its economy, the physical condition and cleanliness of its environment, the quality of its housing stock, its facilities for young and old people, and its rate of recorded crime and racial harassment, it is among the very worst-off localities in the whole of England and Wales. Despite this, many more respondents thought their area to be a good (60 per cent) rather than a bad one (28 per cent) to live in, and ethnic minority respondents rated the area considerably more highly than white ones. 55 per cent of white respondents said that the area was a good one, compared with 65 per cent of Asians and 70 per cent of Africans and Afro-Caribbeans.

Respondents were then read a list of things 'that are a problem in some areas', and were asked to what extent they themselves felt each were a problem. The things most likely to be seen as a big problem in the area were rubbish and litter (51 per cent), crime (44 per cent), and unemployment (32 per cent). 29 per cent of the sample thought that racial harassment was a problem—12 per cent thought it a big problem and a further 17 per cent a bit of a problem. As expected, ethnic minorities were more likely than white people to think that racial harassment was a problem.

Views about racial harassment in relation to other problems

Respondents were also asked what they thought to be the three greatest problems in the project area (see Table 11.1). Crime was considered the greatest problem, followed by rubbish and litter, unemployment, and housing conditions.

Ten per cent of the sample said that racial harassment was one of the three greatest problems in the area, ranking eleventh out of a list of fifteen problems. Racial harassment was for the sample *as a whole* more important only than police service provision, racial discrimination, noisy neighbours, and public transport. As expected, this picture changed substantially when desegregated by ethnic and gender group. Now, racial harassment emerged as a problem second only to crime and on a par with rubbish and litter for Asian women and as the third greatest problem for Asian men. Other ethnic and gender groups ranked racial harassment much lower—seventh for African and Afro-Caribbean women, thirteenth and twelfth for white men and women, respectively and fifteenth (bottom of the list) for African and Afro-Caribbean men.

Table 11.1 Respondents' opinion of the greatest 3 problems in the area (%)

	All	WM	WF	ACM	ACF	AM	AF	V	MV
Crime	48	48	51	41	30	60	52	57	61
Rubbish/litter	43	44	52	30	40	31	28	31	30
Unemployment	24	26	22	25	28	20	20	14	11
Housing conditions	19	19	21	24	19	14	15	11	6
Youth facilities	18	18	25	11	19	9	6	12	11
Leisure facilities	15	19	15	11	12	10	6	12	12
Rowdy youths	14	16	10	14	15	31	14	14	11
Council services	13	11	14	17	18	13	9	18	21
Schools	12	11	11	14	15	13	14	14	11
Graffiti	12	16	13	8	9	4	6	11	13
Racial harassment	10	8	5	3	16	22	28	27	36
Police service	9	9	5	16	10	14	12	18	14
Race discrimination	8	7	3	6	15	17	23	16	15
Noisy neighbours	8	10	5	11	9	10	5	2	2
Public transport	6	7	6	6	10	4	3	2	2
Rank order of racial harassment	11th	13th	12th	15th	8th	3rd	2nd	3rd	2nd

Note: Tables 11.1–11.6
WM = white male
WF = white female
ACM = African/Caribbean Male
ACF = African/Caribbean Female
AM = Asian Male
AF = Asian Female
V = racial harassment victim
MV = multiply victimized

Views about problems relating to law and order

Narrowing the focus somewhat, the survey next asked respondents to say whether or not they found specific forms of crime and disorder to be a problem in their area (see Table 11.2).

As might be expected, a large proportion of African and Afro-Caribbean and Asian respondents considered 'racial attacks on Afro-Caribbean and Asian people' to be a problem. Nearly two thirds of Asian women and men, about half of African and Afro-Caribbean women and men thought it was either a big, or a bit of a, problem in the area. However, there was also a considerable degree of concern among the white majority community about attacks on ethnic minorities; one quarter of white women and one third of white men said they thought that racial attacks *on Afro-Caribbeans and Asians* were a problem in the locality.

Table 11.2 Respondents' opinion of the greatest 3 'crime' problems in the area (%)

	All	WM	WF	ACM	ACF	AM	AF	V	MV
Burglary	55	49	57	57	61	57	61	63	68
Street robbery	39	40	39	30	39	50	39	37	37
Vandalism	35	37	34	43	36	31	21	35	32
Car theft	35	36	33	33	39	42	29	39	37
Sexual assault	21	19	29	25	7	13	14	21	22
Youth misbehaviour	17	18	15	19	9	18	20	21	25
Women pestered	16	14	24	13	15	6	7	18	20
Racial attacks[1]	15	7	11	11	25	28	33	27	28
Fights in street	9	11	9	6	6	8	9	5	3

[1] The question referred to 'racial attacks on Afro-Caribbean and Asian people'.

Views about police priorities

Views about policing priorities reflected, to some extent, beliefs about the greatest crime problems, although some forms of crime and harassment (e.g. sexual assault and pestering) were rated higher as police priorities than as crime problems (see Table 11.3).

Racial attacks were the third highest police priority for Asian men and women (after burglary and street robbery), fourth for African and Afro-Caribbean women, sixth for African and Afro-Caribbean men, and seventh for white men and women. Despite the differences in views among ethnic groups, some white people thought that racial attacks on African and Afro-Caribbean and Asian people were one of the three most important police priorities. The proportions of white people believing that racial attacks on

Table 11.3 Which crime should the police concentrate on most? (%)

	All	WM	WF	ACM	ACF	AM	AF	V	MV
Burglary	50	45	49	54	55	57	58	52	49
Street robbery	36	38	34	25	42	42	40	34	32
Sexual assault	32	30	39	32	31	20	20	24	22
Car theft	27	27	26	27	28	32	25	32	24
Vandalism	26	26	24	32	28	23	24	26	26
Women pestered	21	20	30	21	15	10	7	16	18
Racial attacks[1]	19	16	13	21	28	33	39	30	30
Youth misbehaviour	10	11	8	16	1	12	14	15	21
Fights in street	8	9	7	10	6	7	10	7	8

[1] The question referred to 'racial attacks on Afro-Caribbean and Asian people'.

ethnic minorities are a problem (32 per cent) and should be a policing priority (14 per cent) suggests that there is considerable concern about such attacks among the white majority community.

Fear of racial harassment

Fifty-eight per cent of Asian women worried either a great deal or a fair amount about being victimized, compared with 51 per cent of Asian men, 37 per cent of African and Afro-Caribbean women, 26 per cent of African and Afro-Caribbean men, 20 per cent of white women and 13 per cent of white men. Most white men (64 per cent), African and Afro-Caribbean men (57 per cent) and white women (54 per cent) did not worry at all about being victimized, compared with only 12 per cent of Asian women, 20 per cent of Asian men, and 29 per cent of African and Afro-Caribbean women. When asked whether they worried about the possibility of their families being victimized, the number of those fearful rose for each ethnic-gender group. Most worried of all were Asian women, only 10 per cent of whom claimed to live free from this anxiety (see Table 11.4).

Experiences of racial harassment

Respondents were next asked about experience, if any, of racial harassment. Interviewers explained that the term racial harassment referred to 'any form of insult, threat, violence, damage to or theft of property, or any attempt to do any of these things which was racially motivated. By racially motivated I mean an act directed at you because of your race.'

Respondents were then read a list of some types of offences and were asked to say whether any of them had happened to them personally within the previous eighteen months (January 1988–June 1989). 163 of the 1,174 survey respondents said they had experienced some form of racial harassment, about one in five ethnic minority respondents—21 per cent of African and Afro-Caribbean women (14 respondents), 19 per cent of Asian men

Table 11.4 Respondents' worry about themselves becoming victims of racial harassment (%)

	All	WM	WF	ACM	ACF	AM	AF	V	MV
A great deal	10	5	6	10	18	19	29	35	39
A fair amount	15	8	14	16	19	22	29	25	27
Not very much	23	20	24	16	22	33	24	22	13
Not at all	50	64	54	57	39	20	12	18	19
Don't know/not stated	3	2	3	2	1	5	6	*	*

(57 respondents), 18 per cent of Asian women (43 respondents) and 17 per cent of African and Afro-Caribbean men (n=11). A small proportion of white people also said that they had experienced a racial incident—8 per cent of white men (n=14) and 7 per cent of white women (n=21).

Between them, these 163 victims mentioned approximately 831 actual incidents over the eighteen-month period.[2] This figure assumes that respondents' descriptions of the number of times they were victimized was accurate. They may not be able to recall the number and nature of incidents accurately over a period of eighteen months—some may be forgotten; others may have occurred longer ago and 'telescoped' forward into the reporting period; others may have occurred during the reporting period, but 'telescoped' backward and thus not been mentioned by the respondent. Because of the problem of defining racial harassment, some respondents may have defined incidents as *racial* when the motivation was arguable, or when they could not even be certain that a person from another racial group was responsible for the incident. Others may have ignored incidents they regarded as minor or unimportant.[3]

Despite this, it must be concluded that in the eighteen-month period in question, there were many thousands of incidents defined by the victim as racial harassment in North Plaistow. Given that roughly 10 per cent of the adult population of the area was interviewed, as many as 7,000 instances of insulting behaviour, threats of or actual violence, theft, damage to property (or attempts to do any of these things) where the victim believed that the incident was directed at him or her because of their race may have occurred in the eighteen-month period in question.

Detailed description of incidents

The preceding results are based on information supplied by the whole sample of 1,174 people. Of the 163 respondents who said that they had experienced one or more incidents, 114 agreed to provide details of 158 incidents.[4] These were between two thirds and three quarters of all those who stated that they had experienced a racial incident in the previous eighteen months. The information in the following section is based on their accounts of what happened. The victims detailing an incident were slightly more likely to be male than female, were much more likely to be under 45 than over, and were little different from the occupational class structure of the sample as a whole. Of the 158 incidents described in detail, the race–gender breakdown is as follows: fifty-eight Asian males, forty-five Asian females, thirteen African and Afro-Caribbean males, thirteen African and Afro-Caribbean females, fourteen white males, twelve white females, and three others.

By far the most common form of harassment consisted of insulting behaviour or verbal abuse (42 per cent), which the majority of victims suffered (see Table 11.5). Next were actual damage to property (16 per cent), actual physical assault (10 per cent), and actual theft (7 per cent). There were a very large number of 'less serious' incidents and many 'very serious' ones. Some appeared to be one-off events, while others were said to be part of a pattern of repeated attacks and harassment. This is consistent with the views of officers from local agencies who said that persistent door-knocking, egg throwing, damage to property, verbal abuse, threats, and intimidation had a cumulative effect on victims, even though the events may not look serious as individual 'incidents'.

Nearly six out of ten incidents occurred in the immediate vicinity of victims' homes (see Table 11.6). This including incidents which occurred at the home address[5] (23 per cent), those that occurred in the street outside the

Table 11.5 Types of harassment and numbers of incidents suffered by respondents over an 18-month period (weighted figures)

Form of harassment	Incidents
Insulting behaviour/verbal abuse	303
Threatened damage or violence	98
Attempted assault	81
Actual assault	72
Actual and attempted damage to property	114
Actual and attempted theft	53
Actual and attempted arson	3

Unweighted n = 163

Table 11.6 Where the incident took place (%)

Location	All	WM	WF	ACM	ACF	AM	AF	R[1]
In/around the home[2]	23	21	25	31	15	21	31	37
Street outside home	16	14	17	8	8	31	18	10
Inside own building	4	–	–	–	15	2	9	2
Outside own building	12	14	17	15	–	17	11	20
In garages for houses	4	21	–	–	8	4	–	8
All in vicinity of home	59	70	59	54	46	66	69	77
At work	7	–	–	–	31	7	–	3
All others[3]	33	29	42	39	23	28	17	17

[1] Incidents reported to an official agency (e.g. the police or the Housing Department)
[2] Includes attempted break-ins, incidents on the doorstep, material through the letter box.
[3] Includes school/college, in street near work, in/near a pub, at place of work out of doors and place of worship, and 'don't know'/not stated, all of which were very small numbers. The bulk (33% of the whole sample) were 'other' responses.

victim's home (16 per cent), outside or inside the building in which their home was located (12 per cent and 4 per cent respectively), and near their garage (4 per cent).

Incidents happened at all times of the day and night, 29 per cent sometime during the daytime, and a further 13 per cent occurred in the morning, 30 per cent between 6 pm and midnight, 11 per cent between midnight and 6 am, and 4 per cent sometime during the hours of darkness.

Patterns of victimization for each ethnic-gender group

It is evident that a wide range of different experiences have been defined by respondents as racial incidents. The data suggest that there are very different experiences among the various ethnic and gender groups. Thus, it becomes impossible to speak of the *typical* case of racial harassment or attack. The experiences are so varied that one hesitates to include every instance in the same class of events, behaviours, or experiences.

In addition to differences between groups, there are differences *within* groups. Thus, the incidents mentioned in the survey by a single ethnic–gender group appear to cover a wide range of activities, with regard to the characteristics of the victim and perpetrator, or the context of the incident. In the following analysis, the quantitative data from the survey, *selected* quotations from the survey's open-ended questions are used to illustrate specific points as they emerge.[6]

Asian people

Of the 103 incidents mentioned by Asian respondents, no fewer that thirty-nine of them (38 per cent) were directed at Asian council tenants. Only 14 per cent of the Asians sampled were council tenants, suggesting that those living in council accommodation were almost three times as likely to have provided detail about an incident as Asians as a whole. The majority of council estates in North Plaistow are away from the eastern portion of the study site, which has a high proportion of Asian residents (more than 50 per cent). Council housing lies mainly in the centre of the area (e.g. the Chadd Green estate) or on the western edge of the area where there is a low proportion of Asian residents. These facts support the view that the geographical spread of racial incidents reflects the targeting of ethnic minorities living outside the areas of high ethnic minority concentration.

The survey showed that seven out of ten incidents mentioned by Asian women happened close to home, with three out of ten occurring directly on or immediately adjacent to their homes and a further four out of ten in the street, walkway, or passageway outside their home. The remainder occurred elsewhere. The pattern was similar for Asian men, though more were incidents which occurred in the street outside their homes.

Most recent incident:
I was watching TV at home, and a gang of kids come, shouted abuse, and started throwing stones, hitting and breaking windows in my house, and of my car. *What was it about the incident which makes you believe that the attack was racially motivated?* They call me a black fucking Paki, and they said I shouldn't be here, to go home.

Second most recent incident:
It was some kids I chased off earlier in the day, they come and threw stones at my windows breaking them, shouting 'Go away Paki'. *What was it about the incident which makes you believe that the attack was racially motivated?* The fact that they hate anyone who is a 'Paki' as they call us. They tell me to go away.

Third most recent incident:
We were at the back of our garden, and we heard a noise. We come out to find the windows of our car broken. *What was it about the incident which makes you believe that the attack was racially motivated?* Because I'd had trouble with racial harassment before [Indian man].

The survey found that many incidents consisted of racist abuse, graffiti, window smashing, and egg throwing. There are three reasons for considering what are sometimes referred to as 'low level' or merely 'nuisance' incidents, very serious in their impact and their effect on the security of the victim.[7] First, any type of incident becomes serious when it is repeated frequently enough. Repeated or persistent incidents undermine the security of the victim and induce fear and anxiety. The sense of the cumulative effects of repeated instances of stone throwing, name-calling, and harassment are evident from this example:

Most recent incident:
Came in and called me Paki and started throwing bricks at me. They didn't hurt me because I had thick coat on. They called me Paki before they started throwing the bricks at me.

Second most recent incident:
A gang of teenagers started shouting at me 'Paki' go home and abuse. Nothing else.

Third most recent incident:
It's happened so many times—they come up in groups and call me names—they call me rude names and call me Paki. I want to move away from here because I'm frightened to live here now because it happens so often.

A second reason for taking seriously the effect of repeated harassment directed specifically against ethnic minorities is the apparent exclusionary intent and impact of this form of victimization. The two examples cited above illustrate the exclusionary language and practice of the perpetrator. The phrases such as 'go home', 'go back to your own country' challenge the human rights of the people who are victimized (made into a victim) with the obvious effect of undermining their sense of security and sense of belonging (Hesse *et al.*, 1992). The eventual impact is to create fear about living in a particular locality and to inspire a wish to move away. This aspect of racism is what Hesse *et al.* refer to as the 'logic of white territorialism':

> What then is the context and objective of 'white territorialism'? . . . Consider the discursive resonances wrought by expressions like 'Pakis go home', 'go back to your own country', 'alien cultures swamping British identity', 'immigrants colonizing Britain', 'blacks ghettoizing the inner-city' or more recently 'Islamic fundamentalism sweeping the nation'. At least two things should be apparent from these spatial obsessions. First there is heightened anxiety about these 'subordinate', 'other' populations resisting regulation and getting out of 'our' control; and secondly, there is a sense in which 'our' British identity (for 'our' read 'white') is under threat because 'our right' to dominate is being questioned; this is the expressive logic of the desire for racial exclusion [Hesse *et al.*, 1992: 172].

Even the most mundane instances of racial abuse may be seen as an exclusionary practice, one which acts to 'defend . . . space against change and transformation' (Hesse *et al.*, 1992). In this way, spaces are created within which black people are made to feel unwelcome and vulnerable to attack, and from which they may eventually be excluded.

Finally, mundane but persistent attacks *on property* are also attacks on *those inside* the dwelling (whether or not they are present at the time of the incident). Graffiti, window breakages, and other forms of criminal damage on the fabric of the building and physical attacks nearby the building violate the security of the place where an individual is often considered safest. Although an Englishman's home is (metaphorically) his castle, in actual fact the physical fabric of a house (particularly those in localities such as Newham) provides only an illusion of defence against attack from without.[8] Being a static object makes a dwelling an easy target—one which is open to repeated and persistent attack, and one where the potential for escalation is tied specifically to a fixed location (Hesse *et al.*, 1992). Several respondents mentioned instances of attack which resulted in damage to property where their personal security was at great risk. Such instances include shooting a window with an air gun and attempted arson attacks using inflammable fluid squirted through the letterbox:

A bullet came through the bedroom window and broke it bringing the bullet into the room. An air gun was used. *What was it about the incident which makes you believe that the attack was racially motivated?* It's happened several times [involving] the same person. I have got NF written outside my wall and I don't know what to do about it this time. I have been attacked right in my bedroom [Other Asian].

Someone put container of liquid through letter box. Failed to make a fire. Could have been serious. *What was it about the incident which makes you believe that the attack was racially motivated?* Because of the sort of attack putting fire through letter box. Neighbours had one similar incident [Pakistani].

In several cases documented during the study period attacks have occurred in which groups of assailants have smashed their way through the front door and assaulted the victim with weapons (including knives, a hammer, and a pool cue) inside their homes. In other instances, attacks which started in public space led to attacks on the victim's home:

My children went to the park, under the supervision of my sister, and they were set upon, by these white kids, when they finished beating my kids up they followed them to my address, and threw stones at my window, breaking it. *What was it about the incident which makes you believe that the attack was racially motivated?* Because they shouted, abusive names like Pakis and many other insulting words.

Many of the incidents described by Asians in the survey are of a type identified in the Home Office (1981) study and noted by Walmsley (1986 drawing on Brown, 1984):

Many attacks on Asians and West Indians are attacks in the street when there is clearly no background of a prior argument or misunderstanding. In such incidents strangers may simply approach others and hit them, kick them, throw stones at them or even use knives and bottles to assault them [Walmsley 1986: 26].

In North Plaistow, respondents described walking along the street near to their homes or while shopping, going to work or worship, and being unexpectedly verbally abused or being physically attacked or menaced:

Me and my husband were taking our children to mosque in the afternoon. Some young white man just said verbal abuse—'Paki' and things like that [Indian woman].

As I was coming home there were some kids playing on the road—16 or 17 years old. They said 'You Paki. Why don't you go away from here'. Sometimes when I move my car they are there and won't move to let me get out [Indian].

Guy was drunk, he hit me with a piece of [wire]. Line on my face straight through where he hit me then he ran away—I didn't have time to do anything to defend myself. It happened very quickly, he didn't say anything but he wouldn't have done it if I was white. *What was it about the incident which makes you believe that the attack was racially motivated?* We had no conversation—didn't know the guy—first thing that happened was that he hit me. He just wouldn't have done it if I was white. No [Iranian].

I was shopping once [when a] white young girl came and stood in front of me. I told her I am in the queue and you should wait for your turn. But instead she started saying racially names and slapped on my face as well. *What was it about the incident which makes you believe that the attack was racially motivated?* That is quite obvious. If there was another white woman, first thing she would not jump the queue and secondly in the case of white women, if she had protested, this white girl would never slap her or abuse her [Pakistani].

Some incidents mentioned by Asian men (7 per cent) occurred while at work.

Argument over prices. Bloody Indian, bloody immigrant. Fucking bastard! *What was it about the incident which makes you believe that the attack was racially motivated?* Wording racial. Bloody Paki. Bloody immigrant [Indian shopkeeper].

The only Chinese victim in the sample who gave details of their experience also suffered harassment at work:

Most recent incident:
[I work in a] Chinese fish and chip shop. I come to work the next morning to find our shop window smashed. *What was it about the incident which makes you believe that the attack was racially motivated?* Because they smashed my window without stealing anything. [1] must be someone they don't like.

Second most recent incident:
Two kids came in. Got a drink and tried to steal it. I went out of the counter and said 'You've got to pay for the drink'. They started arguing. Finally he paid for it and on his way out, he was very angry and said "I'm

gonna put a brick through that door". *What was it about the incident which makes you believe that the attack was racially motivated?* I just felt it could have been because of us [Chinese] living here.

The majority of the incidents experienced by both Asian men and women involved groups of young white males who were unknown to the victim. Very few incidents targeted at Asian women were one-to-one confrontations, with 85 per cent involving more than one perpetrator. More than one third of the incidents involved a group of four or more perpetrators. Four out of ten incidents directed against Asian men were carried out by a group of four or more. Asian men and women were harassed by a group of males in two thirds of the incidents. Also in two thirds of the incidents the perpetrators were aged 16–25, and in one quarter were school age.

In just over one incident in ten the victim knew all or some of the people involved and, where they were known, they were not known well, most often by sight only. Two thirds of the Asian victims said that their assailants were white, one fifth that they were African or Afro-Caribbean, and one tenth a 'mixed' group.

The question of whether African and Afro-Caribbean people can exhibit racist attitudes or behaviour toward Asian people has been a recurrent one since the emergence of the problem of racial violence as a policy issue in the early 1980s, though many reports simply duck the issue altogether.[9] In North Plaistow there is no doubt that some of the Asians interviewed believed themselves to have been the victims of anti-Asian racism perpetrated by groups composed solely of young men of African or Afro-Caribbean origin, or groups of blacks and white acting together. In some instances, the belief that attacks by African/Caribbeans were racially motivated was simply because the assailant was black. In other instances, African/Caribbean young people were perceived by the victim to engage in anti-Asian racist behaviour that was not readily distinguishable from that perpetrated by their white counterparts:

Most recent incident:
Graffiti. Very abusive and dirty words were written on both the . . . front door and refuse box. All over the front walls. Some words are still visible. It happen[s] . . . frequently. *What was it about the incident which makes you believe that the attack was racially motivated?* It must be done by white or black kids. We are only two [Asian] families in this block. Everybody know[s]. That is why making our life very hard.

Second most recent incident:
My husband was coming back. A group of young kids push my husband and started kicking him. *What was it about the incident which makes you believe that the attack was racially motivated?* Because the gang was

mix[ed] group. Two white and one black youth. They were awaiting for him [Indian woman].

There are also instances of African/Caribbeans echoing the racist epithets more commonly associated with white racism:

A couple of whites and a couple of blacks called me racist names. They pushed me around . . . *What was it about the incident which makes you believe that the attack was racially motivated?* The verbal abuse. That's all [Pakistani].

Just came and asked me for money. They punched me—black and white gang—there were lots of them. They threatened me but I didn't give them anything. They were carrying knives and a screwdriver. *What was it about the incident which makes you believe that the attack was racially motivated?* Paki—they called me a Paki—if I'd been white I don't think they'd have stopped and asked me for money. Nothing else. No [Bangladeshi].

One Indian person said that he had been assaulted by 'eight black people' who held him to the ground and kicked and hit him. When asked what was it about the incident which made him believe that the attack was racially motivated, he said, 'because they told me it was. There you bloody Paki that will show ya'.

For both Asian men and women, the most common reason for believing that the incident was racially motivated—in 54 per cent of those directed against men and 40 per cent against women—was that the perpetrator had referred to their actual or supposed race. This racial ascription was very often wrong, with people of Indian origin frequently called 'Paki'. The second most common reason, in about one fifth of cases, was the victim's belief that such attacks would not happen to them if they were white. In one in ten incidents directed against Asian men, the victim was told to 'go back to where you came from', or 'to your own country'. Often these racist epithets were combined, such as '[t]hey call me a black fucking Paki, and they said I shouldn't be here, to go home'. In other instances, the victim ascribed a racial motive to the perpetrator because of the circumstances of the incident. This was sometimes because the incident had occurred without prior history, warning, or provocation: '[w]e had no conversation— didn't know the guy—first thing that happened was that he hit me. He just wouldn't have done it if I was white.' On other occasions, this perception stemmed from the fact the victim was one of a few or the only Asian family living in the block; that similar incidents had occurred to minority families living nearby; or that other expressions of racist antipathy had occurred in the past.

Africans and Afro-Caribbeans

About half of the incidents mentioned by African and Afro-Caribbean men (54 per cent) and women (46 per cent) took place at, around, or near their home addresses. All the incidents mentioned by African and Afro-Caribbean respondents involved white perpetrators. In common with the experience of the Asian respondents, most of these incidents consisted of insults and verbal abuse (54 per cent for women and 69 per cent for men) involved unprovoked abuse or harassment:

> *Most recent incident:*
> A white guy came out of a pub and started abusing me. He called me a 'wog' and a 'nigger'. He first called me a wog and when I challenged him he called me nigger. It nearly turned [in]to a fight but a police car drove by and we broke it up. It ended in just words between us. *What was it about the incident which makes you believe that the attack was racially motivated?* Well his words. Wog and nigger. If that isn't racial, what is?

> *Second most recent incident:*
> I was walking down this road. I had a suit on as I was going for an interview when a blue van drove past and a white guy threw an egg at me. It was a fresh egg. Well the egg broke and stained my suit. I . . . had to go back home to change. I was late for the interview and didn't get the job [African].

> Two white boys in a car slowed down as they passed me and shouted 'get out of the way stupid nigger'. *What was it about the incident which makes you believe that the attack was racially motivated?* Well, they shouted nigger didn't they and they were white. So it's obvious isn't it [Afro-Caribbean].

A number of other incidents arose out of a conflict with neighbours:

> We had a party. Neighbours were informed before hand. My neighbours threw a bag of rubbish at my guests. *What was it about the incident which makes you believe that the attack was racially motivated?* The person involved was white. The type of language used by the man [African].

> The woman's [neighbour] dog kept on barking and barking that it was so loud my baby couldn't sleep so I went to the woman and complained. She told me to get lost, called me a black bastard and slammed the door in my face. The dog was so disturbing that I reported it to the council. *What was it about the incident which makes you believe that the attack was racially motivated?* She said I was a black bastard and that I shouldn't bother her. Yes, she's white so it was a racial thing wasn't it? [African].

African and Afro-Caribbean men were the most likely of all ethnic–

gender groups to mention threatened or actual property damage (in 46 per cent of cases).

> Petrol was poured through the letter box and set alight. That's all [Afro-Caribbean].

> Came home from college and found damage on my door and it has been set on fire, with graffiti on the wall calling me names.

> *First Incident:*
> Someone smashed my car windscreen. Nothing was taken. It happened in the evening or night. *What was it about the incident which makes you believe that the attack was racially motivated?* All over the car was written 'Out, out Paki' [*sic*].

> *Second Incident:*
> I came back in my car with children from shopping. I parked my car. Then the youngest son from next door (about ten) went to my doorstep, took down his trousers and urinated in front of me and my children. *What was it about the incident which makes you believe that the attack was racially motivated?* In relation to all the other things that they had done like cutting my telephone wires at least twenty times, stealing my son's glasses and me and my children were racially abused every single day [African].

African and Afro-Caribbean men mentioned incidents perpetrated by other males either in a group (60 per cent) or alone (40 per cent). In just under half of the incidents (45 per cent) the perpetrators were aged between 16 and 25, one fifth were school age, and one in three older people.

When explaining the basis for their perception that the incident was racially motivated, African and Afro-Caribbean men most often said that the perpetrators had referred to their race (54 per cent). They also mentioned that damage had been done to their property with no apparent motive other than racism, that they were told to 'go back to your own country', and that they were the only black people in the neighbourhood and were being singled out as victims of crime. Three out of ten respondents said that they felt that the incident was racially motivated, but had no proof.

About one in three of the incidents mentioned by African and Afro-Caribbean women occurred in their place of work. They were also more likely than any other group to know the perpetrator involved, suggesting that some of these incidents involved co-workers. In six out of ten incidents they were harassed by a sole male perpetrator and in more than half of them they knew the perpetrator involved. In more than half of the incidents described by African/Caribbean women, their race was mentioned and in one incident in ten they were told to 'go back to your own country'. 15 per cent of the incidents were said to have been part of a process of harassment over a longer period.

White people

In many ways the incidents mentioned by white women were similar to those mentioned by Asian and Afro-Caribbean women. A large proportion occurred in the vicinity of their home; many involved unprovoked abusive language and insulting behaviour. However, one very important difference between the incidents mentioned by white women and other groups was the likelihood of it involving theft. Those mentioned by white women were twice as likely to involve theft as those mentioned by Asian women and four times as likely as those mentioned by African and Afro-Caribbean women.

A striking feature of the incidents described by white women is the large proportion of cases in which white perpetrators were involved. White people were said to have been involved as aggressors in more than four out of the ten incidents directed at white women when the race of the perpetrator was known. In three incidents the perpetrators were *all* white and one other involved a mainly white group. Of the remaining six cases, four involved African/Caribbeans, one Asians, and one involved a mixed but mainly black group.

It is evident from some of the things said by white women when asked to describe their experience that some, and perhaps all, of the incidents in which other whites were the aggressors were directed against them because of their association with black or Asian people. The question of violence directed against people in mixed race relationships is explored below.

The types of incidents mentioned by white men diverged considerably from those mentioned by other ethnic–gender groups. Just under half of the incidents described in full by white men (43 per cent) involved theft of property. People of all ethnic and gender groups mentioned incidents of theft from their person or home which they thought to have been racially motivated. However, the rate for white men was at least twice that for any other group and over five times that for African/Caribbean women. The extent to which an incident involving economic gain can also be said to be partly or fully motivated by racism is problematic. That so many of the incidents involving white men involved theft suggests that their experience of 'racially motivated' crime is rather different from those for which no such economic motive was involved. The majority of incidents mentioned by white men involved black perpetrators (78 per cent), a mixed but mainly black group (11 per cent), and Asian (11 per cent).

The transcripts of the open ended questions in the survey reveal a range of types of incidents. Some incidents involve theft from the person, burglary, and theft from cars where the victim did not know who the perpetrator was, but believed that he or she was black. The belief that the incident was perpetrated by a black person carried with it the ascription of racial hatred for several respondents, even when the race of the offender was not known:

Most recent incident:
Car window was smashed. Cassette was stolen. Car smashed. *What was it about the incident which makes you believe that the attack was racially motivated?* Car was parked in front of this block. . . . people know my car. I think it was done purposely.

Second most recent incident:
Somebody tried to break in. An attempt to break in through front door. When I came home the front door lock was [broken]. Nothing stolen. *What was it about the incident which makes you believe that the attack was racially motivated?* That I can't say. Not sure. But I think it may be racially motivated.

I'd had words with a black man earlier for trying to steal my geraniums. At 3 o'clock in the morning I had a brick put through my window. *What was it about the incident which makes you believe that the attack was racially motivated?* A lot of the young blacks in the area always hate whites. They whisper as you go by and I feel their hatred.

In some cases, a racial motive was ascribed simply because the offender was black:

About three of them. One of the pulled on my [chain]. [I didn't] have much money on me . . . they took my money, jewels, watch, beat me up. *What was it about the incident which makes you believe that the attack was racially motivated?* The group were all blacks. Nothing else.

In one case, the respondent complained of being wrongly accused of doing damage to the home of some of his black neighbours:

Most recent incident:
She just used to shout up the stairs. Things like you fucking white trash. All this type of thing, I can't remember every thing she call us. *What was it about the incident which makes you believe that the attack was racially motivated?* Because of the names she called us, white bastards and white trash. She said we did things to her home because we didn't like coloured people.

Second most recent incident:
Down stairs this time smashed the place up, tore light fittings wrote NF on her wall . . . said we done it because we didn't like black [people]. *What was it about the incident which makes you believe that the attack was*

racially motivated? She blamed us because she said we were against her because she was black.

In several incidents detailed in full, white respondents described being unexpectedly set upon by a group of black people:

> Eight people jumped out of a car and started hitting me and my mates. One of them had a bar. They just started hitting. With a bar. On my head and that. *What was it about the incident which makes you believe that the attack was racially motivated?* They had no other reason. I was just in the street and they started, with my mates, hitting you know, with a bar.

> Three guys attacked me. Later took off and went to the pub. Physical damage. Cuts and bruises on my face and chest. What *was it about the incident which makes you believe that the attack was racially motivated?* Because the attackers were black people.

In another instance, the respondent complained about being harassed by the next-door neighbours' 'all-night party' and of being called names when they protested:

> They had a very noisy all night party next door. They kept banging and making noise. When they saw I was disturbed by it they called me names. Whitey Honkey, etc. and started banging on my front door. What *was it about the incident which makes you believe that the attack was racially motivated?* They kept banging on my door and wall. Then they covered up my spy hole so I couldn't see them. They were all blacks and they called me honkey and that.

It is evident that a not insignificant group of white people perceived themselves to have been victim of racially motivated incidents. This finding contradicts conventional wisdom in a number of respects. First, even those official reports which have included white people as potential victims of racial attack have found that such experience is rare. The Home Office (1981) report found that white people were fifty times less likely than Asians and thirty-six times less likely than Afro-Caribbeans to be victims of a racial attack. This figure is the most widely quoted finding of the study and, arguably, on the subject more generally. A replication of this study conducted in 1987 found the differential victimization rate to be even more pronounced, with that for Asians being 141 times that for white and for black people forty-three time that for whites (Seagrave, 1989: 20). Secondly, the experience of violent racism must be considered in the context of the historicity of violence against ethnic minorities in Britain, the connectedness of behaviour and experience to the ideas and practices of racism, and unequal power relationships between white and 'non-white' peoples.

White people's perception that crimes committed against them by blacks were 'racially motivated' cannot be dismissed out of hand, however. Rather, these findings present a challenge to orthodox definitions of violent racism. First, they suggest that *white people may be exposed to* **anti-black** *sentiment and violence because of their association with people from ethnic minorities.* Secondly, the data suggest that white people do perceive themselves to be vulnerable to offences committed against them by black people and that they do sometimes attribute 'racial' motives to such experiences. As one white survey respondent put it:

> This harassment thing you are doing is too one-sided. How come you only ask about racial attacks on Asian or Afro-Caribbeans, how about on we whites? Anything could have happened that day [after complaining about a neighbour's party], fire, rape anything, the police should keep their eyes on the block.

Two linked explanations of the perceptions of white people may be developed. First, the ascription of a racial motive to black crime against whites may be, itself, simply a form of racism. Secondly, these experiences may reflect a real sense of vulnerability experienced by white working-class inner-city residents.

It is important to note that ideologies linking (black) immigrants with crime have a long history in British society (Solomos, 1988: 88–118), and since the 1970s the involvement of black people in 'street crime' has been an important theme in popular language and political and policy debates (Solomos, 1988: 106). The co-articulation of black people and crime was a theme propagated and developed in the speeches of Enoch Powell in the 1970s and was reflected in the 'marches against mugging' of the National Front in 1977 and 1978 in Lewisham. For example, when the National Front organized a march through the East End in the 1970s, 'it was specifically directed against *black muggings*—no qualifications, no inverted commas, no hesitation' (Hall *et al.*, 1978: 333).

That many white people understand crime and disorder to be connected with the presence of black people is evident in McConville and Shepherd's (1992) study of neighbourhood watch, which found that although most of their respondents were unwilling to identify a 'criminal type', 'for many, crime is associated with black people, and respondents were without prompting quite willing to identify ethnic minorities as the principal sources of their crime concern' (McConville and Shepherd, 1992: 110).

This 'streak of racism' was most striking in London where 'some 36 per cent of white respondents in all areas spontaneously blamed black people for crime or made overt racist comments in the course of the interviews'. While some were diffident in expressing their views, others gave full vent to their feelings:

> Black people are dangerous animals. I shouldn't say this, but when [a mugging] happens, I hate all blacks. I don't normally allow a black in this house . . . If you say to me who are the first football hooligans, I would say the British; they were the ones slung out of Europe. You say to a black that mugging is a black crime, crash! that's a red rag to a bull. They won't have it.

> They have got no manners and no respect. . . . They still think that they are living in a jungle and they forget themselves that they are living in England. . . . Half the white people have put their tail between their bloody legs and they've run, instead of staying put. Most of what the blacks do is mugging; they are 'steaming' and all that kind of stuff [McConville and Shepherd, 1992: 110–11].

The sense of *vulnerability* of white people to the presence of blacks was also articulated by Enoch Powell. In his infamous 'rivers of blood' speech on 20 April 1968, Powell suggested that '[d]iscrimination . . . was being experienced, not by blacks, but by whites – "those among whom they have come"'. This invocation—direct to the experience of unsettlement in a settled life, to the *fear of change*—is the great emergent theme of Mr Powell's speech' (Hall *et al.*, 1978: 246). It was also on this occasion that Powell spoke of 'the little old lady of Wolverhampton' (the one nobody ever found), who had 'excreta pushed through her letter box' and endured the racialist abuse of 'charming wide-eyed grinning piccanninies' (Hall *et al.*, 1978: 245; Gilroy, 1987: 87).

Mixed-race families and relationships

It was noted above that 40 per cent of the victimization of white women was perpetrated by other white people. It is not possible to explain this finding fully from the survey data, but it is evident that at least some of these incidents were directed at white women because of their association with black or Asian people.[10] Several of the comments made in interviews indicated that white women themselves or their children experienced racist verbal abuse because of the children's ethnic origin. One respondent also complained of the 'negative attitude', manner, and behaviour of a policeman on an occasion when she attended a police station. In this incident, the woman attributed the policeman's manner to the fact that she attended the station with a black male friend. One Afro-Caribbean man also commented that he had been 'given hassle' by a 'white gang' because he was 'with a white girl': 'as I was walking down the street a big posse of white kids said to me; eh! nigger shouldn't be walking with a white girl'.

That a large proportion of the experience of white women should be at the hands of other white people indicates the importance of recognizing the complexity of the problem of racial harassment, and the risk of throwing the baby out with the bath-water. However, given dominant attitudes towards 'racial-mixing', this finding should hardly be surprising. Negative attitudes are evident throughout the discussion of 'race' in Britain. For example, the reaction of parliamentarians to the 1965 Race Relations Act included warnings about the dangers of racial mixing, including the apocalyptic view that 'the English people have started to commit race suicide' (Cyril Osborne); that 'the breeding of millions of half-caste children would . . . produce a generation of misfits' (Mr Sandy), and 'in thirty years we would be a coffee-coloured nation' (Mr Cordle) (Hall et al., 1978: 240). That such attitudes live on, at least among right-wingers, is evident in a leaflet distributed by the explicitly racist organization, English Solidarity, cited in the preface to this volume. Small's study of 'racialized relations' in Liverpool also points to deeply racist attitudes towards racially mixed people and white people who associate with blacks:

> whites who live in Liverpool 8 [the area in which the majority of Liverpool's black population lives] are regarded as suspect, even 'white trash' by whites outside the area (Gifford et al., 1989). . . . Sexual relations between black people and whites [are] viewed by whites as biologically and socially undesirable . . . the white women who are party to such actions—and it is mostly women—are seen as degenerate, even prostitutes, while the black men are seen as sexually wanton, even 'pimps'. . . . Attitudes to what might become of such relations are equally pronounced. 'Black people of mixed origins' are seen as an inferior species, biologically degenerate, psychologically unstable and socially maladjusted, attitudes which have often been systematically elaborated and which reveal deep historical roots. . . . Instead of viewing a pattern of inter-dating as evidence of 'racial harmony', it is better to note that it is confined to a small section of the white population, the participants are regarded with disdain, even disgust, by others and the attitudes and perspectives of black women are not taken into account [Small, 1991: 517–18].

With the exception of a small number of studies, however, the experiences of violence among racially mixed individuals and families have been overlooked. An exception is a survey conducted by the Department of the Environment (DoE), which found that in one local authority, nearly half of the white people living in mixed-race households who were interviewed said they or another member of their household had been racially harassed (see FitzGerald and Ellis, 1990: 54). These observations about the different experiences of white people, their relationships with and attitudes towards ethnic minorities echo the words of David Thomas, who argues that:

> The effect of pursuing a more differentiated approach to the personal racism of whites is that beliefs about whites will cease to be blanket appraisals. Any blanket appraisals that 'racism is a white problem' and 'all whites are incurably racist' are just that—as blankets they keep myths and stereotypes warm, and smother contact, inquiry and exploration. They protect whites and blacks from encountering each other. How can our ideas and actions against personal and institutional racism have any cutting edge if they are based on superficial propositions that homogenise whites and ignore the complexity of their personal dispositions towards blacks? [Thomas, 1986: 83].

The process of racist victimization and surveys of incidents

Attempting to break down the dynamic of violent racism into a set of discrete incidents and to disconnect them from other social processes is problematic. To illustrate this point, what follows is a description of the experience of one Asian family and of a white woman.

The A family

The A family, comprising mother, father and eight children, have their origins in the Gujerat region of India though they were settled in East Africa for two generations. In 1973, following political and social upheaval in Kenya (Mr A's birthplace) and Uganda (Mrs A's birthplace), Mr. A gave up his job as an accountant and the family moved to London. After a period in which 'no one wanted to let [them] a flat', they found rented accommodation, but were harassed by their Pakistani landlord to the point that they were, effectively, evicted. In 1977 the family moved into their current home, then a new, council-owned three bedroom 'townhouse' in the south western corner of the North Plaistow area. Mr A believes they were the first black or Asian people to move into the neighbourhood, arriving some years before any other Asian families moved in. There were still very few Asian families living in this part of North Plaistow at the time of the study.

Immediately, some local people began to harass the family, making it clear that they did not want Asian neighbours. On the day that they moved in, a brick was thrown through a first-floor window. Over the period that they have lived in this house Mr and Mrs A and their children have suffered several physical assaults, have been threatened repeatedly, and have suffered regular racist abuse. People would bang on the door saying 'come out Pakis, we want to kill you'. On one occasion someone telephoned to say that they were going to put a bomb through the letterbox with the intention of killing the family. In 1977 Mr A was attacked from behind while in a public telephone box near his home by an assailant wielding a twelve-inch blade. Although a young man was arrested for the offence and the knife was recovered, the case was dropped after twenty white families gathered outside the local police station, calling for the boy's release, claiming that they were witnesses and that nothing had happened.

Local children and young people throw eggs and stones at family members and their home. They repeatedly kick a football against the front of the house and bang the garage door. The family have had rubbish thrown into their garden, external plumbing broken, and 'Pakis out' painted on their garage door. On one occasion a visitor to the house was beaten up and had his spectacles smashed. Mr A attributed many of the incidents to two 'hardened' and 'notorious' families (one next door and one across the street). The adults would abuse the family and encourage the children to throw stones at them and engage in nuisance behaviour. Over the past fourteen years their windows have been broken no fewer than twenty-six times. Now, Mr A says:

> we have to put a metal plate across our letter box every night. We can't leave the house empty, we are afraid to go out. We have been imprisoned in our own home. . . . When the police come they say they can't do anything. They ask 'have you been injured? then we can take action'. We have had 15 years' experience, how can we tolerate this? . . . No authority is prepared to help until someone is murdered. . . . The only time we tried to defend ourselves from boys throwing stones, both me and my wife were arrested [leaving their children alone in the house], locked up and charged with assault.

The outcome of the court case was that Mr A was bound over to keep the peace.

Counting incidents: attempting the impractical

It is evident from this vignette that the attempt to count all the 'incidents' involved would, at the very least, be impractical. Initially, a somewhat arbitrary decision would have to be made about what constituted an 'incident'. Certainly a very large number of events which contravene the criminal law have occurred; there have been numerous incidents of 'assault', 'threat', and 'criminal damage'. The attempt to record as a series of incidents the experience of harassment which extends over a period of years would be impractical. Even if it were possible to record all these events it is highly unlikely that the 'victims' would be able, or prepared, to sit down with a survey researcher fully to detail each and every 'incident'. Most likely, many of these relevant 'criminal incidents' would not be disclosed to survey researchers and would simply be defined out of the investigative process.

In the event that respondents were able to recall and disclose all the events involved in their victimization the survey would face the choice of either accurately recording all these events or 'normalizing' the data. If all these 'incidents' were recorded they would have the effect of inflating 'average' rates of victimization which are, often, what surveys are aiming to produce. The alternative, and most frequently chosen, route is to place a limit on the number of incidents that can be recorded. For example, the BCS limits the number of 'series' incidents (i.e. involving the same people under similar circumstances) to an arbitrary five occurrences (see Genn, 1988). From Mr A's perspective such a record of his victimization would be quite meaningless.

Ms J

Ms J is a white woman who was born and grew up in the East End. Her second marriage was to an Afro-Caribbean man and she has three mixed-race children as well as one white daughter. Although her experience as a child and young adult was that of a white East Ender, in later years she found herself victimized by white racism. Her first 'shattering' experiences of racial harassment were of verbal abuse, being spat at, and pelted on one occasion with eggs and on another with golf balls from passing car windows while in the company of black friends or with her mixed-race children. One of the most serious incidents which occurred during the life of the project was directed at Ms J and a friend of African origin. What follows is a description of her experience as recorded by a local housing officer:

> I moved into [a house in a road on the south western edge of the study area] during late 1988 and moved out March [1990]. I did then, and still do live with my four children. My first daughter aged 13 is white, and is from my first marriage. My last 3 children aged 9, 8 and 6 are all mixed race and from my second marriage.

> From the beginning I was not welcomed and the neighbours made it obvious to me that they did not like having me in the area. I could always sense tension in the atmosphere when I went out. They did not really talk to me or smile back at me, but would give me bad looks, so I decided that it would be best if I kept myself to myself. After some time some of the children would shout out verbal abuse at me, because of my half West Indian children. They would say things like 'wog meat, wog lover' and the like. On other occasions they would say 'we don't want any niggers on our patch, this is our Manor and we don't want those wogs here'. They were referring to my younger children, and my black friend who would visit from time to time.

> When I would go and use the public telephone box, the boys in the area

would gather round and try to intimidate me, and be abusive. I soon learnt that it was a close community of hardened racists, who had lived and been brought up in the area, and did not take very kindly to new or black people moving in.

My next door neighbour once invited me to her party, I knew that she wanted me to attend, because she kept checking with me whether I was going to be there. When I attended the party [the neighbour] was dressed up as a golliwog, and her grown-up children and a couple of others were dressed up in the full Ku Klux Klan uniform, with the lettering on their backs. I became afraid and wondered what was going on. They gathered round me and asked me what I was doing there, so immediately I left.

[In] March 1990, at about 6pm I was playing some reggae records, with the window open, but I kept the volume rather low. At this point Mr N from [several doors up the road], who I would classify as the ring-leader of the group of boys that constantly intimidate me, banged several times on my front door. I had previously noticed that he was working on a car directly outside my house. He was holding a hammer and said that, 'a wog friend of yours called my brother something'. He was referring to my friend called E, who used to visit me sometimes with his girlfriend. I had a mind that Mr N was making it up, and decided to disturb me because of the music I was playing. I did not like the fact that he repeatedly called E a wog, so I pretended not to understand what he was talking about. My children were standing behind me at this point and became threatened by his remarks. He then started to wave the hammer at my face and said, 'if I see any more wogs around here I will be back'. I then shut the door and he returned to the car.

At 7pm that evening E came round, and I told him about what had happened earlier, and he confirmed that he had never spoken to anyone around here, apart from me. Then all of a sudden I heard crashing and the smashing of glass, coming from the front of my house. Mr N and two other boys all bout the age of 19 or 20, smashed their way into my house. They were smashing everything in sight, with the hammers they were carrying. E and I quickly grabbed hold of the children and tried to take them upstairs. It was all happening very quickly. The boys got hold of E and was beating him about the head and the body with the hammers. E was hurt very badly, and my children were just screaming. [The next-door neighbour] informed the police, who came after the boys had left.

Before E was taken to hospital he was able to identify the perpetrators to the police, as they were still in the area. When the police returned [the neighbour] verbally identified the boys.

The day after the incident, I left the house with my children, as we were all afraid to live there. A couple of days later I returned to the house to collect a few things for the children. I noticed that the front door was open. I had been burgled and the whole house was in a mess, things were just thrown around everywhere and everything which remained had been smashed up. All our clothing had been ripped and cut to bits. The television, video and Hi Fi had all been taken, and all the other large electrical equipment had all been broken up. All the bedding and mattresses had been cut open. My children's jewellery had been taken. All my children and black friends had been cut out of my photographs, just leaving me, or any other white people behind. There was nothing in my house that was able to be re-used, due to the total destruction that had taken place. I called the police, and action is still pending[11] [Statement made by victim to Plaistow North Housing, July 1990].

These two incidents—the first assault on the house and the second aggravated burglary were, in and of themselves, traumatic for Ms J. However, the process of victimization was by no means concluded once the incidents had occurred. On the contrary, these incidents merely marked the beginning of an ongoing process which took more than eighteen months to resolve.

In the immediate aftermath of the attacks, Ms J felt 'devastated and bewildered' and as though her 'world was crumbling'. Having had her house invaded and eventually made uninhabitable by burglars in a context in which it had been made clear that her presence would not be tolerated, Ms J was, effectively, homeless. After two months, however, she was found a new home elsewhere in the borough.

When her case came to court initially, she had high hopes that 'justice would be done': The case appeared to her to be clear cut; the perpetrator had violated her house, smashed ornaments and furniture, and physically assaulted her friend. Moreover, the defendant was already in custody charged with six further offences. Although the police warned Ms J that the defence would almost certainly involve an assault on her character and allegations against her and E, Ms J recalls: 'I felt confident. I had nothing to hide. E was a law student attending Thames Polytechnic. What could go wrong. We were 100% in the right.'

In the event, however, it was not a clear-cut case. First, the defending barrister completely destroyed the credibility of Ms J and Mr E in the eyes of the jury. From the outset the defence stressed the assertion that Ms J had regular visits from Afro-Caribbean and African people. Throughout the trial, and particularly in his final speech, he referred repeatedly to the incident occurring in an 'unusual household' which 'instinctively' gave us, he said, some indication of the background to the case: '[t]he picture you get is of an unusual household. . . . A large number of African or West Indian friends come and visit [Ms J]. This seems to be a fact. The inferences are up to you.'

Although Mr E was of good character and had never been in trouble with the police, he was alleged to have been a 'crack dealer' who had attempted to sell 'crack' and 'ecstasy' to Mr N's younger brother. It was inferred that the incident in question had occurred because Mr N was incensed about Mr E's behaviour and that Mr E had a crack-dealing accomplice with him at the time of the incident.[12] At one point the prosecution objected to the 'obvious attack on the character of the witnesses', arguing that it was now relevant that Mr N's character should also be assessed on the basis of his previous convictions and six outstanding charges, including offences against the person and misuse of drugs. The defence countered that since the allegation against Mr N was one of racism, he could produce the front page of a newspaper which showed him as a hero who had saved a family of Indians from burning alive in their home in March 1989. The judge commented that with regard to the defence defamation of the character of witness, 'technically the line may have been crossed [but] I will use my discretion to deny this application'. The effect was to give the prosecution licence to use explicit and coded references to the fact that Mr E was black and that Ms J had black friends in its presentation of the case.

Secondly, the defendant and defending counsel had an alternative version of events. In this version, 'coloured people' had, over the previous six or seven months, made sexual remarks to Mr N's stepmother, stolen a radio and tools from his car, and offered 'crack cocaine' to his younger brother. Rather than being an unprovoked attack on Ms J and E, Mr N described the incident as a fight resulting from Mr E saying 'come in the crack house'. According to Mr N, the fight started outside the house, involved Mr E and an accomplice, and the damage was caused by the struggle between him and his two black assailants. This version of events was assisted by an unexplained item of evidence—a cut on the top of Mr N's head. This was used by the defence as evidence that a fight had taken place during which Mr N himself was injured. Mr N's evidence included comments to the effect that he had been hit over the head from behind by Mr E's accomplice. Although the attending police officers stated specifically that they had seen no blood on Mr N at the time of the offence, the evidence of the police surgeon who attended showed that Mr N did indeed have a cut by the time he was in custody. In fact, it appears that this injury occurred after the incident while he was in police custody.[13]

Thirdly, not only was the element of racism in Mr N's language and stated purpose not brought out in the case by the prosecution, it was explicitly down-played. Mr N and witnesses for the defence consistently denied that the incident was racially motivated, claiming to treat black people 'the same as everyone else'. The disappearance of racism from the case was assisted by the appearance in the witness box of a young man, described by the defence as 'mulatto, half-caste', who testified that he was 'best of mates' with Mr N who treated everyone the same and had no bias or hatred towards black people.[14] In his summing up the judge commented that racism was not relevant and questioned the need for a specialized racial incident squad. He commented that, '[w]e live in what is now a multi-racial society. This brings problems and we must work to overcome these problems. . . . I put it to you that the racial element should not loom too large in the case. . . . In anger many words are said.'

In sum, in the courtroom the case was by no means clear-cut. Rather, there were two competing accounts of events which were completely at odds with one another. The defence evidence was not strong and there were conflicts between that provided by Mr N, and his brother and another friend who were witnesses to the incident. But Ms J and Mr E had not been 'good' witnesses either. There were points at which their evidence conflicted (Ms J said there were three assailants; Mr E thought there were two). Their characters were destroyed by the defence. The police evidence was also not strong. There was no forensic evidence; no pictures of the damage done to the house. There was conflict between the police evidence and the evidence of the police surgeon with regard to Mr N's head injury. The defending barrister was sharp and used a range of subtle and blatant strategies to good effect. The prosecution, by contrast, was slow, failed to bring out some important factors in the case, and concluded its case weakly. The racial motive was deemed irrelevant and, indeed, was destroyed in the eyes of the court. As a result, it was not possible for the jury to be any more convinced that Ms J and Mr E were telling the truth than that Mr N was. They had to be sure beyond reasonable doubt that Mr E and Ms J's story was the true one before they could convict. In the event, they did not. Mr N was acquitted on all three counts of aggravated burglary, assault, and criminal damage.

As we left the court, the housing officer who had attended the case was in tears. The police officer was furious, although the outcome of the case had been apparent since the day before the end of the trial. He said:

> its a total f—ing travesty of justice; that's the only words for it. The judge was totally biased. Allowing the defence counsel to defame the witnesses in this way was totally outrageous, disgusting. I feel very angry. Being called an unusual household simply because many of your friends are black shouldn't have been allowed. Basically, if you're black you are either a drug dealer or a whore.

Ms J's immediate emotional reaction was that of anger: 'tears welled in my eyes, anger burned within and Mr N grinned. If I had a gun, he would have died with that expression.' Later I asked Ms J how she felt about the outcome of the court case:

> Immediately after it I kind of felt numb and felt that I had always been led to believe this was a democratic country and that justice would be done . . . I felt awkward about the fact that I was condemned for having black

friends, cause that was what it felt like. It felt like, throughout the trial, that I had an 'unusual household' because I had black friends and I was condemned for that. It then made me worry about my own identity, and where I actually fitted in. And it also gave me an inward strength that made me feel like I was going to fight.

What about the court officials, how do they make you feel?
Particularly the defending barrister and the judge. Well, they made *me* feel like I had something to be guilty for. That I had done some terrible thing. That I wasn't a normal person. That's kind of how I felt. I felt very angry and very embittered.

Would you . . . I mean, maybe this is too much of a leading question, but . . . would you say that the courtroom experience was another form of victimisation?
Yeah. I was victimised. I was condemned for having black friends.

Conclusion

The two case studies presented above draw together some of the themes addressed in this chapter. The key point is that the experience of violent racism is not reducible to an isolated incident, or even a collection of incidents. Victimization and racialization—the processes by which a person *becomes* a victim of this form of crime are cumulative, comprised of various encounters with racism, some of which may be physically violent, some lying only at the fringes of what most people would define as violent or aggressive. Some of these experiences are subtle and amount to no more than becoming aware that someone is annoyed or disgusted by the presence of black people or fleeting instances such as a half-heard racist joke or epithet. At the other end of this continuum are the more easily remembered instances when racism is coupled with physical aggression or violence. Changing the emphasis from racial violence to violent racism allows the experience of becoming its victim to be connected to other process of racialisation and exclusion. As Paul Gordon (1993) argues:

A society that wishes to deal effectively with racist violence must face the uncomfortable and inconvenient fact that such violence, while a serious problem in and of itself, is also a manifestation of something larger: it is an expression of racism, in particular of white exclusionism or territorialism, and if it is serious about wanting to do something about it, rather than mere remedial work, then it must address that racism. In Britain, this is the racism that for more than three decades has defined black people as a problem for white society, whose entry must be controlled; which has time and again expressed its concern, in the clichés of the racist imagination, at possible 'swamping', 'flooding' and 'invasion' by Third World immigrants. Racist violence, on the streets, in the housing estates, at work and in schools and colleges, is the everyday expression—and consequence—of this policy of white exclusionism.

It is evident from the discussion of the local context that the experience of living in Newham differs among different ethnic groups. For white East Enders, East London is their 'natural' home, one over which they are able to exert a territorial imperative and which they act to defend. The literature reviewed above bears witness to the sense of territoriality, racial exclusivity, and hostility to 'interlopers' felt among the white community in the area. This provides white East Enders with a sense of place, identity, and security which does not automatically extend to North Plaistow's ethnic minorities. It must be added that hostility to 'interlopers' may extend to their white associates. Ms J's experience illustrates that white people are not immune to challenges to their identity and security as East Enders.

The opposite side of this coin for ethnic minority communities is the experience of being defined as 'out of place' in the neighbourhood where they live and, quite likely, were born. The language described by the ethnic minority victims in the survey—being told that they are 'not wanted here', to 'go home' or 'back to where you came from'—illustrates the point. Sadly, even at a time when the majority of the ethnic minority community in Newham will be *indigenous*, the very notion of a 'real East Ender' carries racially exclusive connotations.

The pattern of violent racism directed specifically against black and brown minorities[15] which emerges in the history and contemporary experience is dialectically related to racist ideologies. Black and Asian people have been identified as a problem (or more accurately a set of problems (Gilroy, 1987)) which justifies or promotes exclusionary practices including intimidation, harassment, and attack. The exclusionary racist rhetoric accompanying the incidents mentioned above by Afro-Caribbeans and Asians resonates with that of political and common-sense racism.

Some account must also be taken of the power relationship between white majority and ethnic minority communities. This cannot, however, consist in a reductionist notion of racism. In particular, the formulation that racism = power + prejudice in which black people can be the only 'victims' of racism and whites the only 'perpetrators' does not withstand empirical or theoretical scrutiny. This position and the 'municipal anti-racism' which was its author have been criticized from a number of perspectives and exposed as simplistic and impotent in terms of both politics and policy, however well-intentioned (Gilroy, 1987: 136–51; Gilroy, 1990). The problems with such a formulation, according to Gilroy, are that it endorses the idea that racial groups are *real* in the sense of being fixed and exclusive, as an unproblematic common-sense category which can be taken for granted (Smith, 1989;

Solomos, 1988). The political problems which attend it are thereby reduced to prejudice:

> Races are political collectivities not ahistorical essences. 'Race' is, after all, not the property of powerful, prejudiced individuals but an effect of complex relationships between dominant and subordinate social groups. If whites have shared the same job centres, schools, police cells, parties and streets with blacks, in what sense can we speak of them having additional power? [Gilroy, 1987: 149].

Despite this critique of a reified notion of 'races' and racism, however, it is necessary to retain an understanding of power relationships between ethnic minority and majority communities. Most obviously, the fact that the ethnic minorities in Britain make up only a very small proportion of the population (6 per cent in total) place them in a vulnerable position. Even in Newham, with one of the highest concentrations of ethnic minorities in the country, white people are still in the majority. In North Plaistow, wherein some specific localities have more than 50 per cent concentration of ethnic minorities, white people remain the largest ethnic group. This experience of being a minority introduces an important element of experiential context:

> In contrast to his or her black counterpart who encounters white majorities daily, the white person rarely, if ever, finds himself in a wholly black situation. The experience is not a comfortable one, at least not at first. One feels isolated and self-conscious and acutely aware of looks or glances cast in one's direction. One becomes extremely sensitive to half-heard comments or any suggestion that one is being mocked [Parkes, 1984; cited in Thomas, 1986: 80].

In addition to being a small minority of the British population, people of African, Caribbean, and Asian origin are economically weak relative to their numbers. Ethnic minorities are under-represented in national and local political institutions. Even in localities with a high proportion of ethnic minorities, political and economic resources lie mainly within sections of the white community. Land, industry, and commerce which are in private hands are owned principally by white individuals, corporations, and institutions. The local and central state bureaucracies which own or control a large proportion of economic resources are also controlled, by and large, by white people. Although Newham have pursued equal opportunities policies at the level of political representation and the composition of the workforce, the balance remains tipped in favour of white people. Newham's three parliamentary representatives are white and the elected members of the local council do not represent the ethnic mix of the locality. In 1986, the London Borough of

Newham still employed only 300 black people out of a workforce of 11,000, most of whom were in the lower grades in the organization.[16]

Finally, power may also be seen in terms of access to a discourse which defines individuals as superior/inferior, insider/outsider, in/out of place, in/out of one's own country, one of 'us'/one of 'them', white/non-white. As Gilroy and others have argued black people have been historically, and are contemporarily, defined as other than European, British, English, or East Enders. Such inclusionary/exclusionary ideologies give rise to a form of personal power to which only white people have recourse. As Hall *et al.* suggest: '[t]he assumption of superiority over all other peoples is often a quiet, unspoken one, but it is largely unquestioning; and it is especially strong with respect to former "natives"—colonised or enslaved peoples, especially if they are black' [Hall *et al.*, 1978: 147].

What then of Gilroy's rhetorical question whether white people who have grown up alongside and enjoyed the same impoverished circumstances as blacks can be said to have additional power. The answer is that whites, however marginalized socially or economically, have the ability, by dint of their ethnicity, to connect with a form of discursive power from which black people are excluded. Some white people may be unaware of their recourse to racist discourses or the practices of racial exclusion. Others are aware of the discursive practices of racism but refuse to utilize them. What is significant is that such ideas and practices are available to be used at any time. That is, at any moment, racism, expressed most perniciously in violence, can exclude the 'other'.

Notes

1 *Sun* 9 October 1989. Respondents were asked, 'If people want to, should they be given financial aid to help to return to their country of origin'. Rather different from 'Send us back' and repatriation, both of which imply expulsion.
2 Because Asians were believed, *a priori*, to be those most likely to be victimized, they were deliberately oversampled in order to have enough 'victims' in the sample for meaningful analysis. As a result, the number of incidents in the sample reduced to 724 when weighted to correct for oversampling.
3 An attempt was made to offset this problem by explaining to respondents that: 'I don't just want to know about serious incidents, I want to know about small things too. It is often difficult to remember exactly when the small things happened so please try to think carefully.' Nonetheless, the well-documented under-reporting of incidents to the police may also apply to reporting incidents to survey interviewers. The authors of the ICS, for example, concluded from one interview that 'some segments of the population are so over-exposed to [racist assaults]

that it becomes part of their everyday reality and escapes their memory in the interview situation' (Jones et al., 1986).

4 118 when weighted to compensate for oversampling Asians.

5 This includes actual and attempted break-ins, damage to property (including window breakages), incidents on the doorstep, and offensive material through the letterbox.

6 Most of the survey items were precoded, leaving open-ended only questions such as what actually occurred in the incident, why the respondent believed the incident to have been racially motivated, why the incident was not reported to the police and other local agencies (in cases where it was not), and what happened as a result of a police detection (in cases where perpetrators were detected). The responses to these questions as recorded by the interviewer were transcribed in full. Because details were not recorded in every instance and because of the poor quality of some of what was recorded it must be stressed that the quotations selected for inclusion in the text are intended only to *illustrate* the quantitative survey findings.

7 See also FitzGerald and Ellis, 1990: 59; Hesse et al., 1992; Sampson and Phillips, 1992.

8 Some of the quotations provided in this section illustrate the vulnerability of houses and flats to attack through windows, glass door fronts, letterboxes, etc. Local authority flats, in particular, have been shown to be quite penetrable. In several instances which came to the author's attention while working in Newham, flats had been entered by perpetrators jumping through the thin ceiling of top floor flats having gained access to the eaves.

9 FitzGerald and Ellis (1990), for example, state that: 'Initial perceptions of the problem (which was first brought to light in respect of Asian communities in the East End of London) have tended to frame the assumptions on which discussion has taken place and to limit the categories covered by surveys. Political pressure (with a small "p") has also been brought to bear, with strong exception being taken in some quarters to the notion that black people can exhibit racial hostility either towards whites or towards each other. . . . With regard to the survey data, it will be noted that even the Home Office (1981) report does not cover harassment between Afro-Caribbeans and Asians, while most of the other surveys implicitly deny that whites could be victims of racial harassment at all' (*ibid.*: 58). Small notes that 'conflicts between sub-groups, ethnically or otherwise, within the black population' are 'a topic of tremendous taboo' (1991: 525).

10 See also the experience of Ms J described in detail below. Several cases of violence against mixed-race families have been reported in the media recently. Of these, the best known targets are the comic actors Lenny Henry and Dawn French. On 6 March 1991 the daily newspaper, *Today*,

reported that the Ku Klux Klan had targeted the couple with offensive material. On this occasion the French-Henrys were sent a 'tile . . . with a picture of St George on the front of it and on the back it said "You have been visited by the Ku Klux Klan". According to the article, "The National Front has always lurked in the background, sending abusive letters and smearing slogans on Dawn and Lenny's home. Last year . . . bigots daubed the NF slogan above the couple's front door using human excrement". Dawn French commented, 'Just yesterday, I got a letter from somebody who writes to me regularly as a "Nigger Lover".'

11 For some inexplicable reason, although the police visited the scene and recorded details of the incident, no forensic evidence was taken. It was not possible, therefore, to link the burglary with the perpetrators of the assault on Ms J's home and on her friend, E.

12 At one point the defending barrister went so far as to ask 'was the person who was there either of the other [black] people who were with you in the court room yesterday', referring to me personally and a plain-clothes black police officer who had been in court the day before.

13 I was informed after the trial that the cut on Mr N's head had been an instance of 'summary justice' inflicted by the door of a police van.

14 I have been informed by a number of police officers that this is a tactic used regularly by defending counsel in racial incidents.

15 As Hesse et al., found in their study of neighbouring Waltham Forest, 'there was absolutely no evidence of a historical pattern of attacks, abuse and violations of white communities. Furthermore, there was no particular region of the Borough which could be identified as a locale where racial harassment of people because they are white regularly took place' (Hesse et al., 1992: 41).

16 Labour Research survey, May 1986, cited in Tompson, 1988.

12

Woman abuse in London's black communities
by Amina Mama

Introduction

This chapter examines the form, severity and extent of domestic violence experienced by the black women in this study, and the time over which they are subjected to violence before seeking to escape it. It also looks at the strategies employed by the women in the study in their attempts to survive or otherwise cope with repeated physical assault and/or mental cruelty. The chapter is based on the results of in-depth interviews with over a hundred women, conducted in London over a period of twelve months (November 1987 to October 1988). This makes it the first detailed investigation of domestic violence in Britain's black communities. The content of the material is of a highly disturbing nature. This is evidenced by the emotional stress experienced by the interviewers taken on to assist with this aspect of the research. Out of four employed and trained to conduct interviews with the full support of the researcher, only two found themselves emotionally able to cope with the depressing and disturbing nature of the subject group's experiences. The two who remained had substantial experience and training (one as a medical doctor and the other as a social worker who had lived and worked in Women's Aid), which enabled them to cope with the task in a sympathetic and highly skilled manner. The material presented here should be considered in the context of the following methodological considerations.

Method note

Sample characteristics

The sample was not a random sample, which means that generalizations about the communities included cannot be drawn from the interview findings. The material reported here should *not* be used as a basis for constructing new, or supporting old, stereotypes about the Caribbean, Asian or African communities, about gender relations, or about the treatment of women by men in those communities . . .

All the women interviewed had been subjected to quite serious degrees of cruelty. As such it should be regarded as an extreme sample, and not representative of connubial relationships in the respective communities. It will become apparent that nearly all the women in the study had experienced high degrees of physical abuse, only two having been subjected to emotional cruelty without physical violence. (In both cases emotional suffering drove them from their marital homes.) This rendered the definitional problems around more borderline cases irrelevant. The emphasis on physical abuse is not intended to minimize the suffering of women subjected to mental cruelty without actual bodily assaults, and we did not set out to exclude such women. In all cases the physical violence that women experienced was accompanied by mental and emotional cruelty, as will become apparent in the examples below.

All the women interviewed self-defined their relational experience as that of domestic violence. To reiterate, in the terms of this project this means physical and mental abuse by current or past emotional and sexual partners: husbands, cohabitees or men with visiting relationships.

Whereas much research has focused on violence against wives – 'wife-battering' – it became clear in the course of this research that a significant proportion of the women we interviewed at refuges had not been legally married. Furthermore, a significant proportion had not been cohabiting on a full-time basis with their partners during the period of violence, and some of the women never had. It was therefore decided to include these two last groups in this study, in contrast to existing research on domestic violence because growing numbers of women (and in this study, women of Caribbean descent in particular) had what we refer to as 'visiting relationships' with the men who assaulted them. Their assailants stayed with them on a part-time basis, while also retaining residential rights with their mothers, or with other women. Domestic violence is not restricted to any particular family form or structure. In a study of black women it was definitely necessary to also include relationships not conforming to the monogamous nuclear form generally depicted in publications that have in any case not dealt with the situation of black women.

No black lesbian women were encountered in the process of contacting people to interview. The problems faced by black women in violent lesbian relationships are not therefore addressed in this study, although it is apparent that lesbian relationships are not free from abuse and violence, and may well be treated even less sympathetically . . .

Marital status, class and ethnicity

It soon became clear that there were a variety of family forms in the sample. The hundred women who were abused by their sexual and emotional partners comprised women who had been married legally and/or according to their cultural tradition, as well as women who had cohabited or had visiting relationships. Some were escaping violent assaults by ex-partners.

Within each of these three relationship categories, numerous variations existed in terms of roles and expectations, duties and responsibilities. It was not possible to go into any finer analysis in this project, but this variation should be borne in mind.

The three relationship categories identified for the research purposes were not independent of ethnic background. In this sample, the women of Asian and African descent were all legal and/or traditional wives, while more than half of the women of Caribbean origin were cohabitees or were engaged in visiting relationships. This may bear some relation to the fact that the Caribbean sample were predominantly born and raised in Britain where a growing proportion of the population cohabit at some stage in their relationship (Barrett and MacIntosh 1982). It may also be strongly related to the material circumstances of the working-class Caribbean communities in Britain. The economic and power relations are very different when one is considering domestic violence against a middle class but financially dependent wife, as compared to domestic violence against a single mother of three in a local authority flat, or violence against a professional working woman. Men who were violent to the women in this study also came from all socio-economic classes, ranging from businessmen rich enough to keep several homes (and women) to working-class men who had never been afforded the dignity of earning a decent wage. What was most striking is that women across a very diverse range of domestic economic relationships and situations can be forced to flee their homes to escape violence from their partners.

This fact raises a major theoretical question about previous research on domestic violence, which has often tended to regard it as part and parcel of male power and women's economic dependence on the men battering them. While this may be true for 'housewives' in the traditional white middle class nuclear family, it was clearly not the case for a significant proportion of the black women in this study. Many were in fact being beaten by men who were dependent on them, regardless of marital status. This and other issues raised by the research findings are taken up in the discussion at the end of this chapter.

Redefining domestic violence

The case material presented here illustrates the enormous diversity in the manifestation of domestic violence. Culture, material circumstances such as bad housing and economic stresses, drug abuse, childhood relational experiences, sexual insecurities and jealousies, deep mistrust and suspicion, misogynistic (woman-hating) attitudes, and lack of communication are just some of the recurring themes of the material. These factors are not specific to domestic violence between black people, since very similar themes recur in European and American literature on the subject (Dobash and Dobash 1980, Yllo and Bograd 1988, WAFE 1981). Orthodox clinical approaches to 'family violence' tend to treat social and economic factors as 'confounding variables' rather than as variables that should be integrated into the analysis of domestic violence (Bolton and Bolton 1987). Yet social and economic factors constantly appear in women's accounts of their partners' violence towards them as rationalizations and reasons given, as women struggle to comprehend their partners' behaviour.

On the matter of race, the existing research is contradictory, focusing on the non-issue of whether black and minority families are more or less violent than white ones and producing reasons for each side of the argument (Bolton and Bolton). Staples's work is more interesting on race and he utilizes Frantz Fanon's (1967) thesis on violence in colonial contexts to go into the analysis of black male violence (Staples 1982).

Cultural analysis does not appear to have been part of existing research on domestic violence, although it is another recurring theme in women's accounts. It seems to manifest itself most commonly in terms of husbands invoking 'tradition' or 'religion' to justify their expectations of and demands for subservient or obedient behaviour from their womenfolk. None of the world's major religious texts condones (or actively challenges) the abuse of women. Rather the issue seems to me to be more about men appropriating religion in their own exercise of power over the women with whom they live. There is certainly no justification for tolerating woman-abuse in black communities on the basis of it being 'their culture', as appears to occur in racist and colonial contexts. In Britain, other crimes are depicted as 'black crimes' and are far from tolerated. For example in the case of 'mugging' or robbery with violence, a disproportionate number of victims are black women, but popular representations imply that it is a crime in which most victims are elderly white women attacked by violent black men (see Hall et al. 1978 for an extended discussion of this phenomenon).

The subject group were all volunteers and no working definition of domestic violence was imposed on the women by the researcher. In addition to their self-definition, women had also been defined as having experienced domestic violence by the agencies through which we contacted them (women's refuges and community groups), so that some filtering by these agencies had also occurred. Beyond this, the range and extent of violence described below indicates the degrees and forms of violence upon which the research project is based. As was noted above, it turned out that the vast majority had experienced at least some physical injury as well as considerable amounts of emotional anguish.

Although the initial research proposal also included the much broader and harder to define category of 'relationship breakdown', it was decided to focus on domestic violence because of the definitional complexities of the wider area of relationship breakdown and the practical constraints on the project. This was felt to be appropriate because of the central concern with housing policy and practice and because our preliminary research indicated that in the present housing climate, relationship breakdown was seldom grounds for rehousing. Where there were written policies on relationship breakdown, these were not being implemented at a time when only homeless persons are being housed in many boroughs. In any case, in terms of local authority rehousing practices and policies, domestic violence is often treated as an extreme instance of relationship breakdown.

Many women would not have been forced to tolerate violence if there had been any possibility of one or other of the couple securing alternative housing in the earlier stages of relationship breakdown. The high incidence of black male and female homelessness resulted in many couples living together more through lack of options than through choice. Since single black men have no access to public housing at all, black male homelessness can be seen in a number of cases to have been a major factor in determining the decision to cohabit in the first place. In this context the nature of relationships themselves is affected. Sometimes men had simply moved in with black women who had local authority tenancies. Many of these had previously been staying with other women and/or their mothers on a semi-permanent basis and had never had tenancies of their own. As such they would constitute part of the 'hidden homeless' population that has no statutory right to housing. Local authorities (in theory at least) are statutorily obliged to house people who have dependent children living with them, so that parents (who do have their children living with them) have a means of gaining entry to public sector housing that is not open to women or men whose children are not living with them.[1] When relationships deteriorated, men in these living arrangements not only became violent, but quite often also refused to leave, so forcing mothers and children out of their local authority accommodation to join the long queues awaiting housing in hostels, reception centres and refuges.

In terms of the assailants, these fell into a number of categories: (a) husbands; (b) cohabitees; (c) men with whom the woman had a visiting relationship; (d) ex-husbands, cohabitees or visiting partners.

A small number of women interviewed had been subjected to violence by other parties. If this was in addition to violence from their sexual partner, cohabitee or husband they were included in the study. Several of the Asian subjects fell into this category, having been multiply abused by in-laws as well as spouses. One older Caribbean woman was assaulted by her son when he grew up, after she had been subjected to years of violence at the hands of her husband.

If however their experience of violence did not include violence from the man they were having or had been in a relationship with, they were excluded from the data analysis. There were six such cases including for example, Lalita a Philipino domestic worker who suffered abuse at the hands of her employer, and Sharon, a twenty-three-year-old woman of European and African parentage who was sexually abused by her stepfather and step-brother and then violently assaulted when she matured and at the age of sixteen tried to resist having sexual intercourse with them. The others were Asian women who were assaulted by in-laws, like Neelim, the thirty-four-year-old Asian woman who had her nose smashed leaving her face perman-ently deformed by her sister's husband, or the teenager who went into refuge with her mother, having been beaten by her father for trying to protect her mother.

While certain themes occur frequently in the data, others are more idio-syncratic. This is not the place to attempt a detailed study of the causes of domestic violence, or to go into the detail that an individual psychological understanding of would require. Rather the case material is presented to highlight some of the ways in which violence has manifested, as recounted by women who have been subjected to assaults by their male partners. These highly disturbing accounts are treated and discussed as authentic descriptive data. They are presented to illustrate the circumstances which lead women to approach existing statutory and voluntary agencies, or to desist from, or delay in approaching outside agencies, even when they are being subjected to extreme and often life-threatening behaviour. Within each unhappy tapestry there also lies a rich undercurrent of courage which testifies to the resilience and resistance these women have shown, often without any of the support that one might expect any humane society to offer, in the face of the most extreme degradation and brutality.

The violence

Domestic violence against women of Caribbean descent

SUKIE was staying at a women's refuge with her two young sons (aged six and three) when we spoke. When she was eighteen she moved into a council flat with the tenancy in her name. Eugene, a casual painter/decorator came to help with the decorating. They related to each other quite well, and a few weeks later he arrived at Sukie's flat, with his baggage and moved in. Things went well until after the birth of their first son, when Eugene started to feel bitterly jealous of the young infant, and Sukie became pregnant and had their second son. Arguments began and continued, with Eugene forbidding Sukie to have her brother visit, and accusing her of having affairs with other men. When she went to visit her aunt, she would return to find her clothes and pictures hidden and clear evidence that he had entertained other women in their bedroom:

> these things were going on because he used to take the children's toys and hide them in the cupboard; take all my things off the dressing table

and put them inside the drawer, and once he pretended that I was his sister . . . when I used to go down to my auntie's he sort of gave this as an excuse for bringing the women there because I wasn't there, which I thought was wrong. If he wanted to do anything I thought he should go outside of the house to do it, not do it inside my house – I've got the children staying there as well. So from there we started fighting every day. One night I had to run out and he came looking for me. While he was looking he got this knife from my cousin's kitchen drawer and slashed me across the face and tore Neville [son] away from me. I've got the scar here [Sukie still bore a number of scars].

The violence got worse, as did her partner's extreme jealousy, with him waiting outside her workplace and deploying other people to trail her and monitor her movements.

He was possessive and the fact that I was working and saving my money really got to him because he's self-employed and every time he wants anything he wants me to help, so I was not getting any benefit out of working. He said that I was working and hiding my money from him, and that I bring up my kids too fancy – I shouldn't dress them up like that. Every time I visit my friends he said they were a bad influence on me, and he banned me from walking down that particular road. If I took the kids to my friend's house he would sort of trail me, and he got people to spy on me after work.

The thing is he wanted to be the ruler of the house. He said there can't be two kings in one house, and on one occasion he said that I musn't cook for the kids and don't cook for him, that he would buy separate shopping and sort of ban me from using the cooker. When we're fighting I wasn't to sleep on my bed, I wasn't to sleep on the kids' bed and I wasn't to sleep on the settee. One night he locked me in the toilet – sort of nailed it down.

When I was pregnant one time he said that he would see that Neville was born crippled.

Sukie's workmates observed what was happening through the heavy bruising to her face and arms, and she saw the doctor on several occasions with her injuries. She suffered from frequent nose bleeds, headaches, developed as a result of frequent blows to the head, and high blood pressure. She also called the police on several occasions and obtained ouster injunctions from the courts. Her reason for not leaving before this stage:

I've always said because of the kids – because of the kids I'll stay with him, so the kids can have a father.

She had left after Eugene had wrapped a cord round her throat in a strangle grip until she almost blacked out. She still bore the scars of that assault on her neck at the time of interview. After that episode, Eugene was convicted for grievous bodily harm and bound over for a year, but it was not safe for her to go near her flat, so she fled. Her local authority acknowledged she was homeless as a result of domestic violence and placed her in a Bayswater bed and breakfast hotel where she bore filth, cockroaches and no cooking facilities for eight months in one room with her two sons, who repeatedly became ill. Eventually she moved into the women's refuge. A year later I met her again at a different refuge, still awaiting rehousing, thinner and even more worn-looking.

ROWEENA is twenty-six years old. She and her three children were staying in one room at a women's refuge at the time of interview. She moved away from him into her own council tenancy in 1983 after he began to drink heavily and subject her to violent attacks, but friends told him where she was. She has been fleeing from one place to another trying to escape the violent attacks of her children's father for the last five years. During that time she has been in four different women's refuges. She has also been rehoused twice, the first time in a flat abandoned by a black family before her who had been subjected to racial attacks by their neighbours. The same racist neighbours forced her to abandon her long-awaited home. She was subsequently rehoused in her ex-partner's old haunts, so that he located her and tried to burn down the flat by pouring petrol through the letter box. Again she went into a refuge. A year after we spoke, I returned to the same refuge and found she was still there, still awaiting rehousing.

CHARLOTTE is a thirty-three-year-old London-born woman who has lived with the father of her two young children for four and a half years. When they established their relationship she put all her own resources into a business with him, which failed – owing to his gambling habits. He became increasingly abusive towards her over the last two years, subjecting her to constant criticism and derision day and night, and then becoming sexually and physically abusive.

> there was mental abuse as well. There were a lot of bad vibes generally. Bad communication, lots of complaints about everything – he would keep me awake all night going on and on criticising everything about me, my family, what I did, how I spoke, how I reacted to everything. That created a sexual problem which would bring out the violence as well . . . he would – you know – rip off my clothes and . . . [in a lowered voice she explained that she was raped].

During her pregnancy with the youngest child she was subjected to extreme emotional and financial neglect. Another woman became pregnant by him at this point. His cruelty and neglect had deep effects on her during her pregnancy;

> It was very depressing. It leaves you inert and with no energy left to do anything. It took me a long time to realise the actual seriousness of the situation. That I was actually in that situation. Might sound funny but it took a long time for me to admit that it actually was a real nightmare.

In retrospect Charlotte describes her partner as suffering from insecurity, and burdened with debts he had incurred. Their flat was in her name, and she also owned the car (which he prevented her from using).

> I think basically his problem is chronic insecurity, which is something I hadn't realised before . . . he comes over as quite arrogant and pushy actually. But he finds any type of rejection totally unacceptable.

She left on two occasions, but returned, having nowhere else to go. Eventually she had to call the police for the second time to escort her to a women's refuge when he became frighteningly irrational one night. One of the reasons she gave for leaving were his threats to kill their children.

ZOEY was twenty-three years old and struggling to start a different life for herself after spending six abusive years with a man much older than her, who operated as a pimp. She spoke clearly and insightfully about her life. Zoey had been raised by an English family in the country and came to London in 'search of the bright lights' at the age of sixteen. She started working as a hostess in Soho clubs, where she met her partner – an influential man, quite different from anyone she had ever met, and who gradually took over control of her life.

> I thought I was in control of the relationship. He never worked – has never worked, so it was a completely different way of life. And I thought it was exciting, free – he showed me all different things, all the runnings[2] and everything . . . He was willing to show me how I'm supposed to be, and where I come from, my roots. I was to stop putting on make-up. I had been very into myself – into make-up and clothes. He was nothing like that. I never thought I would go for a guy like him. I was looking for something different I must admit. But I thought he was sort of soft when I first met him, cuz that style I had never come across – the black man's style. I think I came unstuck because he was so smart. He really worked his brain on me. He was very patient, so he got what be wanted. Everywhere he went everybody just hails him up—he's very popular.

That's what attracted me to him. When I first looked at him I thought no, I was just looking into his wrinkled old face. I don't know what it was – it was his style, and after a while . . .

Zoey had never experienced abuse prior to this relationship:

The first time he hit me I left him. That's the kind of person I was. I was so shocked and appalled. But in the end I thought, well this is it. I'm in the bottom of hell, I can't get out of it. Now I'm the kind of person who gets beaten consistently and doesn't go, so I've gone mad between then and now. I'd gone mental, lost all contacts, and I had his child. And he knew all those things. He knew what he was doing.

She concealed the reality of her situation from her parents and sister:

To my parents I was playing happy families. They never knew the truth at all. Oh no. It would have been too appalling, it would be like a horror movie to them. That's unreal.

Her partner was also violent to other women, and invoked the Old Testament in his general misogyny:

He had no respect for women at all. He'd say that over and over again. Woman is Delilah, Satan. Woman is man's downfall and all this all the time. Woman is down there. He used to go on about Margaret Thatcher running the country – all these women running the country. When I took him to court I won an injunction. So he had twenty-eight days to get out, and all these things just confirmed that it was a woman's country . . . He's got to have somebody to belittle all the time.

The frequency of physical abuse varied:

Sometimes it would be morning and night, morning and night every night for a week. If we was really at each other's throats, really arguing, and then he might not beat me for six months.

She suffered extensive bruising and cuts from punches, kicks and being hit with furniture and other objects that came to hand. On one occasion he broke his toe kicking her. On another she was hospitalized with her head split open, and had to go to casualty on yet another. The police were called approximately thirty times in five years.

Most of their fights centred around money:

He wanted money from me, from my work. He said he wasn't interested in the house because he was a Rasta and he was going to Africa. But he'd be willing to sit down and let me do everything financially – the food, housekeeping, bills and everything. He used to get me to give him money in the beginning, he said he would pay me back because I loaned him some. But then it got out of hand. For years and years – I can't begin to weigh up how much – thousands and thousands.

She had a friend who was in a similar relationship:

Me and my friend used to laugh, for about three years we'd come down and laugh at ourselves. In the end that was our only pleasure. To run ourselves down. When we faced them we'd know that we'd been cursing them stupid – it was like that.

Her friend left the scene and started a new life for herself some time before Zoey did.

His word was God's to me and he knew best. He knew, you see? He was never supposed to be wrong. Whatever he'd encouraged me in, I would have done. That's why I'm here now. Because of sheer disgust in myself. Disgust. That's all I can say, in the end. Absolute disgust.

ELSIE is a twenty-five-year-old woman of Caribbean and European mixed parentage who grew up in a northern English town. She has a particularly extroverted and dynamic character. The violence she was subjected to in her relationship was so bad that it drove her to attempt suicide. She had been in a relationship with Mike, the father of her child, for eighteen months at the time of interview. They had been living with his mother and his sister at his mother's small (two-bed) council flat for the period of their cohabitation. They attempted to get council accommodation of their own on numerous occasions, to no avail.

Elsie has held a wide range of domestic catering and sales jobs, while her partner is a musician who goes for long periods without work, but felt that Elsie should stay at home and be a full time housewife.

He wanted me to be a housey woman and I ain't housey at all. I'd rather be out working – not barefoot and pregnant over the stove ... He used to go out for days on end, yet if I go out for an hour, he used to say – 'where have you been?' I'd be wanting to ask him questions anyway, but alright. And when he comes in its 'Where's my dinner, why aren't my slippers being warmed by the fire?' and all that bit. While I would tend to go about my business. It's a double standard that's been in force since Adam and Eve. I joke about it, but at the time it's not funny at all.

Most of their fights began with verbal disagreements which escalated into him being violent towards her: kicking her in the legs and chest and punching her to the face and head. He fractured her nose twice and she has a number of scars rendered with an iron bar on her arms and legs. At other times he would strike out suddenly over minor issues. Despite the severity of her injuries, Elsie partly blamed herself:

> I'm a very stubborn person, even now. I was partly to blame. But I don't think it was worth getting slapped in the mouth for it. I mean if it was that I'd done something wrong he could have said – 'Elsie you shouldn't have done that,' and that would have been it, I would have just said, 'Yeah, alright then, I'll do it different next time', you know? It could be that I'd put too much salt in the dinner. That to him was a major mistake and I got a punch in the mouth for it. Such little things – okay, I was wrong about it, you know, but I'm not a cook, and I don't think that not being able to cook should get you a slap in the mouth . . . I'm stubborn and he's stubborn, so I wouldn't give in, because I'd been a single woman a long time before I met him, and like I moulded myself the way I like myself and I knew that. I told him before I moved in together that he was not going to like living with me.

The situation got worse after the birth of their daughter, ostensibly because he was jealous of her. When asked what used to spark off these fights, Elsie responded:

> Money and sex. I mean I think he expected it to be like it was when we first met. Even though we were going through a bad patch. He still – he would like hit me at half past nine and at half past eleven when we were in bed he be all lovey and 'Come on let's do it now?' and I'd say 'No', and he'd wonder – but why? What have I done? . . . He wasn't sorry for what he'd done, because he didn't believe he'd done anything.

Elsie explained her suicide attempt as being due to her partner's violence:

> It was hurting me that much I didn't want to give him the satisfaction of killing me, so I thought – well, I'd top myself. But it didn't work – I was unconscious and they tried to put this tube down my throat and I thought – 'Oh God, I'm going to die here.'

On one occasion when he was trying to force her over the balcony, the neighbours heard Elsie's screams of 'Help – he's killing me' and called the police. While she did not have any family support, she had met a number of Mike's friends; indeed he had introduced her to a particular woman friend of his who he had hoped would teach her the runnings, as he put it. As his violence became more and more extreme, his friends attempted to intervene, expressing strong disapproval of his behaviour towards Elsie, so that he refused to have anything more to do with them. Eventually, despite repeated visits and appeals to the council, unable to find anywhere else to live and trapped in a clearly life-threatening situation Elsie grew desperate and contacted the Samaritans for help. She was eventually referred to Women's Aid.

SARAH is twenty-seven and has an eight-year-old son. She had been in the refuge for nineteen months at the time of interview and there was still no sign of her being rehoused. She had been going out with Maurice for about three years when he arrived one day with his bags:

> He virtually just moved in. I mean we were going out, and one day a neighbour came and said – 'He wants you outside.' And when I looked out of the window, he had taken all his things out of the car. He just moved in. We had been going out for about three years, but that didn't entitle him to move in automatically the way he did. But I didn't really say much. I just sort of asked him, you know, what was happening. He said he thought that was what I wanted . . . Apparently he shared a flat with another woman who had a child for him. They had apparently broken up, so I thought – you know – 'what the heck?'. She threw all his clothes out and then he came and said he thought it was what I wanted.

Maurice was a self-employed decorator, while Sarah did full-time office work. Their relationship deteriorated after he had moved into her council flat.

> He started abusing me and being aggressive, you know. I mean he'd never done it before – he always said 'Oh I'll never hit a woman, I'll never hit a woman' and I always believed him. In all the three years I'd known him he'd never hit me before.

They fought over 'silly things' – if she used the car (which was hers) when he wanted to, or being five minutes late to collect him, for example. This resulted in unexpected consequences:

> I went up the stairs to close the door and I just felt one punch on the back of my head. In my flat you go down as you enter the door, so I went flying down the stairs and crashed into the wall. He just started beating me and kicking and swearing – fucking this and fucking that. I couldn't understand it – that I was too out of order, that he don't know who I think I am and all this. Until I was knocked out unconscious. When I woke up I was so mad, I wanted to kill him, but because he was so big and tall I knew that if I hit him I was going to get twice the hit I gave him back. I thought I was due to die that day because Wayne [her son] was at his aunty's. It

was just me and him in the flat. Wayne was gone for the weekend. I was just so mad – I started trembling, I couldn't stop myself, I couldn't control myself. I just started to shake and then he said 'Yeah, you fucking pretend you're sick, you go on and fucking pretend you're sick'. And I said – 'I want some water – can I have some water?' My lips just dried up and I was just trembling. He thought I was joking or something. Then he realised that I was genuinely shaking. I couldn't keep myself still. He ran to get the water and everything. And then they took me to the hospital – he took me to the hospital and everything – he lied to them and told them that I fell over and banged my head. I just told them that I didn't want him in here. He wouldn't leave because he knew that if he left me I would tell them.

Assaults of this sort had longer term effects on their relationship; not only was making up and saying sorry followed by other attacks, but the nature of their relationship changed:

After he started being aggressive I suppose I became afraid of him. But I always pretended – I never showed him that I was afraid of him. If he said anything, I always said it back, and that – 'I'm not frightened of you'. 'Not frightened of me? I'll give you fright' he'd say, and I'd be sitting there thinking, 'Oh God, please don't let him hit me'. He was always threatening before that incident ... On the other occasion he didn't actually get to abuse me much because I jumped out of the window. I mean he would have killed me. He threatened and then slapped me in the face. I ran through the kitchen and locked the door and took the key. He ran round to come in through the front window, and I said to him you just put one foot through – he lifted his foot and I was over the balcony. I had on something skimpy, it was raining, I had nothing on my feet. Looked like a tramp. I didn't care – I just wanted to get away from him.

Sarah explains his violence thus:

I think he was insecure. He was jealous of the fact that – because I've always been independent, like now I'm a student and everything. I've been saving up money because I do people's hair at home and I charge them £50. I'd been saving up my money and I bought a car. He didn't like the fact that I always went out and got my things – whatever I wanted. He detested that you know – he always wanted me to have a baby for him. And I've always said no because I want my career first. 'Fucking career' – he didn't like it. He did not like the fact, he just wanted me to be a slave to him. I don't know. He just seems really insecure.

Things got worse as time went along. He just got over possessive – he wanted me to be under his spell – at his beck and call sort of thing. I don't know why. I suppose because his parents – his mother always cooked for him and washed for him even though he was living with this other girl, he always went to his mother's for dinner. At Christmas everyone goes to his Mum's and she spoils them. And that's what he expected of me. Cook dinner every day and make sure it's no rubbish.

Violence also had a negative effect on her son:

> He was hyperactive. I had to take him to a child psychiatrist because of all the ups and downs; it disturbed him a little bit. Maurice would shout and Wayne was frightened of him. He used to say things like – 'I don't like Maurice because he hits my Mum', you know – things like that. Sometimes when he got violent Wayne would wet his bed. It was obvious that that is what it was. He was frightened for me. When we took him to the child psychiatrist, I didn't go in with him, and the things he told her – I couldn't believe it. At the time he was about five – I thought what does he know about this. He knows everything and it affects him. I cried when she told me that.

Meanwhile, the mother of Maurice's first child had another baby for him, much to Sarah's distress, since he had denied that he was continuing to have relations with her. She explains why she put up with him for as long as she did under those circumstances thus: 'I don't know. I must have loved him.'

MARY was interviewed at her council house in north London where she now lives with her three-year-old son. She has never stayed at a women's refuge. She is a thirty-two-year-old woman of Jamaican origin who had a strictly religious upbringing in her Pentecostal family. She entered the Church and engaged in missionary work in the Caribbean, and describes herself as having had very little experience of life when she met the man she married. She did not live with him before they were married, and they settled in Hackney. Since they could not find anywhere to live, they were grateful to be offered the use of Paul's sister's council flat. At that stage the relationship was far from violent. It was:

> Great – wonderful! It really was. If he swore he used to apologize – It was always – 'oh I'm sorry!'. I think it was because prior to that I had spent seven years in the Church, so I was a total fool. He could see that, but I think that's the reason why he was so courteous and gentle – I think that had a lot to do with it. I jumped out of the Church and into his arms! [laughter].

After four years of highly sheltered married life, Mary found her life had ceased to have meaning for her. She left her husband and went to live in France for two years while they got a divorce. When she returned from abroad, she was again homeless, all her family having returned to Jamaica some time previously. She stayed with her now ex-husband for the time being. While she had been away he had met someone else, who he continued to see – an older woman who kept him supplied with the drugs that he had developed a dependency on.

> He wanted both of us – he didn't want to choose. So he'd be spending some of the time with her and some of the time with me.

He went through violent mood changes and their relationship deteriorated again. On one occasion Paul took Mary's tape recorder to the other woman's house, and she angrily phoned him there. He returned and subjected her to her first serious assault:

> He came home, opened the door – I was in the kitchen and he just laid into me, left, right and centre. That was the very first time it had ever happened. I was in hospital for two days. I was traumatised and shocked. I had a lot of bruises – my eyes were out here, and I was just really lost. I was really dazed. My family had gone back to the West Indies. My mother had gone, my sister had gone – everybody had gone – I was completely alone. Well almost – I have a brother and sister here, but I couldn't really go to them – it was my younger sister and I don't think my older brother would have understood somehow. So I was alone – I did feel alone and more than that I felt ashamed, so I couldn't go to them. That was really bad. It was the shame more than anything. I couldn't understand it. I mean I had never experienced violence of that kind before. It had never happened – I've got five brothers and sisters – a large family, and I'd never known it to happen to them. I'd heard of violence, obviously, but as far as my father and mother – I'd never seen it. I'd never even met anybody who had experienced it. I think it was partly because I was in the Church, and led a very sheltered life. I'd never expected it.

After this painful experience, Mary reacted in a way not uncommon for isolated victims of domestic violence:

> When he realised where I was, where I'd gone, he turned up at 12.00 that night, but the nurse had told him to come and see me in the morning, and he came back the next day. After about three days, he was really contrite, he hadn't meant to do it and what have you. It sounds a really funny thing to say but, even though I knew what he had done, he was the only person I wanted comfort from. Do you understand what I mean? Although he'd put me in this position and what he'd done and what have

you, he was the only person that I really wanted. I didn't feel to reject him. And I went back to him. And then I fell pregnant [laugh].

It was after this that she discovered her partner to be a user of hard drugs, and their relationship continued to deteriorate.

There were instances when we'd be in the car, and he'd just get into a rage – 'why don't they get out of the way!', as if he wanted to kill everybody. Depending on his mood, I couldn't speak to him, without fear of being snapped at. He was on cocaine, and I think that had a lot to do with his violence towards me.

In the end, and after further violence, even in her pregnant state, he agreed to move out. Since it had been his sister's flat however, he continued to visit and disturb her. All Mary's desperate attempts to be transferred by Hackney council failed.

YVONNE is twenty-five years old and has three children. Her ex-partner, Roland, is a British Rail engineer. They cohabited for a couple of years, somewhat intermittently, after he moved into her council flat with her.

He'd say I'm stepping out of line. I'm getting too big for my boots, I must remember I'm only little and things like that . . . I never had any broken bones, but I've been swollen up and bruised, which is enough. He was just sick. I remember one time I ran away, down to his Dad's house, and he even beat up his Dad so he could come in and beat me. He phoned the police. But by the time the police came he [his father] said – 'It's alright – he's calmed down now – it was a domestic affair, it's alright'.

The violent attacks to which Roland subjected Yvonne, particularly when he came out of prison after being remanded for other violent offences, were clearly life threatening. She was rehoused twice by the local council, and spent long periods in reception centres. He found out the address of her second home before she had even moved into it, from the housing department. Yvonne has essentially been trying to escape from his violence for the last four years; this has included being attacked on the streets when he has spotted her. Their youngest son was born two days before Roland was taken into prison on remand for a different violent offence. Roland appears to have had some mental disturbance:

About two days after Mikey was born he went into prison. When he came out he goes to me – 'When did this take place? Where did this baby come from? It's not my baby'. So I said to him – 'During that space of time that you was in prison you have forgotten that I had a baby?' I said

– 'Obviously, as far as I know my two children got the same father, so if this one ain't yours, that one ain't yours'. He told me that it's either his Dad's child because he's got his Dad's name, or his brother's child. And then he started to name untold amount of his friends – it could be any one of them, so I was supposed to have laid down with all of them.

His hostile feeling towards their youngest child erupted in one of his violent attacks:

> He claims he never saw the water boiling. We were having an argument, I was in the kitchen making a bottle for Mikey. I'd just turned off the fire, and the water was still there bubbling and he come in and brought the argument from one room through into the kitchen, and picked up the water and flung it like that. I had Mikey in my arms, I had him in my hand. He didn't hold it over me – he held it over Mikey like that [demonstrates] and the water splashed upon me, but I didn't get burned. Mikey got burned from his head right down to his chest. All they did was give Roland a six months hospital order, and he kept running away, so he only served about three. After a while they said they didn't want him there no more . . . I phoned the ambulance – and I mean this is how stupid he was – he said to me I must tell them I was giving the baby a bath. Now stupid as some women are, they don't put a baby in the bath head first. When the ambulance men came they asked what had happened and that's what he told them. I never said anything in case he thump the ambulance man down and then thump me down afterwards. He wouldn't let go of the eldest one. He said I must go to the hospital with Mikey and get myself treated and Mikey treated and then come back. The ambulance man said – 'It's alright love, I know what's happened', and he phoned the police on his radio thing.

Perhaps the most alarming thing about Yvonne's case is the nature of intervention by the statutory agencies that were repeatedly involved in the case. Her experience highlights the complete lack of protection available to black women, even when their assailants have both criminal convictions for violence and have been subject to psychiatric orders . . .

Domestic violence against African women

MABEL is a thirty-three-year-old Ghanaian with two children: a five-year-old son and a four-year-old daughter. She ran her own small business and lived in a council flat and has lived in London since 1974. Nine years ago she met Kofi, a Ghanaian tailor, who shared her strong Christian faith, and after two years they were married. She attributes some of their problems to his family:

They didn't seem to get on with me. They interfered a lot, and I won't take that, I don't want anybody to tell me what I have to do in my own home and things like that. Kofi was pressurised by the family: they said I was having a good time, taking the money from him or whatever. I don't know what they were thinking of, because I always worked hard. Yes, most of the time I provided everything. And I din't really demand of him. But because of the way they see me – I love to look good, that's me. So when they see me dressing up well, they think that it's from him.

Her husband's violence was irregular:

One week he's alright, and then the next he's like a monster. It was on and off for about ten months.

At other times he was:

a very nice man. A very nice father. He is wonderful. He really cares for his children. But when the monster comes, you know . . . Then he'd cry. Whatever he did, he'd start crying and asking – 'Why did I do it?' – talking to the little boy as if he was a big man and all that . . . He is a believer, a Christian, and he didn't believe in psychiatrists or whatever they call them. He always believed in – well – we do have demon spirits anyway, so that could come in. Like those were behind everything. As far as I'm concerned, because he can be as nice as anybody and can be as nasty as a monster.

He would break down, he would kiss my feet like Jesus did and he would quote from the Bible – 'The Bible says this, the Bible says that'. But yet he'd do it again. I mean what can you do? 'How long would that go on', I always asked him, 'How long?'.

They turned to the Church and to prayer, but to no avail. Instead Kofi went on to inflict quite serious injuries to her, and she saw the effect this was having on her children:

I had to go to hospital for head X-ray. And I was taking tablets for migraines. He left me with bruises almost everywhere, bite marks and all that.

I didn't want my children to see us fighting all the time. It got to a time that whenever the two of us sat down to talk, my little girl, Suzie – at that stage she was only a year old – she would come and stand in front of us and sort of look at Mummy, look at Daddy . . . and the little boy, especially, when he was about four years old would start and shout – 'Don't shout at Mummy, Daddy, stop talking to Mummy, go away! Don't fight

Mummy, you want to kill my Mummy!' I really felt sorry for my son because I didn't want him to grow up and have that kind of thing in his mind at all – that one time my Daddy wanted to kill my Mum, or that he was being Mum all the time. Otherwise he would probably – God forbid – grow up and behave like that. I just couldn't allow that to happen at all.

Mabel persuaded her husband to move out, but could get no peace from him. Eventually she abandoned her flat and her business and went into a women's refuge, where she was staying when we interviewed her.

IYAMIDE was brought over to England by her husband in 1977. He was much older than her, but she had known of him in her community for years. Since living in London she continued her career as a nurse, while he worked in a large department store. They lived in a house they rented from their local authority, once they had the children. Their relationship deteriorated from the time he brought her to England;

> You know African men – when they've brought you here, they think that you are a slave. Especially when they are older than you. They want to make their power over you.

Her husband, a teetotaller himself, took exception to her drinking an occasional glass of wine. She found herself alone, without friends or relatives in this country. Her husband worked and they had no social life at all:

> We go to work during the day. Then he goes to bed. I had nobody to talk to. We had no social life. It was a miserable life actually. Even if he came to sit down, he'd be over there sleeping. Since I joined him, we could never go out. He'd go to work, come and lie down and sleep.

On the other hand:

> If I introduced any friends to him, he would be after them. After I went back home to visit, one of my friends who used to come – we used to be very close – she just cut off. When I asked her what was wrong, what have I done? She said to me – 'Iyamide, you are very good to me, but all the time your husband is harassing me to make love to him'.

> I had three children for him, and the way he insults me! I can never stand it. Each time I thought about it I didn't want to make love to him.

She was beaten and kicked repeatedly, on one occasion until

> My eyes were bleeding. When he saw my eyes were bleeding, saw the

blood, he called the ambulance. By the time the ambulance had come, he had washed everything, cleaned the whole corridor. He didn't want the people to see that. When the doctor attended me he asked if my husband did this – because of the way they saw my eye full of blood. I went back because of the children. Since 1980 I was staying because of the children. They love him so much.

Iyamide had to go to hospital three or four times, where she had X-rays. Her vision has been permanently damaged by repeated blows to her eyes and head.

When the youngest baby was born he beat me. He tried to strangle me. My voice all went. I couldn't even talk. He was on top of me, holding my neck like this [demonstrates]. After that I just tried to hold on to something and I banged him on the head. Otherwise he would have finished me that day. From that time until today we never made love.

Iyamide left her husband shortly after this. I heard her disturbing account of what happened to her after that in what the council call 'temporary accommodation'.

PATIENCE is a Nigerian store manageress who has been in a relationship with Ransome for nine years. They have a young son and got married a year and a half ago. She has left him many times because of his cruelty to her and their child.

Last Easter he took me and stripped me in front of his friends. He was beating me, punching me and pushing me about. I had come in from the kitchen because I heard him saying some nasty things in front of his friends trying to be funny by making fun of me. So I came out from the kitchen and I told him he would regret the things he was doing. As I was going out he started rough-handling me – shouting and pushing me. As he was doing all that my zip had come down, and my breast was coming out – I didn't even notice – I was busy trying to restrain things so as not to display anything to those people. He started slapping my breast and shouting 'Cover yourself!' All in front of his friend and the wife, while they were looking on.

Ransome has been consistently unfaithful to Patience. Probably partly because she grew up in a polygamous home herself, what disturbs her most is his degrading behaviour towards her and his taste for pornography. When she leaves, he begs and cajoles her to come back.

He hasn't spent long in Nigeria. His Dad is here and he's spent most of his years in this country, yet he says to me 'Our tradition is that women should live with their men'. He is not serious!

She has been subjected to pressure from elders in her family (all men) who are concerned that she should have all her children with the one husband. For her own part she does not feel it would be in her interests to get a divorce from her student husband because as she put it, 'I have worked hard for him'. Custody or maintenance rulings in British courts would be of no use to her when they return to Nigeria, where (in her community) taking legal action against one's husband is not an acceptable way of solving marital problems. Her own friends have tired of advising her to permanently leave Ransome. Patience has been multiply abused; not only has her husband injured her on numerous occasions, but on one occasion when neighbours called the police to intervene, they took the opportunity to arrest her and subject her to racially and sexually humiliating ridicule and then assaulted her at the police station.

Discussion

A number of themes emerge from this material. The degree to which violence against women in their homes is tolerated in Britain has long been condemned by the women's movement here, but this has largely been from a Eurocentric feminist perspective. The class, race and cultural dynamics of agency responses to domestic violence have been grossly neglected by feminists, except for the more vociferous Asian women's organizations (such as Southall Black Sisters). Regarding women of African and Caribbean origin, community groups have focused on police brutality, rather than the more sensitive issue of woman abuse. Police brutality is less of a contentious topic within the black communities because it is an oppression delivered by the 'Other' – in this case the state. Woman abuse remains a shameful and buried phenomenon, like other forms of fratricidal behaviour, only made worse by its private nature. This privatization protects the abuser and facilitates further violence. The collusive silence around the issue has the effect of limiting the options that abused women have. Seeking help from the authorities is often regarded as an act of betrayal and several women in the sample who had been forced to seek police assistance as a result of serious violence, now live under threat of death for doing so (as in Roweena's case). Black women are expected to bear their beatings (as if these too were not a betrayal of humanity), and actually to understand that they are a result of the black man's oppression. Yet, as many survivors have pointed out, being beaten by the man one has taken as a sexual and emotional partner is itself a crude and degrading form of oppression.

In October 1988 a black community meeting, entitled 'Violence Within the System' (and billed as the first ever), was held on domestic violence. During this meeting participants exhibited something of a consensual understanding that black men beat black women because they themselves are brutalized by state repression. While it is commendable that such a meeting was held and that discussions took place with seriousness, this kind of analysis can feed into the collective abdication of individual responsibility for brutal and anti-social behaviours. However, many people in the black communities recognize that it is now time to seriously address the problem of violence against black women in Britain, so that more organized collective responses can be developed.

Our findings demonstrate that high levels of violence and cruelty to women by the men they are or have been in relationships with, are being tolerated, by the communities themselves, as well as by statutory organizations.

The occurrence of domestic violence in all the cultural and religious groups we investigated was clearly demonstrated, and this evidence supports the observation that violence occurs in all creeds, cultures and classes. The fact that this practice may have culturally specific content is also evident in women's accounts. In the examples above we saw Muslim and Rastafarian men using religion to assert their patriarchal authority and misogyny.

Women also often referred to tradition, but in their case it was usually to describe how they had tried to conform – to become the ideal wife – only to find that nothing they said or did satisfied their spouse, or stopped the violence. While women of Caribbean origin referred less explicitly to established orthodoxies, it was clear that the men they were involved with often held quite unrealistic expectations about how 'their' women should behave and conduct themselves, and often felt they had a right to use violence to enforce these. Women (who may well have been born and brought up in Britain) were often criticised and beaten for the 'crime' of being 'too Western', sometimes by men who had also been brought up in Britain.

Others did not refer to religion or tradition, but simply held and tried to enforce expectations that the women found to be oppressive and unrealistic, for example not being allowed to have friends or go out, being expected to stay at home and cook and anger over the woman's cooking (as Elsie described) are just a few examples . . .

Within the communities, extended families sometimes intervened positively, although on some occasions, they did not feel able to intervene (for example where the woman's father was dead or absent). In other cases the woman's own relatives made the situation worse.

In some cases (women of African origin in this study) migration had meant being isolated from family and community support, so that violence reached dangerous levels. For example, in Iyamide's case violence began when her husband brought her over to England.

In-laws were often involved in exacerbating conflict (as in Mabel's case where they were jealous of her and wanted greater access to her husband's income), and sometimes as perpetrators of violence themselves, so that some young wives were multiply abused. In Elsie's case, her cohabitee's doting mother used to watch indifferently, so perhaps giving tacit approval, while her son assaulted 'his' woman . . .

In short, double standards which indulge abuse and neglect of women and wives are quite explicitly upheld by families and conformist elements within the black communities. This indulgence of sons of the community has detrimental effects on the women and children, who are expected to live with them while being denied many basic human rights in the name of 'respectability'.

Professionals within the black communities also often appear to condone violence. Recalcitrant responses to domestic violence have been observed in the white community, so it is perhaps not surprising to find that black professionals too, often adhere to patriarchal values and fail to assist abused women. There were incidents in which women were told by doctors from their own communities that 'women should not leave their husbands' . . .

The lack of protection for women in the privacy of their homes and families emerges starkly. This applies even where the police have been, sometimes repeatedly, involved. In Yvonne's case, for example, it is clear that her assailant was mentally disturbed and a danger to both her and her children. Even when he badly scalded the baby, he was still able to return to continue terrorizing her. Other women were being battered by men who had drug addictions or criminal records for other crimes, yet few were encouraged to prosecute, and one woman who had attempted to prosecute (Yvonne, on a different occasion from the one cited here) had had her case thrown out.

This study also found that women are often unprotected from men they have ceased having a relationship with. Ex-husbands and ex-boyfriends were not deterred from assaulting women. This upholds the theme 'that once a woman has engaged in any form of sexual relationship with a man, his social dominance over her is assumed . . . and this includes the right to physically assault her'. In some cases indeed, the man only became more violent at the point when the woman tried to end the relationship or alter the terms on which it would continue. Yvonne and Roweena are only two of the examples where women had been coerced and intimidated for a long period (several years) after they had ended their relationships with assailants who kept seeking them out and returning to further terrorize them and their children.

The evidence from many of the women in this study (particularly those of Caribbean origin, but also from women of African and Asian origin) contradicts the Western feminist analysis of domestic violence which relates it to women's economic marginalization, and concomitant dependence on their spouse's income. Many had been assaulted by men who depended on them. This indicates that men continue to emotionally and physically dominate women even when they depend on those women. Indeed, the evidence is that this can be an exacerbating factor. Many women cited the fact that they were working and had some economic independence, as a source of antagonism.

At one extreme were a number of women whose men contributed nothing to the homekeeping or upkeep of children, and assumed they had rights to the woman's earnings. Recall that Sukie's partner actually resented her using the money she earned, to buy clothes and food for their children. Zoey's cohabitee never worked, but pimped and beat her, accusing her of cheating him while he sold her sex to obtain a car and other material needs for himself.

Not all these men were without incomes of their own, and some exploited the sexism of the cohabitation rule to collect and control social security payments to the family. Sarah's partner earned several hundred pounds a week, and started assaulting her after he had moved into her flat. Only then did he feel confident enough to violently express the resentment he felt towards her for having a career instead of having a baby for him, even while the mother of his two other children had a third for him. Charlotte put all her resources into a business with her man, only to be kept in a state of near starvation during her last pregnancy, while he impregnated another woman.

This material also shatters the stereotype of the 'strong' or 'castrating' black woman. Rather, many black women are both providers and slaves whose labour supports men who then degrade and abuse them. It seems that when women have even a limited material advantage over the men they have relationships with, this in itself may in fact provoke those men to assert their male authority literally with a vengeance, through violence. This dynamic suggests that the frustration felt by men who are unable to conform to patriarchal standards, manifests itself in sadistic behaviour towards the women they live off. Thus we can see that socio-economic jealousy may operate in a way that parallels sexual jealousy and often links up with it.

Notes

1   Parents are not eligible if their children have been taken into local authority care (perhaps – in a cruel irony – because of homelessness or bad living conditions that threaten their health and safety), or are living primarily with the other parent, or abroad with relatives, for example.

2   'Runnings' is a Jamaican term for 'what's going on', and 'how things work' within a particular subculture.

Bibliography

Barrett, M. and MacIntosh, J. (1982) *The Anti-social Family* (London: Voso and NLB).

Bolton, F. G. and Bolton, S. R. (1987) *Working with Violent Families* (London: Sage).

Dobash, R. E. and Dobash, R. (1980) *Violence Against Wives* (London: Open Books).

Fanon, F. (1967) *The Wretched of the Earth* (Harmondsworth: Penguin).

Hall, S., Crichter, C., Jefferson, T., Clarke, J. and Roberts, B. (1978) *Policing the Crisis: Mugging, the State and Law and Order* (London: Macmillan).
Stapler, R. (1982) *Black Masculinity: The Black Male's Role in American Society* (New York: Black Scholar Press).
Yllo, K. and Bograd, M. (1988) *Feminist Perspective on Wife Abuse* (London: Sage).

From *The Hidden Struggle: Statutory and Voluntary Sector Responses to Violence against Black Women in the Home* (London: Whiting & Birch, 1996) (extracts). Courtesy of the Runnymede Trust.

PART 4

Self and discipline reflexivity: ethnic identities and crime

This part places developments within the area of 'race'/ethnicity and crime within the wider context of contemporary Western society, characterised as late modernity. Late modernity does not signify a radical separation from modernity, but rather, consists of the interaction of two contradictory yet inter-related mechanisms: the 'imperative of order' (Lash, 1994) arising out of, and being located within, the framework of modernity, whereby group collectivities are formed around politicised identities in relation to 'race'/ethnicity, faith, gender, sexuality, disability and age, these being underpinned by a belief in emancipation from oppression. At the same time, standing in contradiction to but also interacting with this imperative, is rising individualisation, the growing fragmentation and liquidity of identity attachments, and increasing disciplinary and self-reflexivity.

During the 1980s, 'blackness' as a concept referring to common political participation by non-White people gained hegemony within social and political contexts. The first suggested reading in this part is an article by Modood (1994), who critiqued the notion of 'blackness', claiming that this overlooked the needs and the distinctive experiences of Asian communities. Modood (1994) argues that 'Black' evokes people of African origins, thereby serving to exclude and 'otherise' Asian minorities. According to Modood (1994), 'Black' falsely equates racial discrimination with colour discrimination and thereby obscures the cultural antipathy to Asians and therefore the character of the discrimination they suffer.

More recently, and specifically within although not exclusively to criminology, paralleling postmodern processes that stress the fluidity, fragmented nature and diversity of identities, the use of broad, 'catch-all' 'race'/ethnic classifications has been criticised. Terms like 'Black', 'Asian' or 'Black and Minority Ethnic' (BME) when researching 'race'/ethnicity in relation to crime and victimisation have been criticised for serving to obscure the distinct experiences of specific groups (Garland, Spalek and Chakraborti, 2006).

Phillips and Bowling's (2003) article raises many important issues for criminology, and is therefore a suggested reading in this part. Phillips and Bowling (2003) reject the pursuit and development of a 'Black criminology', contesting its validity as a unifying identity for Britain's ethnic and racial minorities. Phillips and Bowling (2003) propose that criminologists place a greater emphasis upon developing a 'minority perspective' within criminology, one which articulates the experiences of specific communities and takes into account their histories and identities. Phillips and Bowling (2003: 271) also argue that a core component of the development of a minority ethnic perspective within criminology is the documentation of difference, consisting of a movement away from 'essentialist categorisations of racial and ethnic minorities'. Phillips and Bowling (2003) advocate adopting a method that documents people's specific experiences but which acknowledges that aspects of these can be shared by other minorities due to broader structures of 'race', class, ethnicity and so forth – so-called 'unities within diversity'.

A focus upon 'race'/ethnicity has helped to fuel broader concern about the nature of criminological knowledge claims and the extent to which these are dominated by mainstream experiences and understandings, thereby serving to marginalise those perspectives and experiences of groups whose subjectivities lie outside of dominant norms. For instance, Chigwada-Bailey (1997) has argued that feminist perspectives within criminology have not fully taken on board issues concerning Black women, who are over-represented in the female prison population. Chigwada-Bailey (1997: 47) has highlighted how Black women receive fewer police cautions than White women, and that while socio-economic factors are likely to account for this disparity, 'race' is also a factor: 'Black women are the subject of many negative beliefs and attitudes, the victims of racist assumptions which are likely to affect police attitudes towards them'. Chigwada-Bailey (1997) has also argued that common stereotypes of Black women held by the police include that they are over-aggressive, strong, dominant and that such stereotyping can deter police from taking action in cases of domestic violence.

Black feminists have further raised the issue of whiteness as a dominant, and largely hidden, norm that underpins research approaches and knowledge constructions. The invisibility of 'whiteness', whereby being white is not regarded as being a racial identity and a particular lens through which the world is viewed and experienced, but rather, is considered to be what is 'normal', 'neutral' or 'common sense', has led to accusations that researchers have often ignored, misrepresented and misunderstood Black people's, particularly women's, lives (hooks, 1990; Harris, 1997). 'Whiteness' is thus seen as universal and devoid of any particularity, thereby serving to legitimise white power and privilege. As a result, academic discourse is increasingly featuring a focus upon, and making visible, 'whiteness' (Wiegman, 1999). Ferber's (2003) chapter on constructing whiteness, the third suggested reading in this part, highlights how scholars of 'race' have for too long neglected the study of whiteness.

Ferber (2003) explores the project of constructing white racial identity, this being a central component to the contemporary white supremacist movement, which she defines as actively producing racialised and gendered subjects. According to Ferber (2003), within the white supremacist movement equality becomes impossible to imagine because it signifies the denial of difference. For white supremacists, the construction of 'race' and gender and the maintenance of inequality are necessarily linked.

Pursuing the theme of whiteness, Spalek's (2005) article, the fourth suggested reading, consists of a critical exploration of the nature of the researcher's subjectivity and its influence over the research process. This links in with a wider debate in relation to the question of whether minority ethnic researchers are best placed to understand the lived experiences of minority ethnic communities. Some argue that even as 'outsiders' white researchers can legitimately study such issues, but that this requires active involvement with minority ethnic organisations and individuals in order to understand and portray their worldviews and lifestyles (Gelsthorpe, 1993). Others, such as Papadopoulos and Lees (2002), argue that as 'insiders' minority ethnic researchers are better placed to do this work as they have greater awareness and understanding of minority issues and so can provide accounts of experiences and perceptions that are more genuine and legitimate. At the same time, Spalek's (2005) article builds on a point raised by Gelsthorpe (1993), that in order to comprehend how racisms are produced this requires theoretical and personal reflexivity. Spalek (2005) highlights how a white, Eurocentric perspective has underpinned much feminist work, even though Black women writers and researchers have, particularly since the 1980s, produced a large volume of work about their lives. Spalek's (2005) article illustrates how her subject positions – in terms of being a woman, white and a Western researcher – influenced the research process. Spalek (2005) argues that whilst some aspects of the researcher's self can be linked to marginalised, outsider positions, helping to produce oppositional knowledge, other aspects of a researcher's self-identity can serve to maintain and reproduce dominant power relations. Moreover, this article highlights how reflexivity also includes reflecting upon one's emotions during the research process, as this can help to shed light upon a researcher's many different subject positions.

Another emerging area within criminology is that of Pan-African issues in relation to crime and justice. Here, a critique of criminology as orientalist can be found, where orientalism is viewed as the tendency to negativise or idealise the practices of non-Western nations (Cain, 2000). The final suggested reading in this part comprises a chapter by Kalunta-Crumpton (2004), who maintains that the voices of Africans are marginalised from criminological discourse. African perspectives not only have much to offer criminological knowledge, but moreover, concepts developed within criminological discourse are not necessarily applicable to an African or Caribbean context, yet may be exported due to the hegemony of Western criminology. Therefore, more attention should be paid to the significance of cultural relativity as well as 'the existence of a strong African cultural base from which alternative theorising can emerge' (Kalunta-Crumpton, 2004: 18).

A further critique of criminological discourse appears to be emerging from some researchers who have carried out work with Muslim communities in relation to crime and criminal justice, who stress the difficulties of including a focus upon faith identities within a secular discipline. According to Quraishi (2005: 116), there is a commonly shared sense of victimisation amongst the South Asian Muslims taking part in his study, this being linked to the concept of the ummah, which consists of the individual, community and global Muslim population, so that religious oppression and Islamophobia constitute import-ant aspects to Muslims' perceptions as oppressed minorities. This work high-lights the relevance of faith identities, and more specifically Muslim identities, to experiences of crime and victimisation. The emergence of Muslim identities poses some key issues in relation to knowledge constructions for criminology, potentially heralding new areas of research and novel ways of carrying out research. The notions of religiosity and spirituality are increasingly likely to feature in criminological discourse.

Suggested essays

Modood, T. (1994) 'Political Blackness and British Asians' *Sociology* Vol. 28 (4): 859–876.

Phillips, C. and Bowling, B. (2003) 'Racism, Ethnicity and Criminology: developing minority perspectives' *British Journal of Criminology* 43: 269–290.

Ferber, A. (2003) 'Constructing Whiteness: the intersections of race and gender in US White Supremacist Discourse' in B. Perry (ed.) *Hate and Bias Crime: a reader*. London: Routledge, pp. 351–362.

Spalek, B. (2005) 'Researching Black Muslim Women's Lives: a critical reflection' *The International Journal of Social Research Methodology* Vol. 8 (5): 1–14.

Kalunta-Crumpton, A. (2004) 'Criminology and Orientalism' in A. Kalunta-Crumpton and B. Agozino (eds) *Pan-African Issues in Crime and Justice*. Aldershot: Ashgate, pp. 5–22.

Further reading

Cain, M. (2000) 'Orientalism, Occidentalism and the Sociology of Crime' *British Journal of Criminology* Vol. 40: 239–260.

Carby, H. (1997) 'White Women Listen!' in H. Safia Mirza (ed.) *Black British Feminism: a reader*. London: Routledge, pp. 45–53.

Chigwada-Bailey, R. (1997) *Black Women's Experiences of Criminal Justice*. Winchester: Waterside Press.

Frankenberg, R. (1993) *The Social Construction of White Women, Whiteness Race Matters*. London: Routledge.

Garland, J., Spalek, B. and Chakraborti, N. (2006) 'Hearing Lost Voices: Issues in

Researching Hidden Minority Ethnic Communities' *British Journal of Criminology* Vol. 46: 423–437.

Gelsthorpe, L. (1993) 'Approaching the Topic of Racism: Transferable Research Strategies?' in D. Cook and B. Hudson (eds) *Racism and Criminology*. London: Sage, pp. 77–95.

hooks, b. (1982) *Ain't I a Woman: black women and feminism*. London: Pluto Press.

13

Political Blackness and British Asians[*]
by Tariq Modood

Abstract

In the 1980s a political concept of blackness was hegemonic, but is increasingly having to be defended, even within the sociology of race. This is to be welcomed and seven reasons are given why the concept harms British Asians. The use of 'black' encourages a 'doublespeak'. It falsely equates racial discrimination with colour-discrimination and thereby obscures the cultural antipathy to Asians and therefore of the character of the discrimination they suffer. 'Black' suggests also a false essentialism: that all non-white groups have something in common other than how others treat them. The fourth reason is that 'black', being evocative of people of African origins, understates the size, needs and distinctive concerns of Asian communities. Fifthly, while the former can use the concept for purposes of ethnic pride, for Asians it can be no more than 'a political colour', leading to a too politicised identity. Indeed, it cannot but smother Asian ethnic pride – the pride which is a precondition of group mobilisation and assertiveness. Finally, advocates of 'black' have tried to impose it on Asians rather than seek slower methods of persuasion, with the result that the majority of Asians continue to reject it. The new emphasis on multi-textured identities is therefore encouraging, as long as we are not simply exchanging a political for a cultural vanguardism.

Introduction

In 1982 Salman Rushdie wrote:

> Britain is now two entirely different worlds and the one you inherit is determined by the colour of your skin.
>
> (Rushdie 1982)

He described such a condition as 'the new empire within Britain'. Since then he has come to see himself as battling within a different colour-dualism: this time rallying the forces of light against the forces of darkness (Rushdie 1989), in the process of which he has re-evaluated his view of the British Empire ('we were lucky to be ruled by Britain' (Mortimer 1992: 2)).

Others with easier circumstances or more political steadfastness continue to see Britain in terms of the first colour dualism. For most people who have been active in British race relations debates over the last decade or so, whether at political, academic or administrative levels, have participated or acquiesced in the idea that an, perhaps the, important social fact about non-white people in Britain is their common participation in a political 'blackness'. The single most important and common manifestation of this idea has been the use of the term 'black' to describe people of African, Caribbean and South Asian origins in Britain. Sociologists have been both at the forefront of this development, and amongst the slowest to abandon it. At one of the sessions of the 1992 British Sociological Association Annual Conference, in response to a query about terminology the Chair announced, without any consultation, that she was sure that most of those present were in favour of the term 'black' to cover all non-white people, so that is how she wanted the term used.[1] She was probably right about her colleagues (most of whom were of course white like herself), yet the need for such a ruling from the chair is an indication that even within the confines of sociology of race there is growing recognition that the concept of 'black' is in serious trouble.

Yasmin Ali, following the lead of Stuart Hall (1992: 252), has described the fortunes of the concept of 'black' in the following way:

> At the beginning of the 1980s 'communities originating in some of the countries of the old empire' would have been expressed unselfconsciously as 'black communities'. At the end of the decade 'black' is a much more contentious label than it was previously. 'Black' in its British usage was intended to convey a sense of a necessary common interest and solidarity between communities from the old empire (or the New Commonwealth); it was a usage predicated on the politics of anti-racism. As such 'black' 'became "hegemonic" over other ethnic/racial identities' in the late seventies and early eighties. The moment was not to last. From within marginalized communities and from without there was, in the 1980s, a steady assault upon this fragile hegemony.
>
> (Ali 1991: 195)

As one of the people cited as responsible for contributing to the defeat of this hegemony (Ali 1991: 207), I would like to return to this topic to consider an aspect of why this hegemony was so vulnerable to criticism. It is important to be clear, of course, that what has been defeated is *not* the concept of 'black' but its hegemony, and even then, as far as terminology is concerned, the effect of the change in political writing and academic research is negligible. Hence, while the Commission for Racial Equality in December 1988 ceased to recommend that 'black' as an ethnic monitoring category encompassed Asians (CRE 1988), British academic writing on race has continued with the older terminology. While some explicitly acknowledge that 'black' is a political or ideological term that many of those to whom it refers 'would not accept it as referring to themselves' (e.g. Sarre 1989: 127), increasingly academic writers have been justifying their terminology, though this usually takes no more than a footnote, with the claim that they are merely observing conventional or standard usage from which no politics can be inferred (e.g. Nanton 1989: note 1; Mullings 1992: note 1; Saggar 1992: xii; Smith 1993: note 1).[2] Yet if one compares the 'quality' British newspapers and weeklies and the radio and television current affairs coverage in the years 1984–1988 with the years thereafter one will find, I believe, that in the majority of cases where 'black' was used in the earlier period to mean non-white people, the terminology in the later period is likely to be 'ethnic minorities' or 'black and Asian'. That is to say, that in quality current affairs reportage and discussion the inclusive and political term 'black' comes to the fore in the earlier period and is replaced in the later period by a more specific ethnic usage where 'black' means sub-Saharan African origins or phenotype. I therefore understand the loss of the hegemony of 'black' to mean a pushing back from the mainstream public discourse to its original location, left-wing politics and race sociology, where, of course, it still flourishes.

Because my primary concern is with the kind of current affairs reportage I have referred to, together with the speeches and documents produced by political parties, trades unions, big employers, central and local government officials and professionals and so on (this is what I mean by 'mainstream public discourse'), I would date the hey-day of the concept of 'black' differently from Ali. For her the high-point was the late 1970s and early 1980s (Ali 1991: 201) and others would confine it yet again to the earlier of these two periods when the concept of 'black', devised by New Left radicals to mark a transcendence of ethnicity and origins in favour of a new colour-solidarity and political formation, is said to have been taken up by Afro-Caribbean and Asian communities who found that their separate struggles were actually bringing them together; a moment that was soon to be lost when the concept was appropriated by the set of race professionals that emerged in the local and central government responses to the riots of 1981 (Sivanandan 1985; Gilroy 1989: 25). Yet it was the incorporation of these anti-racist pressures into the British polity that led to the ascendancy of the inclusive concept of 'black' within the mainstream (Banton 1987; Anthias and Yuval-Davis 1992: 159). For with the enactment of the 1976 Race Relations Act and particularly with local government racial equality initiatives after the 1981 riots a tranche of radical activists were brought into work with the state, with 'the system' (Dhondy 1987). It was their anti-racist rhetoric, often contradictorily mixed up with the very different 'black is beautiful' rhetoric of *ethnic* pride, which came together with the more social scientific and administrative language of statistics and policy recommendations, which, too, favoured a white–black tidiness, to create the favoured consensus which was around the term 'black' in early to mid-eighties, first within the specialist lobby and then more widely.

Hence, the important mainstream hegemony came to be established just as the original left-wing, extra-state radicalism and the consequent Afro-Caribbean-Asian solidarities that arose from community self-defence from skinheads or police harassment, were giving way to struggles within the Labour Party and the (local) state in which Afro-Caribbeans and Asians lobbied for ethnic or sub-ethnic interests (usually the distribution of jobs, social grants and control of state-aided community centres and projects) which belied the increasing and uncritical use of the rhetoric of political colour-unity. The contrast, then, between radicals, like Sivanandan, Hall, Gilroy and Ali, dating the hegemonic period as the late 1970s and early 1980s, and my dating it as early to late 1980s is primarily a difference in our respective interests in radicalism and mainstream discourse. For those whose starting-point was extra-state agitation as a way of amplifying and connecting with idealised histories of class struggle and global anti-imperialism could not help but see the transformation of their 'black' movements into 'the race relations industry' and competing ethnic lobbies as, to use Sivanandan's phrase, a 'degradation'. For those like me whose community relations work perspective was, in the period of the 'degradation', increasingly obliged to adopt a 'black' discourse perspective which (as the radicals note) was inconsistent with the emerging ethnic realities, the problem was not about the decline of the concept of 'black', but how such a concept was ever foisted upon the various ethnic minorities.

Why 'black' harms Asians

While the concept of 'black' became part of the race relations discourse orthodoxy (even if this concept was a degraded version of earlier radical hopes), such that, as I can personally testify, it became a taboo to question it within certain activist, administrative and, even, research contexts, nevertheless it did attract several different kinds and source of criticism. Yasmin Ali groups these as 'debates encompassing black cultural politics, anti-racism/multiculturalism, the growth of ethnicism, the laments for England of both the sentimentalist left and the social authoritarian right, and the rhetoric of "popular capitalism" ' (1991: 195). My concern here is very specifically focussed. My argument is that whatever strengths and flaws, good and harm, there may be in the hegemony of the concept of 'black', it has at least one critically undesirable aspect: it harms British Asians. I am aware that other groups too claim that it harms them. For example, cultural Africanists reject

the term 'black' because they believe it strips members of the African diaspora of their African roots (e.g. Yekawi 1986; Dennis 1989); while in Britain
this debate is only gradually reaching beyond poets and artists, it is a recurring topic of debate in the popular London Afro-Caribbean paper, *The Voice*,
and it is interesting to note that parallel debates among black American intellectuals a decade or more ago have now led to the political replacement of the
term 'black' in favour of 'African-American' (as before 'black' replaced
'negro' which previously had replaced 'coloured'), (Martin 1991). A more
politically fractious example is that of the two African-origin councillors in
the London Borough of Brent who, arguing that under cover of 'black', jobs
and resources were going to Afro-Caribbeans at the expense of the less
numerous and visible Africans, have successfully replaced 'black' as an equality monitoring category in favour of categories of origins such as 'African'.
Again, having been persuaded that mixed-race children and teenagers would
suffer from low self-esteem and identity confusion if not told they were
'black', social workers are now finding that the majority of such persons reject
an exclusivist identity and yet have no special identity problems (Tizard
and Pheonix 1993). I offer no comment on these other debates but focus on
my single argument, for it is in the case of British Asians that I can speak
with some personal authenticity, and it is an argument rarely found at any
length in race relations writing.

Given, then, that the origins of 'black' lie in the egalitarian desire of
grouping those people together who suffer similar forms of discrimination
and marginality, so that their condition can be highlighted and remedial
action taken, including ethnic mobilisation, law and policy, how can I argue
that 'black' is harmful to Asians? I offer seven reasons below, most of
which depend upon the fact that the term 'black' is not neutral amongst
non-white ethnic groups. It has a historical and current meaning such that
it is powerfully evocative of people of sub-Saharan African origins, and
all other groups, if evoked at all, are secondary. It is not an empty term
that can be picked up and given a meaning such that any group other than
those of African origins can be the core group (just as masculine vocabulary,
even when intended to be gender-neutral, as in legal and academic language, cannot but put the image of the male gender in the reader's mind).
Some of the negative effects for Asians, in extending an Afro-based term to
describe Asians are as follows (for a related viewpoint, see Hazareesingh
1986).

Doublespeak

Asians are sometimes 'black' and sometimes not depending not upon the
Asians in question (i.e. upon whether they accept the terminology), but upon
the convenience or politics of the speaker or writer. Examples are so commonplace that a report or conference on race in Britain where this did not

occur would be most unusual, and I will illustrate my point with two examples. An expert Labour Party committee on racial equality argues:

> Too often when the party discusses membership of *black and Asian* people it centres on the level of public representativeness, magistrates and MPs, rather than on ways in which *black* people can play a role in the party without necessarily aspiring to hold office; this is not to diminish the important point that many more *black* people should hold such offices.
>
> (Labour Party 1985: 20, my italics)

A sentence which boldly begins with one meaning of 'black' immediately gives way to an entirely different meaning without any suggestion of having done so. Consider also the example of when local authority job advertisements proclaim a desire to attract applications from 'black and ethnic minorities'[3] or 'black and Asian people'. That in each case the second half of these conjunctions is very definitely secondary, an irritating addition, is clear from the fact that regardless of how often these conjunctions are used their order always follows strict precedence. Rare indeed in these contexts would a statement be made in terms of 'all ethnic minorities including black people'. And to expect a phrase such as 'Asian and Black' might not seem unreasonable given the size of the respective populations, or even the convention of alphabetical precedence, let alone the variety normal in the use of language; but it is an expectation which will invariably be disappointed.

It may be thought that these examples, being examples of mere language, are rather trivial and inconsequential. I hope to demonstrate, as I proceed, that this is not so, but at this stage it is important to note the *personam* point that advocates of the all-inclusive term 'black' cannot make this objection. For they believe no less than I do that the language and imagery of public identity is integrally linked with inequality, discrimination and exclusion on the one hand, and with group pride, mobilisation and liberation on the other hand. Hence the energy they put in opposing some words, e.g., 'coloured' and in advocating their favoured term 'black'. I also call upon the growing consensus for not using exclusively masculine language to describe situations which could equally apply to both genders: if 'men' were substituted for 'black' and 'women' for 'Asian' in the examples I have quoted above, we would have sentences that many will agree exemplify marginalisation or the making invisible of the second group. Just as such sentences would be sexist, so my examples are examples of anti-Asian language.

Too narrow a conception of racial discrimination

A focus on 'colour' as the basis of uniting and mobilising those who suffer from racial discrimination falsely equates racial discrimination with colour-discrimination. While there is good evidence that in the case of *face-to-face* discrimination, for example in the context of seeking accommodation or employment, colour is a decisive factor (Brown and Gay 1985; Commission for Racial Equality 1990; Foyster *et al.* 1990), this is really only the ground floor of racism rather than the whole building. It is generally recognised that class is a factor which contributes to racial discrimination and to racial disadvantage. Inferior treatment on the basis of colour can create a subordinate class which, by virtue of its socio-economic location, could continue to suffer comparative disadvantage even were colour prejudice to wane. Thus, for instance, employers who prefer a public school, Oxbridge background will disadvantage the majority of society, but may have a disproportionately greater impact on racial minorities, and this fact is acknowledged in the British legal concept of indirect racial discrimination.[4] While proponents of the concept of 'black' recognise how class is interrelated with race, they overlook how cultural differences can also disadvantage and be the basis of discrimination, e.g., in employment on the grounds of one's dress, dietary habits, or desire to take leave from work on one's holy days rather than those prescribed by the custom and practice of the majority community. An emphasis on discrimination against 'black' people systematically obscures the cultural antipathy to Asians (and, no doubt, others), how Asian cultures and religions have been racialised, and the elements of discrimination that Asians (and others) suffer. If colour (or colour and class) were the sole basis of racism in British society it would be impossible to explain the finding of all the white attitude surveys over more than a decade that self-assigned racial prejudice against Asians is higher, sometimes much higher, than against black people (e.g. Brown 1984: 290; Jowell *et al.* 1986: 150 and 164; *Today* 14 March 1990; Amin and Richardson 1992: 19–21). Moreover, explanations to do with length of settlement and mutual familiarisation belie the fact that the difference in the prejudice against the two groups may be growing (Young 1992: 181).

The emphasis on colour-discrimination and colour-identity denies what otherwise would be obvious: the hostility of the majority is likely to be particularly forceful against non-white individuals who are members of a community (and not just free-floating or assimilated individuals), which is sufficiently numerous to reproduce itself as a community and has a distinctive and cohesive value system which can be perceived as an alternative to and a possible challenge to the norm; this phenomenon is currently growing in Britain and disproportionately impacts upon Asians. It is what explains some of the contradictions in contemporary racism, such as the observation that white working class youth culture is incorporating, indeed, emulating, young black men and women, while hardening against groups like South Asians and Vietnamese (Cohen 1988: 83; Boulton and Smith 1992; Back 1993). A glance at the newspapers will quickly reveal that as many race relations battles turn on issues of culture and minority rights as on colour discrimination and socio-economic deprivation. 'Black' obscures this and prevents Asians from fully articulating and mobilising against the nature of their oppression.

One of the ways of appreciating how the condition and concerns of British Asians are overlooked and distorted because of a doctrinaire assumption about the nature of racial discrimination, is by observing and drawing an analogy from how 'black' British activists approach the issue in Europe. The observation I am referring to has been excellently put by Ann Dummett, who deserves to be quoted at length:

> There is a widespread belief among black people in Britain that you have to be black to be oppressed. This is putting crudely an assumption that is often not spelt out, but it is evident that this assumption is held from the way many black people who have become concerned about 1992 talk about racism on the continent. Instead of showing especial concern about Turks in Germany, who suffer anti-Turkish prejudice and discrimination in ways that are at least as oppressive as the way British blacks suffer, they often concentrate on the situation of black Germans – children usually of black American servicemen and German mothers – and of black immigrants to Germany like Ghanaians, Mozambicans and so on. These latter suffer frightening degrees of hostility and, in places, violence, but to single them out and ignore or give only secondary importance to the Turks is to take a seriously distorted view of racism in Germany.
>
> (Dummett 1992: 8)

A false essentialism

Talk about 'black' people, especially where this is supposed to be or in practice becomes the predominant way of conceptualising the people in question, suggests a false essentialism, namely, that all non-white groups have something in common other than how others treat them. The harm to Asians is that usually what happens in the manufacture of a 'black' commonality is that a set of features are plucked from Afro-Caribbean history or contemporary experience and said to be paradigmatically 'black' (Bonnett 1993: 43–44); Asians are then shown to approximate to this paradigm, or sometimes the writer fails to show any approximation and simply insists that if one looks hard enough one will find it. In my original discussion I cited the much-praised Paul Gilroy's, *There Ain't No Black in the Union Jack*, as the worst case of this (Modood 1988a: 400). A more extended critique of that text along the same lines has been made by Robert Miles. In an article published in French, Miles argues that Gilroy, having:

> posited the existence of a 'black' social movement involving people of Afro-Caribbean and South Asian origin . . . ignore[s] the nature and

content of cultural forms of South Asian origin. As a result, we are left with an analysis in which it appears that people of South Asian origin are granted a 'walk-on' part in a cultural context shaped largely, if not exclusively, by young British people of Caribbean origin.

(Miles 1991: 150–151; p. 14 in English typescript version, kindly supplied by the author)

'Black' obscures Asian needs and distorts analysis

Because 'black' is powerfully evocative of people of African origins, its usage inevitably gives prominence to Afro-Caribbeans, to the point that it obscures the fact that amongst non-white groups in Britain, Asians form an ever-growing majority. While this is not usually quite as gross as the two recent academic assertions that, of non-white groups, people of West Indian origins are most numerous (McIlroy 1989: 235; Waldinger *et al.* 1990: 85), this error does represent a genuine state of mind in this country, not least amongst race egalitarians. Ken Young and Pat Gay's claim of an Afro-Caribbean under-representation amongst Community Relations Officers is typical of occupational analyses which are only coherent on the false assumption that Afro-Caribbean and Asian populations are roughly of the same size (Young and Gay 1988: 83–84 and 95). I have elsewhere given examples of how this marginalisation of Asians is widespread in research and political literature (Modood 1988a: 399–400), so it is not therefore surprising that it should also exist at the level of practical action. For example, Bonnett found that 'most of the "Black Studies" courses introduced in inner-city schools in the early 1970s were dominated almost exclusively by African, Afro-Caribbean and Afro-American self-image and history' (1990: 4). Of course this is a 1970s example and therefore pre-dates the institutional use of the inclusive 'black'; but what, then, is the explanation behind the following two 1989 examples. Linbert Spencer, a prominent race equality professional, managed to get through a whole BBC Radio 4 programme on case-studies of racial discrimination in employment without a single Asian appearing, and the TUC workbook, *Tackling Racism*, much of which was in the form of photographic cameos, was notable (except that nobody noticed it) too, for a virtual absence of Asian faces. Perhaps these are all errors and over-sights that can be corrected in due course. What, however, is one to make of the deliberate and institutionalised expression of this inequality in the Labour Party's Black Sections' resolution in early 1989 that, despite their over 2:1 population ratio, Asian and Afro-Caribbean MPs should be in equal numbers?

Where there is a mental and numerical marginalisation, it naturally follows that the distinctive concerns of the Asian communities will be marginalised. It is notable, for example, that despite the high levels of attacks on Asians and their property from the 1960s onwards, attempts to get the police and policy makers to address this basic issue of security had, till very recently, been less effective than the attempts to get them to focus on the equality of treatment of offenders by the criminal justice system, an issue up to now of far less importance to Asians. Immigration rules, transmission of parental culture to children, minority religious observance in schools, support for large families and self-employment are a number of issues which are of greater importance to Asians than to others, but because Asians have not been in a position to push them to the top of the agenda, these have received relatively less attention in the race equality movement than Asians have felt they deserved. The shock of the Rushdie Affair to this movement is a very good example of the lack of understanding there is of Asian community concerns (Modood 1989 and 1990). Yet, as we all know, it is shocks such as these, though the Rushdie Affair was far more peaceful than is usual with anti-racism explosions, that lead to paradigm-shifts, and I am pleased to note that the point I am making here has begun to get recognition. Malcolm Cross (1991) in a *New Community* editorial has asked for the putting aside of simple social science conflations and for a new agenda for policy and research built out of the self-expression of ethnic minorities and their own critiques of their oppression. More specifically, John Rex, whose perspective is well known for giving primacy to metropolitan social structures and distributive processes over ethnicity, has recently stated:

> It can be argued that amongst social scientists and policy makers, the structure of the various Asian communities and the problems which Asians face have been seriously misunderstood because of the focus on the disadvantages suffered by, and discrimination against, Blacks (1991: 93).

A too politicised identity

Asians (and for that matter any other group) need a richer and more rounded public identity than one focussed on politics can allow. People of African origins can use the concept of 'black' with a historical depth and a cultural texture through freighting it with an African diasporic ethnic pride, as famously captured in the 'Black is Beautiful' slogan, or in the newer idea of 'black Atlantic' (Gilroy 1993). For Asians, 'black' can be no more than 'a political colour', a reference to a limited aspect of their being, which inevitably requires them to give greater prominence to an aspect of their political being than is important to them or than they consider sensible; and, willy nilly, it gives a leadership role to those Asians who, whatever their standing in or commitment to the various Asian communities, can identify with and internalise the politics of anti-colour discrimination. This is too gross a straitjacket for Asian community concerns and qualities which Asians may wish to promote.

Interestingly enough, as a result of *The Satanic Verses* affair, some Muslim activists are simplifying the range and variety of Muslim values and practices into a simple oppositional, political Islamism, so that the very term 'Muslim' becomes identified with their own political causes. It is interesting that many of those who have been at the forefront in homogenising non-whites under 'black' now forcefully criticise Muslim activists for manufacturing, out of a Muslim heterogeneity, a homogeneity to suit their political ends! Thus the Southall Black Sisters responded to the political Islamism of the Rushdie Affair by setting up Women Against Fundamentalism 'to challenge the assumption that minorities in this country exist as unified, internally homo-geneous groups' (Women Against Fundamentalism 1990: 2; see also Yuval-Davis 1992: 284), and in particular to oppose the 'seemingly seamless (and supra-racial) Muslim consensus in Britain' (Connolly 1990: 6). In a similar vein, the ESRC Centre for Research into Ethnic Relations at the University of Warwick has deemed that ethnic mobilisation around Islam is 'potentially negative' because it offends liberal and secular values and distracts from work towards colour-equality, while 'social and political action based on racial considerations' is thought to be 'creative' (CRER 1990: 4–5). My point is not simply to show how a pro-'black' point of view can easily become an anti-'Muslim' one; the critical point is that those who deployed, or went along with a coercive, essentialist, political concept of 'black' have no principled argu-ments against a coercive, essentialist, political concept of 'Muslim' – hence their opposition must turn on a secular prejudice against religious mobilisa-tion despite all their arguments about the dangers to heterogeneity (Modood 1994).

Not conducive to ethnic pride

Even if there is a descriptive, sociological concept of 'black' based upon statistically inferred colour discrimination (and I have already suggested that the concept of racial discrimination is more complex than colour discrimin-ation), this concept is of a negative condition, of how *others* treat oneself, not the basis of a positive identity likely to foster pride in one's origins and establish a secure psychological platform for active participation in British society. For, while mobilisation to secure rights requires a dynamic of group pride, 'black' serves to obscure Asian identities and smother the basis of ethnic pride.

The crux of the issue here rests on a distinction between the values, aspirations, and community structures of an oppressed group (its mode of being) and the social structures and ideological forms which oppress that group (its mode of oppression). A cardinal error of 1980s anti-racism is to substitute mobilisation around opposition to a mode of oppression (racism) for the freedom to be what one is and aspires to be, for one's mode of being. By understanding minorities such as Asians *primarily in terms of racism and anti-racism*, anti-racists in effect create group identities exclusively from the point of view of the dominant whites and fail to recognise that those whom white people treat as no more than the raw material of racist categorisation have, indeed, a mode of being of their own which defies such reduction (Modood 1990a). Many anti-racists' interest in Asians is not in Asians but in the condition of victim; Asians who experience racial discrimination are reduced to discriminated beings ('blacks') who happen to be Asians, and who should publicly proclaim their mode of oppression as their primary identity, while confining the symbolic power of their mode of being to secondary occasions. But this is too superficial a view of oppression and of ethnic mobilisation against racial subordination. We need a concept of race that enables us to understand that any oppressed group feels its oppression most according to those dimensions of its being which *it* (not the oppressor) values most; moreover, it will resist its oppression from those dimensions of its being from which it derives its greatest collective psychological strength. We see this very clearly with working class Asians (and other) Muslims. Despite being the most racially disadvantaged group in Britain, measured in terms of unemployment, over-representation in manual work, educational qualifications, poor housing, attacks on person and property and so on (Jones 1993), they have borne this marginal and oppressive condition with stoicism and kinship self-help, but exploded on an issue of religious honour, when it was perceived that *The Satanic Verses* not only limited one's material opportunities but attacked the very core of one's being (Modood 1990a, 1990b). It is most revealing that the Muslim protesters neither looked for nor were offered any 'black' solidarity and that one of the leaders of 'black' politics, Paul Boateng MP, dismissed Muslim anger as having nothing to do with 'the black discourse' (Kramer 1991: 75). It has been argued that as all identities are situational, individuals are capable of identities of several sorts, and that Asians can be found who have a strong Asian identity and a sense of political blackness, even if not fully acknowledged by themselves (Drury 1990). Drury offers as evidence that 92 per cent of a sample of about a hundred teenage Sikh girls in the early 1980s rejected the term 'black' as a self-description, but a significant number thought there were commonalities of experience between all non-white people. Yet this surely confirms that a sense of being 'black' is for most Asians a forced identity, on the periphery of their conception of themselves and not a source of pride or even of self-defence. The general point I am making is not peculiar to Muslims or Asians. Materialistic theories of anti-racism typically underestimate the defence of group dignity and the positive role of ethnic pride. The 'black is beautiful' campaign in the long term reached far more American blacks than the civil rights campaign and, indeed, provided a personal and collective psychological dynamic which fed into the latter, and which enabled blacks to take advantage of the socio-economic opportunities created by the politics.

Some advocates of 'black' have themselves latterly argued that British anti-racism has been overconcerned with a white audience and too little concerned with understanding, relating to, or giving space to, the rich history of black self-emancipation, especially in respect of forms of expressive culture, and yet these forms of black resistance are critical to racial equality, broadly conceived (Gilroy 1987). This could perhaps be an important bridge for the acceptance of a parallel argument on behalf of Asians.

The coerciveness of the advocates of 'black'

The final reason I offer is perhaps not inherent in the concept of 'black' but rather the way it has been promoted by its advocates. Given the various reasons why I think the concept is harmful to Asians, it was perhaps not likely that the majority of Asians would embrace it; and yet, with its simple appeal of political mobilisation and inter-group unity directed at a pervasive dimension of constraint affecting all non-whites, it was not impossible that Asians could be persuaded of its merits. The advocates of 'black', however, understandably impatient to build political power and effect change, operated as if the consent of Asians (and perhaps others) could be taken for granted and that the selling of the concept to the grass roots was unnecessary. This, however, while typical of a certain kind of militancy, may have been a fatal error (Bonnett 1990: 8–9). Working in racial equality administration and training in the mid and late 1980s, I have witnessed at first hand how 'black' has been, and continues to be, imposed in these contexts. I have had race equality activists and professionals flatly deny that there is an issue here to discuss, and have been ostracised for persisting with my argument and have been called, including in print, a trouble-maker and an anti-black racist.[5] Moreover, I know many Asians, blacks and whites who have said they have been intimidated from questioning the appropriateness of the concept of 'black'.

The charge of coercion is difficult to substantiate (hence my resort to anecdotal evidence), but one way in which it could be done is to demonstrate that the majority of Asians did not embrace the concept that the majority of the professionals and activists were promoting; if this could be shown it could suggest not only that Asians did not support the professionals, etc., but that the Asians' failure to register their dissent in any major way was because they felt intimidated. When I first elaborated my critique, I naturally contended that the majority of Asians did not accept 'black' as a public identity. Yet I had to recognise that there was very little evidence to support my view (though I noted that those who could have gathered the evidence, namely, race relations researchers and those who fund them, had a vested interest in not doing so), though someone of the authority of Professor Bhikhu Parekh, Deputy Chairman of the Commission for Racial Equality (1985–90) had explicitly stated that 'the term black is rejected by the bulk of the Asians'

(Parekh 1987: xii). No one had thought the issue worthy of an opinion survey, in the absence of which Parekh has estimated that 'about 70 per cent resent it, 10 per cent identify themselves as black, and the rest do so with qualifications' (Roy 1988). This has so far proved to be an extremely insightful estimation. For when the BBC Asian television programme *Network East*, the audience of which is weighted towards the young, carried in March 1989 an item on this issue, even though several speakers accused Asians who objected to be called 'black' of being racist, stupid and divisive, this did not prevent nearly two-thirds of the over 3,000 who took part in the subsequent telephone poll rejecting the term 'black' for Asians.[6] A battery of questions on identity are included in the PSI-SCPR Fourth National Survey of Ethnic Minorities which will be the first time that the issue of 'black' and Asians will have been surveyed nationally. Till these findings are published in 1995 nothing superior to the BBC poll is available.

New identities

These then, I suggest, are some of the reasons why the hegemony of 'black' over other ethnic/racial identities was doomed. If one single remark combines and epitomises these criticisms it is Yasmin Alibhai's contention that when most Asians hear the word 'black', they are unlikely to think of themselves, so many fail to apply for jobs where advertisements specifically welcome black people (*Woman's Hour*, BBC Radio 4, 17 November 1988). It is, therefore, not surprising that in 1988 some Asians decided that an anti-racism which was so out of touch with or defiant of basic Asian community concerns had to be challenged. The year began with the National Association of Asian Probation Staff boycotting the Home Office staff ethnic monitoring exercise because it classified Asians as a sub-division of Black, and was followed by an on-going debate in the minority press, especially in *New Life, Asian Herald* and the Afro-Caribbean *Voice*, with occasional overspills into the national media (Modood 1988b; Roy 1988; Uppal 1988; Kogbara 1988; *Heart of the Matter*, BBC TV, 10 July 1988) and academic journals (Modood 1988a).

This critique bore fruit when in December of that year the Commission of Racial Equality (CRE) decided to cease to recommend that people of Asian origin be classified as Black and in the following month the Office of Population Censuses and Surveys (OPCS) announced that they were proceeding to the next stage in the ethnic question trials for the 1991 Census with the same categories as the CRE. It is perhaps an open question as to the significance of these administrative decisions: were they just petty terminological changes or did they mark an important milestone in the philosophy of race relations? The CRE, which was disinclined to read too much into them, was told by a *New Statesman and Society* editorial that it 'should be publicising its decision with confidence instead of weakly whispering out an important decision, almost hoping nobody will notice' (23 December 1988). Phillip Nanton has argued that 'these attempts to capture an acceptable ethnic categorisation suggest that a fundamental change has taken place in the definition of ethnicity, for ethnic categories can no longer be regarded as "given" but are open to interest group pressure and negotiation' (1989: 556). I would go further.

Race equality thinking consists of a number of different ideological strands. I have in mind ideological outlooks such as universalism which emphasises uniformity of treatment; or social utilitarianism which focuses on remedial state action to overcome racial disadvantage; or the anti-racism which is a dimension of class struggle; or the ethnic pluralism which emphasises the diversity of values, the cultural dimension of oppression and the non-political ways in which ethnic groups contribute to social outcomes including racial equality. Each of these is an important ingredient of egalitarian theory and practice, but different times and situations will see a different balance between them. With the possible exception of multi-cultural education, the balance in the 1980s was in favour of universalism and social utilitarianism wrapped in a rhetoric of anti-racism, and one of the expressions of this mix was the acceptance of the political 'black' into the mainstream. In taking the decision that utilitarian and anti-racist perspectives are not decisive on the question of ethnic monitoring, for monitoring classifications should harmonise with people's self-perceptions, the CRE and OPCS has limited these perspectives in favour of the principles of ethnic pluralism and respect for ethnic identities. It may be that this is an intimation of a new balance amongst the competing and complementary strands of our concept of racial equality. It may be that the decision to cease to officially impose the term 'black' upon people of South Asian origin will in retrospect be seen as marking the limit of the influence of militant anti-racism and the opening towards a new balance in the concept of racial equality.

One response of theorists such as Hall and Ali to the end-of-the-hegemony-of-'black' has been to shift attention from organised politics and social structures to cultural identities and their manufacture and communication, from 'a struggle over the relations of representation to a politics of representation itself' (Hall 1992: 253). With this goes a celebration of 'new ethnicities' and cultural hybridity, and a critique of 'ethnic absolutism' – the idea that ethnic identities are simply 'given', are static and ahistorical and do not (or should not) change under new circumstances or by sharing social space with other heritages and influences. The emphasis on the *historical* nature of ethnicity (as opposed to conformity to an atemporal essence or an imagined golden age), on hybridity without loss of integrity or self-respect, on cultural openness and multi-textured identities, rather than on the coercive simplicities of 'black' absolutism, is to be welcomed, and may allow Asians to develop a more authentic repertoire of self-images than 'black' allowed. Yet this new turn is not without its dangers. If 'new' simply comes to describe the *avant-garde*, then it is clear that most British Asians will once again suffer marginalisation. A rejection of theories of primordial ethnic absolutism should not prevent us from accurately describing where most Asians are, regardless of whether it seems sufficiently 'new' or progressive. We must not pit 'new' and 'old' ethnicities against each other: we must avoid the elitism of cultural vanguardism that devalues and despises where the ordinary majority of any group or social formation is at – an elitism so thoughtlessly exemplified in Salman Rushdie's *The Satanic Verses*, to the loss of us all, new and old. And yet in the loss of hegemony there may be wisdom. For in place of a 'two-worlds' Britain, Rushdie now urges that we must stop thinking in binary, oppositional terms for 'the them-and-us rhetoric of victimisation, no matter how legitimate it may seem, creates as many cultural problems as it addresses' (Rushdie 1993).

Notes

*   This article is based on a paper given at the conference on 'The Mobilisation of Ethnic Minorities and Ethnic Social Movements in Europe', University of Warwick, 3–5 April 1992.

1   The British Sociological Association's 'Anti-Racist Language: Guidance for Good Practice', states that 'some Asians in Britain object to the use of the word "black" being applied to them', but most British sociologists of race feel that an insufficient reason to seek a more appropriate terminology.

2   Interestingly, the two British academics who have been stimulated to discuss the issue at any length have decided to abandon the term 'black'. One favours the less convenient but more descriptive, 'people who are not white' (Mason 1990), and the other has adopted 'Asian, black and other minority ethnic' (Cole 1993). Goulbourne's book (1991) is perhaps the first on British race relations to systematically replace 'black' with 'non-white'.

3   This formulation is used by, for example, the London Boroughs of Haringey and Hackney. In private correspondence they have informed me that 'ethnic minorities' in the formula refers to Cypriots and Turks. Other uses of the formula mean the phrase to include Asians.

4   Not that the position of non-whites in higher education is one of uniform under-representation, even at Oxbridge (Modood 1993).

5   Ali herself makes this charge against me (Ali 1991: 207); indeed, it was also made at the conference where this paper was given. It might therefore be appropriate for me to say that while I am aware of the mutual antipathies between Asians and Afro-Caribbeans (as described, e.g., in James 1986, and Bains 1988) I have always opposed them, treating them as no less a form of racial prejudice than that of whites for non-whites, and have endeavoured to develop my argument without conceding

anything to them. For anyone interested in seeing how textual analysis can degenerate into misattribution, criticism by innuendo and character assassination, see Goulbourne 1993: 186–189.

6　A researcher with extensive knowledge of Asians, especially youth, in Southall was greatly surprised that as many as a third of all callers said 'Yes' to 'Black' and wonders whether all of those callers were Asians (Baumann, MS 1994).

References

Ali, Y. 1991. 'Echoes of Empire: Towards A Politics of Representation', in J. Cromer and S. Harvey (eds), *Enterprise and Heritage: Cross Currents of National Culture.* London: Routledge.

Amin, K. and Richardson, R. 1992. *Politics for All: Equality, Culture and The General Election 1992.* London: The Runnymede Trust.

Anthias, F. and Yuval-Davis, N. 1992. *Racialised Boundaries.* London: Routledge.

Back, L. 1993. 'Race, Identity and Nation within an Adolescent Community in South London'. *New Community* 19:217–233.

Bains, H. S. 1988. 'Southhall Youth: An Old-Fashioned Story' in P. Cohen and H. S. Bains (eds) *Multi-Racist Britain.* London: Macmillan.

Banton, M. 1987. 'The Battle of the Name'. *New Community* 14:170–175.

Baumann, G. (MS 1994). *The Politics of Identity: Two Discourses of 'Culture' and 'Community' in a Suburb of London*, Monograph in Preparation.

Bonnett, A. 1990. 'Urban Struggle in Language: The Word "Black" ', unpublished, available from author at Department of Geography, University of Newcastle-Upon-Tyne.

Bonnett, A. 1993. *Radicalism, Anti-Racism and Representation.* London: Routledge.

Boulton, M. L. and Smith, P. 1992. 'Ethnic Preferences and Perceptions Among Asian and White British Middle School Children'. *Social Development* 1:55–56.

Brown, C. 1984. *Black and White Britain.* Third PSI survey. London: Policy Studies Institute.

Brown, C. and Gay, P. 1985. *Racial Discrimination: 17 Years After the Act.* London: Policy Studies Institute.

Centre for Research into Ethnic Relations. 1990. *Research Programme 1989–1993.* Occasional Paper in Ethnic Relations, no. 6.

Cohen, P. 1988. 'The Perversions of Inheritance: Studies in the Making of Multi-Racist Britain', in P. Cohen and H. S. Bains (eds) *Multi-Racist Britain.* London: Macmillan.

Cole, M. 1993. 'Black and Ethnic Minority' or 'Asian, Black and Other Minority Ethnic: A Further Note on Nomenclature', *Sociology* 27:671–673.

Commission for Racial Equality. 1988. 'Ethnic Classification System Recommended by CRE'. Press Statement, 7 December.

Commission for Racial Equality. 1990. *Sorry, It's Gone: Testing For Racial Discrimination in the Private Rented Housing Sector.* London.

Connolly, C. 1990. 'Washing Our Linen: One Year of Women against Fundamentalism'. *Women Against Fundamentalism* 1:5–8.

Cross, M. 1990. 'Editorial'. *New Community* 17:307–311.

Dhondy, F. 1987. 'Speaking in Whose Name?'. *New Statesman*, 24 April.

Donald, J. and Rattansi, A. (eds) 1992. *'Race', Culture and Difference*. London: Sage.

Drury, B. 1990. 'Blackness: A Situational Identity', paper given at New Issues in Black Politics conference. University of Warwick, 14–16 May.

Dummett, A. 1992. 'Problems of Translation'. *The Runnymede Bulletin*, February, 8.

Foyster *et al.* 1990. 'I Landed Twice as many Jobs as my Two Friends – But Then *They* Are Black'. *Today*, 11 September.

Gay, P. and Young, K. 1988. *Community Relations Councils: Roles and Objectives*. London: Commission for Racial Equality.

Gilroy, P. 1987. *There Ain't no Black in the Union Jack*. London: Routledge.

Gilroy, P. 1993. *The Black Atlantic: Modernity and Double Consciousness*. London: Verso.

Goulbourne, H. 1991. *Ethnicity and Nationalism in Post-Imperial Britain*. Cambridge: Cambridge University Press.

Goulbourne, H. 1993. 'Aspects of Nationalism and Black Identities in Post-Imperial Britain' in M. Cross and M. Keith (eds) *Racism, The City and The State*. London: Macmillan.

Hall, S. 1992. 'New Ethnicities' in Donald and Rattansi (eds), *op. cit.* 252–259.

Hazareesingh, S. 1986. 'Racism and Cultural Identity: An Indian Perspective'. *Dragon's Teeth* 24:4–10.

James, W. 1986. 'A Long Way from Home: On Black Identity in Britain'. *Immigrants and Minorities* 5:258–284.

Jones, T. 1993. *Britain's Ethnic Minorities*. London: Policy Studies Institute.

Jowell, R. *et al.* 1986. *British Social Attitudes: The 1986 Report*. Social and Community Planning Research. London: Gower.

Kogbara, D. 1988. 'When is a Black not a Black?'. *The Independent*, 30 November.

Kramer, J. 1991. 'Letter from Europe'. *New Yorker*, 14 January, 60–75.

Labour Party. 1985. *Positive Discrimination: Black People and the Labour Party*, London.

Martin, B. L. 1991. 'From Negro to Black to African American: The Power of Names and Naming'. *Political Science Quarterly* 106:83–107.

Mason, D. 1990. 'A Rose by any other Name . . .? Categorisation, Identity and Social Science'. *New Community* 17, 1:123–133.

McIlroy, J. 1989. 'The Politics of Racism' in B. Jones (ed.) *Political Issues in Britain Today*. Manchester: Manchester University Press.

Miles, R. 1991. 'Le Jeunes d'Origine Immigrée en Grande-Bretagne'. *Les Temps Modernes* 540–541:133–165.

Modood, T. 1988a. ' "Black", Racial Equality and Asian Identity'. *New Community* 14:397–404.

Modood, T. 1988b. 'Who is Defining Who?'. *New Society*, 4 March, 4–5.

Modood, T. 1989. 'Religious Anger and Minority Rights'. *Political Quarterly* 60:280–284.

Modood, T. 1990a. 'Catching Up with Jesse Jackson: Being Oppressed and Being Somebody'. *New Community* 17, 1:87–98.

Modood, T. 1990b. 'British Asian Muslims and the Rushdie Affair'. *Political Quarterly* 61, 2:143–60.

Modood, T. 1992. *Not Easy Being British: Colour, Culture and Citizenship*. London: Runnymede Trust and Trentham Books.

Modood, T. 1993. 'The Number of Ethnic Minorities in British Higher Education'. *Oxford Review of Education* 19, 2:167–182.

Modood, T. 1994. 'Establishment, Multiculturalism and British Citizenship'. *Political Quarterly* 65:53–73.

Mortimer, J. 1992. 'A World Apart', An Interview with Salman Rushdie. *The Sunday Times*, 16 February.

Mullings, B. 1992. 'Investing in Public Housing and Racial Discrimination: Implications in the 1990s. *New Community* 18:415–425.

Nanton, P. 1989. 'The New Orthodoxy: Racial Categories and Equal Opportunity Policy'. *New Community* 15:549–564.

Parekh, B. 1987. 'Preface' in J. W. Shaw *et al.* (eds) *Strategies for Improving Race Relations*. Manchester: Manchester University Press.

Rex, J. 1991. *Ethnic Identity and Ethnic Mobilisation in Britain*. Monograph in Ethnic Relations No. 5. Centre for Research in Ethnic Relations, University of Warwick.

Roy, A. 1988. 'Asians Protest, we are not Black'. *The Sunday Times*, 26 June.

Rushdie, S. 1982. 'The New Empire Within Britain'. *New Society*, 9 December.

Rushdie, S. 1989. 'Choice Between Light and Dark'. *The Observer*, 22 January 1989.

Rushdie, S. 1993. 'Muslim World Needs Progressive Voices, Not A Culture Frozen in Time'. *The Independent*, 7 July, 21.

Saggar, S. 1992. *Race and Politics in Britain*. London: Harvester Wheatsheaf.

Sarre, P. 1989. 'Race and the Class Structure' in C. Hamnett *et al.* (eds) *The Changing Social Structure*. London: Sage.

Sivanandan, A. 1985. 'RAT and the Degradation of the Black Struggle'. *Race and Class*, XXVI(4).

Smith, S. J. 1993. 'Residential Segregation and the Politics of Racialisation' in M. Cross and M. Keith (eds) *Racism, The City and The State*. London: Routledge, 1993.

Tizard, B. and Pheonix, A. 1993. *Black, White or Mixed Race?* London: Routledge.

Uppal, I. S. 1988. ' "Black": The Word Making Asians Angry'. *Daily Mail*, 28 June.

Waldinger, R., Aldrich, H. and Ward, R. 1990. *Ethnic Entrepreneurs*. London: Sage.

Women Against Fundamentalism 1990. 'Founding Statement'. *Women Against Fundamentalism* 1:1.

Young, K. 1992. 'Class, Race and Opportunity' in R. Jowell *et al.*, *British Social Attitudes*, the 9th Report. Aldershot: SCPR.

Yuval-Davis, N. 1992. 'Fundamentalism, Multiculturalism and Women in Britain' in Donald and Rattansi *op. cit.*, 278–291.

Biographical note: **DR TARIQ MODOOD** was a lecturer in political theory before entering racial equality policy work, including at the Commission for Racial Equality. Subsequently he has been a research fellow at Nuffield College, Oxford and University of Manchester, and is now a Senior Fellow at Policy Studies Institute. His publications include *Not Easy Being British: Colour, Culture and Citizenship* (Runnymede Trust, 1992), *Racial Equality* (Institute of Public Policy Research, 1994) and (co-author) *Changing Ethnic Identities* (PSI, 1994).

14

Racism, ethnicity and criminology
Developing minority perspectives

by Coretta Phillips and Benjamin Bowling*

In empirical and theoretical criminology references to racism and ethnicity are commonplace, although much discussion has centred on the narrowly defined 'race and crime' debate. In an attempt to move beyond this debate, which is focused on whether certain ethnic minorities are over-represented in the prison population because of elevated rates of offending or because of discriminatory treatment in the criminal justice system, this paper proposes the formulation of minority perspectives in criminology. These would be concerned with empirical, theoretical, practical and policy issues and address matters of representation, knowledge production, the historical contextualization of minority experiences in theory development, and the ethical duties of criminologists working within a minority perspective.

Stating the case for minority perspectives

References to 'race' and ethnicity are commonplace in empirical criminology. As key socio-demographic variables empirical criminologists routinely use them to describe victims of crime and offenders, and less commonly, criminal justice practitioners. At the theoretical level, the notion of 'race' or ethnicity has infused many schools of criminological thought throughout the history of the discipline. Much of the focus of this empirical and theoretical attention has centred on official statistics which reveal an overrepresentation of certain minorities among those arrested and imprisoned for some criminal offences. On the other hand, self-report studies of offending and drug use have challenged the validity of these empirical 'facts', as have studies which

* Coretta Phillips, London School of Economics and Political Science; Benjamin Bowling, King's College, London. The authors would like to thank David Downes, Bonny Mhlanga, Karim Murji, Ken Pease, Katheryn Russell and Andy Zurawan for their helpful comments on an earlier draft of this paper.

have documented discrimination in criminal justice processing (see Bowling and Phillips 2002). Nevertheless, Braithwaite (1989: 44) has contended that a credible criminological theory ought to be able to explain, among other things, elevated rates of offending (according to official statistics) among oppressed racial minorities, since this is one of several 'strong' and 'consistently supported associations in empirical criminology'.

A primary objective in formulating minority perspectives in criminology is to move beyond the so-called 'race and crime' debate that has preoccupied us. It is the need to refine this debate, extend its parameters, and to raise concerns about the nature of the discipline itself which has spurred us to propose a different approach. Taking our cue from Braithwaite (1989) it is clear that there are many other 'consistently supported observations' in this sub-field, which hitherto have been neglected by mainstream criminology. The findings that black people have been disproportionately the victims of excessive physical force by police, prison and immigration officers and to die in custody, that almost all judges are white even though a significant minority of those who appear before them are not, that Asian people have lower rates of imprisonment than white and black people, that there are few senior minority criminologists in the UK, are but a selection of such observations (Bowling and Phillips 2002). This remark should not be seen, however, as a rallying call for the development of an over-arching theory which can explain all of these phenomena, although there are likely to be common explanatory themes; the point is simply that criminological theory should not solely be dominated by the polemical and now sterile debate centred on elevated rates of offending versus discriminatory criminal justice processing.

A more multidimensional approach to understanding minorities' experience of victimization, offending, criminal justice processing and working within the criminal justice field is necessary. A starting point is the need to *reconcile* criminological data with the 'lived experiences' and subjectivities of minorities. This is crystallized by Shallice and Gordon (1990: 31) when they refer to the disjuncture between empirical research findings on sentencing practices which show no 'race effect' and 'the large numbers of people who readily assert the opposite, largely (though not unimportantly) on the basis of anecdotal, personal and collective experience'. Similarly striking were the differences in perspective expressed during the evidence taken in the inquiry into the murder of Stephen Lawrence. On the one hand, representatives from minority communities—churches, community relations councils, local monitoring groups and activists—referred to their experiences of racist violence, the weakness of the police response to this victimization, and oppressive policing. On the other hand, senior police officers made reference to how seriously they viewed racist violence, describing initiatives in place to respond to this victimization, and evidence showing either increased public confidence in the police (evidenced by increases in reported incidents) or a decrease in the extent of the problem (evidenced by decreases in reported incidents) (Macpherson 1999).

Reconciling these conflicting perspectives can be partially achieved through *both* improvements in the collection, analysis, interpretation and dissemination of such criminological data *and* by making central to our understanding the knowledges provided by minority communities themselves. This, however, does not go far enough. There must also be a critical deconstruction of the process of knowledge production *about* minorities, which in its current state means squaring up to the discipline of criminology itself.[1] These can be addressed through the formulation of minority perspectives in criminology which operate at the level of empirical data collection, theoretical development, practice and policy formulation.

In explicating a distinctive minority perspective for British criminology, our framework builds on that proposed by Katheryn Russell (1992) in developing a 'black criminology' in the United States. The twin crises of an underdeveloped theoretical criminology around race and the underrepresentation of minorities in the discipline referred to by Russell are echoed in the British experience. A second major influence for this paper has been the development of feminist perspectives in criminology. Can the canon of criminological theories be adequately applied to minorities' experiences assuming 'white' is the norm or standard against which minorities are to be judged? Is there evidence of institutional racism in the criminal justice system and the discipline? What is the role of ethnicity ('whiteness', 'blackness', 'Asianess', or some 'otherness') in explaining offending, victimization and criminal justice practices? These are all questions previously raised by feminist criminologists in conceptualizing women's experiences in mainstream criminology (Gelsthorpe and Morris 1990; Morris and Gelsthorpe 1991). The time is ripe for these questions to be explored in relation to 'race' and ethnicity.

Intellectual caution: the criminological taboo, essentialism and the thorny issue of representation

Before discussing some of the directions for minority perspectives in criminology, a few words of caution and clarification are necessary. Russell's (1992: 669) discussion of the twin crises facing US criminology is prefaced with a discussion of the 'long-standing criminological taboo against discussing any relationship between race and crime' (Russell 1992: 669). It can be traced back to genetic theorizing and the Moynihan Report of 1965 which was seen as pathologizing female-headed black families and blaming them for high

---

[1] In time, other sources of knowledge or 'truths' about minority experience will need to be scrutinized; those with currency at present are those primarily within administrative and academic criminology and cultural studies.

levels of crime and delinquency. While acknowledging the reluctance of minorities to engage with these issues because of the negative history of race and crime research and the inadequacy of minority rights in the United States, Russell laments the neglect of this important area.

We share these concerns, not least because of the overwhelming evidence of criminalization among certain minority groups in Britain (see Bowling and Phillips 2002). Yet it is essential for criminologists to examine critically official data on offending (such as arrest and imprisonment rates) since these are commonly taken, regardless of their well-documented flaws, as 'facts' about 'ethnic' or 'black crime'. While we agree that such data relating to offending within minority communities are of questionable validity and are probably worthless in isolation, ignoring them needs to be balanced against the concerns that serious crimes have generated within minority communities themselves (see for example *The Voice*, 22 May 2000: 1–3). Whilst there appears to be no taboo concerning the relationship between ethnicity and crime among the lay criminologies articulated by the media, criminological analyses in the UK have, like their US counterparts, avoided detailed explorations of the inter-relationships between ethnicity, racism, crime and other aspects of social and economic life. Nevertheless, we are sensitive to the dilemma of engaging with debates about minority victimization and offending and contributing to the creation of false pathologies which might then serve to naturalize and reify images of certain minorities as inherently criminal, the risk of 'collusion and treachery-by-default' referred to by Alexander (2000: 227).

A central component of a minority perspective in criminology is to embrace difference by moving beyond crude and essentialist categorizations of racial and ethnic minorities. The 'new ethnicities' literature, for example, has stressed the need to move beyond a black-white dualism in conceptualizing difference and understanding cultural hybridity in the post-colonial period. In the 1990s both hegemonic 'black' and 'Asian' identities have been politically contested because of diverse historical, cultural, political, religious and socio-economic experiences among minorities in Britain. As Stuart Hall (1988: 258) argues, individuals 'speak from a particular place, out of a particular history, out of a particular experience, a particular culture', but they should not be contained by that position. We think this should be taken into account in any research endeavour; examining 'unities within diversity' is our preferred approach.[2] However, Sharma (1996) warns against a celebration of

---

[2] Of course, some research necessarily requires aggregation. Large-scale surveys such as the British Crime Survey, for example, have attempted to disentangle the victimization experiences of people of Indian origin from those of Pakistani and Bangladeshi origin, despite the challenge of small sub-sample sizes (see for example, Kershaw et al. 2000). Less successful has been the disaggregation of the 'black' ethnic group which encompasses those whose ethnic origin is from the Caribbean or Africa, and a significant group categorized as Black Other who, on at least one criterion, imprisonment, appear to have quite distinctive experiences (see Home Office 2000).

difference and marginality which fails to take account of racism, violence, the dominant structures of power and global and national socio-economic inequalities, which, as Spivak (1993) notes, structures the forms in which the 'voices' of minorities can be heard. Neither should this approach obscure the importance of other subjectivities such as gender, class, ethnicity, sexuality and religion (see also Smart 1990; Rice 1990; Daly and Stephens 1995).

This, in part, explains why we advocate the terminology of a 'minority' perspective. We have rejected the term 'black criminology' used by Russell in the United States and Rice (1990)[3] in the British context, because of its contested validity as a unifying identity for Britain's racial and ethnic minorities (see Modood 1988, 1997). We have also rejected the use of the British equivalent of 'African-American perspectives' (for example African-Caribbean) as used by Young and Sulton (1996), in part because it represents an exclusive focus on one minority group. Instead we adopt Takagi's (1981) and Mann's (1993) usage of 'minority', since this recognizes and emphasizes the marginal and excluded status of both visible and other racial and ethnic minorities. Although not the focus of this paper, the term also allows a consideration of other minority groups' experiences as gay, lesbian, bi-sexual, transsexual, or transgendered people.

This leads us to consider representation in minority criminological perspectives. For Russell (1992) a black criminology should, at least initially, be the preserve of black criminologists. The rationale for this is that black criminologists, unlike their 'non-black' counterparts, have a familiarity and understanding of black community experience which will bring legitimacy to the sub-field (see also Young and Sulton 1996 for a more forceful statement on this; and Ferdinand 1994). In time when it has become established, Russell asserts that a black criminology will need white academics/researchers to maintain its momentum.[4] Their role will also be essential in undertaking certain types of research with white people, such as perpetrators of racist harassment and violence.

Recognizing the pioneering role of black criminologists in formulating a black criminology may also go some way to reversing the under-representation of blacks in the discipline to which Russell also makes reference. It should also help to address any resentment that minorities may feel about white academics being the only experts on issues relating to 'race' and ethnicity (see Sharma et al. 1996; Parham 1993; Mio and Iwamasa 1993; Stanfield 1993 in relation to cultural studies and anthropology, psychology

---

[3] Rice (1990) provides a critique of 'black criminology' in Britain, which is identified as the body of work on criminality and race undertaken by black and white criminologists/sociologists, but which has exclusively focused on the causes of crime among black *men*, or their treatment within the criminal justice system, and has not discussed the experiences of black women.

[4] Similarly, Parham (1993), for example, has acknowledged the need for white psychologists to advocate a culturally diverse perspective, for if it is just minority psychologists doing so, they can easily be dismissed or marginalized by white psychologists.

and sociology). This should seem no more controversial than the development of feminist perspectives in criminology which in the early stages fell to female scholars, in part to redress the imbalance of men being the primary producers of knowledge. Indeed, Gelsthorpe and Morris's (1988: 105) position, for example, was that 'women should be given the time and space to develop feminist perspectives in their own way, using their own language and not the categories and concepts provided for them by men and in traditional methodologies'.

The argument that black criminologists are best placed to understand and explain 'black life', if accepted, has implications for both empirical and theoretical criminology. There is, of course, a danger that such thinking falls into the essentialist trap which assumes a definitive, intrinsic, core 'black experience' which assumes universal oppression, and is something that only minorities can speak about. Nonetheless, we tend to agree with Jhappan (1996: 30) when she says 'our material situations, life opportunities, social positionality, and dominant discourses do profoundly mould our experiences and understanding of the world and our places in it', and it is this which provides some measure of authenticity to our articulation of minority experiences. It is here that the concepts of strategic essentialism (Spivak) or contextual essentialism (Jhappan) may be helpful, in that they allow the forging of a political resistance to racist oppression in criminology and criminal justice, whilst acknowledging the contingent and shifting nature of racial and ethnic identities.

However, put simply, our position is that all criminologists, regardless of their ethnic identity, can contribute to minority perspectives in British criminology; our notion of minority positions is an inclusive one. This avoids excluding white academics and researchers because they cannot 'speak for' minorities—a form of 'race credentialism' according to Jhappan (1996), and also promotes a responsibility to confront social positioning in research, policy and practice. Rather the key requirement is a conscious stance and commitment to a number of guiding principles which, in the beginning, bearing in mind positionality, may be more easily conceptualized and operationalized by minority academics and researchers. The guiding principles for a minority perspective are subsumed under approaches which operate at the empirical and theoretical level, and at the level of practice and policy, and it is to these that we now turn.

Empirical approaches

The importance of considering empirical issues relating to 'race' and ethnicity is attested to by a huge literature in this area, particularly in the disciplines of anthropology, sociology, and psychology, and there is a focus in much feminist scholarship too. Despite the centrality of 'race' and ethnicity to its domain, such concerns have received relatively little attention in empirical criminology. It is therefore incumbent on empirical criminologists adopting a minority perspective to borrow from this body of knowledge, so that criminological research does not misrepresent the lived experiences of minorities. Research in this field must embrace a number of principles which are commonly applied in research variously referred to as 'anti-discriminatory', 'anti-racist', or just plain 'good' (Troyna 1995; Gelsthorpe 1990; Hammersley 1992).

First and foremost is a recognition that the research process is structured by power relations between researcher and research participants. This can have the effect of introducing bias in knowledge production from the front end of developing research questions to ways of answering them, particularly where these processes are informed by prejudices about the behaviour under study. Feminist standpoint epistemologies have been developed in response to this problem, taking as their starting point, that knowledge comes from experience. By adopting the standpoint of research participants, feminists have sought to produce a 'truer' version of 'reality' by engaging in reflexive struggle intellectually and politically to understand distinctive social experiences (Harding 1987). A reflexive position should critically analyse the complex social locations, identities, and subjectivities of the researcher and those participating in the research, to see how they bear on the research itself (Cain 1990; Reid and Kelly 1994; Stanfield 1993), although as Maynard (2002) maintains, this is only ever likely to be partially achieved in practice. This provides a challenge to traditional ethnography adopted by the Chicago School which relied on the empathy of *verstehen*. According to Valier (2003), this empathetic approach can have the effect of silencing minorities by masking differences between them and researchers, and not recognizing the 'foreign within oneself'. Further along this continuum has been the post-modern rejection of a search for ultimate truths, away from authenticist accounts of experience (particularly through ethnography) to producing subjective knowledges which are temporally and spatially located but shifting and mediated through researcher interpretation (see for example Alexander 2000).

These approaches attempt to transcend the extremes of the Insider and Outsider doctrines described by Merton (1972). In this context the former posits that minorities have monopolistic and privileged access to empathic knowledge about the socially shared realities of minority experiences because of their continued socialization. For Rhodes (1994), this approach cannot accommodate complex and multifaceted realities which are shifting and likely to vary according to context and topics being discussed in the research situation. In contrast, the Outsider position assumes that knowledge is only accessible to non-members of minority groups who are untainted by prejudice and therefore more objective. As Johnston's (1974) scathing critique of Merton notes, however, this assumes that it is possible to arrive at an absolute truth from objective scientific inquiry, a claim which is roundly rejected in recent discussions of how knowledge about social life is produced. However, rather than fully rehearsing the detail of this epistemological blind-alley, we begin with Merton's (1972: 36) appeal to 'consider the[ir] distinctive and interactive roles in the process of truth seeking', but extend this proposal to seeking truths or 'multiple knowledges', drawing on the work of white and minority feminist scholars (see Harding 1987; Hill Collins 1998).

Building on Merton's call for collaborative work, joining together exponents of the Insider and Outsider doctrines offers the most promising path for minority perspectives, although this may not be straightforward in itself (for examples see Daly and Stephens 1995; Mio and Iwamasa 1993). It will be predicated on inclusionary practices which avoid exploitation in the research process, although whether this can be achieved is open to question (see for example Alexander 2000; Reay 1996; Dyck, Lynam and Anderson 1995). This should not prevent us trying, however, not least because in criminology the status of the researcher and the research participants will be particularly significant with the vast majority of principal investigators on funded research projects being white academics or consultants. An inclusive approach can be partially engendered by recognizing that those participating in research should be encouraged to assist in the production of knowledge about their experience by contributing to the design of the research. This may mean minorities themselves, or informed practitioners or activists working with minorities at the grassroots level. Often such individuals will be the first point of contact in gaining access to a group, particularly for qualitative work. Monitoring groups, law centres, minority professional or support organizations, community groups, religious organizations, are all examples of agencies who could be encouraged to assist with the design of research with minorities. Community consultation could include determining the location of the research, how to approach minorities directly, the framing of research questions, how to use culturally appropriate measures, decisions about the research methods to be used, and the languages in which the research might need to be conducted (see Takagi 1981; Marín and Marín 1991; also Hughes and DuMont 1993 on the use of focus groups).[5]

It is desirable for minorities also to play a part in the collection of data. Building on Russell's (1992) point, it is likely that 'ethnically matched' data collectors will enhance the rapport and trust between researcher and participant, and thus increase the willingness to disclose sensitive information in a qualitative research setting (see for example Bhopal 2001). Recounting incidents of racist harassment or discrimination to white researchers, where minorities may fear being accused or perceived to have 'a chip on their shoulder' is one example where ethnically matched data collectors may enhance the documentation of minority experiences (see FitzGerald 1993:

---

[5] The organization's own documentary material about minorities' experience may indeed contribute to the formulation of research questions and understanding.

49). Nonetheless, the multi-ethnic and hybrid nature of 'minority identities' in Britain, alongside the complexities of the multiple identities of researchers and research participants may preclude total ethnic matching and 'simplistic symmetry' (Mirza 1998: 90). However, researching 'an-other' minority community may still enhance the research process where shared experiences of racism and minority status exist and are perceived between the researcher and research participant. Egharevba (2001), a researcher of African descent, for example, claimed 'insider status' in her study of South Asian women, based on their common placing in England, and despite differences of ethnicity, religion, geography, culture, language, marital status and life experiences. Rhodes (1994), on the other hand, questions assertions that 'race' will dominate other differences between researcher and participant and alerts us to the potential exploitation of minorities, where they are required only for data collection duties and not involved in the entire research process (see also Phoenix 1998). At a minimum, identification with research participants ethnically, culturally and socially, is a necessary first step to ensuring that the resultant data is experientially grounded, whether qualitative or quantitative.

The counter-argument would be that an Outsider researcher could act as a detached stranger in asking questions about behaviour which an ethnically matched researcher may take for granted and then not interpret as important to the study (Simmel 1921). Similarly, Rhodes's (1994) account suggests that in certain contexts, 'cross-racial' interviewing may stimulate rather than block communication in the research encounter. It can even be argued that an Insider position may be exploitative as Reay (1996: 65) notes when referring to 'the thin dividing line between identification and exploitation' and the 'dangers of proximity' which emerged in her research with similarly socially located women. Nonetheless, the legitimacy of the research will probably be enhanced by using 'ethnically matched' field staff or those from within the studied community. It is becoming increasingly common, for example, for ethnographic research on drugs and gangs in the United States to include former drug users, gang members, 'homeboys' and 'homegirls' alongside academic researchers (Joe 1993) or even 'well-connected' undergraduate students (Mieczkowski 1988). Such individuals must identify ethnically, culturally and socially with the research participants and be 'street aware' if the research requires it (see for example Dunlap et al. 1990).

Collaboration should not end when data collection is complete. The interpretation and construction of minority experiential accounts may be culturally different and even inaccessible to white researchers. For as Landrine, Klonoff and Brown-Collins (1992: 149) observe 'the label/meaning we attribute to behavior is a projection of what the behavior would mean if we engaged in it, irrespective of whether "we" are black, white, Latino or Asian'. Similarly, as Gelshorpe (1990: 102) observes in a criminal justice context, 'what appears racist or sexist to me (as a white, middle-class academic) might be completely wide of the mark when compared with the experiences of defendants'. For this reason, it is imperative that research participants and similarly located individuals can contribute to the data analysis and interpretation stages of the research process (see Myrdal 1944 for an example). Even then what is produced as knowledge is still 'simply one version of events', as Alexander (2000: 47) herself acknowledges in her ethnographic account of the experiences of Asian young people and their 'gang'. She describes her position as still one of marginality in some senses, even after nearly five years of study, and in spite of her own Asian origins.

A minority perspective also requires that social research does not exploit those who participate in research. Part of conducting non-exploitative research is to ensure that the research encounter minimizes harm by supporting research participants. This could involve providing contact details for appropriate support or advice organizations, or even providing payment for participation to acknowledge the likely disproportionate impact of research participation on minorities' time. Ethical practice by project managers also requires the protection and support of field staff. Indeed, the British Society of Criminology's Code of Ethics emphasizes the need for research managers to protect the physical and emotional well being of research staff in research environments. 'Insider' researchers may face personal doubts and ethnical dilemmas, for example, in part from being in the unusual role of having always to be accountable to the community being studied (see Zavella 1993; Tuhiwai Smith 1999; Mirza 1998; Wright 1998). Moreover, where minority researchers do face prejudice and racist behaviour in the field, either observed, discussed, or directed at the researcher, research managers should be prepared to assist with debriefing sessions and by monitoring fieldwork experiences (Phillips and Brown 1997). Assuming that these types of experience are only important for the research purpose: 'just write it down, it'll make good fieldnotes' is an inadequate response.

Exploitative practices can be far-reaching. Gordon (1973) has been heavily critical of the way in which academics have conducted numerous studies in poor and black communities in the United States, providing themselves with publications, grants, consultancies, and other prestigious appointments, without improving the life circumstances of those studied; as Spivak (1993: 296) opines, the issue is really about 'getting your backside in gear and working for your constituency'. This raises important questions about the impact of social research on political and social change more generally which falls outside the scope of this paper. However, a minority perspective does make it the responsibility of empirical criminologists to engage in research in a responsible way. Honesty requires an acknowledgement that empirical research is the bread-and-butter of Ph.D. students, academics and consultants—publications, grants, and consultancy work—the number and quality of which reflect on the way we are perceived by the academy.

We have already outlined some guiding principles for undertaking social research with minorities. Researchers working within a minority perspective should also be committed to making their research accessible by disseminating their research findings directly to research participants in parallel with the traditional approach of publishing in academic journals or books. This could be through oral presentations or short articles in practitioner publications or in the minority press. It should reach those who participated directly and those on whom it may impact, in terms of media attention, or changes in policy or practice.

Theoretical approaches

For Russell (1992) a primary objective in developing a black criminology in the United States is to remedy the absence of a sub-field within criminology which is sufficiently sophisticated to explain patterns of offending by black people who are disproportionately arrested, convicted and incarcerated. She argues that there is a need to move beyond the abundant descriptive analyses of the relationship between race and official offending to develop critical theoretical analyses which go beyond tests of existing criminological theories.

For Russell (1992), a black criminology sub-field would encompass theoretical perspectives formulated at the micro and macro levels of analysis, and spanning the political spectrum. It is only with the latter point that we would take issue with Russell. In our view, it is hard to envisage any minority perspectives in criminology which are conservative in orientation, since such approaches usually locate the causes of crime at the individual or sub/cultural levels.[6] While there may be conservative approaches taken by minority criminologists, a minority perspective should not, as Russell suggests, incorporate conservative positions which do not explicitly criticize and challenge the empirical basis for ethnic differences in official involvement in crime, or locate the lived experience of minorities within structural contexts.[7]

Furthermore, the structural context of life within minority communities cannot be understood without incorporating an historical perspective. 'Race' and ethnicity, for example, are not ahistorical essences; racist ideas drawn from the philosophies of the European Enlightenment have been translated into modern ideologies of racial supremacy based on these socially constructed categories. Humanity is presumed to be divided up into distinct 'races' arranged hierarchically with 'whites' or 'Aryans' positioned at the top, above darker-skinned Europeans and Asians, who are, in turn, superior to blacks, who are seen as inherently inferior—in attractiveness, intelligence, cultural form, and capacity for progress (see Bowling and Phillips 2002).

---

[6] For example, see Herrnstein and Murray (1994); Wolfgang and Ferracuti (1967).

[7] Valier's (2003) critique of the Chicago School of Sociology is insightful here, in highlighting its failure to take account of institutional racism and structural forms of exclusion.

Both explicitly and implicitly these ideas have been normalized and insti-
tutionalized to justify the enslavement of minorities, the extermination of
native peoples, and the acquisition and rule of territories as part of the British
empire.[8] Although the impact of slavery and colonialism cannot be viewed in
a unidimensional way, it is apparent that its effects can be seen in the late
twentieth century British context. Denial of citizenship and immigration
rights, exclusion from certain residential areas, concentration in poor housing, and negative educational and employment experiences have all occurred
as state agencies' practices have operated through a racialized filter informed
by notions of inferiority and 'undeservedness' (Smith 1989). The end result
of these discriminatory social practices has been the social, economic and
political exclusion of many minority groups, including some white ethnic
groups (for a brief discussion see Bowling and Phillips 2002).

This historical contextualization of minority experiences has a direct
bearing on our understanding of victimization, offending and criminal justice
in the contemporary period.[9] Thus, structural theories would predict that
people from ethnic minority communities would be disproportionately likely
to be found in 'criminogenic' contexts, since deviance is more commonly a
viable solution for minority communities than for the ethnic majority population. Furthermore, deviant behaviour among socially and economically marginalized people is much more likely to be labelled as criminal, to result in
formal sanctions by the state, and to lead individuals to be propelled through
the criminal justice process towards imprisonment. Thus, processes of social
and economic marginalization not only have consequences for involvement
in deviant behaviour among minority groups, but these are compounded by
policing and criminal justice processes. Indeed, it is noticeable throughout
the work of minority researchers in the United States, that the historical
experience of minorities under the law and the operation of the criminal
justice system, particularly their oppressive and racist impact, clearly informs
current accounts of *both* offending *and* discrimination at various stages of the
criminal justice process (see for example French 1979; Takagi 1981; Mann
1993, 1994).

Linked to the need for minority perspectives to be steeped in an historical
understanding of minority experience in Britain is the central importance of
the explanatory role of *racisms* in a minority analysis of victimization, offending, and criminal justice. By racisms we are referring to direct, indirect, institutional and contextual racisms which may on their own or together assist in
explaining a variety of criminological phenomena involving minorities.

---

[8] It is acknowledged that the relationship between ideologies of superiority and exclusionism
and the actual practices of ethnic exclusion are neither direct nor simple, but it is important to
recognize that the two are linked.

[9] Williams and Murphy's (1995) minority account of the evolution of American policing, for
example, is insightful for its use of historical material to understand a modern context, and for its
reinterpretation of a majority view of the emergence and development of American policing.

Hood's (1992) study of sentencing practices in the West Midlands, for example, found evidence of direct racial discrimination in Crown Courts; black defendants had a 5 per cent greater probability of being sentenced to immediate custody than white defendants, once all legally relevant factors had been taken into account. Direct discrimination was also identified in the biased decisions made by prison staff in Genders and Player's (1989) study of work allocations in prison, where black prisoners were stereotypically perceived to be lazy, work-shy and incompetent.

Probably as important in explaining unequal outcomes is the role of indirect discrimination. This refers to the process whereby the seemingly equal treatment of minority groups has a discriminatory effect despite the application of neutral formal criteria. The minimum height requirement for appointment as a police officer in some jurisdictions is an example of indirect discrimination. Clearly, people from some minority groups (and women) are less likely to be able to meet the minimum requirement, while height is irrelevant to the job of being a police officer. Perhaps the most significant example of indirect discrimination is the effect of remand status on subsequent sentencing decisions; studies of prosecution and sentencing show that a defendant who has been remanded in custody during the court process is more likely to be sentenced to custody if convicted (Hood 1992). Ethnic minorities often fall into the category of people remanded in custody because of their increased chances of being homeless, unemployed or in 'disrupted' families, all of which may be perceived as being linked to failing to appear at court. Thus, the seemingly neutral criteria relating to the likelihood of court appearance is loaded against ethnic minorities because of social inequalities, which are themselves often the result of racially discriminatory social practices in housing and employment, for example.

The Macpherson Report (1999: 28) into the death of Stephen Lawrence has also brought to the centre of the political and policy landscape a new language of institutional racism, defined as 'the collective failure of an organization to provide an appropriate and professional service to people because of their colour, culture, or ethnic origin. It can be seen or detected in processes, attitudes and behaviour which amount to discrimination through unwitting prejudice, ignorance, thoughtlessness and racist stereotyping which disadvantage minority ethnic people'. In the case of the investigation into the racist murder of Stephen Lawrence, the inquiry team concluded that officers negatively stereotyped the victims at the scene assuming they were protagonists in a fight, treated the Lawrence family in a patronizing way following the murder sometimes using inappropriate and offensive language, and were critical of the beliefs of some five investigating officers that the murder was not a racist one. A further example of institutional racism lies in the use of stop/search as a performance indicator. In the context of a history of strained relations between minority communities and the police, the power is used disproportionately and in many instances in a discriminatory fashion against minorities because of prejudice and negative stereotyping. The promotion of stop/search (that is, the more the better) to demonstrate effective job performance in areas of high minority concentration must be seen as further evidence of institutional racism in the police service.

Drawing on the findings from research in the United States indicates the need to consider the role of contextual racism and discrimination. As Walker et al. (1996) note, African Americans are subject to the abuse of discretion in the criminal justice process in certain circumstances but not in others. It is evident that prosecutors, judges, and juries with sentencing recommendation powers, even in death penalty cases, choose a more lenient outcome for African American offenders when the victim is also African American, than in any of the other three victim-offender dyads (Baldus et al. 1990; Gross and Mauro 1989). This is especially true of cases involving sexual assault, rape and homicide (LaFree 1989; Spohn 1994; see also Hudson 1993).[10]

It is also becoming increasingly common in the United States to view the differences in arrest and imprisonment rates of African Americans, Hispanic Americans and white Americans as the product of social and structural contexts. Chiricos and Crawford (1995), for example, point to the need to disaggregate imprisonment data and its link to 'race' according to region (South vs NonSouth), percentage of blacks in the population, percentage of blacks residing in urban locations, and area levels of unemployment. An attempt to consider such structural contexts was undertaken by Jefferson and Walker (1992) in Leeds in their study of arrest rates in areas where there were high and low concentrations of black and Asian residents. Similarly, Hood's (1992) study in the West Midlands highlights the need for a contextualized analysis of sentencing practices. Hood found that, once all legally relevant variables were controlled for, for every 100 black males sentenced to custody in Birmingham, 130 were given a custodial sentence in Dudley and even more at Warwick and Stafford Crown Courts. This suggests that the basis for decision making in sentencing varied in each of the courts. The idea that criminal justice patterns cannot be understood as being determined by 'generalized racism' as Smith (1997) posits, points us towards a recognition that prejudices and their influence on behaviour vary over time, in different places, and in specific contexts. In the case of Hood's research, for example, there are some obvious differences between Birmingham and the other research sites that an historical analysis would have unveiled. In the 1960s and 1970s, for example, it was in West Midlands satellite towns as Dudley, Smethwick and Wolverhampton, that the strength of racist sentiment was most strongly expressed by mainstream racist politicians such as Enoch Powell and Peter Griffiths, and where the National Front and other openly racist political parties have had their strongest showing (see Bowling 1999).

---

[10] The extent to which this is true of female offenders, charged with property and violent offences has not been established.

The type of quantitative analyses required to uncover these contextual complexities are currently difficult to do in Britain because of the paucity of routinely collected national data. However, expanding the parameters of empirical research must be a focus for a minority criminological perspective in order to produce a more nuanced understanding of minority experiences which also draws on qualitative techniques.

Practice and policy within criminology

Ethical duties

There is a public role for criminologists whose work is informed by a minority perspective. First, there is a responsibility to be vigilant in critically assessing and monitoring policy developments to assess whether new policies and initiatives have a specific detrimental effect on minorities, either as victims, offenders, or practitioners. It is part of criminologists' public duty to forewarn policy makers of the type of 'malign neglect' referred to by Tonry (1995) in his book of the same title. In it he sketches the role that the US War on Drugs policy played in the social destruction of minority communities, which Tonry argues was completely foreseeable by politicians and policy makers (see also Miller 1996).

Second, the public service responsibility should also extend to what Russell (1998: 94) refers to as 'an affirmative duty on researchers today to take responsibility for the research claims put in the public domain'. She contends that researchers are duty-bound to put forward clarifications or rebuttals where inaccurate or false representations are made, especially where they are claimed to be based on social science research. In particular, Russell argues for a research community response to the misuse of social science research concerning the relationship between race, ethnicity and crime. A case in point would be a response to the FitzGerald (1999: 22) study of stop/search patterns in the Metropolitan Police to underline that a statistical 'link between the fall in searches and the rise in street crime' was not of a causal nature. Russell suggests that such clarifications could include an official statement from professional associations (such as the American Society of Criminology), a response from a group of experts in the field, and a public response through the media.

Third, there is also an ethical imperative to criticize existing work which is based on ill-considered stereotypes and is guilty of cultural pathologizing. Indeed, it is incumbent on criminologists operating within a minority perspective to ensure proportionate interest in minority experience. The over-representation of some minorities as offenders in official statistics does not negate the fact that the vast majority of offences that are detected are committed by white offenders. That the proportion of white male and female British nationals in prison in 1999 was 86 and 85 per cent respectively should not be overlooked in academic and public debates about offending (Home Office 2000). A critical understanding of the hegemonic nature of white ethnicity and its relationship to victimization and offending is required.

A research agenda

Criminologists working within a minority perspective can contribute to theory, research, practice and policy by opening up a new research agenda which focuses on diverse minority groups in British society. Research topics such as anti-semitic violence and how it is policed, the victimization, offending behaviour, and social control of refugees and asylum-seekers, Irish, Turkish, Chinese and travelling communities are all necessary to broaden our criminological knowledge. Indeed, as Pearson (1983) has shown, historically, various white ethnic groups have been perceived as problematic visiting specific kinds of crimes on the indigenous English and requiring special measures of control (see Bowling and Phillips 2002 for a brief review). However, we are not proposing a project which serves simply to expose the dynamics of 'Other' cultures, since this itself has the potential to pathologize, exoticize, or even to open them up to new forms of surveillance and scrutiny (see Hutnyk 1996). The call is instead for an understanding of the lived experiences of minorities other than those traditionally studied in criminology, and in a way which recognizes the dynamic nature of ethnic identities which are bound up with other sources of identity such as gender, age, class, religion and sexuality. The role of white ethnic identities in understanding racist violence, football and alcohol-related violence should be a key part of this project too (Back et al. 1999).

A balanced programme of research of both comparative and single-group case studies is needed to ensure that racial categories are not reified beyond their social construction (Stanfield 1993). Thus, for example, a qualitative study of the offenders' perspective in relation to robbery (which has the starkest difference in officially recorded rates of offending) could be a comparative study of white and minority offenders convicted of robbery offences. This could chart trajectories into offending, motivation for type of crime, techniques for committing crime, reactions to criminalization and so on. A complementary approach would be to include an analysis of official crime reports and interviews in custody to examine how the police come to charge robbery offenders. It is worth exploring empirically, for example, whether there is a tendency for the police to overcharge minorities with robbery rather than with less serious and non-violent offences (see Blom-Cooper and Drabble 1982). Given the negative stereotyping of young black men as threatening and violent, which undoubtedly contributes to their increased likelihood of being excluded from school, and to have their infractions in prison treated more harshly than their white and Asian counterparts (see for example Ofsted 2001 and Genders and Player 1989), this would seem to be a fruitful avenue for research. Here we are also reminded of Becker's (1967: 242) question and its relevance for minorities: 'Most research on youth, after all, is clearly designed to find out why youth are so troublesome for adults, rather than asking the equally interesting sociological question: Why do adults make so much trouble for youth?'

Both minority and feminist perspectives share a desire to make the interest group visible, but the focus of this visibility is somewhat different. Whereas feminist criminologists have sought to expose the neglect of women as offenders and victims and to understand their treatment in the criminal justice system, minority perspectives will seek to redress a criminological imbalance. Empirical criminology has been overly concerned with minorities, particularly black minorities, as offenders. Less attention, until recently, has centred on minorities as victims of racist crimes (see Bowling 1999 for a review). Clearly there is further scope for extending analyses of victimization to minority experiences of policing and custody where minorities are victimized by agents of the criminal justice system. There is little recent empirical research, for example, which contextualizes the experience of minority prisoners from the perspective of those who experience discrimination, harassment and victimization by prison officers. Similarly, where are the criminological studies of minority prison officers, probation officers, lawyers or policy makers?[11]

A further proposal for empirical criminology informed by a minority position is to extend the boundaries of existing research. Most will be aware of the multitude of methodological difficulties that bedevil attempts to assess the role of direct or indirect racial discrimination in criminal justice processing, making it a futile exercise according to some criminologists (Reiner 1993; FitzGerald 1993; see also Holdaway 1997). In part because of a growing interest in minority experiences of crime and criminal justice, but also because of section 95 of the Criminal Justice Act 1991, it is likely that research will continue to expand in this area. An innovative methodology for rigorously examining the decision making of criminal justice agents, particularly those who have been traditionally less accessible to researchers and less open to public scrutiny, such as judges, will be required.

It is hoped that challenges to the common approach of using regression analyses to statistically model the complex decision making of judges (Hood 1992), crown prosecutors and police officers (Mhlanga 1997; Phillips and

[11] It has often been left to the media to bring to public attention the racism faced by minority staff in the criminal justice field. For example: 'An Asian lawyer who claimed that a culture of racism prevented her from being promoted within the Crown Prosecution Service was awarded £30,000 damages yesterday', *The Daily Telegraph*, 2 February 2000; 'The head of the prison service is to apologize to a black worker who was humiliated and abused when he returned to work after winning damages for racial discrimination' (*The Times*, 20 April 2000); 'North Wales Probation Committee must pay £3,500 after being found guilty of racial discrimination against the area's only black probation officer', *Daily Post*, 23 March 1996.

Brown 1998) to find a direct 'race' effect will be accepted and taken forward. The US approach could assist here. Frazier and Bishop (1995), for example, used their quantitative data—which showed that the 'race' of offender had an independent effect in formal juvenile justice system processing—to explore whether the results were consistent with officials' experiences in the juvenile justice system. The researchers gave a two-paragraph description of the quantitative findings to judges, prosecutors, public defenders, and intake supervisors, and asked them whether the findings were consistent with their experiences. This was an attempt to explore the processes whereby 'race' and racism are socially constructed in routine decision making (cf. Holdaway 1997). Similarly, Gelsthorpe (1993) has emphasized the importance of using qualitative data to examine the organizational context for report-writing practices, to flesh out the superficial data which comes from statistical analyses of ethnically monitored outcomes. These types of studies have shed light on the way in which family assessments determining a lack of 'good parenting' (as assessed against white middle-class norms) impact disproportionately on minorities and are an example of indirect racial discrimination.[12]

Minority criminologists

We touched on the question of who should contribute to a minority perspective in criminology earlier and do not intend to repeat the discussion here, except to consider the professional dangers of partiality (or bias) when minority criminologists study minorities' experience of victimization, offending and criminal justice. Feminists and anti-racist researchers in other disciplines have been accused of lacking objectivity (see Gelsthorpe and Morris 1988; Troyna 1995; Russell 1992), but as Becker (1967: 245) observed, it is inevitable that research is 'contaminated' by personal and political sympathies, 'there is no position from which sociological research can be done that is not biased in one or another way'. It is, in our view, possible and desirable to 'balance commitment with scholarship' (see Waddington 2000).

Associated with claims of damaging subjectivity is the concern with marginalization whereby minority academics/researchers are warned of the danger of topic limitation by focusing exclusively on 'race issues'. Yet as Blaikie (2000) notes, social research is often carried out to pursue personal interests or commitments, to satisfy curiosity or to solve a personal problem. Moreover, regardless of whether the racialized status of minority criminologists does or does not influence their research interests, this should not take

---

[12] See also Frazier and Bishop (1995) who reported that juvenile justice officials used more severe sanctions where they perceived that minority families were incapable of providing good parental supervision. Where parents were expected to be interviewed by juvenile justice personnel, those without telephones, cars or with inflexible jobs were less accessible, and were implicitly deemed to be less capable of providing good parental supervision.

away from any significant contributions to the body of criminological knowledge that minority criminologists make, in whatever area. Finally, as the section on empirical approaches and the next section make clear, it is imperative that minority scholars undertake work in this area.

The establishment of the *Racism, Ethnicity and Criminology Round Table* website and discussion forum has been spurred on by the need to discuss these types of issues in a supportive environment.[13] Arising from a round table discussion held at the 1997 British Criminology Conference, its subscribers include minority and white researchers, academics and practitioners in the criminological community. Its purpose is to inform public opinion, and to aid practitioners and policy makers in their work surrounding issues of racism, ethnicity and criminology. It has been used to discuss new work, emerging ideas, advertise conferences, and to announce employment opportunities in the field (see http://www.kcl.ac.uk/depsta/law/research/rec/index.html).

Looking within the discipline

If a minority perspective is to confront practices within the discipline of criminology itself the question 'is British criminology institutionally racist?' must be faced. The Home Secretary and Minister of State for Prisons publicly acknowledge institutional racism in the Home Office and Prison Service, but there appears to be little consideration of such issues within academia more generally.[14] Borrowing from the definition provided by the Lawrence Inquiry, we have to ask whether British criminology fails to provide an appropriate and professional service to people because of their colour, culture or ethnic origin through discrimination, prejudice, ignorance, thoughtlessness and racist stereotyping?

A starting point to answering this question would be to examine whether the lower salary, seniority and poorer tenure position found for minorities by the Association of University Teachers (2000) using Higher Education Statistics Agency data for 1998/1999 is mirrored in criminology/criminal justice. What are the levels of representation and seniority for minority and white criminology/criminal justice academics and researchers, as well as those serving on the editorial boards of criminological journals, personnel employed within funding agencies such as the Home Office, and those tasked with the governance of the British Society of Criminology? Such basic information needs to be supplemented by a more qualitative assessment of

---

[13] Minority-established support organizations have also been set up in the police service, legal field, probation and prison services, and more recently the Home Office (see Bowling and Phillips 2002).

[14] A new study on institutional racism in universities is being conducted by the University of Leeds Centre for Ethnicity and Racism Studies (http://www.leeds.ac.uk/CERS/research.htm).

minority experiences in the discipline, including the extent of perceived prejudice and discrimination in the academic setting, policy-making environment or in research settings. Is there evidence of prejudice, direct, indirect, institutional or contextual discrimination in student recruitment, in teaching and learning, on work placements, for contract research jobs or other points of access to the field? Are minorities included in the informal networks and patronage that typically feature in a successful academic career (see Heward et al. 1997)? Are discriminatory practices evident in the centres of criminology and criminal justice in universities and the Home Office, in terms of career development and work experience?

While there are obvious limitations to comparing the US and the UK experience, such as the relative size of minority populations, research in this area could usefully draw on what is known about the experience of minority criminologists in the United States. They have painted a largely pessimistic picture of the excluded status of minorities in the criminology/criminal justice field. Young and Sulton (1996), for example, have described the invisibility of minorities in influential positions within American criminology. They feel excluded from reviews of theory, providing expert opinions to the media, as recipients of major grant awards, on policy groups or task forces, on policy-making boards of criminology organizations, and on editorial boards of journals. They note that only two of 157 members of editorial boards of the ten leading refereed journals in criminology/criminal justice were African American. Taylor Greene and Gabbidon (2000) have also criticized mainstream criminological discourses for ignoring the work of pioneering and contemporary African American scholars such as Du Bois and Hawkins.

Some positive solutions have been sought in the field, however, including three American Society of Criminology Fellowships for ethnic minorities, the National Institute of Justice W. E. B. Du Bois Fellowship Program, and the Andrew W. Mellon Foundation/Vera Institute of Justice Postdoctoral Fellowship on Race, Crime and Justice. In 1995 the American Society of Criminology established a Division of People of Color and Crime to facilitate research and advance multiple perspectives about people of colour and crime and criminal justice, to stimulate teaching in the field, to raise awareness within the American Society of Criminology, as well as serving as a resource network for those in the field, alongside internet-based discussion groups. There has also been the devotion of journal issues to minority scholars or work on 'race' and ethnicity. Professional workshops for minorities are also included at conferences in the United States. A minority perspective could carefully consider whether any of these options are appropriate for the UK context. Indeed, following the US lead, the Arlene Mundle Postgraduate Scholarship has been established by the British Society of Criminology, with applications encouraged from minority students.

Just as one response to the Macpherson Inquiry has been a widespread consensus that more minorities need to be recruited into criminal justice services as employees, claims can be made for improving the representation of minorities within criminology and criminal justice. Those working in academic or administrative criminology should reflect the local communities of which they form a part. As Russell (1992) suggests, minority lecturers may also encourage minority students into the field, an essential development for the future of the discipline. The role of minority lecturers, according to Russell, may also be to diversify the criminology curriculum. Indeed, the way in which 'race', ethnicity and racism are covered in criminology must also be examined. The potential for conflict in confronting such academic practices is highlighted by Erasmus (2000) in discussing tensions in the South African academy as minorities challenge liberal white academics' positions on interpreting the stories of minorities, racism, and white dominance post-apartheid.

Conclusion

The current political climate is more receptive to seeing crime and criminal justice from a minority perspective than it has ever been. The government acceptance of the Lawrence Inquiry's finding of institutional racism in the Metropolitan Police Service, the acknowledgement that it is present in many social institutions, including the Home Office and the Prison Service, and the promotion of minority professional associations in the criminal justice professions (the National Black Police Association, Society of Black Lawyers, National Association of Asian Probation Staff, Home Office Network to name but a few) are evidence of this changed environment. The arguments presented in this paper have explored some of the guiding principles for minority perspectives in criminology. It is very possible that they will face the same marginalized status as feminist perspectives have in criminology (Gelsthorpe and Morris 1988). At the very least, however, we hope that its impact will be felt at the front-line, so to speak; that is, in the interaction between researcher and researched.

References

Alexander, C. (2000), *The Asian Gang: Ethnicity, Identity, Masculinity*. Oxford: Berg.
Association of University Teachers (2000), *Ethnicity, Pay and Employment in Higher Education 1998/99*. http://www.aut.org.uk/pandp/documents/ethnicitypayand employment.doc.
Back, L., Crabbe, T. and Solomos, J. (1999), 'Beyond the Racist/Hooligan Couplet: Race, Social Theory and Football Culture', *British Journal of Sociology*, 50/3: 419–42.
Baldus, D. C., Pulaski, C. and Woodworth, G. (1990), 'Comparative Review of Death Sentence: An Empirical Study of the Georgia Experience', *Journal of Criminal Law & Criminology*, 74: 661–73.

Becker, H. S. (1967), 'Whose Side Are We On?', *Social Problems*, 14/3: 239–47.

Bhopac, K. (2001), 'Rescarching South Asian Women: Issues of Sameness and Difference in the Research Process', *Journal of Gender Studies*, 10/3: 279–86.

Blaikie, N. (2000), *Designing Social Research*. Cambridge: Polity Press.

Blom-Cooper, L. and Drabble, R. (1982), 'Police Perception of Crime: Brixton and the Operational Response', *British Journal of Criminology*, 22: 184–7.

Bowling, B. (1999), *Violent Racism: Victimisation, Policing and Social Context*, revised edition. Oxford: Oxford University Press.

Bowling, B. and Phillips, C. (2002), *Racism, Crime and Justice*. Harlow: Longman.

Braithwaite, J. (1989), *Crime, Shame and Reintegration*. Cambridge: Cambridge University Press.

Cain, M. (1990), 'Realist Philosophy and Standpoint Epistemologies or Feminist Criminology as a Successor Science', in L. Gelsthorpe and A. Morris, eds., *Feminist Perspectives in Criminology*. Milton Keynes: Open University Press.

Chiricos, T. G. and Crawford, C. (1995), 'Race and Imprisonment: A Contextual Assessment of the Evidence', in D. F. Hawkins, ed., *Ethnicity, Race and Crime*. Albany: State University of New York Press.

Daly, K. and Stephens, D. J. (1995), 'The "Dark Figure" of Criminology: Towards a Black and Multi-ethnic Agenda for Theory and Research', in F. Heidensohn and N. Rafter, eds., *International Feminist Perspectives in Criminology: Engendering a Discipline*. Buckingham: Open University Press.

Dunlap, E., Johnson, B., Sanabria, H., Holliday, E., Lipsey, V., Barnett, M., Hopkins, W., Sobel, I., Randolph, D. and Chin, K. (1990) 'Studying Crack Users and Their Criminal Careers: The Scientific and Artistic Aspects of Locating Hard-to-Reach Subjects and Interviewing Them about Sensitive Topics', *Contemporary Drug Problems*, Spring: 121–45.

Dyck, I., Lynam, J. M. and Anderson, J. M. (1995), 'Women Talking: Creating Knowledge Through Difference in Cross-Cultural Research', *Women's Studies International Forum*, 18(5/6): 611–26.

Egharevba, I. (2001), 'Researching An-"Other" Minority Ethnic Community: Reflections of a Black Female Researcher on the Intersections of Race, Gender and Other Power Positions on the Research Process', *International Journal of Social Research Methodology*, 4/3: 225–41.

Erasmus, Z. (2000), 'Some Kind of White, Some Kind of Black: Living the Moments of Entanglement in South Africa and its Academy', in B. Hesse, ed., *Un/settled Multiculturalisms*. London: Zed Books.

Ferdinand, D. (1994), *Towards A Black Perspective in Research*, unpublished MA dissertation. Goldsmiths College, University of London.

Fitzgerald, M. (1993), *Ethnic Minorities in the Criminal Justice System*, Home Office Research and Statistics Department, Research Study No. 20. London: HMSO.

Fitzgerald, M. (1999), *Searches in London under Section 1 of the Police and Criminal Evidence Act*. London: Metropolitan Police.

Frazier, C. E. and Bishop, D. M. (1995), 'Reflections on Race Effects in Juvenile Justice', in K. K. Leonard, C. E. Pope, and W. H. Feyerherm, eds., *Minorities in Juvenile Justice*. London: Sage Publications.

French, L. (1979), 'The Minority Perspective on Violence', *International Journal of Comparative and Applied Criminal Justice*, Spring: 3/1: 43–9.

Gelsthorpe, L. (1990), 'Feminist Methodologies in Criminology: A New Approach or

Old Wine in New Bottles', in L. Gelsthorpe and A. Morris, eds., *Feminist Perspectives in Criminology*. Milton Keynes: Open University Press.

Gelsthorpe, L. (1993), ed., 'Minority Ethnic Groups in the Criminal Justice System', papers presented to 21st Cropwood Roundtable Conference 1992. Cambridge: University of Cambridge, Institute of Criminology.

Gelsthorpe, L. and Morris, A. (1988), 'Feminism and Criminology in Britain', *British Journal of Criminology*, Spring 28/2: 93–110.

Genders, E. and Player, E. (1989), *Race Relations in Prison*. Oxford: Clarendon Press.

Gordon, T. (1973), 'Notes on White and Black Psychology', *Journal of Social Issues*, 29/1: 87–95.

Gross, S. R. and Mauro, R. (1989), *Death and Discrimination: Racial Disparities in Capital Sentencing*. Boston: Northeastern University Press.

Hall, S. (1988), 'New Ethnicities', in K. Mercer, ed., *Black Film/British Cinema*. London: Institute of Contemporary Arts.

Hammersley, M. (1992), 'On Feminist Methodology', *Sociology*, May 26/2: 187–206.

Harding, S. (1987), 'Conclusion: Epistemological Questions', in S. Harding, ed., *Feminism and Methodology*. Indiana, BL: Indiana University Press.

Hawkins, D. F. (1994), 'Ethnicity: the Forgotten Dimension of American Social Control', in G. S. Bridges and M. A. Myers, eds., *Inequality, Crime and Social Control*, 99–116. Boulder, CO: Westview Press.

Herrnstein, R. J. and Murray, C. (1994), *The Bell Curve: Intelligence and Class Structure in American Life*. New York, London: Free Press.

Heward, C., Taylor, P. and Vickers, R. (1997), 'Gender, Race and Career Success in the Academic Profession', *Journal of Further and Higher Education*, 21/2: 205–18.

Hill Collins, P. (1998), *Fighting Words: Black Women and the Search for Justice*. Minneapolis, MN: University of Minnesota Press.

Holdaway, S. (1997), 'Some Recent Approaches to the Study of Race in Criminological Research: Race as Social Process', *British Journal of Criminology*, 37/3: 383–400.

Home Office (2000), *Statistics on Race and the Criminal Justice System: A Home Office Publication under Section 95 of the Criminal Justice Act 1991*. London: Home Office.

Hood, R. (1992), *Race and Sentencing*. Oxford: Clarendon Press.

Hudson, B. (1993), *Penal Policy and Social Justice*. Basingstoke: Macmillan.

Hughes, D. and DuMont, K. (1993), 'Using Focus Groups to Facilitate Culturally Anchored Research', *American Journal of Community Psychology*, 21/6: 775–806.

Hutnyk, J. (1996), 'Repetitive Beatings or Criminal Justice?', in S. Sharma, J. Hutnyk and A. Sharma, eds., *Dis-Orienting Rhythms: the Politics of New Asian Dance Music*. London: Zed Books.

Jefferson, T. and Walker, M. A. (1992), 'Ethnic Minorities in the Criminal Justice System', *Criminal Law Review*, 81/140: 83–95.

Jhappan, R. (1996) 'Post-Modern Race and Gender Essentialism or a Post-Mortem of Scholarship', *Studies in Political Economy*, Fall, 51: 15–63.

Joe, K. (1993), 'Issues in Accessing and Studying Ethnic Youth Gangs', *The Gang Journal*, 1/2: 9–23.

Johnston, L. O. (1974), 'A Black Perspective on Social Research: In Response to Merton', *Issues in Criminology*, Spring, 9/1: 55–70.

Kershaw, C., Budd, T., Kinshott, G., Mattinson, J., Mayhew, P. and Myhill, A. (2000), *The 2000 British Crime Survey*, Home Office Statistical Bulletin 18/00. London: Home Office.

LaFree, G. D. (1989), *Rape and Criminal Justice: The Social Construction of Sexual Assault*. Belmont, CA: Wadsworth.

Landrine, H., Klonoff, E. A. and Brown-Collins, A. (1992), 'Cultural Diversity and Methodology in Feminist Psychology', *Psychology of Women Quarterly*, 16: 145–63.

Macpherson, W. (advised by T. Cook, J. Sentamu and R. Stone) (1998), *The Stephen Lawrence Inquiry*. London: HMSO.

Mann, C. R. (1993), *Unequal Justice: A Question of Color*. Bloomington, IN: Indiana University Press.

Mann, C. R. (1994), 'Minority and Female: A Criminal Justice Double Bind', *Social Justice*, 16/4: 95–114.

Marín, G. and Marín, B. V. (1991), *Research with Hispanic Populations*, Applied Social Research Methods Series, Vol. 23. Newbury, CA: Sage.

Maynard, M. (2002), 'Studying Age, "Race" and Gender: Translating a Research Proposal into a Project', *International Journal of Social Research Methodology*, 5/1: 31–40.

Merton, R. K. (1972), 'Insiders and Outsiders: A Chapter in the Sociology of Knowledge', *American Journal of Sociology*, 78/1: 9–47.

Mhlanga, B. (1997), *The Colour of English Justice: A Multivariate Analysis*. Aldershot: Avebury.

Mieczkowski, T. (1988), 'Studying Heroin Retailers: A Research Note', *Criminal Justice Review*, 13/1: 39–44.

Miller, J. G. (1996), *Search and Destroy: African-American Males in the Criminal Justice System*. Cambridge: Cambridge University Press.

Mio, J. S. and Iwamasa, G. (1993), 'To Do, or Not to Do: That Is the Question for White Cross-Cultural Researchers', *The Counselling Psychologist*, April, 21/2: 197–212.

Mirza, M. (1998), ' "Same Voices, Same Lives?": Revisiting Black Feminist Standpoint Epistemology', in P. Connolly and B. Troyna, eds., *Researching Racism in Education: Politics, Theory and Practice*. Buckingham: Open University Press.

Modood, T. (1988), ' "Black", Racial Equality and Asian Identity', *New Community*, 14: 397–404.

Modood, T., and Berthoud, R. (1997), *Ethnic Minorities in Britain: Diversity and Disadvantage*. London: Policy Studies Institute.

Morris, A. and Gelsthorpe, L. (1991), 'Feminist Perspectives in Criminology: Transforming and Transgressing', *Women and Criminal Justice*, 2/2: 3–26.

Myrdal, G. (1944), *An American Dilemma: The Negro Problem and Modern Democracy*. New York: Harper.

Office for Standards in Education (2001), *Improving Attendance and Behaviour in Secondary Schools*. London: Ofsted.

Parham, T. A. (1993), 'White Researchers Conducting Multicultural Counseling Research: Can Their Efforts Be "Mo Betta"?', *The Counselling Psychologist*, April 21/2: 250–6.

Pearson, G. (1983), *Hooligan: A History of Respectable Fears*. London: Macmillan.

Phillips, C. and Brown, D. (1997), 'Observational Studies in Police Custody Areas:

Some Methodological and Ethical Issues Considered', *Policing and Society*, 7: 191–205.

Phillips, C. and Brown, D. (1998), *Entry into the Criminal Justice System: A Survey of Police Arrests and Their Outcomes*, Home Office Research Study 185. London: Home Office.

Phoenix, A. (1998), 'Practising Feminist Research: The Intersection of Gender and "Race" in the Research Process', in P. Connolly and B. Troyna, eds., *Researching Racism in Education: Politics, Theory and Practice*. Buckingham: Open University Press.

Reay, D. (1996), 'Insider Perspectives or Stealing the Words out of Women's Mouths; Interpretation in the Research Process', *Feminist Review*, 53: 57–73.

Reid, P. and Kelly, E. (1994), 'Research on Women of Color: From Ignorance to Awareness', *Psychology of Women Quarterly*, 18: 477–86.

Reiner, R. (1993), 'Race, Crime and Justice: Models of Interpretation', in L. R. Gelsthorpe, ed., *Minority Ethnic Groups in the Criminal Justice System*. Cambridge: University of Cambridge Institute of Criminology.

Rhodes, P. J. (1994), 'Race-Of-Interviewer Effects: A Brief Comment', *Sociology*, 28/2: 547–58.

Rice, M. (1990), 'Challenging Orthodoxies in Feminist Theory: A Black Feminist Critique', in L. Gelsthorpe and A. Morris, eds., *Feminist Perspectives in Criminology*, 57–79. Milton Keynes: Open University Press.

Russell, K. (1992), 'Development of a Black Criminology and the Role of the Black Criminologist', *Justice Quarterly*, 9/4: 667–83.

Russell, K. K. (1998), *The Color of Crime*. New York and London: New York University Press.

Shallice, A. and Gordon, P. (1990), *Black People, White Justice? Race and the Criminal Justice System*. London: Runnymede Trust.

Sharma, A. (1996), 'Sounds Oriental: The (Im)possibility of Theorizing Asian Dance Music', in S. Sharma, J. Hutnyk and A. Sharma, eds., *Dis-Orienting Rhythms: The Politics of New Asian Dance Music*. London: Zed Books.

Sharma, S., Hutnyk, J. and Sharma, A. (1996), 'Introduction' in *Dis-Orienting Rhythms: the Politics of New Asian Dance Music*. London: Zed Books.

Simmel, G. (1921), 'The Sociological Significance of the "Stranger" ', in R. E. Park and E. W. Burgess, eds., *Introduction to the Science of Sociology*. Chicago, IL: University of Chicago Press.

Smart, C. (1990), 'Feminist Approaches to Criminology or Postmodern Woman Meets Atavistic Man', in L. Gelsthorpe and A. Morris, eds., *Feminist Perspectives in Criminology*. Milton Keynes: Open University Press.

Smith, D. (1997), 'Ethnic Origins, Crime, and Criminal Justice in England and Wales', in M. Maguire, R. Morgan and R. Reiner, eds., *The Oxford Handbook of Criminology*, 2nd edn. Oxford: Oxford University Press.

Smith, S. J. (1989), *The Politics of 'Race' and Residence: Citizenship, Segregation and White Supremacy in Britain*. Cambridge: Polity.

Spivak, G. C. (1993) 'Subaltern Talk: Interview with the Editors (29 October 1993)', in D. Landry and G. MacLean, eds., *The Spivak Reader: Selected Works of Gayatri Chakravorty Spivak*. London: Routledge.

Spohn, C. (1994), 'Crime and the Social Control of Blacks: Offender/Victim Race and the Sentencing of Violent Offenders', in G. S. Bridges and M. A. Myers, eds., *Inequality, Crime and Social Control*. Boulder, CO: Westview Press.

Stanfield, J. H. (1993), 'Epistemological Considerations', in J. H. Stanfield II and R. M. Dennis, eds., *Race and Ethnicity In Research Methods*. London: Sage Publications.

Takagi, P. (1981), 'Race, Crime, and Social Policy: A Minority Perspective', *Crime and Delinquency*, 27/1: 48–63.

Taylor Greene, H. and Gabbidon, S. L. (2000), *African American Criminological Thought*. Albany, NY: State University of New York.

Tonry, M. (1995), *Malign Neglect: Race, Crime, and Punishment in America*. New York: Oxford University Press.

Troyna, B. (1995), 'Beyond Reasonable Doubt? Researching "Race" in Educational Settings', *Oxford Review of Education*, 21/4: 395–408.

Tuhiwai Smith, L. (1999), *Decolonizing Methodologies: Research and Indigenous Peoples*. London: Zed Books.

Valier, C. (2001) 'Foreigners, Crime and Changing Mobilities', *British Journal of Criminology*, 43/1.

Waddington, P. A. J. (2000), 'Review of Violent Racism: Victimization, Policing and Social Context', *British Journal of Criminology*, 40/3: 532–4.

Walker, S., Spohn, C. and DeLone, M. (1996), *The Color of Justice: Race, Ethnicity and Crime in America*. Belmont, CA: Wadsworth.

Williams, H. and Murphy, P. V. (1995), 'The Evolving Strategy of Police: A Minority View', in V. E. Kappeler, ed., *The Police and Society—Touchstone Readings*. Prospect Heights, IL: Waveland Press.

Wolfgang, M. and Ferracuti, F. (1967), *The Subculture of Violence: Towards an Integrated Theory in Criminology*. London: Tavistock.

Wright, C. (1998), ' "Caught in the Crossfire": Reflections of a Black Female Ethnographer', in P. Connolly and B. Troyna, eds., *Researching Racism in Education: Politics, Theory and Practice*. Buckingham: Open University Press.

Young, V. and Sulton, A. T. (1996), 'Excluded: The Current Status Of African-American Scholars In The Field Of Criminology And Criminal Justice', in A. T. Sulton, ed., *African-American Perspectives On Crime Causation, Criminal Justice Administration and Crime Prevention*. Newton, MA: Butterworth-Heinemann.

Zavella, P. (1993), 'Feminist Insider Dilemmas: Constructing Ethnic Identity with "Chicana" Informants', *Frontiers*, 8/3: 53–73.

15

Constructing whiteness
The intersections of race and gender in US white supremacist discourse

by Abby L. Ferber

In *Playing in the Dark*, Toni Morrison observes that historically, there is a pattern of thinking about racialism in terms of its consequences on the victim—of always defining it asymmetrically from the perspective of its impact on the object of racist policy and attitudes ... But that well-established study should be joined with another, equally important one: the impact of racism on those who perpetuate it. It seems both poignant and striking how avoided and unanalyzed is the effect of racist inflection on the subject (Morrison 1992, p. 11).

Scholars of race have too long neglected the study of 'whiteness'. Over the past decade, however, sociologists and historians have begun to explore more systematically the construction of white racial identity (Saxton 1987; Roediger 1991; Frankenberg 1993; Harper 1993; Ignatiev and Garvey 1996).

This article contributes to this growing body of research. I explore the project of constructing white racial identity which is central to the contemporary white supremacist movement. This research contributes not only to our understanding of the white supremacist movement, but to the process of the construction of racialized identities, as well as to the interconnections between the construction of race and gender.

The white supremacist movement has largely been studied as an issue of race relations, and most research has failed to address issues of gender within the movement (Ferber 1995b). The work of Kathleen Blee (1991a; 1991b) represents the only attempt to document the role and activities of women in the US white supremacist movement, focusing on women's involvement in the Ku Klux Klan in the 1920s. Blee also provides an analysis of gender in the ideology of the Klan at that time. The recent work of Suzanne Harper (1993) further contributes to a feminist analysis of the movement, exploring the intersections of race and gender in depictions of white men and women, black men and women, and Jewish men and women in contemporary white supremacist discourse.

Rather than reading white supremacist discourse as one which is *descriptive* of race, I am reading it as the *construction* of race. Research on white supremacist movement traditionally defines the movement as one which attempts to represent white interests while espousing hatred towards blacks, Jews, and other non-white racialized groups, taking the given reality of race for granted. Instead, I read this movement as actively producing racialized and gendered subjects.

Contemporary racial theory, moving beyond earlier biological and assimilationist conceptualizations of race, refuses to take racial categorizations for granted, exploring instead the social construction of race (Omi and Winant 1986; Balibar and Wallerstein 1991; Goldberg 1993; Ferber 1995a). While it is popular today in academia to study racial 'diversity', this approach often ends up reifying racial categorizations (Carby 1992; Webster 1992). Alternatively, a social constructionist approach emphasizes the critical need for researchers to 'read the processes of differentiation, not look for differences' (Crosby 1993, p. 140). As Omi and Winant suggest, the meaning of race and racialized meanings are politically contested, and it is this contested terrain which needs to be explored.

Contemporary feminist theory has followed a parallel trajectory, asserting the social construction of gender and refuting essentialist, biologically-based explanations (Butler 1990; Hubbard 1992). A growing body of feminist research is documenting the historical and cultural construction of gender (Riley 1988; Higginbotham 1992; Ware 1992; Frankenberg 1993).

Because race and gender are social constructs, they are not constructed in isolation, but often intertwine with other categories of identity. Feminists of colour have criticized single-axis theories which try to separate race and gender, and emphasize the need for theories which account for both race and gender to explain adequately the lives of women of colour. Single-axis theories have assumed that the experiences of white women show us the meanings of gender, distinct from race. This approach, however, has reinforced the notion that race only shapes the lives of victims of racial oppression. My research, however, argues that we must also explore the interaction of race and gender in the construction of white identity and privilege.

This analysis provides a deconstructive textual analysis, revealing the discursive production of race and gender. Deconstructing rigid categories of race and gender in white supremacist discourse can contribute to our understanding of the construction of race and gender more generally, as well as the intersections between race and gender.

The contemporary white supremacist movement in the US

Throughout this article, I examine white supremacist publications from the Keith Stimely collection, in the special collections of the University of Oregon's Knight Library (for a complete list of publications, see Appendix).

This collection was the private collection of Stimely, who donated his holdings to the library. The collection contains the newsletters of a wide variety of white supremacist organizations in the US, as well as miscellaneous paraphernalia, including flyers, leaflets and membership materials of various organizations. The material I examined was published between 1969 and 1993. I examined all the publications contained within the collection in order to ensure that I covered a wide range of organizations, with differing ideological frameworks and aimed at different audiences.

While there are significant differences between the various white supremacist organizations, there are also sustained efforts to forge shared objectives. As Raphael S. Ezekiel found in his study of members of the movement, 'the agreement on basic ideas is the glue that holds the movement together, . . . the ideas are important to the members. The white racist movement is about an idea' (Ezekiel 1995, p. xxix). Most white supremacist organizations share a number of unquestioned beliefs. They believe that races are essentially and eternally different, not only in terms of visible characteristics, but also behaviourally and culturally, and that races are ranked hierarchically based on these innate differences They believe that the white race is superior and responsible for all the advances of Western civilization. While these are the core beliefs of the movement, they also mobilize against a common threat: they believe that the white race faces the threat of genocide, orchestrated by Jews, and carried out by blacks and other non-whites. White supremacist discourse asserts that this genocidal plan is being carried out through forced race-mixing, which will result in the mongrelization and therefore the annihilation of the white race. Interracial sexuality is defined as the 'ultimate abomination' and images of white women stolen away by black men are the ever present symbol of that threat (Ridgeway 1990, p. 19). The protection of white womanhood comes to symbolize the protection of the race, thus gender relations occupy a central place in the discourse.

Because of the similarities and shared concerns of these organizations, there is a great deal of overlap among their memberships (Anti-Defamation League 1988b, p. 1; Langer 1990; Harper 1993). As Harper observes, divisions within the white supremacist movement often have more to do with personality differences and clashes than with divergences in belief and ideology (Harper 1993, p. 56).

The contemporary US white supremacist movement is part of a broader backlash against the perceived gains of equality-based social movements. As Michael Omi explains, the Civil Rights movement and the subsequent shift in racial politics ushered in a period of desegregation efforts, "equal opportunity" mandates, and other state reforms. By the early seventies, however, a "backlash" could be discerned to the institutionalization of these reforms and to the political realignments set in motion in the 1960s (Omi 1991, p. 78).

The contemporary white supremacist movement depicts these shifts as an attack on whites and has been able to attract a large number of disillusioned white people, primarily male, who now believe that their interests are not being represented. As Ezekiel suggests, 'white rule in America has ended, members feel. A new world they do not like has pushed aside the traditional one they think they remember' (Ezekiel 1995, p. xxv). As an article in *White Patriot* asserts, 'the White people of America have become an oppressed majority. Our people suffer from discrimination in the awarding of employment, promotions, scholarships, and college entrances' (*White Patriot* no. 56, p. 6).

While the contemporary white supremacist movement is concerned with re-articulating a white identity in response to the challenges of racial and ethnic social movements, this white identity is most certainly a gendered identity. The contemporary white supremacist movement is also a response to the second wave of the feminist movement and the challenges it has presented to traditional gender identities. Responding to what is perceived as a threat to both racial and gendered certainties, the contemporary white supremacist movement is primarily concerned with re-articulating white, male identity and privilege. In stark contrast to the images of active, sexually independent women put forth by the women's movement, white supremacist discourse depicts white women as passive victims at the hands of Jews and blacks, and in dire need of white men's protection.

Despite commonly held assumptions that white supremacists are uneducated, or especially hard hit victims of economic upheaval, research confirms that, like earlier incarnations of the Klan, contemporary white supremacist group members are similar to the US population in general, in terms of education, income and occupation (Aho 1990; Harper 1993; Ezekiel 1995). Additionally, there are white supremacist periodicals which target highly educated audiences (including *Instauration*, reviewed here).

Since the early 1970s a wide range of radical white supremacist organizations have been founded. In 1994 Klanwatch identified 329 white supremacist groups in existence throughout the US (Woods 1994, p. 5D). It is difficult to estimate the membership of these groups, which is often concealed. Harper suggests that the general membership in white supremacist organizations is conservatively estimated to be around 40,000, while Ezekiel reports that hard-core members number 23,000 to 25,000, another 150,000 purchase movement literature and take part in activities, and an additional 450,000 actually read the movement literature, even though they do not purchase it themselves (Harper 1993, p. 43; Ezekiel 1995). The Anti-Defamation League [ADL] estimates that fifty white supremacist periodicals continue to publish (Anti-Defamation League 1988b, p. 1).

Since the early 1980s the movement has become increasingly violent. Numerous organizations have established camps for paramilitary training, preparing members for the coming 'race war'. Tracking organizations like the ADL have provided documentation of many murders and attempted murders committed by white supremacists, culminating in the 1995 bombing of the Murrah Federal Building in Oklahoma City (Anti-Defamation League 1988b, pp. 11–15). While certain arms of the movement have become increasingly violent, other white supremacists, including the well-publicized case of David Duke, have moved further into the mainstream, entering traditional American politics.

White men make up the bulk of the membership of the movement, and serve as the writers, publishers, and editors of white supremacist discourse. Ezekiel notes that the organizations he observed remain almost exclusively male, and tasks within the organizations are strictly segregated by gender. He notes, 'a few women are around, never as speakers or leaders; usually they are wives, who cook and listen. Highly traditional ideas of sex roles, and fears of losing male dominance, fill the conversation and speeches' (Ezekiel 1995, p. xxvii). Kathleen Blee's recent work on the contemporary movement, however, documents the efforts of many organizations to recruit women into their ranks. 'As a result,' Blee suggests, 'women now play a highly visible and significant role in the racist movement, constituting about 25% of the membership (and nearly 50% of the new recruits) in some Klan and neo-Nazi groups' (Blee 1995, p. 1). I suspect that these divergent accounts suggest that women's movement into the movement is uneven, and largely dependent upon the recruitment efforts of specific organizations. Women have been targeted for recruitment by various organizations as a strategy to increase membership and help stabilize the membership by bringing entire families into the fold. The discourse of the white supremacist movement remains highly gendered and patriarchal, and it will be important and interesting for future analysts to explore if and how the discourse changes in response to the growing numbers of women in these organizations.

Deconstructing racial and gender difference

Deconstruction emphasizes that while binary oppositions present two terms as oppositional, they are, instead, interdependent; each side of the dichotomy derives its meaning from the contrast, its relationship with the other side (Derrida 1974; Weedon 1987; Scott 1988). A number of binary oppositions are central to white supremacist discourse, including male/female and white/black. According to Derrida, the binary relationship in Western thought is always hierarchical: the first terms are always accorded greater value and worth, the second terms subordinate and derivative (Derrida 1974; Scott 1988, p. 37; Hekman 1990).

The central binary opposition, however, which grounds all these others in white supremacist discourse is the difference/equality dichotomy. Throughout white supremacist discourse, race and gender are constructed as innate differences, and because binary oppositions are always hierarchized, difference in white supremacist discourse is equated with inequality. The other side of the opposition, then, is equality, which subsumes sameness. The difference/equality dichotomy recasts equality as necessarily requiring sameness, whereas difference necessarily requires hierarchy.

As Scott (1988) suggests, the difference/equality dichotomy makes certain meanings possible, and others incomprehensible. Within this discursive framework, racial and gender differences in contemporary white supremacist discourse are constructed as necessarily hierarchical, so that *any attempt to question inequality is represented as a threat to difference itself.* All arguments in support of equality are defined as attempts to erase difference and make everyone the same. An equality that recognizes differences is impossible within this framework. The difference/equality opposition is central to white supremacist discourse, and an analysis of how this dichotomy works to construct meaning will allow us to both understand and call into question this system of meaning.

Producing racial essence

While white supremacist discourse adamantly supports the notion that race is a biological and/or god-given essence, a review of the discourse reveals the *social construction* of that essence. As Diana Fuss points out, 'there is no essence to essentialism . . . essence as irreducible has been constructed to be irreducible' (Fuss 1989, p. 4). Exploring contemporary white supremacist discourse reveals the construction of race and gender as an inner essence rooted in nature and immutable.

Throughout white supremacist discourse, whiteness is constructed in terms of visible, physical differences in appearance. According to one article, true whites are Nordics, 'the thin, fair and symmetric race originating in Northern Europe' (*Instauration*, February 1980, p. 13). In another article, Nordics are described as:

> the only cleanly chiselled faces around. And there are other ways they stand out. The world's finest hair and finest skin texture are in Scandinavia. Some of the world's tallest statures, largest body size and most massive heads are also found in Northern European regions.
>
> (*Instauration*, January 1980, p. 15)

Jews are also constructed as a race in this discourse, made identifiable by physical markers such as 'long kinky curls and typical hooked nose, thick fleshy lips, slant eyes and other typical Jew features' (*Thunderbolt*, no. 301, p. 6).

A great deal of effort is put into physically distinguishing races from one another. Both the book and film entitled *Blood in the Face* take their name from some white supremacists' supposition that Jews cannot blush and only true whites show 'blood in the face' (Ridgeway 1990). Rather than revealing race as a biological essence, this discourse reveals the continued effort required to construct racial differences. Judith Butler suggests that identities are constructed through 'the reiterative and citational practice by which discourse produces the effects that it names' (Butler 1993, p. 2). The construction of identity is not a singular act or gesture but, rather, a process or performance as Butler calls it, which must be continually repeated. The construction of racial and gender difference must '*repeat itself in order to establish the illusion of its own uniformity and identity*' (Butler 1991, p. 24).

The process of repetition and reiteration which constructs race and gender also reveals the construction of these identities, thereby putting this

> identity permanently at risk . . . That there is a need for repetition at all is a sign that identity is not self-identical. It requires to be instituted again and again, which is to say that it runs the risk of becoming deinstituted at every interval. (Butler 1991, p. 24)

As we find in white supremacist discourse, even though racial identity is posited as a biological or god-given fact of nature, the definition of whiteness is in constant flux, and there is disagreement among groups and individuals over who is or is not white, and what characteristics define whiteness.

As Harper observes, 'What it means to be white and who qualifies as white, is forged within the discourse of the publications' (Harper 1993, p. 69). In some of the discourse white skin and European heritage are the only requirements to be included in the category white (Harper 1993), while elsewhere Aryans are defined as strictly *Northern* Europeans, and there is much debate on where exactly to draw the line in Europe. As one white supremacist claims in the film *Blood in the Face*, 'We're more Nazi than the Nazis were!'

Because the visible characteristics constructed as markers of race are not always evident, discerning the race of individuals is of the utmost importance. Articles such as 'Racial Tagging' in *Instauration* reveal surprises in the racial identity of public figures. As this article explains:

> Racial identification is a tricky game. As we keep our eyes open, we stumble across the most surprising information. Recently we have been looking into the Portuguese origins of public figures considered to have been solidly Northern European in racial makeup.
>
> (*Instauration*, October 1976, p. 10)

As these periodicals construct racialized subjects, they construct race as existing in nature prior to their discourse. Racial identity is constructed as an

essence within each person which merely needs to be discovered. The discovery of race, however, is the *production* of the racialized subject.

White supremacist discourse gains the authority to construct race as an
origin and essence partly through citational practices which invoke the
authority of science. Steven Seidman suggests that the power of discourse to
create normative conceptions of race derives from the extent to which it can
invoke 'the intellectual and social authority of science. A discourse that bears
the stamp of scientific knowledge gives its normative concepts of identity and
order an authority' (Seidman 1991, p. 135). Just as eugenic policies in the
early twentieth century drew upon the supposedly scientific racial studies of
anthropologists and ethnologists, contemporary white supremacist discourse
invokes the authority of science to support its political ends. Discussion of
racial difference almost always includes references to named scientists and
doctors. For example, a typical article reports that

> Dr. Audrey Shuey of Northern Illinois University states that the average
> negro has an I.Q. 15 to 20 points lower than that of an average White
> individual . . . Dr. Robert Gayre has conducted many studies which
> show that the negro brain is on the average 10 milligrams lighter than the
> White brain . . . Dr. Carlton Putnam . . . says that the convolutions and
> thickness of the suprannual layer of the negro brain cortex is 14% thinner
> than the Whites . . . Professor Donald Swan of Hattiesburg University
> states that the difference between the races is up to 75% caused by
> heredity (*The Thunderbolt*, August 1979, p. 8).

Exploring white supremacist discourse raises difficult questions regarding
just where to draw the line between white supremacist extremism and the
'mainstream'. Scientific studies of racial and sexual differences, including the
work of contemporary sociobiologists, are often cited as justification for
white supremacist goals within the discourse.

While a great amount of effort and written space is devoted to delineat-
ing physical racial differences, these physical differences are always interpreted as signifiers of deeper, underlying differences. In this discourse,
physical characteristics and culture are linked, both determined by race and
unchanging. For example, *The Thunderbolt* proclaims that

> The White Race has created and developed most of the world's present
> and past civilizations . . . responsible for almost all of the scientific,
> engineering and productive know-how that has raised the world's stand-
> ard of living . . . the only race which has been able to maintain a free
> democratic government. Liberty, justice and freedom only exist in White
> nations . . . culture, art, humanities . . . The charity and goodness of
> the White Race have time and again saved the non-White peoples of
> the world from famine and plague. The White Race in the past has

established moral codes, rules and laws, and educational systems for the advancement of society that have been unsurpassed by any other race of the world (*The Thunderbolt*, 30 May 1975, p. 8).

Additionally, this racial essence is represented as immutable. As an *NSV Report* article about Jews claims,

We fight for things that they cannot understand because of their nature; and because of their nature, they can never understand because they are aliens. Even if they changed their religion, they will not be a part of our Folk. They can never be a part of our Folk for they are aliens. They might as well be from another planet because they are not of our world. (*NSV Report*, October/December 1987, p. 1)

Because racial differences are posited as inherent, immutable essences, attempts to question, modify or change these differences are ridiculed and depicted as fruitless. For example, a *New Order* article explains,

Negroes are best suited for and succeed best in the roles of servants and entertainers. Remove the White liberal from his traditional position, that is kissing the negro's posterior, and what happens to the negro? [He] clumsily shuffles off, scratching his wooley head, to search for shoebrush and mop. In the final debate, an ape will always be an ape.
(*New Order*, September 1979, p. 14)

Similarly, a *White Power* article admonishes:

Perhaps the crudest hoax is the liberal lie of telling the Negro he's the equal of the White man and expecting to make an instant White man out of him by sending him to college, giving him a federal handout . . . Let's have the honesty and decency to recognize the Negro for what he is, and not make impossible demands of him . . . This has nothing to do with "hate" or "bigotry". I love my dog, for example, but I'm not about to recognize her as my equal (*White Power*, March 1973, pp. 3–6).

The recognition of difference, here, is depicted as merely common sense.

Within the equality versus difference framework, equality necessarily entails the denial of difference. The *National Vanguard* refers to equality as 'Man's Most Dangerous Myth' because it denies 'the essence of the inner nature' (*National Vanguard*, no. 68, p. 3). An *Instauration* article entitled 'The Hoax of all the Centuries' warns that 'the real hoax is the equalitarian hoax, the hoax of hoaxes, the universal lie that there are no differences in racial intelligence'. In order to counter this hoax, further documentation of racial differences are then provided. Within the equality versus difference framework, it is impossible to have equality while also acknowledging differences. Meaning here is constrained so that difference assumes inequality, and any attempt to increase racial equality is recast as a threat to difference.

Producing gender difference

Like racial difference, gender difference is posited as rooted in nature and biology. Throughout this discourse, great effort is made to constantly reiterate, and thereby produce the 'reality' of, sexual difference. It is common for many of the periodicals to invent new words in order to distinguish symbolically between males and females and naturalize difference. For example, there are frequent references to Jewesses, Negresses, Mulatresses, WASPesses, Shebrews, etc. (*New Order*, March 1979, p. 2; *Instauration*, December 1979, p. 13; *Instauration*, February 1981). Throughout the periodicals, female versions of words are created, exemplified by one article's reference to 'proditors and proditresses' (*Instauration*, December 1979, p. 13). As Cynthia Fuchs Epstein suggests, inventing female versions of words serves as a form of symbolic segregation, reifying gender difference (1988).

Like racial difference, gender difference is posited as not merely differences in physical and biological characteristics, but differences in character and personality as well. For example, a *White Power* article explains that 'our ancestors wisely realized that women were different from men not just biologically, but psychologically and emotionally as well. They recognized that the sexes had distinct but complementary roles to play in society . . . ordained by natural law' (*White Power* no. 105, p. 4).

The concept of gender equality, like racial equality, is ridiculed as a denial of innate differences. For example, a typical article entitled 'The One-Hemisphere Sex' wails:

They never stop beating the nurture drum! A Purdue professor recently came up with the silly notion . . . that one reason for the superior mathematical ability of boys is they "are encouraged from an early age to do activities which develop spatial performance" . . . So to eliminate the different learning capabilities that separate the boys from the girls, Dr. Wheatley tells us the latter must learn to do more cogitating with their right hemispheres. That they don't do this and have never done this has nothing to do with genetics, of course. It has been the fault of their teachers—or a residue of Paleolithic prejudice—or male chauvinism (*Instauration*, September 1979, p. 19).

This article ridicules those who refuse to accept what is posited as the simple fact that males and females are biologically different, and suggests that all other reasons for gender differences are simply excuses.

Both race and gender are constructed as immutable essences in this discourse, and they are often interdependent. Gender difference is posited as a key component of racial difference. Drawing upon the unfounded claims of nineteenth-century evolutionary theories, a number of articles point out that: 'Sexual dimorphism [the difference between the sexes] is greatest in the Caucasoids' (*Instauration*, January 1980, pp. 14–15; *Instauration*, March 1981, p. 7). Differentiation is posited as the key to advancement, and the more pronounced degree of differentiation between white men and women is read as a sign of white superiority. Similarly males are posited as more differentiated than females, establishing white males, then, as superior to white women and to non-white men and women. As one article explains, 'Sexual dimorphism is greatest in the Caucasoids. We know further that women are less varied (smaller standard deviations) on most physical components, such as height, weight and intelligence (relative brain size)' (*Instauration*, March 1981, p. 7). This matrix of differentiation perches white males firmly on top.

In addition to the degree of gender difference within each race, the differences between white and non-white females is also emphasized as a feature distinguishing the white race and signalling its superiority. The belief that white women represent the ideal of female beauty is widespread and considered common-sense knowledge in this discourse. An *Instauration* article credits '25,000 years of tough natural selection on the edge of glaciers' with producing 'these beauteous products of a very special kind of evolution . . . these magnificent-looking women' (*Instauration*, May 1981, p. 36). Further reflecting this sentiment, another article claims

> the White woman stands at the apex of beauty . . . But what about the Black woman? Alas, she is truly a pitiable creature. Whites have never found her attractive, and Blacks began to scorn her after they caught a glimpse of a White woman (*National Vanguard*, May 1979, p. 11).

Attempting to establish the permanence and immutability of these differences, another article claims

> Chinese archaeologists unearthed an ancient tomb containing a mummy of a female. They describe her as follows: "The shape of her body was extremely beautiful and she was tall. She had blond, long hair that flowed to her shoulders. On her comely face was a pair of big eyes. You could still count her long eyelashes. Beneath her high nose were her tiny, thin lips." The date of the remains indicated that gentlemen preferred blondes as early as 4480 B.C. (*Instauration*, May 1981, p. 23).

Gender is central to white supremacist discourse because the fate of the race is posited as hinging on the sexual behaviour of white women. Harper suggests that images of white women in this discourse depict them either as breeders of the race, or as traitors. They are defined solely in terms of their reproductive and sexual availability. Throughout this discourse, all discussions of interracial sexuality revolve around images of white women and black men, so interracial sexuality also represents a threat to white male authority, usurping his control over both white women and black men.

Interracial sexuality serves as the ultimate threat to racial and gender difference. Eliminating all racial differences and leading to 'mulatto zombies', interracial sexuality threatens the existence of the white race. Additionally, however, interracial sexuality is posited as a threat to gender differences. For example, an *Instauration* article depicts a fictional white survival demonstration where protestors chant:

> "Sweden is going brown." "No more Ingrid Bergman." "America is going brown." "No more Cheryl Tiegs." "France is going brown." "No more Catherine Deneuve." . . . "What is the solution?" "White separatism!" (*Instauration*, 'White survival', 1980, p. 18).

If beauty is what makes white women unique, it is threatened by race-mixing. As another article asserts, 'As the race goes, so goes beauty'
(*Instauration*, 'Black Infusions', 1980, p. 19).

Conclusion

The production of racial and gender difference is central to the project of white supremacy and the construction of race and gender are intertwined. Every white supremacist publication spends a great deal of space and effort producing and reiterating racial and gender difference. The difference versus equality framework links difference to hierarchy, that any threats to difference or hierarchy are posited as leading to sameness. Interracial sexuality serves as the central metaphor of this threat. Any movements for equality are therefore recast as threats to difference. The civil rights movement, the women's movement, and all policies designed to redress inequality are ridiculed for ignoring the 'natural fact' of difference and simultaneously perceived as a threat to white identity.

Exploring the construction of race and gender within the framework of the difference versus equality opposition reveals how meaning works in this discourse. The construction of difference within this binary framework makes certain meanings possible, while rendering other ideas incomprehensible. Within this system of meaning, equality becomes impossible to imagine, because it signifies the denial of difference. The construction of race and gender and the maintenance of inequality are necessarily linked for white supremacists, and it is therefore increasingly important that researchers explore the construction of race and gender, rather than taking these identities for granted as prediscursive realities to be studied. This analysis suggests that we cannot comprehend white supremacist racism without exploring the construction of white identity. White identity defines itself in opposition to inferior other; racism, then, becomes the maintenance of white identity. The construction of whiteness is maintained through racist and misogynist discourse.

In order to delegitimize and resist white supremacy, we must explore the construction of race and gender within the white supremacist movement as well as within our own disciplines. When researchers fail to explore the construction of race, they contribute to the reproduction of race as a naturally existing category. In representing race as a given foundation, we obscure the relations of power which constitute race as a foundation. Rather than taking race for granted, we need to begin to explore the social construction of race, and the centrality of racism and misogyny to this construction.

References

Aho, James A. 1990 *The Politics of Righteousness: Idaho Christian Patriotism*, Seattle, WA: University of Washington Press.
The Anti-defamation League of B'nai B'rith 1988b *Hate Groups in America: A Record of Rivalry and Violence*, New York.
Balibar, Etienne and Wallerstein, Immanuel 1991 *Race, Nation, Class: Ambiguous Identities*, London: Verso.
Blee, Kathleen 1991a "Women in the 1920's ku klux klan movement', *Feminist Studies*, vol. 1, Spring, pp. 57–77.
Blee, Kathleen 1991b *Women of the Klan: Racism and Gender in the 1920s*, Berkeley, CA: University of California Press.
Blee, Kathleen 1995 'Engendering conspiracy: women in rightist theories and movements', in Eric Ward (ed.), *Conspiracies: Real Grievances, Paranoia, and Mass Movements*, Seattle, WA: Peanut Butter Publishing.
Butler, Judith 1990 *Gender Troubles: Feminism and the Subversion of Identity*, New York: Routledge.
Butler, Judith 1991 'Imitation and gender insubordination', in Diana Fuss (ed.), *Inside/Out: Lesbian Theories, Gay Theories*, London: Routledge, pp. 13–31.
Butler, Judith 1993 *Bodies That Matter: On the Discursive Limits of Sex*, New York: Routledge.
Carby, Hazel 1992 'The multicultural wars', *Radical History Review*, vol. 54, Fall, pp. 7–18.
Crosby, Christina 1992 'Dealing with differences', in Judith Butler and Joan Scott (eds.), *Feminists Theorize the Political*, New York: Routledge.
Derrida, Jacques 1974 *Of Grammatology*, Translated by Gaytri Chakravorty Spivak, Baltimore, MD: The Johns Hopkins University Press.
Ezekiel, Raphael S. 1995 *The Racist Mind: Portraits of American Neo-Nazis and Klansmen*, New York: Viking.
Ferber, Abby 1995a 'Exploring the social construction of race: sociology and the

study of interracial relationships', in Naomi Zack (ed.), *American Mixed Race*, Lanham, MD: Rowman and Littlefield Publishers, Inc.

Ferber, Abby 1995b ' "Shame of white men": interracial sexuality and the construction of white masculinity in contemporary white supremacist discourse', *Masculinities*, vol. 3, no. 2, pp. 1–24.

Frankenberg, Ruth 1993 *White Women, Race Matters: The Social Construction of Whiteness*, Minneapolis, MN: University of Minnesota Press.

Fuchs Epstein, Cynthia 1988 *Deceptive Distinctions: Sex, Gender, and the Social Order*, New York: The Russell Sage Foundation.

Fuss, Diana 1989 *Essentially Speaking: Feminism, Nature and Difference*, New York: Routledge.

Goldberg, David Theo 1990 *Anatomy of Racism*, Minneapolis, MN: University of Minnesota Press.

Harper, Suzanne 1993 'The Brotherhood: Race and Gender Ideologies in the White Supremacist Movement', PhD dissertation, The University of Texas, Austin.

Hekman, Susan 1990 *Gender and Knowledge: Elements of a Postmodern Feminism*, Boston, MA: Northeastern University Press.

Higginbotham, Evelyn Brooks 1992 'African American women's history and the metalanguage of race', *Signs: Journal of Women in Culture and Society*, vol. 7, no. 2, pp. 251–274.

Hubbard, Ruth 1992 *The Politics of Women's Biology*, New Brunswick, NJ: Rutgers University Press.

Ignatiev, Noel and Garvey, John 1996, *Race Traitor*, New York: Routledge.

Langer, Elinor 1990 'The American neo-Nazi movement today', *The Nation*, July 16/23, pp. 82–107.

Morrison, Toni 1992 *Playing in the Dark: Whiteness and the Literary Imagination*, New York: Vintage Books.

Omi, Michael 1991 'Shifting the blame: racial ideology and politics in the post-civil rights era', *Critical Sociology*, vol. 18, no. 3, pp. 77–98.

Omi, Michael and Winant, Howard 1986 *Racial Formations in the United States: From the 1960s to the 1980s*, New York: Routledge.

Ridgeway, James 1990 *Blood in the Face*, New York: Thunder's Mouth Press.

Riley, Denise 1988 *'Am I That Name?' Feminism and the Category of 'Women' in History*, Minneapolis, MN: University of Minnesota Press.

Roediger, David R. 1991 *The Wages of Whiteness: Race and the Making of the American Working Class*, New York: Verso.

Saxton, Alexander 1987 *The Rise and Fall of the White Republic*, New York: Routledge, Chapman and Hall.

Scott, Joan W. 1988 'Deconstructing equality-versus-difference: or the uses of posttructuralist theory for feminism', *Feminist Studies*, vol. 14, no. 1, pp. 33–50.

Seidman, Steven 1991 'The end of sociological theory: the postmodern hope', *Sociological Theory*, vol. 9, no. 2, pp. 134–36.

Ware, Vron 1992 *Beyond the Pale: White Women, Racism and History*, London: Verso.

Webster, Yehudio 1992 *The Racialization of America*, New York: St. Martin's Press.

Weedon, Chris 1987 *Feminist Practice and Post-structuralist Theory*, Cambridge, MA: Blackwell.

Woods, Jim 1994 'Rhetoric of hate groups same, rights lawyer says,' *Columbus Dispatch*, 6 March, 5D.

Appendix: White supremacist publications

Crusader no dates 1970s Metaire, LA: Knights of the Ku Klux Klan.

The Fiery Cross 1979 Robert Shelton (ed.), Swartz, LA: The United Klans of America (UKA).

Instauration 1976–1983 Wilmot Robertson (ed.), Cape Canaveral, FL: Howard Allen Enterprises Inc.

The National Alliance Bulletin 1978–1980 William, Pierce (ed.), Mill Point, WV: National Alliance.

National Socialist 1982–1983 The World Union of National Socialists.

National Vanguard 1978–1984 William Pierce (ed.), Mill Point, WV: National Alliance.

New Order 1979–1983 Gerhard Lauck (ed.), Lincoln, NE: National Socialist German Workers Party.

The Northlander 1978 Neither the Southern Poverty Law Center nor the Anti-Defamation League have information on this publication.

NS Bulletin 1974–1983 Matt Koehl (ed.), Arlington, VA and New Berlin, WI: National Socialist White People's Party (The New Order after 1982).

N.S. Kampfruf/N.S. Mobilizer 1974–1983 Russell R. Veh (ed.), National Socialist League.

NSV Report 1983–1993 Rick Cooper and Dan Stewart (eds.), National Socialist Vanguard.

The Spotlight 1986 Willis A. Carto (ed), Liberty Lobby.

The Thunderbolt 1974–1984 J.B. Stoner and Edward Fields (eds.), National States Rights Party.

The Torch 1977–1979 Thomas Robb (ed.), The White People's Committee to Restore God's Laws, a division of the Church of Jesus Christ.

Voice of German Americans 1977–1980 editor and publisher unknown.

The Western Guardian 1980 Roanoke, VA: Western Guard America.

White Patriot 1979–1984 Thomas Robb (ed.), Knights of the Ku Klux Klan.

White Power 1969–1978 Matt Koehl (ed.), Arlington, VA and New Berlin, WI: National Socialist White People's Party.

16

Researching black Muslim women's lives

A critical reflection

by Basia Spalek*

This chapter consists of a critical reflection of a research study carried out by a white researcher documenting black Muslim women's experiences of victimisation and the management of their personal safety. It is argued that whilst some aspects of the researcher's subjectivity can be linked to marginalised, outsider positions, which helped to produce oppositional knowledge, other aspects of her self-identity served to maintain and re-produce dominant racial and cultural discourses and power relations.

Introduction

The dominance of a white, Eurocentric perspective underpinning much feminist work has been extensively documented, illustrating how black[1] women have been overlooked by the wider feminist movement, through 'gender essentialism', the view that there is a monolithic women's experience (Harris, 1997, p. 11). Although feminist research principles call for reflexivity over the research process, so that the values and characteristics of the researcher are made visible, mainstream (white) feminists have often assumed that there is no power differential between themselves and black women, since as an oppressed group they have not viewed themselves as also being likely oppressors, even though black feminist researchers have accused them of adopting theoretical positions and research strategies that take a racist perspective and reasoning (Amos & Parmar, 1997; Collins, 2000).

This paper consists of a critical reflection of a research study that was carried out by a white woman researcher wishing to add diversity and

* Basia Spalek is a Lecturer in Community Justice Studies at the University of Birmingham. She can be contacted at the Institute of Applied Social Sciences, University of Birmingham, Muirhead Tower 11th Floor, Edgbaston, Birmingham, B15 2TT, UK. Tel: +44 121 415 8027; Email: B.Spalek@bham.ac.uk

specificity to a research area dominated by the documentation of white women's experiences. Muslim women living in Britain, of Pakistani and Bangladeshi heritage, were interviewed at length and questions were asked about the management of their personal safety. The findings of this study have been documented elsewhere (Spalek, 2002). Three phases of the research project will be looked at in some detail, these being the sampling, interviewing and analysis stages. By using the notion of 'reflexivity' that is common to feminist research, this paper will explore the nature of the researcher's subjectivity and its influence over the research process. Whilst some aspects of the researcher's self that can be linked to marginalised, outsider positions, helped to produce oppositional knowledge, other aspects of her self-identity served to maintain and re-produce dominant power relations. This ultimately resulted in a research project which, despite attempting to document difference, stressed similarity between different groups of women. This study highlights the multitudinous and situated nature of self-identity, which can significantly influence data collection and analysis. Although western scientific authority has encouraged and legitimated binary, oppositional, either/or categories (Collins, 1998), one can be both oppressor and oppressed, as the following article will outline.

Black feminist critiques of western feminism

In questioning the many taken-for-granted assumptions underpinning so-called scientific, objective work, which failed to take into account gendered experiences, feminist work has made a substantial contribution to social scientific research. However, the dominance of white, middle-class analyses in feminist work is well documented:

> Much of the work undertaken in the 20th century by feminists was still in English and had largely been written for white, middle-class authors and readers . . . The global hegemony of western feminism, together with its access to the tools of cultural imperialism, has meant that its conceptualisation of world territory and of women's issues has tended to be very narrowly and parochially perceived. (Afshar & Maynard, 2000, p. 809)

The invisibility of 'whiteness', whereby being white is not regarded as being a racial identity and a particular lens through which the world is viewed and experienced, but rather, is considered to be what is 'normal', 'neutral' or 'common-sense', has meant that western feminists have ignored, misrepresented and misunderstood black women's lives. The notion of a monolithic 'women's experience' has been predominant, so that black women have been viewed as only women, and their experiences of racist structures viewed as being part of black men's experiences:

> We are rarely recognised as a group separate and distinct from black men, or as a present part of the larger group 'women' in this culture. When black people are talked about, sexism militates against the acknowledgement of the interests of black women, when women are talked about racism militates against a recognition of black female interests. When women are talked about the focus tends to be on white women. Nowhere is this more evident than in the vast body of feminist literature.
>
> (hooks, 1982, p.7)

This has been underpinned by a research approach whereby white researchers have rarely acknowledged differences between themselves and the women that they research. Where difference has been acknowledged in feminist work, black writers point out that difference has often been viewed negatively, so that racist conclusions have been made in which black women's liberation is seen to come from the adoption of western values, for example, by the entry of women into waged labour (Aziz, 1997; Carby, 1997; Collins, 2000). Even when difference is viewed positively, white women's lives and the norms that govern those lives occupy a central position against which black women's experiences are compared and analysed (hooks, 1990). Harris (1997) refers to this as the 'nuance approach' in which white researchers claim that they can be sensitive to differences between women by offering statements about 'all women' in general but qualifying these with the particularities of experience of specific groups of women, these often appearing in footnotes.

A white perspective governs what kind of research is conducted and how it is interpreted and white women 'become the norm, or pure, essential Woman' (Harris, 1997, p. 14). When black women have struggled to voice their hidden experiences and to create new narratives, white feminists have viewed these purely through the framework of racism, thereby maintaining their hegemony within the women's movement (hooks, 1990). The interconnected sources of black women's oppression, relating to structures of race, gender and class, have thereby been unexamined by white feminism (Carby, 1997). Black women writers and researchers have, particularly since the 1980s, produced a large volume of work about their lives, suggesting that feminism must increasingly contend with the heterogeneity of women. However, many argue that this has had little impact upon mainstream academic disciplines, with black women remaining invisible and silenced (Bolles, 2001; Collins, 1998; McClaurin, 2001).

A study about black Muslim women's 'fear of crime'

The impetus for the study presented in this paper arose from a realisation that although feminist work has made a substantial contribution to the 'fear of crime' debate in criminological and other social scientific arenas, revealing that underpinning women's anxiety about crime is a fear of sexual danger posed by male intimates, acquaintances and strangers (Kelly, 1988; Stanko, 1990, 2002), feminist analyses have insufficiently taken into account the notion of difference. As a result, little is known about the specific anxieties (and their meanings) of specific groups of women, particularly those who have different cultural, religious and racial heritages from those of 'mainstream' British society. This study was an attempt to introduce greater diversity and specificity into feminist work on women's fear of crime. It is also important to note that national crime surveys, which explore crime-related anxiety, tend to use very general categories when classifying minority ethnic groups, so that important religious and cultural differences are thereby omitted (Spalek, 2002).

Ten Muslim women living in the Birmingham area who wear the Hijab were interviewed at length and questions were asked about their personal safety, their views on crime and any experiences of victimisation. The reason for choosing women who veil to take part in the study was that the researcher was interested in documenting the role that veiling plays in the management of the women's personal safety. Veiling is a symbol of Islam, a physical signifier of difference, so that these women might become targets of hate crime. At the same time, the researcher wanted to explore the role of the Hijab in terms of women's lives in relation to men. The women who were interviewed were aged between 19 and 30. The interviews were conducted between May 2001 and December 2001 and thus the terrorist attacks in the US of September 11th took place whilst the research project was being carried out. These attacks had serious repercussions upon Muslim communities around the world, and many individuals were attacked (and killed) or subjected to abuse, and mosques also became the targets of hate crime. The interview data therefore also include the women's experiences of harassment and violence in the aftermath of September 11th. The following quotation is an example of how some Muslim women changed their behaviour as a result of an increased perceived and actual threat following September 11th:

> During the first few days after the attack on America my family was very cautious. My mother began to pick me up from work as I work in the city centre and when I am going home I pass by many pubs and clubs where people go to spend their evenings. My mother was also wary that the people whom I work with might also become prejudiced, but thankfully this has not happened . . . The event has definitely changed the way my family and I move around. My mother avoided going into central town to shop until she had no choice. (Spalek, 2002, p. 64)

The Muslim women's anxiety was explored and the multifaceted aspects to veiling recorded, including the Hijab as liberational since many of the women argued that the Hijab frees them from the male (sexual) gaze:

If you take that away from the equation, the women's body, that's one
less thing for men. If they do look at you they are not looking at you in a
bad sense, they're looking at you because of what you are wearing as in a
scarf or a veil. (Spalek, 2002, p. 68)

The importance of exploring the researcher's subjectivity in the research process

Feminist research principles call for reflexivity over the research process, this
being seen as a key way of ensuring rigorousness and reliability when carrying out research. The fallacy of so-called value-neutral or objective research
has been exposed and feminists have successfully claimed that the beliefs and
behaviours of social scientists influence the perception and documentation of
social experience. As a result, it is considered to be important to articulate the
often hidden values and characteristics of the researcher and their impact on
the research process so as to enable the research to be fully scrutinised
(Edwards & Ribbens, 1998; Harding, 1987).

Work carried out by black critical feminists particularly illustrates the
multitudinous nature of subjectivity, since black women's lives are marked by
a multitude of race, class and gender positions, thereby highlighting the
multiplicity of subject locations and the simultaneity of oppression that can
be experienced:

> Those of us who live on the margins of society have always embodied
> multiple roles, straddled multiple social arenas, negotiated multiple
> effects of power and fashioned multiple identities to survive.
>
> (McClaurin, 2001, p. 55)

The notion of 'double consciousness' has been raised, highlighting how distinct aspects of self can co-reside, and so as well as there being aspects of the
self linked to marginalised positions, there may also be parts of the self
that can be linked to the perpetuation of centres of power (Collins, 1998;
McClaurin, 2001). This suggests that different aspects of a researcher's self-
identity will influence the research process at different times. Exploring which
aspects of self-identity become dominant during research and examining the
impact that these aspects have on the study being undertaken can enhance
our understanding of the relationship between self-identity and research, and
can highlight the micro-processes involved in perpetuating dominant knowledge constructions and power relations. The following account of a research
study that was carried out by a white researcher examining black Muslim
women's lives illustrates how different aspects of self were played out by
the researcher during the course of the study, some of these serving to perpetuate dominant knowledge constructions, thereby marginalising minority
experiences.

Sampling decisions: deciding which black Muslim women to interview

A subject position that I held throughout the research study, and which had a significant impact upon the sampling approach that was taken, was that of the 'western researcher'. According to Collins (1998), western scientific discourse has created the illusion of binary oppositions, so that human differences have been viewed simplistically in opposition to each other. My sampling approach resembles this compartmentalised view of the world, since I operated according to the binary of 'free choice' versus 'no choice'. I tried to target women to take part in the study who, in my point of view, were likely to have 'freely chosen' to wear the Hijab. For me, 'free choice' meant that the women were under no pressure from their families and wider communities to veil but rather, had decided to do so for themselves. Women attending the university at which I was based were asked to take part in the study, the rationale here being that these women were less likely to experience patriarchal authority at home, and, being educated, were more likely to belong to an increasing number of young Muslim people in Britain who resort directly to the Qur'an and hadiths as a resource in Islam rather than accepting the traditional views passed on to them from their parents (Joly, 1995). Preliminary discussions were conducted with Muslim female students and those women who talked about veiling in relation to their own interpretations of Islamic doctrine were selected to take part in the study.

However, in pursuing the approach outlined above, rather than valuing Muslim women's lives, I served to perpetuate a demonised Other. This is because by constructing the binary opposition free choice/no choice this served to perpetuate dominant western misrepresentations of Islam, relegating the 'no choice' side of the binary to a deviant, oppositional Other. A more sensitive approach would have been to interrogate western perceptions of 'free choice' and to explore how Muslim women understand 'choice' in relation to veiling. A particularly worrying aspect of this discussion is how unquestioningly, subconsciously even, I assumed that concepts readily in use in my own everyday life, and in wider western society in general, were applicable to documenting the experiences of black Muslim women. I would argue that professional western training in social scientific research methods fails to sufficiently encourage researchers to critically explore the inherent biases in the socially constructed worldviews that underpin research. An approach that asks questions about the researcher's place in an academic discipline's intellectual discourse should be actively pursued (Edwards & Ribbens, 1998; McClaurin, 2001).

A focus upon the emotions experienced by a researcher as they carry out their work can help to illuminate her/his subject positions. An emerging body of feminist work considers emotionality to be a central part of documenting and examining the nature of the researcher's subjectivity (see Pickering,

2001). Traditionally, this form of introspection has not been pursued, amid concerns that researchers who explore their feelings might attract accusations of 'unhealthy absorption' or 'emotional exhibitionism' (Pickering, 2001, p. 486). Nonetheless, this work suggests that by analysing emotionality, there is the potential to reveal hidden decision-making processes which can be linked to power hierarchies inherent in research (Pickering, 2001). As part of this process, researchers examine the emotions that they experience as they carry out their work. The emotions that are identified are then used as markers which can help reveal aspects of both the researcher's and participants' biographies that have a significant, if hidden, effect upon the research process. By reflecting upon the emotions that I experienced as I interviewed black Muslim women, I found that this helped to illuminate the multitudinous nature of my subjectivity and its influence over the research process, as will be outlined below.

Emotionality when interviewing black Muslim women

The semi-structured interviews took place at locations convenient to the participants, on university premises and also in quiet cafes in Birmingham city centre. The women's reasons for veiling, their feelings of personal security and their experiences of victimisation were explored and recorded on a tape recorder, and then later transcribed. Edwards (1993) writes that many feminist researchers have claimed that a special woman-to-woman connection exists between female researchers and female interviewees, enabling interviewees to disclose personal and sensitive information. Nonetheless, Edwards (1993) questions this claim, arguing that divisions between women in terms of race and/or class can undermine any such link or understanding.

After reflecting upon the feelings that I experienced as I interviewed the women, and after reading through the interview transcripts, it is clear that I was engaged in 'emotion management' (Williams & Bendelow, 1998), whereby I tried to suppress some emotions whilst actively encouraging others. The emotions that I experienced as I conducted the interviews related to my positions of being a 'woman', being 'white' and being a 'western academic' and my interaction with the interviewees. Uncomfortable feelings, such as guilt and anxiety, were suppressed whilst other, more reassuring and comforting emotions were pursued. Negative emotions arose from my position of 'white' 'western' researcher. Having never experienced racial abuse myself, it was difficult to know how to approach the issue of racial violence with the interviewees, as I had no personal experience to draw from which could be used to increase rapport. At the same time, I felt acutely aware of my privileged racial position over the interviewees, where being white is 'constituted in opposition to its subordinate other, the not-white, the not-privileged' (Lewis & Ramazanoglu, 1999, p. 23). This deep-rooted awareness of racial privilege, one which wasn't openly acknowledged but which nevertheless influenced how I felt as I conducted the interviews and therefore influenced the data that I gathered, can be linked to the racial structuring of my material environment. I can remember a number of instances whereby I have occupied a racially privileged position, for example, as a teenager taking the bus to school and seeing white pupils verbally and physically abuse black pupils. Rather than intervening and helping the black students, however, I was relieved that I was not the object of such violence. These sorts of experiences have shaped my 'white' identity, leaving behind complex feelings towards racial Others (see Frankenberg, 1993).

As a feminist researcher, struggling against patriarchal power, it is difficult to acknowledge that women can, as well as being oppressed, be oppressors. Mama (1996) cogently argues that violence against women is not intrinsically 'male', as many white feminists have portrayed, but rather, white women (as well as white men) have participated in race attacks. As a feminist researcher, I was extremely uncomfortable with the notion that due to my white identity I might belong to the category of oppressor. So I focused upon an aspect of my identity that I could claim constituted 'the oppressed', which means that instead of examining the racial dimensions to the interviewees' lives, I directed the line of questioning towards the women's general experiences of violence from men. This means that although I recorded some instances of racial abuse, these were not explored in any depth as I did not use 'follow-up' questions to enable the women to elaborate further upon these experiences.

I was also acutely aware of my position as 'western academic' and of the negative stereotyping of Muslims in western discourses. Many white, non-Muslim social commentators and journalists have propagated false images of Islam, and so the interviewees may have viewed me as being a part of this 'white, western, establishment', and so may not have fully revealed their experiences to me. Moreover, due to the verbal and physical abuse suffered by Muslim communities in the aftermath of the September 11, 2001 terrorist attacks, the interviewees may have distrusted my interest in their lives, which means that although I documented some examples of the women's post-September 11th worries, I cannot be sure how adequately and thoroughly I did this. As Gorelick (1991, p. 464) observes, 'a subject population does not tell the truth to those in power'.

Through 'emotion management' I also suppressed the cultural and religious dimensions to the black interviewees' lives. This can be illustrated by the following example. One of the interviewees argued that:

> I used to get approached quite a lot before, hassled on the street by men pointing and shouting names and all that sort of stuff. But since I've worn the veil I've not had any problems. None at all, absolutely none, it's been two years. I mean even in the street when I used to walk down I used

to get Asian men whistling or pointing fingers or whatever it was and I haven't had that since two years.

(Quoted in Spalek, 2002, p. 61)

As can be seen above, this woman clearly refers to the abuse she suffered from Asian men, yet my subsequent questioning did not explore why in particular this woman highlighted that it was Asian rather than white men that were bothering her. Researchers have previously cautioned against constructing the lives of people of different ethnicities as being deviant or bizarre (Maynard, 2002). My fear of 'otherising' the research subjects, as well as my wish to emotionally 'bond' and establish rapport with them, led me to stress the commonalities of experience of the interviewees as women. In doing so, however, my work can be criticised on the basis that I insufficiently captured the ethnic and cultural aspects to these women's lives. Yet as Mama's (1996) work on domestic violence against black women shows, there is often a specific cultural context to the violence, as in the case, for example, where some men use religion to assert their control over women. Perhaps one way of avoiding stigmatising Muslim communities when documenting the abusive aspects of some Muslim women's lives would be to carry out a project that examines the experiences of a wide range of women from many different cultures, including white women's experiences, so that women's plight as a result of the actions of men would not appear to be solely a 'Muslim issue'. This type of cross-cultural approach has the added advantage of enabling researchers to document how certain experiences are shared across different communities, as well as allowing for differences to be acknowledged (Maynard, 2002).

In contrast to the anxiety that I felt in my position of white 'western' academic, I drew comfort from my position as 'woman', due to feeling an intimate connection with the interviewees with respect to the issue of men. National and local crime surveys reveal that actual and potential harassment and violence from men frames many women's lives (Kelly & Radford, 1998; Mooney, 2000; Stanko, 2002). I have, for example, encountered many difficult and frightening situations with men. I have been called abusive names by men, I have experienced physical and sexual intimidation, and indeed, a whole array of disturbing instances has punctuated my life. These situations have left behind strong emotions. It is these emotions that I used to help me to establish rapport with the interviewees and to uncover and record their anxiety about men, as the following transcript data illustrates:

Most women, I mean if I was walking down a dark alley and I saw a man I would instantly feel scared, I'd fear for my life. Most women feel like that. It's always in the back of your mind. Even in the daytime not necessarily in the dark so I do have that fear all of the time.

(Quoted in Spalek, 2002, p. 58)

Williams and Bendelow (1998, p. xvi) define emotion as 'existentially embodied modes of being which involve an active engagement with the world and an intimate connection with both culture and self'. Williams and Bendelow (1998) argue that not only do emotions reflect individual experience, but also, they point to the reproduction of wider social structures. Through my emotional management, I would suggest that I was reproducing the invisibility of black women in feminist discourses, thereby maintaining the hegemony of white feminism. Being 'white' involves existing in a structurally located position of oppressor, a position that is rarely identified and acknowledged, its invisibility helping to reproduce racism. I would argue that through managing my emotions I was reproducing racist structures:

> In a racially hierarchical society, white women have to repress, avoid and conceal a great deal in order to maintain a stance of 'not noticing' colour.
> (Frankenberg, 1993, p. 33)

By pursuing reassuring feelings during the interview situation, feelings which were linked to my position of 'woman', this led me to stress the commonalities of experience between the black Muslim interviewees and women in general. This would suggest that in cases where a researcher claims to have an affinity with her research interviewees she may be engaged in 'emotion management', either consciously or subconsciously. This means that she may be overlooking important differences between herself and her research subjects and instead stressing their similarities so as to avoid uncomfortable feelings. This then becomes part of the process of feeling:

> Emotions always involve the body; but they are not sealed biological events. Both the act of 'getting in touch with feeling' and the act of 'trying to feel' become part of the process that makes the feeling we get in touch with what it is. In managing feeling, we partly create it.
> (Hochschild, 1998, p. 11)

This would suggest caution when claiming any kind of 'rapport' or 'understanding' between the researcher and the research participants. Comfortable feelings may be the product of successful emotional management rather than any valid relationship between interviewer and interviewee. At the same time, it is also important to note the cultural dimension to the articulation of emotion, since according to Hochschild (1998), people draw upon an 'emotional dictionary' in order to articulate their feelings, this dictionary being culture-dependent:

> Each culture has its unique emotional dictionary, which defines what is and isn't, and its emotional bible, which defines what one should and should not feel in a given context. As aspects of 'civilising' culture they

determine the predisposition with which we greet an emotional experience. They shape the predispositions with which we interact with ourselves over time. Some feelings in the ongoing stream of emotional life
we acknowledge, welcome, foster. Others we grudgingly acknowledge
and still others the culture invites us to deny completely.

(Hochschild, 1998, p. 7)

A wide range of emotions is likely to be experienced during a research study,
and so cultural and social factors will influence how comfortable a researcher
is with experiencing and acknowledging certain feelings. Emotion management can take place not only during an interview situation but also in the
write-up of a study, when decisions (conscious and subconscious) are made
regarding which feelings the researcher decides to reflect upon and how
those feelings are re-presented. Particularly negative emotions may be filtered
out from the write-up of research studies, due to their powerful potential of
revealing aspects of our subjectivities and power positions that we dislike.
Hollway and Jefferson (2000) use the psychoanalytic theory of Melanie Klein
to argue that the researcher, as well as the participant, is a 'defended subject',
meaning that the self is forged out of unconscious defences against anxiety.
When reflecting upon a research project, then, researchers may be avoiding
addressing the particularly difficult or uncomfortable emotions that they
experience. So the nature of the researcher's subjectivity and its influence
upon the research process may never be sufficiently exposed or analysed.

Some researchers advocate an approach in which participants should be
given a greater role in the research process by allowing them to express their
emotions and views about taking part in a particular study. Special characteristics of race, class, gender and so forth influence the nature of the relationship between researcher and the researched and so it is argued that it would
be useful to explore how research participants view the researcher and the
likely impact of this on the study (Edwards, 1993). However, this stance is
problematic if, as Collins (1998) cogently argues, a collective secret knowledge can be found in marginalised groups, which is only shared in private,
away from the surveillance of elite groups. So in terms of the study set out in
this paper, it is debatable whether or not the black Muslim women would
have shared their perceptions of the research process with me, and whether
they would have openly expressed any views that they might have of me in
terms of my representing an elite that serves to commodify difference rather
than create oppositional knowledge.

Analysing the interview data generated by black Muslim women

Turning now to the data analysis stage of the research project outlined in this
paper, again I faced certain challenges and dilemmas. Many of the women
who were interviewed argued that the Hijab frees them from the male gaze:

> I think I'm dressing like this because I don't trust men but also I feel
> confident and comfortable in my clothes . . . I think that most men, all
> men are like potential rapists. You can't trust any man, I wouldn't trust
> them. (Quoted in Spalek, 2002, p. 58)

Some women believed that by veiling they reduced their risk of being the
victims of harassment or physical or sexual assault:

> It gives me a sense of that maybe they won't attack you because I am
> covered. (Quoted in Spalek, 2002, p. 59)

Looking at western feminist accounts of women's management of their personal safety, it has been argued that under the dominant system of male
heterosexuality, women stand before the male panoptical gaze (Bartky,
1998). Certain expectations are therefore placed on women in terms of how
they look and how they behave, which in turn translate into women's self-
policing. Women who do not conform to the expected behaviour of the Good
Woman to avoid harassment and violence from men may be judged as
undeserving of societal protection (Stanko, 1997, p. 486). Feminist writers
seek to challenge the ways in which society holds women responsible for
men's behaviour, arguing that it is men's behaviour that needs to be changed
(Dobash & Dobash, 1998).

When trying to analyse the data generated from the interviews that I
conducted, my first reaction was to see if I could frame the women's accounts
within the literature outlined in the above paragraph. So one interpretation of
the interview data could be that these women wear the Hijab as a result of
community expectations about how they should dress, since they have
internalised community values regarding how the Good Woman should
behave in order to avoid physical and sexual violence. Indeed, a study by
Ghazal Read and Bartowski (2000) illustrates how some Muslim clergy and
Islamic elites prescribe veiling as a custom in which 'good' Muslim women
should engage as they are held responsible for their families' honour. However, I was uncomfortable in interpreting the women's accounts in this way,
as by solely focussing upon the role of societal and cultural traditions in
Islamic practices, this would ignore the centrality of faith. For many followers
of Islam, the Qur'an is the actual word of God that was recorded by
Muhammad during the early part of the seventh century (Watson, 1994).
For many followers of Islam, there is thus a legitimate, moral authority
upon which the lives of men and women are based. In the Qur'an women
are told:

> And tell the believing women to lower their gaze and guard their mod-
> esty, and not to display their adornment, except that which ordinarily
> appears thereof; and to draw their veils over their necks and bosom,

and not to reveal their adornments except to their own husbands, fathers (24: 31). (Yacub, 1994, p. 32)

And:

> O Prophet, tell your wives and daughters and the believing women, that they should cast their outer garments over their persons (when out of doors): That is most convenient, that they should be known (as such) and not molested (33: 59). (Yacub, 1994, p. 32)

The representation of female and male sexuality in the Qur'an and the responsibility placed upon women to manage men's behaviour means that issues of personal safety cannot be separated out from their religious beliefs (Spalek, 2002). Thus, one of the interviewees in the study reported in this paper argued that:

> If you present yourself in a way that is not very modest then in a way you're making them (men) cause sin of looking at you with bad intentions so if you protect yourself you protect them from sinning.
> (Quoted in Spalek, 2002, p. 60)

It seemed inappropriate, therefore, to utilise western feminist frameworks to make sense of these Muslim women's lives, as by referring solely to societal traditions and expectations this would serve to undermine the authority of the Qur'an and the importance of faith. Indeed, the women taking part in my study agreed with the differences between men and women that are set out in the Qur'an, arguing that in many situations these distinctions serve to empower women. My findings thus echo Afshar and Maynard's (2000) contention that:

> Muslim women have contested the mainstream feminists' quest for equality, arguing instead for the need to achieve a balanced gender complementarity . . . They have used the theological basis of Islam to carve their own path towards freedom . . . They have argued that Islam, as a religion, has always had to accommodate women's specific needs. Islamist women have chosen to reject some of the most important goals of mainstream western feminism. (Afshar & Maynard, 2000, p. 811)

This illustrates the potential danger of trying to frame the voices of particular groups of women within a dominant academic discourse. Edwards and Ribbens (1998) argue that women's voices may be silenced or misunderstood through the utilisation of academic disciplinary procedures and categories. Yet they also maintain that a researcher must inevitably translate research participants' stories in order to present them in a way that is understandable to a Western audience. In order to minimise the potential for re-shaping and re-defining participants' experiences, Edwards and Ribbens (1998) suggest that it is important to listen carefully to participants' accounts. This would suggest the need for western feminists to adopt a greater sensitivity when learning about the lives of women who occupy other standpoints. This is both time-consuming and demanding work. One of the most challenging aspects of the study reported here was attempting to understand Islamic beliefs. Meeting the interviewees on more than one occasion in order to discuss religious doctrines and practices was particularly helpful.

Although the interview data produced themes that were common to many of the interviewees, the generalisability of my work was limited due to the heterogeneity of people who follow Islam, and the many different schools of Islamic thought that exist (Joly, 1995). This means that I felt I should try to avoid making knowledge claims about Muslim women in general. Nonetheless, adopting such a relativistic stance proved to be problematic as certain oppressive structures frame many Muslims' lives. For example, Islamophobia was heightened in the aftermath of the September 11th attacks, and so I would argue that generalising about how Muslim women's lives had been affected after the terrorist atrocities could serve as an important political tool to gain adequate responses to the women's plight. This illustrates the political power in highlighting the shared experiences of groups of women, so that using a wholly relativistic position is undesirable, a point which has also been argued by other researchers like Moi (1990) and Luff (1999), and demonstrated by critical black feminists (Collins, 1998; McClaurin, 2001).

Conclusion

This paper suggests the need for increased reflexivity over the nature of a researcher's subjectivity and its relationship to research, since the discussions featured here illustrate the complex, multitudinous and situated nature of self. Adopting a feminist methodological and political position is insufficient in protecting against biases from critically influencing a research study, and consideration must be given to aspects of self that are linked to the perpetuation of dominant structures of knowledge. This article further highlights the limitations of western feminist critiques when applied to cultures different from mainstream western society. It illustrates the need for the development of analytical tools which are culturally sensitive and which do not evolve around western feminists' understandings of patriarchy and female empowerment. Finally, when interviewing research participants who hold different racial, ethnic and cultural positions, the researcher needs to be sensitive to the possibility that due to their (conscious or subconscious) wish to establish rapport with the interviewees, they may be overlooking, or insufficiently exploring, importance aspects of the interviewees' lives, aspects which are linked to racial/religious/cultural/class power hierarchies of which the researcher may be a part. The researcher therefore needs to critically reflect upon their 'emotion management' during the interview situation and in the subsequent write-up of a study.

Note

1   The term 'black' used in this article takes Mirza's (1997, p. 3) approach as consisting of the shared space of postcolonial migrants of different languages, religions, cultures and classes through the shared experience of racialisation and its consequences.

References

Afshar, H., & Maynard, M. (2000). Gender and ethnicity of the millennium: From margin to centre. *Ethnic and Racial Studies*, 23(5), 805–819.

Amos. V., & Parmar, P. (1997). Challenging imperial feminism. In H. Safia Mirza (Ed.), *Black British feminism: A reader* (pp. 54–62). London: Routledge.

Aziz, R. (1997). Feminism and the challenge of racism. In H. Safia Mirza (Ed.), *Black British feminism: A reader* (pp. 70–77). London: Routledge.

Bartky, S. (1998). Foucault, femininity, and the modernisation of patriarchal power. In R. Weitz (Ed.), *The politics of women's bodies* (pp. 25–45). Oxford: Oxford University Press.

Bolles, A. (2001). Seeking the ancestors: Forging a black feminist tradition in anthropology. In I. McClaurin (Ed.), *Black feminist anthropology* (pp. 24–48). London: Rutgers University Press.

Carby, H. (1997). White women listen! In H. Safia Mirza (Ed.), *Black British feminism: A reader* (pp. 45–53). London: Routledge.

Collins, P. (1998). *Fighting words*. Minneapolis: University of Minnesota Press.

Collins, P. (2000). *Black feminist thought: Knowledge, consciousness, and the politics of empowerment* (2nd ed.). London: Routledge.

Dobash, R., & Dobash, R. (1998). Violent men and violent contexts. In R. Dobash & R. Dobash (Eds.), *Rethinking violence against women* (pp. 141–168). London: Sage.

Edwards, R. (1993). An education in interviewing: Placing the researcher and the research. In C. Renzetti & R. Lee (Eds.), *Researching sensitive topics* (pp. 181–196). London: Sage.

Edwards, R., & Ribbens, J. (1998). Living on the edges: Public knowledge, private lives, personal experience. In J. Ribbens & R. Edwards (Eds.), *Feminist dilemmas in qualitative research* (pp. 1–24). London: Sage.

Frankenberg, R. (1993). *The social construction of white women, whiteness race matters*. London: Routledge.

Ghazal Read, J., & Bartowski, J. (2000). To veil or not to veil? A case study of identity negotiation among Muslim women in Austin, Texas. *Gender & Society*, 14(3), 395–417.

Gorelick, S. (1991). Contradictions of feminist methodology. *Gender & Society*, 5(4), 459–477.

Harding, S. (1987). *Feminism and methodology*. Milton Keynes: Open University Press.

Harris, A. (1997). Race and essentialism in feminist legal theory. In A. Wing (Ed.), *Critical race feminism* (pp. 11–18). London: New York University Press.

Hochschild, A. (1998). The sociology of emotion as a way of seeing. In S. Williams & G. Bendelow (Eds.), *Emotions in social life* (pp. 3–15). London: Routledge.

Hollway, W., & Jefferson, T. (2000). *Doing qualitative research differently*. London: Sage.

hooks, b. (1982). *Ain't I a woman: Black women and feminism*. London: Pluto Press.

hooks, b. (1990). *Yearning race, gender and cultural politics*. Boston: South End Press.

Joly, D. (1995). *Britannia's crescent: Making a place for Muslims in British society*. Aldershot: Avebury.

Kelly, L. (1988). *Surviving sexual violence*. Cambridge: Polity Press.

Kelly, L., & Radford, J. (1998). Sexual violence against women and girls. In R. Dobash & R. Dobash (Eds.), *Rethinking violence against women* (pp. 53–76). London: Sage.

Lewis, B., & Ramazanoglu, C. (1999). Not guilty, not proud, just white: Women's accounts of their whiteness. In H. Brown, M. Gilkes, & A. Kaloski-Naylor (Eds.), *White? Women* (pp. 23–62). York: Raw Nerve Books.

Luff, D. (1999). Dialogue across the divides: Moments of rapport and power in feminist research with anti-feminist women. *Sociology*, 33(4), 687–703.

Mama, A. (1996). *The hidden struggle: Statutory and voluntary responses to violence against black women in the home*. London: Whiting & Birch.

Maynard, M. (2002). Studying age, 'race' and gender: Translating a research proposal into a project. *International Journal of Social Research Methodology*, 5(1), 31–40.

McClaurin, I. (2001). Theorizing a black feminist self in anthropology: Toward an auto ethnographic approach. In I. McClaurin (Ed.), *Black feminist anthropology* (pp. 49–76). London: Rutgers University Press.

Mirza, H. (1997). Introduction: Mapping a genealogy of black British feminism. In H. Mirza (Ed.), *Black British feminism: A reader* (pp. 1–28). London: Routledge.

Moi, T. (1990). Feminism and postmodernism: Recent feminist criticism in the United States. In T. Lovell (Ed.), *British feminist thought* (pp. 60–84). Oxford: Blackwell.

Mooney, J. (2000). *Gender, violence and the social order*. London: Palgrave.

Pickering, S. (2001). Undermining the sanitized account; violence and emotionality in the field in Northern Ireland. *British Journal of Criminology*, 41, 485–501.

Spalek, B. (2002). Muslim women's safety talk and their experiences of victimisation: A study exploring specificity and difference. In B. Spalek (Ed.), *Islam, crime and criminal justice* (pp. 50–71). Devon: Willan.

Stanko, E. (1990). *Everyday violence: How men and women negotiate their personal safety*. London: Pandora Press.

Stanko, E. (1997). Safety talk: Conceptualising women's risk assessment as a technology of the soul. *Theoretical Criminology*, 1(4), 479–499.

Stanko, E. (2002). Searching for the meaning of violence: The limitations of theory and data in our understanding of violence. In E. Stanko (Ed.), *Violence*. Dartmouth: Ashgate.

Watson, H. (1994). Women and the veil: Personal responses to global processes. In A. Ahmed & H. Donnan (Eds.), *Islam, globalisation and postmodernity* (pp. 141–159). London: Routledge.

Williams, S., & Bendelow, G. (1998). *The lived body: Sociological themes, embodied issues*. London: Routledge.

Yacub, A. (1994). The woman must veil herself but not so the man. Defend the case of Islam. In *Muslim students scholarship awards* (pp. 25–58). London: Fosis the Islamic Foundation.

17
Criminology and orientalism
by Anita Kalunta-Crumpton

Introduction

Mainstream criminological knowledge as we know it is reflective of a western view of the social world. It represents a hegemonic position of western conceptualisation of crime, criminality and criminal justice. What the dominant criminological enterprise is slow to represent is a process of doing criminology from the standpoint of 'others' outside the West. For one, the voice of Africa and Africans is a long way short of being embraced into the centre of the defining process of western criminology, which fundamentally assumes a divide between the definer and the defined. These two categories mirror firstly, the dominant position of those who define as represented in the western perspective and secondly, the subordinate position of those (that is, non-westerners) who are recipients of definitions popularly pursued in criminological inquiry. It is an arrangement that builds on concepts of race and which transcends domestic boundaries to reach global parameters. Within the domestic context, this divide cannot manifest itself any better than in the ways in which race has been dissected within academic analyses of crime. In North America and Western Europe for example, 'race', a term inundated with negative meanings, is commonly utilised to apply to non-whites. More revealing of this racial demarcation is the position of people of African descent as often the subject of inquiry in debates about crime. For instance, to study race and crime is to fundamentally explore such issues as the patterns and causes of black peoples' engagement in criminal acts; to study race in law enforcement is to primarily parade black people's encounters with agencies of the criminal justice system. Regardless of any differences in objectives embraced in such debates, whether it purports to establish a conservative or a radical or a liberal stance, the race-specific approach normally features the existence of a problem worth examining and defining. Addressing race therefore is particularly about analysing, defining and understanding the 'problematic' of blackness.

As already noted, the influential place of hegemony in criminological approach to studying black people is not confined to scenarios in western societies but can also be transposed onto situations outside the West, that is in 'black' societies across the globe (Cain, 2000). This of course is not to claim that criminology holds much positive interest in pan-African issues outside the West. Western criminological interest in 'black' societies in Africa and the Caribbean, for instance, is very limited perhaps due to a belief that these societies have nothing worthwhile to contribute to international comparative criminological research. Such belief could naturally stem from a historical backdrop of white hegemony through which western criminology has itself tended to adopt an absolutist position in defining pan-African issues against western perspectives and standards. As such, any conceptions that black societies have nothing useful to offer criminology can seem to coincide with centuries of ethnocentric viewpoints, which have defined and still define various facets of 'blackness' as inferior to the superior whiteness of the West. It is from this standpoint that we can relate to criminological neglect of, and/ or 'interest', in people of African descent around the world.

This chapter firstly presents a review, by no means exhaustive account, of criminology's relationship with issues relating to people of African descent. It draws attention to the place of race in the criminological journey from the classical period to contemporary times, and in doing so, demonstrates the intersection of theory and practice. And as a case study, it reviews the workings of the UK (United Kingdom) criminal justice system to exemplify the practical significance of criminology *vis-à-vis* race. Secondly, the chapter searches for a criminology, which exists outside the dominant western framework, and concludes by calling for a criminological recognition of pan-African concerns, particularly from the point of view of people of African descent around the globe.

Understanding crime and justice

Criminology developed principally out of western culture and therefore it is reflective of western perspectives. From classical to postclassical criminologies, the place of people of African descent in the range of criminological endeavours has varied in significance. Classical perspectives and their core notions of social contract, utility and rationality held principles that displayed no direct application to race. Explicit questions of race started to arise in the 19th century with the development of positivist criminology and its scientific approach to the study of criminal behaviour. Under this criminological stance, popularly associated with the Italian school founded by Cesare Lombroso, it was claimed that criminal behaviour was biological determined (Lombroso, 1876; Ferri, 1895). By linking crime to certain physical characteristics, Lombroso concluded that criminals were genetic throwbacks to more primitive forms of human species, which he referred to as *atavistic*.

This conclusion drew upon his study of criminals in which he observed that criminals shared many anatomical similarities with savages and non-whites. Examples of those physical similarities were voluminous ears, receding forehead, fleshy lips, darker skin colour, small skull, and thicker and curly hair. Lombroso's ideas were widely received and influential. As Garland (1985) observed, positivist criminology 'developed from the idiosyncratic concerns of a few individuals into a programme of investigation and social action which attracted support throughout Europe and North America' (cited in Roshier, 1989, p.20).

The positivist theories that differentiated the 'criminal type' from the 'noncriminal type' were premised on assumptions of superior and inferior races representing white and non-white races respectively. For one, the principles of biological positivism were centrally beneficial to Europe's move towards the colonisation of the supposed inferior non-white territories following the end of the slave trade in the 19th century. Slavery itself had thrived on notions of white racial superiority articulated by European philosophers of 'The Age of Reason' (Eze, 1997). The belief that intelligence, reason and civilisation can only be found among the white race justified the subjection of Africans to hostile and savage slave labour since as was perceived, their stupidity, lack of intelligence and indolence meant that they were not suited for anything requiring the application of reason (Walvin, 1971, 1973; Fryer, 1984). Biological positivism was greatly influenced by biological evolutionary theories upheld by theorists such as Charles Darwin. Darwin's (1859) *On the Origin of Species* and his concepts of *natural selection* and *the survival of the fittest* not only implied a natural divide between superior and inferior races. It also denounced contact between the two for fear of contamination of the former by the latter. For the 'superior' race to therefore maintain its purity and superiority, it must resist any forms of threat of racial degeneration. Those assumptions were utilised to justify the need for colonialism and the subordination of the 'lower' races in Africa, the Caribbean and elsewhere; they were linked to the idea of trusteeship, which also underlined the philosophies of colonial domination by the 'superior' race.

Within western nations in North America, Europe and elsewhere, the establishment of the eugenics movement founded by Francis Galton towards the latter part of the 19th century (Galton, 1869; Goring, 1913) was to pave the way for the practical implications of Darwin's theory of natural selection. The fundamental mission of the eugenics movement to purify the genetic stock of the white race had from the late 19th century entailed formulating ways of causing the extinction of social categories, defined as socially unfit, undesirable and of low intelligence, through selective breeding. Essentially this involved preventing those 'inferior' categories from reproducing as exemplified in the programme of involuntary sterilisation practised in southern states of the United States (US). Among those included in the eugenicists' list were black people (Miller, 1997). Incidentally, the eugenics movement gained a great deal of its strength from the growing interest in the relationship between crime and intelligence amongst North American and European psychologists. Works on intelligence testing popularly claimed that intelligence was not only biological and fixed but was also related to criminality whether directly or indirectly (Goddard, 1912, 1914; Jensen, 1969; Eysenck, 1971; Hirschi and Hindelang, 1977; Wilson and Herrnstein, 1985).

The implications of these observations for race have been more obvious than not. Psychologists have used IQ scores to uphold the view that white Americans have by far more superior intelligence than their African-American counterparts. And this difference in intelligence is largely attributed to genetic differences between the two groups. Relatedly, differences in crime rates between African-Americans and European-Americans have attracted explanations within this intelligence-biology framework, with the overall argument linking the perceived low IQ among African-Americans to the recorded higher crime rate for this racial group (Gordon, 1976; Hirschi and Hindelang, 1977). Despite the fact that the IQ-race-crime studies stood to invite an array of controversial debates and criticisms (Kamin, 1977), including evidence of methodological shortcomings such as the lack of clarity and consensus as to what IQ scoring measures, and the influence of cultural bias on IQ tests, it is a line of thought that has resurfaced in recent years. Herrnstein and Murray's (1994) book, *The Bell Curve* is a recent reminder of the IQ controversy. The authors reiterated that intelligence is largely a biological factor; that differences in IQ scores coincide with differences in class and racial origins; and that crime and delinquency are conversant with low IQ.

Both Lombrosian biological positivism and its offshoot, psychological positivism, locate the causes of crime in the individual. Notwithstanding the sensitive nature of these theories, their philosophies of individualising crime continue to surface. Explicitly and implicitly, race continues to be a part of this process of understanding criminal behaviour. Such racial influence is further illustrated in the conservative theory of the *underclass*, another major individualistic approach to crime (Murray, 1984, 1990). Here, the underclass are identified by their 'culture of poverty' caused because they possess certain 'unconventional' cultural features (that of poverty), which are passed on from one generation to another, and which prevent them from taking advantage of available opportunities to escape poverty. Such cultural features, which include above all illegitimacy and single-parenthood, unemployment and welfare-dependency, and crime, are commonly found amongst the lower-class sections of society. In the United States, these are known to be largely composed of African-Americans and Hispanics; in Britain, the 'emerging underclass' can include black communities (Murray, 1996).

Alongside psychological explanations of crime, Lombroso's legacy of positivism also evolved into various social theoretical strands that have overtly or covertly manifested the race ingredient in our understanding of

crime and criminality. The Chicago School's influential social disorganisation theory demonstrates a strong relationship between crime and poorer
areas of society. Referred to as the *zones in transition*, those 'crimogenic
areas', often occupied by immigrant populations including high numbers of
African-Americans, were characterised by low levels of social integration,
high levels of socio-economic deprivation and relatedly high rates of crime
(Shaw, 1929; Shaw and McKay, 1942). Merton's (1938) anomie and strain
theory, also influential, focused on the crime-producing effects of social
structural factors. His central argument sees crime as a product of problems
of *strain* that arise out of a disjunction between culturally defined goals and
the legitimate means of achieving those goals. Herein, the lower class is
clearly predicted to be more likely to resort to crime as a response to situations of anomie and strain caused by the contradiction between the two
elements. This prediction is even more apparent for black and other visible
minority ethnic communities given their higher levels of socio-economic
deprivation across nations in North America and Europe, for example
(Sampson and Wilson, 1995; Massey and Denton, 1993; Commission on
Systemic Racism in the Ontario Criminal Justice System, 2000; Brown,
1984; Penal Affairs Consortium, 1996).

Notwithstanding the notable shift of positivist accounts of criminal
behaviour from the 19th century individualistic theories to the 20th sociological perspectives, race has remained a significant feature, particularly in its
implicit connection to the class basis for understanding criminality. Within
the series of attack on sociological positivism that emerged in the middle of
the 20th century and other subsequent criminological advances that were
to follow, the impact of race has been felt. Like the practical illustration of
the individualistic approaches instanced in the eugenics movement, the
sociological pursuits and their offshoots have also had practical implications
for race.

Sociological theory and implications for race, crime and criminal justice with particular reference to the United Kingdom

By the 1950s, the sociological aspect of criminology developed in the United
States had started gathering influence in the United Kingdom (Tierney,
1996). The US impact showed itself more clearly in the popularity that the
North American subculturalist tradition had gained in the UK sociological
studies of crime during the 1950s and 1960s. The specific area of interest to
UK subcultural theorists was the delinquency of lower-class youth (Mays,
1954; Morris, 1957; Downes, 1966), and in this endeavour, the primary
focus of UK subcultural theories was white working-class males. Not only
was the cultural context of black youth's actions relatively marginalised in the
literature but also what existed, as Hobbs (1997, p.811) observed, tended 'to
be presented in terms of its relationship to the police, as a social problem,

rather than as an entity in its own right; a courtesy afforded to white youth, whose every stylistic nuance was pored over by academics'. Implicit in Hobbs' observation is that while UK criminological interest in black youth was relatively insignificant at the time, the black presence was generally felt in other more powerful discursive sites such as the political, media and criminal justice arenas. For example, societal reactions to the urban disorders of the post-1945 period symbolised race within the various images that brought together issues of black immigration, inner-city deprivation, and law and order in political and popular discourses (Solomos, 1988, 1993). At those influential discursive levels, the descriptions of black people as a 'problem' also harboured potential and actual practical implications for this racial group, especially in terms of policing and other criminal justice responses to crime (Hunte, 1966; Humphrey and John, 1971; Humphrey, 1972).

The relatively minimal recognition assigned to issues relating to black people and crime in sociological criminology started to change towards the late 1970s when academic concerns about police-black community relations and black over-representation in crime figures started to grow and attract importance (Hall et al., 1978; Demuth, 1978). Until the 1990s when the compilation of arrest statistics assumed a national status following the intro-duction of section 95 of the 1991 Criminal Justice Act, information on arrest figures had since the late 1970s been gleaned from London-based arrest data put together by the Metropolitan Police. Findings from those series of arrest data show arrest rates for black people to be disproportionate in comparison to the London population and also to be higher than that for other racial groups in every category of offence. For example, under the now defunct 'sus'[1] law, arrest figures for 1975 showed that black people comprised 40.4% of all 'suspected persons' arrests in the London Metropolitan District; in 1977 and 1978, the 'sus' arrest figures for blacks were 44% and 43% respect-ively (Roberts, 1982; Demuth, 1978). Moving into the 1980s, the problem of black disproportionate presence in crime figures had become a crucial debat-able subject in sociological questions about crime and criminal justice. The 'race and crime' debate as it is commonly termed welcomed the dominant influence of sociological criminology, which by the 1960s was supposed to have severely marginalised the influence of biological positivism. It was an inquiry principally pursued by the disparate approaches taken by critical criminology/sociology and left realism. The former highlights the impact of race and criminalisation on the black crime rate, and in doing so prioritises the role of micro- and macro-level processes of racialisation of crime through which racial imageries associating black people with crime are constructed (Gilroy, 1987a, 1987b; Centre for Contemporary Cultural Studies, 1982). Conversely, the latter underplays the place of race by centralising the role of class in attempts to understand black crime figures (Lea and Young, 1984).

This latter approach seemed to have received more recognition at least within 'administrative' or 'governmental' criminology due to its tendency to lean towards the cause-and-effect positivist paradigm of mainstream criminology. By advancing the argument that the marginalised and disadvantaged socio-economic position of black people is consistent with high black offending and invariably reflective of the high black crime rate, left realism adopts the stance of sociological positivism. Doubtless, the black community suffers an adverse and complex form of socio-economic marginalisation not experienced by other racial groups (Oppenheim, 1993; Penal Affairs Consortium, 1996). Given theoretical justifications, stemming from the strain theories put forward by Merton (1938), Cohen (1955), and Cloward and Ohlin (1960) for locating crime prevalence amongst those at the lower-end of the social strata, left realism sees black people as making the crime choice in response to their deprived socio-economic circumstances (Lea and Young, 1984, 1993). To denounce allegations of racism levelled against it by critical theorists, left realism referred to the high crime victimisation rates experienced by the black community, arguing that the majority of crime is both intra-racial and intra-class. Even though this perspective acknowledges the wider influence of structural factors such as the role of the political economy and racial discrimination on the black community's socio-economic situation, it nonetheless conceptualises and promotes elements of individual pathology by somewhat shifting blame of racial discrimination away from influential criminal justice apparatuses.

These left realist conceptions imply that crime figures are accurate indicators of offending rates. In effect, discretionary powers of stop and search accorded the police bear no racially based impact on the high black arrest rate or on other policing decisions around cautioning, charging and bail. This is despite the preponderance of evidence pointing to the determining role of race at various stages of policing – from stop and search (Willis, 1983; Jones et al., 1986; Skogan, 1994) to charging decisions (Landau, 1981; Landau and Nathan, 1983; Commission for Racial Equality, 1992; Home Office, 1998). At other stages of criminal justice, the race effect is undermined by invoking the class framework not simply in its causal link to criminality but also in how it constitutes a strong determining ingredient in criminal justice practices relating to bail and sentencing decisions, for instance. Within this context, legally-provided decision-making criteria such as employment and status of residence are claimed to disadvantage black people in light of their overall marginalised socio-economic position (Crow and Simon, 1987; National Association for the Care and Resettlement of Offenders (NACRO), 1993).

The class context of understanding black people's encounters with the criminal justice system and its seemingly primary objective to wholly or partly dismantle the race factor that often grounds accusations of discrimination is evident across western nations. This approach is not confined to academic circles but can also be found amongst other powerful discourses and practices. In Canada where black people are also over-represented in arrest and prison figures (Commission on Systemic Racism in the Ontario Criminal Justice System, 2000), the class explanation, whether as a precursor to crime or as an integral part of criminal justice decision-making, is known to find significant favour among criminal justice officials. The US crime figures also present the disproportionate presence of people of African descent, particularly for drug offences (Lusane, 2000). Popular attempts to dissect this problem have also drawn on intersections of race, class and crime. For example, Steffensmeier and Demuth (2001, p. 152), having summarised some of the negative and criminal stereotypes of African-Americans, point out that amidst the stereotypical images, 'black offenders are socio-economically disadvantaged and are presumed to lack the resources they need to thwart the imposition of legal sanctions . . .' They add:

> For these reasons, the lack of resources, coupled with attributions that associate black offenders with a stable, enduring predisposition to future criminal activity or dangerousness, is thought to increase sentence severity for black defendants.

Clearly, theorising the black deprivation-crime connection in the UK context has placed some explanations on the wider structural political, social and economic forces, which produce socio-economic inequality, and which in turn leads to crime (Pitts, 1986; Scarman, 1981). Some others have explicitly individualised the link by adopting the 'blaming the victim' approach. The latter, popular within administrative criminology, exhibits notions of conservative theory outlined above. According to Ryan (1976), such an individualistic approach is often used to hide the injustices suffered by the marginalised sections of society. For people of African descent, one notable instance of the 'blaming the victim' strategy is shown in alleged handicaps in black families. In the UK, explanations for black youth involvement in unlawful acts have made strong references to the supposed failure of the black family to adequately socialise their young ones due principally to the high numbers of single-parent families within this racial group. Black families have been known to make up the highest percentage of one-parent households (see Hall, 1989) headed by a black woman (Chigwada, 1991). The perceived failure of the black family to instill fatherly responsibilities in black males is viewed as a pathological characteristic and an expression of family breakdown – features which are seen to sit comfortably with criminality and subsequent involvement with the criminal justice system. Furthermore, as single parents, black women are believed to violate the traditional English family structure and values.

To a significant extent, such notions about black women are evidenced to influence their encounters with the criminal justice system (Chigwada, 1991; Chigwada-Bailey, 1997; Agozino, 1997) where they, like their male counterparts, are over-represented in relation to crime figures (Home Office, 1993, 1998). The disparity that unfavourably confronts black men in the criminal justice process is also witnessed, albeit doubly, by black women who are disadvantaged by their gender position as women and their racial background as black. Black women face greater likelihood of being subjected to police suspicion, stopped and searched, denied a police caution and arrested than their white counterparts (Chigwada-Bailey, 1997; Agozino, 1997). At other stages in the criminal justice process, black women's experiences of differential and discriminatory treatment is evident. They face a higher possibility of being refused bail but instead remanded in custody; their chance of receiving a custodial and a lengthier prison sentence is higher than that of their white counterparts in similar circumstances (ibid.). This picture of black females' (and other minority females') relationship with the criminal justice system is by no means unique to the UK as Sudbury (2002, pp.59–60) highlights:

> Aggregate rates of increase in prison populations under-represent the impact of the prison boom on black women, women of colour and indigenous women. In all the countries mentioned above (which are Britain, Australia and Canada, *my emphasis*), oppressed racialized groups are disproportionately represented. For example, in New South Wales, while all women's imprisonment increased by 40% in five years, aboriginal women's incarceration increased by 70% in only two years. In Canada, aboriginal people comprise 3% of the general population and 12% of federal prisoners . . . African Canadians are also disproportionately policed, prosecuted and incarcerated . . . In the U.S., Latinas and African-American women make up 60% of the female prison population. And despite their small numbers in the population, Native Americans are ten times more likely than whites to be imprisoned . . . Finally 12% of women prisoners in England and Wales are African-Caribbean British passport holders compared to 1% of the general population . . .

Very important to note is that foreign nationals charged or sentenced for drug importation largely influence the disproportionate presence of black women in prisons in western societies such as the UK and the US. In June 1997, black foreign nationals made up 80% of the UK female foreign nationals serving a prison sentence for a drug offence (Home Office, 1998). In the US, the war waged on drugs has had a disproportionate impact on black women from around the globe, who serve longer sentences in US prisons than their white counterparts. As Sudbury (2002, p.60) states: 'The crisis of women's prisons can . . . be read as a crisis for black women and women of colour worldwide'.

Clearly, the US-led war on drugs, which emerged in the 1980s is one of the most glaring contemporary endeavours by the West to extend and impose a western-initiated crime and justice agenda on non-western societies. Assigning blame on the drug trafficking role of non-western nations for the drug problem of the West has been a popular and highly favoured political rhetoric in the drug war demonstrated in North America and Britain in particular (Green, 1998). The Jamaican 'yardie', the Colombian 'cartel' and the Nigerian drug baron/courier instance popularised images of drug trafficking as an imported phenomenon. These images are translated into practical implementations of repressive punitive measures, especially aimed at drug traffickers from the Caribbean, West Africa, South America, Asia and those of visible minority ethnic groups resident in western societies, despite the fact that a vast number of them are located at the bottom-end of the drugs trade (Green, 1998; Lusane, 2000).

Outside the domestic scene, the West's influence is instanced in the use of US-led foreign policies to coerce drug producer and transit countries into complying with the West's drug policy. Green (ibid.) refers to how the West's economic assistance to such countries has tended to balance against their performance in fighting the West's drug war. Responsibilities assigned to drug producer countries have included eradicating and replacing drug crops with alternative 'licit' crops; for transit countries such as Nigeria, their duty is concerned with strengthening their domestic drugs law enforcement policy and practice in order to control international drug trafficking. Nowhere in the drug war agenda is significance given to the drug victimisation experiences of non-western societies. The link between the drug trade and the devastating effects of the strained political economy of the developing world on its people has not been of concern to the West (ibid.). Similarly, the drug-related health plight of people of African descent is insignificant in the West's drug policy agenda. According to Lusane (2000), there is a high number of drug-related HIV/AIDS cases in Caribbean societies, similar to the situation in the US where great numbers of African-Americans are affected by the spread of HIV and AIDS caused by intravenous drug use. A similar scenario is also seen to affect blacks in other societies such as sub-Saharan Africa. Meanwhile, the situation of people of African descent as victims of the drug problem is a fact that is sidetracked in the ongoing global drug war that makes them a convenient scapegoat.

Overall, the recognition accorded the position of black people as victims of crime is one that is far outweighed by the relevance given to their perceived position as perpetrators of crime in western societies. This is demonstrated in other forms. Take for example the issue of racial violence and harassment in the UK. The sequence of political responses to white perpetration of racial violence and harassment towards minority ethnic groups is one of the glaring illustrations of how black peoples' experiences of victimisation tend to be relegated to the bottom of political priorities. Despite the fact that incidents of racial attacks on black and other visible minority ethnic groups had become obvious as far back as the early 20th century (Gordon, 1983; Hiro,

1992), and had shown a dramatic increase by the 1990s (Hesse et al., 1992; Virdee, 1995), political intervention was insignificant. According to Solomos (1993, p.192), the 'nature of the response to racial attacks both by the government and the police for most of the past decade' remained 'low key'. This, he adds:

> . . . contrasts sharply with the oft-expressed views of the police and government on the criminal activities of young blacks, and the amplification of images of black crime in the popular media on an almost daily basis. By contrast, the policy response to racial attacks and related phenomenon has been muted and at worst non-existent.

Although the legislative intervention in the form of the 1998 Crime and Disorder Act has given significant recognition to this problem, it was a legislative transition that owed a great deal to the widely publicised 1993 racist murder of the black youth, Stephen Lawrence. This incident was sustained at the centre of official and political controversy due principally to the perseverance of the Lawrence family. Across the Atlantic, the relative neglect of black victimisation is evident. For example, in the US this can be illustrated in the way cases of rape victims are interpreted within the context of race and gender. Rapes by black men on white women are more likely to be reported, to be dealt with seriously in the legal process, and to attract extensive publicity (Cuklanz, 1996; Chancer, 1998). Such black-on-white rapes 'are most likely to result in severe prison sentences . . .' (Ferraro, 1989, p.156). Conversely, the victimisation of black women receives no such recognition (Chancer, 1998).

Criminology beyond the West?

Criminology originated, survives and prospers on a western platform. Relatedly, understandings of crime and justice have found favour from that angle. Amidst this scenario is a pan-African viewpoint, which is yet to gain significant recognition within mainstream frameworks of western criminology. This is despite the advent of postmodernism and its denunciation of universalism. While the pan-African voice in a western domestic context can be said to be struggling to be significantly heard, that which is based outside the West seems to be almost excluded from the criminological pursuit. Under these circumstances, pan-African issues are popularised from a non-African perspective, which itself is primarily western, absolutist and hegemonic in its interpretations.

Cain's (2000) paper on *Orientalism, Occidentalism and the Sociology of Crime* offers some illuminating illustrations of the above scenario. In a critique of western criminology and its 'hegemonic tendencies', she analyses the orientalist and occidentalist orientations adopted in western criminology towards crime and justice interpretation at a global level. Whilst orientalism negativises and/or idealises the practices and cultures of non-western nations, occidentalism 'presumes the "sameness" of key cultural categories, practices and institutions' (p.239) and denies the existence of a difference. The policy, economic and scholarly implications of information based on these approaches for both the informers and the recipients are unveiled by Cain who on the basis of research-based data drawn from the Caribbean preaches the importance of giving recognition to diversity in its own right. Thus, included in Cain's (2000, p.258) advice to criminologists are:

– avoid orientalism in both its negative and its romantic guises . . .

– avoid occidentalism, both in its denial of difference and in its self regarding interpretation of all difference as resistance . . .

– encourage the capacity to see the Other as her own subject; use other people's writings about their situation to feed into improved abstractions . . .

Of particular interest to this essay is Cain's detailed illustration and analysis of the issue of occidentalism, which I see as the most apparent and a major driving force behind the hegemonic ideals of criminology. By way of example, Cain refers to issues of 'age', 'victimization and poverty', and 'community safety and neighbourhood watch' to show the theoretical and practical representations of occidentalist criminology in the Caribbean context. In doing so, she observes that these concepts are not cultural universal entities. The points of difference between the Caribbean and the West include: (1) the relationship between age and crime is different, and show that unlike the West, the crime rate in the Caribbean is lower among young people; (2) unlike western societies where crime victimisation (including personal and household crimes) is shown to be prevalent amongst the socio-economically deprived, the Caribbean situation shows crime victimisation to be more evident amongst the higher income groups; and (3) the Caribbean agenda for neighbourhood watch is informal in practice with no links to a state agency unlike the more official neighbourhood watch scheme practised in the West.

The reasons for the differences lie principally with the differences in the societal contexts within which those entities occur. However, as Cain importantly points out, these are differences that have been ignored in western occidentalist models upon which Caribbean discourse and practice towards crime and justice have *themselves* rested. For example, the Caribbean response to crime victimisation is that which thrives on 'the export of a model of community policing based on an inappropriate presumption of the generalizability of western victimization patterns' (ibid., p.245). Those 'western victimization patterns' allege the greater vulnerability of the deprived and this theory consequently amounts to the over-policing of the deprived in the Caribbean crime scene.

What Cain describes as 'hegemonic tendencies' of occidentalist (and orientalist) criminological discourses are rooted in a historical backdrop of ethnocentric conceptions of white superiority and non-white inferiority. As partly shown in earlier sections above, those images were useful to the slave trade and colonialism. To most people, slavery and colonialism have been and gone. But in reality their practical embodiments are still lingering, albeit indirectly, in the form of neocolonialism. And criminology is no exception to exposure to this new form of colonialism. Neocolonial criminology not only sidetracks diversity at both domestic and global levels but it also has the tendency to impose its mainstream definitions upon those whom it aims to define. This has, for instance, meant that within the domestic settings of western nations, critical approaches to the treatment and experiences of black people in the criminal justice system have often been met with those popular responses which overtly or covertly construct black people as *the problem*. Broadly speaking, either that the lable on black people as 'the problem' is justified in biological and psychological terms as an inherent quality, or it is interpreted in sociological terms, which tend to patronise or pathologise their circumstances. The latter stance invokes, for example, the class status and single-parent arguments as justifications while the IQ account can exemplify the former. Herein, no significant interest seems to be assigned to black people of middle-class background, those in stable coupled relationships or those with 'high' IQ levels, who in any case are also susceptible to the theoretical and practical ramifications of these negative lines of thinking (Kalunta-Crumpton, 2000).

In her essay entitled *The Color of Crime: External and Internal Images*, Russell (2000) provides some description of the absence of a divide and rule strategy in analyses of black criminality. With reference to the US, she narrates how the amount of media focus on crime committed by a minority of black people far outweighs the recognition given to the law-abiding black majority. As she argued, statistical inferences often claim that 'one in three young black men is under the jurisdiction of the criminal justice system', and in so doing 'what . . . goes unacknowledged is that if 33.3% are in the justice system, then 66.7% are not' (p.19). But what do we know about the '66.7%'? Russell appropriately states that the black 'noncriminal majority is an untapped resource' (p.25); this category is 'frequently overlooked as a resource for analyzing crime and justice issues' (p.19). Instead, familiar images of black people, which have surfaced uppermost in race-crime debates, regardless of western geographical boundaries, are reflected in portrayals such as 'inherently criminal', 'aggressive', 'anti-authoritarian', 'violent', 'threathening' and 'dangerous'. Such labels, which sometimes accompany anti-racism campaigns by black people, serve to promote what

Cain (2000) describes as occidentalist 'interpretation of all differences as resistance'. Through ongoing reproductions of such representations in both theoretical and practical criminological concerns, this common trend in understanding the position of black people has tended to abnormalise and subordinate their differing standpoint.

Examples abound to unveil hegemony in criminology's attitude towards pan-African issues in the western scene. The global context of hegemonic criminology is an extension of the situation in the West, and is seemingly more damaging principally because its occidentalist approach sustains and thrives on the relative absence of western awareness, or even western denial of alternative non-western theorising. In fact, from the outset of contact between Europeans and Africans on the coasts of Africa, cultural relativity was denied by scholars, travellers and traders alike amidst their ignorant assumptions of a cultural universal premised on western ideals. Thus, while Africans were besotted with their physical features and cultural make-up, Europeans in contrast described and treated those characteristics with contempt (Husband, 1982). Alleged sexual abnormality ascribed to polygamous relationships in Africa and the Caribbean, and the interpretation of African traditional religion as heathenism instance negative representations that dominated European ideological constructions of Africans (Walvin, 1973; Barker, 1978) and subordinated any relevance of cultural difference and diversity. Although more subtly, contemporary times have carried on this traditional line of reasoning about African issues including attempts to ignore them. Within the discipline of criminology, the relative absence of non-western African experience is a further sign of western apathy towards difference. This is not to say that the African experience has nothing productive to offer mainstream western criminology.

Interestingly, while it seems that ethnocentrism about difference is a western creation and a right specific to the West, the fact remains that it is not. Non-western societies hold racially-based ideologies differentiating them from others. Fenton (1999, p.85) cites Dikotter (1992, p.5) as stating that 'every civilisation has an ethnocentric world image in which outsiders are reduced to manageable spatial units'. Referring to the Chinese, Dikotter narrates how as far back as the 8th century, the Chinese viewed non-Chinese as barbarians; white Europeans were defined as 'deathly white' with sub-human physical qualities (Fenton, 1999). Such ethnocentric views are also found in Africa as revealed in the following two observations:

> As early as 1621 one writer told of the 'jetty coloured' negroes, 'who in their native beauty most delight, / And in contempt doe paint the Divell white' (cited in Husband, 1982, p.45).

> Unlike the Afro-Caribbean, the West African did not undergo a traumatic uprooting nor did he suffer the indignity of slavery. Hence he had

not developed the feeling of 'intimate enmity' towards the British the Afro-Caribbean had. He did not suffer from the anxiety and neurosis about his colour that was part of the Afro-Caribbean subconscious. He did not wish to be white, nor was he a product of a 'white-based' society. Indeed, in his culture white was the colour of death. He did not suffer from self-contempt, nor did he wish to run away from his past. Quite the contrary. West Africans were rooted in their past and their own socio-cultural tradition (Hiro, 1992, p.65).

These instances demonstrate the crucial significance of cultural relativity and the existence of a strong African cultural base from which alternative theorising can emerge, and influence western criminology and related disciplines. It is now a question of whether criminology is willing to tap into that culture as a resource in its own right.

Conclusion

Relegating pan-African experience to the margins of criminology crucially deprives the mainstream the opportunity to benefit and learn from the culture of Africans, and especially its origins in Africa. The African continent presents a very fertile ground with rich and interesting information that criminologists around the globe can utilise with a view to broadening and enhancing their theoretical and empirical knowledge. To achieve this would mean dismantling the hierarchical structuring of differences in order of their normality and abnormality; refraining from undermining the importance of difference in its own right; and refraining from simply studying and presenting 'other' subjects as passive recipients of definitions. Instead criminology needs to aim at encompassing *all* as active expressions in criminological definitions.

In short, Cain's (2000) suggestion for 'interactive globalization, rather than hegemony' for the purpose of 'mutual and reciprocal learning' captures an important way forward for criminology.

Note

1   Refers to the arrest of a person under s.4 and s.6 of the 1824 Vagrancy Act for loitering in a public place with intent to commit a crime.

References

Agozino, B. (1997), *Black Women and the Criminal Justice System*, Ashgate, Aldershot.
Barker, A. (1978), *The African Link*, Frank Cass, Britain.
Brown, C. (1984), *Black and White Britain*, Heinmann, London.
Cain, M. (2000), 'Orientalism, Occidentalism and the Sociology of Crime', *British Journal of Criminology*, vol. 40, pp.239–260.

Centre for Contemporary Cultural Studies (1982), *The Empire Strikes Back*, Hutchinson, London.

Chancer, L. (1998), 'Gender, Class and Race in Three High-Profile Crimes', in Miller, S. (ed.), *Crime Control and Women*, Sage, London.

Chigwada, R. (1991), 'The Policing of Black Women', in Cashmore, E. and McLaughlin, E. (eds), *Out of Order*, Routledge, London.

Chigwada-Bailey, R. (1997), *Black Women's Experiences of Criminal Justice*, Waterside Press, Winchester.

Cloward, R. and Ohlin, L. (1960), *Delinquency and Opportunity*, Free Press, New York.

Cohen, A. (1955), *Delinquent Boys*, Free Press, New York.

Commission for Racial Equality (1992), *Cautions v. Prosecutions: Ethnic Monitoring of Juveniles by Seven Police Forces*, Commission for Racial Equality, London.

Commission on Systemic Racism in the Ontario Criminal Justice System (2000), 'Racism in Justice: Perceptions', in Neugebauer, R. (ed.), *Criminal Injustice*, Canadian Scholars' Press, Toronto.

Crow, I. and Simon, F. (1987), *Unemployment and Magistrates' Courts*, NACRO, London.

Culkanz, L. (1996), *Rape on Trial*, University of Pennsylvania Press, Philadelphia.

Darwin, C. (1859), *On the Origin of Species, The Works of Charles Darwin*, vol. 15, John Murray, London.

Demuth, C. (1978), *'Sus': A Report on the Vagrancy Act 1824*, Runnymede Trust, London.

Dikotter, F. (1992), *The Discourse of Race in Modern China*, Hurst and Co., London.

Downes, P. (1966), *The Delinquent Solution*, Routledge and Kegan Paul, London.

Eysenck, H. (1971), *Race, Intelligence and Education*, Temple Smith, London.

Eze, E. (1997), *Race and the Enlightenment*, Blackwell, Oxford.

Fenton, S. (1999), *Ethnicity*, Macmillan, London.

Ferraro, K. (1989), 'The Legal Response to Woman Battering in the United States', in Hamner, J., Radford, J. and Stanko, B. (eds), *Women, Policing and Male Violence*, Routledge and Kegan Paul, London.

Ferri, E. (1895), *Criminal Sociology*, Fisher Unwin, London.

Fryer, P. (1984), *Staying Power*, Pluto, London.

Galton, F. (1869), *Hereditary Genius*, Macmillan, London.

Garland, D. (1985), 'The Criminal and his Science', *British Journal of Criminology*, April.

Gilroy, P. (1987a), *There Ain't No Black in the Union Jack*, Hutchinson, London.

Gilroy, P. (1987b), 'The Myth of Black Criminality', in Scraton, P. (ed.), *Law, Order and the Authoritarian State*, Open University Press, Milton Keynes.

Goddard, H. (1912), *The Kallikak Family: A Study in the Heredity of Feeble-Mindedness*, Macmillan, New York.

Goddard, H. (1914), *Feeblemindedness*, Macmillan, New York.

Gordon, P. (1983), *White Law*, Pluto, London.

Gordon, R. (1976), 'Prevalence: The Rare Datum in Delinquency Measurement and its Implications for the Theory of Delinquency', in Klein, M. (ed.), *The Juvenile Justice System*, Sage, Beverly Hills, California.

Goring, C. (1913), *The English Convict*, Home Office, London.

Green, P. (1998), *Drugs, Trafficking and Criminal Policy*, Waterside Press, Winchester.

Hall, S., Critcher, C., Clarke, J., Jefferson, T. and Roberts, B. (1978), *Policing the Crisis*, Macmillan, London.

Hall, T. (1989), 'Black People, Crime and Justice', in Russell, E. (ed.), *Black People and the Criminal Justice System*, The Howard League for Penal Reform, London.

Herrnstein, R. and Murray, C. (1994), *The Bell Curve*, Free Press, London.

Hesse, B., Rai, D., Bennet, C. and McGilhrist, P. (1992), *Beneath the Surface: Racial Harassment*, Avebury, Aldershot.

Hiro, D. (1992), *Black British White British*, Paladin, London.

Hirschi, T. and Hindelang, M. (1977), 'Intelligence and Delinquency: A Revisionist Review', *American Sociological Review*, vol. 42, pp.572–587.

Hobbs, D. (1997), 'Criminal Collaboration: Youth Gangs, Subcultures, Professional Criminals, and Organised Crime', in Maguire, R., Morgan, R. and Reiner, R. (eds), *The Oxford Handbook of Criminology*, Clarendon Press, Oxford.

Home Office (1993), 'The Prison Population in 1992', *Home Office Statistical Bulletin*, 7/92, Home Office, London.

Home Office (1998), *Statistics on Race and the Criminal Justice System*, Home Office, London.

Humphrey, D. (1972), *Police Power and Black People*, Panther, London.

Humphrey, D. and John, G. (1971), *Because They're Black*, Penguin, Handsworth.

Hunte, J. (1966), *Nigger Hunting in England?* West Indian Standing Conference, London.

Husband, C. (ed.) (1982), *Race in Britain*, Hutchinson and Co Publishers, London.

Jensen, A. (1969), 'How Much Can We Boost IQ and Scholastic Achievement?', *Harvard Educational Review*, vol. 39, pp.1–123.

Jones, T., MacLean, B. and Young, J. (1986), *The Islington Crime Survey*, Gower, Aldershot.

Kalunta-Crumpton, A. (2000), 'Black People and Discrimination in the Criminal Justice System: The Messages from Research', in Marlow, A. and Loveday, B. (eds), *After MacPherson*, Russell House Publishing, Dorset.

Kamin, L. (1977), *The Science and Politics of IQ*, Penguin, Harmondsworth.

Landau, S. (1981), 'Juveniles and the Police', *British Journal of Criminology*, vol. 21, no.1.

Landau, S. and Nathan, G. (1983), 'Selecting Delinquents for Questioning in the London Metropolitan Area', *British Journal of Criminology*, vol. 28, pp.128–149.

Lea, J. and Young, J. (1984), *What Is to Be Done About Law and Order?* Penguin, Harmondsworth.

Lea, J. and Young, J. (1993), *What Is to Be Done About Law and Order?* (2nd edn), Pluto, London.

Lombroso, C. (1876), *L'Uomo Delinquente*, Fratelli Bocca, Turin.

Lusane, C. (2000), 'We Are the World: Race and the International War on Drugs', in Henry, C. (ed.), *Foreign Policy and the Black (Inter)National Interest*, State University of New York Press, Albany.

Massey, D. and Denton, N. (1993), *American Apartheid*, Harvard University Press, Cambridge, Mass.

Mays, J. (1954), *Growing Up in the City*, Liverpool University Press, Liverpool.

Merton, R. (1938), 'Social Structure and Anomie', *American Sociological Review*, vol. 3.

Miller, J. (1997), *Search and Destroy*, Cambridge University Press, Cambridge.

Morris, T. (1957), *The Criminal Area*, Routledge and Kegan Paul, London.

Murray, C. (1984), *Losing Ground*, Basic Books, New York.

Murray, C. (1990), *The Emerging British Underclass*, Institute for Economic Affairs, London.

Murray, C. (1996), 'The Underclass', in Muncie, J., McLaughlin, E. and Langan, M. (eds), *Criminological Perspectives*, Sage, London.

NACRO (1993), *Evidence of the Links Between Homelessness, Crime and the Criminal Justice System*, Occasional Paper, NACRO, London.

Oppenheim, C. (1993), *Poverty: The Facts*, Child Poverty Action Group, London.

Penal Affairs Consortium (1996), *Race and Criminal Justice*, Penal Affairs Consortium, London.

Pitts, J. (1986), 'Black Young People and Juvenile Crime: Some Unanswered Questions', in Matthews, R. and Young, J. (eds), *Confronting Crime*, Sage, London.

Roberts, B. (1982), 'The Debate on "Sus"', in Cashmore, E. (ed.), *Black Youth in Crisis*, George Allen and Unwin, London.

Roshier, B. (1989), *Controlling Crime*, Open University Press, Milton Keynes.

Russell, K. (2000), 'The Color of Crime: External and Internal Images', in Neugebauer, R. (ed.), *Criminal Injustice*, Canadian Scholars' Press, Toronto.

Ryan, W. (1976), *Blaming the Victim*, Vintage, New York.

Sampson, R. and Wilson, W. (1995), 'Toward a Theory of Race, Crime and Urban Inequality', in Hagan, J. and Paterson, R. (eds), *Crime and Inequality*, Stanford University Press, Stanford, California.

Scarman, Lord (1981), *The Brixton Disorders 10–12 April 1981: Report of an Inquiry by the Rt Hon. the Lord Scarman*, HMSO, London.

Shaw, C. (1929), *Delinquency Areas*, University of Chicago Press, Chicago.

Shaw, C. and McKay, H. (1942), *Juvenile Delinquency and Urban Areas*, University of Chicago Press, Chicago.

Skogan, W. (1994), *The Police and Public in England and Wales: A British Crime Survey Report*, HMSO, London.

Solomos, J. (1988), *Black Youth, Racism and the State*, Cambridge University Press, Cambridge.

Solomos, J. (1993), *Race and Racism in Britain*, Macmillan, London.

Steffensmeier, D. and Demuth, S. (2001), 'Ethnicity and Judges' Sentencing Decisions: Hispanis-Black-White Comparisons', *Criminology*, vol. 39, pp.145–178.

Sudbury, J. (2002), 'Celling Black Bodies: Black Women in Global Prison Industrial Complex', *Feminist Review*, vol.70, pp.57–74.

Tierney, J. (1996), *Criminology*, Prentice Hall/Harvester Wheatsheaf, London.

Virdee, S. (1995), *Racial Violence and Harassment*, Policy Studies Institute, London.

Walvin, N. (1971), *The Black Presence*, Orbach and Chambers, London.

Walvin, N. (1973), *Black and White*, Penguin, London.

Willis, C. (1983), *The Use, Effectiveness and Impact of Police Stop and Search Powers*, Home Office, London.

Wilson, D. and Herrnstein, R. (1985), *Crime and Human Nature*, Simon and Schuster, New York.

Part 5

Ethnic identities, institutional reflexivity and crime

In late modernity, criminal justice institutions intentionally and rationally reflect upon the part that they play in the perpetuation of identified social problems, as well as reflecting upon ways in which they can intervene and act so as to minimise harms (Lash, 1994; McGhee, 2005). Agencies like the police, probation and prison services regularly engage with issues of 'race' and ethnicity, particularly following the publication of the 1999 Macpherson Report, which found evidence of 'institutional racism' in the Metropolitan Police Service. Following the racist murder of 18-year-old Stephen Lawrence on April 22nd 1993, in Eltham, South London, a public inquiry, led by Sir William Macpherson, found the police to be institutionally racist, which was defined as (1999: 6.34):

> The collective failure of an organisaton to provide an appropriate and professional service to people because of their colour, culture or ethnic origin. It can be seen or detected in processes, attitudes and behaviour which amount to discrimination through unwitting prejudice, ignorance, thoughtlessness and racist stereotyping which disadvantages minority ethnic people.

This stimulated fresh examinations of racism within the criminal justice system, with agencies of the criminal justice system being regularly monitored and inspected for their performances in relation to 'race'/ethnicity. At the same time, agencies of the criminal justice system reflected upon the ways in which different 'racial' and ethnic identities are represented in their workforces. Indeed, the British government has placed a significant emphasis upon improving the representation of minority ethnic communities within the workforce of the criminal justice sector. This is partly due to the belief that by creating a criminal justice system that more accurately reflects local communities, this will improve public confidence in criminal justice.

With respect to policing, the HM Inspectorate of Constabulary report

(2000), *Winning the Race*, gave heightened focus to the need for greater attention to be paid to the recruitment, retention and career development of minority
ethnic police officers. Prior to this, the Scarman Report, which was published in
the aftermath of the Brixton urban disturbances in 1981, highlighted the under-
representation of minority ethnic communities in the police service. Included
within the Scarman Report was an acknowledgement that police racism and
political exclusion were factors helping to account for the Brixton disturbances
(Taylor, 1984). Much emphasis has been placed upon improving the minority
ethnic representation of police officers. Although following the Macpherson
Report police services have sought to improve the retention and progression of
minority ethnic staff, by rooting out racism and creating an environment in
which racist attitudes and behaviour are freely and openly challenged, it seems
that racism continues to be a feature of minority ethnic police officers' working
lives, detrimentally impacting upon recruitment strategies (Rowe, 2004). A further question that arises here is whether criminal justice employees' identities
can powerfully challenge the working practices of criminal justice agencies. In
relation to the issue of police-community relations, for example, the notion that
an improved representation of minority ethnic groups within the police service
will lead to better relations has been challenged, as researchers have argued
that police occupational culture may transcend the ethnic (or other) identity of
police officers and so minority ethnic police officers may not necessarily employ
different tactics than their white counterparts (Holdaway, 1996; Rowe, 2004).

The issue of minority ethnic representation in the police service needs to
be placed within the wider policing context. The first suggested reading in this
part is a brief chapter by O'Byrne (2000), which looks at both the Scarman and
Macpherson inquiries, asking the question of whether Macpherson can succeed where Scarman failed. For O'Byrne (2000), the essential difference
between Scarman's and Macpherson's approaches is that whereas Scarman
saw the responsibility for change being shared equally between the police
and Black communities, Macpherson placed responsibility squarely upon the
police. For O'Byrne (2000), the Macpherson Report has given the police a clear
direction and focus.

Turning to the probation service in England and Wales (now a part of the
National Offender Management Service, NOMS), a 'race' equality agenda has
gained increasing significance over the last few years. Following the inquiry into
the murder of Stephen Lawrence, HM Inspectorate of Probation published a
thematic report entitled, *Towards Race Equality*, in June 2000. The report examined the extent to which the probation service promoted and achieved race
equality in employment practices and work with offenders. It contained 19
recommendations that addressed policy development, improving the quality of
service delivery to offenders, the recruitment and training of staff and performance monitoring. Its publication led to the formulation of a national action plan.
According to Heer (2008: 2–3), whose article is the next suggested reading in
this part, there is insufficient representation of minority ethnic groups in senior

positions in the probation service. Less than 1 per cent of Senior Probation Officers are from minority ethnic groups, and there are no minority ethnic Chief Officers or Deputy Chief Officers, although there has been an increase in the percentage of minority ethnic middle managers, for example, 2.77 per cent of area managers are from minority ethnic groups (Heer, 2008: 3). According to Heer (2008), the National Association of Asian Probation Staff (NAAPS) arose out of a need for Asian staff to assert themselves as separate from Black groups and attempting to address and dismantle stereotypes associated with Asian culture. A study undertaken in 2004 investigating the experiences of Asian employees in the probation service, which included a sample size of 140 Asian staff, indicates that some respondents thought that their religious practices, including wearing cultural dress to work, impacted upon their promotional prospects. At the same time, some respondents indicated that they had experienced racist comments or behaviour based on stereotypical views of Asians. Many also indicated that they felt prejudice in relation to their faith, language, dress and culture, causing them to feel marginalised within the workplace (Heer, 2008). This latter finding illustrates the multiple sites from which prejudice can be experienced, and indeed, according to the HM Inspectorate of Probation Report (2004: 53), *Towards Race Equality*, one fifth of minority ethnic staff have indicated that they experience 'dual discrimination', meaning that they feel discriminated in ways not only related to racism but also in relation to other aspects of their identities, like their faith.

With respect to the prison service (now a part of NOMS), in 2005 the Chief Inspectorate of Prisons conducted an investigation into race relations within prisons, the results of which were published in a report highlighting the key areas that need to be developed in order to implement a race action plan more effectively. This report was entitled, *Parallel Worlds: a thematic review of race relations in prisons*. Key findings in this report include that there is no shared understanding of race issues within prison settings, there are instead a series of parallel worlds inhabited by different groups of prisoners and staff. For example, visible minority prisoners reported that they did not consider that their needs were met, believing that there is racism in the prison regime which manifests itself in differential access to the prison regime and different treatment by staff. Whilst safety was the predominant concern for Asian prisoners, respect was the predominant issue for Black prisoners. Governors and white race relations liaison officers have the most optimistic, managerial, view that the regime operates fairly, although at the same time acknowledging that more work needs to be done (HM Inspectorate of Prisons, 2005: 6).

Suggested essays

M. O'Byrne (2000) 'Can Macpherson Succeed where Scarman Failed?' in A. Marlow and B. Loveday (eds) *After Macpherson: policing after the Stephen Lawrence Inquiry*. Lyme Regis: Russell House Publishing, pp. 107–112.

Heer, G. (forthcoming, 2008) '(In)visible Barriers: the experience of Asian employees in the probation service' *Howard Journal of Criminal Justice.*

Further reading

Beckford, J., Joly, D. and Khosrokhavar, F. (2005) *Muslims in Prison: challenge and change in Britain and France*. Basingstoke: Palgrave.

HM Inspectorate of Probation (2004) *Towards Race Equality: follow up inspection*. London: HMIP.

HM Inspectorate of Prisons (2005) *Parallel Worlds: a thematic review of race relations in prisons*. London: HMIP.

Macpherson, Sir W. (1999) *The Stephen Lawrence Inquiry: Report of an Inquiry by Sir William Macpherson of Cluny*. London: HMSO.

Report of the Zahid Mubarek Inquiry (2006) Volume 1 & 2, June 2006. London: The Stationery Office.

Rowe, M. (2004) *Policing, Race and Racism*. Cullompton: Willan.

Spalek, B. (2005) 'Muslims and the Criminal Justice System' in *Muslims in the UK: policies for engaged citizens*. Budapest: Open Society Institute, pp. 253–340.

Wardak, A. and Lewis, C. (2006) (eds) *Race and Probation*. London: Willan.

18

Can Macpherson succeed where Scarman failed?
by Michael O'Byrne

Introduction

The essence of the argument to be presented, in this chapter, is, that since both inquiries examined essentially the same issue, if Scarman had succeeded, then Macpherson should not have been necessary. What then are the factors that will ensure a different outcome? In examining this question the issue will be approached by looking at three factors:

1   The two inquiries; examining the differences of approach and outcome.
2   The sustainability of the solutions; the usefulness and dangers of targets and a performance-management led approach.
3   The political climate; the effective implementation of the recommendations which is crucially dependent on the presence or lack of political will.

The inquiries

Both of the inquiries were set up by the Home Secretary in order to report on what was essentially a breakdown in confidence between the black community and the police. With the Scarman Inquiry it arose out of the riots which occurred in Brixton in April, 1981 together with similar disturbances in the same year in Liverpool, Manchester and the West Midlands. The Macpherson Inquiry examined the investigation of the racist murder of Stephen Lawrence which occurred in April, 1993, only 12 years after the Brixton riots and the Scarman Report. The Scarman Report was lauded at the time as being ground-breaking. It set the agenda for the development of a better relationship between the police and the black community. It also made a significant number of recommendations for other social agencies whose policies impacted upon life in the inner-city. In theory therefore, the successful implementation of the Scarman recommendations should have prevented the need for the Macpherson Inquiry.

Methodology of the inquiries

Both inquiries used essentially the same methodology. Part One looked at the facts of the case: in Scarman the riots, in Macpherson the investigation of the murder. Part Two examined the issues which underpinned those facts, taking evidence on the causes and effects of racism, discrimination and the policies which were in place for dealing with them. Both inquiries also invited any interested party to submit written evidence. A key difference was that Sir William Macpherson used a panel of three lay advisers whose participation he clearly valued; he stated that:

> . . . their contributions to the report and to the conclusions and recommendations made have been imaginative, radical and of incalculable worth. Without their advice and support the Inquiry would have been infinitely less effective.
>
> (Macpherson, 1999)

Advantages enjoyed by Lord Scarman

The key advantages enjoyed by the Scarman Inquiry were:

- Speed. The riots took place in April, 1981; both parts were completed and the report submitted to Parliament by November in the same year. This meant that memories were fresh and the recommendations had a nexus to the events which gave them additional weight and relevance.
- The absence of other litigation. At the time of this inquiry society was significantly less litigious than now and there were no criminal or civil cases being pursued against potential witnesses. This meant that witnesses to fact and policy could be examined rigorously and there was a greater expectation for openness.
- It was easier for the inquiry to focus more objectively on the facts as there were no deaths resulting from the riots and there was not that highly personal focus faced by the Macpherson Inquiry.
- The unchallenged authority of Lord Scarman. He had carried out the Red Lion Square Inquiry to general acclaim and was a Law Lord of considerable standing.

Advantages enjoyed by Sir William Macpherson

The key advantages enjoyed by the Macpherson Inquiry were:

- The Kent police investigation. Sir William Macpherson had available to him the inquiry carried out under the supervision of the independent Police Complaints Authority by the Kent police. This provided a solid foundation for the examination of the witnesses and its findings of fact were not questioned.

- Mr and Mrs Lawrence. There is no doubt that the way that both of these intelligent and articulate parents were able to describe the way that they had been treated by the police, and other agencies, and to put that experience into a black context, had a significant, if not the most significant, impact on the overall outcome of the inquiry.

- Immunity for witnesses. The fact that the Attorney General granted a general immunity to witnesses for evidence given to the inquiry significantly helped to remove barriers to witnesses being open and honest. The pity was that key witnesses did not take up the challenge that this presented.

Key issues

As already stated, the fundamental issue was a breakdown in the relationship between the police and the black community and the way that this was reflected in the lack of confidence which that community had in how it was policed. In comparing the effectiveness of the outcome of both inquiries it is necessary to look at how this issue was expressed.

Scarman

> Two views have been forcefully expressed in the course of the Inquiry as to the causation of the disorders. The first is that of oppressive policing over a period of years, and in particular the harassment of young blacks on the streets of Brixton. On this view, it is said to be unnecessary to look more deeply for an explanation of the disorders. They were 'anti-police'. The second is that the disorders, like so many riots in British history, were a protest against society by people, deeply frustrated and deprived, who sought in a violent attack upon the forces of law and order their one opportunity of compelling public attention to their grievances. I have no doubt that each view, even if correct, would be an over-simplification of a complex situation. If either view should be true, it would not be the whole truth.
>
> (para 1.4)

. . . the policing problem is not difficult to identify: it is that of policing a multi-racial community in a deprived inner-city area where
unemployment, especially among young black people, is high and
hopes are low. It is a problem which admits of no simple or clear-cut
solution.

(para 1.6)

I identify the social problem as that of the difficulties, social and economic, which beset the ethnically diverse communities who live and
work in our inner cities.

(para 1.7)

Lord Scarman was clearly a creature of his time and saw the problem as
being one which was shared equally between the black community and the
police rather than one in which the police carried the major responsibility in
creating conditions where change could come about. It took little or no
account of the fact that those agencies which had the power and resources to
bring about change had the consequential responsibility to ensure that the
conditions were created which would guarantee that those changes would
occur. This is shown in his description of discrimination, its effects and his
proposals for a remedy:

. . . much of the evidence of discrimination is indirect rather than direct;
but I have no doubt that it is a reality which too often confronts the black
youths of Brixton . . . It was alleged by some of those who made representations to me that Britain is an institutionally racist society. If by that it
is meant that it is a society which knowingly, as a matter of policy, discriminates against black people, I reject the allegation. If, however, the
suggestion being made is that practices may be adopted by public bodies
as well as by private individuals which are unwittingly discriminatory
against black people, then this is an allegation which deserves serious
consideration, and, where proved, swift remedy.

(paras 2.21–2.22)

He was later to reject the allegation that institutionalised racism existed
and his remedy was in the main an exhortation to make better use of the
existing law and procedures.

Changes in legislation are not the principal requirement if discrimination
is to be rooted out. What is required is a clear determination to enforce
the existing law, and a positive effort by all in responsible positions to
give a lead on the matter.

But again he goes on to show that he thinks that the need for change is an evenly shared responsibility rather than one in which government agencies have the major responsibility by stating:

> Pride in being black is one thing, but black racialism is no more accept-able than white. A vigorous rejection of discriminatory and racialist views is as important among black people as among white if social har-mony is to be ensured.
>
> (para 6.35)

Macpherson

> Unwitting racism can arise because of lack of understanding, ignorance or mistaken beliefs. It can arise from well-intentioned but patronising words or actions. It can arise from unfamiliarity with behaviour or cul-tural traditions of people or families from minority ethnic communities. It can arise from racist stereotyping of black people as potential criminals or troublemakers. Often this arises out of uncritical self-understanding borne out of an inflexible police ethos of the 'traditional' way of doing things. Furthermore, such attitudes can thrive in a tightly knit com-munity, so that there can be a collective failure to detect and to outlaw this breed of racism. The police canteen can too easily be its breeding ground.
>
> (para 6.17)

> The failure of the first investigating team to recognise and accept racism and race relations as a central feature of the investigation of the murder of Stephen Lawrence played a part in the deficiencies in policing which we identify in this report.
>
> (para 6.21)

> It [institutional racism] persists because of the failure of the organisation openly and adequately to recognise and address its existence and causes by policy, example and leadership. Without recognition and action to eliminate such racism it can prevail as part of the ethos of the culture of the organisation. It is a corrosive disease.
>
> (para 6.34)

> There is no doubt that recognition, acknowledgement and acceptance of the problem by police services and their officers is an important first step for minority ethnic communities in moving forward positively to solve the problem which exists. **There is an onus upon police services to respond to this.**
>
> (para 6.48, author's emphasis)

> Things [in the investigation] obviously went wrong from the start, and **it was a duty of the senior officers in particular to take their own**

steps to ensure that alternative methods were followed in order to see that the family were kept properly informed and that their relationship with the investigation team was a healthy one. This they signally failed to do. Whatever the difficulties and **whatever their cause the onus clearly lay upon Mr Weeden and his officers to address them.**
(para 14.74, author's emphasis)

The essential difference between the Scarman approach and that of Macpherson is that Scarman saw the responsibility for change as being shared more or less equally between the black community and the police. Macpherson is clear that the responsibility lies with the agency which has the power, resources and legal accountability for the equal delivery of services to all of the communities, and that this responsibility lies with them totally, regardless of their views and perceptions of the responses and reactions of those communities. This reflects a sea change in the way in which the police and other agencies will be held accountable in the future.

Proposed remedies

There were two major differences in the recommendations which the inquiries made.

In Scarman, the allegation of institutional racism was rejected and he focused his major attention on changes to the police discipline code and system; the strengthening of the independent element in the investigation of complaints against police; lengthening of police training with a clearer community relations element and changes in tactics in dealing with public order. It can be said that he dealt with the system issues very effectively but that he avoided, or failed to deal with, the underlying cultural issues. As far as discrimination is concerned he merely called for a determination to enforce the existing law and for all in responsible positions to give a lead on the matter. His belief clearly was that the existing law was adequate and that exhortation was enough to bring about the necessary cultural changes.

Macpherson on the other hand puts cultural issues at the heart of his recommendations. There is a clear implicit acceptance of the fact that there were reasonably good systems in place and that the major failure in the Metropolitan Police investigation was that these systems had not been applied. This strengthens the impact of the report as far as other forces are concerned as they too would have been critical of the Metropolitan Police investigation, and would have been confident that the same approach, in terms of the investigation, would not have been taken in their force. Crucially, exhortation has been replaced by prescription. Key issues such as recruiting, the exercise of powers to stop and search, strategies for the prevention, recording, investigation and prosecution of racist incidents, multi-agency co-operation and training are now to be monitored and measured in terms of their implementation and effectiveness. The probable effect of this approach will now be covered in detail.

Sustainability

In the last ten years the police service, and public service as a whole, have been slowly but surely introduced to performance management systems which require the setting of hard targets. The effectiveness and efficiency of forces are increasingly judged by their ability to achieve these targets. At the time of the Scarman Inquiry this was not accepted practice in the public sector although it was well-established in commerce.

The key difference that target-setting makes is that it is no longer possible to disguise or hide failure, or to live with failure by ignoring the lack of success. For example, Scarman advocated increasing the number of police officers to be recruited from the visible ethnic minorities. The idea was accepted in principle by the government of the day and by the Association of Chief Police Officers, (ACPO). However, no targets, no matter how general, were set and the fact that the numbers increased by very small amounts over a very long time was not a matter for review or apparent concern. This has been fundamentally changed by the fact that the Home Secretary has now set targets, not just for the police but for all the major agencies in the criminal justice system. Whether or not all of these targets are achievable, and what can be done if they are not, will be a matter for debate later in this article. The crucial issue is that failure will be public and the agencies will need to account to their political masters for it and come forward with proposals to correct the situation.

Performance management is, however, a triple-edged sword. The effect of the first edge is as described above. The second edge is best encapsulated by the old maxim, 'what gets measured, gets done'. The difficulty that this presents it is that the corollary is also true, i.e. what is not measured is ignored. This means that any approach must be broadly based and ensure that *all* of the factors which can contribute to the success or failure of an approach to major issues are subject to both measurement and management: too often measurement alone is mistaken for management. It is not enough to know what is going on. It is also necessary to have in place a positive management ethos which seeks to use that information to make a difference.

The second element of this factor is that the selection of priorities becomes critical to overall success. It is a truism that there can only be a limited number of priorities, but it is a truism which tends to be ignored in the heat of the debate whilst politicians are being forced to deal with a complex situation on an issue by issue basis and where the soundbite rules supreme. A classic example of this is the current debate around NHS waiting lists. The priority being given to time has led to treatment for serious and even life-threatening conditions being delayed in favour of patients with less serious conditions who have been on the waiting list for longer than the targeted period.

To put this in a police context, it is clear that the government is now nervous about the coincidence of a predicted upswing in crime, especially property crime, and the timing of the next general election. Pressure on the police to improve crime reduction and crime detection could easily lead to a willingness to be less demanding on the way that issues such as 'stop and search' are managed if there is a possible penalty in the growth of crimes such as burglary, theft of and from motor vehicles and street robbery. A large number of forces still have relatively primitive information systems and fairly crude approaches to performance management. It is not clear if they have the capacity to quickly develop this into the sophisticated performance management systems required to deal with the complexity that the problem presents.

The third edge is the general experience that when performance management comes in the door, ethics go out the window. Where targets are difficult or impossible to achieve there is a tendency, in the first instance, to massage the figures rather than work on the problem. There are examples in recent police history where forces have engaged in exactly these practices. The danger is that these forces will be tempted to go further than mere massaging and will actually engage in corrupt practices in order to achieve targets. In order to avoid this, it is necessary that everyone concerned, from the constable to the Home Secretary, is aware of these dangers and is committed to the development of effective systems working within a corruption-intolerant culture.

Political will

The Scarman Report could not have been published in a less favourable political climate than was the case in 1981. The economy was about to enter into the deepest and longest recession since the 1930s, during which manufacturing industry would be decimated. This made many of Scarman's recommendations on housing, education and employment in the inner cities difficult, if not impossible, to implement for a government committed to the reduction of public spending. Michael Heseltine was the honourable exception to this while in government as he did try to target resources on inner cities, especially Liverpool. In addition, this was a government which denied the connection between crime and social conditions and put an emphasis on individual rights and responsibilities whilst trying to minimise the role of government, both on grounds of dogma and of fiscal necessity.

The debate on the issue, such as it was, was soon displaced by the overwhelming concerns that the public had with the economy and then by the country's engagement in a war. As the 1980s developed, both the government's approach to crime, and its role in sustaining society became more and more focused on the individual and less on the community. It became more and more committed to reducing the tax burden, gradually transferring the responsibility for issues such as health and education from the state to the individual. In addition, the prolonged involvement with the miners' strike led to the politicisation of the police and the whole issue of changing the nature of the relationship between the police and the ethnic minority communities was allowed to effectively wither on the vine.

In comparison, Macpherson has both the wind and the tide behind it. Jack Straw agreed to do what at least two previous Home Secretaries had refused to do by the setting up of the inquiry itself, and, as discussed above, he has set targets in most of the key areas and has put his personal weight and the considerable weight of his office and that of other cabinet ministers behind the issue.

That said, this is also a government which appears to be committed to at least contain and perhaps reduce public spending as a proportion of GDP. This means that there is no commitment to additional resources should they be required. This tempts the commentator into stating that whilst talk is cheap the real test of commitment is shown by action and that is most clearly shown by the commitment of resources, be it the ring-fencing of current resources or the promise of additional resources where they are proved necessary.

The litmus test on commitment will be recruiting, where the government has required the service to significantly increase the number of police officers recruited from the black and Asian communities. This requirement must be seen in the light of the government's current approach to police spending. The Comprehensive Spending Review is committed to providing the police with a 2.7 per cent increase in the current year and 2.8 per cent in 2000/2001. Actual police inflation runs at between four and six per cent. This means that a large number of forces are suffering year-on-year cuts. Since most of the budget where cuts are possible involve staffing, it is inevitable that they will be reflected in reduced police numbers. For some forces this has already meant a freeze on recruiting with the prospect for the coming year being just as bleak.

It is a statement of the obvious that if there is no recruiting there can be no improvement on the overall position in terms of black and Asian officers. For those forces with large ethnic minority communities the existence of targets will mean not only a continuing failure but that the scale of failure must increase as the proportions to be recruited will increase year-on-year as a result of recruiting generally being reduced. It is difficult to see how this circle can be squared other than by some form of additional funding specifically to support recruiting. The money committed by the Home Secretary for an additional 5000 officers does not seem to be the answer as its real effect is questionable and the promise has been rightly described as a trick with 'smoke and mirrors'.

It is inevitable that the black and Asian communities will use this very visible measure to gauge the seriousness of the police intention. No matter what improvements are made elsewhere in issues such as the use of stop and search powers, improved effectiveness in dealing with racist crimes and incidents, it is likely that the views of the ethnic minority communities will be heavily influenced by progress in the area. It is important that the government realises that the visibility created by targets and monitoring also applies to them and that the debate will encompass their willingness to fund the changes that they have demanded.

Conclusion

The persistence of the Lawrence family and the courage of Jack Straw led to the setting up of the Macpherson Inquiry. Its conclusions and recommendations gave a clear direction and focus to all public agencies, but especially the police, on what must be done in order to change the underlying and undermining attitudes, processes and procedures which sustain racism and create and sustain inequality in England today. The problem is now clearly defined, the beginnings of a solution are clearly described, the creation of targets means that success and failure will be visible and that a continuing and informed debate on how best to progress the issues is now possible. In this light it is clear that Macpherson can succeed where Scarman failed. The police service and other agencies must now show that they have both the commitment and the imagination needed to translate this into a more equal future. For its part the government must deal with the issue as one which is complex and which cannot be resolved by soundbite policies. It, too, must be willing to 'walk the talk' by providing the support and resources necessary for success.

References

Macpherson, Sir W. (1999). *The Stephen Lawrence Inquiry*. London: Home Office.
Scarman, Lord J. (1981). *The Brixton Disorders, 10–12 April, 1981*. London: HMSO.

19

(In)visible barriers: the experience of Asian employees in the probation service

by G. Heer

Abstract

This article is based on research conducted in the UK investigating the experience of Asian employees in the probation service and considers wider issues of attitudes towards Asians in the UK. Key findings include a lack of confidence among Asian staff with regards to how management addresses diversity issues; a perception of change in attitudes towards Asian staff directly related to the events of 9/11; a lack of understanding from other black and minority ethnic (BME) and white staff regarding Asian culture and concern about promotion chances and job security. There has been little research on the culture of the probation service, specifically with regard to how management implement policy and how much attention is paid to diversity issues. This research highlights the need for further exploration of these issues, on a wider scale, especially in light of more recent events impacting on attitudes towards Asians, particularly from the South and East of Asia, namely, India, Bangladesh, Pakistan and China.

Introduction

The focus of studies looking at racism in the criminal justice system has to date been concerned primarily with the over-representation of black and minority ethnic (BME) groups in all stages, as offenders and also as victims of crime (e.g. Bowling and Phillips, 2002; Commission for Racial Equality, 2004; NACRO, 2003). In terms of working in the criminal justice system, there has been a greater focus on policing compared with other agencies, that is the courts, Crown Prosecution Service, prisons and probation. In the probation service, Home Office statistics have shown BME groups are proportionately represented, but there is still concern over the lack of BME groups working in senior positions, in both the probation service and the criminal justice system as a whole (Home Office, 2005). Research has so far focused on the experience of BME clients in the probation service and evaluating various programmes to aid resettlement and reduce re-offending (Calverley et al., 2004; Harper and Chitty, 2005; Powis and Walmsley, 2002; Hollin et al., 2002; Rex and Gelsthorpe, 2002).

For staff in the probation service diversity training has been introduced to address the different cultural needs presented by BME groups, and to increase awareness among staff about diversity issues. The difference here is the training undergone specifically by trainee probation officers (TPOs) and that of all staff at a general level. Reference is made to both aspects of training offered to employees which is delivered by probation staff. Overall, it is generally geared towards how staff in public services treat clients, and the focus in recent years directly stems from recommendations from the Stephen Lawrence inquiry (MacPherson, 1999, Recommendation 54), which specifically considered the treatment of BME groups by the police. There has been little evaluation of its impact, in terms of how staff view this training and the experiences of BME staff working in the probation service.

The Home Office RDS report identified four key components to diversity training, which are outlined below:

- Philosophy, i.e. what elements of diversity does it cover: racism, racial stereotypes and prejudice, and racial harassment; equality of opportunity; or diversity?
- Level, i.e. is it aimed at changing individuals, groups, the entire organisation or a sector?
- Target, i.e. whether the training is directed at internal or external relationships.
- Aims and objectives, i.e. what the training is designed to do; training can aim to provide information; to increase knowledge, awareness and understanding about particular groups; to challenge and change assumptions, beliefs and attitudes; to change behaviour; and/or change culture.

(Tamkin et al., 2002, Home Office RDS Report)

These components present a wide range of issues, all of which may need addressing. Emphasis is placed upon the need to be aware of the experiences of staff in criminal justice agencies, in order to ensure any training provisions are relevant and have a realistic prospect of advancing changes. There are clear parallels identified among BME staff in the police, prison and probation services, in terms of the organisation, culture and treatment they receive from colleagues and managers. This is evidenced by lower retention levels among

BME staff and numerous cases of racial discrimination at work, which resulted in damages being awarded to BME staff (Bowling and Phillips, 2002). Her Majesty's Inspectorate of Probation reported marginalisation among BME staff, especially in predominantly ethnic white majority areas and also a failure of managers to address unacceptable behaviour (HMIP, 2004).

The following data, taken from a recent Home Office Report, represents some facts and figures relating to BME staff in the probation service as of 31 December 2005:

- 11.79% BME staff are employed nationally
- 9/10 regions have improved their BME staff recruitment over the past 12 months
- 7.06% define themselves as 'black'
- 2.79% are Asian staff
- 1.48% is of 'mixed heritage'
- 0.46% defines themselves as 'other'.
  (Home Office Workforce Report, Issue 3, June 2006)

The number of Asian staff is identified as:

- 53.17% Indian
- 30.63% Pakistani
- 4.12% Bangladeshi
- 12.08% Other

The ethnic breakdown by job category indicates that the number of TPO recruits has increased dramatically, up by 3.07%; whereas the number of PO staff has remained static and there is a less than 1% increase in the SPO and PSO roles. The number of Chief Officers and Deputy Chief Officers is nil, reflecting a drop from the previous year, but there is an increase in the number of middle management (ACO and area managers) by 2.85% and 2.77% respectively (Home Office, 2006). Such data is reflected in the findings of this research, although the probation service has exceeded its targets in terms of BME recruitment, there still is inadequate representation in senior level positions despite an increase in lower level recruitment. Further scrutiny of the data reveals that there is more Asian staff in support roles than operational positions, 3.08% and 2.70% respectively, with the majority in the role of Board members (8.57%) or psychologists (5.26%). What the report does not highlight is the number of Asian staff leaving the service, as that would have provided a useful form of comparative data for the purpose of this research, particularly when looking at retention levels as well as recruitment and progression.

The Asian experience of racism in the UK

Islamophobia in the UK has long been identified, prior to the events of 9/11 in the USA, and is linked to key points in history which include the Salman Rushdie affair and the first Gulf War, both of which raised issues concerning Islamic religion, such as perceived lack of integration of Muslims in western society and

> Stereotypical assumptions and pronouncements regarding selected customs and, above all, the inherently fanatical, violent and irrational tendencies of Muslim leaders and their followers.
>
> (Werbner, 2000)

It also reflects the alarmist tendencies of the media and public in the perceived threat posed by Muslims to the West, along with the simplification of Asian cultures, in that the diversity within it is not fully recognised (Halliday, 1997). However, since 9/11 and 7/7, there is no doubt that Islamic and Muslim communities have been thrust once again into the public arena, along with a large number of 'ill-informed analyses of Islam and approaches to Muslim communities (which) still dominate the media' (Küçükcan, 2004). This is further reflected in a 600% increase in hate crimes, directed predominantly at Asians from 2004–05. In the three weeks since the 7 July attacks, 269 incidents occurred, compared to 40 in the same period for 2004 (Institute of Race Relations, 2005).

For people of Asian descent working in the criminal justice system, racist views and prejudice about their culture may well be present among their co-workers, and could have implications for their treatment and promotion prospects. This particular form of prejudice has its roots in general racism towards Asians, but recent events around the globe, and their representation in the media, have perhaps perpetuated the extent of negative feeling and suspicion targeted at such groups. For example, the media response on the activities of Al-Qaeda and the Muslim cleric, Abu Hamza, focus concern regarding the Islamic faith as a whole, even though among Asians in the UK, there are other groups, with different cultures and practices to Muslims, such as Sikhs and Hindus (IRR, 2005). Also, this focus gives the public the perception that all those who follow Islam are fundamentalist and do not wish to integrate with others in society.

The Criminal Justice Consultative Council report on race and the criminal justice system highlighted the need to provide more and better opportunities for BME groups and ensure that equal opportunity policies, developed in the 1970s and 1980s, are adhered to (CJCC, 2000). Other groups within the criminal justice system have been set up to improve services for BME staff, such as the Black Police Association, the Association of Black Probation Officers (APBO) and in 1987, the National Association of Asian Probation

Staff (NAAPS). The latter was directly related to the need for Asians to assert themselves as different to 'black' ethnic minority groups and to promote support for Asians and encourage them to seek promotion within the service. It attempts to address stereotypes regarding Asian culture among probation staff and recognises that racism towards Asians is not just about skin colour, but also about religion and culture, all of which impact upon their experience of working in the probation service.

Methodology

This study utilised both quantitative and qualitative methods, and its key aims were:

1 To seek the views of Asian staff in relation to issues of recruitment, retention and progression to allow these to be considered by NAAPS and the NPS.

2 To inform NAAPS funding bids and expenditure plans.

3 To offer a NAAPS response to issues of recruitment, retention and progression in terms of the home secretary's ten-point plan.

4 To offer an informed response to recruitment, retention and progression to the senior managers of the probation service.

5 To consider an Asian perspective, based upon culture, religion, language and dress code in the work of the probation service.

The focus of this paper relates primarily to aims 1, 4 and 5. An Advisory Group was set up, comprising representative interested agencies and departments who could assist in the overall initiative and to provide expertise and experience of specific issues and guide the research. The advisory group was to meet on three pre-planned occasions: prior to a conference where the questionnaire was to be distributed; after the results of the questionnaire had been analysed and, finally, after a draft version of the report had been prepared for comment.

The researchers chosen to conduct this piece of work were selected on the basis of their experience of working with the probation service over a number of years, also being from an Asian background was a factor as they are both bi-lingual which was useful at times when interviewing respondents, in addition having a familiarity with their culture seemed appropriate as there was a direct level of empathy.

The questionnaire was prepared and agreed with the group after some general consultation and it was designed to ensure maximum completion returns at the annual conference in May 2004. In addition, NAAPS allowed a member of the research team to present the project at the conference on the first day. This opportunity to explain the aims of the work and how it might be used to offer and inform the NPS of an Asian perspective was successful in ensuring returns. Participants were informed that all responses would be confidential and that the primary aim of the study was to ascertain an overall view.

140 questionnaires were distributed at the conference. It was pleasing to note that 80 were returned on the first day and a further 25 returned by post. In addition and to ensure that Asian staff members of NAAPS and indeed Asian staff who were not members of NAAPS would have an opportunity to offer their views, further copies were sent out to staff at their place of work. This exercise increased completed questionnaires returns by 35; that is, a total of 140 completions from 190 sent, or 74% returns. Of those returns, 107 were NAAPS members and 33 were not. Demographic data relating to age, gender, specific ethnicity, grade and general location within the UK was collated, to determine if any specific issues were related to the different groups within the sample. The questionnaire then proceeded to address the following issues: recruitment and expectations of the service; induction and general training provided; diversity training and equal opportunities; retention and progression opportunities; work with offenders; job security; support from management and colleagues; and their religious and cultural needs. The questionnaire also gave participants the opportunity to comment on the particular issues raised.

It also included a request at the end for further participation in the research stating:

> Please indicate whether you would be interested to participate in a more detailed interview for this project. This would be a confidential discussion lasting approximately an hour, with a project researcher. Please note that this research is supported by the national probation service.

This was important to allow staff to volunteer information and would give them a forum to voice their opinions in more detail. A total of 50 staff responded to this and 38 interviews were conducted across a range of staff grades and probation areas, as well as diversity of age, gender, location and experience. The one-to-one interviews took place over a four-month period and consisted of open-ended questions in order to allow respondents to express themselves on the general theme of 'recruitment, retention and progression'. Such a technique of 'purposeful sampling' (Patton, 2002) was valid to gain an insight into the views of staff who had, more importantly, volunteered to participate in this form of research. The interviews took place during office hours and in the respective office of the respondent. Some did express a sense of caution when speaking to us, as they were concerned how colleagues and managers would perceive them for being involved in this research (20% of respondents expressed this concern). We had to reinforce the confidential nature of our research but did state that the findings would be given to NPS on a general level. This assisted in alleviating their concerns.

It was disappointing that not as many senior staff volunteered to participate in this stage of the research, but we still managed to obtain some views of senior staff as well as a range of other graded staff.

Both I and the co-researcher were mindful of the impact our own characteristics and how this may influence the responses to the questions asked. Myself being an Indian female not working within the service, and my colleague being a Sikh male who is himself an SPO working in the Midlands region, were key factors that we were aware could not only work to our benefit but possibly to our detriment in terms of the responses we would get. We tackled this factor by tape-recording some fieldwork in order to create more of an informal chat than a formal interview. Comparing the notes of our respective interviews we found we had similar findings which reassured us that such an approach did assist and we hope the data obtained is deemed reliable and of value for analysis and further development.

Results – key findings

From the individual interviews undertaken, respondents identified themselves as:

22% (8)   POs
44% (17) PSOs or equivalent
28% (11) Administrative staff
4%   (2)   SPO and ACO

Of these 55% were female and 45% were male.

The findings below highlight some issues that require further exploration, on a wider scale. This section will be divided up to reflect the main

Table 19.1 Demographic constitution of the sample

Gender	
Male	40%–56
Female	60%–84
Role	
Probation officers	25%–35
PSOs or equivalent	54%–76
Admin staff	15%–21
SPOs/ACO	6%–8

issues addressed by the research, and also the findings from both the questionnaire and one-to-one interviews.

Section 1 – recruitment

Feedback received indicated that respondents joined because they wanted to work in the community in general and, more specifically, to work with offenders. Having heard about the service from friends and family, many were encouraged to join the service on the basis that it employed people from different cultural groups.

> I was told about probation from a friend [who] has a sister who was a probation service officer, I applied and with their (sic) help got a job as a hostel shift worker, since that time I have helped another person into a job with probation.

Working locally was also an incentive, as respondents did not have to uproot and leave their families, and were able to maintain community ties, which they reported as particularly important for their cultural needs.

> Having a chance to work in the community and locally was a key factor in my decision-making to join the service, as my family would not be keen on me moving to another city for work, neither would I really.

A real incentive for applying to join was based upon a genuine desire to help people from the community in order to make a difference in their lives, by working with offenders this was considered as a positive way to contribute towards a good cause.

> I wanted to make a difference in my community locally and the criminal justice system seemed a good way to do that, I like helping people and I feel that is a positive aspect of the Asian culture.

Training and induction

There was widespread criticism over the lack of training for those staff that had not undergone the TPO programme, approximately 30% of respondents felt this area was under resourced; for example, one officer commented:

> I did not receive any formal training in my role – I was just thrown in the deep end and expected to get on with it. (IT support officer)

Also, criticism was targeted at the content in terms of how it dealt with diversity issues whilst on the TPO programme:

Training on diversity is lacking in depth and realism, also it needs to be run regularly to reinforce the commitment to equal opportunities that the service claims it has. (PO)

Diversity training is needed for interviewers especially on the complexities of the differences within the Asian communities. (Administrator)

This point was made by a number of respondents (approximately 45%) who expressed concern about how the training was run, by whom it was delivered and the actual purpose of it (i.e. was it genuine or just a tick box exercise?).

Section 2 – retention

The majority of the respondents (125) felt that the work was interesting and varied and provided career progression opportunities, some internally as well as externally. However, half of the respondents acknowledged that although there were Asian staff in their respective areas, there could be more to reflect the communities that they serve. During the trainee probation officer (TPO) programme many respondents felt that the trainers did not necessarily deal adequately with racist comments made during the sessions, leaving them feeling marginalised during the course:

I was told by a white colleague that my appointment as an Asian was about increasing the numbers of Asians in the service.

Although enjoying the work, the majority of respondents felt uneasy with the introduction of the National Offender Management Service (NOMS), in terms of their job security, as they were unsure what the practical impact of this new role would be on them, at ground level.

Almost two-thirds of employees did not feel valued at work based upon their culture, as many felt that African-Caribbean, White and European staff's stereotypical views of Asians prevailed and they did not seek to clarify them. Such views were expressed in some conversations, such as the assumption that all Asians have arranged marriages, they do not have a social life and they only eat curries:

Colleagues have made remarks at lunch time that my food is smelly. (TPO)

I do not seem to fit in as I do not go out drinking with others or visit pubs and clubs on weekends. (PO)

Comments were made by colleagues (white and black) that my career within the service would be short as I would have to get married soon and raise children as that is what we Asians do. (TPO)

At times some staff did not clarify such assumptions as they felt they were wasting their time on the ignorance of colleagues, others who did clarify issues felt that it did raise some form of awareness but that it was not necessarily their role to dispel such myths. The quote below illustrates this point:

> At my office we celebrated Black History Month; there was no reference to Asian issues. I felt dismissed as it was assumed that I was in agreement with it all, I believed that by complaining to my manager who is black it would cause me greater problems. (PO)

Hence, this stems back to the earlier point of training on diversity and how such forums could be used more effectively to challenge views and stereotypes of staff, which not only reflect upon each other as colleagues, but also to the client group.

> There is little appreciation of Asian religious or cultural events as my Chief Officer organised an event for the local community which fell on the same day as Diwali . . . I did tell him to save embarrassment. (PO)

> I feel isolated from my white and black colleagues based upon my religious observance. (Administrator)

Section 3 – progression

Most of the sample interviewed (32) felt that although there were some Asian staff in senior positions, this was not enough to reassure them that they would progress well based upon merit. Additionally, some respondents thought that their religious practices impacted upon their promotional prospects, including wearing cultural dress to work.

> I think that management feel that offenders will give me a hard time and because of this they will not give me greater responsibility. (Administrator)

> The service tends not to encourage Asian staff to apply for management jobs as far as I can tell. (PO)

> I feel management in my service are not ready to have traditionally dressed Asian women in charge of a white or indeed a black group of people. (PO)

From the responses of the PSO staff in particular, it was noted that most did not wish to progress to PO because they would have to take a pay drop in order to carry out the TPO course, which they were not prepared to do. But also other graded staff felt less motivated to progress due to a perceived lack of support or encouragement from management. There was a degree of consensus amongst most interviewees (35) that management did not view Asians with credibility, particularly in light of current events which tends to portray Asians in general but Muslims specifically as being suspicious, untrustworthy and passive.

> There are limited opportunities for progression within the administrative grades and especially difficult to break into as an Asian. (Receptionist)

> It would help if there were more Asian staff in senior management positions, and then would I see the service taking us seriously professionally. (PO)

Generation gap

There appeared to be a generational difference between the interviewees' attitudes towards dealing with racist behaviour. Differences of opinion occurred between those coming to the UK but were born in the Asian continent (first generation), and those that were born in the UK (second and third generation). This distinction was raised during the interview as this appeared to have a bearing upon how they responded to discriminatory behaviour.

The first generation seemed to 'expect it' and not complain, whereas the second and third generation respondents were more likely to challenge it. For example, a respondent who is 60 stated that he 'expected to get some form of verbal racial abuse' from both staff and clients due to the time he joined the service (in the 1980s) because 'that is what society was like anyway, so why would the workplace be any different'. He further commented below:

> I did not consider racist remarks to be an issue; I expected that kind of behaviour from white staff when I joined the service as I have been brought up in such a climate so it was the norm for me.

In contrast, another PO based in the same office, aged 24, stated:

> When colleagues make generalisations about my culture I will correct them as I am not scared of them and will not tolerate negative comments when I am proud of my cultural heritage.

Experiences of racism within the probation service

There was a general consensus from the interviewees who felt the major problems stemmed from lack of awareness and understanding about how racism impacts their day-to-day life, for example:

I feel I have to explain my religious beliefs unnecessarily to white colleagues on a regular basis.

Having worked in an all-white office and geographical area, I would advise against this practice as it further isolates people of colour; safety in numbers helps so I would have felt better if at least another non-white staff member was there.

Others cited direct racist comments or behaviour based on stereotypical views of Asians, such as:

I believe my opinions are not sought by African-Caribbean and white staff as they may perceive me as being passive and non-opinionated which is disheartening in itself.

When asked how they felt about being defined as 'black' we found that the majority of respondents did not accept this definition;

The term 'black' says nothing about my culture, identity, language or dress code so why use it?

People usually see this to be about skin colour rather than about religion or cultural identity.

Such responses reinforce the reasons why some staff chose to join NAAPS and others are members of ABPO, with a pool of staff not belonging to either.

Most respondents (75%) reported that there was a clear impact on their working relationships as a result of the events of 9/11, specifically the view that Asians as a whole were supportive of terrorism:

It has created a black/white against Asian divide.

I was surprised at how quickly colleagues – both black and white – deemed that I agreed with the bombings or had sympathy for the attacker.

People's perceptions of Muslims has changed to the detriment of those from the Muslim religion.

Examples were given during interviews of the negative effects that sensationalist media reporting had, exacerbating the difficulties they faced and increasing concerns regarding the perceived inaction of senior staff and management to address this issue. There was a degree of consensus that such matters should be addressed within teams via training or team meetings to ensure that these matters were discussed openly in order to minimise the negative impact upon staff relations and perceptions.

Interviewees had little confidence that the policy and practice guidelines that cover race and diversity issues currently in place would really offer them the intended support, or achieve the required changes to make them feel totally comfortable within the workplace. In fact, many (30) felt that prejudice relating to religion, language, dress and culture and those which still cause them to become marginalised. This lack of support was further emphasised with suggestions made by staff that asserting their religious and cultural needs was an 'uncomfortable process'.

Many recognised the aims of diversity training and the resources allocated to improving relationships between BME and white groups, but still felt there was work to be done in order for them to feel accepted within the wider service, as an employee and as a service provider.

Key issues from the interviews

In all, 38 interviews were conducted, the sample included 11 males and 27 females and in terms of religious/ethnic background, 9 Sikh, 6 Hindus, 1 Chinese and 22 Muslim. All came from Ealing, Bradford, Nottingham and Leicester.

The key perceptions of this group were that, in terms of progression, many felt that all 'senior jobs appear to go to white colleagues', and that there are limited opportunities for progression within the administrative grades, especially for Asians. Some felt they were not encouraged by their line manager to apply for promotion and many believed the 'barriers of institutional racism' were clearly evident (20 interviewees expressed this concern). Not socialising with colleagues was seen as a negative trait, in that Asians were perceived as not integrating with the team, which also impacted on their promotion chances:

> You really need to be drinking and socialising with the right people – otherwise you don't get a look in.

The general working atmosphere among administrative staff was described by one participant as:

> Unhealthy, unprofessional and unproductive.

Others cited a clear hierarchy amongst staff, based upon ethnicity. This issue was further complicated with one administrative worker in particular stating that:

> I have an Asian female manager, but she is a real 'power-tripper' being

the only Asian in her position within our office, but also because she is Hindu and I am Muslim, this causes further divisions between us – she has a real problem with that.

Such a view was reinforced by her colleagues, but nothing was done to address it as there seemed to be 'little that can be done about it'. (During this research some comments were made about the inter-racial problems between Asians; however, for the purpose of this report this has not been focused upon due to the limited evidence drawn from the research. Yet, it is certainly a growing concern that should be looked into more specifically at a later date.)

There was a general reluctance to complain to management regarding inequalities, due mainly to a lack of faith in their professionalism in dealing with the situation appropriately, and also a fear of being victimised. Geographical variances were found amongst staff as those in the North experienced more overt racism from white colleagues, whereas in the South, Asian staff have more overt racist experiences from African-Caribbean staff.

An example of this happened in Bradford after the riots in July 2001, which caused an emotive division within the office. A female probation officer informed me that:

I clearly heard a European member of staff blaming the whole incident on the Muslim community, when I confronted her, she didn't back down, on the contrary, she raised her voice further and even personalised the issue blaming it on 'my community' . . . the matter was not addressed by management as a number of comments were being made by white staff during this sensitive time.

Polarisation of staff based upon their ethnicity did occur after the riots right up until the defendants were sentenced. Quotes such as that above reflect the findings of the Cantle Report (*Community Cohesion in Britain*) which highlighted such segregation. The 'parallel lives' that people led was reinforced from the findings, and can be related to the hostility experienced by staff within the probation service.

Additionally, the events of 9/11 had a particularly detrimental impact on working relationships, and contributed to an 'unproductive working atmosphere'. One participant reported:

I have experienced more racism from staff than clients – at least with clients they feel that we are helping them so my race or gender is not always an issue; however, staff carry deep-rooted generalisations, assumptions and these are sometimes shown at times like 9/11 – which is worrying.

Such a comment is reinforced by the findings of the HMIP 2004 report.

Conclusions

The findings from the research led to a number of recommendations, relating to the recruitment and promotion process, retention, training and diversity issues.

Specifically, the working group considered the following:

- reviewing the current support provisions for Asian staff
- managing staff and service provision in line with equal opportunities and increasing awareness of diversity issues via training
- reviewing the current area race and diversity policy in light of the research findings
- ensuring current recruitment approaches make the effort to have representative services
- reviewing local service responses to local and national events; ensuring that any changes to recruitment, retention and progression are linked into the Home Secretary's Employment Targets and include greater involvement from probation areas in terms of ownership of the Asian perspective
- encouraging Asian staff to go for promotion through an approach that does not perceive to give special treatment of any sort such as positive action
- providing a more detailed analysis of probation area recruitment targets, in order to ensure that issues of staff marginalisation/discrimination are acknowledged and addressed.

Some of the comments reflected existing research findings, such as the perception among BME groups working in probation that they were marginalised and suffered from distinct lack of support from management (e.g. HMIP, 2004). Many were aware of the hostility from white colleagues stemming from the use of 'positive discrimination', that is employing or promoting more staff from BME groups to satisfy performance indicators and targets associated with equal opportunities policy. Again, this has been reflected in previous research studies, primarily in the police service (Holdaway and Barron, 1997).

Participants also commented on the identification of Asians as different to 'black', in terms of religion and culture, and also the need for a better understanding to see race issues as going beyond skin colour, that is to increase awareness about what it means to be a member of a BME group, living in the UK. The development of associations to offer support to BME groups working in the criminal justice system and specifically with probation (ABPO, NAAPS) reflect this.

Events such as the Bradford riots, 9/11 and 7/7 have highlighted the general attitudes towards the Muslim faith in particular, which again was reflected in this research as a problem. Muslim staff felt a distinct change in attitude towards them which reflects the notion of Muslims as fundamentalist and 'fanatical followers' (Werbner, 2000). Although many complained about the lack of management support, others attributed this to media reporting, which simplified Asian culture and represented the Islamic religion in an ill-informed and alarmist way (Küçükcan, 2004), and also the lack of support from senior officials in responding adequately to such reports.

The HMIP Report 2004, which looked specifically at race equality, found similar issues of concern for minority staff. Focusing on the recommendations to human resources in particular, the report highlighted the proportion of staff experiencing racism from staff was higher than the level of racism experienced from offenders (HMIP, 2004: 11). Also staff expressed feelings of isolation in the workplace although the availability of support groups was offered to them (ibid.). Concerns expressed by staff on issues of induction, recruitment and retention reflect similar comments made by those staff in this research thus indicating how, for example, advertising in minority ethnic press for vacancies, providing consistent induction programmes which reflect diversity and to promote NAAPS to staff are important factors (HMIP, 2004: 52–3).

The issue of (in)visible barriers, is a matter of interpretation. Some staff made clear references to 'visible' discrimination when having to deal with racist comments, whereas others would perceive their experience as having 'invisible' barriers which have not been significant enough to pinpoint exactly why they have not been given opportunities for progression within the service.

This research suggests that there is a clear need to acknowledge the experience of Asians working in the probation service. Their treatment from colleagues and managers relating to recruitment, retention, progression and the experience of racism highlights a number of problems which are currently not being adequately addressed. They stem from a lack of awareness of Asian culture and the diversity within it, perceptions based on media reporting of global and national events and also the lack of detailed, in-depth analysis of the reality of being an Asian working in probation, which goes beyond recruitment and retention targets.

With reference to the recent findings of the Zahid Mubarek inquiry, we can draw a similar conclusion to that of the report, particularly where it refers to 'parallel worlds' that exist between service users and service providers (Mubarek Inquiry Report 2006). This point is illustrated further by the Inspectorate:

Few BME staff think that their prison is tackling race effectively, although most believe some progress has been made. A few speak of overt racism, and many talk of subtle racism on the part of non-BME colleagues, about which they are reluctant to complain. In some establishments they do not feel they are sufficiently supported when they apply for promotion, and overwhelmingly they are looking for visible and robust support from senior managers.

(Part 5, Ch. 62.6; 2006)

Diversity training was also raised within the Mubarek Inquiry report, which suggested that there should be 'training in cultural awareness for staff, which builds awareness of the different perceptions and experiences of different visible minority groups' (ibid.). This is clearly relevant to the issues that arose from this research as staff questioned the level of genuine interest in this training, and whether it was merely lip service that had to be paid as opposed to a real need for such training.

Recommendation 83 from the Mubarek Inquiry should also be considered here as it refers to the definition of a racist incident stemming from the Stephen Lawrence Inquiry, so that when dealing with racist incidents it is the victim's definition of the action which is of paramount importance – not that of colleagues, managers or personnel (Race Relations Amendment Act 2000). By implementing the definition this will give complainants some faith in the system.

Findings from the Home Office report in June 2006 based upon the workforce profile should also be taken into account as the recruitment, retention and progression of Asian staff needs to be monitored regularly, with due attention being given to areas of not only weakness but also strength. Regardless of whether targets are being met, it is the 'real experiences' faced by Asian staff that must be given a priority at all stages of their employment, particularly if the probation service wants to continue to employ staff from this sector of the community. This can be achieved via meaningful training sessions coupled with constructive debates to dispel myths and embrace the diverse make-up of both staff and service users.

It is evident that there is clearly a need for a more in-depth exploration of these issues, and with regards to diversity training in the public sector. It is unclear how often such training occurs in the probation service, and how well it responds to current events and demands for a better understanding of race, religion and culture in society.

References

Bowling, B. and Phillips, C. (2002) *Racism, Crime and Justice*. London: Longman.
Calverley, A. *et al.* (2004) 'Black and Asian Offenders on Probation', HORS 277. London: Home Office.

Cantle Report (2001) *Community Cohesion in Britain.* London: Home Office.

Commission for Racial Equality (2004) *Implementing Race Equality in Prisons.* London: CRE.

Criminal Justice Consultative Council: Race Sub-Group (CJCC) (2000) *Race and the Criminal Justice System: Joining up to promote equality and encourage diversity.*

Goodey J. (2001) 'The Criminalization of British Asian Youth: Research from Bradford and Sheffield', Journal of Youth Studies, 4 (4): 429–450(22). Carfax Publishing.

Halliday, F. (1997) 'Islamophobia reconsidered', in *Islamophobia: A challenge for us all.* London: The Runnymede Trust.

Harper, G. and Chitty, C. (eds) (2005) 'The impact of corrections on re-offending: A review of "what works"' (2nd edn) Home Office Research Study 291. London: Home Office.

Her Majesty's Inspectorate of Probation (2002) *Towards Race Equality: Thematic Inspection.* London: Home Office.

Holdaway and Barron (1997) in B. Bowling and C. Phillips (2002) *Racism, Crime and Justice.* London: Longman.

Hollin, C., McGuire, J., Palmer, E., Bilby, C., Hatcher, R. and Holmes, A. (2002) 'Introducing Pathfinder programmes into the Probation Service: an interim report,' Home Office Research Study 247. London: Home Office.

Home Office (2005) 'Race and the Criminal Justice System: An overview to the complete statistics 2003–2004'. London: Home Office.

Home Office (2006) *NPS HR Workforce Report* (Issue 3). London: Home Office.

Home Office (2006) *The Zahid Mubarek Inquiry Report.* London: Home Office.

Kent, D.R., Donaldson, S.I., Wyrick, P.A. and Smith, P.J. (2000) 'Evaluating criminal justice programs designed to reduce crime by targeting repeat gang offenders', *Evaluation and Program Planning*, 23 (1): 115–124, Elsevier Science.

Küçükcan, T. (2004) 'The making of Turkish-Muslim diaspora in Britain: religious collective identity in a multicultural public sphere', *Journal of Muslim Minority Affairs*, 24(2): 243–258, Carfax Publishing.

Macpherson, W. (1999) *The Stephen Lawrence Inquiry*, by Sir William MacPherson of Cluny. London: Home Office.

NACRO (2003) *Race and Prisons: Where are we now?* London: NACRO.

Patton, M. (2002) *Qualitative research and evaluation methods.* London: Sage.

Piquero, N.L. (2003) 'A recidivism analysis of Maryland's community probation program', *Journal of Criminal Justice*, 31 (4): 295–307, Elsevier Science.

Powis, B. and Walmsley, R.K. (2002) 'Programmes for black and Asian offenders on probation: Lessons for developing practice', *Home Office Research Study 250.* London: Home Office.

Rex, S. and Gelsthorpe, L. (2002) 'The Role of Community Service in Reducing Offending: Evaluating Pathfinder Projects in the UK', *Howard Journal of Criminal Justice*, 41 (4): 311–325(15).

Tamkin, P. *et al.* (2002) 'A Review of Training in Racism Awareness and Valuing Cultural Diversity'. London: Institute for Employment Studies.

Werbner, P. (2000) 'Divided Loyalties, Empowered Citizenship? Muslims in Britain,' *Citizenship Studies*, 4 (3): 307–324, Routledge.

Appendix: Questionnaire

Recruitment

1. What attracted you to seek employment in the probation service? E.g.

   Pay ☐   Challenges of the job ☐   Terms and conditions ☐

   Other (Please give details)_____

2. Prior to joining the service, did you have any knowledge about the work of probation?

   Quite a lot ☐   A little ☐   None ☐

3. Who gave you information about jobs in the probation service? E.g. (friend, family member, job fairs, media or other, please give details)

4. Do you feel that there was any form of discrimination during the recruitment process?

   No ☐

   Yes ☐   (Please give details)_____

5. How did you rate your induction into the service as an Asian?

   Very good ☐   Good ☐   Satisfactory ☐   Poor ☐
   Very poor ☐

6. What would you improve, if anything, in relation to the above? (Please give details)

7. How well does your service adhere to its equal opportunities and diversity statement?

   Very well   ☐
   Quite well ☐
   Quite poor ☐
   Very poor ☐
   Not at all ☐

8. Would you recommend the National Probation Service to other Asians as an employer?

   Yes ☐   No ☐   Unsure ☐

   If Yes (Please give details)_____

Retention

9. For what reasons do you remain an employee of the National Probation Service? (Please tick more than one if necessary)

   Pay and conditions   ☐
   Interesting and challenging work   ☐
   The best available job locally   ☐
   Career development opportunities ☐

10. How would you rate the probation service in terms of job security?

    Very High ☐   High ☐   Poor ☐   Very Poor ☐

11. Do you feel valued as an employee?

    Yes ☐   No ☐   Sometimes Valued ☐   Not Valued ☐

12. Is your line manager aware of your religious needs?

    Yes ☐   No ☐   Sometimes ☐   Not applicable ☐

13. Do you feel that your cultural values/norms are given appropriate attention?

    Yes ☐   No ☐   Sometimes ☐   Not applicable ☐

14. Do you believe that your area actively promotes race equality?

    Yes ☐   No ☐

15. Have you suffered discrimination from white or black colleagues?

    No ☐
    Yes ☐

16. Have you suffered discrimination from white or black offenders during the course of your work?

    No ☐

    Yes ☐ (Please give details)_____

17. How likely are you to leave probation within the next 12 months?

    Very Likely ☐   Likely ☐   Not Sure ☐   Not at all ☐

18. If you decided to leave, what type of work would you do?

19. As an Asian employee do you receive support on issues of race, religion and culture? Please answer in relation to the following categories (Please tick more than one box if necessary)

    a. Immediate line management

       Yes No

       ☐   ☐

    b. Senior line managers

       Yes No

       ☐   ☐

    c. Chief officer grade

       Yes No

       ☐   ☐

    d. Colleagues

       Yes No

       ☐   ☐

20. Does your area have policy and practice guidelines to protect you from harassment or bullying from colleagues, offenders and/or visitors?

    Yes ☐   No ☐   Don't Know ☐

21. Is the policy enforced?

    Very well ☐   Quite well ☐   Very Poorly ☐   Quite Poorly ☐

22. Are you encouraged to attend support group meetings?

    No ☐

    Yes ☐   (Please give examples of support – e.g. workload relief, work shift cover)

23. How do you feel about being defined/referred to as 'black' by the probation service? Do you:

    Approve ☐   Disapprove ☐   Not concerned ☐

    Please give reasons_____

24. Are you managed fairly by immediate line management?

    Very fairly ☐   Quite fairly ☐   Not at all fairly ☐

25. Since the events of 11 September 2001, do you feel that you have been adversely affected in any way?

    No ☐

    Yes ☐   (Please give details)_____

Progression

26. Are you confident in the system of promotion?

    Yes ☐   Not sure ☐

    No ☐   (Please give details)_____

27. Do feel that your religion or your religious practice will in any way impact your promotional opportunities?

    Yes ☐   No ☐   Not sure ☐

28. What do you think about your promotional prospects?

    Very good ☐   Good ☐   Limited ☐   Very Limited ☐

    Please give reasons_____

29. Do you think you may have been by-passed for promotion on any aspect of your lifestyle? E.g. religion, dress, language, culture

    No ☐   Possibly ☐

    Yes ☐   (Please give details)_____

Please indicate whether you would be interested to participate in a more detailed interview for this project. This would be a confidential discussion lasting approximately an hour, with a project researcher. Please note that the National Probation Service supports this research.

    No ☐

    Yes ☐

If yes, please leave your email address and phone number:

Thank you for your time and co-operation

Conclusion

Clearly, issues in relation to 'race'/ethnicity and crime are numerous and multifaceted. Statistical information about 'race'/ethnicity in a criminal justice context is partial and incomplete, as 'race'/ethnicity are socially constructed phenomena. Nonetheless, statistical information reveals that Black, particularly African Caribbean, men and women are over-represented in penal institutions, raising questions about the social and economic deprivation, and social exclusion, experienced by Black communities, as well as individuals' experiences of direct and institutional racism.

It is important to stress that at different points in the criminal justice system, at different periods of time, different communities will become more prominent in policy, research and media arenas. Whereas in the 1970s and 1980s relations between the police and Black communities deteriorated, in a post-9/11 context, when many terror attacks have been committed around the world by extremists, Asian men, in particular young Muslim men, have attracted attention and have been viewed as constituting a 'problem group'. In a post-9/11 context, faith identities in relation to crime, criminal justice and victimisation are therefore increasingly likely to feature in research and policy arenas.

The experiences of minority ethnic communities as the victims of crime are generating growing research and policy attention. Victimisation by race and religious hate crime is increasingly being focussed upon, particularly as it has been suggested that hate crimes impact not only upon direct victims, but also upon the wider communities to which individuals belong. At the same time, accounts of the process of victimisation feature the ways in which cultural, religious and other factors can influence how individuals experience crime. This work illustrates that social differences are increasingly being taken into account in criminological and victimological work, partly as a result of personal and theoretical reflection, with reflexivity being a constituent part of contemporary Western society.

Reflexivity is a key characteristic of work focussing upon 'race'/ethnicity and crime. In relation to criminological and victimological knowledge production around 'race'/ethnicity, researchers are questioning the applicability of the terminology used to categorise minorities. Also, researchers' reflection involves debates in relation to the racial/ethnic identities of the researcher and the researched, and how these influence the research process. At the same time, the issue of the marginalisation of minorities' experiences and claims to knowledge is increasingly being reflected upon, with some researchers arguing that perspectives within criminology/victimology have insufficiently taken into consideration the voices and individual, as well as group collective, experiences of minorities. A focus upon whiteness is a further aspect to growing reflexivity, where 'whiteness' might be viewed as consisting of what is considered to be 'normal', serving to oppress Black and Asian, as well as other, minority groups.

Reflexivity can also be seen in the work undertaken by agencies of the criminal justice system. With respect to 'race'/ethnicity, agencies of the criminal justice system routinely assemble information to help monitor disadvantage, so as to ensure that their policies and practices are not disadvantaging minority ethnic communities. 'Community participation' and 'community engagement' are phrases that are often found in government and criminal justice policy discourse, and agencies have targets that they are expected to meet in terms of, for example, minority ethnic representation within their workforces.

To summarise, 'race'/ethnicity in relation to crime raises many important issues. The five parts that comprise this *Reader* constitute an attempt to capture this broad, and theoretically rich, area. Future developments are likely to reflect the key issues emerging from each of these five parts, containing theoretical, methodological and policy dimensions.

Bibliography

Agozino, B. (2003) *Counter-Colonial Criminology*. London: Pluto Press.

Alexander, A. (2000) *The Asian Gang*. Oxford: Berg, pp. 1–26.

Bauman, Z. (1989) *Modernity and the Holocaust*. Cambridge: Polity Press.

Beckford, J., Gale, R., Owen, D., Peach, C. and Weller, P. (2006) *Review of the Evidence Base on Faith Communities*. London: Office of the Deputy Prime Minister.

Bowling, B. and Phillips, C. (2002) *Racism, Crime and Justice*. Harlow: Longman.

Bridges, L. and Gilroy, P. (1982) 'Striking Back' *Marxism Today*: 34–35.

Cain, M. (2000) 'Orientalism, Occidentalism and the Sociology of Crime' *British Journal of Criminology* Vol. 40: 239–260.

Castells, M. (2004) *The Power of Identity* (2nd edn). Oxford: Blackwell Publishing.

Chakraborti, N. and Garland, J. (2004) 'Justifying the Study of Racism in the Rural' in N. Chakraborti and J. Garland (eds) *Rural Racism*. Collumpton: Willan, pp. 1–13.

Chigwada-Bailey, R. (1997) *Black Women's Experiences of Criminal Justice*. Winchester: Waterside Press.

Collins, P. (1998) *Fighting Words*. Minneapolis: University of Minnesota Press.

Davis, D. (1997) 'The Harm that Has no Name: street harassment, embodiment and African American women' in A. Wing (ed.) *Critical Race Feminism: a reader*. New York: New York University Press, pp. 192–202.

Fawcett Society (2004) *Women and the Criminal Justice System*. London: The Fawcett Society.

Ferguson, R. (1998) *Representing 'race': ideology, identity and the media*. London: Arnold.

Garland, D. (2002) 'Of crimes and criminals: the development of criminology in Britain' in M. Maguire, R. Morgan and R. Reiner (eds) *The Oxford Handbook of Criminology* (3rd edn), pp. 7–50.

Garland, J., Spalek, B. and Chakraborti, N. (2006) 'Hearing Lost Voices: Issues in Researching Hidden Minority Ethnic Communities' *British Journal of Criminology* Vol. 46: 423–437.

Gelsthorpe, L. (1993) 'Approaching the Topic of Racism: Transferable Research Strategies?' in D. Cook and B. Hudson (eds) *Racism and Criminology*. London: Sage, pp. 77–95.

Gilroy, P. (1993) *The Black Atlantic: modernity and double consciousness*. London: Verso.

Hall, S., Critcher, C., Jefferson, T., Clarke, J. and Roberts, B. (1978) *Policing the Crisis: mugging, the state, and law and order*. London: Macmillan.

Harris, A. (1997) 'Race and Essentialism in Feminist Legal Theory' in A. Wing (ed.) *Critical Race Feminism*. London: New York University Press, pp. 11–18.

Her Majesty's Inspectorate of Constabulary (2000) *Winning the Race: embracing diversity*. London: HMIC.

HM Inspectorate of Probation (2000) *Towards Race Equality*. London: HMIP.

HM Inspectorate of Prisons (2005) *Parallel Worlds: a thematic review of race relations in prisons*. London: HM Inspectorate.

Holdaway, S. (1996) *The Racialisation of British Policing*. London: Macmillan.

hooks, b. (1982) *Ain't I a Woman: black women and feminism*. London: Pluto Press.

hooks, b. (1990) *Yearning race, gender and cultural politics*. Boston: South End Press.

Imtoual, A. (forthcoming, 2008) 'Cover your Face for the Photograph Please': Gender Issues, the Media and Muslim Women in Australia' *Journal of Australasian Studies*.

James, Z. (2006) 'Policing Space: managing New Travellers in England' *British Journal of Criminology* Vol. 46 (3): 470–485.

Jary, D. and Jary, J. (1999) *Unwin Dictionary of Sociology* (2nd edn). Glasgow: Harper Collins.

Johnson, B., Jang, S., Larson, D. and De Li, S. (2001) 'Does Adolescent Religious Commitment Matter? A re-examination of the effects of religiosity on delinquency' *Journal of Research in Crime & Delinquency* Vol. 38 (1): 22–43.

Kennedy, P. and Roudometof, V. (2004) 'Transnationalism in a Global Age' in P. Kennedy and V. Roudometof (eds) *Communities across Borders: new immigrants and transnational cultures*. London: Routledge, pp. 1–26.

Lash, S. (1994) 'Reflexivity and its Doubles: structure, aesthetics, community' in U. Beck, A. Giddens and S. Lash (eds) *Reflexive Modernization: politics, tradition and aesthetics in the modern social order*. Cambridge: Polity Press, pp. 110–173.

Lombroso, C. (1876) *The Criminal Man*. Turin: Fratelli Bocca.

Lyon, D. (1999) *Postmodernity* (2nd edn). Buckingham: Open University Press.

McClaurin, I. (2001) 'Introduction: forging a theory, politics, praxis and poetics of black feminist anthropology' in I. McClaurin (ed.) *Black Feminist Anthropology*. London: Rutgers University Press, pp. 1–23.

McGhee, D. (2005) *Intolerant Britain? hate, citizenship and difference*. Maidenhead: Open University Press.

Macpherson, W. (1999) *The Stephen Lawrence Inquiry*. London: HMSO.

Mirza, H. (1997) 'Introduction: mapping a genealogy of Black British feminism' in H. Mirza (ed.) *Black British Feminism: a reader*. London: Routledge, pp. 1–28.

Morrison, W. (1995) *Theoretical Criminology: From Modernity to Post-modernism*. London: Cavendish Publishing Limited.

Moss, B. (2005) *Religion and Spirituality*. Lyme Regis: Russell Publishing House.

Neville, H., Oh, E., Spanierman, L., Heppner, M. and Clark, M. (2004) 'General and culturally specific factors influencing black and white rape survivors' self-esteem' *Psychology of Women Quarterly* Vol. 28: 83–94.

O'Beirne, M. (2004) *Religion in England and Wales: findings from the 2001 Home Office Citizenship Survey*. London: Home Office.

Papadopoulos, I. and Lees, S. (2002) 'Developing Culturally Competent Researchers' *Journal of Advanced Nursing* 37 (3): 258–264.

Phillips, C. and Bowling, B. (2002) 'Racism, Ethnicity, Crime, and Criminal Justice' in M. Maguire, R. Morgan and R. Reiner (eds) *The Oxford Handbook of Criminology* (3rd edn), pp. 579–620.

Phillips, C. and Bowling, B. (2003) 'Racism, Ethnicity and Criminology: developing minority perspectives' *British Journal of Criminology* 43: 269–290.

Phillips, C. and Bowling, B. (2007) 'Ethnicities, Racism, Crime and Criminal Justice' in M. Maguire, R. Morgan and R. Reiner (eds) *The Oxford Handbook of Criminology* (4th edn), pp. 421–460.

Pitts, J. (1993) 'Thereotyping: Antiracisms, criminology and Black young people' in D. Cook and B. Hudson (eds) *Racism and Criminology*. London: Sage, pp. 96–117.

Poynting, S. and Mason, V. (2006), ' "Tolerance, freedom, justice and peace"?: Britain, Australia and anti-Muslim racism since 11th September 2001', *Journal of Intercultural Studies* 27 (4) November: 365–392.

Quraishi, M. (2005) *Muslims and Crime: a Comparative Study*. London: Ashgate.

Rew, A. and Campbell, J. (1999) 'The Political Economy of Identity and Affect' in J. Campbell and A. Rew (eds) *Identity and Affect: experiences of identity in a global world*. London: Pluto Press, pp. 1–36.

Rowe, M. (2004) *Policing, Race and Racism*. Cullompton: Willan.

Shute, S., Hood, R. and Seemungal, F. (2005) *A Fair Hearing? ethnic minorities in the criminal courts*. Devon: Willan Publishing.

Sivanandan, A. (1981) 'From Resistance to Rebellion' *Race and Class*: 111–152.

Taylor, S. (1984) 'The Scarman Report and Explanations of Riots' in J. Benyon (ed.) *Scarman and After*. Oxford: Pergaman Press, pp. 20–36.

Taylor, I., Evans, K. and Fraser, P. (1996) *A Tale of Two Cities: global change, local feeling and everyday life in the North of England: a study in Manchester and Sheffield*. London: Routledge.

Taylor, M. (2004) 'Sociohistorical constructions of race and language: Impacting biracial identity' in Jean Lau Chin (ed.) *The psychology of prejudice and discrimination: Ethnicity and multiracial identity* (Vol. 2). London: Praeger, pp. 87–108.

Waddington, P., Stenson, K. and Don, D. (2004) 'In Proportion: race, and police stop and search' *British Journal of Criminology* Vol. 44 (6): 889–914.

Walklate, S. (2003) 'Can there be a Feminist Victimology?' in P. Davies, P. Francis and V. Jupp (eds) *Victimisation: theory, research and policy*. Hampshire: Palgrave Macmillan, pp. 28–45.

Webster, C. (1997) 'The Construction of British Asian Criminality' *International Journal of the Sociology of Law* Vol. 25: 65–86.

White, R. and Haines, F. (2000) *Crime and Criminology*. Oxford: Oxford University Press.

Wiegman, R. (1999) 'Whiteness studies and the paradox of particularity' *Boundary 2* 26 (3): 115–150.

Williams, P. (1997) 'Spirit-Murdering the Messenger: the discourse of finger pointing as the Law's response to racism' in A. Wing (ed.) *Critical Race Feminism: a reader*. New York: New York University Press, pp. 229–236.

Glossary

Black – consisting of the shared space of postcolonial migrants of different languages, religions, cultures and classes through the shared experience of racialisation and its consequences (Mirza, 1997: 3). This terminology has, however, been contested. For example, Modood (1994) argues that 'Black' evokes people of African origins, thereby serving to exclude and 'otherise' Asian minorities.

Black and Minority Ethnic – a 'catch-all' term for minority ethnic communities, that has found currency amongst many statutory and voluntary organisations in England since the late 1990s (Garland, Spalek and Chakraborti, 2006).

Colonialism – 'associated with European, White Christian, wealthy rulers who have attempted to impose cultural values over the ruled' (Jary and Jary, 1999: 95).

Community – communities are units of belonging whose members perceive that they share moral, aesthetic/expressive or cognitive meanings, thereby gaining a sense of personal as well as group identity (Kennedy and Roudometof, 2004: 6).

Diaspora – this has both a global and local dimension. In diasporas individual members gain a sense of belonging, devising narratives about themselves and their origins, about how they are linked to broader global religions, nationalities and/or ethnicities as well as to localities which are 'simultaneously home and a place of exile' (Rew and Campbell, 1999: 167).

Double consciousness – the notion, developed from critical Black feminist perspectives, that distinct aspects of self can co-reside and so, as well as there being aspects of the self linked to marginalised positions, there may also be parts of the self that can be linked to the perpetuation of centres of power (Collins, 1998; McClaurin, 2001).

Enlightenment – when reason emerged as the dominant paradigm through which to view the emancipation of humans from the pre-modern static order, the 'ancien regime' (Lash, 1994: 112).

Ethnicity – 'a shared (perceived or actual) racial, linguistic, national, religious or cultural identity' (Jary and Jary, 1999: 206).

Orientalism – this might be viewed as the tendency to negativise or idealise the practices of non-Western nations (Cain, 2000).

Race – 'a scientifically discredited term previously used to describe biologically distinct groups of persons who were alleged to have characteristics of an unalterable nature' (Jary and Jary, 1999: 540).

Religiosity – the degree to which an individual expresses a sincere and earnest regard for religion, which might be understood as including church attendance, giving donations to religious institutions and/or reading theological and/or sacred material (Johnson, Jang, Larson and De Li, 2001).

Spirituality – according to Moss (2005: 12) spirituality has both an inward-looking and outward-looking dimension, the former being a pathway through which individuals seek to find a sense of meaning and purpose in their lives, the latter fostering a sense of responsibility for others.

Whiteness – a dominant, and largely hidden, norm that underpins research approaches and knowledge constructions. Being white is not regarded as being a 'racial' identity and a particular lens through which the world is viewed and experienced, but rather, is considered to be what is 'normal', 'neutral' or 'common sense' (hooks, 1982).

Useful websites

Commission for Equality and Human Rights
http://www.cehr.org.uk/
Commission for Racial Equality
http://www.cre.gov.uk/
HM Inspectorate of Constabulary
http://inspectorates.homeoffice.gov.uk/hmic/
HM Inspectorate of Prisons
http://inspectorates.homeoffice.gov.uk/hmiprisons/about-us/
HM Inspectorate of Probation
http://inspectorates.homeoffice.gov.uk/hmiprobation/
Home Office
http://www.homeoffice.gov.uk/
Ministry of Justice
http://www.justice.gov.uk/

Index

Locators shown in *italics* refer to figures and tables.

Valier, C., 332
Van Dijk, J., 225–6
victimization (concept)
  evolution of study of, 208–10
  impact of regression analysis on
    interpretations of, 36
  in relation to punishment, 69–70
  role in explaining crime trends, 391–2
  social geography of, 210–18
  see also territorialism
victimization, racial
  experiences of, 262–3, 264–9
  patterns among ethnic minorities,
    247–62
  scenarios of, 218–22
victims, of crime
  characteristics of support service
    provision of racial harassment
    services, 225–32
  focus on as barrier to successful racist
    violence monitoring, 195–6
  practical and psychological needs of
    racial harassment victims, 235–7,
    236
  relevance of support service provision,
    222–5
  see also blame; charters, victim; rights,
    victim
Victim Support Scheme (Waltham
  Forest), 222, 224
Victim Support Schemes, 226–8, 233
Victorian Multicultural Commission
  (VMC) (Australia), 141
violence, domestic
  case studies of African women, 292–9
  case studies of African-Caribbean
    women, 280–92, 296–9
  methodology of survey of, 275–80
violence, racist
  adequacy and function of
    criminological research, 205–7
  definitions and interpretations,
    186–90
  European Union trends, 194–5
  extent and nature within European
    Union, 193–4
  failure of EU to monitor, 195–8
  information sources, 190–92, 198–201

Voice, The (magazine), 311, 320
Von Hentig, H., 208

Waddington, P., 2
Walker M., 7
Walklate, S., 205, 209, 231
Waller, I., 232
Walmsley, R., 204
Waltham Forest
  extent and relevance of local victim
    support agencies, 222–5
  racial victimization scenarios within,
    218–22
Waltham Forest Association for People
  with Disabilities (WFAPD), 223–4
Warwick
  racial bias within sentencing process,
    57–63
Weber, M., 72–4
Webster, C., 2, 173
Werbner, P., 129, 420
West, C., 176
West Indians see African-Caribbeans
West Midlands
  racial bias within sentencing process,
    57–63
  see also towns eg Birmingham; Dudley;
    Leeds
WFAPD (Waltham Forest Association
  for People with Disabilities), 223–4
What is to be Done About Law and Order?
  (Lea and Young), 123
White Patriot (journal), 355
White Power (journal), 360, 361
whites (skin colour)
  patterns of racial victimization among,
    256–60
  treatment within criminal justice
    system, 7–30, 10, 11, 13, 14, 18, 19,
    21, 22
  see also movements, white supremacy
Williams, S., 376
Winant, H., 353
Winks, J., 158
Winning the Race (HMIC), 403–4
Witte, R., 187
Wolfgang, M., 208
women see females

Related books from Open University Press

Purchase from www.openup.co.uk or order through your local bookseller

UNDERSTANDING THE MANAGEMENT OF HIGH RISK OFFENDERS

Hazel Kemshall

> This is an extremely important and timely book written by a pre-eminent scholar in the field. Hazel Kemshall has a proven track record not just of exceptional scholarship but, equally importantly, of engaging effectively with policy and practice. Given the damaging synergies between media hype and public insecurities about 'dangerous' offenders, the evidence-based, measured and thoughtful analysis provided in this book provides a vital counterpoint to increasingly punitive and exclusionary discourses around public protection. In promoting a more balanced, humane and integrative approach to risk, the book deserves to influence not just scholars but also policy makers and practitioners facing the complex challenges of managing risk and dangerousness.
>
> *Fergus McNeill, Associate Fellow of the Centre for Sentencing Research,*
> *Strathclyde University, UK*

High risk offenders have attracted much media, policy and practice interest in recent years. New legislation and extensive multi-agency partnerships have been initiated to improve the assessment and management of these offenders in the community.

Drawing on a wide range of cross-national literature and original research by the author, this timely book reviews current approaches to the community management of high risk offenders. The book examines in detail a range of risk management techniques, including:

- Community protection measures (such as sexual offender registration and community notification)
- Restorative and re-integrative measures (such as Circles of Support and Accountability, pro-social modelling, public health campaigns and environmental risk management approaches)

Hazel Kemshall argues for a 'blending' of these two approaches to provide risk management interventions for the 'protective integration' of high risk offenders back into the community. In addition, the book examines contemporary difficulties in risk assessment, effective multi-agency partnership working, and recent policy and legislative initiatives in this challenging area of work.

Understanding the Management of High Risk Offenders is a vital resource for criminology and criminal justice students and stimulating reading for probation officers, social workers, police and prison staff, among others.

Contents

Dedication – Acknowledgements – Introduction – Framing the problem: Contemporary responses to high-risk offenders – Differing perspectives on an old problem: How do we know the dangerous? – Risk assessment: Difficulties and dilemmas – Protection through partnership – Risk management – Key issues in managing high risk offenders – Concluding comments – Glossary – References – Acronyms – Figures – Index.

2008   192pp
978–0–335–21998–8 (Paperback)   978–0–335–21999–5 (Hardback)

RESEARCHING CRIMINOLOGY

Iain Crow and Natasha Semmens

> . . . what makes the book stand out is the inclusion of real research into various criminal justice institutions that have actually been undertaken by the authors. In doing so, what is produced is a book that stimulates interest and injects research passion, as well as offering research 'know how' into what can often be a difficult and sometimes dry area of research.
>
> *Tina Patel, Liverpool John Moores University*

> This book provides an essential tool for undergraduate students embarking upon their own research projects in Criminology. It provides clear and informative guidance on a range of research methods and designs to assist students in their own criminological endeavours.
>
> *Jacki Tapley, University of Portsmouth*

- How do criminologists go about studying crime and its consequences?
- How are programmes for offenders and communities evaluated?
- How can you collect and analyse criminological material?

Research on crime and criminality is often referred to by the media, policy makers and practitioners, but where does this research come from and how reliable is it?

Designed especially for students on criminology and criminal justice courses, and professionals working in the field, *Researching Criminology* emphasises the importance of research as an integrated process. It looks at the ways in which a mixture of investigative methods can be used to analyze a criminological question.

Written by two experienced researchers and lecturers *Researching Criminology* is a comprehensive introduction to the aims, principles and methods of doing criminological research. The book covers all the key topics that you will encounter when researching crime. Individual chapters include material on:

- The research process
- Principles of researching criminology
- How to design criminological research
- Evaluation research
- Researching ethically
- A glossary of essential key concepts

Structured in three parts, addressing the principles of criminological research, how to collect and analyse material and providing detailed examples of real world research, *Researching Criminology* will be of benefit to all students of criminology and criminal justice, for practitioners interested in criminological research, and for those undertaking criminological research for the first time.

Contents
Part one: The principles of criminological research – *The research process* – *The principles of researching criminology* – *Designing criminological research* – *Criminological evaluation* – **Part two: Collecting and analysing material** – *Researching by reading* – *Researching by looking* – *Researching by asking and listening* – *Analysing criminological research* – **Part three: Real world research** – *Researching offenders and employment* – *Researching the youth court* – *Researching a community safety programme* – *Researching the fear of crime.*

2007   312pp
978–0–335–22140–0 (Paperback)   978–0–335–22141–7 (Hardback)

GENDER AND CRIME
A READER
Karen Evans and Janet Jamieson (eds)

Focusing explicitly on questions of gender and crime, Evans and Jamieson guide the reader through a range of classic and groundbreaking studies, highlighting key contributions and debates and providing an indication of the new directions an engendered criminology may take us in coming years.

This engaging reader is divided into five sections, mapping the theoretical, empirical, and practical developments that have endeavoured to identify the ways in which gender informs criminology. Issues addressed by the readings include:

- Female offending
- Gendered patterns of victimisation
- The gendered nature of social control
- Masculinity and crime
- Placing gender in an international context

Evans and Jamieson's powerful concluding chapter clearly sets out the achievements and the challenges that the gender and crime question has posed for criminology. They argue that unless the question of gender remains at the forefront of criminological endeavours, criminology will fail to offer an agenda informed by an understanding of social justice that strives to be attentive to both victims and offenders, whether they be male or female.

Gender and Crime is key reading for students of criminology, criminal justice and gender studies.

Readings by: *Jon Bannister, Susan Brownmiller, Beatrix Campbell, Pat Carlen, Meda Chesney-Lind, Ruth Chigwada-Bailey, Richard Collier, Jock Collins, Jason Ditton, R. Emerson Dobash, Russell P. Dobash, Stephen Farrall, Lorraine Gelsthorpe, Elizabeth Gilchrist, Annie Hudson, Ruth Jamieson, Nancy Loucks, James W. Messerschmidt, Allison Morris, Greg Noble, Lisa Pasko, Scott Poynting, Lorraine Radford, Marcia Rice, Carol Smart, Laureen Snider, Elizabeth A. Stanko, Paul Tabar, Kaname Tsutsumi, Anne Worrall.*

Contents

June 2008   352pp
978–0–335–22523–1 (Paperback)   978–0–335–22522–4 (Hardback)